Mobile Forensic Investigations

Mobile Forensic Investigations

A Guide to Evidence Collection, Analysis, and Presentation

Lee Reiber

New York Chicago San Francisco
Athens London Madrid Mexico City
Milan New Delhi Singapore Sydney Toronto

Cataloging-in-Publication Data is on file with the Library of Congress

McGraw-Hill Education books are available at special quantity discounts to use as premiums and sales promotions, or for use in corporate training programs. To contact a representative, please visit the Contact Us pages at www.mhprofessional.com.

Mobile Forensic Investigations: A Guide to Evidence Collection, Analysis, and Presentation

1234567890 DOC/DOC 109876

ISBN 978-0-07-184363-8
MHID 0-07-184363-9

Sponsoring Editor
Brandi Shailer

Editorial Supervisor
Janet Walden

Project Manager
Kritika Kaushik,
Cenveo® Publisher Services

Acquisitions Coordinator
Amy Stonebraker

Technical Editor
Michael Robinson

Copy Editor
Lisa Theobald

Proofreader
Lisa McCoy

Indexer
Ted Laux

Production Supervisor
Lynn M. Messina

Composition
Cenveo Publisher Services

Illustration
Cenveo Publisher Services

Art Director, Cover
Jeff Weeks

Cover Designer
Jeff Weeks

This book is dedicated to my wife, Amy, my biggest critic,
who has put up with 20 years of geek speak and talk about writing a book,
along with the last several months of staring at my laptop composing the book manuscript.
You inspire me.

About the Author

Lee Reiber started his journey as a member of the Boise Police Department in Boise, Idaho, where he conducted digital forensic investigations until 2009 after almost 15 years of service. During the last few years at the police department, Lee's training company, Mobile Forensics, Inc., became one of the most prominent training companies in the United States for mobile forensics, training hundreds of students from law enforcement, Fortune 500 companies, and academia. MFI specialized in instructing its students on how to interpret and analyze mobile device data collected with multiple tools. It was Lee's research that produced discoveries in data formats, date and time configurations, and file system artifacts that are still used in training today. Due to the reputation of MFI, based upon the company's success in research, development, and training in mobile device forensics, MFI became a part of a global software company in 2009. Lee was promoted to Vice President of Mobile Forensics and he created and developed the mobile forensic curriculum and mobile forensic software solution, both of which are still a part of the company's offerings. In 2015, Lee departed the company and became the COO of one of the most recognized mobile forensic software companies in the world, specializing in deep data analysis of mobile device artifacts.

Lee has testified as an expert in mobile forensics in both criminal and civil cases during his 20-year career and consulted for both international and domestic companies requesting mobile forensic assistance, mobile device collections, data analysis, and data interpretation. Due to his aptitude for deep analysis, Lee is frequently called upon to assist in high-profile cases involving data from mobile devices when alien data is encountered. Lee has written more than 50 articles on mobile forensics, has been featured in both national and international magazines and print, and has lectured around the world on mobile forensics and cyber security. This book, *Mobile Forensic Investigations: A Guide to Evidence Collection, Analysis, and Presentation*, is a product of the 20 years spent staring at HEX and ignoring the push button philosophy.

About the Technical Editor

Michael Robinson is a senior cyber threat analyst and digital forensic examiner for a large international company, where he specializes in mobile device forensics, computer forensics, and intrusion analysis. Prior to this role, Michael was a senior digital forensic examiner for customers in the U.S. intelligence community, where he performed computer and cell phone exploitation and analysis. Previously, Michael performed computer forensic examinations in the FBI's Investigative Analysis Unit, where he assisted special agents with counterintelligence and criminal cases. Michael is the former CIO of the U.S. Department of Defense's Business Transformation Agency, where he oversaw all information technology and information assurance operations for the agency, including overseeing all incident response and forensic investigations.

Michael is the Program Coordinator and Adjunct Professor for Stevenson University's Master of Science in Cyber Forensics. At Stevenson, he was the recipient of the Rose Dawson Award for outstanding adjunct faculty member of the year. He is also an adjunct professor in George Mason University's Master of Science in Computer Forensics. He teaches courses in mobile device forensics, intrusion analysis, and cyber warfare. He holds a Bachelor of Science in Chemical Engineering, a Master of Science in Information Assurance, a Master of Science in Forensic Studies (concentrating on computer forensics), and a graduate certificate in Applied Intelligence. Michael has presented at numerous national and international conferences, including DEF CON, the DoD Cyber Crime Conference, U.S. Cyber Crime Conference, CEIC, InfoSec World, and the BCISS Conference on Intelligence Analysis. He has authored more than a dozen journal articles and a book on disaster recovery planning for nonprofit organizations.

Contents at a Glance

Contents

Introduction

Mobile Forensic Investigations: A Guide to Evidence Collection, Analysis, and Presentation is a comprehensive, how-to guide that leads investigators through the process of collecting mobile devices, analyzing the data, and disseminating their findings. This book was created from the many questions received during training courses, lectures, and interviews over many years and a desire to impart the answers to new, seasoned, and advanced digital forensic examiners.

Until now, no direction or guidance has been available to students and practitioners other than a few manuscripts and many vendor-specific training courses. Unfortunately, examiners have been left to figure out mobile forensic procedures and techniques for themselves, and often, at least in the digital forensic circles, mobile forensics is referred to as the "wild west" of digital forensics—just point and click. By trusting only in the automated tool, most examiners today do not fully understand the methods and processes used, so this term often fits. It is the goal of this book to change this mentality and move the examination of a mobile device into today's required standards.

This book is intended not only to educate new students coming into the field or those looking for a career in mobile forensics, but examiners who have been conducting mobile forensics for years. It helps both student and examiner understand what constitutes processes and procedures, how to formulate an examination, how to identify the evidence, and how to collect the various devices, and it culminates with advanced tools and methods the examiner can use to uncover data that most tools forget.

This book can be read from cover to cover, but it can also be used to consult individual chapters during an examination. With the many tables and figures outlining mobile device file systems, targeted files, and digital gold, the student and examiner can use *Mobile Forensic Investigations: A Guide to Evidence Collection, Analysis, and Presentation* for reference during many examinations.

The first two chapters help expose the reader to the world of mobile forensics and clearly define the differences and similarities between mobile forensics and computer forensics. Chapters 3 through 6 outline the steps an examiner should take when coming into contact with mobile device evidence, including how to handle the evidence, and it ends with a discussion on the types of mobile forensic tools and the multitool approach. Next, Chapters 7 and 8 begin the exploration into the first examination by setting up the collection environment and defining what problems can be encountered, along with ways to fix them for both collections and data analysis. The last part of the book in Chapters 9 through 13 is all about the data. This includes determining what type of data should be expected within the various mobile device file systems, what type of data is expected in a standard collection versus an advanced collection, and how to decipher and decode advanced data from iOS, Android, Windows Mobile, and BlackBerry devices. Chapter 14 discusses how to present the data and how to become a mobile forensic device expert. This chapter explains that without proper documentation detailing the process from collection to analysis, the recovered evidence is often confusing and could be inadmissible.

A student or examiner in mobile forensics must be prepared for tomorrow today. *Mobile Forensic Investigations: A Guide to Evidence Collection, Analysis, and Presentation* provides a tremendous start.

1 Introduction to the World of Mobile Device Forensics

In 2014, Cisco's Visual Networking Index (VNI) Global Mobile Data Traffic Forecast Update indicated the number of mobile devices in use exceeded the world's population. Mobile device sales have outpaced PC sales three to one since 2003, as reported in a study conducted by the National Institute of Standards and Technology (NIST). Statistically, the examination of mobile device data should be similar proportionally, but unfortunately this is not the case. In actuality, computer evidence is still more prevalent in civil and criminal cases, but mobile device evidence is on the rise, though not at the rate of induction of the actual devices.

A common theme with mobile forensic experts in both law enforcement and enterprise is the overwhelming inundation of electronic evidence from mobile devices, which is increasing at an alarming rate—so much so that the groups I've surveyed from both law enforcement and corporate organizations indicate they had to hire or assign a specialist who would examine and collect data only from mobile devices. What is truly alarming is the fact most of these examiners also indicated that little consideration is given to the actual content of the mobile device when a computer is also part of the electronic evidence scene. When an American adult spends an average of 34 hours on the Internet using a mobile device, versus only 27 hours using a PC (as reported by Nielson, a global research company), shouldn't a forensics examination reflect that? This mentality is based primarily upon the limited amount of information available on correctly processing, analyzing, and reporting on the data from a mobile device, whereas computer forensics has been time tested and is accepted by examiners and courts across the globe.

The proliferation of mobile devices will only increase with the world's population growth and as this population's dependency on technology accelerates (see Figure 1-1). Now should be the time to accept and understand that the information contained on a mobile device details, documents, and exposes the thoughts, actions, and deeds of a user substantially more than any data stored on a personal computer.

With this unprecedented amount of electronic evidence comes the need for highly skilled mobile device forensics investigators. This book is a comprehensive, how-to guide that leads investigators through the process of collecting mobile devices, analyzing the data found, and disseminating their findings. This holistic approach to mobile device forensics will not only feature the technical approach to data collection and analysis, but it will also explore

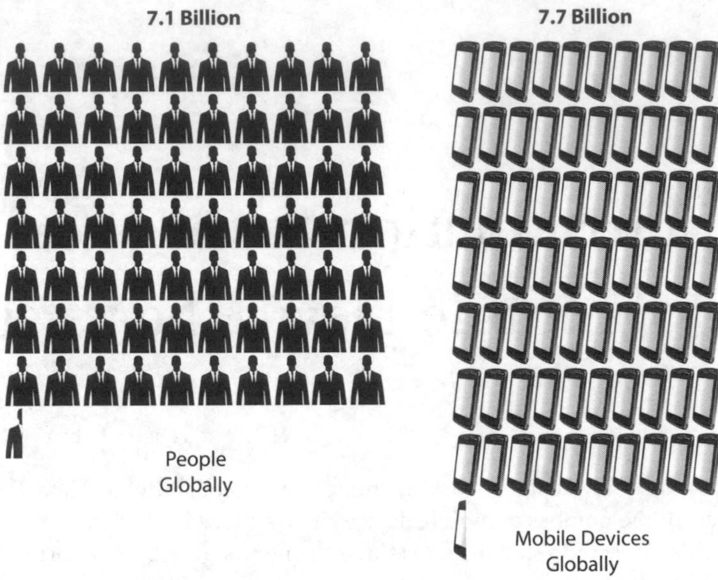

FIGURE 1-1 **There are currently more mobile devices on Earth than people.**

the legal aspects of mobile device forensics. It is widely known that today's digital forensics examinations have been "dumbed" down with a heavy reliance placed on using tools to extract and collect data. These methods have bred a systemic influx of "data collectors," rather than mobile device forensic examiners. This book attempts to counter this trend as it approaches and readies not only the newest examiners, but seasoned digital experts as well, with skills and knowledge that surpass the simple "easy button" approach.

The successful examination of digital evidence from a mobile device requires the intimate understanding of the medium that produced it. This fact is especially important when it comes to the examination of the artifacts left behind by a mobile device. Often the unique aspects of mobile devices are overlooked by examiners and students when encountering these small-scale digital devices because their first impressions are often clouded by the actual size of the device. It is a common belief that the small size of the device implies that it contains only primitive and rudimentary data, which equates to the belief that the examination of the device should be consistent with its physical size. In practice, many believe it should be as easy as inserting a flash drive and hitting the "find evidence" button. However, it is typically due to this tactic that most examiners, and quite honestly the majority of examinations, fail at the critical part of the evidence lifecycle—the dissemination of the facts.

An examiner who must testify to his or her findings will quickly realize that it is not acceptable to testify to the fact that he or she pushed the "get evidence" button and then believe that reasoning/explanation will suffice. An examiner must be ready to answer the question, "Where did the phone book come from?"—and not answer, "From the phone."

The true expert digital forensics witness will be ready to give the location of the phone book's contents as they relate to the phone's file system and to specify how the user data was not altered during the examination. Unfortunately, for most, this is a daunting task because it takes additional training, for which many admit they have neither the time nor the resources. By reading this book, understanding the principles, and, most importantly, working through the various scenarios, your experience as an examiner will have already surpassed the majority of the people conducting mobile device examinations today.

The primary goal of this book is to suggest methods and procedures for the collection and analysis of digital data from a mobile device so that your examination will stand up to the scrutiny of court. This book also aims to dispel the mobile device size myth and to prove that today's mobile devices contain more relevant and transactional data than a personal computer 100 times its size. Armed with a full understanding of the wealth of information available for discovery contained in this book, you will be prepared with not only the knowledge of how to use mobile device forensics tools to conduct investigations, but also with a holistic understanding of how and what these tools are doing.

A Brief History of the Mobile Device

Welcome to the world of mobile device forensics. The examination of data is no different from the examination of the words in any book or manuscript. To understand the words in a book, the reader must have an understanding of the letters that form the words and the words themselves to form a thought or sentence. Without this initial understanding, reading would not be possible. The same goes with understanding a mobile device. To be a truly good forensic practitioner, the examiner must understand the specimen. Before we begin a discussion of mobile forensics, let's begin with a history of the evolution of mobile devices themselves.

Mobile phones for cars and other vehicles preceded the handheld mobile phone and by all accounts were initiated by Bell Labs in 1946 in St. Louis, Missouri. This book will focus on the handheld mobile device that followed a little more than 26 years later.

Martin Cooper

In 1973, Martin Cooper from Motorola began developing a device that would enable a person to walk the streets while making calls without the need for attached wires—a portable handheld mobile phone. On April 3, 1973, Cooper demonstrated the portable phone with a call to Joel Engle of Bell Labs, Motorola's main competitor, to let Engle know he was calling on a portable handheld phone from the streets of New York City. The call was routed via a base station Motorola installed atop the Burlingame House into the AT&T landline telephone system. Cooper had been working on the development of a radio phone for many years. Ten years after he used this device to call his rival, it was brought to the mainstream market. This radio phone employed the same technology used by the military to communicate on the battlefield.

Cooper developed the DynaTAC (DYNamic Adaptive Total Area Coverage) 8000x portable phone, which allowed users to call another portable phone, landline, or radio phone. This device was approved by the U.S. Federal Communications Commission (FCC) on September 21, 1983, and was offered commercially in 1984. It weighed 2.5 pounds, with the battery contributing the majority of the size and weight. The talk time was approximately 20 minutes, and it took approximately 10 hours to charge the device between uses. This first device was, by today's standards, impractical due to its size and weight. Picture the 1980s TV show *Miami Vice* and the main character played by Don Johnson, with white cotton pants and matching jacket, with a large, angular phone and protruding black antenna—that was the DynaTAC 8000x.

The price tag of the device made it extremely impractical for widespread use against the prevalent pager or beeper of the age. When mobile radio devices came to market, prices ranged from U.S. $2000 to 4000, and they seldom worked outside of only a few major markets. The DynaTAC 8000x was priced at $3995.

Despite the introduction of the DynaTAC, car phones continued to be more popular, mainly because of the large mobile phone price tag. By 1984, the car phone was a large device with a very heavy base and typically a curly cord that ran to the handset. These devices had much better transmission and reception rates because of the constant battery power that exceeded the current ranges of the DynaTAC. Car phones were typically mounted and hardwired in vehicles and looked like a normal kitchen phone of the day. Users wanted phones that were more portable, however, so manufacturers began making the devices capable of being removed from the vehicle. The *bag phone* was born. ("Bag phone" was not the official name, but it stuck simply because the device could be carried in a zippered bag.) Impractical and extremely heavy, this device was not around for long. Who is to say what the impact of the electrical radiation might be?

Size Evolution

Shortly after the DynaTAC, cellular devices began to be manufactured in smaller form factors. In 1989, the Motorola MicroTAC was released. This device was much smaller than the DynaTAC series but still large and expensive enough that mainstream consumers were not buying. It was not until 1996 when the StarTAC series entered the market that things changed. The first cell phone to make a sizable impact with consumers was the full clamshell feature phone, which could be carried around in a pocket or small purse. The price point for the Motorola StarTAC was $1000. Because these portable devices only made and received calls, the price tag versus necessity was still out of reach for most consumers, however, so the progression away from the landline to the cell phone was not immediate.

The price for the mobile device started to drop when the technology, components, competition, and assembly became cheaper. In the mid to late 1990s, there was a shift to make the smallest device possible, but in the early 2000s, the size paradigm started to shift the other way. Today, consumers are speaking into mobile devices the size of small laptops, conveniently termed "phablet" for phone tablet. What has become important is the type and amount of data that can be transmitted, as well as what components are inside.

Data Evolution

Cell phone users quickly saw the need to send messages that they could type into a QWERTY keyboard or pound down the keys in a series of taps instead of speaking to someone. From this need, Short Message Service (SMS) was born. Limited to 140 characters, SMS enabled users to express themselves via a short sentence to other mobile device users. Today, 140 characters is still the limit. Concatenated SMS, or what some call Protocol Data Unit (PDU) mode SMS, is more widely used and provides 160 characters by changing from using 8 bits per character to 7. This was a significant advancement that moved the pager away from the businessman's belt loop and to the eventual demise of this type of communication service. The cell phone soon advanced away from the simple walkie-talkie. Mobile device users next needed storage for these text-based messages, and soon for pictures, videos, calendars, and e-mails as well—who would have foreseen the application revolution?

Note The walkie-talkie, invented by Donald L. Hings, was first used as a portable field radio for pilots flying around Canada. In 1937, when the first walkie-talkie was built, Hings referred to the device as a "two-way radio," and it has been used ever since.

Storage Evolution

Most of the original mobile phones did not contain a media type that would support the storage of data, because most were engineered to use the space as a scratch pad to run the needed process, remove the process, and move to the next process. Storage of *nonvolatile* data, or data that would continue to exist without constant power, onto a device's memory chip was not possible initially. This meant that any data that was visible on the device would not be stored, and as soon as the device was shut down, all the data disappeared. Because initially the mobile phone was used only to make and receive calls, this was not observed as a limitation.

Because of this, no phone book storage or any other settings could be maintained. The first cell phones were merely a block of circuitry that had the same combinations of buttons included on the well-known landline. The functionality was the same—attempt to recall the number of a contact from memory and key in the number (think about that—having to remember all of those phone numbers).When TDMA (Time Division Multiple Access) devices in the United States began to transition to GSM (Global Systems for Mobile Communications), which had already arrived in Europe, device information such as a phone book and SMS could be stored onto the SIM (Subscriber Identity Module). Storage areas for contacts, SMS, and last numbers dialed had already been built into the SIM standards developed by the ETSI (European Telecommunications Standards Institute), where this data could be written to and stored to the smart chip.

Since SIM cards were already storing phone data that was used in the authentication process, why not add values that stored the contacts, SMS, and last numbers dialed? The SIM card was already being used in the device as a "key" to the cellular network, assisting in the authentication of the device using stored values. TDMA devices could store a set number of contacts that users could look up and select to be dialed, plus a limited number of SMS (15–25 typically; that's it!) that could be reread, even if the device was shut off. Other carriers that did not have SIM cards started to develop devices that used nonvolatile memory so data could be stored and saved even if the device was turned off completely or the battery was removed or drained. The older feature phones used an acronym—*nvm*, for nonvolatile memory—to designate this type of data within their file systems and prefix the file and/or folder name.

This was where data was actually written to the phone and the start to the recovery of a goldmine of data.

Volatile Memory and the Visor PDA

A great example of volatile memory and mobile devices is the Visor personal digital assistant (PDA). With the technology of all PDAs at the time, most had a whopping 8MB of RAM and did not store data for long if no power was supplied.

On to the story.

A Visor seized in a search warrant was brought in for examination. The power cradle had been left at the scene, and it was a Friday, so the device was going to have to sit in the evidence locker until the following Monday. Upon arriving back at the lab on Monday, the examiner tried to start the device, but it was immediately apparent that the device had lost all power—it would not boot up. A power cradle was located for the device at a local store and the device was charged. When there was significant power to the device, the examination continued. To the dismay of the examiner, there was nothing on the device—no user content anywhere. What was puzzling was the fact that a substantial amount of data *had* existed on the device and was outlined and documented by the officers who seized it. Had someone broke into the lab over the weekend and deleted the data from the device? Had the officer somehow deleted the data or caused it to self-destruct?

The Visor documentation was consulted, as well as manufacturer's documentation, which indicated that PDAs drew constant power to keep the data on the devices populated. If the device was allowed to be completely drained of power, the data would no longer be available. Because the data resided in the device's RAM, the data was volatile, and, as such, when power was lost, the data stored in RAM was also lost. It was a hard lesson to learn but a great example of the limitations of volatile memory.

Moving forward, all devices had to have their power maintained, if possible, and most training courses on mobile forensics began to preach this lesson as well. Instruction on the use of portable charging units during transport as well as during storage began to be included in training courses and digital forensic examination kits.

Mobile Device Data: The Relevance Today

Mobile devices have come a long way since their inception. Data contained on a mobile device can now be compared to the written notes of a daily diary (often with pictures and videos), containing a company's most secure documents, our financial status, and most importantly our everyday habits, patterns, and routines. If a picture of an individual were painted with the personal data recovered from a PC, the picture would be a blurry representation with no clear edges. If, however, the data recovered from a mobile device were examined, it would most likely paint a very personal, and potentially embarrassing, picture of the individual.

Mobile Devices in the Media

Every day, the world media reports cases solved using evidence from mobile devices or a how a mobile device was involved in a crime—either a text message or chat was sent or received; a social media post was sent or interpreted; or a voicemail was heard, recorded, or hacked. In 2014, the Pew Research Center reported that 90 percent of U.S. adults owned a cellular phone, which translates to about 135 million cell phone users. It is no wonder that law enforcement digital examiners are looking to these devices as an evidence treasure trove. Mobile device data is today's equivalent to yesterday's DNA evidence.

One day, a mobile device that shows up in the lab or in the field may hold data that has never been seen by the world—the grassy knoll, the shot heard 'round the world, the missing plane's last communication, and the smoking gun. Quite simply, you can fill in the blank to determine what a mobile device might be involved in when contemplating the events of today.

Digital data from a mobile device holds the key. To the forensic examiner, this data is critical in many investigations. The following story, "Mobile Devices on the Scene," details the relevance of data on a mobile device and how its recovery is critical.

Mobile Devices on the Scene

In 2009, a fight was reported on a congested Bay Area Rapid Transit train platform. After officers responded to the scene, an officer shot one of the subjects, who later died at a nearby hospital. At the time, there were no news crews on the scene or closed-circuit television cameras in the area. What *was* on the scene were multiple people with cell phones, who captured the event both in still and video formats. These videos were uploaded and disseminated to media outlets and the Web. It is reported that the raw video of the event was downloaded more than 500,000 times in a single week! Videos from the cell phones taken from many different angles were critical to the case. The videos were irrefutable evidence of the transpiring events—a police officer was subduing an individual at the train platform, shots were fired, and the account of what happened was clear. The individual who was being subdued was shot as onlookers watched. What is different about this case is that it was not a witness's perception of the event, but the actual event caught on video in real time. Six videos were known to exist prior to the case and were subsequently used in the court cases. By all accounts, the videos from the mobile devices were critical evidence used by both prosecutors and the defense during testimony at the criminal trial, but also the civil trial.

The stories of eyewitness accounts captured with a mobile device are endless. In a traditional investigation, investigators would have to rely on an actual person recalling the event—which, as most know, can be susceptible to many different perceptions, views, and beliefs. The always on, always ready, and always filming video camera in today's mobile device has revolutionized and forever changed what an eyewitness is and will ever be.

The Overuse of the Word "Forensic"

NIST describes "forensic science" as "the application of science to the law." Forensics can include the scientific examination of fossils, a crime scene, metals, vehicles, post-mortem bodies, and of course, digital data that can be in many different forms. Digital examiners get lost in this meaning and sometimes interpret forensic science to indicate that a software application or a hardware device is forensically sound. But according to the NIST definition, the use of the tools by the examiner in a way conforming to known scientific processes and procedures is the forensic science, not the tool itself. A perfect example is the use of a write blocker when processing digital data.

Write Blockers and Mobile Devices

NIST and its Computer Forensic Tool Testing Program specifically states that the central requirement of a proper forensic procedure is that the examined original evidence must not be changed or modified in any way. One of NIST's listed requirements for a layered defense is to use a hard disk write-blocker tool to intercept any inadvertent disk writes.

Note Many different kinds of write-blocking equipment have been created by many different companies. Any mention of a specific unit here is not an endorsement of the tool; it simply indicates that the tool was used in the case or test.

A *write blocker* is a software or hardware device that stops specific communication from a computer to a mass storage device. Write blockers come in many different types. Software-based write blockers can use a simple Windows Registry change; hardware units are sophisticated boxes that are coupled to the examination computer via cables and the device to be examined attached to the other side. Some allow a connection directly to the pins located on the actual hard drive and then to the computer conducting the forensic analysis, while others have USB connections to plug a removable USB hard drive or flash drive into an available port.

Hardware tools can be used to protect disk access through the interrupt 13 BIOS interface of a PC. Because the mass storage device is attached to the hardware write blocker, all input and output (I/O) commands sent from the PC are monitored. Any commands that could modify the hard drive are not passed onto the hard drive, but intercepted by the write-blocking device. Software write-blocking tools also block the writing to attached drives plugged into the USB drive, mounted drives, and by device classes, if needed. This can be changed by editing the Registry of the Windows PC or using many of the available software tools.

Essentially, the write blocker acts as a traffic signal to data requests made by the computer. The computer makes requests to receive data from the connected device, which are accepted and processed; if a request to write data to the protected device on the other side of the write protector is made, these requests are stopped and not allowed to reach the device. The write-blocking hardware or software tool is not considered forensically sound, but the employment of the device and methods as part of the process is. To test this theory, obtain any write-protecting hardware device and attach a mobile device; then follow along with the example in "Real-World Example: Testing the Theory."

Real-World Example: Testing the Theory

This research example was conducted while I was preparing for testimony on a mobile device case in which a computer forensics expert was challenging the lack of usage of a write blocker when conducting an examination of a mobile device.

Using a Tableau USB write blocker and a Motorola Razor V3 mobile device, I began the experiment. The object of the research was to test my theory on write-protection devices and mobile devices. My theory was that since a mobile device is not observed by a PC's operating system as a mass storage device, the Tableau USB write blocker would not stop writes targeting the mobile device. (Note that this is not a limitation of the Tableau USB write-blocker product. This product, as well as all others, will operate the same as outlined in this example.)

I plugged the mobile device into the USB port of the Tableau write-blocking device. I then plugged the USB write blocker into a USB port located in the PC running Microsoft Windows.

The Tableau device immediately identified the device in the digital readout: "Motorola." Using P2K Commander, a free tool for browsing a Motorola PK device, the device's file system was read into the software. The entire device's file system was available. With the options in P2K Commander, I created a new folder within the device's file system. Since a write protector was in place, it would seem plausible that the folder would not be created. Unfortunately, however, the folder was created in the device's file system.

With the write-protector device still in place, I copied a file called *WriteProtector.txt* into the device file system and into the folder that I had created. The file showed that it was successfully transferred. I then shut down the software and collected data from the device using AccessData MPE+. The file system, as expected, contained the folder and the file that I had previously moved onto the phone with P2K Commander while the write protector was in place.

What did this mean for the write blocker used in this test? Did this mean that the write blocker did not operate as it should? Did this mean the test was not forensically sound? Of course not, but you must understand that these devices protect for writes only to mass storage devices, not devices viewed as something else by the computer's hardware. Because the Motorola was viewed as a modem, the connected computer could write any data it wanted to the attached media because writes to the modem were not halted.

As an examiner entering this field, you need to understand that the process you use to examine the mobile device and comprehend what has changed on the device is what makes the examination forensic. It is neither the software nor the hardware you use, but solely the process that you use during examination that makes it truly forensic. This concept applies not just to mobile device examinations, but also to the examination of all digital data in today's electronically driven world.

Mobile Device Technology and Mobile Forensics

Mobile device forensics is likely the most rapidly advancing discipline that digital forensics has ever seen or ever will see, primarily because of the rapidly changing environment of the actual devices. Device operating systems have become more advanced, and the storage capacity on the current devices is astronomical. Today's devices are mobile computing platforms, but accessing the data contained on these devices is much more difficult than accessing data from any other digital device. Communication to these devices with software is much different from communicating with other mediums containing digital data. Users must use tools specifically designed for mobile devices, and they use many different software tools on one device. This brings a new wrinkle in the examination process. A lot of seasoned digital forensic examiners are disappointed and turned off by the limitations imposed by software to these mobile devices, believing that mobile devices should behave like a computer's hard drive. Also, many mobile device forensic software products have their roots in the sync software world and not in the forensics world. This does not help their credibility with examiners coming from the computer forensic lineage.

From Data Transfer to Data Forensics

Mobile sync software enables the user to add or delete items such as contacts and calendars from a mobile device. This is extremely satisfying to the standard mobile device owner, because it allows the easy addition of hundreds of contacts and contact details. No longer does the user have to key in every contact via the keypad; now, with the assistance of PC software and a cable, this information can be quickly added to the device.

Adding and deleting user data would never be something a forensic examiner would desire, a fact that was realized by companies developing sync/data transfer software. So these companies began to create models and versions that were intended for the forensic examiner. The software and hardware were no different from the sync software, with one exception: The write/transfer button or selection was not enabled. These devices and applications simply allowed the data to be read from the device, not written to it. Sometimes the forensics updates involved a removal of a button, and sometimes it was merely adding new instructions in the manual. The underlying code base in the equipment or software was the same; only the implementation was different—along with the MSRP.

Field Note: From Commercial Tool to Forensic Tool

This story was passed along to me when I first started training examiners in the mobile forensics world as I began researching emerging software.

While I was training law enforcement officers in early 2007 on tools such as Cell Seizure; Data Pilot; and free programs such as BitPim, Oxygen Nokia Phone Suite, and SIMCon, a student retold a story of two people who worked at a nonprofit company who ventured into a cellular telco store and saw a black box that was communicating with a phone and transferring the data to an SD card. They had previously seen this device at a trade show for electronics and law enforcement and asked the company if they could try it out. The nonprofit had trained law enforcement officers on digital forensic examinations and conducted mobile device collection research, and the employees believed this tool might assist law enforcement. But the nonprofit employees had been turned away, so they purchased the same unit that they had seen used in the telco store.

This is how the device worked: The customer's old mobile phone data needed to be transferred to the new purchased mobile device. So the old phone was connected and the data was copied to an SD card. The new phone was then connected and the data from the SD card was transferred to the new phone. It later progressed to attaching one phone to the left and another to the right and moving the data from one to the other. This enabled a user to come into the store with an old device and transfer contacts, call logs, and anything else to the new phone. Law enforcement officers were interested in the technology because they had been conducting data recovery from mobile devices, and the ease of use was captivating. By word of mouth, more law enforcement officers started purchasing the data transfer version as used in the store. Soon the device manufacturer realized the demand and interest, and using new ideas from the officers, began to manufacture a new forensic model of the tool. This model was nearly the same tool used by the telco to transfer data between phones, but now the device transferred data from a device to a removable USB stick and the term *forensic* was assigned.

Shortly thereafter, many other companies began designing forensic versions of their data transfer software. Companies such as Cellebrite, Compelson, Oxygen, and Susteen all migrated to the forensic software business from their initial start in the phone data transfer market. It has been said that Compelson began to manufacture MOBILedit Forensic based on its data transfer software MOBILedit prior to any of the other companies.

Processes and Procedures

If automated tools will be used in any forensic examination of digital data, examiners must have a set of processes and procedures in place; using an automated tool without such direction could be a detriment to the entire process. An understanding of the processes and procedures of mobile device forensics is required in this age of mobile computing because of the many automated tools, variances of each, lack of complete coverage, and diverse training levels. Ultimately, understanding the processes and the steps needed, interpreting results, analyzing output, and documenting the data, all while maintaining case integrity, should be the goal.

People use mobile devices every day to buy groceries, send birthday wishes, break up with a lover, transfer millions of dollars, and unfortunately commit crimes. Gaining an intimate knowledge of how to collect valuable data from these devices, uncover valuable data, and present the data will put you ahead of the rest. Chapter 2 will discuss how to compile standard operating procedures for collecting the physical mobile devices and accessing data on those devices. Your understanding of the device and the progression into the actual digital investigation is critical for a successful outcome.

Examination Awareness and Progression

When mobile devices contained volatile data storage, the only examination of the mobile device consisted of removing the SIM card and reading the information stored on it. This made for a quick examination of the smart chip, and the device was seldom examined forensically. So essentially the first introduction anyone had to the examination of a mobile device started at the SIM card. The first software for mobile device collection also read the data from a SIM card. (In Chapter 8, you will be shown the various collection methods and software used for SIM cards.) As mobile devices advanced in terms of how data was stored, the methods used to collect the data from the internal memory, or nonvolatile area, did not progress in tandem.

The awareness of the data was there, but collecting it by means other than scrolling through the device and documenting the information was extremely limited. The first examinations of data by law enforcement on a Motorola StarTAC or Nokia 1610 Plus involved simply turning on the device after reading the data from the SIM, scrolling through the menus, and writing by hand the calls made and received and the contact information. This information was then transferred to a report, and the first mobile device examination was out the door. This worked well, since the devices held a limited number of calls and contacts, but imagine using this process with a mobile device of today! Imagine documenting 5000 contacts into a spreadsheet by hand, including all the associated e-mail addresses, phone numbers, and addresses, not to mention scrolling through the "selfies."

Cameras eventually began to play a role in the documentation of data for mobile devices. Important SMS messages, images, or contacts could be documented using a webcam or digital camera. These images were then placed into a report for review. Several companies built systems to allow the examiner to lay out the evidence, document the size, and more.

Soon the examination progressed to using software as a few software applications became available. The early mobile device software applications used in the examinations of cell phones were developed by engineers to deal with their own personal mobile device problems—such as how a phone book could be saved, edited, changed, modified, and exported without having to use the phone's dial pad to reenter information.

Software applications such as BitPim, initially developed by Roger Binns, is a perfect example. Binns created an application that would allow him to transfer data, primarily his contacts, from an old phone to a new phone. He explained that it had been extremely tedious to add contacts, get pictures, and move information on and off an LG phone, so he decided to write an application to make it easier, and BitPim was born. At first, BitPim allowed data to be written and read from the cell phones supported, which was forensically sound. At the time, Binns had not seen the need to allow only data to be read, but soon he was contacted by a mobile forensic examiner and asked if he would allow users to turn off the ability to write data to the phone. BitPim software was being used in Mobile Forensic, Inc., courses and primarily for law enforcement officers, so Binns kindly accepted the reasoning and soon he added a Block Writing Anything To The Phone checkbox to the settings, as shown in the following illustration. BitPim was limited mostly to CDMA devices, but because protocols were based upon the Qualcomm chipset, some Samsung GSM devices could be supported as well. GSM devices, however, were never officially supported by BitPim, and the software's last official build was on January 24, 2010.

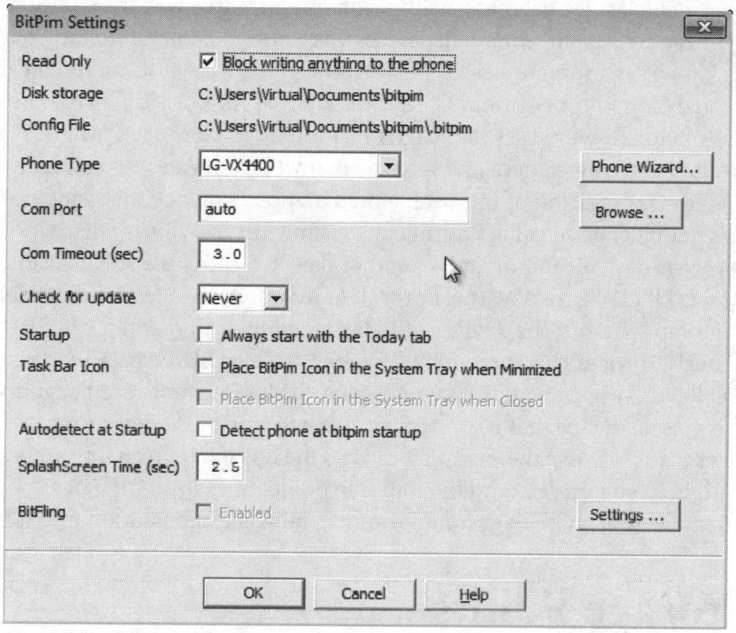

More and more developers began to contribute, and more and more devices were added. More applications from actual cell phone manufacturers such Nokia and Samsung were developed for the transfer of user contacts, SMS, and more. These proprietary software suites began to be used regularly by law enforcement officers to perform extractions and collections so they did not have to go "commando style" on a cell phone to get the information manually. Applications such as Paraben Cell Seizure, TULP2G, SIMCon, and MOBILedit began to be used in training courses and forensic labs around the world. These applications gathered data from mobile devices by using the same protocols reverse-engineered from tools such as Nokia Suite and Samsung PC Suite. Today, as in the beginning, the same problem exists: not all mobile devices are supported by a single solution. There is not and will not be a single solution to extract and collect data from all mobile devices, simply because there are too many devices and new devices are being added and changed continuously.

Tip Using multiple tools to examine digital data from a mobile device should never be observed as poor practice. Quite the opposite, using multiple tools will allow not only verification of data, but more importantly, it enables you to uncover additional data the initial tool either did not support or simply missed.

Examiners at this point in the mobile forensic timeline had two types of evidence to process: a SIM card and the mobile device. Sometimes the only data that could be collected from a mobile device came from a SIM card. There were, and still are, many variables to be considered: Did the actual device even have a connection to communicate with the software? Did the device store data internally? More importantly, was the device even supported? At this time, a new trend emerged; devices were now capable of holding data on a removable card, known as a memory card. Yes, the first cards were not microSD cards, but large PCMIA (Personal Computer Memory Card International Association) cards primarily used for PCs. These obviously were very large, so transitioning to CompactFlash (CF) cards moved them from the PC to the camera and into the many PDA devices for storage.

With the addition of removable media, mobile device forensics expanded to three pieces of evidence to collect during any examination. (This is where mobile device evidence types are today, but tomorrow is another day.) CF cards are still available, but the Secure Digital (SD) cards are now most prevalent in mobile devices. These small SD cards range in storage capacity, but the devices of today are limited to reading 128GB—on a single SD card! Obviously, devices can contain multiple SD cards or SIM cards, but the items to be examined and collected will remain the same: device, SIM, removable media, and sometimes a backup of the mobile device that is located on another type of media, such as a PC. Today's mobile devices primarily use the microSD card as the de facto external storage medium.

To help you understand the multiple points of examination of a mobile device, let's take a general look at these data storage points and what information might be stored on each.

Data Storage Points

With multiple places to store data, the examination of mobile devices has become more advanced as the years have progressed, much like the cellular technologies (see Figure 1-2). It is important that you understand the various terms that will be used before you read more about using storage points for evidence.

Mobile Technology Acronyms

Acronyms are used throughout the book and also in most digital forensic reference materials. Technological terms, reference documents, and government agencies all use acronyms, and the following list includes the most prevalent terms in the industry. Some terms describe cellular network functions and transmission techniques.

The following provides an overview, rather than a complete, detailed description. There are entire books describing these transmission methods in great detail. This book is intended to expose these terms generally, so, if needed, you can conduct further research on your own.

AMPS/NMT/TACS

In the 1980s, the Advanced Mobile Phone System (AMPS) was the analog standard used in the United States, Nordic Mobile Telephone (NMT) was the analog standard in the Nordic countries, and Total Access Communications Systems (TACS) was the analog standard in the

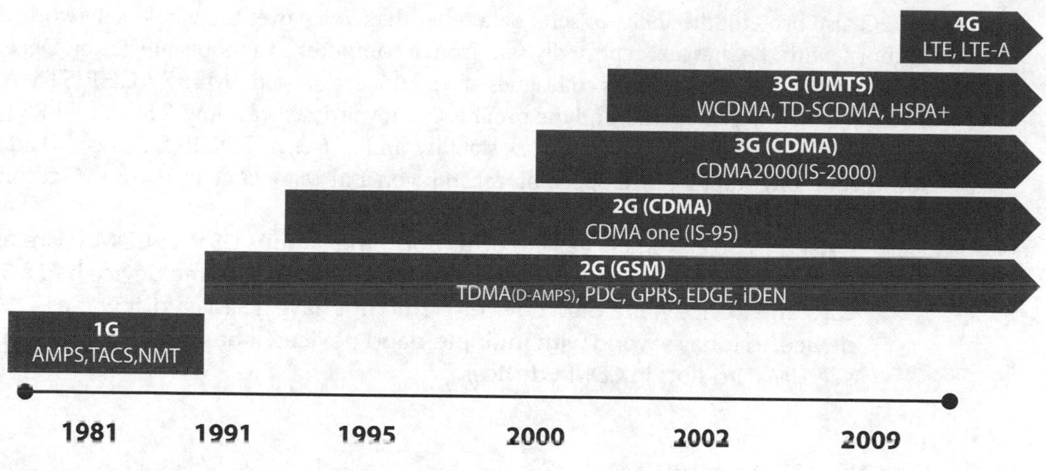

FIGURE 1-2 **The cellular generational timeline represents the various transitions in technology related to mobile devices from 1G to our current LTE-A.**

United Kingdom. Analog transmissions operated in the 800MHz band between the frequencies of 824MHz and 894MHz in the United States, 450MHz and 900MHz in the Nordic countries, and in the 900MHz range for Europe. The transmission and the reception of the data ranged from 20kHz to 50kHz so transmissions did not collide. Obviously, with the limited number of devices that could operate simultaneously, it was easy to listen to conversations on radio devices tuned to the same frequency. This technology was later termed 1G, for first-generation, cell phone transmission technology.

Governing bodies for mobile device transmission understood that additional data should be included in the transmission, such as text messages, while also allowing for more mobile devices to use the same frequency channel. For this reason, analog would need to transition to digital data. Mobile devices purchased for use that were labeled single band indicated that the device could use only a single cellular band. Because of the varying frequency differences among countries, the device might not work in another country if the cellular band was not the frequency band within which the device was capable of operating. Because of this limitation, device manufacturers began to add hardware capabilities to allow for multiband frequency support, moving first to dual-band, then tri-band, and eventually quad-band support.

TDMA/GSM/CDMA

TDMA and Code Division Multiple Access (CDMA) are 2G (second-generation) technologies, and devices entered the handheld wireless scene in the 1990s. The main standards for 2G are GSM, Interim Standard 95 (IS-95) (CDMA), IS-136 (digital amps), and iDEN (Integrated Digital Enhanced Network). The biggest change was from analog to digital with the advent of 2G systems, along with digital encryption of the transmission. The first commercial 2G network on the GSM network was first made available by Radiolinja, a Finnish operator.

2G also brought the ability to send data other than voice over the wireless network; SMS was born, with the first text reportedly sent from a computer to a mobile device on December 3, 1992, from Neil Papworth to his colleagues at Vodafone, that said, "MERRY CHRISTMAS." 2G technologies slowly improved, and the progression toward 3G was slow. 2.5G, or GPRS (General Packet Radio Service), improved network stability, and 2.75G, or EDGE (Enhanced Data rates for GSM Evolution), improved the speed of transmission and was a large leap from 2G technologies.

Note It used to be extremely easy to distinguish the various GSM or CDMA wireless companies simply by looking under the device battery. If the device had a SIM card, the device was a GSM device; if it did not have a SIM card, it was a CDMA device. In today's world with multiple-band devices, it has become common to see SIM card slots in CDMA devices.

UMTS/CDMA2000

Universal Mobile Telecommunications System (UMTS) and IS-2000 (CDMA2000) are the 3G, or third-generation, cellular systems established by specifications outlined in IMT-2000 (International Mobile Telecommunications), which introduced large gains with Internet access and video and data streaming in the early 2000s. The Third Generation Partnership Project (3GPP) standardized UMTS, and 3GPP2 (Third Generation Partnership Project 2) standardized CDMA2000. UMTS uses W-CDMA (wide-band CDMA) for transmission and CDMA2000 using EV-DO (Evolution–Data Optimized). UMTS was used with GSM devices in Europe, China, Japan, and most other areas of the world, while CDMA2000 and CDMA devices were used primarily in North America and South Korea.

UMTS upgraded to HSDPA (High-Speed Downlink Packet Access) and was combined with HSUPA (High-Speed Uplink Packet Access) to form HSPA (High-Speed Packet Access), which is still the most widely deployed technology globally. What might be referred to as 3.5G is debated as HSPA+ and also LTE (Long Term Evolution). LTE is often mentioned with regard to 4G technologies, but the data upload and download rates do not meet the standards set forth by the ITU (International Telecommunication Union) to call it 4G. The first commercial LTE networks were launched in Norway and Sweden in 2009.

LTE-Advanced

LTE-Advanced (LTE-A) is also defined by the ITU, and it is a true 4G system. LTE-A was standardized in 2010 by the 3GPP and is dependent not only on the infrastructure of the underlying cellular network, but also on the processors within the mobile devices.

Mobile Device

The mobile device evolved from a simple handheld device to communicate via voice into a mobile computing device capable of transmitting large amounts of data instantly. The movement in technologies and the air-side of the network was never intended to create a clearer conversation, but to increase how much information one could send or receive in the shortest amount of time.

A mobile device can contain many pieces of information—from devices that stored contacts, SMS, and call logs in the first years, to today's devices that are actually small computing devices containing any type of digital data—from documents, media, SMS, MMS, call logs, e-mail, calendar, notes, and contacts to actual applications. These built-in applications can store additional data types, communicate with the Internet, launch rockets, play music, map a house, direct a vehicle to a destination, know internal body vitals, and conduct bank transactions. There is almost nothing that a person cannot do with these smart devices—including activities that only 10 years ago required devices thousands of times their size. Today's current smart devices come with standard applications, but a user can also install one of a million applications available on various mobile phone application distribution points, which makes a "standard examination" of the contents of mobile devices a nearly impossible exercise.

Mobile devices come in all shapes and sizes and have progressed from holding circuits to more than 128GB of storage space. What is most important for the mobile device forensic examiner is the underlying operating system. Knowing the type of operating system will help you determine the course of action you should take in the examination. Knowing this will also determine the actual software that you should use to complete the collection. As you read through this book, you'll read more about these devices, and it will become apparent that your examination should start with an understanding of various types of evidence.

SIM

Subscriber identity modules, or SIM cards, were developed to enable portability and, more importantly, to store information to enable authentication on the cellular network. *Authentication* in this sense meant that the device could register and allow users to make and receive calls. With the SIM card acting as the key to the network, a user could switch equipment by removing the small smart chip and inserting it in a different GSM device. As SIM cards began to allow the storage of user data such as contacts, SIM removal also meant that users could take their contacts with them to the new device. When the SIM card was inserted into the new device, the user could access contacts and make and receive calls. Storage on the SIM card made it easy to move from one device to another. Along with contacts, SMS were also stored, as were the last numbers dialed.

All data types on a SIM card are not infinite, and the amount of data that can be stored is a static value determined by GSM standards. As outlined in the initial documents by ETSI (European Telecommunications Standards Institute) and later adopted by 3GPP, the "Technical Specification Group Terminals Specification of the Subscriber Identity Module" outlines the type of data along with how many records can be stored for each type of data. The SIM cards in today's GSM and CDMA devices are called UICCs (Universal Integrated Circuit Cards) and assist in the operation of the UMTS, HSPA, and LTE systems.

Some say, incorrectly, that a SIM card is the same as a USIM (Universal Subscriber Identity Module) card. Although technically SIM cards are physical cards that operate only on 2G GSM systems, a USIM is an application on the UICC. The USIM application enables the mobile device to be identified on the UMTS, HSPA, and LTE systems. UICCs also contain a SIM application that allows for backward-compatibility to the 2G networks and may also contain another application called the CSIM (CDMA SIM), which allows access to CDMA networks and an application called ISIM (IP-multimedia Subsystem Subscriber Identity

Module). The ISIM allows for secure use of the Internet Protocol multimedia subsystem and is the backbone of the LTE network. This means support for voice over IP (VoIP), SMS, and emergency calls without a network can occur securely.

Note Earlier CDMA SIM cards were called R-UIM (removable user identify module) cards and contained a primitive version of the CSIM application and a SIM application for GSM.

Like the SIM, the UICC also allows for the storage of contacts, SMS, and other user histories. What has not changed from the SIM to the UICC or USIM application is the ability to store more SMS messages or more call detail data. The reason behind that has to do with the understanding that today's devices default to storing data to the handset, not the SIM card. Along with the velocity and volume of this data, this is not likely to change. In Chapter 7, you can read about the actual structure and the evidence locations for specific UICC data.

Media Storage Cards

SD cards were created in an effort to expand the available storage for mobile devices. SD cards are of four different types: Standard-Capacity (SDSC), High-Capacity (SDHC), Extended-Capacity (SDXC), and a newer type not used currently with mobile devices, called Input-Output (SDIO). These four types come in three different form factors: the original, which measures 32-by-24 mm; the mini, which measures 21.5-by-20 mm; and the micro, which measures 11-by-15 mm.

Tip External micro-sized SD cards typically come with an adapter that enables the cards to be read using a standard-size SD card reader. Important to remember is that most SD card full-size adapters have a "lock" that disables writes to the SD card media. When processing these storage mediums, you must set the card to locked to enable the write-protection feature built into the card.

Today, mobile device equipment often contains a slot to accommodate a small storage card that stores saved images, videos, or other media, but can also store documents, applications, and more. Important to remember is the fact that external media cards are another form of evidence. In the early years of mobile devices, external media cards were sized at 256 to 512MB. The most prevalent type and form factor used in today's devices are the original and microSDHC cards. The SDHC standard, released in 2006, supports a total capacity of 32GB and the micro size is the most prevalent type of card with mobile devices. The SDXC, released in 2009, supports up to 2TB of data by using Microsoft's exFAT (Extended File Allocation Table) file system, and some current mobile devices support these cards in the micro size up to 128GB.

Note To grasp just how much data can be stored in a gigabyte, let's discuss just what a gigabyte is. A gigabyte is equivalent to a device's ability to store 10,000 one-page documents in the Times New Roman font, 12-point, single-spaced; 520,000 text messages; 1074 regular sized photos; and approximately 250 songs that are each

4 minutes in length. With the sheer volume of data that can be stored on media smaller than a postage stamp, it becomes apparent that omitting this type of evidence from your mobile forensic exam could be catastrophic.

Many new devices, especially those running the Android operating system, also have internal microSDHC and SDXC cards soldered to the internal circuitry to add internal storage capacity. This is an inexpensive way to expand the capacity of a device. Understanding and recognizing that a device has internal microSD storage is very important during your digital exam. This internal storage is in the range of 16GB, which can hold an astronomical amount of data. More devices today contain both internal and external microSD cards. During a proper examination, if possible, you should collect and analyze both storage locations.

Tip To determine if a device contains both internal and external SD card components, research the device before starting your examination. This information can be obtained from web sites covered in the coming chapters.

Mobile Device Backups

The last type of associated data for mobile devices is the backup that some devices create on media such as PCs, MACs, and other operating systems. Devices are now also using the Cloud to store backups. Devices such as Apple iPhone and iPad and the new BlackBerry create backups that can later be analyzed. Apple iOS devices create a backup using the Apple software iTunes. These backups can be found in different locations depending on the type of computer operating system and version.

For Windows computers, the backup default location for an Apple iOS device will depend on the operating system version.

- **Windows XP** \Documents and Settings\<*username*>\Application Data\Apple Computer \MobileSync\Backup\
- **Windows Vista, Windows 7 and 8** \Users\<*username*>\AppData\Roaming\Apple Computer\MobileSync\Backup\
- **Mac** ~/Library/Application Support/MobileSync/Backup/

These areas contain valuable data and can also contain multiple backups of the same device. For an iOS device, the data that is typically backed up as outlined by Apple in the support wiki (http://support.apple.com/en-us/HT4946) is listed here:

- Camera Roll photos, screenshots, images saved, and videos; for devices without a camera, Camera Roll is called Saved Photos
- Contacts and Contact Favorites
- Calendar accounts and subscribed calendars
- Calendar events
- Safari bookmarks, cookies, history, offline data, and currently open pages
- Autofill for web pages

- Offline web app cache/database
- Notes
- Mail accounts (mail messages aren't backed up)
- Microsoft Exchange account configurations
- Call history
- Messages (iMessage and carrier SMS or MMS pictures and videos)
- Voicemail token (This is not the voicemail password, but it is used for validation when connecting; restored only to a phone with the same phone number on the SIM card)
- Voice memos
- Network settings (saved Wi-Fi hotspots, VPN settings, and network preferences)
- Keychain (includes e-mail account passwords, Wi-Fi passwords, and passwords entered into web sites and some apps)
- App Store app data (except the app itself, its tmp, and Caches folder)
- App settings, preferences, and data, including documents
- In-app purchases
- Game Center account
- Wallpapers
- Location service preferences for apps and web sites you've allowed to use your location
- Home screen arrangement
- Installed profiles
- Map bookmarks, recent searches, and the current location displayed in Maps
- Nike + iPod saved workouts and settings
- Paired Bluetooth devices (only if restored to the same phone that did the backup)
- Keyboard shortcuts and saved suggestion corrections
- Trusted hosts that have certificates that cannot be verified
- Web clips

Note A series of files and folders are created for the iOS device backups at these storage positions. If the user has elected to encrypt backups via the iTunes interface, the backups will not be readable unless the iTunes password is known.

BlackBerry also creates backups using the BlackBerry Desktop Management software, or Link as it is known today for some new BlackBerry devices. These backups are also located in a default location.

- **Windows** My Documents\BlackBerry\Backup
- **Mac** /Users/<*name*>/Documents/BlackBerry Backups

Note A user can always change the backup location using the BlackBerry Backup Software.

Depending on the version of BlackBerry software that was used to create the backup, the file will either have an .ipd or a .bbb extension. Files with an .ipd extension will have been created with earlier versions of BlackBerry Desktop Manager (versions up to 6), while .bbb files are created by BlackBerry Desktop Manager version 7 and the new Link software. The .bbb files that are created by Link are fully encrypted, and known BlackBerry user information must be used to decrypt the data.

Tip Both iOS and BlackBerry backups contain very valuable data that you can analyze in commercial tools such as AccessData MPE+, Oxygen Forensic Detective and Analyst, MSAB XRY, and Cellebrite Physical Analyzer, along with free tools such as iPhone Backup Browser and MagicBerry. The collection and analysis of backups can assist your investigation if the device cannot be located or accessed, but examinations of the backups are also a way to compare the data from the backup to the actual device for a historical perspective.

BlackBerry Enterprise Server (BES) technology was the first platform that allowed an enterprise to store data from a mobile device in a central location on the company premises. This added great security to a company's critical and confidential data by allowing local storage of e-mail, documents, messages, event data, and company materials. This information could be accessed by company enterprise security teams to ensure compliance and gain visibility into the device if law enforcement requested data not stored on a device or data that had been deleted. Security administers of the BES can also remotely unlock a device if it is under control of the enterprise, which is also of great benefit to law enforcement. BES12 is an endpoint mobility management (EMM) tool and can contain data that is not accessible on the physical device, so don't overlook this information while conducting an investigation of a BlackBerry device.

As mentioned, devices can also create backups in the Cloud. iOS devices use a service called iCloud, which launched in October 2011 and currently has more than 320 million users. iCloud's service enables the user to store user data, applications, documents, pictures, and more on a server maintained and owned by Apple. This information can be retrieved using tools such as iPhone Backup Extractor with the user's Apple ID and password. Because of many security concerns with unauthorized access to iCloud backups, Apple has now made two-factor authentication available to users. This security update has added another hurdle for law enforcement when legally obtaining information stored using the iCloud service. In December 2014, Apple's two-factor authentication had been hacked, and a tool was made available to obtain a user's iCloud backup without knowing the username and password. Storing backups on the Cloud has moved to Android with onboard applications downloadable from the Google Play Store; BlackBerry has moved new devices to BlackBerry Protect. With many new devices moving to the Cloud, investigators have to be cognizant of these locations as well.

Educational Resources

Any investigation should begin with research of the device to be examined. Knowing as much information about a device as possible will ensure that you won't miss internal and external components. Knowing, for example, that a device has a built-in 16GB internal SD card is very good information to know before you start an examination. Several resources online can assist you in identifying the many nuances of the millions of devices available.

Phone Scoop

Phone Scoop (www.phonescoop.com) contains valuable information to assist in the identification and research of the device to be examined. You can search by device model, make, or operating system to see information such as the current operating system and version; processor; memory (both internal and external); whether or not there is a SIM card; and the type, memory slots, and the FCC ID.

Phone Scoop has images of the device to help the investigator quickly identify the device visually and also contains links to query the FCC database. Querying the FCC database provides detailed summaries of the internal components, what the original equipment looks like, and where the label should be located and what it should look like.

Phone Scoop stores information on devices for North America only. Using this resource will help you as you research to gain a better understanding of the device, its features, and how to begin an examination.

GSMArena

GSMArena (www.gsmarena.com) is much like Phone Scoop, but this site contains only GSM devices and is primarily for devices outside of North America. GSMArena is an information repository for reviews of the devices; phones searchable by model number, manufacturer name, and common name; and mobile device specifics. Mobile phone manuals are available for most devices, along with all the specifications, including but not limited to, size, memory, SIM type, operating system, hardware specs, USB port, and detailed images of the device.

Forums

Although Phone Scoop and GSMArena are valuable resources, obtaining information about what software might have been used on a specific device, tricks that you should know, and processing ideas all come from real experience. Forums are a way to connect with examiners and ask specific questions, search large databases for a device to see what software works best with that particular device, and so much more. The key to gaining experience and knowledge is by gathering as much intelligence prior to starting the actual examination of the device.

Here is a list of several forums that are good sources for information.

Forums with Databases

These forums contain databases that you can query in search of a device and the software to use.

- **Mobile Forensics, Inc.** (http://forum.mobileforensicsinc.com/) Register with Mobile Forensics, Inc., to become a member and search the vast database for a device. Once you locate the device, you'll find detailed information, including the cable to use, the data extracted, and the software.
- **Mobile Forensics Central** (www.mobileforensicscentral.com/mfc/) Use Mobile Forensics Central by searching its database to locate a phone report that lists the mobile device software and additional information needed for processing. MFC is a free site but requires registration.

Technical Information Forums

Use these forums to ask and search for mobile forensic technical questions.

- **Forensic Focus** (www.forensicfocus.com/computer-forensics-forums) This forum is for general forensic comments and questions based in Europe. This forum has a subforum for mobile forensics and contains tips, tricks, software information, and more.
- **Android Developers Forum** (http://developer.android.com/index.html) In this forum you'll find developer information on the Android operating system; you can also obtain all drivers for Android devices and download the Android Emulator along with prereleases of the Android operating system.
- **XDA Developers Forum** (www.xda-developers.com/) This site contains a forum along with development resources for smart devices, primarily Windows and Android. In 2010, a sister site, iPhone-Developers.com, was launched. The XDA name represents the first device, a Windows PDA, for which the site was developed.

Preparing for Your Journey

Mobile device forensics is no different from any other technical discipline. All demand a respect of the details along with an effort to understand every variable and contingency that you might encounter. There will be many bumps in the road with respect to tools and devices and, more times than not, a mixture of both. Working through each and every problem for a solution will arm you with knowledge that many others in today's mobile forensic world relegate to a tool.

Mobile devices will continue to be involved in the lives of nearly every human being on this Earth. They will continue to be used in some way in crimes, conversations, transactions, meetings, and Internet access for years to come and beyond. Mobile device examinations are not like any other digital examination discipline. To conduct thorough mobile device examinations, you need a constant appetite for research and training with this rapidly evolving discipline. Be patient, but more importantly, question the tools, understand what is under the hood, and prepare for anything!

Chapter Summary

Mobile device forensics is nothing like any discipline in the range of digital data examination because of the many different types of mediums associated with the single device (SIM, device, SD card, and even backups). Furthermore, the ways of acquiring the data from the devices is atypical to the standard digital forensic exam. The standard device collection is not the "bit-by-bit" image you would expect in other disciplines. Having a firm grasp on the basics will give you a strong foundation that will withstand the staunchest critique and challenge. Without having an underlying foundation, your examination will surely crumble under the scrutiny of an opponent.

2 Mobile Devices vs. Computer Devices in the World of Forensics

Mobile device forensics is a very specialized, and at times frustrating, discipline, especially for a new mobile forensic examiner crossing over to the discipline after years of service as a computer forensic examiner. With typical file system formats and well-documented operating systems and system processes, understanding a computer and its relevant artifacts is straightforward. With a legacy Nokia Series 40 (S40) mobile device, however, with its S40 operating system and no official documentation outside of Nokia, uncovering structure and artifacts may not be so straightforward. Mobile device storage media or internal flash is similar to the solid state drives (SSDs) in today's computers, but the file formats and, most importantly, the way to access this data as an examiner is much different. Additionally, the ability to create and obtain a physical image of a mobile device is much different from, and at times extremely more difficult than, creating a physical image of a mass storage device or traditional hard drive.

Note When speaking about a physical image of a hard drive or mass storage device, most practitioners refer to obtaining every bit and byte from the first sector (or start of the hard drive) to the last sector (or end of the hard drive). Obtaining an exact copy of the media is the truest form for a computer forensic examiner.

Most seasoned computer forensic examiners struggle with the limitation of obtaining an exact, unaltered form of a mobile device's internal storage media. For this reason, many examiners say they will not conduct a collection or examination of a mobile device and cannot refer to it as a "forensic exam." Some have even refused to refer to this as "mobile device forensics," instead calling it "mobile device collection or extraction." This mentality will last only so long, however, especially when an examiner conducting a mobile forensic exam becomes an expert. As soon as an examiner is held to be an expert in the field, his or her testimony will be weighed against the *Daubert* or *Frye* standard, depending upon the current jurisdiction.

Note *Frye* is based upon *Frye v. United States*, 293 F. 1013 (www.law.ufl.edu/_pdf/faculty/little/topic8.pdf), which states that expert testimony must be based upon scientific methods that are sufficiently established and accepted. *Daubert* is based upon *Daubert v. Merrell Dow Pharmaceuticals*, 509 U.S. 579 (https://supreme.justia.com/cases/federal/us/509/579/case.html), which states, among other things, that scientific knowledge can be established if it can demonstrate that the conclusion is the product of sound "scientific methodology" derived from the scientific method, and the decision as to scientific knowledge laid out by Federal Rule of Evidence 702 will rest on the shoulders of the trial judge.

The world is quickly moving to mobility, and mobile devices are becoming more like small computers, with no end in sight. Examiners must begin to understand that the forensic process is more important for the examination of a mobile device than for traditional computer forensics, based upon the many differences and hurdles that currently exist with these devices.

The forensic process is important in the examination of a mobile device for several reasons. The greatest impedance to the forensic process is overcoming and recognizing that write-protected devices are ineffective to protect the integrity of mobile device evidence. When corners are cut, training is insufficient, and a full understanding of the process is relegated to pushing a button, case law and precedence are often set. If the examiner has a concrete understanding of the process and follows it and understands the theory behind mobile device communication via software, then the evidence recovered will stand up to challenge. The flip side is uncovering a significant amount of useful information by not following or understanding the process and then being informed in court that recovered data cannot be used. What could be worse is that the evidence is used in the proceeding, but during the proceeding the validity is disputed because the practitioner used improper collection methods or did not follow a formulated scientific process. This concept is difficult to accept for examiners with many years in the computer forensic discipline.

Computer Forensics Defined

The examination of digital data from a computer's storage medium, either the traditional hard drive or the SSD, is a discipline familiar not only to law enforcement, but also to enterprise and academia. In every vocation, digital data from computers has been examined to verify, confirm, and attempt to determine users' intentions by investigating their actions and history. Processes and procedures govern the way a computer forensic examination and, more importantly, an examiner should proceed throughout the investigation. When you understand how prominent organizations define computer forensics and know the minimum requirements for a successful digital investigation, you can establish proper processes and procedures, implement plans, and establish a structure to facilitate mobile forensics.

International Association of Computer Investigative Specialists (IACIS)

IACIS is an international volunteer-based non-profit corporation that provides training and education in forensic computer science and grants the Certified Forensic Computer Examiner (CFCE) certification. The organization membership was originally limited to law enforcement but is now open to computer forensic practitioners who qualify. The CFCE core competencies document describes computer forensics as the acquisition, reconstruction, examination, and analysis of data stored on electronic media. To become certified, the examiner must address seven competency areas in the CFCE program, obtain peer review, conduct practical examinations, and pass a written examination. The seven areas are pre-examination and legal issues, computer fundamentals, partitioning schemes, Windows file systems, data recovery, Windows artifacts, and the presentation of findings.

International Society of Forensic Computer Examiners (ISFCE)

ISFCE is a private organization that conducts research and development of new and emerging technologies in the science of computer forensics. ISFCE grants the Certified Computer Examiner (CCE) certification, which also requires that core competencies be met in the certification process. These competencies include ethics, law, software, hardware identification, networks, operating systems, seizure process, forensic examination procedures, file systems, other media, media geometry, preparing media for imaging, forensic boot disks, low-level analysis, processing issues, and practical examination skills. To be accepted into the CCE testing process, a candidate must have completed at least one of three requirements: attended a CCE Boot Camp from an authorized training outlet, possess at least 18 months of verifiable digital forensic work, or have documented self-study in the field of digital forensics deemed appropriate by the CCE board. Once this requirement is fulfilled, the candidate can apply to the CCE testing process and must pass both an online written assessment and practical examinations.

Applying Forensic Processes and Procedures

Both IACIS and ISFCE follow similar processes and procedures in their competency requirements before a candidate can become certified to examine computer digital evidence. The following sections cover specific parts of both organizations' competencies along with supplemental information obtained from the U.S. Department of Justice (DOJ) on electronic evidence. By understanding the following areas of concentration as outlined for computer forensics methods, you can formulate strategies to build the best approach for a mobile forensic examination. Having a competent examination process that is repeatable and that subscribes to the scientific method at the onset of the journey will help you create a firm foundation and reliable process. This foundation and process must hold the weight of the facts when you testify to the results of any examination.

Seizure

Any investigation into electronic evidence must start with the legal seizure of the device that is holding, was holding, received, or transmitted the electronically stored information (ESI). The proper legal steps will be determined by the situation. Is the ESI in a place that a search warrant must be obtained, that permission must be given by the owner, or that is corporately owned? If the seizure of the device and subsequent data is tainted by questions on the legality of how it was obtained, the information collected will be dismissed in subsequent proceedings. You must exercise extreme care at the onset.

Collection

You must extract data from a digital device in a manner that enables you to show that the ESI did not change, was not altered, and is the same as when it was collected. The collected data typically contains an electronic fingerprint. If any data is changed, added, or removed from the collected data container, the electronic fingerprint will change. The integrity of the collection of digital data and the validation and verification of the software that collected the device are the responsibility of the person conducting the collection.

Analysis/Examination

Analyzing the data that has been collected from the seized device is often the most tedious part of an examination. Looking into many gigabytes of information is labor intensive even with automated tools. Because of the volume of data, typical digital examinations are predicated by the type of investigation the data will be used to support. Using the DOJ's "Electronic Crime Scene Investigation" document as a guide, the examiner can steer the examination of digital evidence by the crime or incident being investigated. By using this type of direction, an examiner's time can be better used in the analysis of pertinent information on a case-by-case basis. For example, the guide states that for crimes against persons, investigations and electronic data examinations should focus on the recovery and analysis of images (pictures), Internet activity logs, legal documents, and wills, along with any research the suspect conducted on the victim. The analysis and examination of the digital data can take significant time, but if the examiner has a clear picture of what information might be required for a particular investigation, the time can be minimized.

Presentation

Once the analysis is completed on the seized and collected data, the examiner must present the information, typically via a written report. The presentation is the most important piece for those who will review and most likely act on the information that has been recovered and analyzed. The presentation must outline the entire process, including any problems encountered, from the seizure to the analysis. The analysis portion must be clearly documented as to the request, the methodology, and findings. The examiner may have the most difficulty at this stage because technical examiners often do not communicate well with nontechnical people. The presentation stage defines the entire examination, however, since those who review the process will use this information to determine the validity of the examination and its results.

Approach to Mobile Device Forensics

Using well-tested and clearly defined forensic procedures can be a great start to creating a process and procedure for mobile device forensics. First, however, you need to understand several items that are at the heart of the scientific debate over the validity of mobile forensics.

One of the major debates by seasoned computer forensic examiners has to do with the integrity of image creation. Because a write-protect device cannot be used in the examination of a mobile device, the image cannot be substantiated as a true representative of best evidence—or can it? Most computer forensic examiners consider mobile device forensics *nonscientific* because of this single limitation. As discussed earlier, a write blocker stops writes to a mass storage device, thus maintaining the integrity of the device from which the image is being created. The hardware device or software switch inhibits writes to ensure that data is not overwritten and allows for a duplicate image of the storage device. Thus, the examiner can obtain a *hash*, or mathematical fingerprint, of all the data on the device. Because a mobile device is not recognized as a mass storage device and a write blocker cannot be used, some examiners believe the image must be labeled unreliable. However, when you fully understand the nature of the software used to connect to and collect data from the mobile device, you realize that the image can be reliably captured, even without involving a write-protect device.

When plugged into a computer, mobile devices initiate a change in the computer's operating system, which recognizes that a mobile device has been plugged into the system. Furthermore, the mobile device also makes changes to its operation to allow for communication with the computer. Mobile devices can be tethered to a computer using several means: infrared (IR), Bluetooth, Wi-Fi, serial cable, and USB cable. Connection with the device will always need a way to communicate, and this requires a driver—a conduit, command set, or program for a particular device or device set that allows communication between the device and the computer. In essence, a driver "bridges the gap" between the devices. Drivers are used not only for mobile devices, but also for any hardware attached to a computer system. If a driver is not installed properly, communication cannot occur. Drivers are the primary "pain points" when it comes to processing a mobile device. The correct driver must be installed correctly for communication to work while processing a mobile device. The communication between a mobile device and a computer system could involve the transfer of data to and from the device to the computer, creating an Internet hotspot, installation of applications, and many other things.

The word *communication* is important. For the mobile device to be recognized and communicate with the system via the driver, the mobile device typically must be powered on, and this fact brings up another point of contention with computer forensic examiners. If the device is powered on, then it is possible that data is constantly changing on the device from the cellular network or Wi-Fi network to which it is connected. Would not the clock on the device continue to update along with various other running processes on the mobile device? Invariably, the data is in constant flux, but ultimately it is the responsibility of the examiner to determine what data has changed, if any. Isolation techniques will be covered in later chapters, but for now you can assume that data will change on the device when it is powered on. This is an incredibly difficult concept to comprehend for a computer forensic examiner coming into mobile forensics. Both IACIS and ISFCE specifically state that nothing should change on a device during the collection process, and if it does, the recovered data cannot possibly be used as best evidence.

In today's modern world, however, we have software tools that recover volatile memory from a running computer. *Volatile memory*, memory that goes away if a computer is powered off, includes Random Access Memory (RAM). RAM can contain very valuable information such as passwords, keywords, media, and files, along with many other great forensic items. Because RAM is volatile, if the computer is shut down, the data would cease to exist, purged from the system, and recovery would be impossible. So to collect this data, the computer must be live and powered on, and a forensic application is run to target the machine, capturing the volatile data.

This live technique is in fact much like mobile device collection. Files are changed on the mobile device just as the files on the computer change during a live collection. It is up to the examiner to understand and comprehend what is taking place from start to finish, and most importantly, to ensure that no user data is altered by the software during the collection.

Communication between the mobile device and mobile forensic software occurs via the driver connection using the device's protocols, and the communication must first be in the language (protocol) accepted by the device. Different protocols are used for different devices, and sometimes multiple protocols are used, depending upon the access needed to the device. Some devices must even have small applications installed via their operating system onto their internal storage to collect the required data during the forensic examination. When you consider the many different devices available to the consumer and the various protocols used, it is apparent why some mobile devices cannot be examined using communication via a USB cable, serial cable, Bluetooth, or Wi-Fi. It is important that the examiner develop a thorough understanding as to what communication is occurring between the software and the mobile device so that he or she can maintain the integrity of the image and the mobile device's contents can be verified as best evidence and untainted during the mobile forensic examination.

In 2008, NIST published a document entitled "Forensic Filtering of Cell Phone Protocols" (NISTIR 7516), which describes ways to use phone manager software tools believed to be non-forensic in forensic examinations. The document describes a protocol filter that can be applied to the software to intercept communication that poses a risk to the integrity of the investigation. The document, although dated, contains valuable information as to how forensic tools of today combat the limitation imposed when a write-protection feature cannot be used. The document explains that the underlying functionality of forensic mobile device tools is based upon the same protocols used by the manufacturer's phone management tools. Furthermore, the forensic software tools inhibit or restrict the protocols used to issue commands or instructions that will read data from the device, along with other functions that impose little risk to the integrity of the evidence. This is done, as NIST explains, using a filter between the software and the device—much like how hardware and software write blockers work.

Validating the mobile forensic software and verifying that it uses forensic filtering of common mobile device protocols are the responsibility of the examiner. The ability to add, remove, or change records on a mobile device during or after a collection and subsequent analysis of the device should not be available to the examiner or in the software available today. Of course, as will be explained later, there are certain instances in which writes do occur to the connected device. These writes are not indiscriminate to the device, but targeted writes to temporary storage in the form of an application that assists with the extraction of the user data.

After the examiner collects the data from the mobile device, the analysis of the data, much like in computer forensics, is the most time-consuming part of the process. At this phase, some examiners and examinations falter. A lack of knowledge on the structure of a device's internal file system, critical artifact locations, system values, and critical file types means most examinations target the "lowest hanging fruit." WYSIWYG data typically satisfies the majority of examiners, not because of lack of motivation, but because of a misunderstanding of the device's storage areas and operating system characteristics. Know the device, its capabilities, and its file system, and you can substantiate any challenge to the examination.

Unlike computer forensics examiners, those who conduct mobile device forensic investigations have no globally recognized standards, as outlined earlier in the chapter.

Simply put, as long as the data from the mobile device is included in a report, there is no regard as to how that data was collected from the mobile device. It is because of this "Wild West" approach that most computer forensic examiners see mobile device forensics as mobile device *extraction*, which is inherently wrong if you understand what it really means to be *forensic*. Mobile forensics do, indeed, have processes, like computer forensics, but typically they are seldom adhered to by those conducting examinations.

This disparity is one of the main reasons the Mobile Forensic Certified Examiner (MFCE) curriculum was created and formulated by the training company Mobile Forensic Inc. (MFI). The MFCE requires that a candidate receive training on mobile forensic practices or have verifiable work in mobile forensics to apply for certification. If accepted, the candidate then undergoes six practical exercises and a written test to receive certification. The MFCE has not been widely accepted, however, primarily due to its limited reach and resources. For that reason, in late 2014, the MFCE was incorporated into the IACIS advanced mobile device training as a certification process, where it will be maintained and governed by a board of examiners.

Most software vendors also provide training on the software that they develop and sell. This type of training is important because the examiner must fully understand the tool to use it correctly during mobile forensic examinations. Training also provides credibility when examiners testify in court. These vendors also provide certification, which typically involves showing competence via written examinations, practical experience, or both.

Note **If you are unsure about whether to receive a mobile forensic certification on your overall understanding of the process or based on a particular tool, my best recommendation is to work toward a cumulative certification on overall processes and procedures.**

As shown in Figure 2-1, the current approach to mobile forensics and the analysis of a mobile device is a bit upside down. The foundation shown in the figure is the tool, which is supporting the weight of the procedure, process, and training. But having only a tool-based foundation in mobile forensics will never support your conclusions. A foundation based on training, however, which represents the largest area of the pyramid, along with a core centered on processes and procedures, will support a tool-based approach. To be successful in the mobile forensic field, you will invert the current examination pyramid and rest your knowledge foundation on what will support the approach covered throughout this book.

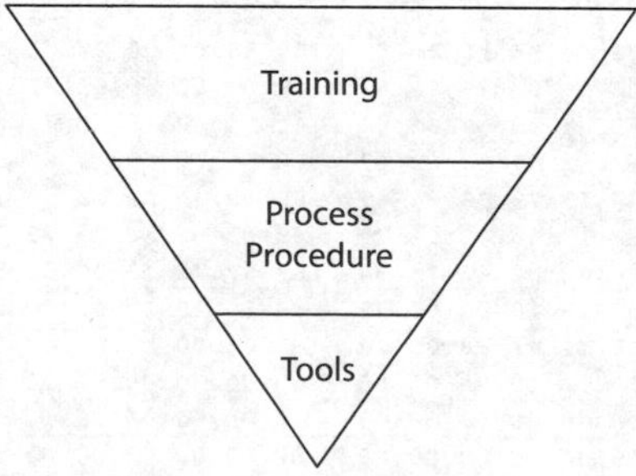

FIGURE 2-1 **The backward approach to mobile forensics**

Tool Understanding: Should It Be Painful?

When I first began in forensics, I attended several training courses. The most prominent other than my two-week IACIS training course was BDRA (Basic Data Recovery and Analysis) conducted by the National White Collar Crime Center (NW3C). In the week-long BDRA course, students started at the hard drive disk level. We learned about disk geometry, how the aperture arm worked, how the platters are configured, how the 30-pin ribbon cable worked, and the jumpers used to make one a master or a slave. We also learned how to create an image of a 3.5-inch floppy drive containing possible evidence. We then examined the image using a tool called a *disk editor*. The disk editor enabled students to examine the information at the data level, which helped us identify files by the file header and the file footer to determine the actual file type. The following screenshot shows what I was exposed to during the initial training phase and using a disk editor to examine the data on digital media.

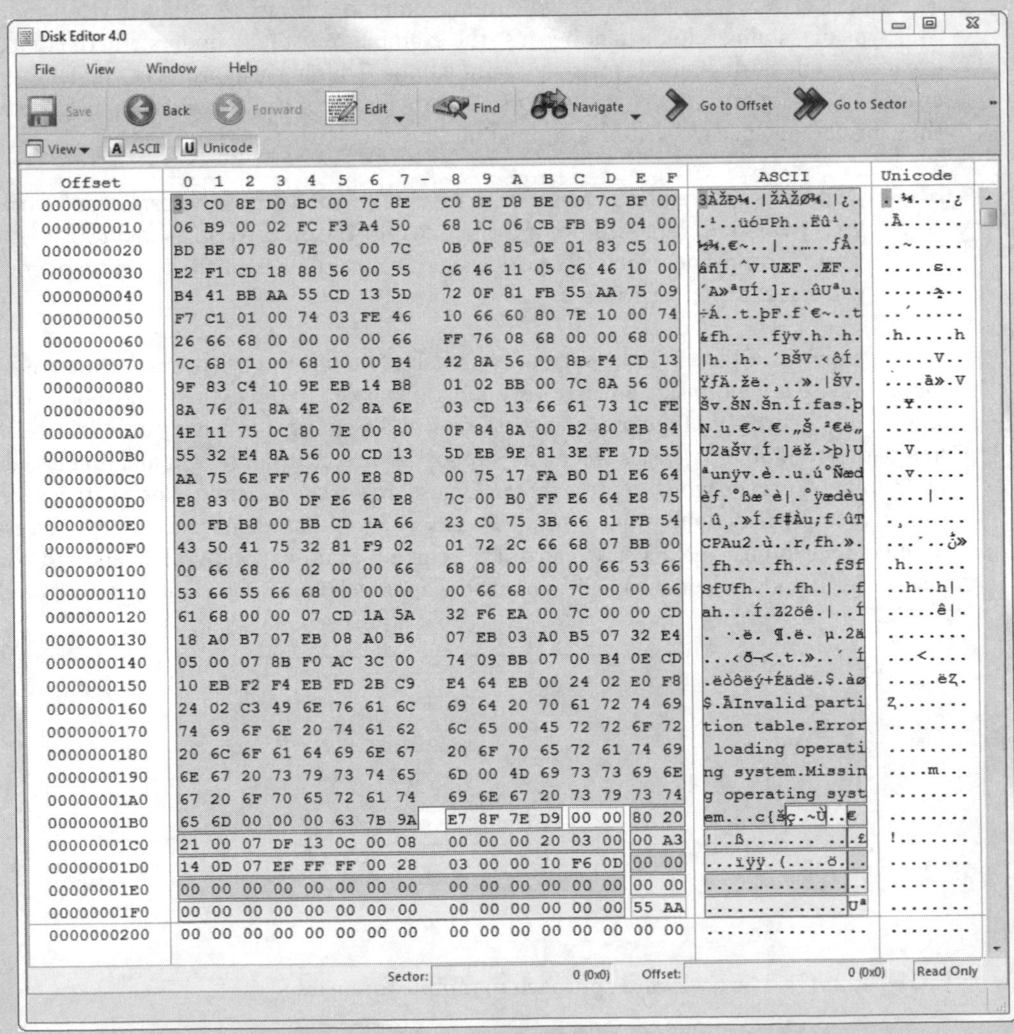

Using the disk editor, we were instructed to find a JPG by identifying its header and footer. We would then take the first byte and move to the last byte, copying the data from the disk to its own file, assigning it a .jpg extension. Clicking the file we just created, we immediately saw the product of our labors—a picture of a cat. It was amazing, carving an image from a blob of hexadecimal data, to produce an actual file! It was not until the last day of the course that we were allowed to use automated tools again to carve the data from the floppy disk. What!? Automation? Why was this tool not given to us the first day of the course? This would have saved a tremendous amount of time and shortened the five-day course into two. I was beginning to think that the instructor was a masochist and was questioning his intentions, but then the epiphany came.

The countless hours of explaining the architecture of the media, the structure of the file system, and formation of files finally made sense to me. We, in simple terms, were the tool—first finding the header of the file and carving from the header to the footer—just as an automated tool was doing. So when we are requested during testimony to qualify what *carving* is and how a tool can find and extract the forensic file data, we fully comprehend and can explain how this process takes place within a software solution.

The foundation of a mobile forensic exam should be a sound understanding of the operation and output of any automated tool used. Organizations and academia have now changed the "computer forensic" label to include digital forensics in an effort to cover small-scale devices such as mobile phones and tablets. As discussed, mobile devices have inherent differences in the way information is obtained from the device, but the examination of the collected data should be complementary.

NIST and Mobile Forensics

In its executive summary on mobile forensics (NIST Special Publication 800-101, May 2007: "Guidelines on Cell Phone Forensics"), NIST clearly explains that the digital forensic community faces the biggest challenges when it comes to mobile devices and investigations. Mobile devices are constantly changing to improve technologies, and investigative techniques must evolve with each new introduction. As stated, the key to understanding and answering the questions of today's investigator is having a firm understanding of the mobile device's software and hardware. A clear understanding of the limitations and the functions of forensic tools is important, but a clear and documented process and procedure are paramount.

Note NIST has since updated the special publication (NIST Special Publication 800-101, May 2014) after seven years, with revision 1 and a change in the title to "Guidelines on Mobile Device Forensics," along with content to cover new devices and procedures. The importance of a key understanding of a device's software and hardware is again stressed and reaffirmed.

Process and Procedure

Every job or discipline requires a set of processes and procedures that clearly define what is expected of the work and that aid in the workflow and ultimately a successful outcome. Procedures in forensics should never comprise a mere list of items to accomplish, starting at A and ending at Z. Adhering to a list and simply missing a step between A and Z would mean the entire process would fail. In forensics, and in technology investigations in general, the process-and-procedure document should be used only as a guide. There will be many different variables to consider, ranging from the actual physical device, to the type of software used, to the type of investigation the mobile device evidence will support. Processes used for one device might not be relevant to another or to a particular type of examination. What is important is that a clear set of procedures to conducting a mobile forensic collection and examination be established prior to the first examination to be used as a guide.

However, even before a set of processes and procedures can be created, you must consider several objections to the notion of a process in conducting mobile device collections and thorough examinations. Following are two of the more prominent objections.

Lack of Time

To complicate the process further, examiners began to incorporate a four-letter word in forensics: T-I-M-E. Time is the excuse that is typically used in the mobile forensic community when it comes to undergoing a full examination of the extracted data from a mobile device. "We do not have enough time in our job to look at every application or file system file." The person conducting the collection has to move on to another case, another device, or another responsibility. But conducting the examination with this attitude is a critical deficiency in mobile device forensics, especially in the age of the smart phone, and can prove to be detrimental and costly in the long run. A hasty examination of digital data is like reading the first and last chapters of a book and then trying to write a review. The overall premise and how it might fit together could be garnered from the pages read, but without reading the entire book, the opinion is based upon 20 percent of the overall information contained therein. The examination is without substance. Although mission-critical data is often needed in the shortest time possible, the examiner should never ignore an opportunity to examine every byte, if given the chance.

The Importance of Time and Training

Back in the day when the first floppy drives were seized at an electronic crime scene, they were stored to be analyzed later because they had something to do with a computer's data—and the same goes for a laptop, PC, or any other storage/processing device found at the scene. It was understood, and still is, that these devices may contain data relevant to the case. First responders were not trained in the examination of the data, so they collected and held the devices until the computer forensic examiner could conduct a proper investigation. Floppy drives held a maximum of 1.44MB of data, and the devices of the day could have contained only a 528MB hard drive for storage. Today's mobile devices can store 16, 32, or

64GB of data. (To put this into perspective on sheer storage capacity, a single gigabyte can hold data from 711, 1.44MB floppy disks and the data from almost two of the 528MB hard drives.) First responders, patrol officers, narcotics officers, and school resource officers are collecting and holding mobile devices every day because they need actionable intelligence quickly, but they still consider a mobile device just a phone, not a computer.

Collections by first responders should be supported, however, as long as the collections adhere to a predefined and vetted process. The examination of the data must be conducted by a person who has both the *time* and the *training* to peel the skin from the onion and peer into the many subcutaneous layers.

Simplicity of the Tool Equates to No Training Needed

Mobile forensic software and hardware tools have been designed and marketed to express to the purchaser that little to no training is needed to conduct a mobile forensic examination. Simply push this button and out comes the evidence; no need to add training or comprehend what is actually occurring when the button is pushed. The inverse is true, however, because the simpler the tool, the more training will be needed to testify about what is really occurring. Did the software on the device, once the button was pushed, query a database to retrieve the contacts and SMS? If that is the case, what database did it query? If the examiner can answer these questions, then using an automated tool for mobile device collections will stand up to scrutiny.

Standard Operating Procedure Document

What should be a part of the mobile forensic process? Much like the computer forensic process, it must start with a written document outlining the mission—a standard operating procedure (SOP) document. The SOP procedures cover not only the person or persons conducting the examination of data, but also those who are collecting and seizing the device or devices holding the digital data. The SOP should outline the process and procedures to be followed, from the seizure to the reporting of the data.

When starting a forensic lab or beginning to examine mobile devices, creating this document should be your first step. SOP processes and procedures for mobile forensics are much like those for computer forensics. The Scientific Working Group on Digital Evidence (SWGDE) maintains that a proper SOP (such as its template, version 3.1) will assist in maintaining the best practices for collecting, acquiring, analyzing, and documenting data in digital forensic examinations. Using the outline, suggestions, and information in the following sections, you can develop a SOP that will be specific to the enterprise, agency, or company.

Purpose and Scope

The mobile device forensic SOP should outline the purpose and scope of each possible location at which a mobile forensic device or collection could occur. The *purpose* explains why the section or SOP is being used and identifies the goal of the SOP or section, and it should be detailed enough so that the reader will recognize what the document or section will cover. Several purpose statements can exist in a single SOP, with only one purpose statement per SOP section. The *scope* identifies who will be following this procedure and what the procedure covers. The scope can also explain what will be needed or covered in the SOP or the section. The scope should be very clear and identify areas that are and are not going to be covered or that are outside the scope of the document. The writer of the SOP should not assume that the reader will understand that something is or is not part of the document or procedure; this must be implicitly stated.

Here are examples of both purpose and scope for a mobile forensic off-site request.

> ***Purpose:*** The purpose of this procedure is to seize, secure, and collect digital data from a mobile device at an off-site location to maintain the integrity of the device and contents for further analysis and processing.
> ***Scope:*** This SOP outlines the process and procedures to follow when you are conducting mobile forensic assistance at an off-site location. This SOP is not a training document, but a set of procedures to follow at an off-site location.

After listing the purpose and scope, the SOP will continue with the actual equipment, specific knowledge data, and procedural items. Recommended areas to cover include definitions, materials and equipment, general information, procedures, and references and related documents.

Definitions

The definitions paragraph should list and define all acronyms and technical words included in the procedural part of the SOP. When creating an SOP, the writer must understand that the reader might not understand the technology—for example, assuming the reader knows what WCDMA or UICC means could cause on-site problems if these are unfamiliar terms. Defining any term that is related to the technology is recommended. Here is a sample definitions paragraph that could be used for an on-site or lab SOP.

> ***Definitions:***
>
> **Mobile device:** Portable devices that use network communication (cellular or Wi-Fi) and have digital storage capabilities. Examples include a cellular phone or tablet.
> **Mobile device external media:** Digital storage media. Examples include microSD cards and SD cards.
> **Mobile device internal media:** Digital storage media that is part of the actual mobile device, typically soldered to the internal components of the device and not removable.

Equipment/Materials

The equipment statement should include all the items that are needed to accomplish the listed procedure successfully. This should cover every contingency and should be broad enough so that the reader will not have to return to pick up additional items not listed in the SOP. An example of an equipment statement is listed next.

Equipment: The equipment that will be needed includes the following items:

- Digital camera
- Sterilized portable USB hard drive
- Media card write-blocking tools
- Radio frequency (RF)–shielding device
- Mobile device collection tools
- Mobile device cables and SIM card readers
- Evidence packaging materials

General Information

Include general information to define limitations or background information regarding performing the duties outlined in the SOP. Important limitations should be explained directly and clearly to the reader. In a mobile forensic examination, limitations could include information regarding on-site and off-site seizures and collections. This paragraph should set the stage for any contingency the reader may encounter. This area of the SOP can often continue to grow because of constant change in both mobile device and software technology. An example of a section outlining limitations on an off-site seizure of mobile device data is shown here.

General Information – Limitations:

- If a mobile device has network access, data destruction can occur.
- If a mobile device is shut down or loses power, it may lock, essentially eliminating further access.
- If a mobile device is locked upon seizure, further access might not be possible unless a passcode is obtained from the owner or computer with which the device was last synched.
- Some software tools do not collect all of the data on a device.

Procedure

In the procedure portion of the SOP, the reader is walked through the performance of the task. This should include enough detail to enable the reader to perform the duty, but it should not be so detailed that the reader feels compelled to perform each step for success. An SOP is not the exact process that must be used in every instance, but a guide as to the best practices to conduct a mobile forensic examination from start to finish. For example, the following procedure is too detailed to be used in every case:

> Place the device into airplane mode by navigating to Settings > Tools > Network > Airplane mode.

Clearly, this would not work in every instance and would cause confusion. Simply stating, "Place the device into Airplane mode," would suffice. An example of a procedure you could use for an off-site response to a mobile forensic scene is shown here:

General:

- The scene should be secure and safe for all individuals.
- Protect devices and the evidence contained on the devices.

- Identify the areas of the scene to be searched.
- Photograph the area and each potential item of evidentiary value.

Mobile Devices:

- Photograph the device and any data on the screen.
- Block the mobile device from receiving RF signals either by placing the device in airplane mode or using an RF-shielding device.
- If the device cannot be shielded from RF, the device should be turned off.
- The device should be packaged and submitted for processing as soon as possible.

References/Documents

The final category included in an SOP will be references or related documents. The reference area should include other SOPs that are related to the current SOP, such as the SOP for the "Collection of Mobile Device Data On-Site" included within the SOP for the "Seizure of Mobile Device Evidence On-Site." This allows the reader to transition immediately to the SOP to learn how to handle an actual collection of the data if needed. Also, any documents that might aid the reader in performing a task should be included, such as published documents, web sites, or manuals.

Successful SOP Creation and Execution

For mobile forensic SOPs to be successful, they must be categorized in sections or modules according to specific operations. The following sections discuss the recommended modules and content that should be contained within a mobile forensics SOP document. You can add more specifics to these modules after establishing a clear understanding of proper procedures for conducting the seizure, image creation, and analysis. These processes are covered in depth in later chapters.

Mobile Forensic Seizure On-Site Procedures

This module should cover the procedures users will take when preparing for and arriving to a site or scene where mobile devices and evidence relating to a mobile device will be encountered. This module should cover equipment needed, scene safety, identification of a mobile device, SIM cards, external storage mediums (SD cards, microSD cards), USB cables, manuals, location of passwords or PIN numbers for a mobile device, and devices that may hold backups of mobile devices such as a computer or laptop. The proper methods to inhibit a mobile device's network connections, what to photograph, how to package a mobile device upon removal from the site, and the transportation of mobile device evidence should also be included in this module.

Mobile Forensic Image Collection On-Site Procedures

This module should cover the necessary procedures if a mobile device image is to be collected using mobile forensic tools while the user is on the site or scene. Items covered should include, but are not limited to, equipment needed to create a forensic image of a mobile device, SIM card, or removable media; and procedures for proper isolation of a mobile device from network connections. Proper procedures for the recovery of a mobile device image should include determining the type of mobile device and its functions, determining the correct software for the type of device, and conducting an extraction and subsequently verifying that the data extracted can be manually located on the device.

Mobile Forensic Image Collection at Lab Procedures

This module should cover the procedures users should take for forensically processing and analyzing a mobile device in a lab setting. Included should be the steps required to complete the isolation of a mobile device, depending upon the state in which the device was received, with specifications for how device information should be obtained and how to gain a thorough understanding on the device capabilities prior to beginning the extraction. It should include guidance on what to do if the device supports a SIM card and what software will be needed to conduct a forensic examination of the SIM card. If a media card is also located, the appropriate software should be used to create a forensic image of the media card and should be described here. Any software that will be needed to complete an extraction of the mobile device should be identified. Once the correct software for extraction has been determined, the process should be determined by the state of the device. If the device is powered off, this procedure will instruct the lab examiners to begin with data from the SIM and media cards and conclude with the mobile device. If the device is powered on, the reverse process should occur: handset, media card, and then SIM. This information is covered extensively in the processing section.

Creation of a Workflow

The creation of a workflow or flowchart can be of great benefit both to the first responder and forensic examiner to guide them from the seizure to the examination of a mobile device. In 2007, MFI produced a flowchart to assist in processing mobile devices when they come into the lab. During Mobile Forensics World 2008, this flowchart was introduced to students in the MFI Crash Course to Mobile Forensics class that was held at the Chicago police department's training facility in downtown Chicago. The workflow shown in Figure 2-2 was outlined in 2007 and can be followed with today's mobile devices. In chapters to come, additional steps will be added to the flowchart to help expand on different scenarios.

Specialty Mobile Forensic Units

Mobile device forensics can be much more involved than traditional computer forensics. Successful mobile device forensics can be a time-consuming process. Because of the many applications, files, logs, and constantly changing technologies involved, a special unit or a specially trained individual should be in charge of conducting mobile device investigations. With the proliferation of mobile devices and their involvement in every aspect of today's world, the challenge of finding someone who can juggle multiple disciplines could negate the importance of conducting a thorough examination.

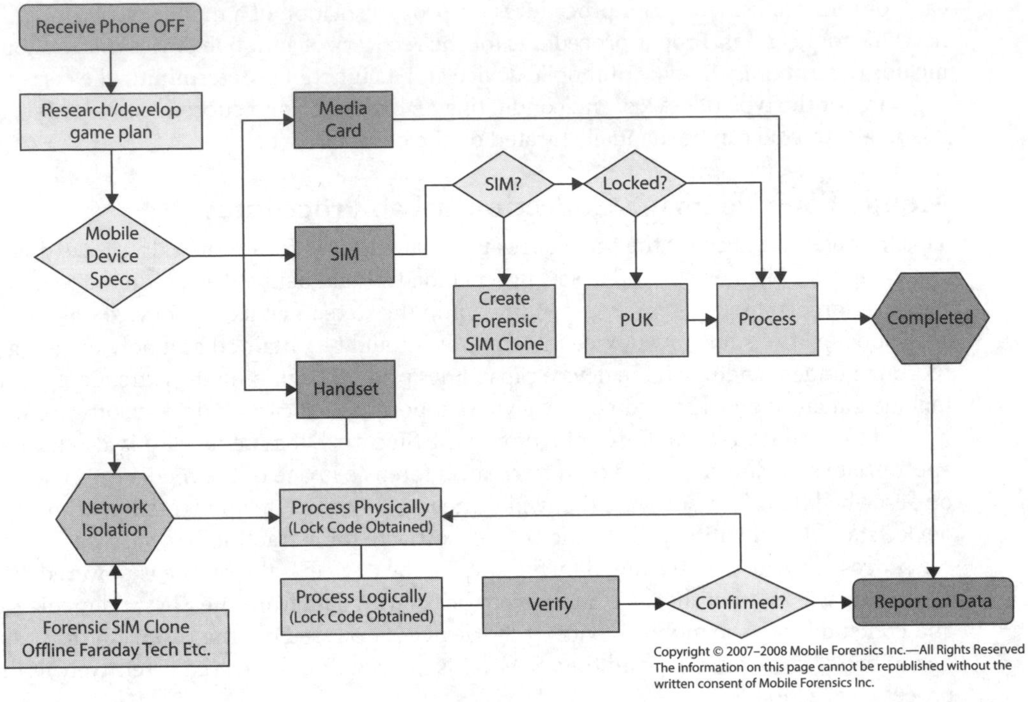

FIGURE 2-2 Processing a mobile device (introduced at Mobile Forensics World 2008)

Mobile Device Examination Priority

When I began working in forensics, I started with a foundation in computer forensics, with proper training in both theory and application. Computers would arrive in the lab and would be categorized and examined based upon procedures that had been established previously. I then moved into the examination of mobile devices, and my world changed—not because I really enjoyed processing mobile devices, but the onslaught of mobile devices was like a broken faucet, releasing 100 gallons per second, as devices began arriving from all over the state. With both computers and 20 to 25 mobile devices per week to examine, I found it almost impossible to juggle both disciplines. To examine both computers and mobile devices effectively and according to the required standards, something would have to give, or the quality of the investigations would degrade. As the number of devices continued to increase, the variety of software continued to change, and the time involved in a proper examination increased, I decided to make mobile devices my priority and focus.

Forensic Software

The U.S. Computer Emergency Readiness Team (US-CERT) defines computer forensics as "the discipline that combines elements of law and computer science to collect and analyze data from computer systems, networks, wireless communications, and storage devices in a way that is admissible as evidence in a court of law." So mobile forensic software, to somewhat paraphrase US-CERT's definition, would be software that is used to collect and analyze data from a mobile device in a way that is admissible as evidence in a court of law.

A software application is a generic set of instructions for a computer. Software used by practitioners is defined by two classes: system software and operational or application software. System software is used by the computer system itself and does not involve the user; it is designed to be used for specific tasks that keep the computer or system running as expected—such as writing of data to a disk drive or displaying a graphic on a computer screen. Application software facilitates tasks the user needs to perform his or her work—such as word processing, image creation, and mobile forensic examinations. All mobile forensics tools are application software. They are not magical things that conduct massive investigation feats with the click of a mouse or that autonomously process a device and output a report. You must understand your application software and interact with it in a way that is admissible in a court of law and to produce a product that can be used to substantiate the entire investigation.

Many different types of mobile forensic software can be used for today's examinations. Mobile forensic software typically differs in functionality and complexity, but it also differs as to the types of devices that are supported. With the many different types of mobile devices that vary not only by manufacturer but also by communication protocols in use, no single mobile forensic software tool supports all mobile devices. What it really comes down to is the type of examination, the goal of the examination, and how the produced evidence might be later used.

Common Misconceptions

With mobile forensics and examiners, many misconceptions must be dealt with—not only when explaining the produced work to the requestor, but also when answering questions during testimony. Being prepared to combat the common misconceptions and head those off before they proliferate will be important to the ultimate success of the examiner.

Seasoned Computer Forensics Examiners' Misconceptions

Examiners who have been conducting only computer forensic exams for many years make up the largest group who misunderstand the validity and value of the scientific examination of a mobile device. These examiners have undergone training that dictates that they must obtain a full duplicate copy of the digital media using a write blocker and ensure that the operating system obtaining the image did not perform any inadvertent writes to the evidence. This produces a copy of the evidence that they later analyze, and they must be able to conclude unequivocally that the data was not tampered with during the collection and analysis.

On mobile devices, writes do occur, simply because the devices are powered on during extraction, with the simple change of the clock or other internal processes. Concurrently, the extraction takes place without a write blocker, and because of this, a mobile device is not viewed as a mass storage device. Also, because a mobile device cannot be imaged as a hard drive, computer forensic examiners have relegated mobile device forensics as merely mobile device extraction.

To combat this misconception, the mobile device examiner must recognize that although data does change on the device during the investigation, user data should never change or be altered by software. This can be shown by locating the actual files from which the data was collected and by verifying the software's results. You must understand that the protocols to communicate with a mobile device limit the collection of the device's internal memory, and that proprietary hardware and software limitations imposed by the hardware manufacturers make it difficult to capture a full image. What makes the examination forensic, however, is not the software, but the process the examiner takes during the extraction and subsequent analysis of the data.

First Responders' Misconceptions

Unfortunately, the majority of mobile device seizures and extractions are conducted by individuals who have not received formal training on forensic processes, but who have received tool-specific training. Most extractions take place at the scene or on-site. Because the majority of the training involves how to conduct the collection of the mobile device, any deviation from the training course material typically means that the mobile device forensic tool will fail. If first responders do not receive training on the software tool, the percentage of failures of that particular device grow dramatically. This does not just have to do with a software tool failing to connect to a particular device, but with the data that is collected. A common misconception is that the software tool did not work if the data is not immediately presented to the user. This is far from the truth, however. Since the majority of today's tools use database files to store data and use common file types, would it not behoove the user to analyze the data rather than the output? This is the conundrum of today's mobile device examiner.

Sometimes Data Is Not Where You Think

I was assisting an officer with an investigation using AccessData's Mobile Phone Examiner Plus software. The officer was extremely frustrated because he had obtained an image of an Apple iPhone and was unable to locate the specific text message from the device's image. Because the device had been returned to the owner, the officer was upset that this evidence was now gone. I asked to see the created image and asked about the case.

The case was simple: a text message was sent to the person requesting some information about a package. The officer pointed to the report and the interface showing the date and the time when it should have been listed, and said, "It is not there." I was shown the initial report outlining the SMS and MMS data and also was told it was not there. He complained, "The tool doesn't work!"

I immediately asked if he had looked into the device file system to determine whether the message was sent from a third-party application. He said that he looked only at the applications that had been automatically parsed by the tool and did not see the message. I explained to him that many applications are released every day, and it is possible that the application had not auto-parsed.

We navigated into the file system and found an application called Facebook Messenger. Inside this application, we located the common SQLite database and immediately located the data he had been looking for. The case was solved—not by a magical application, but by following a process and understanding the underlying file system and file types that made the difference. This was not a failure of the software.

Chapter Summary

The principles of examination are no different between the disciplines of computer forensics and mobile device forensics. To be successful in the discipline of mobile device forensics, the examiner must understand that the process from seizure to analysis is no different from examining anything containing 0's or 1's—in other words, the same process used for a computer forensic examination should be followed and conformed to in mobile device forensic examination.

The user must seize the device legally, collect the device, and conform to common evidence best practices to extract the best evidence image, verify the output and image, and conduct a thorough analysis of the collected data. That information then has to be presented in a way that conforms to industry standards.

IACIS, ISFCE, and SWGDE contend that processes and procedures must be adhered to during the complete evolution of a digital device examination. Furthermore, process and procedure should be part of a set of SOPs for all facets of the mobile forensic lifecycle and location. These SOPs can be successful only if the entire company, department, or agency fully supports them, from top to bottom. With successful implementation of SOPs, along with complementary training, success can be guaranteed.

The many misconceptions—from seasoned examiners to first responders—can be circumvented with training and knowledge of not only the small differences in mobile device forensics, but also with the similarities of successfully gathering and analyzing any digital data.

Now that you understand the similarities to computer forensics and the importance of the SOP for mobile forensics, the next chapter will explain how to begin a mobile forensic examination correctly by properly seizing evidence from the scene.

3 Collecting Mobile Devices, USB Drives, and Storage Media at the Scene

Every successful examination starts with a successful physical seizure of the devices that hold the data and/or the repository (such as iCloud storage). A physical seizure involves taking possession of the container or containers in which the digital data is stored. This could be, but is not limited to, a server, Cloud storage, a computer desktop or laptop, a flash drive, a portable hard drive, and, of course, the mobile device itself.

Lawful Device Seizure

A successful physical seizure of the device along with its contents can be a complicated endeavor. Because the seizure process can be dictated by federal, state, and local laws pertaining to a person's rights, if correct procedures are not followed, your search may be deemed illegal. In general, this hinges on whether or not the seizure and subsequent search were completed by a government agent, an official, or a private citizen. In the United States, a person's Fourth Amendment rights protect them from unreasonable searches and seizures by a government agent, official, or private citizen who is acting on behalf of a government agent or official. That means if a person is not acting on behalf of the government, using a wiretap or other electronic surveillance and searches of mobile devices without a person's consent are legal because searches and seizures by private citizens are not covered by the Fourth Amendment. Of course, the private citizen is not immune from being civilly sued for the invasion of privacy by the subject of the search.

On the other hand, a successful seizure for agents of the government must comply with federal, state, and local laws governing the seizure of personal property from individuals. Any seizure of property must be lawfully authorized prior to the acquisition of the device and the digital evidence. If the seizure or collection occurs lawfully but the actual seizure occurs without lawful authorization, any data collected cannot be used in court and will negate the seizure of the device or devices.

If the location to be searched has been lawfully authorized, the seizure of the device holding the data must be secured. Establishing a chain of custody of not only the device, but also the data, is very important to the entire digital investigation.

Note A *chain of custody* clearly details, in chronological order, every hand that the piece of evidence has been in—from seizure to disposition. Typically referenced in criminal cases during introduction of physical evidence, chain of custody can also play a large role in civil cases and should not be dismissed. The chain of custody should be clearly documented in a report or form that defines the appropriate details.

When it comes to electronic evidence from a mobile device, there are two different chains of custody: one for the physical device and another for the data collected from the device. If the device holding the information is not properly seized and a chain of custody is not established at the onset, any information gathered post collection becomes fruit of the poisonous tree—unusable. What does that mean to you as an examiner? It means that any information gathered at the scene that might implicate guilt or innocence can be dismissed at trial because the physical device that holds the digital gold was not properly seized.

For example, suppose a mobile device's data is collected at the scene without probable cause, but the owner of the device consented to your looking at the call records. You recover the collected data to a portable hard drive, and it is subsequently examined by another forensic examiner, who uncovers a heinous plot that is detailed in photographs and videos stored on the mobile device. The alleged suspect is apprehended and later arrested based upon this new evidence. During trial, the digital evidence that was located on the digital device is used, but it is determined that consent was not given by the owner to collect images and video digital data, so the plot information cannot be used in the trial. The rest of the evidence is considered circumstantial, and the case is subsequently dropped.

Note *Lemons v. State*, 298 S.W.3d 658 (Tex. Ct. App. - Tyler 2009) states that even if consent has been given for call details on the mobile device, photos from the device cannot be observed and subsequently used under the consent initially given.

In another example, suppose a corporate employee is fired for probable policy violations. The mobile device issued to the employee is taken from him upon termination. The employee indicates that he stored personal phone numbers on the device and the company has no right to look at the information. The company does not comply and believes that since the device is owned by the company, it can examine the information even if a formal policy is not in place indicating employees will agree to a search of the device during their employment and upon leaving the company voluntarily or involuntarily. The company security examiner finds data of a criminal nature on the device and summons law enforcement. The law enforcement officer obtains the information and understands that the device is owned by the company; therefore, the information on the device can be examined without a warrant. The law enforcement agency collects the data from the mobile device and determines the employee has committed a crime and subsequently arrests him. The information found on the mobile device is later used as the primary evidence in an attempt to convict the employee of a felony. As the trial progresses and the evidence of the device collection is introduced, it is determined that personal contacts, short messages, and pictures were stored on the device. Subsequently, the device was determined to be equal to a personal device, briefcase, or file cabinet that could not be searched without a warrant, even if owned by a third party. The information was located by the company and turned over to a law enforcement officer, who did not seek a search warrant based upon the device being owned by the company, not the person in question; this was fruit of the poisonous tree and could not be used in the trial. The case was later dismissed.

Tip *United States v. Finley*, 477 F.3d 250 (5th Cir. 2007) stated that even though the cell phone was owned by the company Finley worked for, personal data was stored on the device, and Finely had a reasonable expectation of privacy for the data contained on the device.

Obtaining electronic data using forensic tools should not be the start of the investigation, but the culmination of the successful seizure of the physical device. If the seizure of the physical container is not properly conducted, the examination is inconsequential and worthless should evidence be needed at trial. A proper procedure for mobile forensic examinations should include following a protocol that outlines the seizure of mobile devices in a manner consistent with local, state, and federal laws.

Before the Data Seizure

Prior to the seizure of the physical device or devices, you need to answer several questions:

- If a search warrant has not been executed, has the device owner consented to the search?
- If a search warrant has been executed, is the device included on the original warrant?
- If the device is included on the warrant, are the contents of the device also defined?
- In a corporate situation, is the device owned by an individual or his or her employer?
- Is a corporate policy in place to allow collection and subsequent analysis?
- Could the device contain personal information?

Answering each of these questions is imperative to your successful seizure of the evidence at the scene. Failure to secure answers to these basic questions could lead to the dismissal of evidence recovered at the scene.

The creation of documentation regarding the seizure of the physical devices and other articles related to a mobile device can be different for law enforcement and corporate investigations. What is consistent, no matter whether it is a law enforcement or corporate investigation, is the fact that misinformation typically comes from not asking the correct questions prior to the seizure of the data.

Fourth Amendment Rights

In the United States Constitution, the Fourth Amendment states the following:

> The right of the people to be secure in their persons, houses, papers, and effects, against unreasonable searches and seizures, shall not be violated, and no warrants shall issue, but upon probable cause, supported by oath or affirmation, and particularly describing the place to be searched, and the persons or things to be seized.

This amendment grants a "right to one's privacy." The government or its agents cannot examine a person's digital devices without a court order or search warrant issued by a judiciary arm of government. In other parts of the world, privacy rights are also maintained that do not allow the government to obtain data from a digital device without first complying. In South Africa, for example, a mobile device and its contents are subject to search only after the agent receives a search warrant for the contents of the device, similar to the United States. The United Kingdom also holds in *Malone v. United Kingdom* that numbers dialed by a subject are "protected telephonic communications." In that case, it would be interpreted that any other data that is stored on the device would be protected as well.

The Supreme Court and Mobile Device Data Seizure

Two cases, *Riley v. California* and *United States v. Wurie*, lay the foundation for the change in the doctrine long used when conducting a search of a mobile device.

In *Riley v. California*, a stop for a traffic violation led to Riley's arrest for a weapons charge. Incident to arrest, officers found a mobile phone in the arrestee's pants pocket. The data was accessed, and a repeated reference to a term known to be associated with a street gang was located on the device. Later, another law enforcement officer examined the device's contents in more detail and found media (images and videos) that assisted in charging Riley with a shooting. Riley attempted to suppress all the information from the mobile device on grounds that it was obtained without a warrant, but he was still convicted.

In *United States v. Wurie*, Wurie had been arrested and transported to the police station, where officers removed a mobile device from the arrestee. The officers noticed that several incoming phone calls had arrived, including one message that said "my house" on the screen. They accessed the device to reveal the phone number for the contact "my house," along with an image. The number was investigated, and officers determined that this was the arrestee's residence. A search warrant was then executed on that residence, where officers located drugs, firearms, ammunition, and cash. When Wurie attempted to have this evidence suppressed, he was denied, and eventually Wurie was convicted.

Ultimately, the Supreme Court of the United States (SCOTUS) decided in a historic vote that data on a mobile device should be covered by the same protection outlined in the Fourth Amendment, overturning both of the previous decisions. Furthermore, the opinion read by Chief Justice John Roberts clearly outlined in the decision that law enforcement generally may not search digital information on a mobile device seized via search incident to arrest without a warrant. The decision also stated that digital data from a mobile device does not pose a risk to officer safety. The device itself can be altered into a weapon, but the data itself will not cause harm—so a cursory examination of the physical device is permissible, but not an extraction.

Also, destruction of evidence by remote wiping and even encryption could be circumvented with available techniques used by law enforcement, such as using signal isolation devices and disabling the locking mechanism. The most important decision in summary is by Chief Justice Roberts:

> Cell phones differ in both a quantitative and a qualitative sense from other objects that might be carried on an arrestee's person. Notably, modern cell phones have an immense storage capacity. Before cell phones, a search of a person was limited by physical realities and generally constituted only a narrow intrusion on privacy. But cell phones can store millions of pages of text, thousands of pictures, or hundreds of videos. This has several interrelated privacy consequences. First, a cell phone collects in one place many distinct types of information that reveal much more in combination than any isolated record. Second, the phone's capacity allows even just one type of information to convey far more than previously possible. Third, data on the phone can date back for years. In addition, an element of pervasiveness characterizes cell phones but not physical records. A decade ago officers might have occasionally stumbled across a highly personal item such as a diary, but today many of the more than 90 percent of American adults who own cell phones keep on their person a digital record of nearly every aspect of their lives (pp. 17–21).

As clearly explained in the historic decision, a person's right against unlawful search and seizure by law enforcement extends to a digital device, today's diary. Before conducting a valid examination of a mobile device, get a warrant.

Warrantless Searches

Searching electronic evidence, particularly mobile devices, by civilians who are not agents of the government can occur without a warrant. Individuals may have an expectation of privacy regarding data on a mobile device, but if that expectation is violated by an ordinary citizen, no Fourth Amendment violation has occurred. Ordinary citizens can conduct a search of an electronic device, so long as they have not violated any other laws in order to examine the device—such as breaking into a person's house and taking a mobile device and then conducting an examination. Ordinary citizens do not need the consent of the party to extract data from a mobile device; this is referred to as the "private search doctrine."

In *United States v. Grimes*, 244 F. 3d 375 (5th Cir. 2001), a private citizen searched a computer without consent of the owner and recovered illegal pictures that were later turned over to the police. Because the citizen was not acting as an agent of the government, the search was deemed valid and the recovery of the data was not suppressed. For government actors and agents, however, this is not the case.

Note **Warrantless searches of digital devices, particularly mobile devices, by law enforcement were typically conducted using the "search incident to arrest" doctrine, as outlined in several cases. In 2014, SCOTUS changed the way in which law enforcement and government address search incident to arrest as it pertains to mobile devices. The information in this section provides background to the case law used prior to the SCOTUS decision to lay a foundation for the historic decision.**

Three particular cases govern, to an extent, when officers can search property found in the possession of or near an arrestee. *Chimel v. California,* 395 U.S. 752, states that search incident to arrest is limited to the immediate control of the arrestee when an officer's safety is a concern, along with preventing the destruction of evidence. Another case, *United States v. Robinson,* 414 U.S. 218, used *Chimel* to explain that a search of a pack of cigarettes found on the arrestee was valid because the risks identified in *Chimel* are always present in custodial arrests, even when there is no concern for an officer's safety or loss of evidence. The last case, *Arizona v. Gant,* 556 U.S. 332, deals with the search of a vehicle, where the arrestee has access to the passenger compartment or other places within the vehicle believed to hold evidence of the crime the person had been arrested for. Using the case law outlined in *Robinson*, it would seem that law enforcement had precedent to extend a search to a mobile device incident to a lawful arrest.

Again, the search incident to arrest clause avoided the need for a search warrant for a vehicle or the person after an arrest of the individual is made. This was to secure the person for transport due to officer safety concerns and remove all possible contraband from the arrestee's possession (such as wallet, keys, weapons, and mobile devices) to disallow access to these items that might harm the officer, the arrestee, or others who might come into contact with the person under arrest prior to booking. Subsequently, search incident to arrest also allowed the law enforcement officer to secure a vehicle if it was involved with the arrest. A search would be performed in the "lunge area" of the vehicle to ensure that the arrestee had not stored any contraband there during the initial contact and subsequent arrest.

Most statutes specify that if law enforcement comes into contact with any locked containers during a search incident to arrest, a search warrant would be necessary to look into the container. Laptops and briefcases typically fall into the search warrant clause, but initially mobile devices did not. Mobile devices, because of their small footprint, were searched either manually at the scene of the arrest or using an automated tool. In 2014, the SCOTUS cited this search and the reasons typically voiced to enable a mobile device search were in violation of a person's Fourth Amendment rights.

Another exception to the warrant has to do with *consent.* A law enforcement officer can stop and search, under reasonable suspicion based on "specific and articulable facts," a person for officer safety concerns, as defined in *Terry v. Ohio,* 392 U.S. 1. If the officer located a mobile device on the person's possession, the officer could request consent from the person to look into the device only if several conditions are satisfied. Consent is an interesting exception to the warrant for many reasons. If an arrestee has a reasonable expectation of privacy for a mobile device and a government representative did not have a warrant to access the data, the officer can request for consent. The person who is giving consent must have standing to give consent, must be capable of giving consent, and must understand that the consent can be revoked at any time during the search.

In *United States v. Meador,* 2008 WL 4922001 (E.D. Jan. 7, 2008), parental consent to search a mobile device owned by their son, but under their account, could not be given. Also, the scope to which the consent applies is important. This means that if a government agent requests to search a room and the mobile device is in another room and is seized, the scope of the consent was exceeded *(United States v. Zavala,* 541 F .3d 562 (5th Cir. 2008). In another example, *Smith v. State,* 713 N.E.2d 338 (Ind. Ct. App. 1999), the government agents requested to search a vehicle for several things but did not specify mobile devices. Several mobile devices were seized and subsequently suppressed at trial because the seizure exceeded the scope of the consent.

Obtaining consent to search a mobile device can be extremely delicate, and you should approach it with caution. When obtaining consent to search a mobile device, you must create a document that clearly details ownership, explains what is to occur, lists the tools that will be used, and provides the outcome if illegal information is recovered.

The last exception to a warrantless search is *exigent circumstances*, when there is not enough time to obtain a warrant for fear of physical harm to the government agent or others, the escape of the suspect, or the destruction of evidence. *United States v. Parada*, 289 F. Supp. 2d 1291 (D.Kan. 2003), indicated that because a mobile device has limited storage, there is a possibility that the information contained on the mobile device could be deleted or overwritten, so a search to retrieve the data was needed immediately to preserve the evidence. To argue, training in today's mobile forensic courses focus on maintaining the device in an isolated state, so that network connections are not allowed. This action would negate this type of exigency in most situations. In another case, *United States v. Morales-Ortiz*, 376 F. Supp. 2d 1131 (D. N.M 2004), it was also argued that access had to be made to the address book under exigent circumstances, but unlike *United States v. Parada*, which involved call logs, this search and seizure was not justified. (There are, of course, exigent circumstances related to national security, but those instances are beyond the scope of this discussion.)

A somewhat murky area surrounds lost or abandoned property. If a subject leaves a mobile device in a store's restroom, for example, and the owner of the store turns it over to police, can officers search the device? In *People v. Schutter*, 249 P.3d 1123 (2011), an iPhone was left in a gas station bathroom and subsequently searched after the business owner gave the phone to police. Because Schutter returned to try to find the device, it was never lost or abandoned, and the information the government agent recovered was suppressed. In another case, *State v. Dailey*, 2010 WL 3836204 (Ohio Ct. App. 3 Dist, Oct. 4, 2010), a person caught after shoplifting fled the scene, leaving behind a jacket. Inside the jacket was a mobile device, which was later examined by government agents, who discovered an address book that was used to find the suspect. The suspect was located, and the evidence was allowed into the trial since the suspect had abandoned his property when he fled the store.

Always, the best course of action for a government seizure of data is to obtain a search warrant. Warrantless searches, unless by a private citizen, should be approached with caution. If a warrantless search is to occur, it must be clearly documented and outlined as to how consent was obtained or what necessitated the exigency. Without that information, it is highly unlikely that the evidence obtained will be usable in a criminal proceeding.

Location to Be Searched: Physical Location

When creating a legal document to search a physical place (residence, business, or site), the *affiant*, or officer who signs an affidavit to obtain a warrant, must describe the physical place, the address, and what should be searched for. This information is gathered after investigation and intimate knowledge based upon probable cause that the items exist at this location and in the particular place defined. This process protects the person and place to be searched from unnecessary searches and seizures—and, more importantly, the neighboring homes immediately to the right and left of a residence to be searched.

When developing an affidavit for a search warrant at a residence, the affiant must explicitly define clearly, but not be limited to, the color of the home; the type of home exterior construction (brick, wood paneling, and so on); color of any accents (shutters, trim, windows); the address of the residence; any trees, toys, and vehicles in the front of the residence; features unique to the target residence; and what is to be searched for once at the location. Not including this amount of detail in the search warrant upon the execution could have disastrous results.

Location to Be Searched: Mobile Device

Describing the location to be searched when completing the affidavit to obtain a search warrant for a mobile device should include ample detail. Simply identifying the device as a "Verizon, black, Android smart device" could lead to questions as to what device the original search warrant was drafted to cover. When drafting court paperwork to recover data from a mobile device, the affiant must specifically describe the place and property to be searched. Prior to seizure and subsequent search of a mobile device, the place (the device) and the property to be searched (data) should be defined. You must understand what should be at the scene and how it might relate to the overall mobile device examination.

It is best to document, when available, the following information regarding the "place to be searched":

- The mobile device manufacturer
- The mobile device model
- The mobile device serial number (not the device's phone number; it can be changed easily to another device)
- The color of the device
- The type of cover for the device—even if not unique
- The wallpaper visible on the device screen or lock screen wallpaper
- The presence of a camera on the front and/or on the back
- The presence of a headphone jack—top or bottom or side
- Description of any specific details unique to the device (scratches, broken screen, and so on)

The key is to be very specific, to define clearly to the reader and person conducting the seizure that there is no doubt that the device described in the warrant is the device to be seized. Accomplishing this task with precision in a warrant will lead to better results when challenged on the validity of the item to be searched.

Items to Seize

The second part of the warrant for the mobile device should include the items to seize, which can vary immensely depending on the type of device that is being examined, but more importantly on the circumstances of the seizure. The scope of the warrant will dictate exactly what can be searched for during the examination. Scope is typically dictated by the type of event that constituted the search of the device as described in the affidavit. For example, if investigating an embezzlement case, the mobile device is collected forensically for images, but audio data might not be within the scope of the warrant if it was not included when writing the affidavit. The same would be true if conducting a collection of a mobile device for voicemails if the investigation was dealing with an image-related crime. Every circumstance, if articulated correctly in an affidavit, should involve every piece of data to be collected from a mobile device.

One fact is crystal clear: data contained on a mobile device should cover the gamut of an individual's actions, regardless of the case. Mobile device data is relevant to each and every investigation in today's electronic investigations. The seizure of mobile device data ultimately comes down to the articulation and understanding of today's communication and its relevance to the investigation.

When specifying the data to be seized from a mobile device, follow these guidelines:

- Research the device and the data types that can be located on the device. Using sites such as phonescoop.com and GSMArena.com can help you locate the user data types. Also, use the device manufacturer's site to ascertain the types of data that may be contained on the specific mobile device.
- Understand that today's communication occurs via third-party apps, so all cases should involve seizure of this information.
- Documenting everyday life, capturing business documents, or storing important notes is often done using the device's built-in camera or microphone. These images, including both video and audio, are saved to the device and can also be uploaded or transmitted via the built-in media viewer, a third-party app, and even near field communication (NFC). Generalizing this information to include not only transmission but reception data is critical for every type of collection.
- Text messaging and multimedia messaging can transmit and receive notes, passwords, keys, company information, threats, confessions, audio notes, images, videos, social media shares, and much more. Every investigation should include a search of messaging.
- Personal information manager (PIM) data can include, but is not limited to, call logs, contacts, calendar, and notes. Typically, mobile device users store reminders, monikers, and important dates in these areas, which can constitute influential material for any investigation.
- Installed applications and "stock" applications, or apps, extend the use of the device to allow for access to the Internet, remote servers, gaming, and more. Apps also allow for the transfer of money, images, documents, audio, video, and much more. Understanding what is installed and what has been accessed is very important during any mobile device collection.
- Including deleted data in all mobile device warrant applications should be substantiated by indicating the type of data category (such as SMS, MMS, apps) and why this is needed. Today's devices store data on flash memory, and nonvolatile flash memory stores data even if it has been deleted by the user. Also, applications used by smart devices use database files that can store data previously deleted by the user.

Note Today, far more text messages are sent than voice calls every day. Pew Research Center states that the number of calls made and received per day in 2010–2011 averaged 12.3 voice calls per day for an average adult. The average number of text messages per day during the same period was 41.5 for an average adult.

Articulating why the data is needed from the device is also key to a successful examination, analysis, and eventual presentation. In today's world, everyday life is stored electronically on handheld devices; it could be debated that search warrants could merely indicate "all data on the phone" and be unchallenged. This mindset, however, will eventually lead to case law mandating that collections and examinations be governed by a set of standards. If the standards are not met, the examination and collection cannot be used in a court proceeding. On the other hand, articulating the reasoning for the collection and examination of the various types and formats of data from mobile devices will do two things: the examination and analysis will have meaning, and the focus of the investigation will be clearly defined to assist subsequent examinations.

The Federal Judicial Center (www.fjc.gov) and U.S. Department of Justice (www.justice.gov) web sites provide sample search warrant applications for electronic evidence along with specific guidelines.

Securing the Scene

No matter where the crime scene is located, it must be safe—this goes for a law enforcement scene, corporate location, or enterprise situation. The safety of the people at this location is paramount. Just showing up at a location to conduct a routine collection of a mobile device could be very stressful for the person or persons who own the mobile device. The data contained on a device is often compared to the information written in a person's diary; this information typically does not see the light of day, and any seizure of that information can be traumatic. Make sure the collection location is free from outside distractions, including the owners of the digital devices. Prior to requesting that the occupants leave the premises, you must conduct a guided discussion about the mobile device and any other details that might assist. Sometimes securing the scene is as easy as locking the residence or location; in other cases, you might need to request that the scene be monitored by security while the search is taking place.

Digital data on mobile devices is extremely volatile, and announcing the probability of arrival to conduct an examination of a mobile device will typically lead to dismal results. With most of today's devices, the user can quickly wipe the device of data by navigating to a menu location or even sending a remote signal to the device. It is imperative that you take steps immediately once the scene is secure to secure the device or devices that are to be collected.

Data Volatility at the Scene

As discussed, a mobile device can be wiped of data either by the owner manually navigating the appropriate menu or remotely using the device, manufacturer, or telco software. You must take several steps to ensure that this does not occur. Simply removing the device from the possession of the user may ensure that data cannot be manually removed, but what about remote access to the device on the scene?

Cellular transmissions occur via radio waves, and data transmissions can originate and terminate at the device via the cellular signal or a Wi-Fi network. A remote wipe signal can be

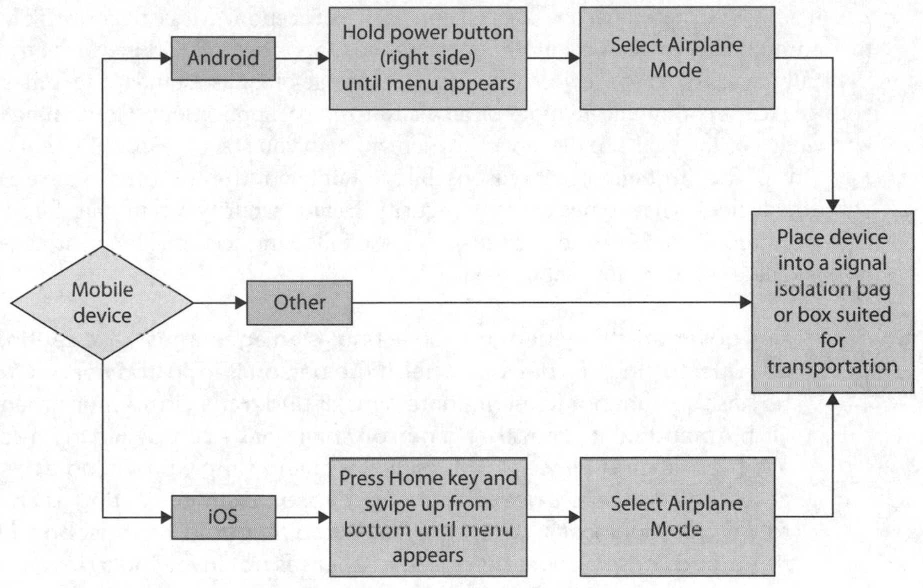

FIGURE 3-1 Device isolation response for a scene when an examiner is not available

sent to the device via a cellular signal. Inhibiting the reception of this signal can ensure that the device will not be remotely wiped, thus protecting the data. Also, by inhibiting the cellular signal and Wi-Fi, you can ensure that the device cannot receive additional transmissions such as calls, texts, and other data-related deliveries.

When a mobile device is located, isolation of the device must occur immediately. Figure 3-1 outlines steps that should be taken for a mobile device depending upon the type of device. By using this simple flowchart, you can be sure to isolate the device by using airplane mode, if available, or, in the case of a legacy mobile device, a signal isolation bag.

Note Newer devices using Bluetooth can also receive data from NFC devices.

Asking the Right Questions

The security of the scene and the mobile device is extremely important, but if the device is locked with a passcode, the investigator at the scene should speak with the device owner, which may help to elicit information that can help with unlocking the device should the need arise.

The owner of the device can also paint a picture of daily usage; indicate what applications she uses on a regular basis; and indicate how often she uses text messaging, who she most often speaks to, and how many images the device can hold. These questions may seem ordinary, but they can be used to direct the analysis of the information once it's collected from the device.

If an owner states that she uses an app such as Facebook Messenger or Kik Messenger to communicate, you can begin by analyzing those apps before working with any others. Typically, users of smart devices who are over the age of 20 use standard text messaging; younger users communicate more often via third-party applications. Combining this with knowledge of the habits of the device owner can help you steer the examination later.

One of the most important reasons, but certainly not the only one, to have a conversation with the device owner comes down to security. Device security can inhibit the collection of data from mobile devices and is discussed in the following section, along with alternative possible data locations for mobile device data.

Note Any government agent or person acting as an agent must take caution during any questioning of a device owner. If the person is in custody or not free to leave, he has the right not to incriminate himself under the Fifth Amendment. The Fifth Amendment states that "a person shall not be compelled in any case to be a witness against himself." This could involving simply providing a password to access the device to a government agent or an examiner acting as an agent. Prior to any questioning, if a subject is in a custodial setting, he must be advised of his rights and consent must be in place. For cases not involving a government agent or actor, the implications of self-incrimination do not apply.

Device Security

Mobile device security can be a real problem during collection of electronically stored data. Two types of security can be enabled on a mobile device: user authentication device security and/or data security.

User authentication security mechanisms include passwords, personal identification numbers (PINs), passcodes and passphrases, patterns, and biometrics. Each provide a different level of security for the device, and sometimes multiple measures are used on a single device. Typically, legacy devices use a passcode consisting of numbers, and if a SIM card is available a PIN and/or PIN unblocking key (PUK) can be used. Smart phones can use locking devices ranging from passcodes to biometrics, depending on what the user has set and the type of options available.

Note PINs and PUKs are numbers comprising up to eight digits, but typically four for a PIN and eight for a PUK. A PIN locks a SIM card, and a PUK is used to unblock a SIM that has been PIN-locked. These will be covered in Chapter 9 in more detail.

Data security could also pose difficulty to the examination. If the device and any storage areas (internal or external) have been encrypted, the ability to recover that data could be limited. Most smart phones have a feature that enables users to encrypt their data; this can be a separate code in the settings or the user authentication code for device security. Android 5.0 devices, for example, have data encryption turned on by default to address user concerns over personal information availability should a device be lost. iOS devices also encrypt data on the device by default and enable the user to force the device to produce an encrypted backup where a second password is needed to decrypt. Windows Phones are not capable of using

Windows Phone BitLocker encryption unless the device is a managed device—the device must be under a Mobile Device Management system at the enterprise level to allow for encryption. BlackBerry devices enable users to turn on encryption in the settings of the device for both the device and the media card. A secondary passcode must be used to decrypt an encrypted BlackBerry device to obtain usable data. With the release of BlackBerry 10, the backup files are also encrypted by default.

Whenever possible, consider obtaining security keys from the owner. If biometrics is used, the device must be unlocked by the device owner at the location in which the device has been seized if possible, and all other security measures should be removed. If any other methods of security are used, the agent should request the information and attempt to access it in the presence of the owner. This way, if the code is not correct, the agent can obtain more information and make another attempt. This method may seem to be less than ideal, but with current devices, this may be the only way to collect data from a device forensically. If the agent receives the correct information to unlock the device and remove encryption, he or she should make the setting permanent so that the device can be successfully examined at a later date if necessary.

Backups

Valuable information can also be located from backups of a mobile device. A smart device, such as an iOS device, creates a backup of data from the device on a computer to which it has been connected, either using a USB cable or via Wi-Fi. Other devices, such as a BlackBerry, a Windows Mobile phone, and an Android, can also back up their data. All of these operating systems can also encrypt the information that has been backed up, which adds another level of difficulty when collecting and analyzing the information. Request information on any devices that might have been backed up if the backups are password protected. The collection and analysis of backups are covered in Chapter 10 (BlackBerry) and Chapter 11 (iOS).

Examining the Scene for Evidence

After gathering information from the occupants or the people at the scene, the agent should search the area systematically. Searching can occur in a pattern, by working from the outside to the center of the location, by using a back-and-forth search, or by dividing the location into several smaller portions. The key is to use a method that will not duplicate the work of others or confuse the team conducting the search.

Prior to the search, take photographs of the area from all angles to allow for documentation. In addition, create a sketch of the area to document dimensions and locations of various pieces of evidence. A sketch will also help when you're searching the various portions of the scene. Each search area of the overall scene should be small enough that a single person can search quickly while a second person provides security and can photograph. When dealing with electronic storage devices, particularly mobile device evidence, the pieces can be extremely small. Breaking down the search area into small, consumable portions will help searchers avoid overlooking evidentiary items. On the other hand, if the area is too large, a small SIM card or microSD card can easily be missed. The photographs and scene sketch of the pre-search area can be used to compile a more precise evidence map in the final documentation when creating the report of findings.

Many items related to a mobile device can be found at a scene. These are covered in the following sections. These electronic storage devices and accessories are essential to your investigation's overall success.

USB Drives

Removable USB drives, often known as flash drives or thumb drives, can contain up to 1 terabyte of storage space (as of this writing). An inexpensive way to transfer data from one device to another, these drives are often used to store images, documents, and even mobile device backups. A mobile device typically does not have a USB connection that would allow direct output to the removable device, but a lot of mobile tablets do. Mobile devices do not have much storage on board, and using removable media such as a USB drive can help expand that storage space. Also, data from a mobile device is often sent to a remote location either by messaging, e-mail, or third-party applications and can then be saved to the removable media. Any USB devices collected should be included in the mobile forensic examination.

Chargers and USB Cables

Often during examination of a mobile device, the power for the device becomes depleted. Obtaining the power cable during the seizure of the device can help lower the cost associated with purchasing power cables for every device examined. The search warrant should always indicate seizure of power cables to negate the possibility of losing power once the device is back at the lab for examination.

USB cables are also typically included when the device is purchased and are likely part of the charging unit. USB cables are needed to connect the device to a mobile forensic tool for collection of the mobile device's digital data. Some mobile device units have a unique cable, and if they are not obtained at the scene, processing the device may be postponed until a cable can be located. Most mobile forensic software tools also come with a cable kit, but some do not. If a kit is not part of the mobile forensic solution, a new cable must be purchased for every device that will need to be processed. Make sure the mobile device USB cable is on any search warrant or court paperwork.

SD Cards

Mobile devices do not have infinite storage capacities, so manufacturers have allowed for expandable storage using microSD cards. These cards are extremely small, and locating them can be very difficult if they are not installed in the mobile device. The cards can also be exchanged between different devices—for example, a digital camera SD card adapter could contain a microSD card that was once used in a mobile device. Examiners have reported finding microSD cards with mobile device images that were taken with a digital camera, and vice versa. Because more and more digital devices are using some type of flash storage, you must locate and seize all devices and media storage drives during the scene examination.

SIM Cards

Small SIM cards can be difficult to locate if they are outside of the mobile device. The portability of SIM cards was one of the features that set GSM (Global Systems for Mobile Communications) devices apart from CDMA (Code Division Multiple Access) phones, but this also means multiple SIM cards can be lying around, possibly hidden, at the scene. Old SIM cards, and even SIM cards belonging to different devices, can also be located and collected during the search.

Older Mobile Devices

Often during a search for a particular device, older devices are neglected. But older mobile devices can contain critical data that might be relevant to the current case being investigated. When seizing an older device from the scene, remember to grab the chargers and USB devices that match the old device.

Personal Computers

Computers can contain mobile device backups and information that can be used to unlock a locked device. Apple devices that are backed up to a computer use a property list file that can help iTunes synch data without the user entering the lock passcode. Using this file, the examiner can use forensic software to obtain a backup without knowing the passcode of the device. This information will be covered in Chapter 11 in our analysis of backups and Apple devices.

Conducting a forensic analysis of a computer can also yield passwords for the device, additional synched data from third-party applications, media automatically synched, and documents and settings. Any computers located at the scene should be further analyzed by forensic examiners for additional information that may assist in the examination of any mobile devices located and later collected.

Once You Find It, What's Next?

When searching a scene, excited searchers can forget all their training and work when they locate the specified target item or items. A search should be directed, meticulous, and calculated to avoid this. After each sectioned area has been thoroughly searched, the team can move to the next area. A forensic search is like an archeological dig, where a 3000-year-old bone could be destroyed if people are moving too quickly. Getting overly excited can often lead a person to miss a piece of evidence such as a small microSD card or SIM card in the same area of the iPad or Galaxy S5 that was the primary focus of the search. When items are located to be seized from the scene, follow a set plan for the actual collection; working without a plan can often lead to improper collection and the dismissal of the artifact and possibly the case.

This phase of the search should involve a minimum of two people per team. One person collects the physical artifacts while the other documents the seizure. When at least two people are involved in the exercise, each can realistically monitor the other. This can alleviate any accusations of improprieties. It also enables each individual to focus on his or her assignment. Focus is important when conducting a search and seizure of evidence at any scene. If the people conducting the search are not focused on their assigned duties, things will be missed.

Inventory and Location

The person responsible for documentation should photograph each area from multiple angles. (These photographs are in addition to the overall scene pictures that were taken at the onset of the search.) Once an artifact is located, the searching team must slow down the process to move to the documentation phase. The person conducting the search should identify the location of the artifact without moving it and notify the person in charge of documenting it, who photographs the items in its original position and from multiple angles. If possible, the team should use measurement labels to assist if the area has to be reconstructed and to indicate relational size. If the device is powered on, it is extremely important to photograph the screen that is visible and to document whether incoming messages, calls, photographs, or other data arrived on the device. With some devices, the first few lines of a message are visible and can offer immediate, actionable intelligence. Because a lot of devices can be remotely wiped, documenting data on live mobile devices should be done quickly. Older devices also did not have the storage space available on today's devices, so information on these devices could be overwritten with an incoming message or call.

Once the device is seized and the following information is ascertained, the evidence should be placed into an evidence container or RF-shielding material. Before packaging a piece of digital evidence, answer the following questions:

- Will the device be analyzed at the scene?
- Does the device need latent processing?
- Are there biological concerns?
- Is the device security enabled, or has the security been disabled?
- Is power depletion of the device a factor?

Document all of these questions for later retrieval and to determine the way the digital device will be packaged. If the device must stay powered on because of security concerns (such as locking, encryption, or passwords) and power to the device is not a concern, place the device into a radio signal isolation bag and then into an evidence bag to inhibit radio signals reaching the device. (Isolation techniques are discussed in depth in Chapter 4.) If the device can be powered off, place it into a standard evidence bag. If the digital device has any type of biological material that might be contacted during analysis, you'll need to take additional steps (described in Chapter 4).

Before packaging, consider whether fingerprints or other evidence should be obtained from the exterior of the mobile device. If the device is powered on and has to remain on due to security locks, decide on the necessity of immediate retrieval of the data on the device prior to transporting to a lab or a field recovery of latent fingerprints. If the device is to be transported, place it in a radio signal isolation box or bag and then in an evidence container.

For evidence located at the scene during the search, the individual documenting the collection of artifacts should label each evidence container with the following information:

- Location found
- Evidence description
- State of device (on/off and locked/unlocked)
- Processing need (at scene/at lab)
- Owner name (if known)
- Case number
- Person collecting
- Chain of custody (person, date/time)

This detailed information is critical. With the appropriate data documented on each evidence container ahead of time, the examiner can quickly determine what devices need to be collected at the scene. If the data must be collected at the scene, the examiner can perform the extraction of data from the piece of evidence while maintaining an unbroken chain of custody.

Note Establishing a chain of custody is one of the most important details regarding evidence collected at a scene. This is extremely important in cases when the evidence is located at the scene by one person, who hands that evidence to another, who then takes that device to the person who will conduct the device extraction. As described, the chain of custody would be extremely difficult to maintain without documentation. If documentation is not captured correctly, the entire process and the admissibly of the evidence will undoubtedly be questioned.

Proper handling of digital evidence will be covered in greater detail in Chapter 4.

Data Collection: Where and When

Determining where to collect a mobile device's electronically stored information and the duration of collecting and completing the collection are typically dictated by the type of investigation that is underway. If possible, collect the mobile device in an environment where distractions are at a minimum, safety is not of concern, and time is sufficient. The collection of the data using forensically sound methods and techniques is just as important as the physical collection of the evidence from the scene. Having the luxury of collecting data and examining it in a lab setting is not always possible. More often, data collection, especially for law enforcement, occurs at the scene. Collection circumstances can vary broadly, ranging from a device that locks if power is depleted, to an owner who grants consent to search but will not allow the device to be removed from the location, to the need for immediate actionable information.

If power is depleted or a device is turned off, security settings can render collection of the device data impossible. If the possibility of the device locking will hamper the investigation and device collection, the extraction should occur immediately at the scene.

Consent to search a device is often requested by law enforcement if the device is not part of the original search warrant, the device is on the person under arrest, or the device is at the scene of a call for service. A consent search is an exception to the search warrant rule, as explained earlier. If the person giving the consent has proper authority and waives his or her rights, you can safely obtain information from a mobile device. The person giving consent can also revoke the consent at any time, however, so it is imperative that the data be collected at the scene.

In a corporate situation, a policy can be in place to allow a search of a personally owned mobile device at the workplace without employee consent. Such a policy should be clear, much like the Texas Workforce Commission policy that states the following: "Make it clear to the employee that the employer reserves the right to search any devices, with storage or memory capabilities that they might bring to work and can make copies of any files found therein." For a corporately owned device, the employee doesn't usually expect privacy, and the company can collect the data whenever reasonable.

In either situation, the company will benefit by your searching a mobile device in the most effective way to decrease the time the device will be out of service. Collect a personal device as quickly as possible to help mitigate an employee's emotional response, and collect a corporately owned device as soon as reasonably possible.

At times, the device data is recovered and collected at the scene to be used immediately in the investigation. For law enforcement, that could mean gathering contacts and SMS messages from a device to locate stolen property that is due to arrive that same day. It could also mean they need to locate an accomplice in a crime using the person's contact list. For corporate mobile device collections, it could mean recovering SMS messages of a threatening nature, sexual harassment allegations, or pictures of a refinery fire that need to be collected immediately to gain as much intelligence as possible at the onset of the investigation.

Whenever possible, however, the collection and subsequent examination and analysis should occur away from the scene and in a controlled environment.

Chapter Summary

Creating a detailed plan on the location and seizure of the device is just as important as a detailed plan on the collection and analysis of the data. Understand that privacy rights exist not only regarding a person's place of residence or workplace, but also regarding the contents of a mobile device. Recent court decisions state that a mobile device is the equivalent of a person's private history, and as such it should be treated as a locked file cabinet. If, for example, a significant text message for a case is intertwined with a year's worth of unrelated personal data, and segregating that data is not possible, a search warrant for the content of the device should be obtained. Understanding that in corporate situations, a person's personal data can be stored on the same device with company data makes retrieval of information even more difficult if policies are not in place for collection.

When you are conducting a search of the area, making sure to document the scene prior to seizure and identifying where a particular piece of evidence is located will assist later when you complete your report. While on the scene, be aware of items such as storage devices, computers, and media cards because mobile device data can be stored on each medium. Passwords and encryption may be enabled, so speak to the device owner and look around the scene for any documents that might contain password bypass information. During the search and seizure, clearly document every person who contacts the evidence to maintain a solid chain of custody, no matter whether it is a law enforcement or a civil case. Finally, understanding that the examination of the data cannot occur if the physical device is unlawfully obtained will help you guide the initial states of the mobile device examination.

While you're at the scene, all evidence, including the device, must be packaged correctly depending on how and in what state it was located and what type of examination will take place. This information is covered in the next chapter.

4 Preparing, Protecting, and Seizing Digital Device Evidence

Conducting a proper initial investigation is a vital part of any forensic examination. How the evidence is prepared, seized, and then packaged after the proper seizure can be just as important, however. Data can be easily destroyed by improperly preparing and packaging a device.

The old adage "don't sweat the small stuff" does not apply to the investigation of digital devices—particularly mobile devices. The small things are extremely important to the overall success of every investigation. "Bagging and tagging" the device using the proper procedures is not the only concern; the state of the device at the time of seizure and during property transportation and storage is also important. You must also understand the ways in which a mobile device communicates and the types of security used with mobile devices so that you can determine the most appropriate ways to protect the device before and after it is seized.

Data from a collected device can be suppressed during a trial, even after a proper seizure, if it was improperly documented regarding the chain of custody. If investigators fail to package the electronic evidence properly because they are in a hurry, they know the device data will be collected immediately, or they are unaware of the problems associated with an active or security-enabled network, their hard work and the investigation can be inadmissible in a court procedure.

Finally, the way in which a device is transported from the scene to a lab or storage facility is also important.

Before Seizure: Understanding Mobile Device Communication

A mobile device is an *active device*—in other words, a mobile device is attached to several networks that can allow outside communication to interfere with physical collection and subsequent extraction of data. A mobile device can be connected to a cellular network, a Wi-Fi network, Bluetooth, or a near field communication (NFC) device. How you deal with an active device can determine the success of the evidence collection. The physical collection of the actual mobile device and any accessories can also determine the validity of the introduced evidence if used in a legal proceeding.

In the early days of mobile device forensics, the cellular network was the only communication method examiners typically had to eliminate when collecting a digital device. Today's mobile devices communicate in several ways. Eliminating the risk of contamination of important digital data can be extremely challenging. Those involved in seizing mobile devices must understand how the devices communicate—not only with the cellular network, but with other devices as well. Understanding device communication can help examiners choose the appropriate forensic equipment for use in various scenarios in the lab and in the field, and it can help inhibit a mobile device from all communication to avoid data loss and image integrity issues.

Cellular Communication

A mobile device uses radio frequency to transmit and receive cellular communication and data. Several factors determine the radio frequency used by the mobile device and also affect the way an onsite team and an examiner approach a device to eliminate the possibility that it will initiate or receive communication during or after seizure. Determining factors include the type of device, the cellular telecommunication company, and the allocated frequency band used by the country in which the mobile device is operating.

Chapter 1 discussed the cellular network and how radio waves travel along the air gap from the cellular system's mobile towers to the mobile device. Because the device transmits and receives information via the cellular network, evidence collectors and examiners must use a signal isolation technique to inhibit the radio waves from being received and transmitted by the device. These techniques can include switching the device off, placing the device in airplane mode, wrapping the device in a material that blocks cellular signals, and placing the device into a radio isolation box. Some forensic examiners use large radio isolation rooms completely devoid of windows and lined with special copper wallpaper.

Note Radio isolation techniques use a principle Michael Faraday discovered in 1836 with the invention of a Faraday cage. Faraday (1791–1867) was a scientist who discovered that electrically charged particles that are approaching a metal object (in this case, aluminum or copper mesh) remain on the exterior of the object. A Faraday cage shields items inside the cage from static electrical fields. All electrostatic charges and electromagnetic radiation are distributed across the exterior of the cage, blocking electric charges and radiation from entering the cage. Similar devices or bags can be used to block radio signals from reaching a mobile device.

Device Frequencies

True 4G devices must use either Frequency Division Duplexing (FDD) or Time Division Duplexing (TDD) Long Term Evolution (LTE). FDD LTE is used globally by more carriers, but TDD is gaining carriers in countries such as China and the Middle East. Newer smart phones are beginning to use both frequencies for communication. The LTE frequency bands extended to 44 with the addition of TDD-LTE. Band 43 in the LTE spectrum runs at 3600–3800MHz, which is not covered by a lot of isolation bags and enclosures.

Tables 4-1 and 4-2 contain the various LTE allocated frequency bands. Current frequency bands used by true 4G LTE must be isolated by signal isolation techniques.

TABLE 4-1 FDD LTE Bands and Frequencies: Frequency Allocation Table

LTE Band	Uplink (MHz)	Downlink (MHz)
1	1920–1980	2110–2170
2	1850–1910	1930–1990
3	1710–1785	1805–1880
4	1710–1755	2110–2155
5	824–849	869–894
6	830–840	875–885
7	2500–2570	2620–2690
8	880–915	925–960
9	1749.9–1784.9	1844.9–1879.9
10	1710–1770	2110–2170
11	1427.9–1452.9	1475.9–1500.9
12	698–716	728–746
13	777–787	746–756
14	788–798	758–768
15	1900–1920	2600–2620
16	2010–2025	2585–2600
17	704–716	734–746
18	815–830	860–875
19	830–845	875–890
20	832–862	791–821
21	1447.9–1462.9	1495.5–1510.9
22	3410–3500	3510–3600
23	2000–2020	2180–2200
24	1625.5–1660.5	1525–1559
25	1850–1915	1930–1995
26	814–849	859–894

(Continued)

TABLE 4-1 FDD LTE Bands and Frequencies: Frequency Allocation Table *(Continued)*

LTE Band	Uplink (MHz)	Downlink (MHz)
27	807–824	852–869
28	703–748	758–803
29	n/a	717–728
30	2305–2315	2350–2360
31	452.5–457.5	462.5–467.5
32	Downlink only	1452–1496

TABLE 4-2 TDD LTE Bands and Frequencies: Frequency Allocation Table

LTE Band	Allocation (MHz)
33	1900–1920
34	2010–2025
35	1850–1910
36	1930–1990
37	1910–1930
38	2570–2620
39	1880–1920
40	2300–2400
41	2496–2690
42	3400–3600
43	3600–3800
44	703–803

Note If a device can be powered off and security has not been enabled, the device should be placed into airplane mode prior to powering it off. By doing this, the device can be powered on at the forensic lab without concerns about isolation. Of course, if the device cannot be powered off, using portable isolation bags rated for new cellular frequencies is highly recommended.

Bluetooth Communication

With Bluetooth technology, a user can move data between a mobile device and a computer and attach headsets, headphones, and wireless speakers to a mobile device. In the SANS research paper "Dispelling Common Bluetooth Misconceptions" (www.sans.edu/research/security-laboratory/article/Bluetooth), author Joshua Wright points out that although organizations typically consider Bluetooth to be short-range technology, class 1 devices can operate at ranges that are typical of a wireless network at 100 meters (328 feet). Granted, to operate at that distance, a class 1 device would have to be at both ends of the communication. Today's mobile devices, including the most prevalent Android and iOS devices, operate as only class 2, at a range of 10 meters (33 feet).

Some companies employ Bluetooth Smart Beacons, which enable retailers to transmit location information to smart devices. The location can then identify and target the device, sending location-specific data immediately to the device to notify it of a retail sale and gather analytics regarding where in the store most people are shopping. Once considered as just a way to transfer data to a device, Bluetooth can now identify a smart device by using location-based technology.

Note Location-based technology actually originated from the first hacking, or "Bluejacking," of a Bluetooth device. Bluejacking involves sending messages and controls via Bluetooth to another Bluetooth-enabled device. (Don't confuse this with "Bluesnarfing," in which access to information on the mobile device is compromised and stolen from the device, or "Bluebugging," which controls the device to become a listening device.) All of the Bluetooth hacking techniques are limited by distance because most mobile devices cannot be accessed from greater than 10 meters. With the use of directional amplified antennas, however, some hackers have been able to penetrate Bluetooth device security at up to 1 mile—this is referred to as "Bluesniping." This technique can be especially troubling because a lot of vehicle communication systems in today's automobiles are class 1 Bluetooth devices.

Apple iOS devices, Androids, Windows Phones, BlackBerrys, and most modern mobile devices allow for Bluetooth connections and maintain a list of devices that can connect with the device, their associated media access control (MAC) address, and other available Bluetooth-enabled devices that were nearby but that did not connect. These lists can be obtained using mobile forensic software to observe the connections made with the device and those that were available and were not connected. These device Bluetooth profiles can be used to assist in performing various functions, including transferring files to and from the device; communicating hands-free; accessing Internet hotspots; using a mouse or keyboard with the mobile device; and sharing messages, contacts, and calendar data with another device. All devices must have their Bluetooth radio turned on for a connection to occur. Androids and Windows Phones must also have their Bluetooth visibility turned on and available to Bluetooth-enabled devices. The device then must be paired to the other device to transmit and receive data. The current Android SDK does not allow for unpaired connections. For iOS devices, the connection to the device must be encrypted and a key must be shared between devices.

Wi-Fi Communication

Wi-Fi is a local area wireless technology (also called a wireless local area network, or WLAN) that enables a device to be connected to an access point that is connected to the Internet and/or a local area network (LAN). The first device reported to have Wi-Fi capabilities was the Calypso Wireless C1250i, demonstrated at the 2006 3GSM World Congress trade show in Barcelona. Most smart devices sold today can connect to a WLAN.

A Wi-Fi connection uses a frequency band identified by the Institute of Electrical and Electronics Engineers (IEEE) using the IEEE 802.11 media access control and physical layer specifications for WLAN communication using the 2.4, 3.6, 5, 6, and 60GHz frequency bands. A Wi-Fi network's range is typically limited, but as the frequency increases, the range increases, with a current maximum range of 70 meters (230 feet).

Mobile devices can also operate as a Wi-Fi hotspot using a cellular signal so that other WLAN-capable devices can be wirelessly attached to the mobile device. Because of the various potential infiltration points, a Wi-Fi–enabled mobile device must be removed from the WLAN as soon as possible at the scene.

Wi-Fi connections, like Bluetooth connections, are stored within a file maintained in mobile devices. This allows for the device to connect immediately to known and authorized sites and devices.

Note Versions prior to iOS 5 maintained a list of all Wi-Fi connections that were available to the device—not just those used by the device. This list was stored in the consolidated.db file in the device file system. When accessed, it identified all the Wi-Fi connections along with their latitudes and longitudes, which could be used to track the device, and the person using it, as it was moved to different locations. This vulnerability was fixed, and the consolidated.db was moved to the operating system partition; however, it's back with iOS 7, but with very limited available information.

Wi-Fi connections contain name and sometimes password information. Android devices are notorious for storing each and every successful connection to the device, information that could lead to security issues if an access point has been compromised. This is true not only for Android devices, but also for most devices set to connect automatically to an access point without notifying the user.

If a device is not properly isolated from a Wi-Fi signal during the initial seizure, the device could become vulnerable to penetration. An individual with network knowledge can exploit the device by posing as a known access point, creating an ad hoc network and identifying the network with the same Service Set Identifier (SSID) used for a legitimate access point. If the device is not disabled from connecting automatically, it can connect with the rogue access point. Some devices, such as the iPhone, come preprogrammed with Wi-Fi SSIDs and can be vulnerable to this attack. A perfect example is an iOS device from AT&T with the "attwifi" hotspot preconfigured. A person posing as a valid AT&T Wi-Fi hotspot could penetrate the device and possibly compromise the data before the device is even examined.

Near Field Communication

Today's devices also can operate as NFC devices that transfer and receive data simply by being near another NFC device or system set up to transmit and receive the signal. NFC is a short-range wireless technology that enables mobile devices to connect by touching the devices together or bringing them within a few inches of each other. NFC enables small amounts of data to be shared between an NFC tag and a mobile device or between two mobile devices capable of communication by NFC.

An NFC tag is based upon the NFC Data Exchange Format (NDEF). Mobile devices that are capable of NFC can make transactions, exchange content, and connect devices. NFC includes a lot of the components of contactless card technology and can be used to control multiple instances of a contactless card (such as hotel keys, work key cards, and so on).

Because NFC is close-proximity based, it is unlikely (though not impossible) that problems will occur during the seizure of a mobile device if NFC is enabled on the device. Attack of an NFC-enabled device would typically occur with another device using a relay system to capture data from the device and transfer it to a proxy card or device that is emulating the actual mobile device and being read by the NFC receiving device, such as a point-of-sale (POS) machine. The technique would allow the relay system to act as the actual POS machine and capture data because the individual's device "believes" that it is communicating with the actual POS device. Software could also be installed on the mobile device to act as a relay system to a fraudulent card emulator communicating with a reader device. Although NFC issues are highly unlikely when you're seizing a mobile device, you should consider isolating the device from the possibility of an NFC attack by turning off NFC.

Understanding Mobile Device Security

As mentioned in Chapter 3, several types of security can be enabled on a mobile device. Understanding these can help you determine the appropriate course of action during and after collecting the device.

If a device is powered on without security enabled, you must collect the device at the scene in a forensic manner to counter any security features that might engage if the power of the device is lost or if the device becomes locked before it can be examined at a lab. After a quick collection, talk with the owner to determine the type of security enabled and any ways to bypass it.

Prior to speaking to the device owner, you must have legal standing even to ask questions. If you are a government agent or actor, the device owner must understand his rights and accept that his testimony could be used against him.

Remember that multiple security settings may be used, such as the device password or PIN, a subscriber identity module (SIM) PIN, an encryption password, and a password for the device's backup if backup encryption will be enabled. If you can conduct a quick forensic collection prior to the conversation with the owner about the device's security settings, there is a far better chance the owner will provide the correct information. If the owner does not provide the security information or subsequently has given information that is later determined to be false, the initial forensic collection at the scene will prove valuable. On the other hand, if you obtain the correct information, the forensic examiner can further examine the device at the lab and compare information to what was collected initially. This comparison can be used to show that information was not altered during or after seizure.

Both scenarios—the owner disclosing or not disclosing information—are much different from the same scenarios in traditional computer examinations, although some drive encryption tools have made computer collections just as challenging. Today, a lot of mobile device forensic collections must occur at the scene because of data volatility and device security. Being prepared for an on-scene collection will help you combat a tremendous number of problems associated with today's device and data safeguards.

Tip **Request the information from the device owner, verify that the information is correct, collect the device on scene if possible, and if the security of the device is not a concern or has been circumvented, power off the device. If the security of the device is a concern for any reason, the device should be collected forensically at the scene.**

Most mobile devices encountered at a scene or forensic lab will be smart devices, but legacy phones can also have security features, including passcode or PIN and/or a SIM PIN. Although the general guidelines outlined here will suffice, the following sections discuss the various smart device security features by manufacturer. Your ability to recognize the type of device and respond in an appropriate way will be important for the follow-up collection.

Apple iOS Devices

Apple iOS device security depends upon the model, OS version, and user configuration settings. First-generation iOS devices used only a simple passcode (a four-digit number) and a SIM PIN. These devices were available only for Global Systems for Mobile Communications (GSM) markets until 2010, when an iOS device capable of running on the Verizon network was released. Subsequent generations allowed for both simple and complex passcodes along with a SIM PIN. With a complex password, the user could enter numbers, letters, and symbols up to 37 characters, providing greater security against brute-force attacks. (About 10,000 possible combinations could be guessed in about 13 minutes at a rate of 12 per second.) The latest generation of iOS devices allows for simple, complex, and biometric (fingerprint scanner) security, according to user settings.

If the passcode is entered incorrectly, a wait period will be required before a user is allowed to access the device. Apple documentation and the passcode screen indicate that the device will be wiped after 10 failed attempts, but it is the 11th failed entry that initiates the wipe. Table 4-3 lists the wait times in relation to failed attempts.

Recognizing the various screens that might be encountered can assist as you document, seize, and further examine the device. Figure 4-1 shows the possible iOS screens when requesting a simple passcode and a complex passcode. For a complex passcode that contains only numbers, the number pad will be available instead of the iOS keyboard, along with the complex passcode text box for the numeric entry.

TABLE 4-3 Failed Attempt Consequences for iOS Devices (from cinnamonthoughts.org and mcafee.com)

Failed Attempts	Added Waiting Time	Total Waiting Time
1 to 5	none	none
6	1 minute	1 minute
7	5 minutes	6 minutes
8	15 minutes	21 minutes
9	60 minutes	81 minutes
10	60 minutes	141 minutes
11	black screen	wiped device

Devices starting with iOS 4 added full disk encryption. This meant that any unallocated space on the device remained fully encrypted even if the password was known. Apple also enabled the user to encrypt backups using an iTunes setting. When enabled, this set a flag on the iOS device when synced to encrypt the data stream as it left the device for backup. So even if the device was not protected by a user password, the data that was collected would be encrypted if the iTunes password was not known. There is no visible setting on the iOS to indicate whether the device has been set to encrypt the backup. To determine whether backup

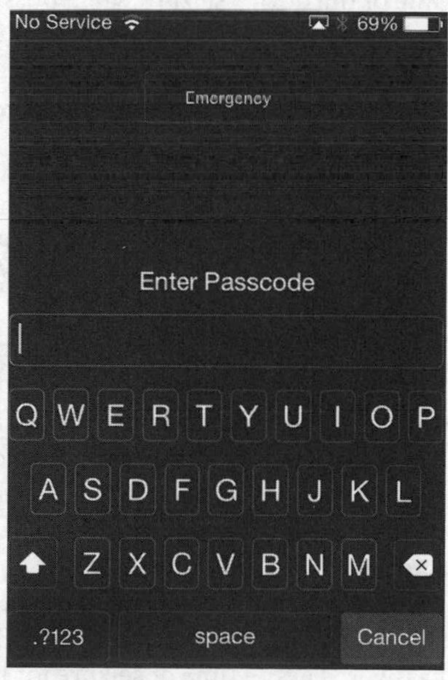

FIGURE 4-1 Simple (left) and complex (right) iOS passcode entry screens

encryption is enabled, you must launch the iTunes application on a computer, plug the iOS device into the same computer, and examine the iTunes software device information screen. The information screen indicates if backup encryption is enabled. Some mobile forensic software solutions such as AccessData's Mobile Phone Examiner Plus will indicate whether backup encryption is enabled during connection.

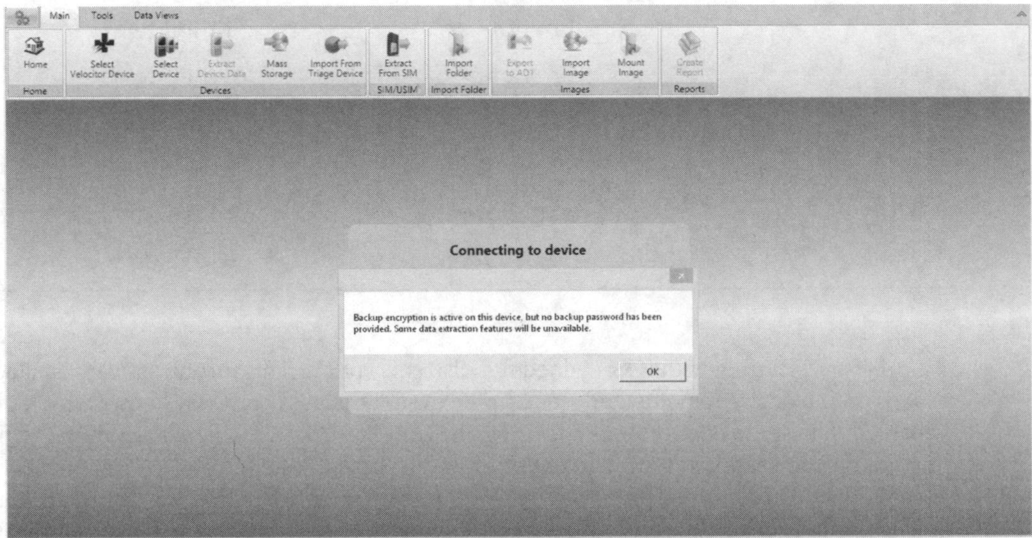

The investigator should request the iTunes password from the user of the device at the time of the device seizure when possible. If the user refuses to provide this information, some mobile forensic tools can be used to bypass and recover limited user data.

Note The iTunes backup password can be different from the device password or code.

In iOS 8.0, released in 2014, Apple changed the way device encryption worked to allow for greater security. The iOS device can use the passcode of the device to encrypt the device so that Apple itself is unable to recover the user data stored on the device if the passcode is not known. Prior to iOS 8, law enforcement officers had been allowed to send locked iOS devices with proper court documents to Apple security analysts, and if specific criteria were met, the officers would receive a disc image of the user partition for analysis. With the changes in iOS 8, Apple no longer uses the same methods and is unable to assist with these types of recoveries. If an iOS device running iOS 8 is locked with any of the security measures described in this section, the device password must be obtained from the user of the device before any type of forensic collection can occur.

The examiner should document any type of security, if enabled, along with the device type and operating system of the iOS device. This information should also include any known passwords at the time of seizure for both the device and iTunes. Having this information will assist with collection at the forensic lab.

Android Devices

Android devices brought a new type of security to the mobile device: the pattern. The first release of the Android OS allowed the use of a four-point pattern within the 3×3 grid, but newer devices allow the use of all nine points. The increased number of points elevated the security for the pattern, but the use of a pattern is still the lowest form of security for an Android device. With a nine-point pattern, about 50,000 restricted (same dot only once) pattern combinations are possible; with a four-point restricted pattern, about 1400 combinations are possible. In fact, a "smudge attack" can typically reveal the pattern of the Android user if the device is held at a 60-percent angle to a light source, as outlined in the article "Smudge Attacks on Smartphone Touch Screens," published by the members of the Department of Computer Information Science at the University of Pennsylvania.

Note A hash is stored in a key file within the Android file system. This file can be extracted and analyzed using forensic tools to reveal the pattern used to secure the device. This will be discussed in Chapter 13.

Because of the various security vulnerabilities, more security options were added to later versions of the Android OS. Android devices now allow the use of patterns; PINs; passcodes; passwords using letters, numbers, and symbols; and biometrics. The user enables security in the device settings, and if the examiner knows the type of security that is enabled, he or she can determine the viability of a bypass during a mobile device collection. More than 12,000 different Android devices are available on the global market, and identifying the exact type of security on these devices is difficult at best.

It is recommended that an examiner look at the device screen for clues as to the type of security in use. As shown in Figure 4-2, a set of dots indicates a swipe pattern, and a dialpad with nine numbers indicates a PIN. If a text cursor and keyboard are shown, a password or passphrase is required. If a fingerprint image is used, the device will show a location for the finger press that will unlock the device. Not shown in the figure is a screen with an active camera, which indicates that facial recognition is required. All biometric security features are backed up with another form of security—typically a PIN. If the device cannot be unlocked by biometrics, a PIN can be used.

No matter what security is used, even if the device is locked, it can be accessed with mobile forensic tools if the Android Debug Bridge (ADB) is enabled. However, ADB is typically not enabled by default. If it is enabled on the device after it is seized, the device can be forensically analyzed even if the screen is locked. (ADB will be covered in depth in Chapter 13.) When an Android device is seized, if access to the settings menu is available, the device should first be placed into airplane mode, and then the device ADB setting should be enabled and applications turned off. These settings will depend on the version of Android. Refer to Table 13-1 in Chapter 13 for version information.

Prior to Android 3.0, full device encryption was not available. With version 4.0, encryption is included in the system settings, and the user can choose settings to encrypt the contents of the mobile device along with data on the external memory card. With Android 5.0, device encryption is turned on by default. Device encryption will not inhibit the standard user data collection of most mobile forensic tools, but it is important that the device be properly placed into ADB mode as soon as possible.

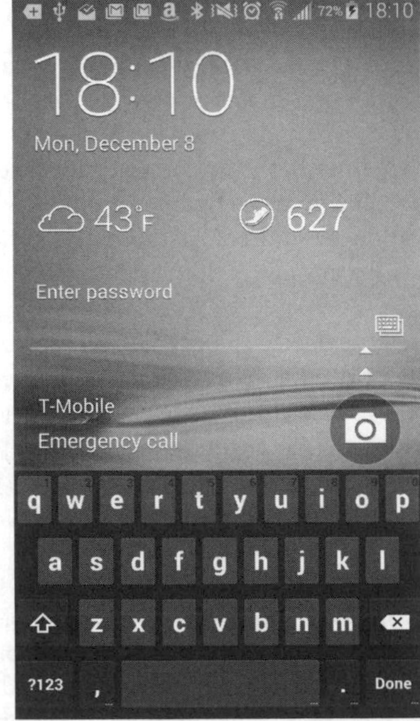

FIGURE 4-2 Android devices showing (clockwise, from top left) a swipe pattern, numeric PIN, biometrics (fingerprint), and passphrase

The type of security enabled, along with the Android device type and operating system, should be documented. This information should also include any known passwords at the time of seizure.

Windows Mobile and Windows Phone

Windows devices have transitioned from simple PIN and strong alphanumeric passcodes in Windows Mobile 6.0 and 6.1 to passwords only in Windows Phone 7 and 8 devices. All devices can also use SIM PINs to block calling features. The security password can be set by the user in the system settings of the Windows Phone 7 and 8. These devices are extremely difficult to examine without knowing the passcode or PIN. This information should be obtained from the user if the device will be later examined.

BlackBerry Devices

BlackBerry devices have always been known for their security, which is not easily bypassed. BlackBerry devices first used a simple PIN and a password or passphrase. Later versions could use a PIN, a passcode, or passphrase, plus a password for data encryption. There is no known way to bypass BlackBerry device security to collect the device's data without the handset's lock code when using forensic tools. A BlackBerry Enterprise Server (BES) can reset the device passcode if the device is part of the BES and that setting has been enabled previously. If the device also has a passcode set for data encryption, this must also be known. Gathering this information from a device user is especially important when dealing with these types of devices.

BlackBerrys can create a backup of their data, which can also be protected by passcodes or PINs. If the device password or PIN and encryption password are known, an unencrypted backup can be produced. If the password or PIN is not entered for the handset lock, a backup cannot be initiated and the device's data cannot be recovered. BlackBerry 10 devices added another tier to the security of the file system backup. Even if a device password is known and entered into the device, and even if the device is unlocked, the username and password for the Blackberry Link software must be entered. The Blackberry Link software is the Research in Motion (RIM) software used to update firmware and software and sync the mobile device with a computer.

Photographing the Evidence at the Scene

Photographing a device prior to the physical collection can be as important as documenting what is found at the scene. When a mobile device is located and it has been determined that the device will be seized as evidence, it should be photographed in place as it was found.

Before taking a photograph, assign an evidence number to the device and transfer that to an agency evidence tag, which is placed next to the device to be photographed and seized. The photograph should include the device along with the evidence number. The photographer should work around the device, shooting at all angles and including as much detail as possible.

Photographing the device in place is important for many reasons. Without this information, questions as to the validity of the extracted data could arise.

- A photograph provides a visual documentation of the device exactly as it was found, including the condition of the device and its screen or keyboard, plus any noticeable scratches or other noticeable anomalies indicative of use.
- Visually documenting this information will help to dispel potential accusations that the device was destroyed or damaged by the person collecting it from the scene.
- Such documentation can also be used to determine whether the device has any evidentiary value.
- If the device is powered on, a screen saver or wallpaper might provide information of interest.
- The date and time that appears on screen is important information as well.

After the face of the device has been properly photographed, the device can be turned over so that the opposite side can be photographed, again including the evidence tag number. The back side or battery side should be photographed to document serial numbers, missing batteries, missing backs, and any damage. After the device has been photographed, it can be placed properly in an evidence bag, as documented in the following sections.

Tagging and Marking Evidence

Each piece of mobile device evidence has unique characteristics and requires specific handling procedures. Mobile device evidence can be sensitive to changes in state, and you must take care when handling, tagging, and marking the evidence. Protect the device and any other mobile-related artifacts by wearing gloves to avoid adding fingerprints. Also, by maintaining the user's finger smudge marks on the capacitive screen, you can determine a passcode or phrase later to unlock a mobile device that uses a swipe or pattern for security. Maintaining the integrity of the user's marks on the device could be extremely important.

Before marking, tagging, and bagging memory cards, you must be grounded electrically to avoid sending electrostatic discharges (ESDs) onto the card. Memory cards and SIM conductors are highly susceptible to damage from ESD. A small static charge transferred from a person to an object can deliver from 3000 to 25,000 volts. A memory card's flash and SIM conductors that operate in the range of 1.8 to 5 volts can be corrupted and even destroyed by as little as 30 volts. Considering the high voltage that can be delivered in the process of identifying and bagging memory and SIM cards, make sure those collecting the artifacts have taken proper precautions.

When tagging and marking mobile device evidence, identify each piece with a unique number. The numbering should include the current year, the department case number assigned to the current event, a location number, and an article number. Maintaining this consistency when collecting evidence to be examined later may seem like overkill, but if the same information is collected as part of the organizational policy, this will be second nature. When an organization follows the same policy and procedure for tagging and marking evidence, every person involved will understand the procedure if requested to assist or take over the assignment. Also, days, months, or even years later, anyone examining the evidence will be able to refer to the documentation for a clear understanding of the event and where the artifact was seized.

The evidence numbering system is straightforward. For example, suppose a mobile device was recovered in a bedroom during an execution of a search warrant. The bedroom had been identified as room 2 of 5 and documented as such during the scene assessment. The departmental report number assigned to the event is 555123. The tag and marking for the piece of evidence would look like this: 2014-555123-2-1. The final 1 indicates the number assigned to this piece of evidence. Using this format clearly defines all the appropriate information about the evidence.

A tag or label should be affixed to every piece of evidence prior to it being placed into an evidence container, which will contain the evidence number as previously described. If an artifact cannot be tagged or labeled, it should be marked. The tag or label should indicate the following:

- Date and time
- Collector's name/identifier (such as badge or employee number)
- Evidence number (year-case-location-artifact)
- Description of artifact following the appropriate guidelines

You may need to mark the evidence directly if the artifact is not large enough to affix a label or tag. In these instances, the following guidelines can help you ensure that these artifacts are properly documented:

- Mark the evidence location and number. In the example "2-34," shown next, the 2 indicates location 2 and 34 is the artifact number. The marking should not cover any unique identifiers (such as the ICCID on a card).

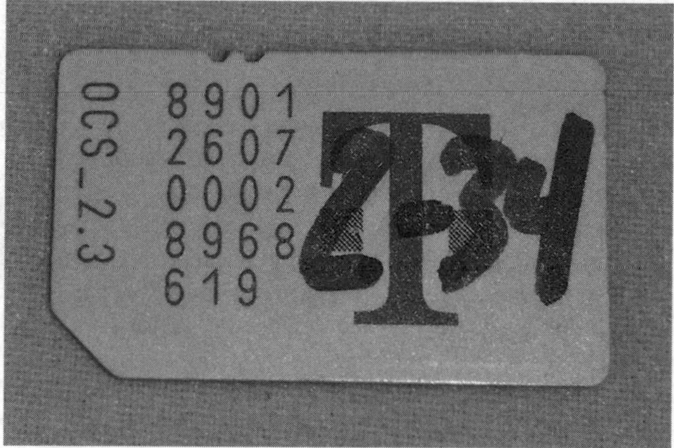

- If marking is made directly on the artifact, document why it was necessary to mark the evidence.
- If the artifact is placed into a container, affix the label or tag to the container.

Documentating the Evidence at the Scene

The documentation of the seizure of a mobile device and any related materials should be very clear and interpretable by anyone in the chain of custody. It can be difficult to keep track of many small items, such as SIM and memory cards, in an evidence bag if the evidence is placed loosely without regard into the bag without accompanying documentation. Instead, every item seized should be documented on a prepared form that includes not only descriptions of the evidence, but also where each object was located on the scene. Furthermore, each article must be described so that it will not be confused with another piece of evidence.

Describing evidence can be challenging, not only because of the volatility of the data and current status of the device, but also because certain types of mobile evidence often do not have discernible features. Detailing any unique attributes will allow for successful identification and can be matched to the completed property/evidence sheet that documents all artifacts seized from the location. Being able to match the item to the property/evidence sheet will be helpful if an item is somehow separated from the evidence container.

The property/evidence sheet should list all items seized from the location for the particular case. The minimum details that should be listed on the property/evidence sheet should include but not be limited to:

- **Item number** This is a unique value assigned to the seized property.
- **Quantity** This will indicate the number of items for a single item type (for example, micro USB cables, chargers, and so on).
- **Property description** This should include serial numbers, markings, and so on. (include serial numbers, markings, etc)
- **Owner**
- **Location found**

Following are some suggestions for documenting various items of mobile device evidence.

Mobile Device

For a mobile device, the documentation should include, but not be limited to, the serial number, make, model, color, size, condition, and the telecom company. The status of the device should also be indicated—that is, whether it is powered on or off. If the device is powered on, does it use cellular service or Wi-Fi? If there is a network connection of some type, it is critical that you quickly isolate the device from the network. Also, take care in retrieving the serial number, since most device serial numbers are printed on a label in the battery compartment area. Obtaining the serial number could involve removing a battery and powering off the device, which in turn could lock the device.

If the device is already powered off, does it contain a SIM card or memory card? If cards are inserted, document only that they are inserted into the device along with any discernible serial numbers. It is not recommended that you remove the SIM or memory card from the device while at the scene unless you're conducting an on-scene collection.

Mobile Device Accessories

The documentation of all items associated with the mobile device can be important should an accessory be needed to charge or connect the device to the hardware while conducting the forensic exam. Document the number of power cables, USB cables, and cases that match the seized device. If the accessory is connected to the device, photograph it prior to disconnecting, and label the connections. This is helpful if the connection will need to be re-created at some point during a detailed exam. This can also help the examiner determine which charger or cable is assigned to each device, especially when multiple devices of the same type are seized.

SIM Card

Multiple SIM cards on the scene may not be inserted into the actual mobile device, but they could contain valuable information and should be seized and documented along with the SIM card inserted into the device. The location of each card should be indicated along with its integrated circuit card identifier (ICCID) number, type (standard, micro, nano, as shown next), color, condition, and the telecom company.

Note The ICCID is the serial number of the SIM card, a unique number assigned to a single SIM card. Using this number can help you positively identify the SIM. The ICCID is discussed in Chapter 9.

Memory Cards

Identifying and documenting a memory card can be difficult because the serial numbers are typically not located on the exterior of the card. Memory cards, like SIM cards, can contain an extremely large amount of stored data and all should be collected, not only the cards installed within the mobile device. The location of the card at the scene should be documented along with the size (512MB, 32GB, and so on), type, color, condition, and brand, as shown next. Any numbering on the exterior should be documented. If multiple identical memory cards are collected, each card should be labeled and marked appropriately so they can be uniquely identifiable.

Dealing with Power Issues: The Device State

After you locate a mobile device, it's critical that you determine whether the device is powered on or off and whether or not the device is password protected. If the device is not locked and does not currently have security enabled, it should be processed immediately by a trained examiner. If the device is powered on and the password is known, do not attempt to enter the password to confirm while at the scene. In both instances, the necessity of immediate processing ensures that information can be obtained prior to the device locking or if the password is not known.

If the device is powered on but security is enabled and the owner will not unlock the device or the password provided does not unlock the device, the device can be powered off and bagged. If the device is powered off, leave it powered off and bag and tag the device as appropriate using an anti-static bag.

If the device will be remaining on, attach a portable power source to maintain a charge. Several portable power sources enable the continuous charge of mobile devices for up to eight hours. The documentation should indicate that the device is currently powered on and that a portable power source is being used. To preserve the device integrity, you must isolate it by placing it in a shielding bag or by putting the device in airplane mode.

The device should remain isolated from the cellular network using both airplane mode and a Faraday bag (see the next section for information on bagging). Understanding the simple fact that the device is currently powered on and system functions are already running will help to alleviate concerns that data is being changed by navigating to airplane mode. If the device is powered on, you should recognize that data is constantly in flux and the changing of a simple device function will not alter the user data, only system information.

Note Criticism for manipulating the device by pushing buttons or pressing the screen in an attempt to locate airplane mode has been included in many documents and at conference meetings for years. However, the practice of inhibiting the device by placing it in airplane mode using the device menu is now referenced as proper procedure in materials from SANS to NIST.

Placing the device in airplane mode will deactivate the cellular signal, Wi-Fi, and Bluetooth connections. (Wi-Fi can be manually enabled while in airplane mode.) The most popular devices and the locations and methods required for placing the devices in airplane mode are listed next.

Apple iOS 7 and Later

Swipe up from the bottom of the iOS device screen depicted in the first illustration. This will expose the submenu with an airplane icon in the upper-left corner, as shown in the second illustration. If the airplane icon is not highlighted, tap it to enable airplane mode. A notification on the top of the screen will then indicate that the device is in airplane mode.

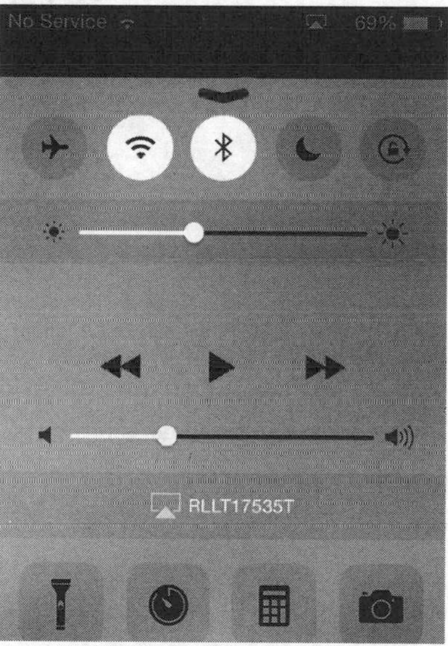

In previous iOS versions, you access airplane mode from the main page of the settings application. To locate the settings application, tap the gears icon. An airplane mode toggle switch will be visible next to the label. Switch the toggle to the OFF position.

Android

Android has not changed the way that users locate and toggle airplane mode on and off with updates to the operating system. In all versions, to activate and deactivate airplane mode, press and hold the power button on the upper-right corner of the phone. You'll see a dialog asking if the device should be powered off, along with an airplane mode setting and other selections, depending on the OS version (as shown). Tap Airplane Mode to isolate the device from network connections.

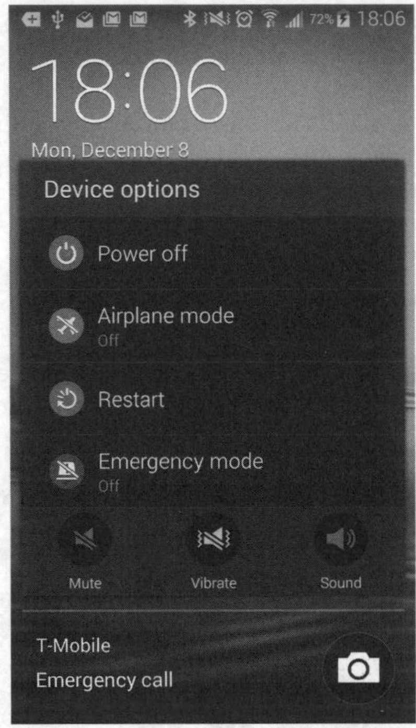

Windows Phone 7 and 8

You place Windows Phone into airplane mode similar to how it's done on a laptop running Windows 8: On the device Home screen, flick left, select Settings, and then tap Airplane Mode.

Why Leave a Device Powered On?

With mobile devices in the personal digital assistant (PDA) era, a constant charge had to be maintained or all the user information would be deleted from the device's volatile memory. The flash memory used in today's mobile devices is nonvolatile—so why should a charge on a mobile device need to be maintained when it is bagged for transport? In the years of volatile memory, all data was lost when a charge was lost. But today's mobile data may be lost for a different reason: If a security-enabled mobile device is allowed to lose its charge, any security measures employed by the user could be enabled, making access to data impossible. Maintaining a charge when a mobile device is powered on and possibly has security enabled or if the device has been unlocked temporarily by the user can be important to maintaining access to the data.

Bagging Sensitive Evidence

Place electronic devices into an evidence bag that is anti-static and protected from electrostatic discharge (ESD). All other mobile device artifacts such as memory cards and SIM cards should be placed in separate anti-static bags. These items should then be placed in appropriate evidence bags or containers specified by the agency, company, or department policy.

Plastic evidence containers or bags should not be used to encase mobile device evidence that has been packaged in anti-static bags. Cardboard or paper bags should be used instead because sealed plastic containers can allow for humidity and condensation to build up, which could damage mobile device evidence.

Both memory and SIM cards are also susceptible to damage from the oils and acids on a person's skin. When handling these artifacts, evidence collectors should wear appropriate gloves and avoid touching the gold portions of memory cards or SIM cards.

Types of Bagging Equipment

When bagging mobile device evidence, you must place the artifacts in the appropriate type of evidence container. Electronic evidence contains data that can be destroyed or corrupted by simple exposure to static electricity, elemental factors (rain, snow, and so on), network transmission (cellular and Wi-Fi), and power concerns. The type of container used should be appropriate to the circumstances.

Use electrostatic bags or anti-static bags during the seizure of mobile device evidence. Anti-static bags are usually used for shipping computer parts and can protect the static-sensitive parts from ESD. There are different types of electrostatic bags, and it is important that you understand the differences and when each should be used.

Some bags simply dissipate electrons across the surface of the bag so the electrons do not build up. By not allowing the electrons to build up, contact charging will not occur. Contact charging can occur if two electrically charged pieces of matter rub against each other. With electronic equipment, this could pose problems with ESD. Typically, the bags that help to dissipate the charge are pink in color but can also be purchased in different colors such as blue or green. The bags should be labeled as anti-static.

Another type of bag protects from and stops an ESD, similar to how lightning rods on top of buildings protect them from damage during electrical storms. These rods are used to stop an ESD from damaging a structure by allowing current to travel safely to ground. The same concept is used when ESD bags stop electrical current from damaging circuits or flash memory. These bags typically are slightly opaque with a mirrored or metal look because of an aluminum coating. They offer both an anti-static and ESD protection and should be used to protect evidence from static shocks when someone is handling the evidence both on the scene and in the lab.

Signal isolation bags, commonly referred to as Faraday bags, are also needed at the scene in case a device needs to be shielded from cellular signals. Several studies have been conducted on the success rate of signal isolation bags, and most show significant weaknesses in protecting a device from network signals. Most weaknesses are related to the proximity of the mobile device to a cellular base station, however. The closer a device is to a tower, the stronger the signal, and the more likely a signal will reach the mobile device even when it's inside the bag. Take care when using signal isolation bags, and test them prior to deployment and use in the field.

Properly Bagging Mobile Device Evidence

Properly securing a mobile device will help to maintain the integrity of the follow-up examination and later presentation of the facts. A mobile device contains various points of vulnerability or compromise. Most modern mobile devices contain headphone jacks, memory card doors, camera lenses, and toggle switches. The state in which the device was found and seized should be maintained and documented. To maintain the state in which the device was found, several things must occur during the bagging process.

All the various settings of the external switches, cameras, and any other exterior observations should be documented and photographed. Then all evidentiary items should be protected using the following methods before covering the items with evidence tape and marking the tape with the collector's initials:

- **Exterior switches** Some mobile devices have exterior toggle switches that turn the sound on and off or up or down. Cover these switches with evidence tape to maintain the position at the time of seizure. If a device must be processed for latent fingerprints, document and photograph the position of these switches.
- **USB port** Cover any exterior ports with evidence tape.
- **Headphone port** Headphone jacks can be used to attach ear buds or a data reader for point of sale (POS) scanners and other commerce tools. Cover this port with evidence tape.
- **Camera lens** Cover all lenses with tape to prevent them from capturing any pictures or video after device seizure.
- **Battery compartment** Access to the battery area would allow access to the SIM card and memory card. Cover the compartment with evidence tape.

Once you've taken steps to ensure the security of the mobile device, place it into the appropriate evidence bag. Then mark the exterior of the evidence bag or containers with the following information, which is similar to the information you placed onto the tags and/or labels on the actual piece of evidence:

- Case/incident identifier
- Item number
- Date
- Location of collection
- Item description
- Serial number
- Collector's information (name and identifier)
- Where is the evidence going? (lab or storage)
- Comments (immediately process, phone on and charging, biohazard, and so on)

Affix the label to the outside of the evidence bag or container, and then seal it properly with evidence tape. The collector should initial the evidence tape to ensure that any tampering will be obvious.

Transporting Mobile Device Evidence

The transportation of mobile device evidence can be just as important as proper seizure, bagging, and tagging the artifacts. Be aware of the following when transporting mobile device evidence:

- Avoid placing evidence in an area that had previously transported materials that contained caustic liquids or other wet materials.
- Mobile device evidence can be susceptible to shock and vibration, so be sure that the evidence is secured prior to transport.
- Mobile device evidence can be damaged by electrostatic discharges and magnetic fields produced by speakers, radios, and large electronics mounted using magnets. Electronic evidence should not be transported or stored in close proximity to these devices. It should be transported either in an enclosure designed to resist ESD and magnetic fields or stored in a location away from devices known to produce electrostatic discharges.
- Extreme temperatures can damage mobile device evidence. Avoid prolonged exposure to extreme temperatures.

Placing any mobile device evidence into the trunk of a patrol vehicle where the radio transmitter and receiver are located can be disastrous. The police radio transmitter can create an electromagnetic field that can destroy the contents of a mobile device.

To Storage

When transporting evidence to be stored for a prolonged period, notify the evidence custodian of any mobile device evidence that might be susceptible to data loss or security measures. For any evidence that needs immediate attention, instruct the evidence custodian to notify the responsible party who will conduct the follow-up on the mobile device evidence.

A property/evidence sheet should have already been completed, listing all of the property that is being transported. During the transfer of the evidence to the storage facility, all evidence containers should be inventoried and matched with the proper property/evidence sheet.

The delivery should be documented, indicating the transportation of the evidence and any problems noted upon inspection after arrival. The documentation should also include to whom the delivery was made, the facility to which the evidence was delivered, the date and time of the delivery, and any other pertinent information.

The mobile device evidence should be stored in the appropriate manner. Ensure that the evidence is not exposed to extreme temperatures, humidity, ESD, and/or magnetic fields.

To the Lab

When mobile evidence must be immediately processed for trace evidence, latent evidence, and forensic digital evidence, the articles will be delivered directly to a forensics lab. It is extremely important that any evidence transported and released to the lab be documented, including details on the evidence transportation and any problems encountered upon inspection after arrival. The person receiving the evidence, along with the time and date and reason for the release of property, should be documented on the exterior of the evidence bag or container; the property/evidence sheet; and any supplementary documentation.

Upon reception, evidence should be stored in an appropriate manner to ensure the integrity of the articles.

Establishing Chain of Custody

As discussed in Chapter 3, the chain of custody document clearly details in chronological order every hand that has been in contact with the piece of evidence, from the seizure to the disposition. Mobile device evidence may have been handled by many different people, from the scene where the artifact was collected and bagged, to the storage area, and to the lab, where the article is analyzed. Documenting this information can be easily accomplished if procedures are in place at the onset.

Requiring all persons in contact with mobile device evidence to identify themselves on a chain of custody form will make the documentation lifecycle much more manageable and inherently invulnerable to later challenge. Failing to document the chain of custody properly for each piece of mobile device evidence can have devastating results if later that evidence is used as a critical piece of the investigation.

Using a simple chain of custody form on each piece of evidence packaging will help to satisfy this prerequisite. Evidence cardboard boxes and bags that contain a preprinted chain of custody form are used by many departments and agencies. If these types of evidence containers are unavailable, using the simple form shown in Figure 4-3 can satisfy this requirement.

Evidence Number: ____________________
Case Number: ____________________

Transferred From	Transferred To	Reason for Transfer	Date/Time	Signature

FIGURE 4-3 Sample chain of custody form

Chapter Summary

Before the collection of the data from mobile device evidence, all the appropriate physical artifacts from the scene must be properly packaged, marked, tagged, and bagged. The mobile device, the device state, and device security must be considered and clearly documented. Knowing whether or not the device will have to be immediately examined and collected is determined by the current state of the device.

Outside environmental influences, including network communication, weather, magnetic fields, and electrostatic discharges, must also be considered throughout the evidence lifecycle. Improper handling or transportation could lead to the destruction of evidence contained on mobile devices.

Before conducting a forensic collection of a mobile device and any accompanying artifacts, the custody of the artifact must be correctly documented. The process of evidence handling is often attacked during both criminal and civil trials because of poor chain of custody documentation. For every piece of mobile device evidence, a completed chain of custody form is required to ensure that every person who comes into contact with the evidence is documented.

5 Toolbox Forensics: Multiple-Tool Approach

After the mobile device evidence has been successfully seized, tagged, and packaged, the next steps involve preserving, processing, and analyzing the data stored on the devices. As discussed in preceding chapters, mobile forensics is different from computer forensics in many ways, and one significant difference has to do with how the devices are processed during examination. With mobile device forensics, using only one tool to process and analyze the evidence can be a detrimental task, although a computer forensics examiner can sometimes get by with using only a single tool. This poses problems for a lot of mobile device investigators for several reasons—in particular, the cost involved in using several software solutions. Mobile device forensic software does not come cheap. Although open source solutions are available, one solution will not provide all the tools necessary to accommodate every type of device, every type of operating system, or all different types of stored user data. This is a limitation of all mobile forensic solutions because of one simple fact: no one tool can process and analyze all mobile devices.

This chapter covers the various reasons you'll need to use a multiple-tool approach to the examination and analysis of a mobile device. To choose the best tools, you need to know not only what a tool is doing to the extracted data, but also what methods are used to validate the tool, the collection, and the process. Examiners will encounter a variety of pitfalls, whether trying to use a single tool or multiple tools. Your understanding and preparation for these challenges will help reduce criticism of either approach and will help you improve your expertise in the mobile forensic field.

Preparing for the challenge of collecting digital data from a mobile device is based primarily on the methods and tools that you use. Of course, most examiners are not capable of financially supporting each forensic solution currently available on the market. With that in mind, you must be knowledgeable of what your current software is capable of and its limitations. More importantly, you must research the available software and purchase the most competent software that will handle the majority of devices to be encountered. Research the types of devices, operating systems, and the available and appropriate technologies; armed with this information, you can make the right decision regarding the best tools to use.

Choosing the Right Tools

A decision as to which tool to use in an examination can be affected by a variety of factors, including price, ease of use, and, more often than not, using what "everyone else" uses. Each of these reasons has its own merits. Studying a tool and using sound judgment can make your decision much easier.

Commercial mobile forensic tools are some of the most expensive software examination tools available. Although their prices are significantly variable, what is included in each is not necessarily related to the price—in other words, the manufacturer's suggested retail price does not correlate to what is actually included with the solution. Commercial tool prices range from $500 to well over $10,000 for a single license for a single year. These prices may then be reduced to approximately 30 to 40 percent for yearly updates. Keeping up with the technology of mobile device forensics is costly, but with wise research on the tools for your mobile forensic toolbox, you can justify the expensiveness of some tools. The astronomical prices of some software solutions in the market are often attributed to the fact that these companies think the money they've invested in research should be passed onto the consumer. Because of the pricing disparity and the variety of technologies available, it is extremely important that you conduct diligent research on each tool prior to purchase.

If some examination and collections will be conducted by first responders or persons who have not been formally trained on forensic practices for the collection of digital evidence, it is important that you look at the tool's ease of use along with how it maintains forensic integrity. Does the tool enable those who are not technologically savvy to perform the steps necessary to recover the required digital data from a mobile device? Maintaining forensic integrity requires a tool that packages the collected data in a format that probably cannot be tampered with or altered. This is typically completed by the software in the form of hashing. Hashing of the overall data in its current form can help to fingerprint the data collected, but not all solutions hash the data the same.

Note In the National Reference Software Library (NSRL), NIST describes hashing as a mathematical technique used to produce a unique signature of a file. Hashing a file involves a one-way computation when the file has been compressed to a fixed length of 0's and 1's into a single string. A unique number is created based upon the mathematical computation and is often referred to as the *digital fingerprint* of the file. If even a single 0 or 1 is changed within the file, the entire digital fingerprint will change.

The way in which the software hashes data can be very important. If the software simply hashes the extracted personal data (such as Short Message Service [SMS], contacts, or call logs) after it has been extracted into a Microsoft Excel spreadsheet, it is doubtful that this hash can be verified using another solution. If the secondary solution extracts the same data, but this solution hashes the file in which the data actually exists, the hash could be entirely different. It would make sense that additional metadata would also be in the overall file where the data had been extracted, which would create an entirely different hash.

Extracting the physical files, hashing them, and producing an overall hash value of the entire collection contained in a single file would be the best method. With this method, all the collected data is contained within a single file, and if any portion of the file is altered, the fact that the overall hash has changed could be immediately identified. Also, to check the integrity of an individual file, the container could be opened and each file's hash could be rehashed to show that the file had not been tampered with since first being collected. To verify the reliability of the collected data, each collection and subsequent analysis must be repeatable. Having tools that will allow for the creation of digital fingerprints, or hashes, of the files and overall container should be a priority when you choose a mobile forensic solution.

What types of mobile examinations are going to occur? Will you examine the actual collected device or the backup, or both? These are important questions to consider when you're selecting a mobile forensic solution, especially if only backups are going to be analyzed. Choosing a software solution that covers the collection of the mobile device when the target is always going to be a device backup obtained from a PC or network server would be frivolous and unneeded. Understand the target of the examination when you're making a determination of the types of solutions to fill your mobile forensic toolbox.

You should also look for software solutions that include support of current technologies. Look for solutions that offer the greatest support of not only the collection of data, but also superior analysis of the underlying structures. Today's devices contain storage databases and configuration files that are loaded with digital information that is often overlooked by software solutions. Choose a tool that can not only collect but also digest and analyze the critical files found within most new smart devices.

Remember that different parts of the world use different types of devices, different parts of a geographic region use different types of devices, and different areas of a company or agency use different types of devices. Tailor your mobile solution toolbox to the devices and, more importantly, the types of devices that are appropriate to your area. If a region deals with Nokia legacy devices exclusively or BlackBerry devices exclusively, don't choose a tool that specializes in iOS or Android devices. If you're conducting examinations in Europe, don't purchase a tool that is primarily used for Code Division Multiple Access (CDMA) mobile devices.

Consider the following facts as you determine the best tool to use in examinations of today's mobile devices:

- More than 50 percent of users globally in 2014 used a smart device.
- In North America, most forensic labs deal with Android and iOS devices in almost 90 percent of their digital investigations.

Supporting global mobile device statistics should not influence your decision as to what type of mobile forensic software you select if these statistics are not consistent with what you will deal with locally.

Using the multiple-tool approach can be limited at the analysis phase simply because various software products do not allow for the analysis of another tool's data. Make sure that the software you use to conduct data analysis can import various types of mobile device data from multiple tools. The ability to import multiple image types will allow for validation of the collected data and will also provide a complement to another tool. This feature will help you uncover even more information that may have been missed by another tool.

Finally, one thing that should *not* influence your decision for a competent mobile forensic solution is the fact "everyone is using it." Just because software is popular does not necessarily mean the software will be useful to all examinations in all regions. Carefully consider and investigate all facets pertaining to a localized tool set. Research the type of software, its features, interoperability, and forensic implications before making a decision as to the software that you will use for mobile device examinations. Most companies allow demonstration copies to be evaluated prior to the purchase of the software; this can be a good way to determine whether the software is right for you before you purchase.

After you've gathered forensic tools, you must properly assess them and learn to use them before conducting a live investigation. Learn about the software's operating functions, features, and limitations. Consider and seek out training on the software, which is often provided by competent companies. Without undergoing training on the tools you will use, you may end up using them in less-than-optimal ways. Moreover, because technology changes quickly, what was once a current method for conducting a collection may no longer be valid.

Note For example, when Apple changed the processor in its iOS devices from an A4 (S5L8930X) to an A5 (S5L8940) chip, it was no longer possible to create a physical image of the iOS device. The exploit that had been used for devices with A4 and older chips was not valid for new iOS devices containing the newer chips.

Analyzing Several Devices Collectively

When you're dealing with many devices and collective evidence, keep in mind that some mobile forensic tools do not allow the analysis of more than one device image or different types of media (such as computers and mass storage devices) at a time. In these instances, you may find it better to use a conventional computer forensic solution for detailed analysis. This will enable you to examine all digital information and multiple devices simultaneously, which provides a very big picture of the collected evidence. Using different types of software (computer forensic), not just different types of mobile forensic software, can help paint a collective picture of the events. More and more mobile devices are becoming mini computers with extended memory, storage, and capabilities. Also, more investigations of a single event will contain multiple pieces of digital devices, so the ability to analyze all of the data collectively and in a single platform will provide digital evidence synergy.

An example of collective analysis of an attack conducted on multiple fronts is provided in the "Collective Analysis" sidebar.

Collective Analysis

In 2010, investigators were zeroing in on a location they believed was the epicenter for narcotics trafficking. This location had been under surveillance for many months until the investigators believed they had enough information to obtain a search warrant of the premises. Believing that computers and other digital devices were on site, the investigators' search warrant included information regarding the collection of the devices and the forensic analysis of the data.

The day arrived, and prior to the investigators' arrival, two vehicles departed the location. Information on the vehicles was sent to a neighboring jurisdiction, and while officers conducted a traffic stop on the vehicles, investigators initiated and executed the search warrant at the location.

The officers who stopped the vehicles communicated with the occupants, who denied any involvement with any persons at the location where the search was being conducted. A records check of both occupants in the two vehicles indicated that they had outstanding warrants, and they were placed under arrest. During the search of the subjects, officers discovered both carried mobile devices. These devices were searched incident to arrest at the scene (this occurred prior to the *Riley v. California* Supreme Court decision, as discussed in Chapter 3) using a mobile forensic solution.

When officers viewed the informational report, it was quickly apparent that both suspects knew one another because the officers located contacts and SMS messages between the two suspects. In the report, no information tied them to the search location, but they were seen leaving the area prior to the search warrant execution. Lead investigators indicated that the subjects had been seen previously at the location, but they were unsure of the subjects' involvement.

Investigators arrived and conducted interviews of both vehicle occupants, who still denied knowing anything about the location at which they were seen leaving. They were shown the report documenting the communication between them that had been collected from the mobile devices. Both indicated that they knew one another and worked together on several projects. At the conclusion of the interview, both subjects were taken to jail for the outstanding warrants. One subject paid the bond on the warrant and was out of jail within two hours.

Simultaneous to the arrests, investigators at the scene of the search warrant seized several computers and flash drives, along with several types of narcotics paraphernalia and a small amount of controlled substance. The lone occupant of the location, who was not listed on the actual lease agreement, was taken into custody on possession of a controlled substance and booked into the local jail after an unproductive interview.

The computers and flash drives were later examined by a computer forensic examiner who was assigned to the case a week after the search warrant was issued. During the forensic examination of a computer laptop, the examiner discovered several fraudulent identification documents, including driver's licenses, Social Security cards, and power bills. He also located a device backup of an iPhone with several SMS messages indicating that the "product was completed and being shipped to the house," "the tracking number is 9102 6537 1256 4987 3098 12," and "the explosives are also purchased." In this backup, the device ID was found along with a very large contact list.

Investigators contacted the U.S. Postal Service with the tracking number to determine the location from which the package was sent. The delivery location was the same place at which the search warrant was initiated, but the sender's location was approximately 2500 miles and several states away.

When a second computer was analyzed, examiners located recipes for explosives, how to make fraudulent documents, and images of a very sophisticated narcotics manufacturing

(Continued)

system, along with images of weapons. This information helped to substantiate the belief that the location was involved in illegal activities, but investigators did not have the primary actors in this investigation—at least that's what they believed, considering the digital evidence the forensic examiner was currently reviewing.

The forensic examiner began to look into the property and noticed that no mobile devices were collected from the scene. He had found a backup of an iPhone on the computer, so he contacted the lead investigator. The investigator met with the forensic examiner and explained that two subjects had left the scene and were stopped in another jurisdiction. Their mobile devices were examined at the scene, and there was nothing to tie them to the location based upon the information in the report created by the mobile forensic software—just the fact that the two subjects had communicated with each other. The forensic examiner asked for a copy of the report.

After he reviewed the report, the examiner immediately recognized the device ID of the iPhone from the backup analyzed on the computer and contacted the lead investigator. Luckily, the device was still in jail property because the subject was still in custody and could not post bond due to the outstanding warrant. The forensic examiner obtained a search warrant for the device based upon the information obtained from the computer backup along with the information obtained in the initial collection of the device after the traffic stop. What the examiner located after conducting a full forensic analysis of the second collection with the computer data was amazing.

The actual iPhone contained several exterior images of a residence that also contained Exchangeable Image Format (EXIF) data with GPS coordinates. These coordinates, when placed into Google Maps, landed right on a house with an address that matched the shipping point identified earlier. Further examination of the iPhone revealed several chat apps that contained information implicating the user of the device in the creation of fraudulent documents found on the examined computers. The same chat app implicated the second driver as a courier for narcotics, and an image of the courier was found on the computer, indicating a fraudulent driver's license had been created for him, plus PDF documents from Dropbox that included ledger information on narcotics transactions.

Armed with this new information from the forensic examiner, the lead investigator and a tactical team from the local law enforcement agency arrived at the site revealed in the pictures on the iPhone and the tracking information from the computer. A seizure of the location was initiated, and what was found inside the residence was a testament to the value of collectively analyzing data from all digital devices. They had found not only the largest narcotics manufacturing plant in the state, but also an intricate lab for manufacturing explosives.

It was determined the iPhone owner was the leader and actually the owner of both locations. The second driver who had bonded out was not located, but an arrest warrant was issued based upon the analysis of the iPhone and the corroborating data from the computers at the scene of the first search, along with the device information obtained at the scene of the traffic stop.

If the digital investigator had not decided to look at the collective big picture, this case could have easily been dismissed.

Verifying and Validating Software

After you have determined the software to purchase and received training to use it, but prior to your first examination, you must verify and validate that the software performs as you expected. A lot of software vendors will explain exactly how the software *should* perform, but ultimately it comes down to how the software actually performs within the environment in which the examiner will be operating.

Verification and *validation* are often used synonymously in digital forensics, but they are two separate processes used in different situations to test a software solution against a predefined set of knowns. International Organization for Standardization (ISO) 9000:2005 outlines quality management system standards and defines both verification and validation separately. In both definitions, *objective evidence* is used, which ISO 9000:2005 defines as "data supporting the existence or verity of something."

- **Verification** Confirmation, through the provision of objective evidence, that specified requirements have been fulfilled.
- **Validation** Confirmation, through the provision of objective evidence, that the requirements for a specific intended use or application have been fulfilled.

In other words, *verification* consists of determining, through testing and examining specific tasks or data, whether the specified performance of a tool is met satisfactorily. *Validation*, on the other hand, involves determining through testing that a tool, when used in a certain way, performs as intended. Applying the concepts of verification and validation within the context of mobile forensic examinations is similar. Verification typically can be performed using a single software solution and observing whether the data that is reported matches what is stated in the guidelines and documents regarding the software. Validation typically involves using multiple tools to show whether or not the initial tool has altered the original evidence while performing a collection as defined by the software manufacturer.

Both verification and validation techniques, along with the results, can be used in other atypical ways. Sometimes these techniques can be used to determine a difference in a control sample, which could indicate compromise, while other methods might be used to determine data integrity compromise. Important to understand is that reliance on what a product developer states should be the output is not as important as what the examiner determines using a *baseline*. The only way to complete this task is by verification and validation of the software solutions in the forensic toolbox.

These baselines should be performed using the same reference device(s) when the software is first installed and configured and also after each major update.

Establishing Baselines

In science parlance, a *baseline* is a point, or a reference point, at which the experiment will be measured. Once a baseline reference point is made, any and all other experiments can be measured against the baseline to determine what changes have occurred. A baseline will shift only if it is created using a different medium, which would create an entirely different reference point.

In mobile device forensics, the creation of a baseline will allow for the verification and validation of the software. By having a reference point, the examiner can quickly identify any changes that have been made by the software to the recoverable data from the mobile device, the mobile device operating system, or even malicious infiltration by malware or unauthorized entities.

How the baseline is created will depend upon the desired result—verification of data changes or validation of the software. If the desired result is to identify the various data that is collected from the baseline device after changes in version, versus what the product literature indicates it will collect, one method should be used. If the desired outcome is to determine if user data has been altered by a forensic tool or by hostile programs or actors, another baseline should be used.

Creating a Baseline Image for Data Verification

When creating a baseline for data verification, your objective is to determine whether collected user data from the mobile device has been altered between updates to a forensic software solution or if data has been added or deleted by malicious, accidental, or hostile means. As indicated, baseline devices should be purchased and populated with data and will be used only for verification of collected data from a mobile forensic solution. If the objective of the baseline is to determine hostile, accidental, or malicious intent, the actual suspected device will need to be collected to create the baseline. Both software verification and device integrity verification should be covered. Pay specific attention to how a baseline is taken, compared, and examined for both types of device verification.

Note Hostile intent could mean the installation of software to monitor the device, such as a rogue application or service, and malicious intent could indicate the installation of an application intended to destroy data.

Software Verification Software verification involves examining the data of a pre-populated device with the forensic software solution that will be used to perform mobile device examinations. Save the collected data in a format that can be easily analyzed and compared side by side to a secondary extraction. This comparison extraction should occur upon any minor and major updates to the forensic software used for examinations. The simple comparison collection should consist of all of the current user data capabilities supported by the software and should be a query of only the logical data contained on the device, not a physical collection.

Note A logical collection, in the context of a baseline, consists typically of only data that can be accessible by simple communication techniques; a physical collection uses more advanced communication that yields entire partitions from a device.

Once data has been pre-populated on the mobile device, the exemplar devices must not be altered after the baseline is created and not until the comparison collection is completed. By using this method, the examiner can determine whether changes have been made during the various updates to the forensic software to verify that the data collected is consistent with data that is within the baseline and to identify any variations to the output. Changes to software occur frequently, and using this method will assist the examiner in determining quickly whether the software conforms to the expectations of a similar collection.

Changes or differences to the collected data can be attributed to the addition of new scoped data artifacts, new capabilities, and alterations to data within an already scoped data set. An example of each of these changes is described next, along with recommendations for each when encountered.

- **New scoped data artifacts** These artifacts are additions to already defined data. This could include the addition of a status to a SMS message indicating a read or an unread message that was not indicated in the previous version, the addition of a work phone number to the contacts table, or the read date in a calendar entry. This should be documented and verified to ensure that the new addition is correct for the exemplar device. If new scoped data artifacts are located, an entirely new baseline should be created after the completion of the verification cycle.
- **New capabilities** These would include an entirely new set of data that was not in the previous release, such as the addition of memos or user applications when the previous forensic software version did not collect this app data. This addition should be documented, and each artifact in each category should be analyzed to ensure that the data conforms to the expected values. A new baseline should be created after the completion of the verification cycle.
- **Alterations to data within an already scoped data set** This alteration occurs to a value that previously existed in an earlier release. Because the actual value of the data has changed, the examiner must research whether the previous value provided by the software was incorrect or the release being evaluated is incorrect. This change is the most important to document and to understand because it can have the biggest impact on the software verification cycle. If you determine that the value was corrected in the software from a previous release, make sure the software company has documented this on release notes. A new baseline should be created using the new version after the verification process has been completed and all changes documented. If the value in the software that is being verified had been correct in previous versions and is now incorrect, immediately notify the software vendor of the inconsistencies. Then document this information and do not create a new baseline.

The baseline comparison method can be tedious. Because of the manual process involved in determining new capabilities and additional artifacts within each capability, it is important that you clearly document data contained on the exemplar devices. To obtain the needed baseline information, you should first export the logical data by data type. Then export each data type to a format that can allow for easy comparison by their hash values. If the hash value of the files is the same, then there is no additional change in values or capabilities. If the hash value does change, this could indicate a change, and those files will have to be manually inspected to determine the changes that have occurred. If a change has occurred, create a new baseline, and the changes in the forensic software should be updated and verified in the release documentation.

Verification Workflow Example Following is the workflow for the verification of software. The tools used in this exercise are not the only tools available to accomplish this task. Mobile forensics tools such as Cellebrite Physical Analyzer, Micro Systemation XRY, Oxygen Forensic

Detective and Analyst, Paraben Device Seizure, and Susteen Secure View can all export collected data in various formats. The following procedure can be used with any of the mobile forensic tools that will allow collected data to be individually exported into single files.

For this example, the tools used are AccessData Mobile Phone Examiner Plus (MPE+) and hashdeep. Using AccessData MPE+ 5.0, all available capabilities from the baseline image are exported into a comma-separated value (.csv) file (see Figure 5-1). (Note that MPE+ will also be discussed in Chapter 6.) Hashdeep is a free program that computes multiple types of hashes against a set of folders, files, and subfolders. It can also be used to compare a known set of values in a text file against a set of files, folders, or subfolders when performing an audit. Hashdeep was developed by Jesse Kornblum and can be downloaded from http://sourceforge.net. It is maintained at https://github.com/jessek/hashdeep.

This exercise involves comparing a baseline created with a previous version of MPE+ with the current version of MPE+ (5.5.6.133). This comparison uses the hashes created from exported files in an effort to identify changes immediately within the files. If a change is encountered, we will determine whether the changes fall into the three categories discussed:

- New scoped data artifacts
- New capabilities
- Alterations to data within an already scoped data set

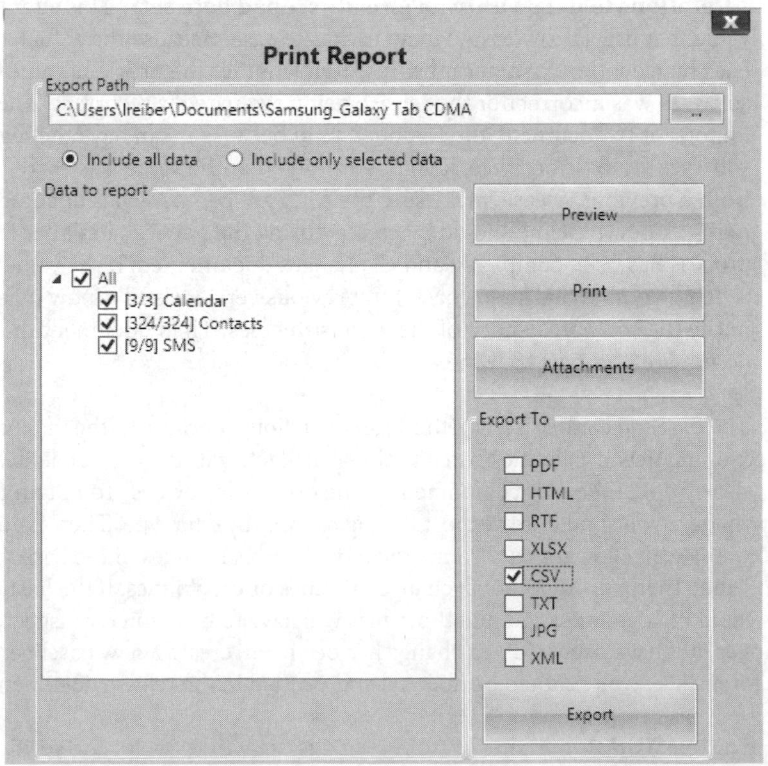

FIGURE 5-1 AccessData MPE+ 5.0 exports data into a comma-separated value (.csv) file.

First, we export the data into a folder and, from the Windows command prompt, hash the contents using hashdeep with the following instructions:

```
C:\md5deep-4.4>hashdeep64 -c md5,sha1,sha256 -b
C:\Users\lreiber\Documents\Samsung_Galaxy_Tab_CDMA\*
```

The format for the command contains a call to the executable (hashdeep64), a flag (`-c`) to enable comma-separated output, the hash formats, a flag (`-b`) to enable bare mode and only show filenames of hashed files, and then the path to the folder with the files that will be hashed.

The result shows the hashdeep dialog, the result format, and the string used to invoke the application and the hashes:

```
%%%% HASHDEEP-1.0
%%%% size,md5,sha1,sha256,filename
## Invoked from: C:\md5deep-4.4
C:\md5deep-4.4> hashdeep64 -c md5,sha1,sha256 -b
C:\Users\lreiber\Documents\Samsung_Galaxy_Tab_CDMA\*
##
2793,233e009e500e778105f76c748264c6ff,605ea51597a9f1f9f63b28a18be1f5aa061c
d6ab,649cfe728c8db68dffb41e387dd2056bdf667f2842b1db3dd4aa944e9c08c351,Sam
sung_Galaxy Tab CDMA-Calendar.csv
135,ee86970c5d481f403b7d56b43b77aacb,246f289ffc8b0855731436ac3e069abafdf8b
32f,e838baa03dfdf65ab2ee926a86f60a084ce757661ee6a2458875110146b2202d,Sams
ung_Galaxy Tab CDMA-Phone Info.csv
877,c6d5b788a7765c00f77c35f6bcbfb248,1223bad888f43a3f7e12649f7354e6f5dd0ce
550,b5e964e28e68702ce03888aebcfefb829c1240aeef018c7182188634bb89d10a,Sams
ung_Galaxy Tab CDMA-Sms.csv
60589,b5693f8d0bb128d5d99944f6f950371c,89bc10f47a71575aaddb9030fc0454a636b
b13c2,
a03795d220374b79d6e732b641eed028f3f4d8bb8701b1b0470a8713c2637acb,Samsung_
GalaxyTab CDMA-Phonebook.csv
```

The result, including the hashdeep dialog, is then saved to the file baseLine-knowns.txt. This file will be used to determine any differences in any image that will be obtained with the newer version of MPE+ so that the values can then be compared to ascertain whether changes have been made to the mobile device data's output.

Using AccessData MPE+ 5.5.6.133, we make another collection on the exemplar device when an update is sent out to users. The capabilities are all exported to a .csv file (see Figure 5-2).

From the Windows command prompt, we use hashdeep again to compare the hashes to show those that match and those that do not match in the baseline hash file baseLine-knowns .txt. This command determines whether any files are the same based upon hashes by using the `-m` and `-k` flags. The `-m` flag specifies to hashdeep to show only the files within the baseline that match the hashes that are within the file identified with the `-k` flag. It returns no matches, which indicates that all the files are different between releases of the forensic software:

```
C:\md5deep-4.4>hashdeep64 -m -k baseLine-knowns.txt
C:\Users\lreiber\Documents\BaseLineTesting\Samsung_Galaxy_Tab_CDMA\*
```

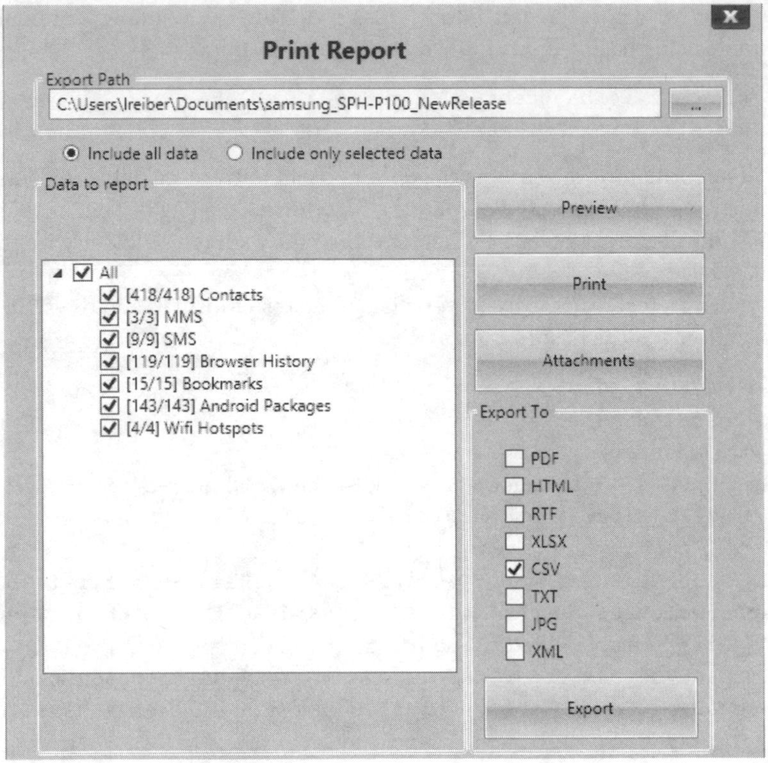

FIGURE 5-2 The second export of the same exemplar device after an acquisition with MPE+

To identify which files are different based upon the known file hashes, we run another command using the `-x` and `-k` flags. The `-x` flag will identify which files within the baseline are different, and the `-k` flag identifies the file of known values. If files are returned, they can then be manually compared to the known files.

```
C:\md5deep-4.4>hashdeep64 -x -k baseLine-knowns.txt
C:\Users\lreiber\Documents\BaseLineTesting\Samsung_Galaxy_Tab_CDMA\*
C:\Users\lreiber\Documents\BaseLineTesting\Samsung_Galaxy_Tab_CDMA\
Samsung_Galaxy Tab CDMA-Calendar.csv
C:\Users\lreiber\Documents\BaseLineTesting\Samsung_Galaxy_Tab_CDMA\
Samsung_Galaxy Tab CDMA-Phone Info.csv
C:\Users\lreiber\Documents\BaseLineTesting\Samsung_Galaxy_Tab_CDMA\
Samsung_Galaxy Tab CDMA-Sms.csv
C:\Users\lreiber\Documents\BaseLineTesting\Samsung_Galaxy_Tab_CDMA\
Samsung_Galaxy Tab CDMA-Phonebook.csv
```

Several hash values have changed, and those files must be examined to determine the differences. This will help us differentiate between the types of changes that have occurred between releases in order to verify the forensic solution. The next illustration shows several changes between versions of MPE+. The large difference was a direct result of the manufacturer changing the application that queries an Android device. This information would not be known if it were not for the verification of the software. The image in Figure 5-3 depicts an additional column of data indicating whether the SMS message has been seen or read, and also changes the format from local time to UTC time, which are both listed in the Sent column.

If any changes between the baseline and the secondary comparison image are detected, a new baseline should be created. In this example, a new image was created with MPE+ 5.5.5, and the files are all hashed. A subsequent extraction was completed with version 5.5.6 and the results compared using the steps previously covered with hashdeep. Here is the process with the new version:

```
C:\md5deep-4.4>hashdeep64  c md5,sha1  b
C:\Users\lreiber\Documents\SamsungBaseLineTest\*
%%%% HASHDEEP-1.0
%%%% size,md5,sha1,filename
## Invoked from: C:\md5deep-4.4
## C:\md5deep-4.4> hashdeep64 -c md5,sha1 -b C:\Users\lreiber\Documents\
SamsungBaseLineTest\*
##
8757,c98329f08a70bb3fb892b8e0d344a385,ebb565ac8430a3a10059cc0bf1fc9fb0ed06
66d9,samsung_SPH-P100-AndroidPackages.csv
```

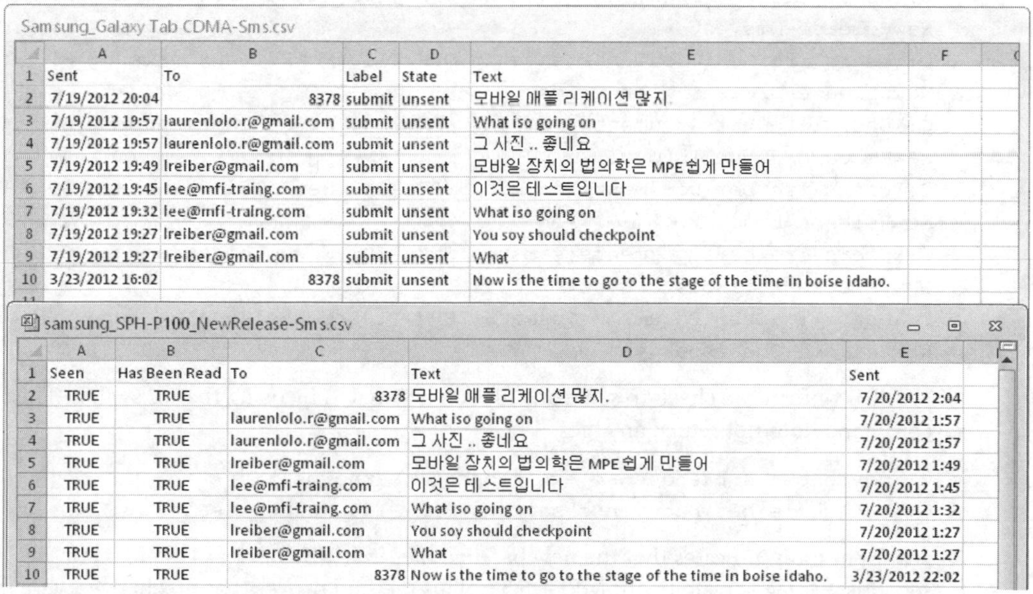

Samsung_Galaxy Tab CDMA-Sms.csv

	A	B	C	D	E	F
1	Sent	To	Label	State	Text	
2	7/19/2012 20:04	8378	submit	unsent	모바일 애플 리케이션 많지	
3	7/19/2012 19:57	laurenlolo.r@gmail.com	submit	unsent	What iso going on	
4	7/19/2012 19:57	laurenlolo.r@gmail.com	submit	unsent	그 사진 .. 좋네요	
5	7/19/2012 19:49	lreiber@gmail.com	submit	unsent	모바일 장치의 법의학은 MPE 쉽게 만들어	
6	7/19/2012 19:45	lee@mfi-traing.com	submit	unsent	이것은 테스트입니다	
7	7/19/2012 19:32	lee@mfi-traing.com	submit	unsent	What iso going on	
8	7/19/2012 19:27	lreiber@gmail.com	submit	unsent	You soy should checkpoint	
9	7/19/2012 19:27	lreiber@gmail.com	submit	unsent	What	
10	3/23/2012 16:02	8378	submit	unsent	Now is the time to go to the stage of the time in boise idaho.	

samsung_SPH-P100_NewRelease-Sms.csv

	A	B	C	D	E
1	Seen	Has Been Read	To	Text	Sent
2	TRUE	TRUE	8378	모바일 애플 리케이션 많지.	7/20/2012 2:04
3	TRUE	TRUE	laurenlolo.r@gmail.com	What iso going on	7/20/2012 1:57
4	TRUE	TRUE	laurenlolo.r@gmail.com	그 사진 .. 좋네요	7/20/2012 1:57
5	TRUE	TRUE	lreiber@gmail.com	모바일 장치의 법의학은 MPE 쉽게 만들어	7/20/2012 1:49
6	TRUE	TRUE	lee@mfi-traing.com	이것은 테스트입니다	7/20/2012 1:45
7	TRUE	TRUE	lee@mfi-traing.com	What iso going on	7/20/2012 1:32
8	TRUE	TRUE	lreiber@gmail.com	You soy should checkpoint	7/20/2012 1:27
9	TRUE	TRUE	lreiber@gmail.com	What	7/20/2012 1:27
10	TRUE	TRUE	8378	Now is the time to go to the stage of the time in boise idaho.	3/23/2012 22:02

FIGURE 5-3 **Using Microsoft Excel, both .csv files from MPE+ 5.0 and 5.5.5 are compared, showing various differences.**

```
739,17282d94f4b5d46fb79237ebe34d6389,1d462456000ecea6bfa2af2e79ff5188612c5
60d,samsung_SPH-P100-Bookmark.csv
2203,9d7e02d0a3eea068007d3b31077f0ff0,345c10e321e7514b52e11d1ecec3ad82a84c
2fc8,samsung_SPH-P100-Mms.csv
28189,2580444096d93033355cd2bf550a3792,0eb9c61d45aefae193faab283de78a3a314
a5b94,samsung_SPH-P100-Browser History.csv
895,e1e725d371b7fa47552236ead450a3a4,2bebef77324eb6e4e587a65d671029233cb7b
2e4,samsung_SPH-P100-Phone Info.csv
849,2e41f603991afab10c58e9d689c73b4e,4b8145ec8619c4615e0a859ac9d7e88734ed1
d9c,samsung_SPH-P100-Sms.csv
34172,34f054e3fe5ee65a9043ce7d114a6124,9f2f5d962cfa21efc1045966b0c3bba0228
5bf2f,samsung_SPH-P100-Phonebook.csv
194,b23190ac69277791f15cfc704a0840f7,d0078e800b464c119ded299440f0caa484c1b
950,samsung_SPH-P100-WifiHotspots.csv
```

Using the `-m` switch this time identifies all files that match within the original data set and the new version:

```
C:\md5deep-4.4>hashdeep64 -m -k baseLine-knowns.txt
C:\Users\lreiber\Documents\samsung_SPH-P100_NewRelease\*
C:\Users\lreiber\Documents\samsung_SPH-P100_NewRelease\samsung_SPH-P100_
NewRelease-Bookmark.csv
C:\Users\lreiber\Documents\samsung_SPH-P100_NewRelease\samsung_SPH-P100_
NewRelease-AndroidPackages.csv
C:\Users\lreiber\Documents\samsung_SPH-P100_NewRelease\samsung_SPH-P100_
NewRelease-Mms.csv
C:\Users\lreiber\Documents\samsung_SPH-P100_NewRelease\samsung_SPH-P100_
NewRelease-Browser History.csv
C:\Users\lreiber\Documents\samsung_SPH-P100_NewRelease\samsung_SPH-P100_
NewRelease-Phone Info.csv
C:\Users\lreiber\Documents\samsung_SPH-P100_NewRelease\samsung_SPH-P100_
NewRelease-Sms.csv
C:\Users\lreiber\Documents\samsung_SPH-P100_NewRelease\samsung_SPH-P100_
NewRelease-WifiHotspots.csv
C:\Users\lreiber\Documents\samsung_SPH-P100_NewRelease\samsung_SPH-P100_
NewRelease-Phonebook.csv
```

To confirm, we check to see if any files do not match by using the `-x` switch. This command does not return any files:

```
C:\md5deep-4.4>hashdeep64 -x -k baseLine-knowns.txt
C:\Users\lreiber\Documents\samsung_SPH-P100_NewRelease\*
```

The result indicates that the new baseline files in MPE+ 5.5.5 are identical to the secondary image created with MPE+ 5.5.6. This method proves that no changes were made to the extraction method and additional software capabilities have not been added between releases.

Device Integrity Verification The baseline steps involved in the verification of the software differ from the steps used for verification of changes to a device. The device integrity verification process does not determine whether the forensic software has made a change, but whether the device has been compromised.

Many global companies rely on mobile devices to keep their employees in touch with one another, to allow for work to be completed remotely, and to keep production up—no matter where employees are located. An employee who is constantly tethered to a mobile device can instantly access files, documents, e-mail, and any other type of electronic data. With this mobility comes the price of data security, however. When you are confronted with the possibility of device compromise, you can take steps to ensure that the compromise can be recognized. You can create a baseline of the mobile device prior to its being deployed in an area where data could be compromised and later examined. This verification can identify malicious applications, injection of foreign data, and other types of espionage.

To complete this process, you must create a baseline of the device just prior to the journey. Of course, data will change in the course of the deployment, simply because the user will be using the device. But by creating a baseline for the device and its contents, you can quickly dissect information to determine whether anything has been compromised on the device. Once the device is obtained, a physical data collection should be completed. If a physical data collection cannot occur, for example, on a new iOS device, a full file system collection along with application files should be obtained. The files are needed in this type of verification because the addition or deletion of files that had previously existed or had not existed will be key to the process.

Tip Not all mobile forensic software can complete this process, but software such as AccessData MPE+, Cellebrite UFED 4PC, UFED Touch Ultimate, Micro Systemation XRY, and Oxygen Forensic Detective and Analyst can create an image that can later be used to conduct a baseline analysis on most smart devices.

Once you have created a baseline for the device partition or file system, you must make an image of the device data along with hashing and indexing all the files within the created baseline image. Indexing involves categorizing, listing, filtering, and sometimes formatting the data to make it easy to search. Once all of the files in the collected image have been hashed and indexed to create each file's unique digital fingerprint, you create a *custom dictionary*, a list that contains all the file metadata along with the hash of each file in the image. Your forensic software should be able to create a dictionary containing all of the file hashes within the baseline image. Then save this dictionary along with the device baseline image to sort the known files against unknown files or alert files contained within the comparison device image once the device is back from the deployment.

This technique is typically used by companies that are operating in different countries and by military employees or contractors. The following example information was culled from the employee travel policy of a major gas company. This policy requires that the security team take a baseline of the contents of the device and create an indexed list of the contents, which can be later compared to the contents of the device immediately when the device is returned.

> Immediately prior to the travel the mobile device designated to be used shall be forensically imaged by the device security team. The image that is created of the mobile device will be indexed and stored.... Upon return, the device will be immediately forensically imaged using the same technique used to create the baseline. The baseline dictionary will be imported and any delta analyzed immediately. Should the delta be identified as a security risk as defined in...the device should be removed from service and further response from the designated security team will be elevated based upon the reported compromise.

In today's world, entire company networks can be infiltrated with a simple rogue malicious app unknowingly embedded on a mobile device. This technique does not have to be used only for travel policies, but can also be used to create a baseline of a device upon distribution to employees. If an employee is terminated, accepts a job from a competitor, or is subject to an investigation, the device data can immediately be compared to the baseline that was created when the device was distributed at hiring.

Using the following process, a device's integrity from a snapshot was examined to determine compromise, data changes, and malfeasance.

First, the images were collected using a Cellebrite UFED Touch device and then examined in AccessData Forensic Toolkit (FTK) as shown in Figure 5-4. FTK is a computer forensic product with built-in functionality for comparing known values that enables the examiner to flag files that match and do not match a known set of hashes.

Note X-Ways Forensics software can also create a set of hashes that can be used against an image created and exported by a mobile forensic tool. EnCase Forensic from Guidance Software can also allow for a set of hashes to be exported and then added to a hash database within the product. EnScripts are also available and can be used within EnCase to enable the examiner to export all files that either match or do not match a known hash within the hash library.

Next, a complete file list was created that contains all of the file hash values, which can be stored in a file and imported into a file database of known file hashes—in FTK, this is called the Known File Filter (KFF). The KFF stored the file hashes and used them to discern the known files from the unknown files when a second image of the device was created and imported into FTK. With this information, the examiner quickly identified which files had been altered and immediately began the examination into the cause of the change to the files.

After the baseline was created, the device was taken outside of the country for approximately three days, where it was used on various networks. The following process was used to determine whether data was altered while the device was out of the country.

1. A file list was created (by choosing File | Export File List Info, as shown in Figure 5-5) with the added evidence using the function within FTK to export file list information. Once exported, it was saved to a .csv file, which was modified to contain only the MD5, SHA-1, and SHA-256 columns.
2. This created a listing of 52,456 file hashes. The hashes were exported and modified, and then the user imported them into a file list to be used by FTK's KFF. (This file list can also be used in other tools such as EnCase and X-Ways Forensics.)

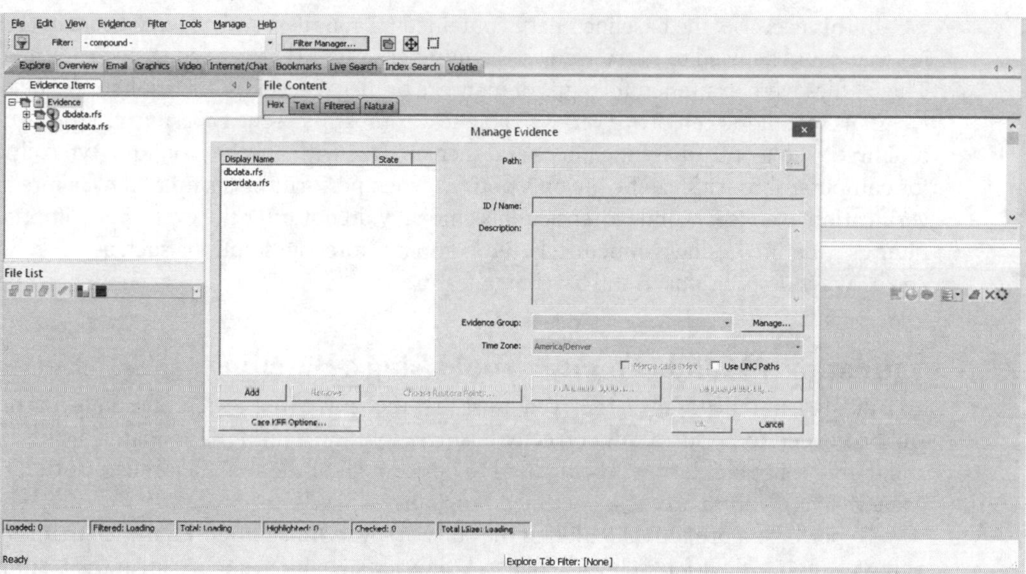

FIGURE 5-4 **A physical image of the device partitions for an Android are imported as evidence into FTK.**

3. A secondary image of the same device was collected using the same software—in this case, Cellebrite UFED Touch. The same partitions used to create the known hashes were used—the userdata partition and the dbdata partition from a Samsung Fascinate. These partitions were again added as evidence into the FTK case.
4. The evidence was processed. Once complete, using the Filter Manager, all files that were identified as KFF Ignorable could be hidden. (KFF Ignorable equates to the files that are identical in hash from the baseline list.) After the files were hidden, only the files that were altered or created sometime after creating the baseline image were shown.

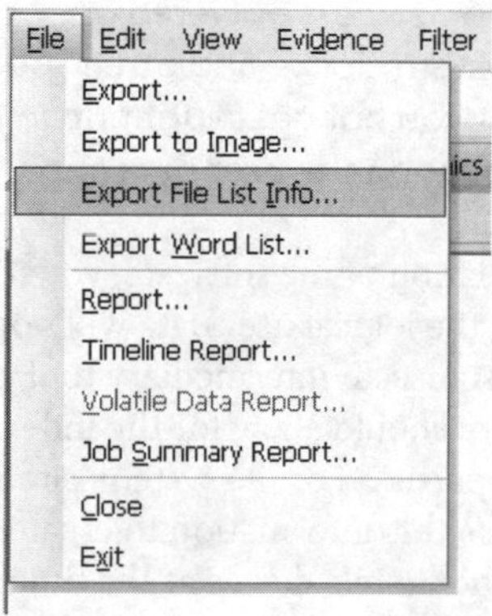

FIGURE 5-5 **Using FTK to export a file list to a .csv file**

In this exercise, the baseline image contained 52,456 files, and all were hashed, creating a list that could be used to narrow down the number of files that needed to be examined to 64. The 64 files were examined for signs of malware or illegal access. The results were negative.

This technique can prove very valuable to a company's security. Using a mobile forensic tool first to collect the baseline image and then analyze with another tool that typically is used for computer forensics can be the only options when performing a similar device integrity verification exercise. Mobile forensic tools currently do not offer the examiner an option to filter user-defined values immediately, but computer forensic solutions such as FTK, EnCase, and X-Ways do offer this useful baselining feature.

Validating a Mobile Forensic Tool Using a Baseline

To validate a mobile forensic tool, you must first recognize that a second mobile forensic tool will be needed to perform this correctly. A single solution cannot be validated against itself, and if only a single solution is being used to perform all of the mobile forensic duties, then using the verification processes outlined previously will suffice.

To perform a proper validation of the software, you must employ a device that is used only as a mobile device baseline exemplar. Using actual evidence to perform the testing could pose problems should the software being validated fail testing. Having device exemplars of the most prevalent devices that are examined in the region will be the best use of the validation principles.

The object of the validation is to determine whether the software is modifying the device data upon extraction. It's important to understand that data on a mobile device will invariably change because communication continually interfaces with an active mobile device. By using one mobile device forensic application to create the baseline, you can use another application to test for possible data corruption. Perform these tests before using any mobile forensic software in an examination and also upon each major release update.

Note As you know, a mobile device cannot be inhibited from being written to simply by employing a typical write-protection device. Furthermore, mobile forensics software interfaces with the device via protocols used to debug, back up, query, and manipulate the data on the device, changing the data in some way. Also, because the device is powered on, working processes such as system maintenance, system clocks, and other processes will continue to operate. It is important that you not get caught up in the changes to the various system processes but focus on the user data and user applications on the device.

To perform the validation of the software, you must collect a physical or file system image. Simply collecting the logical user data will not allow you to correlate and compare the two tools. You should also use an intermediary tool, as described earlier in the verification of software data. This tool should allow for the indexing, categorization, and hashing of each file in the mobile device partition or file system, similar to what was discussed earlier in the chapter. Then you can use this information to create a baseline dictionary of files, using their hashes, that existed on the mobile device at the time of collection. Next, you use the validated tool on the exemplar mobile device to conduct a logical extraction, selecting all capabilities that are supported for a forensic extraction. At the conclusion of the data collection on the mobile device, reacquire the mobile device with the initial mobile forensic software and recollect physical or file system data. It is important that you perform the same type of collection you used during the first extraction. You can compare this image to the initial data collection by using the dictionary created with the baseline data collection. If data has been added, deleted, or modified by the tool being validated, these files will be immediately identified upon completion of the dictionary comparison.

You must examine each file that diverges from the baseline image. These will undoubtedly include system files, which will commonly change because of the active state, and software protocols and changes the examiner may have made to complete a data collection of the device (such as placing an Android device into Android Debugging Bridge mode). Any files that contain user data should be scoured. The forensic software should not alter content in files that contain user data, such as SMS, contacts, call logs, browsing history, user applications, and so on.

If you determine that the mobile forensic software has modified a critical piece of user data, you must further examine the file to determine if the integrity of the user data has been compromised. At times, forensic software can alter a file's metadata during the extraction, which could change the overall hash value, but the data contained within the file has not been altered. If this is the case, although the user data has not been compromised, you should have a clear understanding as to why the file metadata was changed. If at any time you determine that the user data other than the metadata contained within the file has been altered, notify the forensic software company and discontinue use of the software until it is updated to address the problem.

Validation Workflow Example The following example shows a complete workflow using several products to address this type of software validation. This workflow was completed using Cellebrite UFED Touch, FTK, and MPE+.

1. Using the technique described in the section "Device Integrity Verification," we created an image using a single forensic solution—in this case, MPE+. This was the baseline image—a physical image or image that contains a device file system.
2. We created a hash list of the files using FTK, as outlined earlier.
3. Using the software to be validated (UFED Touch) and the same device on which the baseline was just created, we conducted a full extraction of the device; this could be logically or physically or both.
4. After the collection was completed by the UFED Touch of the exemplar device, we performed another collection using MPE+, as with the initial baseline in step 1.
5. We compared the files obtained from the collection by UFED Touch in step 4 to the hashes obtained in step 2 in FTK.
6. We analyzed any files that were different as identified by the hash to determine whether they were a system file or a file that contained user data, which could have been altered by the software being validated. If any new files were identified that were not in the baseline image, we closely inspected the files to identify whether they were collected from the device or added by the software. The software should never add a file that was not extracted from the mobile device. If this occurs, the software should not be used until verified by the vendor software developer.

In this example, the UFED Touch did not add files upon the extraction, but six files showed different hash values. Inspection of the files showed they were system files, with no adverse changes to user data. This test validated the UFED Touch.

Using Multiple Tools to Your Advantage

This chapter described the ways that you can use one software application to complement another for verification and validation. Using multiple tools to perform this very important task is important to ensure the validity of each data collection event and of the overall investigation. Using multiple tools is not just for verification and validation, however, but also for the actual analysis of data. This analysis typically cannot be performed using a single solution for many of the reasons already discussed, and most in the industry agree that there is no single solution that will perform every function an examiner will request or want.

The ultimate goal of any digital investigation should be to uncover and make visible all data available on the device should that data be desired during an investigation. If the data exists on the device and it can be recovered, that data should be presented in some way for further analysis. Simply using a single tool will not suffice because of the inherent limitations known to exist in every mobile forensic solution. In many cases, digital artifacts are easily seen in the data within the forensic tool, but the information cannot be visualized into a report or clearly represented in a way that could be discernible to an average observer. Using a secondary tool to support the analysis and display of the data in a form that can be evaluated and used to convey the investigative message is the ultimate goal of any digital investigation. The actual case example described in the sidebar shows the value in this type of collective tool analysis.

Case Study: Working the Case Using Multiple Tools

A law enforcement agency was involved in the investigation of a homicide that had occurred in a large city—a male had been shot and killed at an unknown residence. The responding officers knew very little since the deceased was found in a neighborhood park by a person walking his dog. A canvas of the area did not assist in gathering leads to the crime, but investigators identified the deceased as a gang member and began questioning known associates. After these people were questioned, limited additional information was collected, which is typical in investigations of homicides when a gang member is involved. Generally, people do not want to get involved for fear of being the next target. A break in the case came when one person came forward and identified a possible witness to the crime. Investigators interviewed the witness, who indicated that the homicide occurred because of an unpaid drug debt and provided the name of one of the people allegedly involved.

Police responded to the potential suspect's residence and began to interview the person they believed was involved in the homicide two days prior. During the interview, the person revealed enough information that he was taken into custody and transported to the detective annex to be further interviewed. A mobile phone was also in the suspect's possession, and this device was taken as evidence. A search warrant for the device contents was compiled, issued, and served.

A device physical image was obtained using Cellebrite UFED. The mobile device data was further analyzed in Cellebrite Physical Analyzer software, which revealed that the subject in custody was involved in the homicide—but, more importantly, another subject was identified based upon text messages that had been sent from the phone. No messages were received by that number on the subject's phone, however. Investigators were unable to locate a carrier associated with the phone number to which the messages were sent, but they did have a name and possible address. Officers responded to the location and took a second subject into custody. This person also had a smart device in his possession, which was seized and ultimately examined after completing a search warrant for the contents based upon probable cause to believe this person was involved in the homicide.

Officers examined the device and collected it with the same software used for the first device. What was puzzling to the officers conducting the examination was the fact that the phone number that was given to them by the first suspect and the one the message had been sent to was not the same phone number for this device. Officers believed that the subject had another device or had purchased a new device. Both of these theories were proved incorrect once they began examining the SMS messages, however. They found that messages were listed with date and time information referencing the time before, during, and after the date of the homicide. The text messages clearly indicated that the subject in custody was the person receiving the messages, which was evident by the use of his name in the conversation.

The mobile forensic examiners had multiple tools and subscribed to the multiple-tool approach. The image of the second device was imported into MPE+ and Oxygen Forensic Analyst in an attempt to uncover information not readily available in Physical Analyzer. Running simple search strings in MPE+ for the text message they believed should be on the device as indicated by the original suspect, they immediately found the message within an application, Google Voice. Inside the Google Voice settings, they found the phone number that the first suspect was referencing and the number to which his text message had been sent. It was starting to make sense. Using a Google Voice number, the suspect was not just receiving voice calls but was receiving and sending text messages. Using additional tools and functions not in the Physical Analyzer, the examiners were able to rebuild the message from the device, indicating the second person's involvement in the homicide, along with two others; the location where the victim had been killed; the motive of the crime; and geomapping evidence that placed the device in the area at the time of the crime.

Had it not been for the usage of MPE+ and Oxygen Forensic Analyst to complement the Physical Analyzer, the data that ultimately solved the case might not have been uncovered. The use of multiple tools in this instance was priceless.

The use of a single solution to handle all mobile devices and contingencies is something that most software vendors realize is not possible. Most practitioners also understand this and believe that more than one tool is needed, as indicated in the case study. What can be clearly observed, however, is that very few examiners actually use multiple tools.

Why is there no single solution that can cover every contingency? The many reasons involve too many mobile devices, too many mobile applications, lack of a specific analysis feature, missing analysis of a specific application, or lack of support for a specific file type. The reasons are many, the solutions are few, but what is clear is that no single tool can rule them all. For this reason, the word that should be used in mobile forensics is *complementing.* To complement one another is to "bring to perfection," as described in one definition of the verb.

When you use a secondary tool to perform analysis of data that works differently from the imaging tool, the solutions truly complement one another and the investigation profits.

As outlined in the actual law enforcement case, the use of multiple tools can be a game changer. Adhering to the philosophy that a single tool is all that's needed is a recipe for disaster.

Dealing with Challenges

Most challenges to the examination of a mobile device will not come from *what* was collected from the device, but from *how* the data was collected. Also challenged will be the software used to collect the data. Questions abound about whether the tool wrote data to the device, whether the tool deleted data from the device, and whether the tool merged data from the previous collection into the current device's data. Also, a lot of challenges can come from questions about the inability of one tool to do one thing while another tool can accomplish the task.

Understanding the many ways in which the processes described in this chapter can be challenged will help you prepare for better examination techniques and for handling these common objections in court. What is quite evident when observing most individuals conducting mobile forensic exams is the fact that few examiners comprehend how important these challenges can be to their cases. Moreover, some current examiners believe that multiple tools are only for validation of the tools and fail to recognize that using multiple tools increases the chance of uncovering additional data from the device.

Overcoming challenges in verification and validation, along with the use of both single-tool and multiple-tool examinations, will forever be challenged.

Overcoming Challenges by Verification and Validation

The reasoning for conducting verification and validation of mobile forensic software is simple: to overcome a challenge before being challenged. Software is created by a software engineer who is a human being, and human beings can make mistakes. Software code is developed to do one thing, but it sometimes does another. Relying on what a software company has stated regarding how a tool should perform is not good practice. It's the responsibility of the examiner to maintain and test any software to be used in the forensic lab or in the field to perform digital data collections and analysis from mobile devices.

When it comes to explaining the various reasons behind the verification and validation of tools in the lab, an examiner must be prepared to support each challenge when presented. If an examiner cannot support the reasoning behind tool verification and validation with credible data, the collection and analysis of a mobile device should not be completed or even initiated.

There are various challenges to performing a proper baseline that mobile forensic tools can stifle. The greatest challenge is typically regarding how the integrity of the device was compromised due to the intrusive methods in the collection of the digital data from the device.

Some claim that mobile forensic software can change, alter, and modify data on the device. Mobile devices typically have their data collected while they are powered on, so data can change even without software interaction. When a device is powered on, its operating system is constantly changing its system files, just as a computer does. The device will update directories and index files, and will allocate memory and monitor the system clock. This even occurs when the device is isolated 100 percent from all network sources.

When testing a forensic application by creating a baseline, you can show that no user data was altered in the collection and subsequent analysis of the data. In baseline verification and validation testing of the software used in the analysis, you can show that no user data was altered, changed, or modified. Based upon the testing of the software and passing results, you can conclude that during the digital forensic investigation, the software performed as described and did not alter, modify, or change the user data as represented in the case.

Typical mobile device collections are conducted via a USB cable connected to a computer and to the mobile device. Using device and manufacturer protocols, communication occurs between the software and the device, which are unlike any other digital device collection method. Unorthodox methods such as using protocols to initiate a data backup of the device, installing a small program and initiating the program to query the device's internal user data repositories, and placing a custom partition on a device to allow for the bypass of security are a few methods used in mobile forensic software. These methods do not alter, modify, or change the user data as determined by the baseline testing conducted using the mobile forensic software.

Overcoming Challenges for Single- and Multiple-Tool Examinations

Another, more personal challenge, can be the attack of the examiner who conducted the collection and examination. Any change from the expected results is said to be caused by a lack of training of the examiner or the improper type of training received, along with the forensic tool used.

Training is necessary to mitigate challenges of the improper use of the forensic software or any device used in the forensic examination of the mobile device. Being certified in the forensic software is not essential to conduct an examination using it, but a certificate can show the examiner's competence to perform collection and analysis of the mobile device. Becoming well acquainted with all of the software that is currently in the mobile forensic toolbox can occur only with proper research, usage, and ultimately training.

Single-Tool Challenges

In many instances, even if the examiner has more than one tool available, he or she will use a single tool from the start to the finish of the examination. This tool will be used to collect the data from the mobile device, create an image, analyze the data, and create a report. This scenario, more times than not, is the criterion. Sometimes an examiner has only one mobile forensic tool in his or her arsenal because of budget issues or for other reasons. In any case, the challenge often cited is that data output cannot be verified using the same tool that created the first forensic collection. This is primarily because an anomaly in the software's collection of data from a mobile device would, in theory, exist each time the collection was performed on an exemplar device, showing no difference.

If the lab has multiple tools, then using a single solution from start to finish can be justified so long as the verification and validation have occurred as outlined previously. What becomes critical when only a single solution is available will be the validation, testing, and identification that no user data was altered over subsequent extractions of a testing device. You must conduct the baseline testing as documented earlier and cover the steps on baselining devices when device integrity is required.

If only a single tool is available for the collection and analysis of data, the examiner should be diligent in every aspect of the examination. Verification of the data must typically be managed by visual verification on the actual exemplar device during verification testing. Challenges to "missing" data that is recoverable with another tool can also occur when using a single solution. When data is missed and consequently critical to the opposing counsel, the examiner who was not able to recover this critical piece is often questioned as to why this data was not disclosed, which questions the credibility of the examiner.

Dealing with this type of challenge involves simply explaining that all software is not created equally, with some having very robust analysis features while others simply report on limited data. In this instance, the software that was used has limited analysis features and does not support the recovery of the indicated information; ergo, the data was not located.

Multiple-Tool Challenges

When you use multiple mobile forensic products for a single device collection, various challenges can involve how the image was created, whether the integrity of the image was maintained, and whether changes were made to the actual data within the case. To overcome these challenges, you can follow several key investigative techniques.

To avoid problems with a challenge to the creation of the image and its integrity, use only one piece of software to create the data image of the mobile device. It is extremely important that you make every effort to extract the mobile device data only once from the evidentiary device. The more times that a device is hooked up to a computer, queried, extracted, and accessed, the more likely corruption will eventually occur. Sometimes collecting the digital data from a mobile device more than once is unavoidable—for example, when the device data is extracted at a scene and then again at the forensic lab. In these cases, to avoid a challenge, make sure you examine and compare the first extraction data to that of the second collection. If you note a difference in the data collected, clearly document all of the changes and the reason the data has changed. If proper procedures have been followed to isolate the device from network connections, the second collection should not contain additional user personal information, but should this occur, provide additional documentation stating how this information was written to the device. Such changes to data will undoubtedly be used later to discredit the data on the device and examination.

Also, challenges can be made against the integrity of the evidence by using a secondary tool when the secondary tool can import and analyze another tool's created mobile device image. It becomes very important that when you create an image with mobile device software, you also create an overall hash value of digital data collected. Most mobile forensic software applications create an overall hash of the evidence image, but for those that do not, the examiner should use a third-party tool that will create a hash value. Several free file hash software applications are available online and can be downloaded to perform this task.

If you're using an online software application, it is important that you create a text file that can be associated with the image file that contains the hash value, the date the hash was created, the person who hashed the file, and the software that was used to create the hash. With this information, if needed, a second person can duplicate the steps to validate the image as well. Once the hash value is obtained, it will be used at the conclusion of the examination

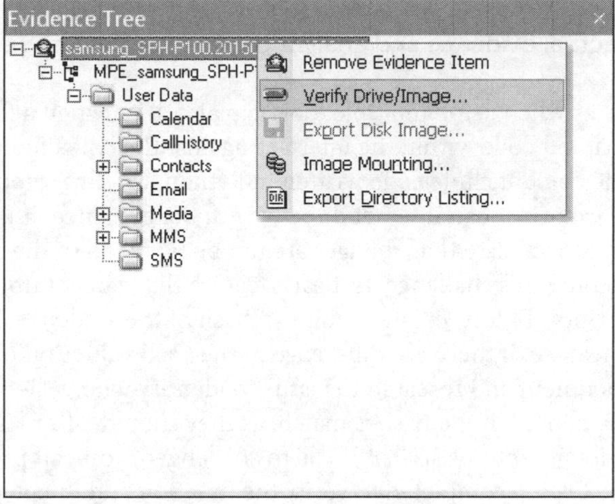

FIGURE 5-6 **Using AccessData FTK Imager, import the created image, right-click the device, and select Verify Drive/Image.**

to verify the integrity of the image after a secondary tool has been used to analyze the primary tool image. Some software titles will actually verify the image's hash upon import, and if it is not identical from the hash obtained at the creation of the image, the user will be immediately notified. Other applications, such as AccessData FTK Imager (Figure 5-6), can run a function to verify the integrity of images created by AccessData products. This hash, as shown in Figure 5-7, can then be used to compare against the image when requested at any time during the evidence lifecycle.

FIGURE 5-7 **The image will be tested and hashed and compared to the hash that was created when the image was made.**

Tip When using a secondary tool to analyze a primary tool's image, make a copy of the actual evidence and analyze the copy of the image using the secondary tool.

Challenges when using multiple tools can also arise when a feature that is used to analyze data runs scripted code within the interface against the collected mobile device evidence. Scripted code could include code written in Python, C#, EnScript, or others. By using these features, the examiner can interact directly with the evidence; it is extremely important that you take steps to validate that changes are not being made to the actual evidence.

To overcome this challenge, test each feature that can act upon evidence with user-generated scripts. To test, create a simple rehash of the evidence containers after the use of the customized feature. If there is a difference in the hash values before and after running a script, you must document and research the issue to identify where the failure occurred and if the evidence was tainted. If the hashes match, as they should, after running the custom scripts, you should also document this so that if you're challenged, you can provide specific information regarding the testing completed to verify the function and image integrity testing.

Tip When conducting any type of analysis, all work should be done on a copy of the actual evidence file. Evidence should not be used for testing or baselining purposes.

Chapter Summary

Data integrity is at the heart of a forensic examination. Maintaining confidence in the resulting output of a mobile forensic collection is critical. To do this, the examiner must be confident in the mobile forensic tools that are being used to perform the data collection and examination. By performing frequent verification and validation techniques, the examiner can be confident that his or her examinations will hold up when challenged. A great byproduct of rigorous testing of the forensic tools in a lab will be tool knowledge. Expanding the examiner's knowledge of the tool from a traditional training curriculum or "I read the manual and web site" track with intimate hands-on work will not only benefit in court, but also in work production. Examinations of mobile data will be much more detailed and pointed, and will contain information that only an examiner very knowledgeable with a product could produce. The more that a tool can be dissected, tested, and used, the better the examiner will become at using the tool, and the actual investigation will reap the benefits.

Although there are many benefits to using multiple tools for mobile device examinations, not everyone has the luxury of using more than one tool. In these cases, you should ensure that the validation process is conducted vigorously. By using a single tool, not only will the examinations be limited to a single set of features and support, but the ability to verify and validate will be much more difficult. Using a single tool to conduct mobile device investigations can be accomplished, but there will always be a bigger risk of a challenge to the operation of the software and the examiner's methods. Also, the location of additional data could be jeopardized simply because the single tool does not support a feature, device, or data set. Selection of the mobile forensic tool, if allowed to have only one solution, is critical.

There are great benefits to using multiple tools to collect and examine mobile devices; nevertheless, with the use of multiple software applications comes risks. The many benefits range from verification and validation, to wider spectrum of device support, to the recovery of additional data by using features and controls of a secondary tool not supported by the primary tool. The risks come from the collection of the same device with different tools, ways in which tools validate the data with hashes, the inability to determine if a tool altered the data, the integrity of the collected digital data, and the lack of correlation of the data between software applications.

Without the examiner having a firm understanding of the tools in his or her toolbox, there will always be risks. Overcoming any challenge to the collection and analysis of mobile device data comes in the form of understanding the operation of the mobile forensic software in the digital forensic toolkit.

6 Mobile Forensic Tool Overview

Selecting a mobile forensic solution can be an extremely difficult task. Understanding the capabilities of each tool can be confusing and at times cryptic. Although lot of mobile forensic software vendors list the vast number of devices that can be supported, remember that even if a product supports 15,000 devices, if it will not help with the single device that you need to collect, or the device is supported but does not extract the data that could be critical to the case, it's not the right tool for you. Vendors in the mobile forensic marketplace use the term "profiles" to describe their support and generally describe support for a "type" of device, loosely based on model. This enables the vendor to claim support for a subsection of the model or profile, even though not all of the carrier's versions may be supported.

Quite honestly, the numbers game used by most mainstream vendors is just that—a game. The examiner should be aware of these types of nuances when selecting a solution that claims to support a specific model of device that will be examined. Most vendors have an online location where the examiner can go to determine if a device is supported. What does it mean when a vendor says the software handles the "logical and physical collection" from an iPhone 4 running Apple iOS7? Such information is often misleading, especially because logical and physical collections might mean one thing to one examiner and mean something entirely different to another.

In this chapter, several mobile device solutions are identified and the types of examinations are discussed—but in a more granular way that departs from the traditional nuances of logical and physical collections. Open source, freeware, and commercial tools all have benefits and limitations. Each piece of software covered here comes from my personal experiences as well as community experiences, but as in everything, one person's experience can differ from another's. Consideration of the level and type of examination required should be one of the deciding factors in the type of mobile device tools to be used for the collection and subsequent examination of recovered data. In some cases, the tool used to collect a mobile device can be entirely different from the tool that completes the analysis of the data.

Just as confusing is the tool progression—the decision to move into another category of examination for a particular device or situation. Not all devices are supported with a simple connection via USB cable, and some are not supported by any traditional methods. Some devices must be examined after the removal of the memory chip, while others can be examined with a physical connection directly to the mobile device printed circuit board (PCB).

Mobile device forensics in today's world does not involve simply attaching a cable, clicking a Go button, and waiting for completion. To conduct a thorough mobile device examination when it counts is to comprehend the tool progression continuum, the risk involved, the training needed, and the available tools.

Collection Types

There is no more confusing discussion in mobile forensics than either listening to or speaking about a logical and a physical collection of a mobile device. This topic is one of the most danced around issues in mobile device forensics. What constitutes a logical collection and what constitutes a physical collection? If a file system was recovered and happens to contain files and folders, is that a logical collection? If the file system contains unallocated space, does it constitute a physical collection? To be honest, there is no clear definition for the difference between logical and physical with regard to mobile device collections, and there are too many variables involved. The following section discusses both terms, some historical data, and what today's working practitioner believes to be the definition.

Logical Collection

As defined in the 2007 publication, NIST SP 800-101 "Guidelines on Cell Phone Forensics," a *logical acquisition* implies a bit-by-bit copy of logical storage objects (such as directories and files) that reside on a logical store (such as a file system partition). In 2013, the Scientific Working Group on Digital Evidence (SWGDE) published the document "SWGDE Best Practices for Mobile Phone Forensics," which removed the bit-by-bit classification proposed by NIST and classified a logical collection in a different way. SWGDE stated that a logical acquisition implies a copy of logical storage of objects (such as directories and files) that reside on a logical store (such as a file system partition). In the 2013 publication "SWGDE Core Competencies for Mobile Phone Forensics," a logical examination is described as a process that provides access to the user-accessible files. Moreover, SWGDE indicated that the logical analysis process will "not generally provide access to deleted data." In a 2014 revision, NIST SP 800-101R, "Guidelines on Mobile Device Forensics," described a logical acquisition as capturing a copy of logical storage objects (such as directories and files) that reside on a logical store (such as a file system partition).

Note The definition is getting closer between both groups, most likely due to the personnel who are now contributing both to the NIST and the SWGDE documentation.

Confusing, isn't it? There appears to be a common theme of files and directories from a mobile device, and honestly, the definitions have become better in describing the data available, but to a layperson reading this information and ultimately applying it to his or her job, it is cloudy at best, and almost mystical. The mysticism comes in the form of one of the terms used in SWEGDE's logical definition: "generally." It is because of this "generality" that the word "logical" has lost some credibility. The problem arises because, within a subset of devices such as iOS and Android devices, a logical file extraction can often contain deleted data. Simply stating that a logical examination is capturing the logical storage objects (such as directories and files) from the file system of a mobile device is *too general* and, quite honestly, in some situations inaccurate. The terms "logical" and "physical" acquisition are throwbacks to computer forensics parlance, and they are more often than not misinterpreted when it comes to mobile device forensics. Data that is not accessible to the user, such as system files, application stores, and deleted data, can often be collected from a device in a currently defined logical extraction. This would contradict some of the definitions mentioned.

A logical collection on its face should be interpreted as the extraction of user data from a mobile device without the collection of a device's file system. This data is extracted from the mobile device using proprietary protocols and queries and displayed in the software user interface. An example of a logical collection as just defined would be using a software tool on an Android device with an Android application package (APK) file. Most forensic software applications use this method when conducting their version of a logical extraction. The APK queries the Android device's internal databases and returns the data to the software interface. The data is then displayed in the software's user interface. This method does not return a file system, but the data that is represented by the contents of the files on the device. This distinction is important because the currently accepted definition makes an assumption that all logical collections and recovered data from a mobile device by software are similar, so long as the device is supported logically. Because of this often-used generality in describing a logical collection of a mobile device with a particular solution, a subcategory of a logical extraction should be discussed—a file system collection. A *file system collection* bridges the gap between what the mobile forensic community believes to be a logical extraction and a physical collection.

File System Collection

A file system collection contains much more information than the defined logical collection and should be considered a step up from a logical collection. A file system contains the files and folders that the device uses to populate applications, system configurations, and user configurations along with user storage areas. The following sections define and explore different types of file system collections.

MSC, MTP, and PTP Mobile devices such as iOS, BlackBerry, Android, and Windows Phones can have "points of storage," which could mean that mobile device file system collection must occur in multiple places. A user storage area can be the location where images, videos, and audio are stored and accessible by the user via a computer and a cable. Another user storage area can be an internal storage point that also stores application data, system log files, and documents.

Mobile devices have long enabled users to transfer data to a PC using "USB Mode," or the USB Mass Storage Class (MSC). Legacy feature phones and devices, when removable media was added as a supported feature, would allow the user to move media from the device to a PC much like transferring data from a flash drive to a computer. In 2008, the Media Transfer Protocol (MTP) mode, originally part of the Microsoft Framework, became a standard by the USB Implementers Forum (USB-IF) as a USB type. This mode is recognizable when a device is plugged into a PC and is automatically mounted as a device, rather than a drive. This access occurs via MTP, a subset of Picture Transfer Protocol (PTP), that adds some enhancements and enables communication between the mobile device and the PC to copy, move, replace, and delete files from and to the mobile device. The move away from MSC to MTP was made in most modern mobile devices because if the device was in MSC mode, it could not store or communicate with the default storage point, making the device useless during an MSC connection. The device could not access applications, take pictures, or otherwise operate, so MTP mode was implemented, which enables the device to function even when tethered to a PC.

The "media" in MTP should not be confused with traditional media such as images, videos, and audio. In the MTP specifications outlined in Media Transfer Protocol v.1.1, the term "media" in Media Transfer Protocol is used to identify any binary data and is not restricted to the audio/video formats to which it is commonly applied. This clearly indicates that any file that is stored can be recovered using MTP. Mobile devices running the Android system, Windows, BlackBerry, iOS, and feature phones of today allow for access to a logical file system via MTP and PTP.

The difference between the operating system, at a basic level, is really to what extent and what types of files can be accessed in this manner. Apple iOS devices will allow access to the media (pictures and videos only) area via a file explorer, such as Windows Explorer and the Finder, using PTP. With an Android device, default in Honeycomb (3.0) and standard in Ice Cream Sandwich (4.0) and above, the device can provide access to the internal storage area of the device, an external media card, or both using MTP. The data accessible includes application files, user documents, and media and system files. A Windows Phone, like the Android, allows for the transfer of files from both the internal and external card (if available) using MTP. Windows Phone data from both locations can contain documents, images, audio, and video. BlackBerry devices starting at version 5.0 allow for MTP as well as MSC. If the BlackBerry is set as a portable device, access to the internal and external card storage areas are available. These storage areas can support multiple file types such as documents, audio, video, images, and system files. Access and recovery of these files should not be overlooked in the examination of a mobile device.

Table 6-1 shows the types of data available on basic mobile devices using MTP and PTP.

Figures 6-1, 6-2, and 6-3 show the various device types and how they are depicted within the desktop operating system.

Although not generally recommended, the files can be copied manually to an evidence location when the device is connected to the examination computer. This is advisable only if the forensic software does not support the collection of these files. To make these accessible to the computer, the device must be unlocked.

Internal System Collection and Display Some mobile device systems can also be accessed from a protocol level to display a represented file system. Feature phones using propriety file systems can have their file systems collected and displayed to show system files, user

TABLE 6-1 Mobile Device OSs and Data Accessible Using PTP and MTP

Operating System	Type	Type of Data
Apple iOS	PTP	Images and videos
Android, BlackBerry 10, Windows Phone	MTP	Images, videos, and media (documents, files, other)

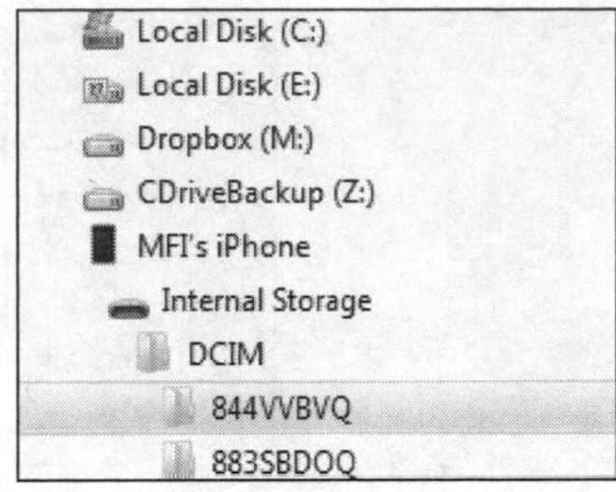

FIGURE 6-1 File system view of an iOS device connected as a PTP device—Digital Camera Image (DCIM) folder is available

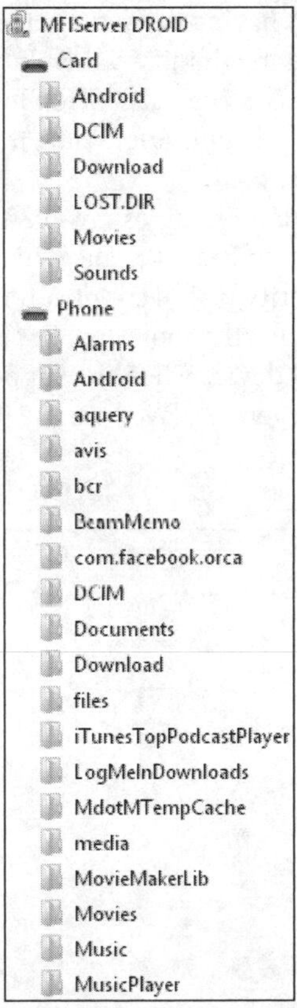

FIGURE 6-2 File system view of an Android device connected as a MTP device—notice the internal and external file systems containing various files and folders

FIGURE 6-3 File system view of a Windows Phone connected as an MTP device

databases, media, user files, logs, user settings, and more, as shown in Figure 6-4. These files are not directly accessible to the user via the device interface, and inside of these file systems are artifacts that, without the use of specialized tools, would not have been available. These files are the actual containers that the logical software queries and parses to display to the user in the software interface. By having the actual file, you can conduct a more detailed analysis, which should be considered much more valuable than what "logical" defines. Similarly, mobile devices, such as Apple iOS, Android, and BlackBerry devices, also can have their underlying file systems collected to reveal application data, media, user files, system files, logs, user settings, and device settings.

All three of the file system examples involve collections that can be lumped into the "logical collection" bucket definition. Because this level of collection is not available to all software solutions that identify logical support for the device, it makes sense to identify a secondary category or level for the tool used. For example, a vendor may describe providing "logical support" for an iOS device when the support is actually a query and return of the database content, which is then displayed via the user interface. In all actuality, an iOS device

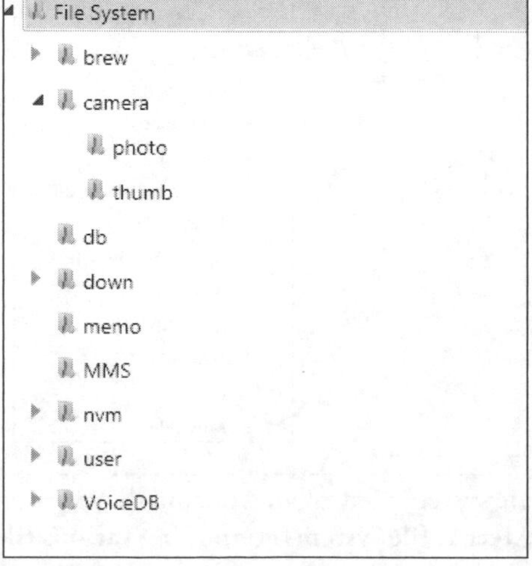

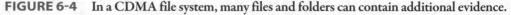

FIGURE 6-4 In a CDMA file system, many files and folders can contain additional evidence.

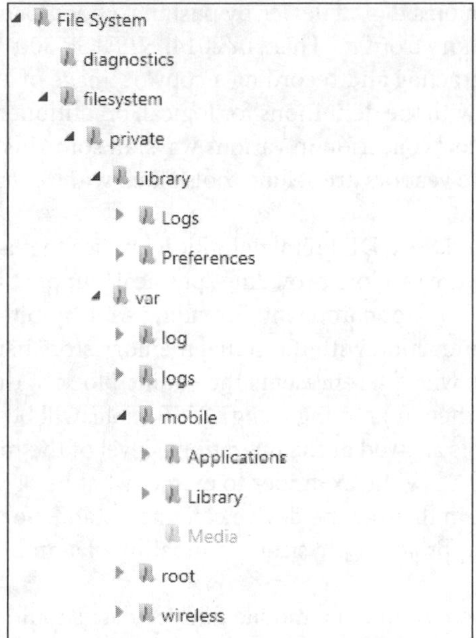

FIGURE 6-5 **In an iOS device file system, many files not represented by a superficial logical collection will be missed.**

contains numerous files, as depicted in Figure 6-5, such as property lists (plists) and SQLite databases that contain user, system, and deleted data at the logical file system level, which is something that the vendor does not support but claims to. This type of recoverable data at the logical level clearly extends the definition of what is often described as a "logical extraction." Chapters 11 and 12 are dedicated to the analysis of these types of files, so you can clearly see that the term "logical" is often misrepresented by software vendors.

When possible, the examiner should make a collection of a device's file system. The information contained far exceeds any data that is collected on the surface. Collecting the "surface" logical data along with file system recovery is what every examination should strive to accomplish. This type of collection should be referred to as a *file system collection*, not simply a logical extraction.

Physical Collection

To some, a physical collection includes application data, system files, and other information that is not available to the user via the handset. NIST SP 800-101 states that a "physical acquisition implies a bit-by-bit copy of an entire physical store (e.g., a memory chip)." In 2013, "SWGDE Best Practices for Mobile Phone Forensics 2.0" used a definition of a physical acquisition that was identical to that of NIST. In 2014, "Cell Phone Forensics in a Correctional Setting: Guidebook" was released and published by the Department of Justice, which described a physical analysis of a mobile device as a "digital forensic examination process that involves reviewing the data on a digital device by pushing a boot loader into the digital device and dumping the memory from it." Then, in 2014, NIST SP 800-101R described a physical acquisition as "extracting and recording a copy or image of a physical store (e.g., a memory chip)." Clearly, as with the definitions for logical, practitioners and researches interpret the definition of physical collection in various ways. In some instances, the definition is so vague that some software vendors are selling tools along with their own idea of supporting mobile devices "physically."

If the NIST and SWGDE literal definition implies that a bit-by-bit copy of a memory chip is used, then software vendors providing "physical" support for legacy devices, or smart devices using a USB cable, are not compliant. Providing a bit-by-bit copy of mobile device memory would entail an interaction with the actual memory store using a tool that can read from block 1 to block *n*, where *n* represents the ending block of the flash memory chip. Inherently, a mobile device, when interacting using a USB cable, will be able to scan and collect data only in a way that is allowed at the operational level of the mobile device. In simple terms, a mobile device will allow the examiner to extract what he or she wants and only if the software can communicate in the way the device can understand. So a change is necessary in how an examiner should approach a physical examination of a mobile device and then define what is taking place.

The physical collection of a mobile device's data should imply that direct communication with a device's internal data storage is made to collect a representation of the data as it is stored on the actual device flash memory. This data is a snapshot of the area of the flash memory store that is accessible using specialized tools and methods. That being said, there are different levels of a physical collection that depend upon the type of specialized tools that are used. In "Best Practices for Mobile Phone Forensics 2.0," SWGDE defines these as "non-invasive" and "invasive" physical collections, which are further explained in the following sections.

Non-Invasive Physical Collections

A non-invasive physical collection, according to SWGDE, "involves a process that provides physical acquisition of a phone's data without requiring opening the case of the phone." With this technique, the software must be able to communicate with the device to allow for a binary data "dump" of the device. In most cases, a collection using non-invasive techniques and software will not yield a physical image as defined by NIST (a bit-by-bit copy of the physical store). However, this method should yield a representation of the data area targeted by the software's communication in the format in which it is stored on the device. The data can then be interpreted and displayed in the software as it was on the device, allowing for advanced analysis techniques.

An example of a non-invasive method is attaching a flasher box to a device's USB port or FBUS connection and dumping the memory from predefined offsets known to contain user information. Another non-invasive example would be collecting an Android device using tools such as Oxygen Forensic Analyst or Detective, UFED, and XRY and selecting a physical option for a particular device that is not currently locked, with Android Debugging enabled. All mentioned tools communicate with the device to obtain partition information using the Android Debug Bridge (ADB), and they subsequently extract the returned partition table and partitions without altering the device partitions or operating system structure, which should be considered non-invasive.

Note Communication does not always necessitate the loading of a boot loader, as some literature indicates, but elevated privileges to the device do need to be obtained by the software conducting the physical collection (such as HEX dump or data dump).

These methods, however, target only what is visible by the communication method. Various partitions are not enumerated by the Android device's operating systems by design and are not accessed or extracted by the forensic software. Again, the partitions that are available are extracted and in the format (file system) found within the actual device, but it is not a bit-by-bit representation of the entire device memory store.

Invasive Physical Collections

An invasive process, according to SWGDE, provides physical acquisition of a phone's data and requires disassembly of the phone for access to the circuit board. For example, JTAG (Joint Test Action Group) allows for communication with a mobile device using the device TAPs (test access points). This is not a direct read of the actual memory module (flash), but a method to communicate with the device processor to access the NAND area of the device and obtain a binary file containing a representation of the partitions on the device. Again, if the software is interacting with the device microprocessor, the microprocessor will dictate what memory stores are available and where to read from. The use of JTAG is classified as invasive primarily because the direct interaction with the mobile device circuit board is necessary when soldering to the TAPs or using specialized connections directly to the circuit board.

Note Usually, a device is still functional after a JTAG procedure.

Another example of an invasive process is the removal of the memory chip from the mobile device, typically referred to as "chip-off." Chip-offs are destructive methods, however, and generally the mobile device will not be functional after using this technique. A chip-off, however, will enable a direct read of the memory chip using specialized hardware and software. The examiner can create a full binary file of the device memory flash without limitations typically imposed by a device microprocessor. This physical collection method would conform to a bit-by-bit representation of the entire device physical store and equates to a traditional hard drive collection. The resultant data must also be interpreted by software and a represented file system compiled from the binary file in order to conduct further analysis. As devices progress along with file systems, the encryption of the device at the file system level will hamper JTAG or chip-off examinations as well.

Collection Pyramid

A "collection pyramid" was developed by Sam Brothers of the U.S. Customs and Border Protection and described in the SWGDE document "Best Practices for Mobile Phone Forensics 2.0" and also later published in "Guidelines on Mobile Device Forensics." This pyramid outlines a tool classification that can be used as a practitioner's approach when conducting mobile device examination; it is a departure from merely classifying a tool as logical and/or physical. Using this approach, the examiner can outline the analysis methods without identifying the differences between a logical and physical acquisition relative to the device or the data, but relative to the actual type of analysis and extraction methods used. This ideology traditionally caused confusion in the mobile forensic community. Because of the various opinions as to what constitutes a logical examination versus a physical examination, the comparison to the definition imposed by computer forensic examiners, and governing bodies of forensic practitioners, the use of multiple analysis methods is recommended. By describing methods of collection of a mobile device, an examiner can predict the outcome of using the available forensic tools and also the training and expertise required for each discipline.

The collection pyramid is visually represented as an analysis ranging from the most invasive and specialized tool to the least invasive and least specialized tool (see Figure 6-6). The tip of the pyramid, or smallest represented part, is the most specialized tool, and the largest and base of the pyramid is the least specialized. These methods are numbered from 1 to 5, with 1 being least specialized and 5 the most specialized. The following sections present the different levels listed by name, as provided by Brothers, with additional information to better explain what each will offer to the examiner when conducting each level of analysis.

Level 1: Manual Extraction Manual extraction, or examination, involves capturing stored device information either by photography or written documentation. Photographing the information would be much more reliable in legal proceedings and therefore is the preferred method. Conducting a manual examination via the "commando method" or by "thumb jockeying" the device involves manual manipulation of the device to locate evidence stored inside. This method involves navigating the mobile device to the user stored areas and photographing or writing down the content observed in the device's viewing area. The first mobile examinations were conducted using the manual examination method, but mobile

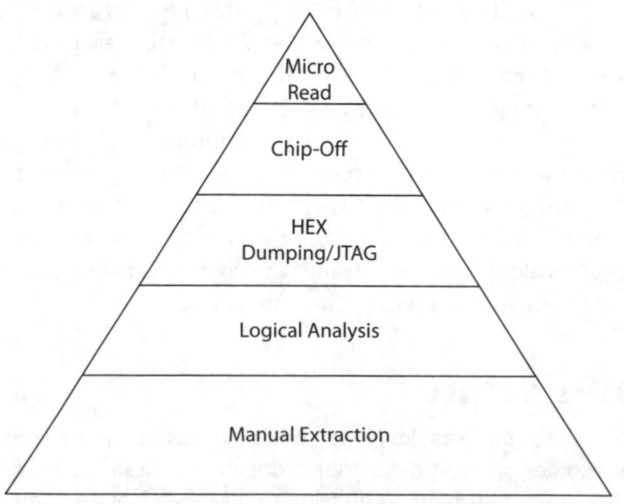

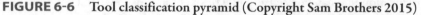

FIGURE 6-6 Tool classification pyramid (Copyright Sam Brothers 2015)

devices at that time were not capable of storing the amount of data that can be stored in today's devices. Conducting a manual examination of a smart device today is a considerable feat when prompted to document thousands of mobile device text messages, videos, or images!

This method may be the most cost effective, and sometimes the only available, option, but it can be difficult at times and dangerous in others. If a mobile device is damaged or locked or data is stored in a foreign language, the documentation can be difficult, if not impossible. Manual examinations of a mobile device can be conducted by examiners without training and with only a digital camera, which involves more people in the examination process. Manipulating the keys and navigating a foreign device could expose the possibilities of unintentional data corruption at a later date, and there may be a complete disregard for the preservation of the data. Tools for conducting manual examinations are further discussed in the "Tools Available" section later in the chapter.

Level 2: Logical Analysis A logical extraction occurs using a built in device transfer method (such as USB, Wi-Fi, IrDA, or Bluetooth) used by the mobile device. A connection is made with the device using a data transfer method, whereas the software can communicate using device protocols to extract data using commands comprehended by the mobile device. The data is returned to the software, which can be further analyzed and reported. This is the type of collection currently offered by most examiners as well as forensic software vendors.

Level 3: HEX Dumping/JTAG This level of collection uploads specialized software into the volatile memory of a mobile device. In doing so, it bypasses built-in security that would typically inhibit access to the device's internal memory store. However, devices that have chip-level encryption enabled will still pose problems for examiners.

Tip This method could be used when conducting an analysis of an iPhone 4. These devices do not allow access to the internal protected stores that contain protected data (for example, Apple's built-in e-mail client) using any of the connection methods and communication described in a logical extraction.

A custom application or package is installed onto the device in an effort to act as the original application, package, or ROM on the device that contained the security measure. Once this vulnerability has been patched with the vendor's own application or package, allowing access to the device that was inhibited by the device file, the examiner can then access the files using commands and procedures used by the mobile device. Typically, a raw file system, represented in the format used on the mobile device, is extracted.

A subsection of this portion of the pyramid also belongs to flasher boxes and JTAG methods. Both will be described in the "Tools Available" section, but to help you understand their placement in this pyramid, they are briefly described here.

By using the JTAG TAPs in a mobile device, the examiner has access to the flash memory. Using specialized tools comprising hardware and software, the examiner uses software to communicate via hardware to the microprocessor of the device that interfaces with the flash storage medium. The examiner accesses the flash area, circumventing password security, to obtain partition information and user storage areas. Using JTAG can be invasive because the device is disassembled and in some instances leads are directly soldered to the TAPs on the circuit board, but in some instances preconfigured jigs can be used. The output when using JTAG is a binary file of the selected partition or memory area.

The output produced by most flasher boxes is represented by what the hardware flashing device has been configured to output. The output can be in an encrypted format, segmented, or altered (boot loader added to start of image), or it can be a flat binary file. This is truly a hexadecimal representation of the data living on a mobile device. Limitations to flasher boxes are numerous, ranging from proprietary output to flash area memory constraints. Data output produced with the use of JTAG methods offers a better representation of the data, with little interference with the digital data output—it is the preferred method, but it can be more physically destructive to the mobile device. The decision to use these devices should be left to examiners with appropriate training and an understanding of the various formats and implications of using the tool and its invasive nature. This type of collection not only involves specialized hardware, but also specialized training and skills.

Level 4: Chip-Off The chip-off examination involves the physical removal of the mobile device flash memory. Using specialized tools and techniques, the examiner disassembles the device and removes the flash memory from the circuit board. Once the flash module is removed intact, it is placed into a specialized component to read memory modules. These memory module adapters are specific to the type of flash memory and its configuration. A binary file is produced upon reading that must be interpreted by software that specializes in the decoding and interpretation of this type of file. An examiner who should be conducting these examinations should be well trained; otherwise, the evidence could be easily compromised. Needless to say, a chip-off examination is invasive, and once the chip is removed from the device, the chip would need to be *reballed* and then reinstalled into the device so it could operate as it had previously. This process is extremely labor intensive and equally expensive. Generally, once a device has been disassembled at the chip level, the device is inoperable.

Note During the removal process of the BGA chip, you must remove the tiny pads that allow for the flow of input and output communication to the PCB; these must be reattached, which is called *reballing*. Reballing involves affixing tiny solder beads to each pad on the memory chip. This is no easy feat, as some flash memory chips have more than 200 pads! These beads, once affixed, are then reheated (reworked) to allow them to become permanently attached to the flash memory, which will allow communication with a chip programmer.

Level 5: Micro Read With this level of examination, the flash memory medium is read by an electron microscope. This type of examination is not only considered theoretical, but it has never been conducted publicly on mobile device evidence. The theory involves using an electron microscope to read and count electrons that occupy a cell on a flash memory chip. If electrons are present, a 1 is represented; if no electrons are present in the cell, a 0 is represented. This is often referred to as "gating." After combining the binary data manually, it can be translated into raw data and interpreted. An example of the work involved to translate the information after reading from a flash chip is shown in this example:

01001101 01101111 01100010 01101001 01101100 01100101 00100000 01000100
01100101 01110110 01101001 01100011 01100101 00100000 01000110 01101111
01110010 01100101 01101110 01110011 01101001 01100011 01110011 00100000
01100110 01101111 01110010 00100000 01110100 01101111 01100100 01100001
01111001 01110011 00100000 01100101 01111000 01100001 01101101 01101001
01101110 01100101 01110010

What is incomprehensible would be the interpretation and decoding of more than 32GB of binary data from a standard Android device using this technique. Most examiners will never experience this form of examination and collection, but those who do this will probably not boast of their exploits, since this work would likely involve matters of national security.

Collection Additions

Although the collection pyramid does capture a vision of classification based upon collection of digital data from a mobile device with a tool, some additional considerations must be addressed and added to the continuum. If classifying a tool and a collection, you must consider a few other methods and subsections involved.

Manual examinations described using a specific tool or method should include a subset that describes using imaging (such as a photograph or video) or not using imaging. Suggested additions include manual extractions, manual with documentation, and manual with photography and documentation. There are obvious differences between simply pushing buttons and writing down the contents versus pushing buttons and then photographing the screen.

Pushing buttons on the device and writing down the contents displayed takes no tool training and is very labor intensive; it should be classified separately from more thorough methods. Methods progressing up the pyramid would involve manually pressing a device's buttons and then photographing or creating a video of the various screens of interest. By using video, the examiner is not only documenting the data on the screen, but also the procedure he or she used. This can help to dispel any allegations of improprieties that may have occurred during the manual examination.

In the logical classification of the pyramid, a file system extraction should be included for defining a tool and the mobile device analysis. Some tools do, in fact, perform a logical extraction, but they fail to support the device file system and should be classified separately. A file system collection will contain data not accessible by the user as well as data that has been deleted by the user, unlike a traditional logical query. Analyzing a mobile device file system can be challenging and time consuming, and extensive examiner training is necessary, which also should be considered in the tool and analysis continuum. Because of the enormous amount of additional data that can be collected in a file system extraction, it is always the preferred method. However, most collections by mobile forensic tools and examiners are logical without an attempt to collect the file system because of a lack of understanding and expertise in the analysis of the resultant collected data.

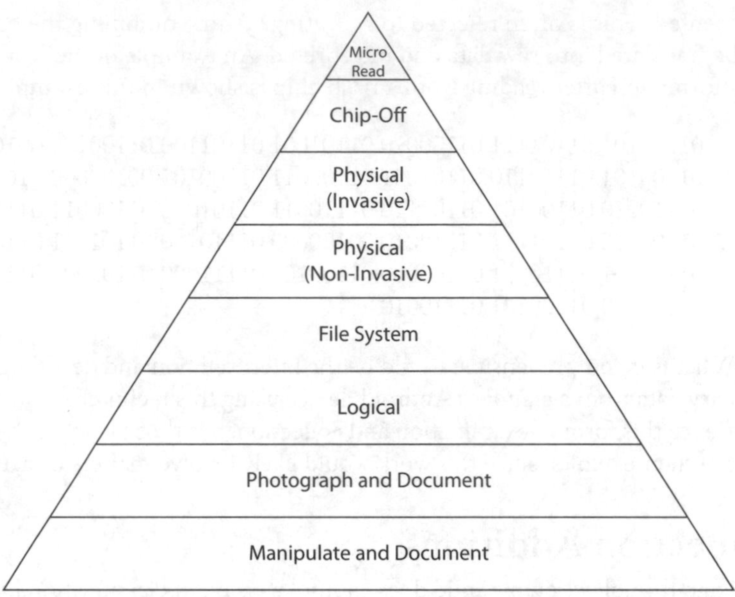

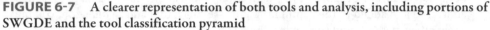

FIGURE 6-7 A clearer representation of both tools and analysis, including portions of SWGDE and the tool classification pyramid

Note SWGDE identifies a file system level of collection in "Best Practices for Mobile Phone Forensics 2.0."

In the pyramid's HEX and JTAG collections level, the term "boot loader" is used to identify a method that satisfies a higher level of tool collection and analysis. Because a boot loader is not always needed to obtain a raw binary dump of a mobile device, a better classification should be used. A new tool and collection pyramid can be created to indicate not only the types of tools that can offer the type of collection required, but also the level of complexity of each tool, as shown in Figure 6-7.

To understand these new categories, you need to understand boot loaders.

Boot Loaders

A boot loader is code that loads in a runtime environment or operating system. Boot loaders can be used in nearly all digital devices that have an underlying operating system. With mobile devices, a boot loader can change depending upon the hardware as well as the device's service carrier. If the boot loader code becomes corrupted, the device either cannot be started or will continue to restart over and over—this is referred to as a "boot loop."

The use of a boot loader to obtain a physical collection of a mobile device is classified in the "SWGDE Best Practices for Mobile Phone Forensics 2.0" as a non-invasive physical classification. Considerable operational differences are involved between using or not using a boot loader. Tool classification should be further expanded to describe that not all collections of binary data from mobile devices will involve using a boot loader, and in some instances, altering a device's boot loader can have dire consequences.

To use a custom boot loader in mobile forensic software, the examiner places the device into a certain mode. For iOS devices, this is called Device Firmware Update (DFU) mode; most Android devices use a recovery or download mode. This can occur operationally by the software, but the examiner typically places the device into this state with a combination of key presses. Once the device is in the correct mode, the examiner selects the device make and model, and the software then replaces the device boot loader, unlocks the boot loader, and in some instances of Android replaces the ROM with a custom ROM. The software then begins the process of calling instruction code to complete the collection of the mobile device's data store. The customized version of the boot loader and/or ROM loaded onto the device has been designed to allow full access to the device's memory store and additional settings relating to data transfer. With a customized version in place, communication can occur with the software to obtain unadulterated access to the device. Typically, on completion of the data collection, if the boot loader or ROM was exchanged, the original boot loader or ROM is returned to the device. In many cases, the customized boot loader is installed in the volatile area of the device's memory and will be released upon restart of the device to remove it. The use of a custom boot loader or ROM is specific to each device, and if used on another device, corruption of the device boot process can occur and render the device useless. For this reason, a classification for "physical non-invasive" should include a subset that describes tools and analysis if using a custom boot loader; otherwise, these techniques should be classified as "physical invasive."

Note Tools such as Cellebrite UFED Touch use a modified USB cable to place a device into device mode without requiring a keypress pattern.

Not all binary collections as described as "physical non-invasive" have boot loaders or ROM altered to obtain a hexadecimal dump of the memory store. Some techniques used in mobile forensic tools also allow physical access to a device memory store by the addition of a code set not available in the device's original code base. The action places a file or files into the temporary space of the device's logical file system. This code then adds commands that are not installed by default to be executed to elevate privileges on a mobile device. With elevated privileges, the software can communicate with the mobile device and obtain access to areas of the memory store that are typically inaccessible. Once this area is accessed, the memory storage can be recovered from the mobile device.

The classification "HEX/JTAG" and even "physical non-invasive" should include these possibilities and not assume that this classification applies only to tools and collections that use a boot loader to access a device memory store. This classification should indicate that the collection involves using customized techniques to allow access to the mobile device memory store that are not accessible ordinarily, because some methods might be non-invasive to the physical device but invasive to the internal operation. This classification would apply to boot loaders, rooting software, customized files, and customized ROMs.

Nontraditional Tools

Other tools can be used in many investigations, but because of their limitations or other concerns, they are considered "nontraditional" tools. Some tools are considered non-forensic, and others are extremely expensive. Having a thorough understanding of how these tools can be used is important because these tools are often discussed throughout the digital forensic community. Likewise, in some situations, nontraditional tools may be the only means of recovering the data.

Manual Examination Tools

A manual examination of a mobile device can consist of taking pictures of a mobile device's onscreen digital content using a tripod and a digital camera. The examiner will move from screen to screen photographing the various pieces of evidence. This technique can be accomplished without specialized training in digital data recovery.

Tip For a manual examination, use a digital video camera at the beginning of the work and allow it to run continuously during the entire process. This entire work can be reviewed either for court, final reporting, or both. Stills from the video can be captured when needed for inclusion in a written report.

Some commercial products enable you to capture images of mobile device evidence. Using these tools, you can immediately document images or video in associated software for later review and reporting. There are, of course, limitations to the type of information that can be obtained using these tools, but little to no training is needed to operate them.

The following solutions are similar and allow the examiner to obtain information from the mobile device that may not be possible using traditional mobile forensic tools. Also, by using a manual solution, the examiner can allow for the documentation of the manual manipulation of a mobile device prior to conducting a traditional examination to show the actual device during testimony or presentation.

- **Paraben Project-A-Phone ICD8000 and Paraben Project-A-Phone Flex** These camera setups allow for both HD video and 8-megapixel pictures. The ICD8000 uses a clamping mechanism that can inadvertently press buttons on the side of the mobile device, including the power button on the right side of most Android devices, and improper clamping could change settings or power off the device. The Project-A-Flex does not use a vise but instead uses a mat on which the device can be placed to photograph the evidence.
- **Fernico ZRT3** This tool combines a camera and HD camera along with materials to hold the device and cameras in place. The device connects directly with software installed onto a PC to capture the photographs, and it uses technology such as Object Character Recognition (OCR) to translate images containing text to searchable text within the report. The device includes a mat onto which evidence can be placed to conduct the manual interrogation of the device.
- **Teel Technologies Eclipse 2** This tool is similar to the ZRT3 and combines a camera, mount, and platform, with a software solution to capture and document the images collected during the manual examination.

Flasher Boxes

A flasher box is a service tool that is typically used by mobile device technicians to fix a nonresponsive device, add features, or unlock a device for unrestricted access with any carrier. The tool's name is derived from the action that the device is built to perform—it flashes a new version of the device firmware, ROM, OS, or settings. The flasher box could also be used to add language packs and even change the serial number of the mobile device. The altering of a mobile device's serial number (IMEI [International Mobile Station Equipment Identity] for GSM and ESN/MEID [Electronic Serial Number/Mobile Equipment Identifier] for CDMA) is illegal, however, and by changing the serial number, some devices can operate on a network blacklisted by their original serial number. Device manufacturers do not endorse the use of these types of hardware tools for these reasons.

These hardware devices were never designed for mobile forensics, but they are frequently used, and their technologies were used to formulate a lot of the current mobile forensic product capabilities. Each flasher box functions, programs, and repairs a specific device—sometimes a specific model of mobile device. Because of the various differences in device hardware and programming, many hardware flashing tools are available to fulfill this need. Not only are multiple boxes available, but these boxes come with multiple cables. Typically, each mobile device must have its own specific cable, and hundreds of cables are available for these boxes.

Because the devices are developed to repair and alter a mobile device's software, the software used to control the flasher box can read and write to the attached device. Because of this ability, most examiners will not use a flasher box to conduct a physical examination of a mobile device; in addition, there is little to no documentation regarding how to use the hardware and software. This type of analysis should be classified as invasive, and the examiner needs specialized training before using this technique.

A flasher box will communicate with the mobile device using serial and USB protocols to recover areas of mapped memory. Memory offsets must be known if not identified by the software to recover the area where user data is stored. The resultant output is a binary file that often must be manually parsed and interpreted to locate evidence artifacts. In some cases, the data that is output is encrypted in a format known only to the flasher software. In this way, the flasher box manufacturers hide methods and procedures from other flasher box manufacturers. This limitation makes it difficult to examine the produced file. Table 6-2 represents some of the common flasher boxes and a general idea of the device support.

TABLE 6-2 Common Flasher Boxes Used in Mobile Forensic Device Collections

Box	Support
Ns Pro	Samsung
Z3x	Various Samsung devices (Agere, Sysol, Swift, Infineon, OMAP, Qualcomm)
Octopus Box	LG and Samsung
SHU Box	Nokia and Sony Ericsson
Advance Turbo Flasher (ATF)	Nokia Legacy, Nokia Lumia Series (SL3)
Vygisoft Toolbox	LG
Infinity-Box	MTK, ZTE, Huawei
IP-BOX	iOS PIN unlock

JTAG

The Joint European Test Action Group (JETAG) was formed in 1985 in Europe as a standard for boundary-scan testing. Boundary scanning the context of mobile devices efficiently tests connections on the printed circuit board in an effort to program or debug the device without needing physical access to the flash. In 1986, members from North America joined, and the group became the Joint Test Action Group (JTAG).

Between 1986 and 1988, the group proposed and published a series of proposals to the IEEE Testability Bus Standards Committee (P1149) with the final JTAG Version 2.0 being accepted. This standard (IEEE Std. 1149.1) was accepted and published in February 1990 and has been updated several times with the current specification identified as IEEE Std. 1149.1-2013. At its core, JTAG is the standardization of TAPs and boundary-scanning architecture.

Note The word "JTAG" has a variety of meanings, from directly programming systems to debugging others, from Xbox hacking to forensics. In the context of this book, JTAG is described as the process of setting and reading values on the test pins accessible on the PCB of the mobile device. By using the TAPs, communication can occur via the boundary-scan path, interfacing with the Boundary Scan Registers (BSR) that interface with components on the PCB. These components can be programmed or read without removal, independently reading or programming each separately.

In order for communication to occur with components, IEEE Std. 1149.1 indicates at a minimum that three input connection and one output connection ports must be on a PCB. Furthermore, the TAP is a multipurpose port that allows access to test support functions built into a component, and the standard outlines that the TAP shall include TCK (Test Clock), TMS (Test Mode Select), TDI (Test Data In), and TDO (Test Data Out) as connections. An optional input port, TRST (Test Reset), can also be used and is covered in the IEEE document. A basic understanding of each TAP is outlined next in an effort to help you visualize what is taking place when conducting a collection using JTAG, which is also represented in Figure 6-8.

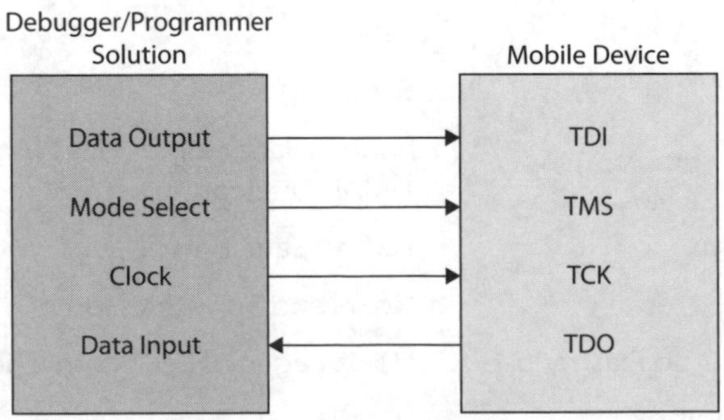

FIGURE 6-8 A simplistic communication model from a software debugger/programmer to and from a mobile device TAP group

- **TCK (Test Clock)** This port enables the synchronization of the internal state of the device between components. Devices are made of many components that could be using different forms of timing. The TCK maintains a standard across the components during a test.
- **TMS (Test Mode Select)** This port controls the TAP controller and relies on the TCK to determine the state of the process.
- **TDI (Test Data In)** This port accepts the data from the software debugger/programmer and sends it to the target
- **TDO (Test Data Out)** This port accepts the data from the target and sends it to the debugger/programmer software.
- **TRST (Test Reset)** This port is optional but can be used to reset the TAP.

The TAPs for mobile devices are not readily documented, and manufacturers are making it more difficult to locate them on the device PCB. Some manufacturers, such as BlackBerry, have gone to massive lengths to hide the TAPs or place them where any access destroys the device. Some software and hardware vendors do have the devices that they support listed within their software showing the TAP locations, and some software can determine the correct TAPs automatically.

JTAG hardware for mobile devices is just another type of flasher box, but the point of communication and interaction is different from the typical box. The difference is the fact that serial communication occurs to and from TAPs located on the mobile device PCB, unlike most flasher boxes that communicate using the traditional USB connector pin-outs on the device.

Note Some flasher boxes used for Nokia models communicate using the Fast Bus (FBUS) or MBus connectors on the PCB, which are early forms of TAPs. These connections were exposed and available under the battery, as shown in Figure 6-9.

JTAG hardware communications occur from the software to the hardware box through a cable or wire attached to the TAPs on the mobile device PCB. The wires to the device TAPs must be in contact for communication to occur. You must locate the TAPs and determine the type of test port in use. Because some JTAG boxes do not auto-detect the port type, this process can be time consuming. To determine to correct test port, you can use a secondary tool to scan the TAPs and identify TCK, TMS, TDI, TDO, and TRST. One such tool, the JTAG Pin Finder from 100RandomTasks, enables the examiner to attach wiring from the JTAG PIN finder to the TAPs on the PCB and use associated scanning software to determine the correct ports. Once the correct ports are identified, the wire can be attached to the JTAG hardware to conduct a collection. Both the scanning of the port and subsequent collection involves soldering the wire to the appropriate TAP, as shown in Figure 6-10. However, in some instances special Molex connectors can be used that snap directly onto a female Molex connector located on the mobile device PCB (Figure 6-11). Using a Molex connection would mean there is no need to solder the wires directly to the TAPs on the device PCB, which can be advantageous when attempting to determine the level of invasiveness that will be acceptable.

JTAG software undergoes communication with the mobile device, and the examiner identifies the type of data to collect. When used correctly, the software can bypass all security

FIGURE 6-9 FBUS connections on a Nokia 1280

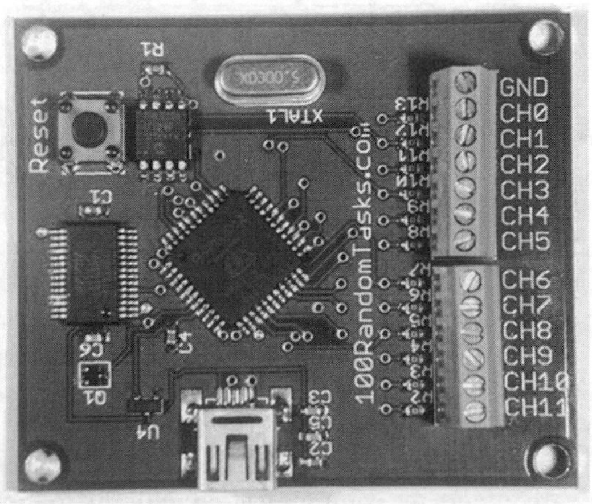

FIGURE 6-10 JTAG Pin Finder for scanning JTAG TAPs

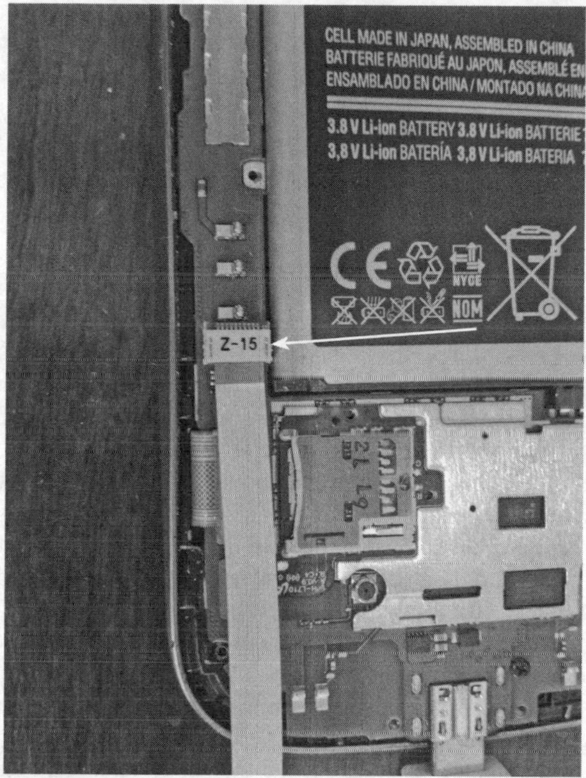

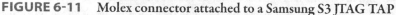

FIGURE 6-11 Molex connector attached to a Samsung S3 JTAG TAP

of a mobile device and obtain entire device images in the file system format that exists in the flash memory. The JTAG software does not interpret the data to allow for a forensic analysis and the rebuilding of the file system, but several tools such as Cellebrite Physical Analyzer, Micro Systemation XRY, and Oxygen Forensic Analyst can import and analyze such images obtained from a JTAG collection.

Again, like using flasher software, JTAG hardware and software was developed to flash, alter, and repair a mobile device. It was never the intention of the JTAG hardware and software designers to offer features that would be used by mobile forensics examiners. Because of this, examiners must be properly trained in using these tools. All associated JTAG software can destroy evidence if not used correctly in a controlled environment, but when used properly, it can yield magnificent results. Table 6-3 lists several JTAG hardware and software combinations with supported device information.

Chip-Off

The removal of a device's flash memory module and analyzing it is referred to as "chip-off." The chip-off procedure is quite labor intensive in both the removal of the actual embedded flash memory chip and reading of the stored data. Because of the various differences between

TABLE 6-3 Commonly Used JTAG Boxes in Mobile Device Collections

Box	Support
RIFF Box	Samsung, HTC, Nokia, Huawei, LG, ZTE, and others
Medusa Box	HTC, Huawei, LG, Samsung, Sony Ericsson, ZTE, and others
ORT JTAG	Samsung, LG, HTC, Huawei, ZTE, SKY, SE, and others
GPG JTAG	Google, HTC, Dopod, and others

phone models and storage types, which could range from Thin Small Outline Package (TSOP) to Fine-pitch Ball Grid Array (FBGA), the purchase of the equipment to read the information from the embedded chips and the time investment can become expensive. However, conducting the imaging of the memory chip using this method is the closest to the bit-by-bit collection a forensic examiner would expect and is similar to imaging a computer's hard drive.

To perform a collection using the chip-off method requires that the examiner have specialized skills in disassembly of mobile devices, repairing of mobile devices, desoldering and soldering of fine electrical components, and forensic procedure. This technique is commonly referred to in electronics as "rework." Depending on the type of chip, TSOP or FBGA, the removal and preparation of the memory chip will require different skills and time investment.

For TSOP chips, the pins that attach the chip to the PCB are exposed and can be easily removed by heating the solder joints. BGA chips must be heated to the correct temperature to remove the solder joints and adhesives and then be carefully removed from the PCB because their solder joints are not accessible along the exterior as are TSOP chips. Both chips must be removed with extreme caution because they cannot be reattached to the mobile device after removal. Upon successful removal, both TSOP and BGA chips must be thoroughly cleaned, examined, and inspected. For BGA chips, once they have been examined, they must also be reballed.

Once properly prepared, both TSOP and BGA chips can then be attached to the appropriate adapter and read in the designated chip programmer.

Tip TSOP chips are not as common as BGA chips in today's devices and are used in mobile devices on limited runs, prototypes, and smaller manufacturers. BGA chips allow for larger data capacities and faster input and output (I/O).

The *chip programmer* is the tool that will allow for the collection of the raw data from the memory chip. The programmer itself can also be a detriment, much like a flasher box or JTAG box, because it can write to and even erase a memory chip if used incorrectly. Examiners must follow proper procedures when using such equipment. Also, typically more than one programmer should be available to an examiner since there are many different types of embedded flash memory types with the many mobile devices, adding even more complexity. In addition, prior to placement in the chip programmer, the memory chips are affixed to unique adapters; each of these can cost upwards of $1800! These adapters must be compatible with the memory chip type—with the many differences in BGA-style chips, this can become extremely expensive.

Once the chip has been placed into the correct adapter and into the chip programmer, the examiner must select the identical chip and model as printed on the memory chip to begin the reading process.

Note The exact chip manufacturer and chip module must be selected and supported by the chip programmer. This step helps to identify unique preferences, algorithms, and settings that might be needed to perform a collection.

The analysis of the file produced by reading the memory chip is often the most tedious part of the process. Because a mobile device memory chip is based upon flash memory (such as NOR or NAND) chips, the inherent advantage of I/O when compared to a traditional spinning hard drive might be the biggest detriment to forensic examination at the chip level. NOR flash memory is older technology that allows for high read performance, but does not allow for high capacities. NAND flash memory allows for both faster programming and erases, but it can consume more power because of its higher functioning and complicated I/O interface. To understand some of the problems that could be encountered, you need a better understanding of flash storage.

How Flash Memory Works

Flash memory in NAND arrays is stored in a series of blocks, which also happen to be the smallest erasable entities on a NAND memory chip. Within these blocks are pages, which are the smallest programmable entities on a flash chip. Pages include sectors, or chunks. Pages contain a data area and an area for memory management called the out-of-band (OOB) data. There is OOB data for each sector or chunk within each page that can contain metadata specific to the page's status (such as valid, invalid, or bad). The OOB area can also contain metadata on the associated page and block and does not have to be immediately following the sector (adjacent), but all can be at the end of the page (separate).

NAND memory chips do not have a finite lifetime, but are measured according to the number of erases that occur. Typically, the number of erases that can occur without a failure of the memory chip far exceeds the lifetime of the mobile device. This measurement is very important when discussing the way the data is often written to the flash memory. Data is written to a flash cell in the form of a 0 or 1; 1 represents empty and 0 represents full. So, if data was written to a block, a 1 can be replaced by a 0, but a 0 can never be changed to a 1 to alter the data. The entire block would have to be written to another block, and the previous block would be erased during another background process. This technique is a function of the flash memory and is typically called "wear-leveling."

Wear-leveling is a way for flash memory to make sure that areas of memory are not exceeding the number of erases too quickly; it "evens" out the erases over the surface of the flash chip. In turn, when a file is updated on the flash, it is not possible to program the current page, so it is completely rewritten to another location (a page, pages, a block, or blocks). This location does not even have to be in the same block or blocks. During this

(Continued)

process, the OOB area is marked as active for the new page and the old page is marked as inactive. Another flash mechanism called "garbage collection" is a function of reclaiming entire blocks if the number of inactive pages exceeds a given threshold. If this occurs, the entire active page or pages are written to a new block, and the entire block is then erased to allow for new data to be written and become available for new data. These processes in turn extend the life of the flash memory.

Various types of traditional file systems (such as FAT, FAT32, VFAT, HFS+, EXT, EXT3, EXT4, NTFS) and actual flash file systems (such as JAFFS2, YAFFS, UFS) can be observed in the data from a chip-off collection. The difference between the two types is whether or not the file system needs a transition layer or whether the file system uses a system of databases to manage flash memory. For traditional file systems, there must be a Flash Translation Layer (FTL) that will operate as the interpreter for the file system and allow it to act as a block file system and emulate a flash file system. Different FTL interfaces use different specifications (such as MMC, eMMC, MSD, ATA). As data is written to various areas of the flash to conduct wear-leveling and other procedures, the FTL presents the information to the traditional file system as though it had been written to a static location, so the traditional file system operates normally. On the other hand, a flash file system handles all the wear-leveling and creates its own data structures without the need of an FTL. These data structures are generally mounted into RAM and will contain flash information such as bad blocks, block erases, and pointers to files for the mobile device. This structure is written to the flash upon shutdown and then rewritten into RAM on startup.

When you put together the ways in which a NAND chip's memory is constructed; the built-in structures, wear-leveling, and garbage collection processes; and the various file system types, it is no wonder that reconstructing the data from a chip-off examination is so difficult. Data collected by a chip-off examination can look disjointed and spread across the entire image. This type of data is commonly referred to as "non-contiguous," and with some mobile device file systems, this makes recovering the data time intensive.

It's important to recognize the way flash memory moves data on the chip surface to prolong the life of the medium. With the function of traditional file systems and the flash translation layer, along with flash file systems, the fact that data is often written multiple times across the medium provides more opportunity for the examiner to recover forensic artifacts.

Traditional Tool Matrix

Table 6-4 indicates logical, file system, physical (non-invasive and invasive), and limited support features of several forensic tools. Limited support means only a small number of devices (such as Android and iOS only). For brevity, only the most popular tools currently in use are listed. NIST maintains a large list of forensic tools on its web site, including most mobile device forensics tools on the market (www.cftt.nist.gov/tool_catalog/taxonomy/index.php).

TABLE 6-4 Traditional Mobile Device Forensic Tool Classification

Tool	Logical	File System	Physical (NI)*	Physical (I)*	Limited Support
BlackLight	X	X			X
UFED 4PC	X	X	X	X	
Device Seizure	X	X	X	X	
EnCase	X	X	X		
Lantern	X	X	X		X
MOBILedit Forensic	X	X			
MPE+	X	X	X	X	
Oxygen Forensic Analyst	X	X	X	X	
Secure View	X				
XRY	X	X	X	X	

*(NI = non-invasive; I = invasive)

Tools Available

A plethora of mobile forensic solutions are available today, from open source software, to freeware, to commercial tools. As previously discussed, the tools used in the forensic laboratory and in the field are those that can be used on the majority of devices observed in the area of operations. The tools discussed in the following sections will cover the majority of devices, have the most robust feature set, and complement one another. These tools will provide the capability and versatility you need when you're conducting mobile forensic examinations.

Open Source Tools

Open source tools allow for the viewing, changing, altering, and sharing of the source code by anyone. Any restrictions depend upon the licensing that accompanies the distribution. Most open source mobile device forensic tools are geared toward smart devices, iOS, and Androids. BitPim and TULP2G, for example, handle feature phones, but both tools are no longer updated.

Let's begin by discussing the actual usage and philosophy of these tools. There has always been a rift in the forensic community regarding the use of open source tools versus commercial and freeware (closed source) tools. In 2003, Brian Carrier published "Open Source Digital Forensics Tools: The Legal Argument," which discusses the forensic community debate that is still ongoing today and hinges on the integrity and reliability of the data and support for the software. There is no clear winner in this debate. Many examiners believe strongly one way or the other and cannot be swayed no matter the argument. However, both types of software can coexist in today's mobile device forensic toolkit.

Using an open source tool for the collection of a mobile device can be of great benefit because the collection of the device is 100-percent verifiable and transparent. That is difficult to say about a closed software solution, and it is often an Achilles heel for the examiner who has no idea how the tool extracted the data from the mobile device—it just simply happened.

Tip At times, the use of open source tools is advisable simply because the mobile device image creation can be closely observed. Because device image creation is often challenged, having the source code to gather specific intelligence as to what is "under the hood" can help you dispel any allegations to discredit the image creation.

iOS Devices

iOS devices can be examined using several open source tools that work for both Windows and Linux as well. These tools all use the Apple Backup service to initiate a local backup of the device, just as a user would if using iTunes. Some tools also use additional Apple services during the collection of mobile device data. All of the tools covered in this section allow access to the device without enabled security—that is, the passcode for the handset as well as the iTunes password must be known, if enabled.

iPBA2 (iPhone-Backup-Analyzer-2) This software was originally developed by Mario Piccinelli and can be used, as the name implies, to decode iPhone backups up to iOS 6.x. iPBA2 does not conduct a collection of the device, but allows the browsing of an iOS device backup. The backup must be obtained prior to using iPBA2. The software has not been updated, as of this writing, since March 2013 and does not contain the latest locations for some of the system databases. The software does, however, allow the user to browse the backup after the file tree has been rebuilt, it parses a number of user databases and a few application databases, and allows for the browsing of complex file types. The most current build is available on GitHub (https://github.com/PicciMario/iPhone-Backup-Analyzer-2).

The following features are supported for auto-parsing:

- SMS/iMessage
- Call history
- Address book
- Notes
- Network information
- Safari history
- Safari bookmarks
- Wi-Fi

Here are the plug-in file and application viewers:

- Binary/XML plist viewer
- SQLite database browser
- HEX/image/text/Exif viewer
- Skype, Viber, and WhatsApp viewer

Santoku Santoku is a suite of tools used for mobile device forensic investigations, mobile malware analysis, and mobile security assessment, all rolled into one interface using a Linux virtual machine (VM). Santoku can be added to a Mac partition to dual-boot, or to use the preferred method and only suggested method for Windows, a virtual machine. The Santoku web site offers online documentation that walks an examiner through the installation of the materials and setup for both Mac and Windows machines. Using the tool, however, requires a lot from the examiner: to use most of the tools in the suite, the examiner must have knowledge of the Linux command line. Because of the degree of user interaction required, use of this tool is not recommended for those not familiar with command-line–based programming. The suite of tools is compiled and all are installed, which allows for easy setup and usage, but, as indicated, it can be intimidating.

Both iOS and Android device collections are supported in the Santoku interface (Android collection is discussed next). For iOS devices, Santoku can collect, parse, and carve data. Collections occur via an iOS backup, using an open source library called libimobiledevice, shown in Figure 6-12, and then uses iPhone Backup Analyzer to conduct the parsing of the iOS backup. iPhone Backup Analyzer is the previous version of iPBA2.

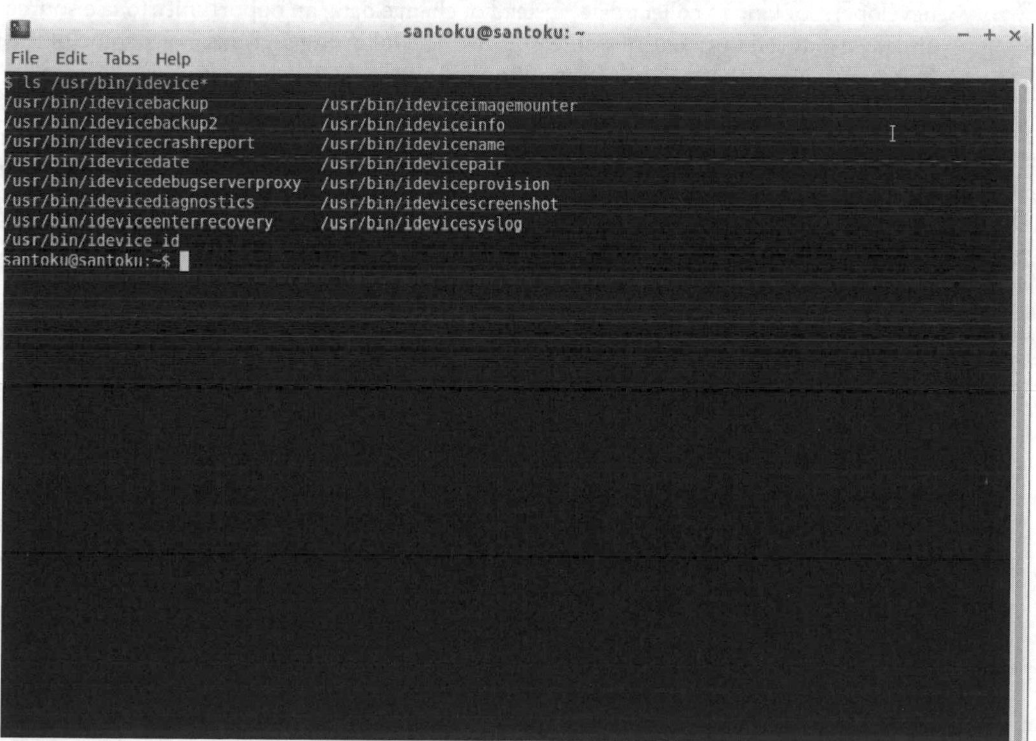

santoku@santoku: ~
File Edit Tabs Help
$ ls /usr/bin/idevice*
/usr/bin/idevicebackup /usr/bin/ideviceimagemounter
/usr/bin/idevicebackup2 /usr/bin/ideviceinfo
/usr/bin/idevicecrashreport /usr/bin/idevicename
/usr/bin/idevicedate /usr/bin/idevicepair
/usr/bin/idevicedebugserverproxy /usr/bin/ideviceprovision
/usr/bin/idevicediagnostics /usr/bin/idevicescreenshot
/usr/bin/ideviceenterrecovery /usr/bin/idevicesyslog
/usr/bin/idevice_id
santoku@santoku:~$

FIGURE 6-12 **Using the Santoku interface to start libimobiledevice to create an iOS backup**

Additional tools for parsing device data also are installed on the virtual machine. Both Scalpel and The Sleuth Kit are included (https://github.com/sleuthkit), which can be used to investigate the file system and conduct data carving methods. Both tools are also command-line tools but can allow for analysis of the file system to locate files by type, create a timeline based on identified files, and check hashes of files against known hash libraries and custom libraries.

Android

Many more open source tools are available for Android devices, probably because Android source code uses some open source language and access to the Android development SDK is available online (http://developer.android.com). Because of the variety of devices on which the Android OS operates and variants of firmware on top of the various builds of the operating system, open source tools are sometimes more reliable for the collection of the device data. Quick code changes and frequent releases, along with high community involvement in addressing a specific problem, also make open source tools popular. These frequent updates and code modifications are necessitated by the openness of the Android device OS. If a carrier uses a specific code base or the device does not operate as the user wants, the user can change it! The "modding" community for Android is larger than any other mobile device community, with a mission to make the phone do what they want. This, in turn, offers open source developers looking to collect data, instead of change data, an opportunity to use source code already produced in an entirely different way. The following sections cover some of the tools that are used frequently in the forensic community.

Santoku As mentioned, Santoku is a Linux-configured VM and is a self-contained mobile forensic, mobile security, and mobile malware suite of tools. For Android devices, many more options are built into the application. For basic logical extractions, AFLogical Open Source Edition (OSE), developed by ViaForensics (changed to NowSecure in 2015), is included in the Santoku edition.

AFLogical OSE enables the collection of contacts, call logs, SMS, MMS, and device information using a small application that is installed to the device via the command line. The user then runs the installed application on the device, which communicates with the content storage and outputs the data to the device SD card. The data can then be examined with built-in viewers, and extracted data, which has been saved into a comma-separated value (.csv) file, can be viewed.

Also included in Santoku are developmental tools that can be used to obtain a non-invasive physical device file system by using exploits such as Odin, Heimdall, and built-in fastboot methods. Note that these methods are extremely risky when used without proper training and guidance and can have catastrophic consequences to the mobile device data and the device itself. Santoku also contains several tools that enable the analysis of mobile device malware, including Androguard and Apktool to decompile Android application files, along with versions of Wireshark that can assist with network analysis of Android applications during dynamic malware analysis. Again, this virtual environment is not for examiners just starting out in mobile forensics because it requires that the user interact with command-line utilities.

All the tools that have been compiled under the Santoku environments are available for native installation and do not need to be run under the prebuilt environment. However, having the system already set up and configured is a plus, especially since control of the built-in applications, device collection, and data analysis often must be configured to run correctly.

Open Source Android Forensic Toolkit (OSAF) The OSAF Toolkit was developed as a project for education by a group of students at the University of Cincinnati. Much like Santoku, this system uses a virtual machine based on Linux that houses different types of tools. The OSAF Toolkit concentrates on the analysis of malware on Android devices both statically and dynamically, but it also contains some mobile forensic tools. OSAF contains APKInspector, which Santoku does not include, which allows for the static analysis of Android APK files in an attempt to identify malware injections. Dynamic malware analysis using OSAF is completed, like Santoku, using Wireshark. OSAF also uses viaForensics AFLogical code and is comparable to extraction using both the stand-alone AFLogical or Santoku versions.

OSAF is not as robust as Santoku for the physical collection of the Android device, but the analysis of malware on an Android device is comparable. Like Santoku, this environment is not for the inexperienced mobile examiner who is not familiar with the Linux operating system and command-line functions.

BlackBerry: MagicBerry

An open source tool (https://code.google.com/p/magicberry/) that allows for the parsing of both IPD and BBB files created using BlackBerry Desktop Manager software. Newer backups that are produced by BlackBerry Link software are not supported by the MagicBerry code or any open source tools. The MagicBerry compile program can be downloaded from the MagicBerry web site (http://menastep.com/pages/magicberry.php). The software supports the parsing of the IPD and BBB file to extract several types of user data, including SMS, contacts, call logs, service book, tasks, memos, calendar, and media (images and audio). The information can then be extracted and exported in various formats. This software was not created with the forensic examiner in mind, but it does enable the recovery and parsing for presentation. The MagicBerry software has not been updated for several years, and with the change in format along with encryption, this software appears to be at end-of-life.

Freeware Tools

Freeware is software that is essentially free to use, but the source code is often not available. Most freeware code cannot be modified by the user, viewed by the community, or updated without the direct involvement of the freeware project software development team. Some of the following tools do have open source components.

NowSecure Forensics Suite (Community Edition)

viaForensics became NowSecure in late 2015 and now has a Community Edition as well as a purchasable forensic suite of tools targeting the Android operating system. NowSecure's documentation indicates that iOS devices will be supported in future releases. NowSecure is based on a fork of the Santoku Linux platform and adds the viaExtract tool suite. The Community Edition is limited to the tools for collecting and analyzing mobile devices, primarily Android. Because NowSecure is encapsulated in Santoku, some iOS tools are still available. The tools for mobile malware and security are also available within the Community Edition VM, just as they were with the Santoku release.

The NowSecure Forensic Suite allows the examiner to connect to and collect data from an Android device using several methods, from a logical file system, to a device backup, to the use of the AFLogical code for a logical query of user data databases.

Note ADB Backup to extract persistent application data from Android devices running version 4.0 and later is contained in NowSecure viaExtract and will be discussed in detail in Chapter 13.

NowSecure viaExtract is also capable of bypassing lock screens on supported Android devices and shell rooting supported devices to enable the extraction of the device partitions for later analysis, as well as different analysis tools such as timeline support, artifact viewing, deleted data recovery, and global searching. With the purchase of the full version, an examiner can get access to the physical non-invasive methods for Android devices.

When you use the viaExtract Community Edition and viaExtract, the collection of an Android device is more straightforward than simply using the Santoku command-line version, which makes it more user friendly for new examiners in the mobile forensic field.

iFunbox

iFunbox is a freeware tool for iOS devices. Apple's iTunes must be installed on the device that is running iFunbox because the software uses Apple's device services and device drivers to communicate with the software. iFunbox enables access to the iOS device applications and media area for all iOS devices, and with devices prior to iOS 8 it enables access to the raw file system. If an iOS 8 or later device has been jailbroken, then a raw file system is also available. This tool is especially useful for gathering the file system data to be examined later using another forensic tool. iFunbox does not conduct any analysis of the device contents; it simply enables the internal contents to be displayed and copied to a storage location without the use of iTunes. iFunbox is also very useful if iTunes cannot recognize the device to conduct a backup. This software is not a standard forensic tool and should be used only after testing and validating the processes used by its communication. All iOS devices are supported, and access to the device and file system are available without a jailbreak.

Commercial Tools

A commercial tool is classified as a closed source application that is available for purchase. Commercial tools covered in the following sections contribute both to the collection and analysis of mobile devices in a single solution. A lot of commercial tools that can be used for mobile device forensics perform several tasks, although an examiner might need to use a second tool to complete the analysis if a feature is not available. This was discussed earlier as a basis for a multitool approach to mobile forensics. An example would be the collection and viewing of property lists from an iOS device. One tool may collect the files, including plist files, but these files cannot be viewed within the application, so a second tool would have to be used. The commercial tools discussed here can also be used generally as a single solution if multiple tools cannot be purchased based upon the supported devices and feature set.

Note The tools discussed here are those that I am well versed with and have personally relied upon for both professional and research collections. The following information is not intended to outline how the tools should be used, provide guidelines on collections using the tool, or describe specific instructions in the analysis of mobile device data. These sections provide an overview of the tools, their features, and their general use for mobile device forensics. Also, the devices are listed alphabetically, not in order of preference. These tools will also be used throughout the processing, artifact finding, and analysis discussions within this book.

AccessData Mobile Phone Examiner Plus

MPE+ was developed by AccessData Group in Lindon, Utah. It can be used to collect data from UICC (Universal Integrated Circuit Card), feature phones (GSM/CDMA), smart devices, and mass storage devices. The collection methods vary depending on the type of device, but support exists to complete standard logical, logical file system, non-invasive physical, and invasive physical collections. The collected device image is saved as its original raw binary file and can also be saved into an AccessData proprietary AD1 image format.

Note The raw binary image file would pertain to a non-invasive or invasive physical collection from an Android device and also a physical collection of an iOS device.

Once the image has been collected, the device information, user information, and other data are parsed and visually displayed within the user interface. Additional tools including a built-in property list (plist) viewer and SQLite database viewer allow further analysis of smart device files. A built-in customizable SQLite query platform, called SQLBuilder, along with a Python platform called pythonScripter, allow for the processing of advanced artifacts or structures that have not been included in the solution's automated parsers. Additional tools such as data carving for mobile device artifacts, conversion of messages to a conversation view, searching, timeline visualization, and column filtering allow for focused data culling when exposed to thousands of records. MPE+ can scan for text, phrases, Unicode characters, or any data entered into the Alert repository across the entire device's data views, alerting the user to areas where hits have been located.

MPE+ enables the import of the created AD1 files along with JTAG and chip-off images, as well as images created with other tools such as EnCase, UFED4PC, UFED Touch, and XRY. These images, once imported, can be parsed and analyzed using all of the advanced features built into MPE+.

Cellebrite

Cellebrite produces several tools—UFED4PC (Logical and Ultimate), UFED Touch (Logical and Ultimate), and (Logical and Physical) Analyzer software—for the collection and analysis of mobile devices and is developed in Petah Tikva, Israel. The UFED4PC, UFED Touch, and

Physical Analyzer software perform differently depending upon the version that the examiner is using. If the examiner is using the Logical version of both the UFED4PC and Touch, the collection support is for UICC, feature phones (GSM/CDMA), smart devices, and mass storage devices. The collected data types are logical only, without file system support. If the examiner is using the Ultimate version of the UFED4PC or Touch, logical, logical file system, non-invasive, and invasive physical collections are possible. Both the UFED4PC and Touch Ultimate solutions come with the Physical Analyzer (PA) software, which is used to conduct the decoding and analysis of the collected data from either tool.

The PA software enables importing and decoding of mobile device images from JTAG, chip-off, and GPS devices, and it can decode and parse collected images created using the UFED4PC and Touch Ultimate. PA software also includes visualization of timelines, link analysis, communication analysis, malware analysis, and watch lists. PA can search globally using strings, text, proprietary device formats, regular expressions, and many other data types across the entire device image and can conduct data carving across the device image to uncover additional data from unallocated and logical file system areas. Custom scripting is via Python, and a built-in shell and plug-in feature are available. PA also has integrated malware scanning using Bitdefender.

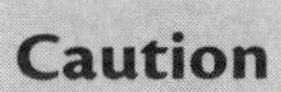

Malware analysis using one vendor can be limited because this type of signature analysis can be easily duped by malware developers. It would be much more prudent to scan the evidence with several types of malware-scanning software to maximize signature analysis.

Oxygen Forensic Analyst and Detective

Oxygen Forensics, Inc., is based in Alexandria, Virginia and develops both Oxygen Forensic Analyst (OFA) and Oxygen Forensic Detective (OFD). Both applications support the collection of UICC, legacy CDMA/GSM devices along with smart devices. Logical, logical file system, non-invasive, and invasive methods are supported.

Images from other tools such as the UFED series, Lantern, and XRY can be imported into both OFA and OFD to further analyze the information. Analytics, password analysis, malware analysis, and mobile app support are available within Oxygen Forensic software as well making it a choice for examiners gathering group intelligence. File carving as well as deleted data and file searching over multiple images is also a supported feature.

Support of JTAG images from Android devices can be parsed for valuable user data within OFA along with a powerful SQLite database viewer. Oxygen Forensic Detective also contains a tool to obtain information from cloud backups from Windows Phone, iOS, and Android devices. All data recovered from any mobile device via the cloud or directly from the device can be visually represented within a time line, social graph, and aggregated view, along with a native user data view.

Chapter Summary

The mobile forensic examiner must have a critical understanding of the different types of collections and what can be collected using each method, and at what level, for success. This becomes clear when considering the various tools that are available. Although tools may indicate the ability for logical collections of thousands of devices, upon closer inspection they do not support a logical file system collection. This limitation can be a detriment when requested to unearth additional data from the mobile device that might be contained only in the mobile device file system. Being prudent in what a mobile forensic tool can accomplish and knowing its limitations before making a purchase or considering it for the toolbox are important. Understand your mission and choose the appropriate tool to accomplish your mission, but also reflect on what might be needed later—such as file system or partitions. Remember that doing one collection at the onset of the investigation is preferred instead of multiple collections due to tool limitations.

The tool classification outlined by NIST is only a guideline, and several recommendations outlined in this chapter should be considered in the same way. Obtaining a device file system is paramount and a subset of logical examinations that enable obtaining a file-system should be included. Additionally, HEX and JTAG should be more clearly defined, as listed by SWGDE, in declaring non-invasive and invasive methods. Furthermore, the terms non-invasive and invasive, as defined by SWGDE, should not describe only physical methods as collecting data by means of removal of the device coverings and internal components, but should also reflect the exchange and replacement of internal software ROMs. Performing a replacement and exchange of a portion of the device operation system to circumvent security and permissions to gain a physical binary image can be just as invasive as performing a chip-off or JTAG procedure.

What is clear in the tool classification pyramid and in the text is the fact the progression up to the top of the chart should be directly related to both the technical training and knowledge needed to perform the analysis. What is also apparent in the tool progression pyramid is the relational size of each level, which can also visually represent the number of examiners conducting the specific types of examination. What can also be gleaned from the pyramid is the need for training as the examiner climbs to the top. For an examiner to be successful at the level of chip-off, for example, he or she must undergo a sufficient amount of training and have sufficient knowledge in the area of device disassembly, flash memory physical architecture, flash memory internal architecture, and digital file systems. Without a level of competency that matches the level of examination, the examiner's success rate will be small, while the possibility of catastrophe is high.

Many tools can be used in a mobile forensic examination, and the use of multiple tools is a necessity. Tools that can be verified and validated more easily could be open source tools that allow the examiner to peer into the actual code to verify what is happening while creating an image or parsing the data. The use of open source tools has always been controversial, but usually the controversy is spurned by commercial tool vendors. As long as the tool can be verified and validated, be it open source, freeware, or closed source, it will be usable in mobile device examinations and will stand up to court challenges. Use of commercial tools is a necessity because these tools cover more devices than typical open source tools. This is primarily due to the concentration of the open source tool on a single operating system and sometimes a single device. This is not due to a lack of understanding in the open source community, but due to a particular developer or group concentrating on the device subset that they actually own! Coupled with the fact that development time costs money, commercial tools will cover more device profiles and file systems.

Several tools are covered at the end of the chapter that will be used for further collections and analysis throughout the book. These software titles are not the only tools available to the mobile examiner, as is plainly evident in the tools table. These tools cover the largest number of devices with the most built-in features. Obtaining a single mobile device solution set that can conduct collections, analysis of internal and external data, and complete reporting is often the preferred solution.

Your understanding of the levels of examinations, along with the levels the tools will support, will help you make the best decision as to which tools will best suit the examination at hand.

7 Preparing the Environment for Your First Collection

If your collection and analysis environment is set up properly, you are far more likely to extract and analyze forensic data successfully. If the environment is set up improperly, however, you can be confronted with many problems throughout an examination. Sometimes, the collection device or computer is different from the analysis computer, and the optimal configurations on the two can be different as well. In a poorly configured environment, software may be ineffective at not only connecting to the device, but also at extracting valuable data, leading to frustration.

Typically, software vendors include specifications on release notes or user guides that detail the computer configurations required to run their software properly. Sometimes, however, vendors' configurations are unrealistic for a working environment in which several different types of software are stored on the computer, and their minimum requirements are insufficient for running all the software. In addition, because forensic software solutions often write critical data temporarily as well as permanently, you need to know the location of this data, especially when you're conducting sensitive investigations.

Device drivers are also critical to a mobile device examination, and when properly installed, they provide the conduit to the device's digital data store. The mobile device examiner is often responsible for setting up the system at a scene location, so it's important that he or she get to know the devices. What happens when a driver is not installed properly? Obviously, communication to the device will not occur. But do all the drivers have to be installed? Many devices can also mean many drivers, which can hinder the computing environment's performance, especially in the Windows environment.

For the many reasons covered in this chapter, examiners often create virtual machines to operate each type of mobile forensic software in their toolboxes. This often eliminates the configuration problems that can be associated with each piece of software. Both NowSecure (which is built on Santoku Linux) and Santoku are Linux virtual machines that have been configured and fine-tuned to help eliminate some configuration problems, but they cannot solve all problems. Some forensic software solutions cannot be run in a virtual machine and must be installed in a traditional, statically installed operating system. Not only do some mobile forensic solutions inhibit their software from running within a virtual machine, devices such as iOS do not work well with virtual machines because of driver issues. When an Apple iOS device is plugged in, a driver installs, but when you're conducting a non-invasive physical collection of the device, additional drivers for Device Firmware Update (DFU) and iBoot must be installed on the fly. This installation flow gets caught up when the device drivers first attempt to connect with the host operating system before the virtualized system can take hold, often causing errors. For this reason, some devices simply cannot be collected using a virtualized environment.

Mobile forensic solutions that offer software installed on hardware, such as Cellebrite UFED Touch and Radio Tactics Athena, are not covered in this section because these units are self-contained hardware units that come preconfigured with device drivers. Other solutions from Cellebrite include the UFED 4PC and Physical Analyzer, which do require that device drivers be installed.

Creating the Ideal System

Computer specifications typically depend upon the analysis functions of the software that is installed on the system. If a software solution contains features such as data carving, database processing, searching, or other hardware-intensive functions, it would stand to reason that a more powerful computer solution should be used. Some software applications that extract data from a mobile device have little or no analysis capabilities, and a less powerful computer solution would be needed. The particular situation or mission will generally dictate the type of hardware and software configuration that a mobile examiner should use.

Most software vendors list the minimum specifications required for the base operating system, but few take into account the installation of other mobile solutions on the system. Experience has shown that the minimum specs that are listed for many vendors are too low for today's devices and, if used, can have negative effects on the overall collection and analysis process—even without the installation of another mobile forensic solution.

For example, consider the minimum specs listed for Micro Systemation XRY Logical on its web site (www.msab.com):

- **Processor** Intel Atom Processor 1.6GHz dual-core
- **RAM** 1GB
- **USB ports** Minimum two ports
- **Operating system** Microsoft Windows 7 or 8

The software will function and run with these specifications, but other processes must take place during the collection of the device, and with the low specs indicated here, operating system performance will be affected and the process can become frustrating.

The following sections offer general recommendations for building a mobile forensic environment that will efficiently run most mobile forensic software without issue. These are recommendations based upon a typical install running three mobile forensic tools simultaneously. Each additional software solution installed on the system will generally degrade the performance of the computer, so you should make adjustments as necessary.

These recommendations are based upon multiple tools installed on the system per the guidelines outlined in this chapter.

Processor (CPU)

The processor, or central processing unit (CPU), type is integral to the success of your forensic software. The CPU runs the computations, functions, and I/O specified by the system, and its performance, measured in gigahertz (GHz), depends on several factors. The higher the *clock speed rate* of the CPU, the more functions it can perform each second. For example, a 3.4GHz processor can perform 3,400,000,000 cycles per second, which is obviously more computations than a 1.8GHz processor that performs 1,800,000,000 cycles per second. Although a higher clock speed rate means more cycles are performed, this should not be the only consideration in choosing a comparable processor, especially when it includes multiple *cores*. A CPU can contain multiple cores that allow simultaneous computations n times, where n = the number of processors. So a computer with more cycles per second (GHz) but with a single or dual core may handle less information and run more slowly than a computer containing a processor with four cores and a slower clock speed.

Another important consideration in processor selection is choosing a 64-bit (x64) versus a 32-bit (x86) processor. A processor that is capable of x64 operations can handle twice as many bits (64) of information with the same clock speed as an x86 processor. A computer with at least a dual core capable of 64-bit processing should be the minimum recommended for mobile forensic software.

Note

Even if the mobile forensic solution can run on a 64-bit machine, that doesn't necessarily mean it operates in 64-bit mode. Some solutions can run as a 64-bit solution but operate only in 32-bit mode. Make sure to check the documentation to gauge your expectations regarding performance.

RAM

Random Access Memory (RAM) enables the processor to run computations on the flash memory rather than on the actual storage disk of the computer. When the processor places data into a computer's temporary memory, faster input and output result, which means data analysis can be completed more quickly. RAM is typically measured in gigabytes (GB) in today's computers. Mobile forensic software running in a Windows environment should have a minimum of 4GB of RAM, based on a single running instance of software at a time. Anything less than 4GB of RAM will not corrupt or invalidate the device collection, but it can cause software solutions to crash from out-of-memory exceptions.

By Microsoft's recommendations, Windows requires at least 1GB of RAM to run on an x86 system and at least 2GB to run on an x64 system, which gives the forensic software approximately 3GB of RAM to conduct the collection, analysis, or reporting—or all these functions simultaneously. If Windows cannot access the required RAM or is left with less than the required memory resources, the operating system will display the familiar "Blue Screen Of Death" (BSOD). If a BSOD occurs during a collection or an analysis, the information will be lost and the collection or analysis will most likely have to be redone.

Most software vendors in the mobile forensic field recommend that a minimum of 2GB of RAM should be used, but with only 2GB of RAM, even a small device containing approximately 10,000 records will have noticeable limitations. With most smart devices having hundreds of thousands of records that need to be processed using RAM, less than 4GB of RAM is not recommended.

Input/Output (I/O)

A computer's I/O throughput can also have a dramatic effect on the success and overall presentation of the forensic software. I/O involves not only the physical USB hub that is part of the computer, but also secondary hubs attached to the computer. I/O is directed by the processor, and it's important that you understand how the controller and processor work together.

The USB controller and its USB hubs on a computer come in three types: 1.0, 2.0, and 3.0. USB 1.0 is the slowest I/O and USB 3.0 is currently the fastest. USB 1.0 is seldom found in newer computers these days, but many mobile devices communicate only at USB 1.0 speeds. It is recommend that at least three USB ports be available in a forensic workstation, including at least one USB 3.0 port. Information specifications from the USB Implementers Forum (www.usb.org) are shown in Table 7-1.

Simply having a USB 3.0 port does not necessarily mean that information will flow at a higher rate from a mobile device to the software during collection. The mobile device and the software conducting the collection will govern the speed of connection and data transfer. As specified, most devices communicate using USB 1.0 protocols. USB 3.0 and USB 2.0 are backward compatible, so the connection between device and computer is not much different from that of USB 1.0 when the device is connected to one of these USB drivers. However, the speed of data output from the device to the collection computer can be noticeable. Obviously, collection speeds using USB 3.0 will be faster than those of USB 1.0 and 2.0, but if the device cannot output at a higher rate, the speed of the computer's USB hub will not matter. The speed is dictated by the device and software, not the computer's port.

TABLE 7-1 USB Speeds as Determined by USB-IF

Type	Speed
USB 1.1 (low bandwidth)	1.536 Mbps
USB 1.1 (high bandwidth)	12 Mbps
USB 2.0	480 Mbps
USB 3.0	5 Gbps
USB 3.1	10 Gbps

Storage

Storage space and storage media are often underestimated by examiners seeking to collect and examine a mobile device, perhaps because the physical size of the device is misleading as to the amount of actual storage available and the number of computations and calculations completed by the mobile forensic solution. Today, the most popular mobile smart device's (iOS and Android) on-board storage averages 16GB. Most mobile forensic solutions need twice the size of the evidence when processing a single device because of the storage of the collected image and any temporary storage used during examination, processing, and analysis. You must consider portability, segregation of forensic tools, and I/O speed when choosing a storage medium for the mobile forensic solution and device processing. The use of multiple hard drives for the forensic analysis of mobile devices is not required, but it is often critical because of the many variables, processing overhead, and growing size of today's mobile devices. Apple devices now come with 128GB storage capabilities, and Android devices can carry 64GB SD cards and soon 128GB cards, so having additional storage available for these devices is necessary.

The operating system, utility software, and forensic software should be installed on a hard drive devoid of any evidence or temporary data collected from a forensic tool. This drive should be used only to run the computer and associated software. By segregating the entire OS and software to a single drive, you can clone the drive and restore a pristine copy without compromising evidence or the integrity of the OS and software. In this way, forensic software and other related software can be maintained, changes and updates to the operating system or restores can be made without compromising evidence, and disk capacity does not shrink due to saving evidence images, temporary files, or other files relating to the processing and analysis of mobile devices. The operating system and software drive can be a traditional spinning hard drive (HDD) or solid state drive (SSD) with a minimum of 250GB of storage.

A secondary drive should be used to store all temporary data, both from the operating system and forensic software. If using Windows, moving the location of the Windows pagefile .sys file to another drive can also increase software performance. The Windows pagefile.sys is used as a virtual memory swap file when a computer's RAM is exceeded and is often set to the same size as available physical RAM installed to the computer. If the pagefile.sys file is moved to an external drive, a crash of the operating system could occur if the drive is removed from the system, so moving pagefile.sys file to an internal drive is recommended if the move is warranted.

The location of pagefile.sys is different between Windows 7 and Windows 8. The following instructions show how to change the location of the pagefile.sys file for Windows 7 and 8.

For Windows 7

1. Press the Windows key.
2. Right-click Computer and then choose Properties.
3. Click Advanced System Settings.
4. On the Advanced tab, under Performance, click Settings.
5. On the Advanced tab's Virtual Memory section, click Change.
6. Clear the Automatically Manage Paging File Size For All Drives checkbox.
7. Under Drive [Volume Label], click the drive where the page file should be stored.
8. Check the Automatically Manage Paging File Size For All Drives checkbox.
9. Click OK.

For Windows 8

1. Press Windows key-x, and then choose System in the pop-up menu.
2. Click Advanced System Settings.
3. On the Advanced tab, under Performance, click Settings.
4. On the Advanced tab tab's Virtual Memory section, click Change.
5. Clear the Automatically Manage Paging File Size For All Drives checkbox.
6. Under Drive [Volume Label], click the drive where the page file should be stored.
7. Check the Automatically Manage Paging File Size For All Drives checkbox.
8. Click OK.

Note Moving the pagefile.sys is not mandatory, and not moving the file will not adversely affect the evidence you obtain during a mobile device collection and analysis. The recommendation to move the file is based on storage and I/O speed when the file is stored on the same disk with the operating system and forensic software.

The effect of temporary storage is not limited to the operating system because it affects forensic software as well. Most software solutions use temporary storage to conduct different transactions against the evidence being examined to maintain a usable level of memory for the solution and the operating system. When the transactions are completed by the software solution, the temporary data is supposed to be removed from the disk by the software using that space, but this is not always the case.

Storing temporary data on a secondary drive enables the examiner to control the data, such as removing and purging sensitive data (company IP, financial records, criminal case evidence, or other data), which is often part of the forensic examination. The drive should be dedicated to the temporary storage of the data from the Windows temp folder and pagefile .sys along with any forensics tools. This area can be sanitized after each forensic examination without compromising the operating system or installed applications on another drive within the forensic workstation. Because this secondary drive will be used by both the operating system and forensic software to store large amounts of data temporarily, a drive that is three times the size of the largest device that will be processed is required. Also, an SSD drive, if possible, should be used, which will provide a noticeable increase in both read and write speed during the collection and analysis of the mobile device data, as analysis tools used by mobile forensic software require large amounts of temporary storage to complete transactions.

A third drive should also be used for the storage of the evidence files from mobile devices either temporarily, semi-temporarily, or permanently. This drive is used only for the files and images classified as evidence: the original mobile device image, the output proprietary image from a mobile forensic solution if applicable, any generated reports, exported native files, case notes, case folders, and anything else that will be needed to complete a final report presentation and later archiving. This drive can be an external drive or internal drive with an HDD or SSD configuration. The appropriate size of this disk depends on its intended use: If it will temporarily house the evidence until the case is completed, the size is determined by the number of cases that will be typically concurrently worked. If the drive will store all of the evidence permanently until it can be deleted, a RAID solution can help protect against failing hard drives and data loss and allows for more efficient I/O functions.

External Storage

External storage is not attached to the device that is conducting the collection, computation, and evidence. It has two specific storage options: temporary and semi-permanent. Both are often required, but this is generally determined by the type of software being used and its features.

Using an external device for temporary storage is usually needed when the tool exporting the collected data sends it to an externally attached drive for later analysis, when the temporary data used by the device is later removed by the tool when the tool has completed its work, or in both cases. Tools such as Cellebrite UFED Classic and Touch, along with AccessData nFIELD software, specify that the examiner plug in a removable drive to complete the extraction, which then deposits the collected image and data to the attached removable storage. UFED Classic, which is now end-of-life, was able to extract only to storage drives formatted with a File Allocation Table (FAT) file system, which often led to a large number of files for high-capacity devices because of the file size limitations for FAT-formatted devices. The UFED Touch and 4PC and Oxygen Forensic Detective and Analyst can perform writes to NTFS drives, which allows for large file writes.

Note Both UFED Touch and Oxygen Forensic Detective and Analyst can also export the data to a network or mapped drive if needed.

Once the data has been collected, it will be available at the location indicated by the examiner. Also, as discussed, having a secondary drive to write temporary data to is advised, and a removable drive can be used much like an internal drive. However, the I/O of a removable disk will be slower than that of an internal drive and, when used as a temporary location, there are noticeable limitations.

Tip Some examiners also use the removable drive to store temporary data and export collected image files. Using this method is not advisable for obvious reasons, however, such as possible evidence contamination or inadvertent deletion when the software solution decides to purge the temporary data.

External storage can also enable archiving. When an image of a mobile device is created, it should be stored separately after a copy has been made. The copy image will then be analyzed. Typically, the storage of any electronic evidence should be on RAID to ensure redundancy and safeguard the image should a hardware malfunction occur with the external storage.

Operating System

Mobile forensic tools usually run on some version of Microsoft Windows. BlackBag BlackLight and Katana Forensics Lantern run on the Mac OS, but BlackLight can also run on Windows.

Note Mac setup is not covered here because most examiners who use Macs for mobile device forensics use a type of virtualization that runs Windows. For those using Macs for mobile forensics, the information in this chapter can be used to set up the Windows virtualized environment, just as a user would on a system running Windows.

Some forensics software still indicates that Windows XP is a supported operating system, but using Windows XP is not recommended simply because newer devices and their associated drivers cannot run on XP. Also, software built using Microsoft .NET Framework versions later than 3.5 will not run on XP. Most mobile forensic software supports both Windows 7 and 8, with a recommendation by most to run Windows 7. Experience conducting hundreds of examinations has shown that Windows 8.1 is much better at communicating with mobile devices in both setting up and then removing drivers as necessary more efficiently. Previous versions, such as Windows 7, did not remove device drivers from allocated COM areas, and some mobile forensic software had difficulty with communication.

As mentioned earlier, with today's forensic processing and its demands on the operating system, if possible, use a 64-bit version of Windows, as long as the forensic software will support it. This will allow for more information to be processed and will address more memory than a 32-bit system.

Allowing automatic updates will also benefit the mobile device examiner; be sure to enable this within the software as recommended. Prior to installing any mobile forensics software, you should install all Windows updates and security patches.

Power functions can also cause difficulties while processing a mobile device. Most communication between a mobile device and forensic software solutions occurs via the USB port and a cable. If the power to the USB port is regulated by the operating system, the forensic solution cannot communicate properly and collection cannot occur. The power to the USB ports for both desktops and laptops is regulated by default in Windows. This allows Windows to turn off the USB ports when the OS believes that there is a need (such as during inactivity, low battery, or hibernation). In theory, Windows should wake the USB ports when a device is plugged in, but experience shows that this is not always the case, depending on the version of Windows installed in the forensic environment.

Tip Troubleshooting this problem within Windows is covered in the "Troubleshooting the Device Connections" section later in the chapter.

Once the operating system has been updated and configured and all supporting software has been installed (but before any forensic software is installed), you should create a restore point. This restore point will allow the user to return to a baseline if needed. The following procedures show you how to create a restore point in Windows 7 and 8.

For Windows 7

1. Press the Windows key.
2. Right-click Computer, and choose Properties.
3. In the left pane, click System Protection.
4. Click the System Protection tab, and then click Create.
5. In the System Protection dialog, type a description, and then click Create.

For Windows 8

1. Press Windows key-x, and then choose System in the pop-up menu.
2. Click Properties.

3. In the left pane, click System Protection.
4. Click the System Protection tab, and then click Create.
5. In the System Protection dialog, type a description, and then click Create.

If possible, use software such as Symantec Ghost to return the forensic computer to a point in time identical to when the image was created, which is unlike the Windows built-in Restore function. I suggest that you create a ghost image after all software is installed, but before the first examination. This way, the machine can be brought back to a "clean" restore point after each examination to ensure a clean version before each new collection.

Device Drivers and Multiple-Tool Environments

Using multiple tools is important for success in the world of mobile forensic investigations, but there can be consequences, particularly issues that occur with the unique drivers used by the various types of software to communicate with different mobile devices. Software vendors, at times, develop their own mobile device drivers that do not work with every piece of software that might also be installed on the system. As such, when a mobile device is plugged in and a software-specific device driver is installed, other software solutions on the computer will be unable to communicate directly using a proprietary driver. This is immediately evident, when an error is returned by the software solution indicating that the software was unable to communicate with the attached device. A quick check of the Windows Device Manager can identify the driver and the manufacturer. If the driver is not the original equipment manufacturer (OEM) version of the driver (for example, the equipment is Motorola but the driver is Susteen), there could be a problem with all other software titles that use the OEM driver to communicate with the mobile device. Changing from the proprietary device driver to the proper OEM driver will typically solve the problem.

Some examiners create independent virtual machines for each software product and then run all the virtual machines on a single machine to combat a software-caused driver conflict. This enables all software to run independently and conflict-free using software-specific drivers. This can be a good solution, albeit a more advanced one, but unfortunately not all software will be able to run within a VM. To complicate matters, some mobile devices, such as iOS devices, which disconnect frequently within the VM, attach to the host operating system, which causes a collection failure.

The key to running a multitool environment, or even a single tool environment, successfully is to understand how to control driver problems.

Understanding Drivers

Mobile device drivers are the gateway that allows hardware or software to communicate with the mobile device. If a device driver is not installed or is improperly installed, communication is generally impossible. Device drivers are not unique to mobile devices; they are also used for printers, scanners, cameras, motherboards, CD/DVD drives, USB controllers, monitors, and other computer peripherals and software. Anything that is not a part of the original operating system code base will need a driver to interact properly with the operating system. Device drivers are used in every operating system available and are undoubtedly one of the most common problems encountered in mobile device forensics.

Device drivers are themselves software applications that allow an operating system or another application to use hardware or other devices with common code and procedures to perform I/O. However, drivers are hardware dependent and also specific to an operating system. This means that, for example, a driver developed for Windows XP will generally not work if it's installed in any other version of Windows, and a driver developed for an LG device will not work with an HTC device.

A driver is like a switching station, where data from the operating system or application is interpreted upon arrival and translated to communicate to the device by way of the device driver. The device sends data back to the application and operating system as requested. A device driver allows a generic set of instructions from the operating system or application to request to read data, perform functions, and send data independent of knowing what device the software will be communicating with.

Here's an example dealing with mobile device forensic tools. Many different mobile devices are supported by a mobile forensic tool, but a single set of instructions is used to read data from a mobile device. Consider, for example, processing an Android device logically, when there are more than 12,000 different Android devices on the market. How could a development team write specific code for each type of hardware? It is possible, but this would be an enormous task! By using a device driver unique to the Android hardware, the communication code is interpreted and translated to a format specific to the hardware connected by the driver. By using the device driver, virtually all the data collected will use the same communication code transmitted from the forensic solution for any Android device attached. The driver allows the forensic software to "speak" to the device using a single set of commands to allow the support of thousands of devices by way of the single driver.

Now that you have a basic understanding of what device drivers are and how they operate, your next challenge is finding the correct driver for the mobile device that needs to be processed.

Finding Mobile Device Drivers

When a mobile device comes into the lab for processing and has not been pre-installed into the mobile forensic solution, the examiner must locate and install the driver manually on the system before collection can occur.

Note Some manufacturers, such as Cellebrite (UFED Touch), have pre-installed the device drivers directly to the hardware device they ship, so generally device drivers are not needed.

There are times when trying to locate mobile device drivers is like trying to find a needle in a haystack. Typically, mobile devices do not ship with a driver on a CD, as most other hardware devices (such as printers and cameras) do, and sometimes drivers are not readily available on the manufacturers' web sites. Nonexistent or missing drivers are more common with older feature phones, but even some newer Android devices do not have available drivers on the manufacturer's site. Often, missing or nonexistent drivers are encountered with newer prepaid devices. In an effort to subsidize the cost of the device, manufacturers will allow the communication port to be disabled. By disabling the port for connections to a personal computer, a company can then offer additional services to transfer media or user data via online services, thus making additional revenue on data transfer that would not be possible if the user could plug the device into a computer and do the same thing. Because some of these drivers are needed and are not available on the manufacturer's web site, a hunt for the driver ensues.

Where does an examiner go to locate drivers if the solution does not have one? The answer is "it depends." It depends on several factors, ranging from the type of device, the manufacturer of the device, and the type of connection required to transmit the data to the operating system. Table 7-2 is not exhaustive, but it contains information on where to find drivers for the majority of devices encountered.

TABLE 7-2 Mobile Device Drivers for Device Manufacturers and Models

Manufacturer	Device Type / Drivers	Credit
Acer	Android www.acer.com/worldwide/support/mobile.html	developer.android.com
Alcatel One Touch	Android www.alcatelonetouch.com/global-en/support/faq/usbdriver.html	developer.android.com
Asus	Android http://support.asus.com/download/	developer.android.com
Dell	Android http://support.dell.com/support/downloads/index.aspx?c=us&cs=19&l=en&s=dhs&~ck=anavml	developer.android.com
Foxconn	Android http://drivers.cmcs.com.tw/	developer.android.com
Fujitsu	Android www.fmworld.net/product/phone/sp/android/develop/	developer.android.com
Garmin-Asus	Android https://www.garminasus.com/en_US/support/pcsync/	developer.android.com
Hisense	Android http://app.hismarttv.com/dss/resourcecontent.do?method=viewResourceDetail&resourceId=16&type=5	developer.android.com
HTC	Android www.htc.com	developer.android.com
Huawei	Android www.huaweidevice.com/worldwide/downloadCenter.do?method=index	developer.android.com

(Continued)

TABLE 7-2 Mobile Device Drivers for Device Manufacturers and Models *(Continued)*

Manufacturer	Device Type / Drivers	Credit
Intel	Android www.intel.com/software/android	developer.android.com
KT Tech	Android www.kttech.co.kr/cscenter/download05.asp	developer.android.com
Kyocera	Android www.kyocera-wireless.com/support/phone_drivers.htm	developer.android.com
Lenovo	Android http://developer.lenovomm.com/developer/download.jsp	developer.android.com
LGE	Android www.lg.com/us/mobile-phones/mobile-support/mobile-lg-mobile-phone-support.jsp	developer.android.com
Motorola	Android http://developer.motorola.com/docstools/USB_Drivers/	developer.android.com
MTK	Android http://online.mediatek.com/Public%20Documents/MTK_Android_USB_Driver.zip	developer.android.com
Oppo	Android www.oppo.com/index.php?q=software/view&sw_id=631	developer.android.com
Pantech	Android www.isky.co.kr/cs/software/software.sky?fromUrl=index	developer.android.com
Pegatron	Android www.pegatroncorp.com/download/New_Duke_PC_Driver_0705.zip	developer.android.com
Samsung	Android www.samsung.com/us/support/downloads	developer.android.com
Sharp	Android http://k-tai.sharp.co.jp/support/	developer.android.com
SK Telesys	Android www.sk-w.com/service/wDownload/wDownload.jsp	developer.android.com
Sony Mobile Communications	Android http://developer.sonymobile.com/downloads/drivers/	developer.android.com

TABLE 7-2 Mobile Device Drivers for Device Manufacturers and Models *(Continued)*

Manufacturer	Device Type / Drivers	Credit
Teleepoch	Android www.teleepoch.com/android.html	developer.android.com
Toshiba	Android http://support.toshiba.com/sscontent?docId=4001814	developer.android.com
Yulong Coolpad	Android www.yulong.com/product/product/product/downloadList.html#downListUL	developer.android.com
Xiaomi	Android www.xiaomi.com/c/driver/index.html	developer.android.com
ZTE	Android http://support.zte.com.cn/support/news/NewsDetail.aspx?newsId=1000442	developer.android.com
Bluetooth	Bluetooth-capable devices www.broadcom.com/support/bluetooth/update.php	
LG	Legacy, Windows Phone, Windows Mobile www.lg.com/us/support	
Motorola	Legacy, Windows Phone, Windows Mobile https://motorola-global-portal.custhelp.com/app/answers/prod_detail/a_id/97326/p/30,6720,9050	
Samsung	Legacy, Windows Phone, Windows Mobile www.samsung.com/us/support/	
Huawei	Legacy, Windows Phone, Windows Mobile http://consumer.huawei.com/en/support/downloads/	
ZTE	Legacy, Windows Phone, Windows Mobile www.zteusa.com/support_page	
Nokia	Legacy, S40, Symbian, ASHA www.microsoft.com/en-us/mobile/support/product/nokia-pc-suite/	
Nokia	Legacy, S40, Symbian, ASHA (after 2013) www.microsoft.com/en-us/mobile/support/product/nokia-connectivity-cable-driver/	
Nokia	Windows Phone www.microsoft.com/en-us/mobile/support/	

Installing Drivers

Once the examiner has located a driver, the next step will be installing it. Most of the drivers located on a manufacturer's web site include an installation program that makes it easy to install the device and then register it on the operating system, which allows the OS to place it into the proper Windows driver location so that when a device is plugged in, it is installed without user interaction. The method used by Windows when searching for and installing a driver for a new device is outlined in Table 7-3.

When a device is plugged into a Windows computer running Windows 7 or later, Windows will automatically check the Microsoft Update Services, and if it cannot locate the driver, Windows will check the driver store. If the driver is not located in the driver store, Windows will look to the default system location of the INF (device information file) as specified in the registry:

HKEY_LOCAL_MACHINE\Software\Microsoft\Windows\CurrentVersion

Note Other operating systems are not covered here simply because most forensic software operates with the Windows OS, which subsequently experiences the most driver issues.

If the driver is located from the Windows Update query or from the default system location for INF files, it is then moved (called *staged*) to the driver store and installed from that location. The driver store, introduced in Windows Vista, is a two-part process comprising staging and installation. In order to be installed, the driver must be staged, which involves moving the INF file and all the files referenced in the INF file and then verifying and validating the package. If all checks pass, the driver is copied into the store and installed without user interaction. If the driver does not pass (for example, files are missing from INF, the user does not have permissions, or the digital signature is not correct), the driver is not installed, and manual installation of the driver must then be handled by the examiner.

Note Manually installing drivers for all versions of Windows involves locating the problem driver via the Device Manager and then updating the device with the proper driver.

TABLE 7-3 Windows Installation Path for Device Drivers (Microsoft Developers Network)

Search Phase	Server 2003 and XP	Server 2008 and Vista	Windows 7 and Later
Without User (Auto)	DevicePath	Driver Store	Windows Update, driver store, DevicePath
With User Interaction	Prompt for manufacturer CD, Windows Update	DevicePath, Windows Update, prompt for manufacturer CD	None

Windows Device Manager

All examiners should be familiar with the Windows Device Manager, an application within Windows that enables the user to view and update device drivers on the system, check to see that the hardware is functioning properly, and modify the hardware's settings. How you navigate to the Device Manager depends upon the version of Windows in use.

Only Windows 7 and Windows 8 are covered here because Microsoft no longer supports Windows XP.

For Windows 7 using Control Panel

1. Click Start, and then click Control Panel.
2. Click Hardware And Sound.
3. Click Device Manager.

For Windows 7 using the command line

1. Click Start.
2. In the search box, type **mmc devmgmt.msc.**
3. Press ENTER.

For Windows 8 on the main Start screen

1. Press Windows key-C, and then click Search in the pop-up menu.
2. Enter **Device Manager** in the search box.
3. Select Apps and then click Device Manager.

For Windows 8 on the desktop

- Press Windows key-X, and then click Device Manager in the pop-up menu.

Once you access the Device Manager, you'll quickly see any existing driver problems. Typically, the yellow exclamation prompt or question mark makes it clear that there is a problem with the installed driver or that a driver is not found. If a driver is not found for a device, the device will be installed in the Other Devices section, as shown in Figure 7-1. If the driver is installed, Device Manager will identify whether a problem exists with it. In both cases, you must install the correct driver before the forensic software can communicate properly with the device. To diagnose the problem and determine what steps will be needed, the Device Manager takes a closer look at what Windows indicates as the problem and the device as described by the operating system.

In the Device Manager, locate the device with the exclamation or question mark—for mobile devices, these are typically located under Ports, Modems, ADB, USB Controllers, and Portable Devices. There are always exceptions, but the most important information will be listed in the properties for the troubled device: Right-click the device and select Properties. A new dialog will open (Figure 7-2) with several tabs and a description of the device that you selected. Directly in the center of the first page under Device Status is the first clue to a

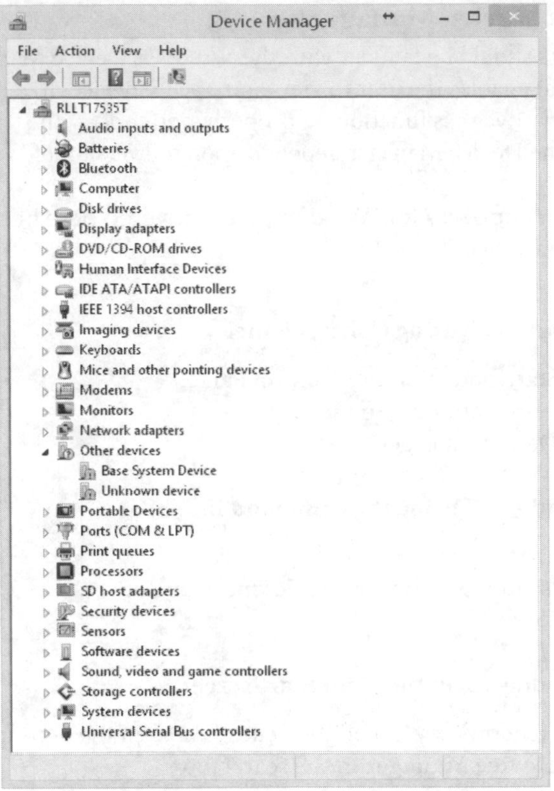

FIGURE 7-1 If devices are not recognized or the driver cannot be found, they are located in the Other Devices section of the Device Manager.

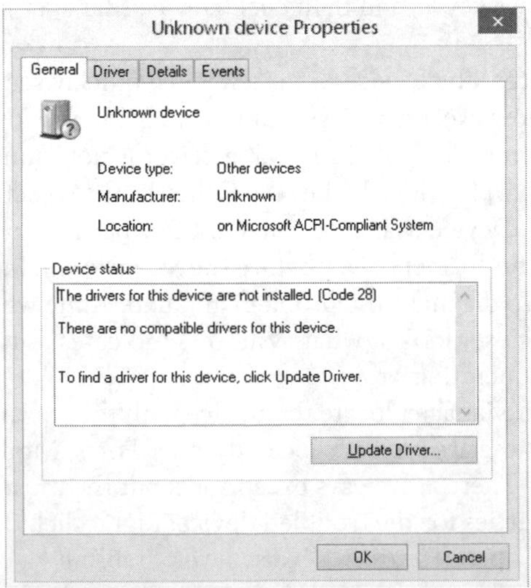

FIGURE 7-2 The Properties dialog for a device in the Device Manager details the device and associated drivers.

problem or problems with the device. The displayed message will provide a short description of the problem and the associated code: In the figure, the message "The drivers for this device are not installed. (Code 28)" is displayed.

Many codes can be listed here, but typically the codes displayed for a mobile device are Codes 10 and 28. Table 7-4 shows a listing of all the codes used by Microsoft to describe problems in the Device Manager. This is not an exhaustive list, but it includes the most prevalent device problems.

TABLE 7-4 Device Dialog for Each Device Describing the Status, Drivers, and Compatibility (http://support.microsoft.com/KB/310123)

Code	Display Status	Fix
No Code	This device is not configured correctly.	Update the device driver.
Code 3	The driver for this device might be corrupted, or your system may be running low on memory or other resources.	Close some open applications. Uninstall and reinstall the driver. Install additional RAM.
Code 10	This device cannot start.	Update the device driver. Driver is for x86 or x64 only.
Code 12	This device cannot find enough free resources that it can use. If you want to use this device, you will need to disable one of the other devices on this system.	Disable the conflicting device.
Code 14	This device cannot work properly until you restart your computer.	Restart your computer.
Code 16	Windows cannot identify all the resources this device uses.	Assign additional resources to the device.
Code 18	Reinstall the drivers for this device.	Update the device driver. Uninstall and reinstall the driver.
Code 19	Windows cannot start this hardware device because its configuration information (in the registry) is incomplete or damaged.	Uninstall and reinstall the driver. Revert to the most recent successful registry configuration.
Code 21	Windows is removing this device.	Refresh the Device Manager view. Restart your computer.
Code 22	This device is disabled.	Enable the device.
Code 24	This device is not present, is not working properly, or does not have all its drivers installed.	Update the device driver. Remove the device.

(Continued)

TABLE 7-4 Device Dialog for Each Device Describing the Status, Drivers, and Compatibility (http://support.microsoft.com/KB/310123) *(Continued)*

Code	Display Status	Fix
Code 28	The drivers for this device are not installed.	Install the device driver.
Code 29	This device is disabled because the firmware of the device did not give it the required resources.	Enable the device in the BIOS.
Code 31	This device is not working properly because Windows cannot load the drivers required for this device.	Update the device driver.
Code 32	A driver (service) for this device has been disabled. An alternate driver may be providing this functionality.	Uninstall and reinstall the driver. Change the start type in the Registry.
Code 33	Windows cannot determine which resources are required for this device.	Configure or replace the hardware.
Code 34	Windows cannot determine the settings for this device.	Manually configure the device.
Code 35	Your computer's system firmware does not include enough information to properly configure and use this device. To use this device, contact your computer manufacturer to obtain a firmware or BIOS update.	Contact the computer manufacturer to update the BIOS.
Code 36	This device is requesting a PCI interrupt but is configured for an ISA interrupt (or vice versa). Please use the computer's system setup program to reconfigure the interrupt for this device.	Change the settings for IRQ reservations.
Code 37	Windows cannot initialize the device driver for this hardware.	Uninstall and reinstall the driver.
Code 38	Windows cannot load the device driver for this hardware because a previous instance of the device driver is still in memory.	Run the Troubleshooting Wizard. Restart your computer.
Code 39	Windows cannot load the device driver for this hardware. The driver may be corrupted or missing.	Uninstall and reinstall the driver.
Code 40	Windows cannot access this hardware because its service key information in the registry is missing or recorded incorrectly.	Uninstall and reinstall the driver.

TABLE 7-4 Device Dialog for Each Device Describing the Status, Drivers, and Compatibility (http://support.microsoft.com/KB/310123) *(Continued)*

Code	Display Status	Fix
Code 41	Windows successfully loaded the device driver for this hardware but cannot find the hardware device.	Update the device driver. Uninstall and reinstall the driver.
Code 42	Windows cannot load the device driver for this hardware because there is a duplicate device already running in the system.	Restart your computer.
Code 43	Windows has stopped this device because it has reported problems.	Run the Troubleshooting Wizard. Check the hardware documentation.
Code 44	An application or service has shut down this hardware device.	Restart your computer.
Code 45	Currently, this hardware device is not connected to the computer.	Reconnect the device to your computer.
Code 46	Windows cannot gain access to this hardware device because the operating system is in the process of shutting down.	No resolution required.
Code 47	Windows cannot use this hardware device because it has been prepared for safe removal, but it has not been removed from the computer.	Reconnect the device to your computer. Restart your computer.
Code 48	The software for this device has been blocked from starting because it is known to have problems with Windows. Contact the hardware vendor for a new driver.	Update the device driver.
Code 49	Windows cannot start new hardware devices because the system hive is too large (exceeds the Registry Size Limit).	Uninstall devices that you are no longer using.
Code 52	Windows cannot verify the digital signature for the drivers required for this device.	Run the Troubleshooting Wizard. Update the device driver.

Your next steps will be determined by the code and/or the description of the error listed in the Device Manager. This could involve finding the correct driver package for the device and running an executable program that installs the driver and reattaches the device. Or it might involve you manually installing the driver when an installation package cannot be located. Whatever the course, becoming familiar with the Device Manager in Windows should be a priority.

Tip Something that has always been suggested, but rarely implemented, is placing a shortcut to the Device Manager on the desktop or taskbar of the analysis machine. By creating a shortcut, the examiner can quickly navigate to the Device Manager if any issues need to be investigated during a mobile device examination.

Identifying the Driver

If a problem exists with the driver and it is determined that the version of the driver is compatible with only a certain operating system version (such as x86 or x64), then generally the device properties will indicate, "This device cannot start. (Code 10)," but it will install. On the other hand, if a driver could not be located by the operating system and the installed device does not have a driver, it will be listed under Other Devices in the Device Manager with a message, "The drivers for this device are not installed. (Code 28)." In either situation, to find the correct driver, you can determine the device information by consulting the device properties, but this time using the Details tab.

The Details tab lists all the information about the device that is connected to the computer system. The important sections and tags for determining the correct driver are Hardware IDs and Compatible IDs. Both will help you locate a suitable driver for the attached device, and both contain valuable information in determining exactly what device is attached to the computer. An example in Figure 7-3 shows a Hardware ID with several lines that are important to the overall meaning; each will need to be broken down. Every USB device has two codes that distinguish it from other USB devices: the Product ID (PID) and the Vendor ID (VID).

- **PID (Product ID)** This is an essential part of every driver and must be used. This is the type of product or a family of products (such as modem, serial port, human interface device). The PID does not have to be unique and can be by anything that a vendor assigns.

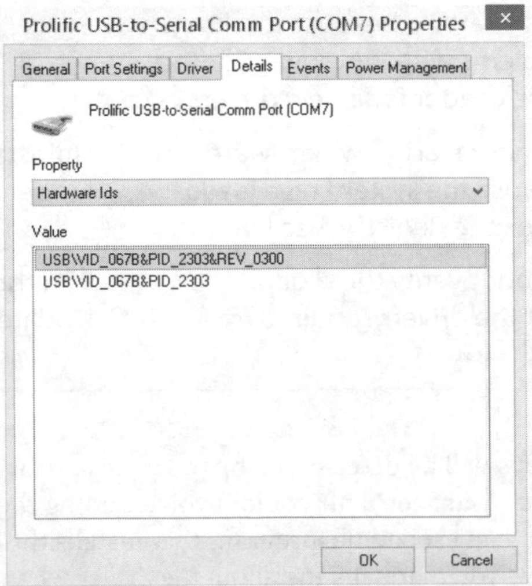

FIGURE 7-3 The Prolific Cable Properties table under the Details tab identifies the assigned PID and VID for the device.

- **VID (Vendor ID)** This is also an essential part of every driver and must be used. A VID must be granted by the USB Implementers Forum, which assigns and maintains all VIDs as part of the compliance program. Sometimes this may not be the vendor of the mobile device. The VID could identify the chip vendor that is either embedded into the cable itself or the silicon chip embedded in the mobile device, but a manufacturer has cooperated with the vendor and conformed to the driver specifications.

Tip You can determine whether a driver is needed for a cable by plugging in the cable without the mobile device attached. If a driver is installed, or a driver install is attempted but fails, then hardware is embedded in the cable. The typical chips embedded into cables are Prolific or FTDI.

Once you've obtained this information, you can search both the VID and PID on the Internet to identify the correct driver needed for the mobile device. When you locate the package, you must download and install the INF and associated files manually.

Troubleshooting the Device Connections

At times, a device will not communicate with the forensic software, even when the correct driver has been installed. This might be encountered in the following situations:

- Multiple tools accessing the same device are running concurrently.
- The computer is allowed to manage the power to the USB hub.
- The computer is using a USB hub with multiple devices attached.
- The mobile device does not have enough power.

When multiple software processes are accessing a device, the device will be able to respond only to one at a time. I call this "COM envy"—if a communication port (COM) is open by one piece of software, it will not be released until that software either completes the tasks or releases the device or the software and processes are stopped and closed. Because of this limitation, another software solution cannot connect to the mobile device. When collecting mobile device data, you must have only one software solution running while initializing a connection and conducting an extraction.

Power management of USB hubs can also cause device connection problems, often disabling the connection and causing a collection error. Windows 7, by default, turns power off to the USB hub when the system senses that power needs to be managed. This is particularly noticeable with laptops that are not plugged in because of their power management profiles. There are two ways to manage the power management, but in all instances, the ability for Windows to manage the USB hubs should be disabled.

For Windows 7 and 8

This should be done for all USB root hub listings.

1. Click Start, or press Windows key-x for Windows 8.
2. Search for **mmc devmgmt.msc**.
3. Navigate to the Universal Serial Bus Controllers section at the bottom of the device listings.

4. Locate all USB Root Hub listings.
5. Right-click and select Properties.
6. Select Power Management.
7. Uncheck Allow The Computer To Turn Off Device To Save Power, and click OK.

A better way for both Windows 7 and 8 will be to change the power settings via the power management console:

1. Click Start, or press Windows key-x for Windows 8.
2. Search for **edit power plan**.
3. Click OK.
4. Click Change Advanced Power Settings.
5. Scroll to USB Settings.
6. Expand USB Selective Suspend Setting.
7. Switch both On Battery and Plugged In to Disabled, and click OK.

Power to a USB device can also be inhibited when the power is distributed across multiple devices attached to a single external hub. When you're processing mobile devices, if you use an external USB hub that is attached to the processing computer, drivers may not be installed, and inconsistent connections can occur to an attached mobile device. If possible, attach a mobile device directly to the computer when conducting the mobile device collection, not through a USB hub.

Lastly, the power of the mobile device being examined can also cause problems with device driver installation. If the mobile device does not have at least 50 percent power, when you attach it to the collection computer, a failure to recognize and install the device driver is possible. During all collections, a mobile device should have at least 50 percent power before you connect the mobile forensic solution and throughout the entire extraction process.

Cleaning the Computer System of Unused Drivers and Ports

Windows, in an effort to be efficient, will cache all devices that have been attached to a Windows computer at one time with its assigned COM port number. What is considered efficient by Windows can have dire effects on mobile forensic software, however. This problem has been improved with the release of Windows 8, but it's still a problem. It boils down to *phantom devices* (or non-present devices)—hidden ports (devices) that are not shown in the Device Manager because the actual device is no longer connected with Windows. By default, users cannot see these hidden devices and will not even realize there is a problem. Even when an error is encounter by the mobile forensic solution because of the presence of a phantom device, most examiners are still unaware of the root of the problem.

The issue that arises with a phantom port and mobile forensic software is called *port enumeration*. Mobile forensic software enumerates through each port number that is used, looking for an attached device, and it will submit a challenge to the port to identify the device so communication can begin. When a computer running Windows has been used for mobile forensics, many devices get plugged into the USB port. When a device gets plugged into the computer and the driver is installed, a COM port is assigned to the device. When the device is unplugged, the device information, including the COM it was attached to, is saved so that when the device is plugged back into the same USB port, Windows will have already identified it and the same COM number can be assigned. This all means a couple of things of the examiner: One, if the device is plugged into any other USB port, it is assigned another COM number. Two, when any other device gets plugged in, a new unique COM number is assigned to that new device even if it had been plugged in to the same computer before. This means some computers can soon be operating with hundreds of assigned COM numbers, which can cause forensic software to timeout while looking through all of the COM ports for a valid device.

These phantom devices should be removed so problems do not arise when you're attempting to connect to a mobile device with a Windows-based forensic solution. You can manually remove the ports from the Windows command line, invoking a Registry change, by navigating to the Device Manager to show hidden devices and then removing each device with a right-click and Uninstall. They also can be removed with several open source automated tools that are currently available, along with CPD PortScrubber and Micro Systemation XRY, which include a port cleaner as part of their solutions.

Removing Non-Present Devices (Phantom Devices)

The manual method is covered here in an effort to help you understand what Windows is doing or the process undertaken by the automated tools when they remove the phantom devices.

For Windows 7

1. Click Start.
2. Search for **Command** and select Command Prompt.
3. At the command prompt, type the following, and then press ENTER:

```
set devmgr_show_nonpresent_devices=1
```

4. Type the following command, and then press ENTER:

```
start devmgmt.msc
```

5. Choose View | Show Hidden Devices, as shown next:

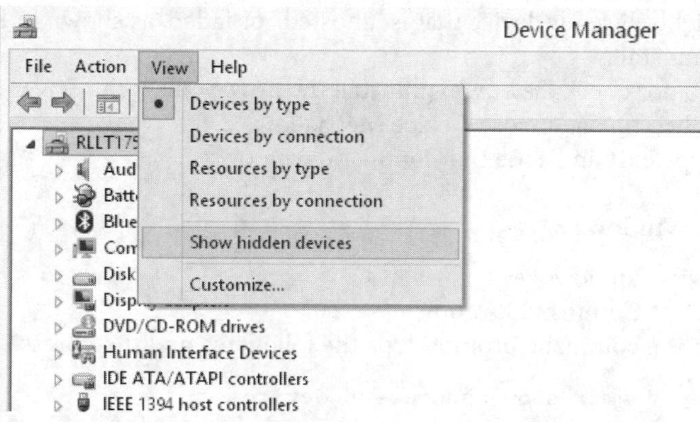

6. Navigate to Ports, Modems, USB Controllers, ADB, and other device areas where mobile devices have been installed.

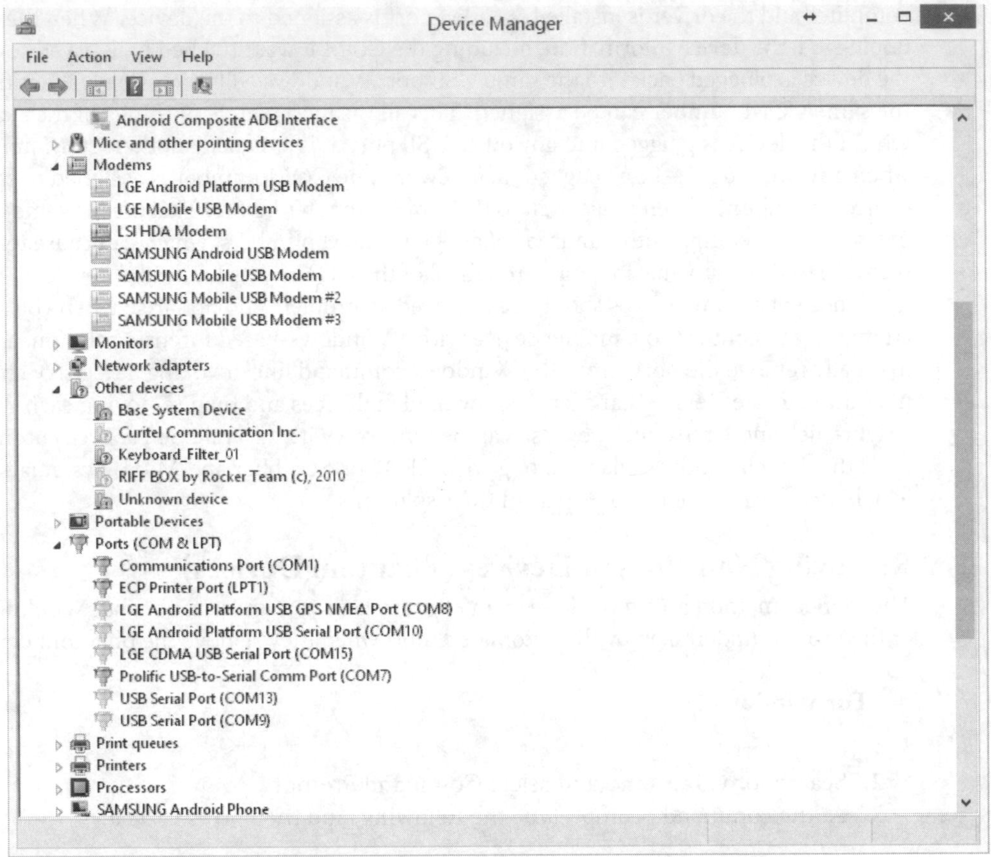

FIGURE 7-4 Several devices are shown as phantom devices under Modems, Ports, and Kindle (for example, Android Composite ADB Interface, Samsung Mobile USB Modem, LGE Mobile USB Modem).

7. Right-click any device that is "ghosted," or faded, as shown in Figure 7-4, and select Uninstall.
8. Do not check the box to uninstall the driver unless the driver is causing a conflict.
9. When finished, close Device Manager.
10. Type **exit** and close the Command window.

For Windows 8

1. Press Windows key-x.
2. Select Command Prompt.
3. At the command prompt, type the following, and then press ENTER:

```
set devmgr_show_nonpresent_devices=1
```

4. Type the following command, and then press ENTER:

```
start devmgmt.msc
```

5. Choose View | Show Hidden Devices.
6. Navigate to Ports, Modems, USB Controllers, ADB, and other device areas where mobile devices have been installed.
7. Right-click any device that is "ghosted," as shown in Figure 7-4, and select Uninstall.
8. Do not check the box to uninstall the driver unless the driver is causing a conflict.
9. When finished, close Device Manager.
10. Type **exit** and close the Command Prompt window.

Several automated tools are available to conduct this process simultaneously on multiple phantom devices, and some are freely available. Phantom device removal applications are generally based upon the Microsoft DevCon (https://msdn.microsoft.com/en-us/library/windows/hardware/ff544707%28v=vs.85%29.aspx) utility. DevCon, or Device Console, is a command-line utility that lists the devices on a computer running Windows. The utility can show phantom devices and remove them using several built-in commands and controls. By using the basic functioning of the DevCon source code, GhostBuster (http://ghostbuster.codeplex.com/releases/view/566397) enables the enumeration of phantom devices and aids in their removal with a GUI. GhostBuster is available for both x86 and x64 Windows systems. Prior to connecting a device to the forensic workstation, make sure that phantom devices are not consuming available COM port numbers. CPD PortScrubber is available from CPDForensics. This is a commercial tool, but does work with Windows x86 and x64 systems up to and including Windows 8.

It is also recommended that you use the same USB port when conducting a mobile device collection. This will ensure that the driver that was installed previously for the same device is not installed again. By using the same port every time, Windows will already have reference to the device and will use the same driver that was used successfully the previous time the device was attached to the computer. If another port is used, Windows will search for the driver using the same process, depending upon the OS version, described in the section "Installing Drivers," and then install the driver to the device store.

Chapter Summary

How a computer system has been set up prior to installing mobile forensic software can ultimately determine the success of the software solution. If the hardware, such as processors, RAM, and hard drives, is not set up correctly, forensic collection and analysis will suffer no matter what type of software is running on the computer system. You can consult the ideal specifications outlined on the vendor's site and then follow the guidelines listed in this chapter to ensure that the software solution will perform well.

Simply using the minimum specifications listed on a vendor's site will generally not allow the software to run at peak performance, typically because the vendor tests when only a single solution, their solution, is running on the machine. A rule of thumb is to multiply the component capacities and requirements by two to get an idea of the ideal size system that should efficiently run the vendor software, but also any other solution that may be used in a multitool environment.

By multiplying the specifications by two and allowing for additional software solutions, along with providing enough storage space for each solution's temporary storage and evidence storage, all solutions should operate well.

One of the most important, and often overlooked, problems with mobile device forensics is the device driver. By first understanding their usage, the examiner can make reasonable decisions as to whether the software solution simply does not support the device or the device is not installed correctly. Too often, examiners blame the software solution for failing to work, when the problem is actually based on a conflict between the operating system and the device. Because some device manufacturers update their device drivers regularly, it is a good idea to check regularly with a manufacturer's web site to make sure that the current driver used by the forensic solution is the newest driver for the device. Using Table 7-2, the examiner can at least have a starting point to identify the problem and then locate a device driver if communication to the device and the software becomes an issue. By understanding that some devices do not have an OEM driver and that each is identified by a PID and VID, an examiner can now search for the driver using other methods. This can help uncover drivers for devices that could not be previously located by simply searching a device manufacturer's site.

When troubleshooting communication problems between software and devices, faulty drivers, software conflicts with other software, or an overabundance of COM ports can be found. The examiner's ability to identify exactly where the problem lies takes a keen sense of understanding the different fault points. For example, when drivers do not install correctly, the forensic solution will be unable to communicate with the device. The examiner must be able to locate and update a driver manually. If multiple software solutions are installed on the same machine and one uses a custom-built driver for a mobile device while another uses the OEM driver, an error will be caused in communication if the wrong driver is installed. Realizing this, the examiner can switch to the compatible driver instead of dismissing the failure as a problem with the forensic software. Lastly, COM ports are a way of life for communication to a connected mobile device. Clearing COM port numbers that are not being used and using the same port for all mobile device connections will substantially reduce the time Windows takes to install a driver and can also fix problems encountered by software solutions that iterate over all COM ports whether the devices are present or not.

Troubleshooting expertise is an important step in becoming a mobile forensic expert and can be a common practice when conducting hundreds of examinations using multiple forensic solutions. Understand a device connection, the proper setup for forensic tools, and common pitfalls associated with drivers, and you can minimize many of the frustrations involved in conducting mobile device forensic collections and examinations.

8 Conducting a Collection of a Mobile Device: Considerations and Actions

Now that the environment has been set and you understand some of the problems that may result, let's get into the actual processing and collection of the mobile device. As covered previously, connecting to the device to complete an extraction can be difficult at times, so starting with a clean system and arming yourself with knowledge of troubleshooting problems can keep your frustrations to a minimum. Once a device successfully connects, you'll find that collecting the digital data from the mobile device will be one of the more straightforward procedures in mobile forensics. Before we get into the connection and extraction of the digital data, let's look at some initial considerations.

As discussed in Chapters 2 and 4, the status of the device when it is received and how the request to process the device is made will often steer the type of examination that will occur and all subsequent steps thereafter. If the device is powered on when it comes to the lab or is located at the scene, the initial steps in the examination as well as the workflow could be much different than they'd be if the device were powered off.

The type of collection (such as logical or physical) of a mobile device is another important consideration. The type of collection required is generally determined by the type of investigation underway, the time needed or given, the device to be examined, the training and expertise of the examiner, and the tools available for the job. No matter what type of collection is used, proper isolation and documentation of the device and its components are necessary because the processing order can be dictated by both. The type of mobile device that is to be examined can also determine how the collection should be approached.

Feature phones, also referred to as legacy devices, add a different dimension regarding preparation before the collection, but the actual extraction of the digital data from these types of devices is no different from that of the latest smart device. The setup of these devices prior to device collection is also important to the overall success of the digital data collection.

Alternative methods for collecting mobile device data are available for some devices such as BlackBerry, Android, Windows Phone, and iOS, and these should also be considered if traditional collection methods do not work or are unsuccessful; however, the initial preparation of the device prior to the data collection should be no different.

Initial Considerations

Before beginning the collection phase on the mobile device, the examiner must reflect on the various aspects of the collection, such as whether the examination will take place on the scene or in a lab. Additionally, the state of the device is important. Most devices arrive at the lab powered off. Sometimes, while on scene, the device is powered on and the examiner must immediately take steps to examine it.

Note In most instances, whatever the state of the device at the time of collection, it must be powered on to be processed.

Prior to processing a mobile device of its digital contents, an examiner must consider other aspects of the examination. From documenting the state of the device in written form and in photographic form, to processing associated evidence, there are many nuances to a mobile device collection, and each must be considered. Also, the type of examination (whether logical or physical), as discussed in Chapter 6, must be considered. Conducting a physical collection outside the lab is not recommended, but it may be necessary based on the situation. To determine the need and urgency of a specific type of collection, the examiner must consider how much time is available to complete the collection along with the type of data that is expected by either the requester or examiner.

Adhering to a sound methodology for all mobile device encounters will help solidify the resultant data and overall examination. The specifics are outlined in detail in the following sections of this chapter.

Isolating the Device

The examiner conducts the initial observation and subsequent processing according to the device state—powered on or off, or even in pieces. Whether the device is brought to a lab or the examiner conducts an on-scene examination, his or her first step should be to make sure that the device is isolated from any network connections. Device access to a network can corrupt and even destroy the data.

If the device is powered on, it must be isolated immediately. Methods and appliances to isolate include but are not limited to mesh, bags, boxes, tents, rooms, and even signal disrupters. After the device is properly isolated, the examiner must be sure to keep the device isolated during the entire examination process.

Note This section is not intended as a guide for the examiner in isolating the device; that information was covered in Chapter 4 and is continued later in this chapter.

If the mobile device is powered off at the scene or when brought to the lab, the examination should commence immediately using a systematic approach. The physical characteristics of the mobile device should be documented, and all peripheral evidence (such as a Universal Integrated Circuit Card [UICC] or media card) should be forensically collected.

It is good practice to keep a device in a signal isolated bag, even if it is powered off. Some devices can turn power back on if an alarm has been set, which could lead to a connection to a network and possible data loss or contamination.

Whether the device is powered on or off, the examiner must research to determine whether the device can be examined physically using a non-invasive method, which could include both software and hardware solutions. Armed with this information, along with the level of the examiner's expertise, the current status of the phone (on, off, or locked), and the software that will be used, the examiner can decide on the next step.

Device Collection Type: Logical or Physical

The status of the mobile device upon reception or discovery often determines whether the device should be processed logically or physically. The type of examination is contingent on the device's power status and whether the device is locked, password protected, or disabled (disassembled or broken). Prior to conducting the initial collection of the device, the examiner must consider operational speed, available tools, and his or her level of expertise and training.

Note Not all mobile devices can be collected physically. An iPhone 5 or 6, for example, cannot be collected physically using non-invasive methods. The following suggestions are offered to the examiner with the full understanding that each type of device encountered must be approached in a unique way.

In general, a physical collection should occur first to provide a representation of the overall data on the mobile device and can validate a logical collection. During a physical examination, any information collected can be used as a foundation for the data from a logical extraction. This foundation is extremely important, because this is the information on which a logical collection will stand. With a physical collection, an examiner can clearly show where the information "lived" when it was extracted during a logical collection.

Tip If a physical collection is not achievable, a logical-file system extraction can suffice.

By the examiner first obtaining the foundational information from a mobile device with a physical collection, any information that subsequent tools or logical extractions produce can be directly compared to the device file system. Comparing the data collected from a logical examination with the data from a physical collection is powerful evidence, especially if data recovered corroborates or contradicts either collection. Having this type of information is extremely powerful to an examination and to the overall outcome of the investigation.

Conducting one type of collection before the other generally does not constitute a disaster or epic failure, but in most situations, conducting one without the other can jeopardize the investigation. What will determine the order of the collection type (physical or logical) are the circumstances dictated by the scene, investigation, or request.

Note Some examiners say that a physical collection should always precede a logical collection because of *wear-leveling*, which arranges flash data so that write/erase cycles are distributed evenly among all of the blocks in the device. Simply reading data would not corrupt or overwrite existing data in a forensic examination, however, so this theory should not be the sole basis for conducting a physical collection of a mobile device prior to a logical collection.

Time Issues

Investigations that are not time sensitive or that have been submitted to a forensic lab should obtain a physical collection prior to a logical collection, when possible. As mentioned, by conducting a physical collection first, the examiner can rely on the underlying data to verify any information collected with the logical collection.

If an investigation depends on the examiner accessing the information quickly and in a format that can allow immediate follow-up, a logical examination should be first. With a logical collection, the investigator can immediately follow up on the information that is extracted from the device. A logical collection is also beneficial if the device loses power or is powered off and a lock is enabled. This quick collection can also assist if the device does not support a physical collection or if a physical collection is not possible for other reasons; the extraction can occur later either when time allows or upon arriving at a location that can conduct a physical collection safely and efficiently.

Device Power and Security Status

The power status of the mobile device should also be considered when determining whether to perform a logical or a physical collection first.

Note The type of investigation should be the primary directive in determining the type of collection, and the power status of the device should be secondary. If the investigation dictates immediate action, then whether a device is powered on or off does not matter. If the device is already powered on, process it logically first.

A physical collection should be attempted first if the mobile device is powered off when it is acquired. This can be accomplished with many feature phones if the connection to the device is via a USB or FBUS cable. These feature phones are often powered off while the device is placed into a special mode (such as flash, download, or boot loader) and cannot connect to a network. Also, if a device is powered off and it is a GSM (Global Systems for Mobile Communications) device containing a UICC, the card should be removed. When the card is removed from an iOS, Android, or Windows Phone, the device will be isolated from the cellular network and the examiner can attempt a physical collection using a USB and other non-invasive methods. With devices such as a Samsung SPH-D710, for example, an examiner can conduct a non-invasive Joint Test Action Group (JTAG) collection relatively easily with the device powered off. In this case, researching the device and the various ways to complete a physical examination are important before the examination begins. The physical collection should be a non-invasive physical technique, but the device can still be examined logically later.

If the device is powered on and unlocked, it should be processed logically first, because if the device is processed physically first and the device battery is removed or the device is turned off, the device can lock and a logical examination could be difficult. After the logical collection, the mobile device can be powered off for a physical collection and a locking mechanism will not be an issue.

A password-protected or locked device typically offers the examiner one initial collection method: physical. During a physical collection of the device, the examiner can hopefully obtain the passcode to access the device logically if required.

Note Sometimes a device may be collected physically but the passcode cannot be obtained to unlock the device and conduct a logical collection. In these instances, a physical collection will suffice.

Device Damage

If a mobile device is damaged (such as by exposure to water, a broken USB connection, or a damaged electrical system or circuit board), the device should first be examined physically using non-invasive methods and then using invasive methods if needed. In some cases, the examiner has only one chance to obtain data from the mobile device, and the only connection that can be made requires using an invasive technique. Because a damaged mobile device is unlikely to be able to be examined both physically and logically, a physical examination may be the only option. However, every attempt should be made to collect the device logically after completing a physical collection.

Initial Documentation

The documentation stage, which should occur just prior to collection, enables the examiner to capture not only the device details, but all associated materials. Having photographic evidence of the device, UICC, battery, and media card not only enables the examiner to complete a detailed report, but it will also help when the device has to be reassembled!

Tip Photographs and documentation of the initial collection should detail every angle so that there is no question as to which device a card or battery belongs with. In addition, when examining multiple pieces of electronic evidence, never pile the UICC cards together, to avoid the tedious task of identifying which UICC goes with which device later on.

Photo documentation should begin as soon as the evidence is received. The outside of each evidence container should be clearly visible in each photograph. In addition, the chain of custody form should be clearly visible, and if an evidence seal is used, it should also be photographed to show it has not been manipulated or tampered with. When the evidence is removed from the evidence container, it should be photographed immediately to include all pieces that are within the container; the associated case number should also be clearly visible, as shown in Figure 8-1. The same procedure should be completed with each evidence container prior to beginning the individual examination of the artifacts; the examiner should

FIGURE 8-1 A Kindle Fire mobile device shown alongside the UICC card, both a part of Case# 15-225, item K

be sure to return the evidence to each container after completing the documentation and examination. This will ensure that evidence items from different containers do not commingle.

Each container may contain multiple artifacts, but a single artifact (such as a mobile device or media card) should be removed from one container at a time. Each item should be photo documented in great detail and examined individually prior to the extraction of data from the device. During the collection phase, only one piece of evidence should be out of the container at a time. This helps ensure that items that are not part of the current case or extraction are not introduced to the evidence for the current case; this can easily occur if multiple devices are lying around with loose UICC or memory cards.

The following sections offer descriptions and information regarding handling the various types of evidence encountered during a mobile device exam and the proper ways of documenting each artifact. Order of documentation depends upon the power status of the device, on or off, and typically defines the documentation phase. A diagram showing the process for documenting mobile device evidence is shown in Figure 8-2.

Device

If the device is powered on and isolated from the network, documentation should include a clear image depicting the device within the isolation environment; if the device is in airplane mode, the image can be taken outside of an isolation environment. Also, a photograph should document the current display of the device that clearly shows the device carrier, date, time, and desktop or main screen. Documenting the date and time on the device is extremely important during the examination phase of the extracted data. This information is often critical in an investigation; the owner of a collected mobile device can change its date and time in an effort to throw off the examiner, for example, if this detail is critical to text messages, e-mails, or device use. Without this information, the collected data from the mobile device can be extremely confusing.

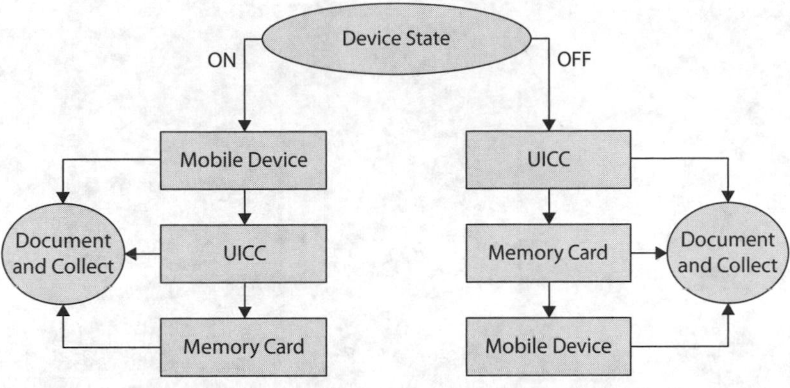

FIGURE 8-2 Using the device state as a cue to the documentation phase can help the examiner develop a systematic approach while maintaining power to the device if needed.

Note Documenting the initial screen was especially important with early-model Nokia mobile devices that lost the date and time and GMT (Greenwich Mean Time) offset when the battery was removed. Documenting the screen would allow the examiner to reset the date and time if needed to the proper time or use the offset information when converting dates that were extracted.

The back of the device and the USB connection should also be photographed to detail any imperfections, damage, or obstructions. This can help to dispel any allegations that the device was damaged during the examination process. Photographs should be taken of the device within its protective case, if applicable, and then outside of the case, including images of the front, back, and sides. It is important that the sides of a mobile device be photographed to show the location of a memory card slot. After a memory card slot is located, the protective flap should be carefully moved to photograph whether a memory card is inserted or not; the card should not be removed. With a device that is powered on, the collection phase of the examination would start at the completion of the device documentation.

Tip Some devices, such as those in the Apple family, show clear model numbers on the exterior rear of the device. Be sure to document these numbers clearly.

If the device is powered off, the order of documentation is considerably different, with the exception of the initial photographs of the exterior of the device. The first few photographs should be of the front, back, sides, and USB connection with the case on (if applicable), and then with the case removed. These images will be used to identify the device and also document the current state of the device. If the device has a battery compartment, it should be opened and photographed. With the battery compartment exposed but the battery not removed, the examiner should locate and photograph the memory card and UICC slot if visible. Sometimes the memory card and UICC slot are under the battery, and the battery will have to be removed. Removing the battery should expose the device serial numbers, device information, the memory card, and UICC if available (see Figure 8-3).

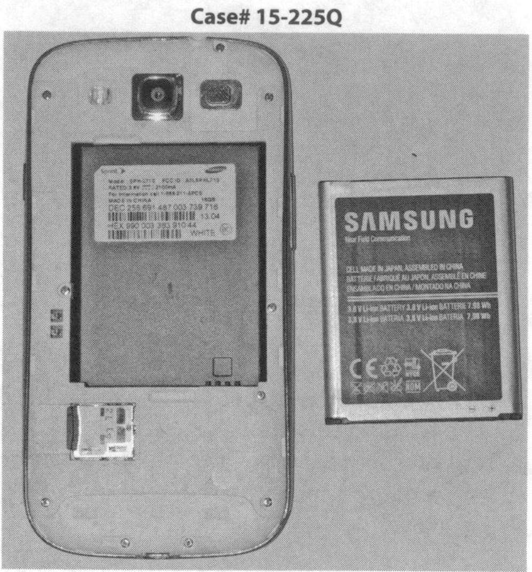

FIGURE 8-3 **The serial numbers of the device should be clearly visible, along with the memory card still in place.**

Tip Some devices, such as those in the Apple family, do not allow the battery to be accessed and do not have memory cards.

Battery

If the device is powered on, the battery should not be photographed or accessed until after the device has been successfully collected logically. If the device battery is accessed while powered on, the device may lose power, and if security is enabled, the device may be locked. After a device that is powered on has been successfully processed, logical access can be made to the battery compartment to complete the documentation, as described next when dealing with a device that is powered off.

If the device is powered off and the battery has been photographed in the device, the battery should be removed and photographed. The front, back, and sides should be photographed, and any distortions to the battery should be indicated. A failing battery should be documented, which is generally noticeable by a bulge in the center of the battery (Figure 8-4).

Note "Thermal runaway" is a phenomenon caused by the battery failing to dissipate heat faster than it is generated, and the increased temperature of the battery distorts the plastic container, causing the battery to appear bloated.

Prior to starting an examination of the mobile device, a new battery should be used because of the possibility that the damaged battery may breach and subsequently damage the mobile device.

FIGURE 8-4 A normal battery (front) and a bloated battery (back). The middle of the back battery is distended and could explode, causing damage to the evidence.

UICC

If the device is powered on, the UICC should not be removed until after a logical collection has been completed successfully. Access to most UICC cards is via the battery compartment, and removing the UICC card may allow the device to lose power. If a device loses power, and if security was enabled, the device may lock and a logical examination would not be possible. After a device has been processed logically, the process to document the UICC card can be followed for a device that is powered off.

Note Some devices can contain multiple UICC slots, and if more than one UICC is located, all should be documented as indicated in this section.

If the device is powered off, the UICC may be in various locations, depending upon the device family. For iOS devices, the UICC slot is located on the top or side of the device. For most other devices, the UICC is in the battery compartment. The UICC location should be photographed in place prior to removal. Once removed, the UICC should be marked with the case number and evidence number if it has not been marked already. This marking should not obstruct the serial numbers on the exterior of the card. The UICC should also be photographed alongside the mobile device it was removed from; the UICC serial number, or the ICCID (Integrated Circuit Card Identifier), should be clear in the photograph. This documentation can help identify that the UICC is associated with the device if this detail is challenged later. Both sides of the UICC should be photographed along with the case number and evidence number. The UICC can then be processed with mobile forensic tools, and a forensic clone can be created, if needed.

Once processed, the UICC should be taped to the mobile device's exterior, not reinserted into the device, because this would allow the device to communicate with a cellular network if the device was somehow powered on when repackaged. If a UICC must be inserted into the device, use the created forensic UICC instead of the original card. By taping the original UICC to the device, the examiner can be sure that the card will not be misplaced during the examination of other evidence and that it is matched with the device to which it belongs.

Memory Card

If the device is powered on, the memory should not be removed until after a logical collection has occurred successfully. Most mobile forensic tools will allow for the collection of data from these memory cards during an extraction, so removing a card while the device is powered on could miss critical data.

Tip Android devices containing external memory cards can corrupt the data on the memory card if it is removed while the device is powered on and not unmounted first. If the device is powered on, unmount the memory card prior to removal.

Access to some memory cards is via the battery compartment, and removing the memory card could allow the device to lose power and lock. After a device has been processed logically, document the memory card in the same way you would if the device were powered off.

If the device is powered off, the memory card location should be photographed prior to removing the card. The memory card slot is on the top or side of the mobile device, under the battery, or in the battery compartment. Once removed, the memory card should be marked with a case identifier and evidence number and photographed alongside the device. The media card can then be physically collected separate of the device and reinserted into the device when complete. If the device is going to be collected physically, the memory card can remain inserted; that way, if a logical examination is also performed, the memory card will be available.

Note Remember that all photographs should contain the case number and evidence number assigned to the article. Clearly photographing the progression of the collection will help for later documentation and also dispel any allegations of evidence tampering, destruction of evidence, or other issues.

JTAG or Chip-Off

If a mobile device examination will be at the level of a JTAG (Joint Test Action Group) or chip-off examination, documenting the internal components is also important. For both JTAG and chip-off examinations, prior to disassembly, the examiner should follow the previously listed steps to photograph the device and its components. Once the device is disassembled, the printed circuit board (PCB) should be photographed prior to making any connections. Once connections have been made to the JTAG test access ports (TAPs), a photograph should clearly document the connections to the ports. At the conclusion of the collection and removal of the connections, the printed circuit board should again be photographed and then again after the device is reassembled. For chip-off examinations, photographs of the memory chip should be taken prior to removal, after removal, after reballing (if applicable), and during a read of the memory chip.

Note The amount of documentation may seem extreme, but by showing the examination's progression and clearly showing that the chip in the device is the same chip that was collected can help immensely later if any challenges occur.

Isolation of the Mobile Device

The techniques or methods for isolating the device are often dictated by the device type. Whatever method or technique is employed, the isolation of the device must remain constant during the entire collection if the device is powered on. If the device can be collected while powered off, it is still a good idea to isolate the device if power is still available to it, because the device could be inadvertently powered on by the examiner or the software.

Several different isolation methods and techniques are covered in this section, from manually changing the device communication, to placing it in rooms devoid of radio waves. When selecting the type of isolation method, the examiner must remember that various factors can interfere with the technique's consistency and coverage. As outlined in Chapter 4, different frequency ranges are used by the various technologies built into a mobile device. The techniques used by the examiner should be tested on all frequencies encountered in the course of the examination.

If a device is not properly isolated from the network, data loss can result, because the cellar network, Wi-Fi network, and Bluetooth network offer a conduit to the device's internal file system—a mobile device can pair with an active Bluetooth device in the examiner's office, or it can authenticate on an open Wi-Fi guest network in the area. There might not be data loss, but the integrity of the data will be changed with the addition of information unrelated to the case. If the device accesses a cellular network or the Internet, a signal submitted to the device can also remotely wipe all the information from the device, making any type of recovery next to impossible. By following the simple steps and techniques covered in this section, an examiner should not have to worry about these types of scenarios.

Covered in detail in Chapter 4 are the various communication methods that are used in today's mobile devices: cellular, Wi-Fi, Bluetooth, and near field communication (NFC) are used for both the reception and transmission of data. These services should all be inhibited during the collection process when possible using one or multiple techniques outlined.

Note Some solutions such as Cellebrite UFED Touch and UFED 4PC, Micro Systemation XRY, and Oxygen Forensic Detective and Analyst, among others, have a function for extracting data from devices using Bluetooth technology. If Bluetooth is inhibited, data transfer cannot occur from the device to the forensic solution. In these cases, the device Bluetooth must be enabled.

Methods, Appliances, and Techniques for Isolating a Device

There are various ways to isolate a mobile device from the network, and their differences are many. Isolation products range in cost from free to thousands of dollars. Some signal isolation products are portable; some are not. Some products require practice to use; others do not. Each appliance the examiner will use must be vetted against real-world scenarios and tested prior to deciding upon the best solution, since many variables can affect even the most expensive appliances. Also, in some cases, an appliance is not needed and a method or technique can be used instead.

Before embarking on any isolation solution train, the examiner must test and retest the solution with live mobile devices where most of the mobile device collections are going to take place. If device collections will be conducted only at a lab, it makes it much easier for testing. However, if the scene of mobile device collections is always unknown, the examiner must ensure that the solution is suited to isolating the strongest signal that may be available. What makes the selection of a signal isolation tool so difficult at times is that the simple installation of a new cellular tower by a local carrier can render a signal isolation device unable to protect the device from unwanted signals. The distance to the nearest tower can affect the usefulness of the solution, simply because the closer the device is to the tower, the stronger and more concentrated the signal will be. Also, if an isolation solution had been successfully tested with a third-generation (3G) device but the device to be examined is capable of using a fourth-generation (4G) signal, the solution might not be rated to block those signals, which ultimately can breach the supported barrier and reach the device. Many free apps for iOS (available from the iTunes Store) and Android devices (on Google Play) can read the radio frequency (RF) signal strength in a particular area. Using these apps can help the examiner determine what course of action to take and whether a particular appliance will be effective.

Tip An app should be thoroughly tested prior to using it in an actual forensic environment, where real evidence will be examined. Also, during testing, the app should be installed to a controlled device, not to the device that is to be examined.

Sometimes, the easiest solution when deciding on a proper appliance is not to use an appliance at all. Several chapters have mentioned placing a device into airplane mode, a technique that is the easiest to use and at times the most difficult to convince examiners to use. It is easy because all modern mobile devices have an airplane function, which inhibits all forms of communication, but it's difficult for some examiners to embrace because the device must be manipulated—that is, buttons are pushed and screens are accessed. Some examiners believe doing this negatively impacts the device collection, but as mentioned in Chapter 4, placing a device into airplane mode is described in NIST and SANS documents as a viable technique to isolate a device.

If airplane mode is not available or the protocol requires that the examiner manipulate the device as little as possible, there could be another option. With GSM smart phones from Apple, Android, Windows Phone, and BlackBerry, the examiner can remove the UICC card and still process the mobile device. Without the UICC card, the device is effectively isolated from accessing the cellular network, but Bluetooth, NFC, and Wi-Fi can still be available. More information on processing mobile devices without UICC cards will be covered later in Chapter 9, but remember that the removal of a UICC card could mean the device must be powered off and any security feature that is active could be enabled. Because CDMA mobile devices operate primarily without a UICC, this method and approach will not work with those devices.

Tip If security is enabled, airplane mode can still be accessed for the smart devices outlined in Chapter 4. Because security is already enabled, the device can simply be powered off, because turning off the device is not going to lock the device further. The examiner should then research the device to determine how to process the locked device effectively.

If a device is powered on, the methods used to isolate it are similar no matter whether the device is GSM or CDMA, but they depend on security. If the mobile device does not have security enabled, both CDMA and GSM devices should be placed into a signal isolation appliance so that the examiner can visually see and manipulate the device.

Once inside the isolation appliance, the examiner can place the device into airplane mode and then remove the device from the appliance. Several available appliances will allow the examiner to see the device, push buttons, navigate capacitive screens, and even photograph it. Table 8-1 lists two appliances that have been used to process and interact with a mobile device in active investigations. Other isolation appliances that do not have the ability to connect to a computer are not listed in the table, but they are typically less expensive. At times, examiners have even used several wraps of aluminum foil or lined and unlined metal paint cans to isolate a mobile device during transport or while awaiting collection.

Note A study, "A Field Test of Mobile Phone Shielding Devices," was conducted in 2010 at Purdue University that tested various RF-isolation appliances and mobile devices. The testing involved sending various messages and content to mobile devices while they were inside an appliance. No appliance tested passed at 100 percent signal blocking 100 percent of the time, so be careful when using any isolation appliance.

A signal isolation appliance enables the examiner to fix portable power, access external USB connections, conform to capacitive screens on today's mobile devices, and view the device through a transparent window. The appliance can be connected directly to a power source and a computer and easily monitored. This technique can be used when the examiner does not want to remove the device from the appliance or navigate the device to locate airplane mode. When the examiner can keep the device in the same isolation appliance, whether at the lab or on scene, outside contamination by both radio signals and the various people who come into contact with the mobile device can be minimized.

Tip Signal isolation bags are made of interwoven metal fibers that degrade over time, leaving gaps where signals can escape and enter. Because this degradation is not visible, it is important to replace these bags frequently and handle them with care.

TABLE 8-1 **Appliances Used to Process and Interact with a Mobile Device in Active Investigations**

Name	Company	Description
STE3000F2	Ramsey Electronics (ramseytest.com)	Hardware case, large enclosure, power, USB 2.0 support, ability to interact with device from exterior
SFP1218	Select Fabricators (select-fabricators.com)	Soft portable enclosure, USB 2.0 support, viewable window, ability to interact with device from exterior

Some techniques and methods are specific to the type of mobile device (that is, CMDA or GSM). Because of these differences, each technology is discussed in a separate section.

CDMA (Code Division Multiple Access) Devices

CDMA devices can be isolated using appliance-based solutions (such as isolation bags and boxes) and airplane mode if they are powered on, but some CDMA devices can also be processed without powering them on, bypassing security. When connected with a USB cable that allows charging and data transfer, CDMA devices—feature phones, in particular—often have enough power to be recognized by the computer. Once the device is recognized, a driver is loaded, and the mobile device can be processed as if the device were powered on.

Tip Carefully monitor the CDMA device when plugging the device into the computer, because some devices will start a boot-up process.

If the CDMA feature phone is powered off, removing the battery and then plugging the device into the computer with a charging cable seldom boots the device. However, when the battery is attached to the device and then plugged in, the phone booting sequence would begin. For smart devices of today, the device cannot receive enough power to allow the computer to recognize the device and load a driver, so this option is not available.

GSM (Global Systems for Mobile Communication) Devices

For GSM devices, creating a forensic subscriber identity module (SIM) clone can effectively isolate a device from the cellular network. Because a feature/legacy CDMA device does not contain a card to access and authenticate on a cellular network, this process will not pertain to these devices, only to GSM. Why not just remove the UICC from the mobile device and in that way isolate the device? This would be the best course of action, and it has already been established that removing the UICC in a smart device such as an Android, Apple, BlackBerry, and Windows Phone still allows for the collection of the device's data. However, this is not always the case, especially with feature phones. By removing a UICC from a feature phone, forensic software is unable to communicate with the majority of handsets, and examiners are forced to take isolation of the mobile device seriously. Because the UICC must stay within the feature phone for a logical forensic examination to be successful, the device must be isolated correctly. This is why a forensic SIM clone is needed.

Note The term "forensic SIM clone" was coined in a paper I wrote in 2008 called "SIMs and Salsa," which outlined the vulnerabilities of U.S. cell carriers and showed how a forensic SIM could be created without the original SIM card. Some of the content is used in this section to describe the process of creating a forensic SIM.

In essence, the examiner will create a SIM card that will satisfy the mobile device's need for specific files, the IMSI (International Mobile Subscriber Identity) and the ICCID. Here's an excerpt from my 2008 paper, "SIMs and Salsa":

> The two files we will focus on in this document are the ICCID … and the IMSI…. We will be focusing on these two important files because these files are needed to complete a Forensic SIM Clone™ and effectively isolate the device from the cellular network. To further elaborate, some handsets only need the IMSI, while some need only the ICCID and in some cases the device needs both the ICCID and IMSI.
>
> Mobile Forensics, Inc. coined the term Forensic SIM Clone because the completion of this method should not be considered in anyway a "clone" in the sense that the card is a duplicate of the original SIM. If that were the case then we have not effectively isolated the clone from the network because if it is a duplicate of the evidence all the network information still resides on the handset. If this network information still resides on the cloned card we know that the cellular network can add, delete or change data on the handset. Hence "Forensic" was added because all the network information is nonexistent.

The question asked by students and examiners alike is, "Why not just place a foreign SIM into the device so the device has a SIM and the forensic software can then process the device logically? Just place a T-Mobile SIM card into a T-Mobile phone, right?" Completing this type of process would result in dire consequences, however, because the mobile device would reject the SIM card and undoubtedly purge data, as the expected files (IMSI and/or ICCID) were not there. Most often, call logs would be deleted, but the deletion of images and videos was also observed on early iDEN (Integrated Digital Enhanced Network) model devices. To create a proper forensic SIM clone, the proper IMSI and ICCID must be obtained from the original SIM. If the examiner does not have the original SIM card or the original SIM card is locked, proper paperwork would have to be submitted to the carrier of record for the mobile device to obtain both the IMSI and ICCID. With both the ICCID and IMSI, a forensic SIM could be created manually onto a GSM test card and inserted into the mobile device. This, however, does not always work for the reasons outlined in another excerpt from "SIMs and Salsa":

> What if the original SIM card is PIN locked? SIM card is gone? Damaged? For starters, if the SIM is PIN locked you are limited by the inability of most logical software to process the device. Again, I say logical, we will discuss physical software shortly. We know if the SIM PIN is locked, the ICCID is still readable. This is due to the fact the ICCID does not need a security condition to be satisfied to be read. Reading the ICCID is easy, but how about the IMSI? Well, the opposite is true for the IMSI. The IMSI does have a security condition, the PIN. Unfortunately if we do not have the PIN we cannot satisfy the condition to read the IMSI. Without the IMSI we cannot in confidence create a Forensic SIM Clone that the device will not think is foreign. So how do we obtain the IMSI?
>
> There are three methods that can help with this dilemma.
>
> - Send court order to cellular carrier
> - Obtain the IMSI from physical memory
> - Or create the IMSI yourself

> I am sure you are aware of the first solution. By sending a valid court order to the carrier they can supply the last IMSI utilized by the device and matches the ICCID you have supplied. The second way mentioned involves using specialized hardware/software to obtain RAW data from the device and then parse the data, recovering the last IMSI or last IMSIs of the SIM. The examiner can then manually type this information into the MFI Forensic SIM Cloner application and create a Forensic SIM Clone. I am sure you are wondering about the third situation, creating the IMSI yourself.

Here's an elaboration on the first condition outlined in the document in reference to obtaining a valid IMSI from the carrier: If a user contacts the carrier to obtain a new SIM card because the old card has been lost, the information from the old SIM will be lost and the information (IMSI) returned will be incorrect for the device. This would mean a failure in creating a forensic SIM clone, so obtaining information from a carrier does not always mean obtaining the correct information to compile a forensic SIM manually. Obtaining the IMSI from physical memory of a device was a better method, and once this was obtained, it could be used to create a forensic SIM card and obtain access to the device.

Note To automate the process of both reading an original SIM and then writing to a test card, I created the MFI Forensic SIM Cloner (which is no longer available). All major commercial mobile forensic solutions now support the creation of forensic SIM cards when needed.

The creation of a forensic SIM card with today's investigations is generally not needed simply because the majority of devices that need to be processed and collected are smart devices. To reiterate, a smart device can be forensically collected without a UICC card, unlike legacy feature phones of the past.

Mobile Device Processing Workflow

As you know, the examiner should follow a process for every mobile device examination. If proper isolation techniques have been followed, the recommended methods for processing a mobile device depend on whether the device is powered *off* or *on*. Several pieces of evidence can be collected with a mobile device, and each must be treated as a single piece of evidence during the processing phase. Figure 8-5 represents the suggested ordering of processing for various situations, and the following sections offer information on how to process the device in various situations.

Device is powered on and unlocked Evidence processing should be conducted in this order:

1. **Mobile device** The mobile device should be processed logically, and when the examiner is satisfied with the results, it should be processed physically, if possible.
2. **UICC** The smart card should be processed, obtaining the complete file system.
3. **Memory card** The memory card should be processed outside of the body of the mobile device and a physical image created.

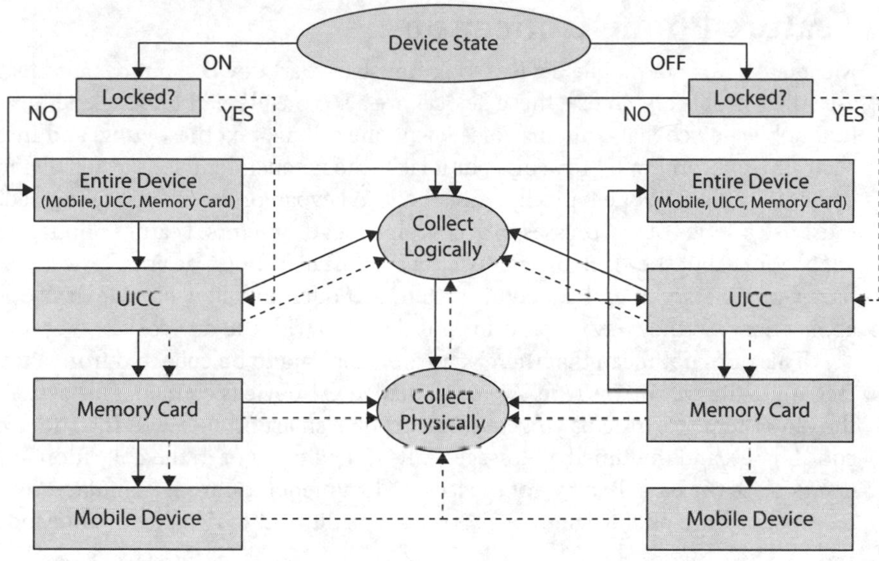

FIGURE 8-5 Mobile device evidence processing workflow

Device is powered on and locked Evidence processing should be conducted in this order:

1. **UICC** The smart card should be processed, obtaining the complete file system.
2. **Memory card** The memory card should be processed outside of the body of the mobile device and a physical image created.
3. **Mobile device** The mobile device should be processed, physically if possible. If a physical image is obtained, obtaining security information for bypass from the physical image may be necessary to then conduct a logical examination.

Device is powered off Evidence processing should be conducted in this order:

1. **UICC** The smart card should be processed, obtaining the complete file system.
2. **Memory card** The memory card should be processed outside of the body of the mobile device and a physical image created.
3. **Mobile device** The mobile device should be powered on and if not locked, the mobile device should be processed logically; when the examiner is satisfied with the results, it should be processed physically.

Device was powered off but is now powered on and locked If the examiner turns on a mobile device and it is locked, the UICC and memory card should have already been processed. The final processing would involve only the mobile device.

- **Mobile device** The mobile device should be processed, physically if possible. If a physical image is obtained, obtaining security information for bypass from the physical image may be necessary to then conduct a logical examination.

Feature Phone Collections

Most collections of mobile devices today involve smart devices, but because feature phones are still available and in use, these devices are also considered here. In general, a *feature phone* is a mobile device that contains voice telephone calling, text messaging, and Internet features such as e-mail and web browsing, but it lacks the independent apps available for a smart device. A feature phone typically uses a built-in keypad or a number dialing pad, and the user must use a series of key presses to access alphabet characters. Feature phones do have built-in applications, but they lack the ability either to install or upgrade apps. These devices generally have a proprietary or embedded file system that does not allow outside developers to create applications, so they rely on built-in apps that ship with the device.

This does not mean that there is no available data to be collected from a feature phone—in fact, quite the contrary is true. As mentioned, these devices contain a file system, and within the file system are artifacts you could expect on a smart phone, with Internet histories, GPS coordinates, and multimedia messages. The difficulty is not in the collection, but in the decoding of the data. Because of the lack of documentation from manufacturers (for obvious reasons), feature phone data repositories can be difficult to decipher and decode.

Note This is not an exhaustive list of feature phones, and some devices may support only the extraction of a small subset of the proposed list. The type of data that can be extracted varies, and the software that is used to complete the extraction should be consulted to see what data should be expected.

Connecting to the Feature Phone

The examiner should research to determine the best way to connect to a feature phone using available forensic software. Connection can be via USB, Bluetooth, or IrDA (Infrared Data Association). If the device has been isolated within an appliance, generally the only available connection method will be USB, so determining the software capabilities could impact the isolation mechanism, technique, or appliance. Once the connection method has been determined, the examiner should research whether or not the device must be placed into a certain mode to conduct a transfer to a mobile forensic solution. For example, to connect to a Nokia 5300 device and many other Nokia feature phones, the device must be placed into Nokia Mode by navigating to the appropriate menu on the device after a USB cable has been attached to the computer and to the phone. If the device is not in the correct mode, forensic software solutions will not be able to connect and collect the user data. The examiner should research data transfer methods and any specific settings by reviewing the model's user manual prior to beginning a collection. These manuals are easily located on the manufacturer's site, Phone Scoop (phonescoop.com), or GSMArena (GSMArena.com). Having a clear idea on how the connection will be made before beginning will save the examiner time when and if problems are encountered during the connection process.

Most connections to feature phones are made via a USB connector on the device. Feature phone USB connections have never been regulated, so many different types of connectors have been used, which can make connecting to the many devices difficult at times. All USB connections, however, communicate using specific pins on the USB head connected to the pins on the exposed USB connection on the phone. If any of the pins on either the cable or device are corroded, missing, or nonoperational, a connection cannot be made. The examiner should carefully inspect both the cable pin connections and the connections on the device to ensure a successful connection and data collection. If any debris is seen inside of the USB connection port, the examiner can use a small wire brush to clear it away. After a successful connection to the computer using a USB cable, the device is recognized and driver installation begins.

Note If a cable with a serial-to-USB converter (such as Prolific or FTDI) is used, the examiner cannot be sure that a successful connection has been made to the device until a forensic software solution is used. Because the installed driver is for the cable and not the device, the examiner may be required to reexamine the device if the software cannot connect.

If a connection cannot be made and a driver does not load, the examiner can check the type of cable that is being used (see Figure 8-6). Some USB cables are for charging only and do not allow data transfer. Because specific pins are used to charge and others are used to transmit and receive data, a faulty cable may be a charging cable that does not have the Tx (Transmit) and Rx (Receive) pins. The examiner can exchange the cable with another cable that is known to be a data transfer cable.

Device State Considerations

In order for a driver to install successfully and a solid connection to be made, the feature phone must be at least 50 percent charged or be connected using a charging cable. A charging cable has an extra pin that allows the device to receive power from the USB hub on the computer while connected. This is a good alternative if the device does not have a 50 percent charge and time is critical.

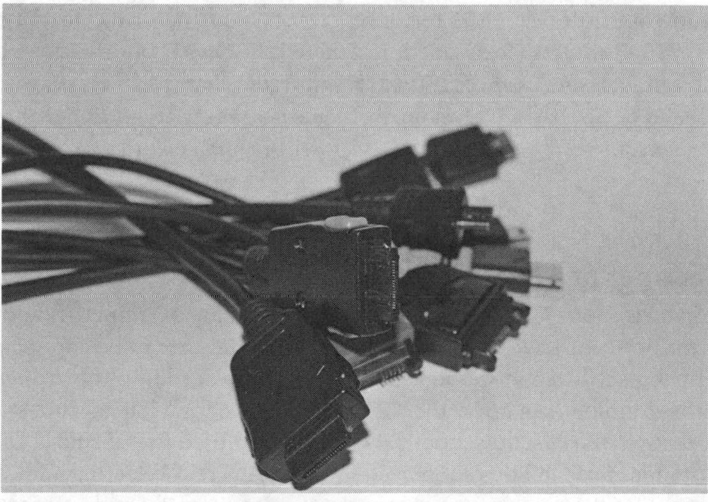

FIGURE 8-6 **The many different types of cables used for feature phones can make collecting data difficult at times.**

If a device does not have enough power when it is connected to the mobile forensic solution and computer, failure during processing may occur, such as the inability to recognize the device driver, collection failure, or a successful collection but incomplete data. A computer communicates with the mobile device through the driver, and if the device does not have enough power to bridge the two devices, run system processes, and keep the phone functioning, this communication will not occur. When power is not sufficient or available, the driver either fails to load or ceases functioning at some point.

A failed collection is obvious to the examiner, because the software crashes or returns information identifying that connection cannot be made to the device and to reconnect and try again. Receiving this error during the collection can be frustrating, but it can be managed. Even if a device is not sufficiently charged, some software will return the collected data as though a successful collection had been achieved, but closer inspection will show that data is missing. This consequence can be devastating, because the examiner believes that no error has occurred and considers the collection complete. In fact, NIST, as part of its testing for mobile forensic software, disconnected a device that is being collected to determine whether this effect can occur to the software. The resulting physical disconnection of the device is similar to the behavior of a device that is 50 percent charged, and, as NIST notes, some software solutions do not indicate to the user a failure has occurred.

Consequences of Insufficient Device Power

During a class, while students were using Paraben Device Seizure, we witnessed a phenomenon that confirmed that battery condition and power really do matter for a successful collection. The mobile devices all contained the same information to allow instruction to flow efficiently for the class, with 25 text messages and 30 contacts. The feature phones used in class were sometimes not fully charged, and after a student reported that he acquired only 15 of the 25 text messages and 8 of the 30 contacts, I made a closer inspection of the device. All 25 text messages could be manually located on the device as well as the 30 contacts. The student reacquired the device, but this time, only 14 messages and 10 contacts were extracted. The student stated that the device battery light was flashing and needed to be charged. Over lunch, the device was charged, and upon returning, the student reacquired the device with Device Seizure and all data was successfully extracted.

Collecting the Device Logically

If the feature phone is powered on and not locked, the examiner should first attempt a logical collection after the device has been isolated. The device can be connected to the computer using the prescribed and supported methods and placed into the proper mode if applicable. Next, the examiner can apply the solution of choice for a logical collection.

A *file system collection* should always be attempted first if such a collection is not a part of the standard capabilities supported by the software. Collecting a file system of a feature phone enables the examiner to demonstrate unequivocally in documentation and testimony where data came from during the logical collection of the phone. Too often, examiners simply allow the software to identify the data (such as contacts, call logs, and Short Messaging Service

[SMS]) without completely comprehending where the actual file that contains this data "lives" within the device's embedded file system. When a file system is extracted from a feature phone, however, this is no longer a limitation, because the file is available for inspection, examination, hashing, and documentation.

If a file system option is not available or has already been completed, the examiner can obtain a *surface collection* of user data—this WYSIWYG extraction uses device protocols to query the device files, parse the extracted information, and present the data to the examiner in the solution interface. This type of logical collection can be compared to navigating the mobile device interface to locate the information and then using the software to extract that same information into the forensic solution. Typical feature phone surface collections include contacts, call logs, SMS, Multimedia Messaging Service (MMS), calendar, notes, and media.

Having this information immediately available can help steer any additional follow-up and also help to identify areas of interest to the examiner during a file system examination and after the device is collected physically. The biggest benefit to conducting a logical collection as a first step with a feature phone is ease of collection and support. Most feature phones that are not disabled by the carrier can be collected logically by most mobile forensic solutions with a USB cable, and most surface data can be parsed. However, obtaining the file system of a feature phone along with the surface data is recommended.

Associated Evidence (UICC and Memory Cards)

Feature phones also can contain a UICC and memory cards. As mentioned, each item should be treated as a separate piece of evidence. Following the recommended guidelines on processing, the examiner should examine the UICC and memory card first if the device is powered off and last if the device is powered on. Collecting each card individually outside the body of the mobile device is important, because it will assist the examiner in collecting much more information that can be used later in the investigation if needed.

UICC With feature phones, the UICC can contain much more evidence than would be found on a smart device's UICC and should not be ignored. Because of the limitations on the internal storage of a feature phone, some valuable information is stored on the UICC, including text messages and contacts. This storage setting can be controlled within the device by the phone's user.

Most mobile forensic tools will allow some information to be read from the UICC from within the mobile device during a standard logical collection. Unfortunately, this information is very limited. The examiner should always collect the UICC outside of the body of the device, to enable the UICC and its complete file system to be collected and later examined. When conducting a collection of a UICC, the examiner should make sure that the forensic tool allows for a full file system collection of the card, not just the surface data. With the file system, the examiner can verify and validate the data that has been parsed and displayed and locate additional information, as outlined in Chapter 9.

Memory Card Generally a memory card within a feature phone contains far less data than a memory card in a smart device, but some newer Nokia feature phone devices contain a 32GB card. Typically the smaller size limitation has to do with the phone's internal capacities to recognize larger memory cards. During a logical examination, the memory card can be read by most forensic software while it is within the phone, so the card should not be removed until this is complete. Once the memory card is removed, the examiner should also physically read the card using a forensic tool that will allow for the creation of a forensic image of a mass storage device. AccessData FTK Imager is a free alternative for creating a forensic image, along with paid commercial tools from Guidance Software (EnCase), AccessData (MPE+), Cellebrite (Physical Analyzer), and several others.

Tip When creating an image of a memory card using one of the mentioned tools, the examiner should be sure to have a write-blocking mechanism or appliance in place. Doing so will disable the abilities of the software to write to the evidence.

The creation of a physical image will allow for a deeper analysis of the memory card, which will include unallocated space and file slack, which generally contains deleted data. This type of data is not recoverable when the memory card is within the device and standard logical collection has taken place.

Collecting the Device Physically

If the feature phone has been powered off and is locked or disabled, or after completing a logical extraction of the mobile device, the examiner should do a physical collection of the device. A physical collection of a feature phone is critical and advisable in all situations if the device is supported for a simple reason: deleted data is almost never available in a feature phone's file system with a logical collection. If deleted data is required for a case, a physical collection of a feature phone is necessary.

Cellebrite supports the most feature phones for both GSM and CDMA physically, with Micro Systemation coming in second because of its limited CDMA support. Unlike a smart phone, a feature phone's physical image includes only a small part of the device's internal memory. With a feature phone's memory measured in megabytes, this does not yield a lot of additional data, but when possible a physical image should be obtained.

When collecting a feature phone physically with a mobile forensic tool, the examiner should remove the UICC and the memory card from the device prior to starting the acquisition. Methods for obtaining a physical collection of feature phones were derived from the methods and code used by service tools, as discussed in Chapter 6. Overheating has been known to occur during acquisition, which could damage the UICC and memory card if they are inserted in the device at the time of the physical collection. Also, the UICC and memory card are not needed, nor are they a part of the area the tool will read to obtain the internal memory area.

If using other means, such as a flasher box, JTAG, or chip-off, the examiner should follow the procedures described in Chapter 6. Prior to the examiner beginning the physical acquisition, it is critical that a logical collection occur.

After a collection is completed, the examiner can analyze the information obtained in the physical collection. This is a labor-intensive process, because a lot of forensic tools currently do not support the decoding of the feature phone's file system. Tools such as Micro Systemation XRY and Cellebrite Physical Analyzer do allow for the decoding of many feature phone file systems. These file systems can then be compared with the logical extraction during the critical data analysis phase. File system and data analysis for feature phones are covered in Chapter 9.

Archiving the Data

During each phase of the feature phone collection, all data collected from the logical collection to the UICC and memory card, to the physical acquisition of each image, along with all associated data, should be securely stored on an evidence drive prior to the examiner beginning the analysis phase. This storage location should use a unique name that pertains to the case or investigation. All subsequent analysis will be on a copy of the data that was collected during the primary acquisition. By doing this, the examiner is never working on the original data from any phase. By archiving data, the examiner can be assured that if the software or computer malfunctions, the original evidence will still be available if a new examination of the data must occur.

BlackBerry Collections

BlackBerry devices were once prevalent in many examinations, but today, in my experience, they account for less than 5 percent of investigations. BlackBerry devices were one of the most easily collected devices by forensic software, but now they are one of the most difficult. Early BlackBerry devices' content, backup, and storage methods were documented and available to developers all the way up to version 7. Because of this level of documentation, software vendors and open source engineers built tools to mimic BlackBerry desktop software to create a local backup of the device and then parse the resultant files. This method drastically changed with the release of BlackBerry 10, an operating system built from scratch. With this new file system, along with the methods a version 10 device uses to create a backup, forensic tools have a difficult time producing usable evidence.

Connecting to a BlackBerry Device

As with all mobile forensic solutions, the connection to a BlackBerry device requires a USB cable—either a mini USB or micro USB connection. Like any other mobile device, the BlackBerry must be isolated using an appropriate isolation method or appliance.

Note BlackBerry was the first reported smart device that could be remotely wiped using settings within the phone. This was first reported on the forums at crackberry.com in 2008 when BlackBerry had not even added the feature to its user guide. However, this feature was used by a criminal to wipe his BlackBerry while it was being transported to be examined, and the story is often used in forensic training classes.

If a BlackBerry is powered on and locked, the examiner must know the password to access the device. Also, if the BlackBerry has encryption turned on, a secondary password might be requested, which could be different from the first. If either password is not known, the examiner will not be able to connect to the device using a USB cable; however, connection to any other associated artifact (such as the UICC and memory card) can still be attempted.

Device State Considerations

If possible, the examiner needs to know the BlackBerry access passwords, whether the device is controlled by a BES (BlackBerry Enterprise Server) or the device is unlocked. By having both passwords (handset and encryption), the examiner will be able to conduct a logical or physical collection. If the device is set up with a BES, the administrator of the BES can disable or enable the password and encryption for the device, if needed.

For BlackBerry 7 and older devices, the examiner will recognize that a device is locked by the padlock icon that is displayed in the lower-right corner of the screen. If the device is also encrypted, another padlock will be visible in the upper left. The device will have to be unlocked using the previous suggestions or by enabling the info.mkf file on the memory card. This file is available only on the memory card at /BlackBerry/system/ if the device is locked and the card has been encrypted using either the BlackBerry Security Password or Device Password mode. If this is the case, the examiner can use the Elcomsoft Phone Breaker tool to obtain the password. This method will not uncover all passwords, especially if they are complex, unless a dictionary has been compiled. The password, if obtained, can then be used to create a backup of the device.

On BlackBerry 10 devices, security is similar to prior versions with device passwords, device encryption, and media card security and encryption. One difference, however, is that locked version 10 devices cannot be accessed using the info.mkf memory card file. If a device is locked, the only way to bypass security and obtain a forensic image is by obtaining the password or the BES 10 admin resetting the password if possible.

Collecting the Device Logically

If the device is powered on and the examiner has access to the device with disabled security, he or she can perform a logical extraction using most mobile forensic software. This involves attaching a USB cable, plugging the cable into the computer, and selecting the device to be collected. The software will perform a backup of the device, similar to the backup functions in the BlackBerry Desktop software, and then parse out the database files for supported user data files. The BlackBerry collection does not contain a typical file system as you would expect, but a listing of all of the database files from the device. In a logical collection, it is important that the software enables the examiner to access each of the database files, regardless of the software's ability to parse out the user information. In other words, the examiner should be able to examine the complete set of files collected from the BlackBerry device to verify and validate the solution's parsing ability as well as uncover additional data the solution might not be currently able to extract.

Note Current mobile forensic tools do not support the collection of a BlackBerry 10 device directly, but some can produce a backup and then conduct an analysis. This method will be explained later in the section.

Much like a feature phone, if the BlackBerry also contains a UICC and memory card, the artifacts should be removed and processed. However, because of the limitations also imposed on a physical collection by a locked device, a physical collection should be attempted before an acquisition of the UICC and memory card if the device is unlocked. If the device is locked or powered off and known to be locked, the UICC and memory card can be processed first as described in the preceding section, making sure a physical collection of the memory card takes place.

Collecting the Device Physically

The collection of a BlackBerry device physically using a USB connection is limited to a small number of devices and even a smaller set of forensic tools. Cellebrite UFED Touch currently supports physical collection of 50 various CDMA and GSM devices, as indicated in its current supported devices list (cellebrite.com/mobile-forensics/support/ufed-supported-devices), but the device password must also be known. Currently BlackBerry 10 devices are not supported for a physical collection by any tools via a USB connection.

JTAG can be used on locked devices if the password is not known, but this technique is relegated to older devices because BlackBerry has made the TAPs extremely difficult, if not impossible, to use. The only alternative method would be an invasive physical examination. The chip-off method can be used on devices up to but not including BlackBerry 10, and the created binary file can be examined and decoded using Cellebrite Physical Analyzer or Oxygen Forensic Analyst. However, even when the chip-off method is used, examining BlackBerry 10 devices is impossible because the data is encrypted at the chip level. So even with a successful binary dump, the data could be unreadable and unusable.

Additional Collection Methods

Both free and commercial mobile forensic solutions use the same protocols used by the manufacturer's software, and at times using the software developed by the manufacturer can be beneficial. However, the BlackBerry software up to version 7.x, BlackBerry Desktop Manager, also allows data to be restored and synced to a connected device, so the examiner must be careful when using a software tool that can synchronize data to a device being examined. BlackBerry 10 devices now use BlackBerry Link, which also allows the device to be backed up and restored. Currently available tools cannot complete a backup of a BlackBerry 10 device independent of using the BlackBerry Link software. Furthermore, the output file that is created by the software is encrypted and unable to be parsed by most currently available software, with two exceptions. Oxygen and Elcomsoft both support the ability to open BlackBerry backups from BlackBerry 10 devices.

BlackBerry Desktop Backup Software To create a backup of a BlackBerry device successfully using BlackBerry Desktop Manager software, the examiner must first install and properly configure the software, which can be downloaded from http://us.blackberry.com/software/desktop.html. Both Mac and Windows are supported. The examiner should make sure to disable automatic syncing upon connection and ensure that auto mount is disabled on the forensic computer so the memory card is not altered by the operating system. When the examiner sets up the device, My Computer's Date And Time With My Device should be unchecked, as shown in Figure 8-7. The BlackBerry can then be backed up.

Blackberry IPD and BBB Backup Files An IPD (Inter@ctive Pager Database) backup file is produced with the BlackBerry Desktop software running on Windows machines up to version 7, and a BlackBerry Backup (BBB) file is produced on the Mac versions of BlackBerry Desktop up to version 7 of the BlackBerry software. The IPD is a single file that contains multiple other database files that make up the content on the BlackBerry device. The Mac BBB file (up to version 7) is a compressed IPD file. At version 7.1, BlackBerry transitioned to

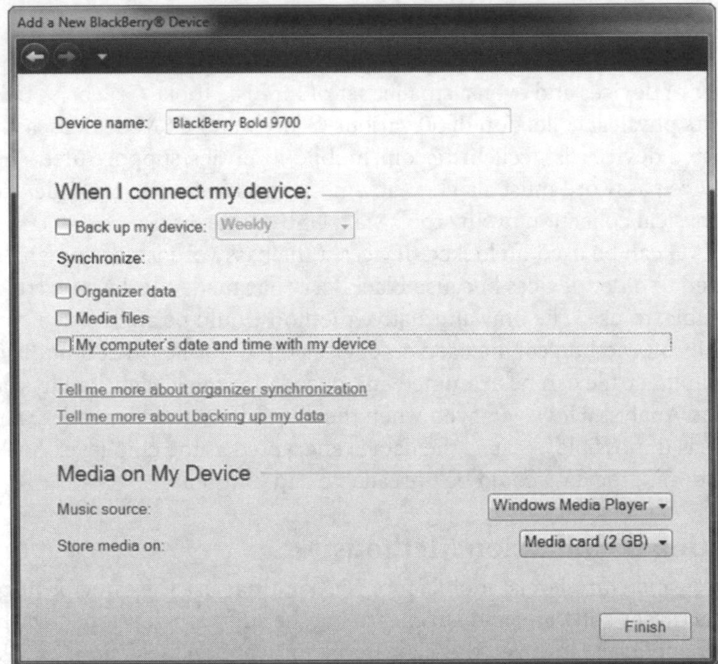

FIGURE 8-7 **Disable the synchronization feature before connecting the device.**

creating BBB files on both Mac and Windows machines using BlackBerry Desktop, and the BBB is still a compressed file, but it now comprises .dat files. Each .dat file contained various data and data types. BlackBerry Desktop is no longer updated by BlackBerry because the company is transitioning users to the BlackBerry Link solution.

BlackBerry Link also creates a BBB file that differs from the Desktop BBB file. The difference is encryption: the newer BBB file is fully encrypted independent of user interaction on the device or within the Link software. This means that if a backup is going to be read within a forensic software solution, the examiner must have a key piece of information: the BlackBerry Link password associated with the BlackBerry user account. Technically, the examiner will need both the user account associated with the device and the password, but current software, like Oxygen Forensic Analyst which supports the analysis of BlackBerry 10 devices, reads the user ID from the manifest and requests only the associated password. What can cause difficulty is the fact that the Link password is completely independent of the device password, so even if the device password is known for the BlackBerry 10 device and it is unlocked, the collected backup might still not be able to be examined if the Link password is unknown. The BlackBerry Link password must be used to decrypt the files to enable the software solution to parse the available user data. Furthermore, the verification of the BlackBerry ID by the BlackBerry server is used for BlackBerry Link and is necessary for the decryption of the backup and restore process. The software solution must be online for this process to be successful.

The BBB file that is produced is similar to the original BBB compressed file, but new BBB files contain a manifest file and informational file that are not encrypted and can offer information about the device. This file is needed by the current software solutions mentioned in previous sections along with the BlackBerry Link password. Mobile forensic software from Oxygen Forensics allows the new BBB files to be decrypted and analyzed with the correct BlackBerry account password for both live and backup collections.

Archiving the Data

Much like a feature phone collection, the BlackBerry data and UICC and memory card information should be securely stored on an evidence drive prior to beginning the analysis phase. This storage location should have a unique name that pertains to the case or investigation. All subsequent analysis will occur on a copy of the data that was collected during the primary acquisition.

Note Even if the BlackBerry 10 device is currently encrypted, the examiner should create a backup if possible. This will allow the examiner to perform an analysis at a later date if a password is eventually discovered or additional techniques are introduced. Software solutions are always advancing with more options available. Having the file at the onset, even if not currently usable, would allow it to be parsed with new technology.

Windows Mobile and Windows Phone Examinations

The Windows Mobile operating system is no longer on the market, and Microsoft has transitioned to Windows Phone, but Windows Mobile systems are still being used. Windows mobile devices, both Windows Mobile and Windows Phone, differ regarding collection, the ability to access user data, and data layout. Today, the Windows Phone holds a small portion of the smart device market share, but it continues to grow. Undoubtedly, an examiner will be requested to complete an examination of a Windows Mobile or, more likely, a Windows Phone at some point.

Windows smart phone devices were released in 2000 as a mobile solution based on Windows CE (Compact Embedded) and saw exposure as Pocket PCs and the Windows smart phone based on CE 3.0. Windows Mobile 2003 was running 3.0, and in 2004, Windows Mobile 5 was released and 6 followed, all progressing on the CE architecture. The last available Windows Mobile version, 6.5, was released in 2009, and Windows Phone 7 became available in 2010, which was not just a complete rebranding, but something completely new.

At the release of the Windows Phone 7, users and examiners alike saw a complete change in the collection and recovery of a Windows mobile device. Windows Phone 7 was not based on previous Windows Mobile functions and accessibility, and as such it created problems for digital forensic examinations. In 2011, Windows Phone 7.5 was released, and version 7.8 added some Windows Phone 8 capability, since 7.8 devices could not be upgraded to Windows Phone 8 due to hardware limitations. In 2012, Windows Phone 8 was released and in 2014 upgraded to version 8.1. The device will again be rebranded as Windows 10 Mobile in 2015 (fall 2015 as of this writing), and more problems will surface for mobile forensic examiners.

Remember that a Windows device can also contain a UICC and memory card, so the correct procedure in processing these pieces of evidence should still be followed depending upon the state of the mobile device.

Connecting to the Device

Communication with a Windows Mobile device and a Windows Phone both generally require a USB cable and computer, but the way and conduit in which the communication occurs differ between the two devices. Communication to the Windows Mobile device occurs using Active Sync or Windows Mobile Device Center (WMDC) protocols. Both operate using a hardware abstraction layer, much like how iTunes operates with an iOS device. Active Sync and WMDC are not capable of the same communication layer with a Windows Phone device, so Microsoft Zune was released to accommodate that. However, the access to a Windows Mobile device using Active Sync and WMDC is considerably more verbose than a connection to a Windows Phone using Zune.

When connecting either a Windows Mobile or Phone device, the software must have preinstalled drivers or the examiner must install drivers for the device. Most forensic software that supports Windows Mobile devices will either have Active Sync or WMDC installed as part of the driver package. Connecting and then collecting with a Windows Mobile device, as mentioned, is similar to an iOS device in theory. The examiner will use the data syncing function built into the Windows Mobile device architecture and operationalized via Active Sync or WMDC, install a file to the device or device SD card, and initiate the card on the device. Connection and logical collection can occur only using an intermediary file, also referred to as an *agent*. The agent, using the Active Sync or WMDC connection, transfers data to the forensics software. Be careful that the loaded file does not overwrite inactive data.

Windows Phone logical collections using commercial and open source tools involve using the Zune software or a derivative.

Note Some commercial tools have harvested some of the functionality from the Zune software to bundle into their driver packages, but these tools will not allow Zune to be installed along with the forensic software. If a Windows Phone cannot be recognized, make sure the forensic software is not conflicting with Zune, if installed.

Collecting the Device Logically

If the device is powered on and unlocked, and after connection has been made to the Windows Mobile device using Active Sync or WMDC, the agent recovery process will begin. Typical data recovered using mobile forensic tools includes contacts, call logs, SMS, media, and other critical user information. On the other hand, a Windows Phone will yield very little user type information with a logical collection. The information that is collected in a logical extraction of a Windows Phone is limited to media and documents. Really, anything that is accessible using a Windows Explorer instance will be collected in a logical collection using modern forensic solutions.

If the device is locked with a password, the only option will be to conduct a physical collection of the Windows Mobile or Windows Phone device.

Collecting the Device Physically

Most Windows Mobile device models can be collected physically using non-invasive methods. Cellebrite, Micro Systemation, and Paraben software include methods to recover a file system from a Windows Mobile device. When the examiner is conducting a physical collection of a Windows Mobile device, Active Sync or WMDC will be used to place an agent onto the device. The agent is then initiated and the recovered data is sent to the forensic software.

Most of the forensic tools are based upon the work by Willem Jan Hengeveld and the open source Remote API (RAPI) tools (www.xs4all.nl/~itsme/projects/xda/tools.html). RAPI is defined by the Microsoft Developers Network as follows:

> The Remote API (RAPI) library enables applications that run on a desktop to perform actions on a remote Windows Mobile device. The functionality that RAPI provides includes the ability to manipulate the file system on the remote device, including the creation and deletion of files and directories. RAPI functions can be used to create and modify databases, either in the device's object store or in mounted database volumes. RAPI applications can also query and modify registry keys as well as launch applications and invoke methods on the remote device. Although most RAPI functions are duplicates of functions in the Windows Embedded CE API, a few new functions extend the API. Use these functions to initialize the RAPI subsystem and enhance performance of the communication link by compressing iterative operations into one RAPI call.

Caution Using RAPI tools and other advanced tools and command utilities without properly understanding and testing them is not advised.

The RAPI tools shown next enable the examiner not only to extract the database and system files, but also dump RAM and entire partitions from Windows Mobile devices with more than 30 different functions. Only two of these functions are discussed in this section.

- **itsutil.dll** This file is copied to the connected device using Active Sync and is used as a helper library for access to the Windows Mobile device. This file can be copied to various locations on the mobile device and is set by using a registry key on the examination computer.

  ```
  HKEY_CURRENT_USER\software\itsutilsdevicedllpath [ "\Storage Card\itsutils.dll"
  ```

  This places the file onto the storage card of the connected mobile device. A log file is also created if set to true, and its location can also be set in the registry of the connected computer. When any item is executed using the itsutil.dll, the examiner will be prompted to accept this function on the mobile device interface.

- **pdocread** This command can be used to make a copy of the partitions on the mobile device. Using this command with a `-l` flag will list the known devices and the active handles on the device. This information will be used by the examiner to identify the correct user partition to be selected and then extracted. Using a `-w` flag when reading the selected partition will specify use of the standard disk API to perform the read. The format and parameters of the command should look like this:

```
pdocread -[flag(s)] -[partition] [starting byte] [ending byte] <path and output file name>
```

After obtaining a list of the partitions using `pdocread -l`, the examiner will see partitions identified as disks with partitions, but more importantly for collection, string handles. Using the partition name (in hexadecimal) or handle number and total size of the partition (in hexadecimal), the examiner can then extract the partition from the device. If the output produced by `pdocread` lists the partition of interest as `handle#3 73efe04a 60.98M (0x3cfc000)`, the command to create a binary image of this partition looks like this:

```
pdocread -w -h0x73efe04a 0 0x3cfc000 D:WindowsMobile.bin
```

A binary file will then be output to the D: drive and can be analyzed by EnCase, FTK, Oxygen Forensic Analyst and Detective, Physical Analyzer, or XACT.

Note On devices containing larger partitions, the standard disk output controlled by Windows can fail to extract the complete disk size specified in the command.

Windows Mobile applications cannot run on a Windows Phone, so a different approach to obtaining a physical image of the device is needed. Several methods for obtaining partition-level information from Windows Phone 7 have been circulated, which are much like the earlier versions of rooting techniques for Android. Still termed "rooting," the level of sophistication and technical work involved with both Windows Phone 7 and 8 devices to obtain root-level access is daunting for most examiners. For both version 7 and 8 devices, the examiner must have a device with an unlocked bootloader, and if the device is not unlocked, he or she must perform necessary modifications to the device to unlock the bootloader. Once unlocked, another application will be run to obtain permission and root the device. ChevonWP7 was frequently used with earlier Windows Phone 7 devices but has since ceased to be developed or used because of the difficulty involved in running it successfully.

With Windows Phone 7 and 8 devices, the most successful methods currently used to obtain a physical level collection use invasive techniques. Both version 7 and 8 devices are supported by JTAG techniques and chip-off. The collected image can then be examined in EnCase, FTK Imager, FTK, Oxygen Forensic Analyst and Detective, Physical Analyzer, or XACT.

Alternative Collection Methods

Windows Mobile devices are supported pretty extensively by all commercial tools. With coverage for both logical and physical level collection, a commercial mobile forensic tool will often be the most reliable. However, alternative applications are available for Windows Mobile devices.

PIM Backup (www.dotfred.net/) has been used in MFI mobile forensic training courses and offers a free alternative to the logical recovery of valuable data from a Windows Mobile device. PIM Backup functions much like the commercial forensic tools and uses Active Sync or WMDC to install an application to the device over a connected USB cable. After the application is installed to the mobile device, it runs and the selected data is exported into individual files (such as CSV, XML, or iCAL).

Windows Phone 7 and 8 do allow for the creation of a backup using Zune, but the backups are encrypted and currently no tool can decrypt the backups. Some third-party tools also allow backups, but they also use the Windows Phone backup service that creates the encrypted backup. Windows Phone 7 and 8 devices allow the examiner to access files and folders that are stored on the internal memory and also the external card. Both versions use external and internal storage areas much like the standard Windows operating system and use these areas to store data that is directly related to the device operating system. If a memory card is removed, a Windows Phone could become unstable, and sometimes the device will have to be reset. This creates a great opportunity for the examiner to recover valuable information simply by moving the data from the memory card into an evidence location. This data could include media types, documents, and other files.

Archiving the Data

All data, including physical images, exported files, backups, and logical images, along with physical images of memory cards and UICC information should be copied to an evidence drive before the analysis phase. The information needed for the analysis phase should then be copied to a temporary location. The storage location should have a unique folder specific to the case and an internal folder that is specific to the device. Any additional evidence recovered as part of the analysis should also be stored permanently at this location once the case is completed.

Apple iOS Connections and Collections

A collection of an Apple device by a forensics examiner can be an almost daily occurrence because Apple mobile devices are some of the most used devices globally. Connections to and collections of these devices are rather straightforward processes. Apple allows the device to communicate with a computer using its proprietary protocols via iTunes. iTunes allows for communication to occur with the attached device, and a user can update applications, media, and device firmware, to name a few. Forensic software vendors use the same type of communication methods used by Apple with iTunes. Forensic software vendors, third-party free utilities, and open source tools use methods and services that have been exposed in Apple's API, enabling the software to simulate an iTunes communication session, but these tools also use methods that are not used in the iTunes application.

Communication with the Apple device is generally straightforward for each solution. What will be the most confusing part for an examiner is understanding the logical versus physical support of an Apple device.

Connecting to the Device

Connecting to an Apple device with most traditional mobile forensic solutions requires a USB cable. Apple mobile devices up to and including the iPhone 4S and iPad 1 will use a standard iPhone 30-pin cable. When the iPad 2 was released, Apple changed the USB cable to an 8-pin Lightning Cable, and now all Apple devices use this cable for charging and syncing.

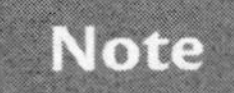

With the cost of the Apple Lightning Cable, many manufacturers released products that violated Apple's patent and produced a non-OEM cable. Most of these cables are recognized by the Apple device when plugged in and will not allow for data transfer or cause failures during data transfer. Using the Apple Lightning Cable for connection to an Apple device is recommended, however.

The cable connection is located at the bottom of the device, and after the cable is plugged into the computer, with devices operating iOS 7 and later, the examiner will see a prompt asking whether the computer should be trusted (see Figure 8-8). This security feature enables the device to create a pairing record with the attached computer if a pairing record has not already been established. (If the device has previously been connected to the computer and unlocked, this prompt will not be shown. The pairing record that is created upon acceptance is discussed a bit later in this section.) Once the device is attached to the computer and the drivers have been successfully installed, the device can be collected using a software solution of choice as long as the iOS device and its OS version are supported by the solution.

If at any time the examiner chooses not to trust the computer, the device will have to be unplugged from the computer and then reattached for the trust prompt to be displayed again. If the examiner does not indicate that the computer can be trusted, the forensic software will be unable to collect the iOS device. If the prompt to trust the computer does not display, either the device is running an iOS version earlier than 7 or the device has already been deemed trustworthy.

Device State Considerations

If the device is unlocked and powered on or off, collection will not be a problem, no matter what the operating system version. If the device is locked by a password and the password is known, the examiner should attach the device to the computer that will complete the

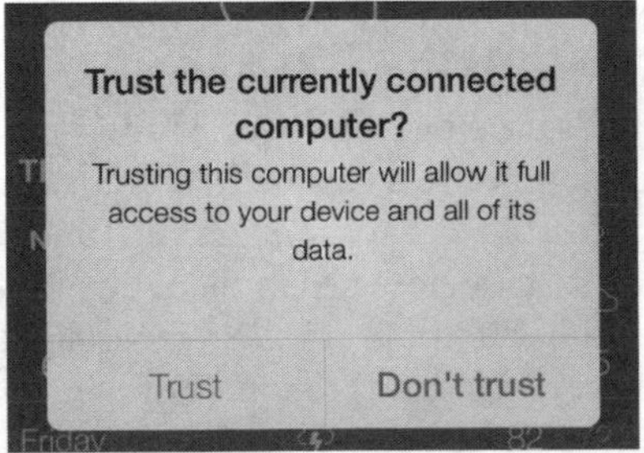

FIGURE 8-8 The Trust Computer prompt is a new feature with iOS 7 and newer iOS devices.

collection, unlock the device, and then accept to trust the computer. Unlocking the device will create a trusted pairing relationship that will be used later during the collection if the device locks. If at any time the device has to be reexamined, a password will not be needed to complete a collection.

If the device is locked and running any version of iOS, the examiner can use the *escrow keybag,* also known as the pairing record. The escrow keybag is created and used for user experience during an iOS device backup-and-restore process. Where the escrow keybag for the iOS device is located depends on the type of computer operating system being used for the examination:

- **Windows** %AllUsersProfile%\Apple\Lockdown\
- **Mac OSX** /private/var/db/lockdown/

Within the lockdown folder is a property list (plist) that is identified using the device UDID (Unique Device Identifier). Using these property lists will be covered when discussing a locked device in the following section.

When a user plugs in an iOS device with a set passcode, he or she is asked to enter the passcode. The device then creates an escrow keybag (pairing record) that contains the same keys that are used on the device, along with a new generated key. The escrow key and the new key are split between the device and the computer to which it is connected. With any reconnects to that same computer, a password does not have to be entered into the device for processing. By using the escrow keybag, the software can bypass the lock and process the mobile device. With iOS 7 and later versions there is a caveat, however: if the device is rebooted and then reconnected to the computer that contains the device escrow keybag, the device could request the passcode to be re-entered, creating a new trusted relationship. Obtaining the lockdown folder from the computer with which the iOS device was last synced can help to process a mobile device that is locked. Using this folder and included property list files, the examiner can use mobile forensic software to use the file to simulate a pairing relationship with the iOS device and conduct a logical collection. Without this pairing record for today's iOS devices, the examiner will be unable to connect and ultimately process any mobile device data.

Collecting the Device Logically

All mobile forensic tools use Apple File Conduit (AFC) and forms of AFC along with Apple Services to conduct a logical extraction of an iOS device, just like Apple's own iTunes. iTunes must be installed on the forensic computer for a logical collection to occur for most software solutions; however, some software solutions that collect iOS devices do not require that iTunes be installed. All iOS logical collections are not created equal, and it is imperative that the examiner understand and research the data that can be extracted with the software solution that will be used. A software solution for an iOS device should be able to collect more data than would be available in a standard iTunes collection.

Note Consulting the forensic software solution's documentation will assist in determining whether iTunes must be installed on the forensic computer prior to conducting a collection.

The connection and logical collection of an iOS device is the same for all devices, with some special considerations. Typically the examiner can connect the USB cable, connect to the computer or hardware device with the collection software, and extract the data. The special considerations come in the form of an iTunes password and encrypted backups. If the device to be examined has the backup encryption set, the backup that is to be collected will not be readable. During the collection phase, the examiner must supply the password for the iTunes backup in order to decrypt the iOS data after it is extracted from the device. Most forensic software solutions offer the ability to decrypt the device backup from an iOS device. If the iTunes password is not known, some data will still be available for collection if the device is not locked, such as media and some application data.

Note A logical collection of an iOS device can include a significant amount of valuable data. Far too many examiners believe that only a small amount of data is available in a logical iOS collection and neglect to perform a collection. In Chapter 10, you'll see why this is not the case.

An iOS device does not have an external media card, but it can contain a UICC, which should be removed prior to the collection. Personal experience has shown little valuable user information on a UICC card from an iOS device, but network information can be observed. However, the UICC should be collected and included in the overall case file as evidence.

Collecting the Device Physically

Probably the most frequently asked question of software vendors, support staff, and training staff has to do with the non-invasive physical collection of an iOS device. The question is always centered around the collection of an iOS device version later than an iPhone 4S from those versed in the limitation, but from new examiners it is more along the lines of questioning why a piece of software that specifically states it supports the physical collection of iOS devices fails on anything above an iPhone 4S or iPad 1. This is not a limitation of the software or of the technology, but a limitation imposed by Apple in an effort to patch vulnerabilities. Devices with an A5 or newer processor (as of today, an A8x) will not support the vulnerabilities exposed by today's forensic software. The iPad 2 was the first device to use the A5, with the iPhone 4S soon following. The A4 and earlier processors can be exploited using the same method by all forensic software vendors that currently support a physical collection of an iOS device.

An iOS device can run in normal mode, DFU (Device Firmware Update), or Recovery mode. The non-invasive physical methods used by forensics tools use DFU or Recovery mode to obtain access to the device via USB. If the device is not running in DFU or Recovery mode, the device typically boots up in normal mode starting with the read-only bootROM as the first stage when powering on. This startup procedure in normal mode is called the "chain of trust." In the chain of trust, the device boots and walks through a series of security checks using signatures for each level. Each level will then check the other level (for example, the LLB [Lower Level Boot loader] checks the iBoot, iBoot checks the Kernel), and if at any time a signature does not match, the iOS device will stop the boot process.

When an examiner places a device into DFU or Recovery mode, the iOS device boot procedure changes to involve second-level boot loaders, iBSS and iBEC. These are stripped-down versions of iBoot that allow for the preparation of the device Restore RAMdisk, but in the case of a forensic collection, the iBSS bootstraps the iBEC to deliver a custom RAMdisk into the volatile memory of the iOS device. The custom RAMdisk allows access to the iOS device and the partitions (OS and UserData) that otherwise could not be accessed when the iOS device is in normal mode. The forensic software will take advantage of the newly granted access to the device's file system and a non-invasive physical image of the device can be collected. Once the device is rebooted after the collection, the custom RAMdisk is removed, and the only trace that something has occurred to the device would be the indication that it had been rebooted.

The HFS+ file system contained within the physical image of the iOS device can then be examined within the forensic software. As outlined in Table 8-2, the custom RAMdisk method is possibly with only a certain set of iOS devices. With the supported devices, Apple added a layer of data encryption for unallocated areas of the user partition. With this layer of encryption, the data can be collected, but the keybag used for the decryption of that area is unavailable. This occurred in devices after and including iOS 4.

All other iOS devices not supported using the bootROM or iBoot exploit and RAMdisk function (such as iPhone 6+, iPhone 6, iPhone 5S, and so on) can also have their internal file systems collected with exposure to protected files not available in a logical file system collection. In this case, the device must be jailbroken using a Userland exploit, which is completely software based and access is available only to the user area without access to the boot process. This means that the entire partition, as in a bootROM or iBoot exploit, is not available for full extraction; only the internal file system can be extracted. When an iOS device is jailbroken, most forensic software will obtain the new jailbroken verbose file system using the standard logical collection methods. This collection, because of the now-jailbroken device, will allow access to files and folders otherwise not available in a standard logical collection. These folders and files include Apple Email, Safari, applications, protected data store, cache, and many other files not accessible by other means.

The most common solutions used for iOS devices, which are constantly updated, are PanGu (http://en.pangu.io/) and TaiG (www.taig.com/en/). Both offer untethered solutions up to and including iOS 8.2. If using a tethered jailbreak, the iOS device must be plugged into a computer every time it is booted so the iOS device can boot with the help of the jailbreak application. Most jailbreaking tools use a tethered solution.

TABLE 8-2 Devices Capable of a Physical Collection Using the Customized RAMdisk Option

iOS Device	Versions Supported
iPod Touch	Generations 1–4
iPhone	iPhone 3G, 3GS, 4
iPad	Generation 1

Note Jailbreaking a mobile device was ruled *not illegal* by the Library of Congress in 2012 (www.copyright.gov/fedreg/2012/2012-26308_PI.pdf), but this does not currently extend to a tablet (such as an iPad). However, jailbreaking can void the warranty by Apple, so using third-party methods to jailbreak a device should be used only in situations where warranted.

An examiner who understands the methods used to obtain physical access to an iOS device, either using bootROM exploits, iBoot exploits, or Userland, can positively impact later testimony and documentation, especially if the method is challenged.

iTunes Collection

If performed correctly, an iTunes collection will yield much of the same information you would expect from a collection with forensic software. However, an iTunes collection backup will contain many files that are represented by a hash of the path of the actual file on the device. Although the collection process and the connection of the device to the computer is no different from what has already been discussed with other operating systems, the collected data's format is much different from the others. The examination and analysis of this data are covered in Chapter 10.

To create a backup successfully using iTunes, the examiner should first download and install the most current version from Apple (apple.com/itunes/download/). After installing and launching the software, and after iTunes is running, the examiner should navigate to Edit | Preferences and click the Devices icon on the tool ribbon. On the Devices screen, the examiner should check the box in front of Prevent iPods, iPhones, And iPads From Synching Automatically. The iOS device can then be connected.

iTunes displays the connected device. On the device information screen, the examiner must clear the checkbox for Encrypt Backup. If this is checked, the device has been set to encrypt the backup, and the examiner, when unchecking the box, will have to enter the password for the iTunes backup that the device owner used. If the password is not known, a backup can still be created, but the data that is produced will be encrypted. An examiner should still create a backup even if the backup password is not known in case the password is later available. Or the examiner could use software such as Elcomsoft Phone Password Breaker (EPPB) or Oxygen Forensic Detective and Analyst to retrieve the password. While still connected, the examiner should right-click the connected device and select Backup. A backup will be created in the predefined default location depending on the operating system:

- **Mac** ~/Library/Application Support/MobileSync/Backup/
- **Windows Vista, Windows 7, and Windows 8** \Users\(username)\AppData\Roaming\Apple Computer\MobileSync\Backup\

First iOS Examination

In 2007, when no forensic tools were making collections of iOS devices, I was asked to complete a forensic examination of a new type of phone—the iPhone. After doing some research, I learned that the device created a backup using software called iTunes. After I installed iTunes and connected the device, it immediately started to sync the information from the device into iTunes (and I learned a valuable lesson: I must disable this option first!).

When the collection was completed, I researched the backup function and initiated a backup of the device onto the computer. When the backup was completed, I was amazed at the amount of information that I could find within the backup file using AccessData FTK software. I uncovered numerous text messages, photographs, and call logs that were needed for the case. As many more iPhones came into the lab and there still was no solution out there for the forensic examiners, I wrote a white paper covering the way I completed my first iPhone collection. This document was later used by both open source developers and commercial developers to create a solution to harness the way iTunes completed a backup and then parse the user data. The initial document I published in 2007, "iPhone Data Extraction," is still available on the Internet at www.mandarino70.it/Documents/iPhoneProcessing.pdf.

Archiving the Data

All data, including physical images, logical file systems, backups, pairing records, and UICC information, should be copied to an evidence drive before the analysis phase begins. The appropriate information should then be copied to a temporary location for the analysis phase of the investigation. The storage location should be a unique folder specific to the case and an internal folder specific to the device. Any additional evidence recovered as part of the analysis should also be stored permanently in this location after the case is completed.

Android OS Connections and Collections

With more than 12,000 Android devices available to users around the world, it is no wonder that connecting and collecting from these devices can be difficult at times. An Android logical collection is much different from an iOS logical collection because the logical file system of an Android is not typically available. Settings on the device must be enabled for proper communication, and this can vary depending upon the device. Not only does it matter what type of Android device is being examined, but the version of the operating system will also determine whether a connection and collection can occur. Other considerations for Android collections include whether the device is powered on or off, locked or unlocked, encrypted or not, and also whether or not security is enabled. A locked device with security enabled can prevent the examiner from turning on settings needed to communicate with an Android device. All of these facts must be considered before the examiner even connects the device to be collected.

The Android device can contain a UICC along with memory cards, and the processing order described in the "UICC" and "Memory Card" sections in the chapter should be followed. These sections cover the connection of the mobile device.

An Android device should be collected with the memory card still inserted in the device to collect and extract the media and file data that are located on the removable media. If the memory card is removed, actual files that are on the external media will not be mapped to data that is contained on the mobile device's internal database.

Connecting to the Device

The Android Debug Bridge (ADB) is used to communicate with an Android device. The ADB .exe command-line tool is part of the Android Standard Development Kit and is used for testing and development of Android apps and applications. This tool offers a computer a way to communicate with a connected Android device. It comprises the client, a server, and a daemon. The *client* is the action or job initiated by the ADB command. The *server* is the management portion that is running on the computer that manages the communication between the client and the ADB daemon that is running on the Android device. The ADB *daemon* is a background process that is running on the device conducting the command and control as given by the client. ADB must be used for all communication to and from an Android device, whether it is a logical or particular non-invasive physical collection. The Android device that is to be collected must have ADB enabled, either manually by the examiner or programmatically by the software. Once ADB is enabled, the proper ADB driver must also be installed and functioning on the examination computer for proper communication.

Tip The only driver that would need to be installed successfully to collect an Android device is the ADB driver; all others are not significant.

Whether the examiner will need to set the Android manually into ADB will depend upon the operating system. Outlined in Table 8-3 are the various ways of setting an Android device into ADB, depending upon the operating system version. All ADB menus are located in the Developer options menu.

Note Up until Android 4.2, Developer options were visible in the Settings menu. Android 4.2 and later versions have hidden Developer options, and to see the menu, the examiner must go to About Phone in Settings and tap Build Number seven times. Developer options will then be visible in the Settings.

In addition, when conducting forensic collections, you need to set the device to allow unknown sources in the Security settings on the Settings menu. Allowing unknown sources will enable the forensic software to "sideload" a special package file, called an Android application package (APK), onto the device. *Sideloading* an app means installing APK files that are not directly from the Google Play store. If the device will not allow unknown sources, the forensic software will not be able to install the forensic package to collect logical data.

Another setting—more of a security feature—is the acceptance of an RSA key when the device is connected to a computer (for devices running Android 4.2.2 and later). This must be accepted on the device, not the computer to which the device is connected. This RSA key acceptance is similar

TABLE 8-3 Ways to Locate the ADB Functions Within Android Devices (http://developer.android.com/tools/help/adb.html)

Android OS Version	To Place a Device in ADB...
2.x and 3.x	Choose Settings, Applications, Development, and then USB Debugging
4.x	Choose Settings, Developer Options, and then USB Debugging
4.2.2 and later	Choose Settings, About Device, and then tap Build Number seven times Choose Settings, Developer Options, and then USB Debugging

to selecting to trust the computer with an iOS device. By accepting the RSA key on the device, the examiner is stating that the connected device is safe to connect with the computer.

Once all settings have been configured, the device can be connected to the mobile forensic software and the collection can begin.

Device State Considerations

If an Android device is unlocked and powered on, unlocked and powered off, or the security is enabled and the password is known, the connection and collection will be typical and straightforward. There are instances, however, when an unlocked Android device cannot be recognized by the software or even the forensic computer or hardware. In such instances, it is important that the examiner determine whether the device's USB port is intended for charging only or whether data can actually be transferred to and from the device via the port.

Here's an easy way to determine this: Upon plugging the device into a computer, if a device can transfer data, the device will be shown as a portable device within the computer's device tree, and a menu will be displayed on the mobile device screen with at least an option to turn on USB mode for the device. USB mode will allow the device to move files on and off the media portion. If the device is capable of doing this, it can be collected using ADB.

Tip Android devices are predominantly collected using a USB cable connected to the computer running the forensic solution. In some situations, however, the use of alternative connections may be warranted.

Locked and Hidden USB Connections

Many "burner" Android phones will not show an ADB driver as being installed in the computer's Device Manager, even if ADB has been enabled in the Developer options menu. Here's a perfect case in point: While assisting an investigator with the examination of an LG VS908 Android device, I found that the phone was not showing up to allow collection. The device was shown as a portable device and all the folders and files could be browsed in Windows Explorer, but ADB was not available in the Device Manager even when it was enabled in the Settings menu.

I had the investigator unplug and then plug in the device again from the computer several times to check for a bad connection. Still, ADB could not be installed, but a menu was enabled every time the device was plugged in. The menu presented three options: Charging Only, Media Sync, and Internet. Knowing that the Media Sync option would allow access only to the media card, I had the investigator select Internet. A submenu became available with Modem and Ethernet as choices. These options are the tethering options for the device, and if either is selected, ADB will be available in the Device Manager. Once he selected Modem, the investigator was able to process the device normally with his forensic software.

The settings to inhibit data transfer are very common with inexpensive Android devices. I have found submenu items on most of these devices that, when activated, will activate ADB that had been previously been turned on in the Developer menu.

If the device is locked by a password and the password is not known, the device must be physically collected or reset by Google (after a court order) to access the data. As mentioned earlier, in order for data transfer to occur, ADB must be enabled. Android devices by default do not have ADB enabled, but an examiner should always plug the device into the forensic solution, even if locked, to see if ADB has been turned on. Users who frequently sideload applications or hack Android devices will have ADB enabled, and when it is available, the device will still be accessible if locked. However, if the device is locked and ADB is not enabled, logical access will not be available and the examiner will be limited to non-invasive physical or invasive physical collections.

Collecting the Device Logically

Once ADB is enabled, a logical collection of an Android device can occur. Forensic software vendors all use a customized APK file to collect this valuable user data. The examiner needs to firmly understand the method and installation of a program onto an Android device to collect data. Because the forensic software is writing to the evidence and altering the internal file system, a challenge could be raised that the evidence is no longer valid. This, of course, is not the case, but without an understanding of the forensic tool and how the process works, an examiner may have a difficult time dealing with such a challenge.

An APK is a compressed file containing uncompiled code. This package contains files and folders that, when compiled on the Android device upon installation, create a port for which the forensic software can communicate and collect the user data from the mobile device. Each software vendor's APK is different: some extract user packages and Wi-Fi settings, while others do not; some remain installed on the device after running, while others do not. What is important, other than what type of data will be extracted, is how the APK is delivered, where it is delivered, and what happens to it once it has been installed and run. Typically, the APK is pushed onto the Android device and placed into the system/tmp folder using ADB. The APK is then installed and compiled onto the device and an instance is initiated, also via ADB.

Note Most forensic software solutions instances are not visible on the device during the collection, with the exception of Oxygen Forensic Detective and Analyst, Compelson MOBILedit, and Cellebrite. These programs display a splash screen on the device while the app is running, collecting data.

While running, the app will be sending data to the forensic software based upon queries to the supported databases. This is an important concept for the examiner to understand, because a logical extraction of an Android device will not include the actual database files where the queries were directed. In simpler terms, if the SMS messages are collected from an Android device, the mmssms.db file is not extracted during a logical collection—only the data from the SQLite database table is extracted. Because the Android protects the data area of the file system, access to these database files is available only with a physical collection and elevated privileges, commonly referred to as *root privileges*. If database files, media files, or other files are extracted in a logical collection, they will be extracted from the internal and/or external storage area using the Media Transfer Protocol (MTP).

Once the collection has completed, the forensic software will issue another command to the installed application to uninstall the software. The software is then removed from the target device and the system/tmp file will be cleaned and purged of any leftover data. If the examiner is unsure whether the forensic software removed the installed APK, he or she can navigate to the applications area on the Android device. If an icon for the forensic software APK is located, the app was not uninstalled and should be uninstalled manually.

Collecting the Device Physically

Collecting an Android device using non-invasive techniques requires *root access* to the device. Typically, if an Android device is supported in a forensic software solution for physical collection using a USB connection, two methods can be used, either *automated rooting* or *custom ROM* installation.

What Is Root Access?

On an Android device, there are levels of user access, much like on a Windows system with users and administrators. Android, based on Linux, has many user IDs that are granted access to perform various tasks on the device, such as run processes and control functions and calculations, but each type of user is restricted to performing particular privileges only. All Linux systems also have a superuser with a user ID of 0, called the root ID. This superuser can perform any task on the device, even if the file, folder, or setting has been marked as read-only. The superuser can change the access to read and write, access the area of the system that has been marked inaccessible, and more. This is called having "root access." With root access to an Android device, the examiner can access any part of the device without limitation. No matter what method is used by a forensic software vendor, if access to the device is via a USB and a physical image is obtained, that software solution "rooted" the mobile device.

Note Different root levels are available on a device. A *shell* root is the most desirable when you're conducting mobile forensics because this can obtain root access to the device. Upon reboot, after the extraction is complete, the device will be back in the unrooted state. With a *permanent* root, on the other hand, a reboot will not remove the root access. Some third-party rooting tools can also "unroot" a rooted tool, and if available this should be attempted after the collection has completed. Leaving evidence in a rooted state could introduce malware or other issues that would not be possible with a secured device.

Automated rooting procedures require an unlocked phone with ADB available and enabled; to perform the rooting process, ADB must be enabled and available. Forensic tools such as MPE+, Oxygen Forensic Detective and Analyst, UFED Touch/4PC, and XRY have built-in functions that will attempt to root the device when conducting a physical collection. If a tool is unable to root a device and no other methods for physical access are available, however, some third-party applications can be used: Wondershare MobileGo supports devices from Android 2.1 to 4.4.4 but does not allow unroot; Kingo Android Root supports devices up to 4.2.2 and includes unroot capabilities; and SRSRoot supports Android versions up to 4.2 and has an unroot option.

If the device is locked and supported for physical collection and ADB is disabled, the forensic software will connect to the device typically by using fastboot, recovery, or download mode. These modes are used to install customized ROM that enables ADB and grants access to the device with root access. Once the collection is completed, the original ROM is returned.

Caution It is extremely important that the specific ROM matches that of the evidence to be collected when using a forensic solution with this type of physical method. Because of slight differences in the ROM for any Android device, using another device's ROM can cause disastrous results. This is primarily why this method fits in the invasive physical collection method category.

JTAG can also be used and has become extremely popular for Android collections. RIFF Box (riffbox.org) is the most widely used JTAG box in the mobile forensic community, but as with most everything else, this single mobile forensics solution does not support every mobile device encountered. JTAG software typically displays the TAPs for the model to be collected in an image within the application. Following the image, the connection to the JTAG hardware can be made either by soldering to the correct port as indicated and then matching to the referenced port on the JTAG hardware, or connection can be made with nonsoldering solutions such as Molex or jigs. When connected and the JTAG software has been configured, a binary image is created and can then be imported into mobile forensic solutions such as Cellebrite Physical Analyzer, Oxygen Forensic Detective and Analyst, and Micro Systemation XACT.

Alternative Collection Methods

As with other device types, Android mobile devices can be collected using other, more raw collection methods. If a physical collection is not available, these alternative methods can be used to gather information from an Android device over and above what a standard logical collection can gather, including file system and app data. These methods do not require having device root.

ADB Backup This function became available in Android 4.0 and allows a backup of individual apps or the entire app catalog along with the application data, cache, and internal storage. This function can be initiated using ADB.exe, available in the Android SDK in the /platform-tools/ folder. In order to use ADB Backup, the device must be unlocked and USB debugging must be enabled. Once an app or apps are downloaded using ADB Backup, the created file will be compressed and encrypted. To uncompress and decrypt the created file, the examiner runs the file through Android Backup Extractor (http://sourceforge.net/projects/adbextractor/), which will create a tarball file that can be examined using mobile forensic software capable of importing and viewing these types of files. Use of ADB Backup involves using a command-line instruction and device interaction once ADB Backup is initiated on the mobile device.

Note ADB Backup does not allow for the backup of DRM-protected applications.

The parameters and flags needed to create an ADB Backup, along with a breakdown of each parameter, are shown next:

```
adb backup [-f <file>] [-apk|-noapk] [-shared|-noshared] [-all] [-system|-
nosystem] [<packages...>]
```

- **[-f <file>]** Specifies the location where the backup will be stored.
- **[-apk|-noapk]** Specifies whether or not the app APK will be backed up. Backing up the APK could allow for later scanning for malicious software. The `-noapk` flag is set by default.
- **[-shared|-noshared]** Specifies whether or not shared memory areas on the internal and external storage media will be backed up. The `-noshared` flag is set by default.
- **[-all]** Specifies all applications on the device. When conducting a forensic backup of the device, use the `-all` flag.
- **[-system|-nosystem]** Specifies whether or not ADB Backup includes system applications in the backup. The `-nosystem` flag is set by default.
- **[<packages...>]** Specifies the app that will be backed up. If this is set, only the specified app will be included (that is, com.android.provider.telephony).

Here are the command parameters and flags for ADB Backup to collect all applications and internal/external media to a file called *backup* without system files at C:\Evidence:

```
adb backup -f C:\Evidence\backup.ab -all -nosystem -shared
```

If the examiner wants to extract all apps and memory contents of internal and external areas and their APKs to scan for malicious applications, the command would look similar to this:

```
adb backup -f C:\Evidence\backup.ab -apk -all -system -shared
```

When the command is complete, the examiner will be prompted with the screen displayed in Figure 8-9. Do not enter a password to encrypt the backup, and tap Back Up My Data. The duration of the process will depend upon the amount of data that is being backed up. Once the process completes, the examiner will be notified on the Android screen. The backup can then be extracted using the Android Backup Extractor and examined in the software solution of choice.

HoloBackup Android collection can be difficult to make via the command line. For that reason, an automated tool was created that features a GUI that can be run from a computer with an Android attached with ADB enabled. HoloBackup (https://github.com/omegavesko/HoloBackup) is available for download on GitHub and can easily perform the required functions. Individual apps, entire sets of apps, and even user data can be backed up and accessed using HoloBackup.

Helium Helium, formally known as Carbon, is an app-based solution that uses the front end of ADB Backup as well. To use Helium on a non-rooted device, install the application on the target device and on the desktop. An examiner can create a backup of select applications or individual applications to the PC; by default, the backup is saved to the SD card.

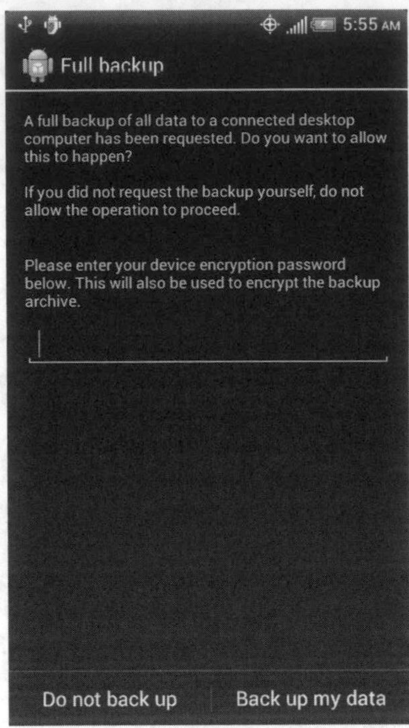

FIGURE 8-9 Screen activated on a connected Android device when running the ADB backup command

Windows Explorer

Android devices are recognized as portable devices by both Mac and Windows systems. If a forensic solution is unable to extract the data from the internal or external memory areas, the examiner can copy the information from the mobile device to the location where the evidence is to be saved. Because dates will probably be altered using this method, it should be used only if there are no other alternatives.

Archiving the Data

All data, including physical images, logical file systems, backups, and UICC information, should be copied to an evidence drive before the analysis phase. The information that is needed for analysis should be copied to a temporary location. The storage location should have a unique folder specific to the case and an internal folder specific to the device. Any additional evidence recovered as part of the analysis should also be stored permanently in this location once the case is completed.

Chapter Summary

The collection of mobile device data is often the easiest part of mobile forensics, but only if device state, drivers, and workflow are considered appropriately. Thoroughly documenting the device, UICC, and memory cards is the first step, but the examiner must also determine what evidence should be processed first, depending on whether the device is powered on or off.

Logical examinations are just as important as physical collections, and both types of collections should always be attempted. Obtaining a logical collection first can usually help the examiner obtain valuable data in case a physical collection is not supported, does not successfully complete, or disables the mobile device. The device type (whether a feature phone, an Android, a BlackBerry, an iOS, or a Windows Phone) can also determine the order of processing and workflow.

Often, mobile device forensic software will use functions and technology to conduct logical collections that have been formulated from the device manufacturer's own backup tools. Because of this, an examiner can use the manufacturer's software to create a backup as an alternative. It is important to understand, however, that some settings might need to be adjusted to maintain a valid backup. Collection methods may not work or may be unsuccessful, but the initial preparation of the device prior to collection of the digital data should be the same, no matter what device is to be examined and what software is used.

By understanding the way forensic software communicates with a mobile device to obtain data, the examiner can be prepared to face many challenges. The expert examiner should know how to determine that an APK file is installed, that the Android device data is placed into a temporary area and later removed, that a custom RAMdisk is created in the iOS volatile memory and later removed upon restart, and that obtaining root to an Android device changes security privileges and not the underlying user data.

9 Analyzing SIM Cards

Previous chapters covered procedures, seizure, and collection of physical and digital evidence on a mobile device. The next several chapters discuss the analysis of the data within the device files and folders. In this chapter, you'll learn about the SIM (subscriber identity module) card, once used only in GSM devices but now found in CDMA devices, and the evidentiary data that may reside within the file system.

SIM cards contain information that can be used by an examiner to locate a device, identify contacts, and see a user's communications. The examiner will need to concentrate on the card's file system—not an easy task, especially because SIM cards often store data in unconventional formats in various locations with different security levels. Nevertheless, the SIM card is well documented, ensuring that the manufacturers and cellular communication companies have a clear set of instructions regarding how to communicate within the GSM/UMTS network. The pertinent standards and documents are discussed throughout this chapter and can be referenced often if the examiner's case involves the analysis of a SIM card.

This chapter covers SIM and UICC (Universal Integrated Circuit Card) smart cards, the SIM file system, and the various artifacts that may be used in any investigation. This chapter does not cover all of the files and folders available on a SIM because many of these are used strictly for network communication—hundreds of files are contained on a single SIM, and covering them all within a single chapter is not possible. You can find more information by consulting the materials mentioned throughout the chapter.

Smart Card Overview: SIM and UICC

The European Telecommunications Standards Institute (ETSI) defines *smart cards* as "microprocessor equipped tokens, able to store and process a diverse range of data and applications" (www.etsi.org/technologies-clusters/technologies/smart-cards). Many examiners use the terms "UICC" and "SIM" interchangeably, though, strictly speaking, UICC (Universal Integrated Circuit Card) is the latest generation of the SIM card. The UICC is the hardware portion of the smart card, while the SIM, USIM, and others are software applications included on the card. Initially, a SIM was used only for GSM networks as the key to the mobile device operating on a cellular network along with both the hardware (mobile device) and software component.

UICC cards now are used in most smart devices, including CDMA devices. UICC covers the gamut of subscriber cards to include the removable user identity module (R-UIM) and CDMA2000 subscriber identity module (CSIM) cards, also part of the CDMA devices that can be used globally.

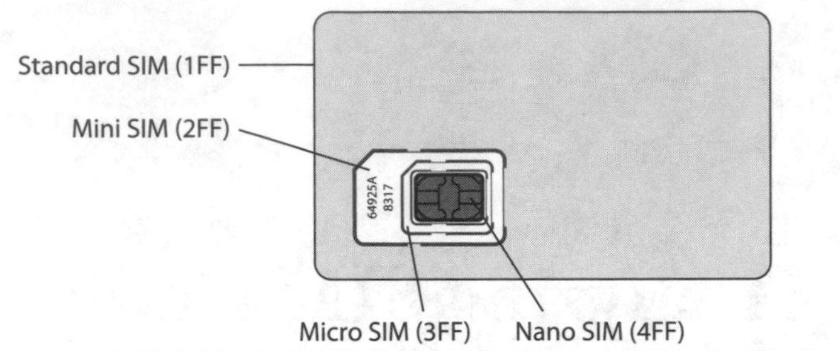

FIGURE 9-1 The evolution of SIM/UICC size

All the applications on the UICC are defined by ETSI and adopted by the Third Generation Partnership Project (3GPP). Applications (such as USIM, SIM, ISIM, and CSIM) contain information and help with flow of information to the mobile device depending upon the network used. If a UMTS network is being used, the USIM application will maintain control of communication and includes the data needed to help the device operate on that network; if a 2G or EDGE connection is needed on a GSM network, the SIM application would be used. A SIM card containing only a SIM application cannot operate on a UMTS-only network, but a UICC with both the SIM and USIM application can operate on either a GSM or UMTS system.

The physical size of a UICC is described in ETSI TS 102 221; version 11.0.0 references both ISO/IEC 7816-1 and ISO/IEC 7816-2 for acceptance. The most significant change to the UICC has been the size of the smart card, and Figure 9-1 shows the various size progressions of the card. The sizes are defined by ETSI as 1FF ID-1 UICC, 2FF Plug-in UICC, 3FF Mini-UICC, and 4FF Nano-UICC. The ID-1 UICC was never used in a mobile device because of its large size (credit card), but the Plug-in UICC is the most commonly referenced and was found in feature phones and early smart devices until 2004. The Mini-UICC was then released and made its way into most smart devices until the Nano-UICC was released in 2012 and adopted in newer iOS, Android, BlackBerry, and Windows Phones.

The actual microprocessor did not change between the SIM and Nano-UICC, but the shell that contained the microprocessor was changed. There was a debate between ETSI and Apple on Apple's ability to change the size of the microprocessor, and Apple finally won. Most UICC cards that are used in today's devices are still the original size for feature phones, but the majority of smart devices use the Nano-UICC.

SIM Card Analysis

Mobile forensic software replicates commands used by the mobile device to communicate with the applications on the UICC. The software can collect various data files using application protocol data unit (APDU) commands. These commands communicate with the mobile device and the UICC to obtain and store data by writing information to the UICC. A UICC is passive and does not initiate contact with the mobile device to begin a transaction, but instead stands by to listen for the APDU commands sent from the mobile device. A mobile device, or the operating firmware on the mobile device, can request the device serial number, the last SMS message, and even the last known location. By replicating APDU commands when using mobile forensic software, the examiner can also request this information to be used for the investigation.

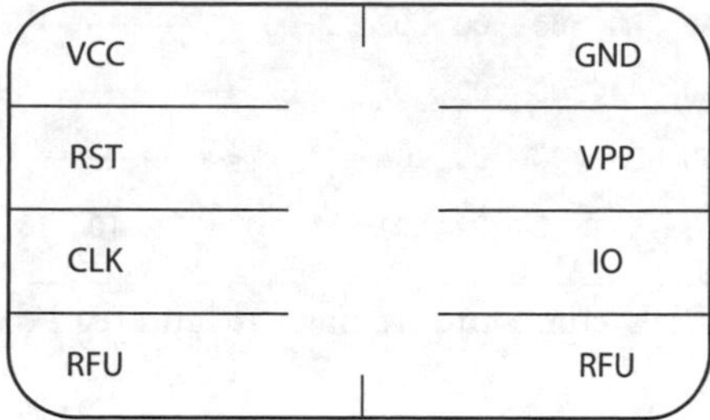

FIGURE 9-2 **UICC smart card contact points: communication to the chip occurs via the I/O contact, which is the pathway to the UICC CPU.**

Before we move into the communication methods from the software solution to the UICC, you should understand the physical characteristics of a UICC. The UICC comprises a microprocessor (CPU), RAM, ROM for firmware, and Electrically Erasable Programmable ROM (EEPROM) for nonvolatile storage. The UICC accepts communication via the I/O contact point (Figure 9-2) from the mobile device, but to operate correctly, the UICC needs all points in contact with the mobile device terminal pins. The UICC surface is contacted by the six or eight points along reciprocal contact points on the mobile device—most UICCs in today's devices have six pins. Reading, querying, and writing to the UICC occurs at these contact points.

As mentioned, the UICC is a passive part of the mobile device and must be contacted with APDU commands for action to occur. An APDU command comprises two components: a command and a response, as shown in Figure 9-3. The command is always initiated outside of the UICC (from forensic software or mobile device firmware) and a response is always returned, even if a command is incorrect. The UICC's response can indicate that a command was successful, unsuccessful, successful with security problems that must be addressed, or successful with a return of data.

An APDU command first needs to navigate the SIM card file system using INS (instruction) commands on the way to the appropriate file ID. During the navigation, if any security or permissions need to be satisfied, they, too, will have to be entered as APDU commands. Security conditions for SIM cards are referred to as ADM (Administrator) or CHV (Card Holder Verification). Once at the file ID, the APDU command must send an instruction (INS) that will tell the SIM what is to occur at the file ID. The instruction codes that can be used

Command

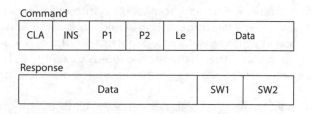

CLA	INS	P1	P2	Le	Data

Response

Data	SW1	SW2

FIGURE 9-3 **APDU command and response structures**

```
A0  A4  00  00  02  3F00 ←———— Select Master File
A0  A4  00  00  02  2FE2 ←———— Select ICCID
A0  B0  00  00  0A       ←———— Read 10 Bytes (Binary)
98  68  32  02  01  00  00  00  10  13 ←—— Returned ICCID
```

FIGURE 9-4 APDU commands to navigate and read the ICCIC

in an APDU are outlined in ETSI TS 102.221 (www.etsi.org/deliver/etsi_ts/102200_102299/102221/08.02.00_60/ts_102221v080200p.pdf). A file ID must then be "selected" to include additional instructions. To "select" a file ID, the APDU command must include `A4` as the INS code. The ID for the file to be acted upon, if using the select INS, would then fill the Data portion of the command structure shown in Figure 9-3. Whatever the length of the data portion in bytes, this number will be added to the Le block of the command. A file ID is made up of 2 bytes, and its specifications are outlined in ETSI TS 131 102 and 3GPP TS 31.102.

The commands that would be issued to a UICC to retrieve the ICCID (integrated circuit card identifier) using a command APDU are shown in Figure 9-4. The first commands navigate to the ICCID via the file system, identifying the file and then sending the instruction code to read the number of bytes located within the record. The return command contains the ICCID indicating success. The ICCID is in a "reverse nibble" format (each byte is flipped to create the actual value—for example, 21 80 48 would be 12 08 84). Response codes are also listed within ETSI TS 102.221. This is the same process forensic software will use to read the UICC ICCID. The reading of various portions of the UICC is covered later in the chapter in the section "User Data Locations."

File System UICC Structure

Obtaining the file system of all pieces of evidence is the goal of an examination, and it's the same with UICCs. Most information on the UICC is used for network communication and authentication, but the card can also contain valuable user information. Most mobile forensic solutions can obtain a UICC file system, with a few known exceptions—MOBILedit Forensic, Oxygen Forensic Detective and Analyst, and Susteen Secure View obtain user data directly from the UICC and import the information into the user interface. Some solutions even query the UICC through the handset rather than via a secondary SIM card reader. This section will not cover these tools, but it will include the artifacts that can be found within the file system and their formats.

Note The examiner will benefit from working through the UICC file system manually in the same way a forensic solution would work automatically. Understanding the method in which an automated tool obtains the data from these smart cards is an important feather in the mobile forensic examiner's hat, and it's a necessity for an examiner who wants to be an expert in mobile forensics.

Understandably, today's mobile devices contain little user information, simply because the data transmitted and received with a smart phone far exceeds the limited storage capacity of the UICC. However, mobile devices, including smart devices, can still store user data to the UICC that would otherwise be missed if the smart card were not examined. It is critical that the examiner obtain a full file system collection from the SIM/UICC and always recommended that the UICC card be collected and examined outside the body of the device, no matter the device, for reasons that include but are not limited to network location, networks accessed, subscriber information, SMS, contacts, and calls, to name a few. Each of these records can also contain information that an automated tool either cannot parse or does not parse correctly, so manual inspection is sometimes necessary.

The UICC file system is made up of several levels that contain four types of files: a Master File (MF) and Dedicated Files (DF), which include Application Dedicated Files (ADF), and Elementary Files (EF). There is only one Master File on the UICC and it is analogous to the root folder of a computer file system. The file ID of the MF is 3F00. There can be several DFs on the UICC (for example, GSM, DCS1800, TELECOM, USIM, PHONEBOOK), and these are analogous to a directory on a computer and files that are identified and described by ETSI TS 151 011 and 3GPP 51.011. The partitions on an SIM have always been described in forensic circles as SIM, USIM, and CSIM, but in reality they are applications that are used depending upon the type of network that is accessible.

Note SIM partitions are actually applications, and within the applications are various files that are referenced by what is commonly referred to as "file IDs."

If a CDMA system is available, the CSIM partition/application is used, but if a UMTS system is available and preferred, the USIM partition/application is used. The UICC file system can be confusing, with several layers within each application and folder system, some containing duplicated information. This information is duplicated in the file system view, but is actually written only once to the smart card, as is clearly observable when using the UICC file ID system. The file ID system simply references the needed record within the application. Because the UICC storage space is finite, a reference to this information must be made, and then, within the application, a pointer to the file ID is made. As mentioned, file IDs for most UICC data are defined and outlined within ETSI TS 131 102 and 3GPP TS 31.102. This does not mean that a file can only be on the UICC if the file ID is defined and listed by ETSI, however. In fact, a file can be created on a UICC that is specific to a particular carrier and used only by the carrier within its supported mobile devices. This is another reason the examiner should make sure to do a file system collection of all UICCs encountered.

Tip If a UICC contains multiple partitions/applications, it is important that each referenced area be examined, because a USIM application can contain additional phonebook entries over and above those in the SIM application.

Network Information Data Locations

Many files reside on the UICC card, most of which are network related. Generally, most files within the file system can be examined manually if needed. They contain information used by the mobile device to communicate on the network in a format that makes sense only to the network of the carrier system engineer. However, the examiner should be aware of several of these network-related files on the UICC when conducting a mobile device examination because they often contain data that could be used in a mobile device investigation.

Some files, such as the ciphering key (Ki), although important and necessary for the authentication process and contained on all SIM cards, are unavailable to the forensic examiner using any forensic software. Although some files are not available for examination, they should still be recognized and their existence documented.

ICCID

The ICCID is analogous to the serial number of the UICC; it represents the unique number assigned to that single UICC—that is, no other smart card on the cellular network uses the same unique number. Typically, this number is located on the exterior of the smart card, but not always. The number can be a maximum of 20 digits. The ICCID must always be available to the mobile device without limitation, primarily because this number will be used for the authentication process. This means that even if a UICC is locked with a PIN, the ICCID can be ascertained, and the examiner can then use the ICCID to obtain the PIN unblocking key (PUK) to change the PIN and access the UICC contents by sending the carrier of record the appropriate court order.

Note The "authentication process" is involved in accepting the subscriber onto a cellular network so that calls, data, and other transactions can occur. Without a successful authentication process, the mobile device will be unable to use the cellular network. Emergency service calls are an exception, however.

Table 9-1 shows valuable information such as the size, number of bytes, file ID, and additional information about the ICCID and its contents. Figure 9-5 shows the actual representation of the ICCID on the exterior of the UICC, and Figure 9-6 shows the output of the ICCID using mobile forensic software. The ICCID is stored in a reverse nibble format within the record found directly under the Master Files in EF_ICCID. So when the examiner is decoding the ICCID, each byte must be reversed to interpret the ICCID digits properly.

The ICCID is made up of 10 bytes that comprise several values. The first two digits are the system code, a constant value for mobile devices, 89, which represents ISO 7812, "Telecommunications Administers and Private Operating Agencies." The next two or three digits represent the country code for the UICC. For the United States, the country code is 01. The next two or three digits represent the Issuer Identifier Number, which for a mobile UICC is analogous to the first two digits on a credit card that identifies the credit card issuer (such as Visa or MasterCard), but for the UICC it would be T-Mobile, AT&T, Vodaphone, and so on.

Tip To find other country codes, refer to en.wikipedia.org/wiki/Mobile_country_code or consult international numbering plans at www.numberingplans.com.

TABLE 9-1 TS 102 221 Information on the ICCID

File ID	Length (Bytes)	Bytes	Need
2FE2	10	1–10	Mandatory

FIGURE 9-5 UICC exterior with a visible ICCID

ICCID	8901260110012177310

FIGURE 9-6 Decoded ICCID

The first three data groups cannot exceed seven digits. The remaining digits represent the UICC number and are made up of the year and month of manufacturing, configuration specs, and the unique UICC number. The final digit is referred to as the *checksum* digit.

Consider, for example, the ICCID number 89310170105113168601:

89310170105113168601 System code
89**310**170105113168601 Country code
89310**170**105113168601 Issuer identifier number
8931017010**51131686**01 UICC number
8931017010511316860**1** Checksum

IMSI

The International Mobile Subscriber Identity (IMSI) is the unique number that identifies the subscriber on the cellular network. This number is used to find a subscriber across the network and deliver calls, data, and other transactional information. Often, examiners think the phone number of the device is important to a cellular network. But it is the IMSI, for both GSM and CDMA networks, that is needed for contact to be made. This is an important file and should always be reported during the investigation. In fact, this record can be used to subpoena the records of the subscriber.

The IMSI is a protected file, and as such, if the UICC is locked with a PIN it will be inaccessible. The IMSI, under GSM/UMTS standards, will be 9 bytes, but the subscriber number can be a maximum of 15 digits. This is an interesting concept when the examiner recognizes that the total number of digits equals 18 when looking at the raw hexadecimal

TABLE 9-2 TS 151 011 Information on the IMSI

File ID	Length (Bytes)	Bytes	Need
6F07	9	1 = Length 2–9 = IMSI	Mandatory

values under EF_IMSI in the UICC file system. The values are also stored in reverse nibble, with the first byte as the length, which will always equal x08. The preceding bytes compose the IMSI in reverse nibble, and in order to decode the digits, you must first reverse them; the first digit, which will always be 9, should be dropped because it is not part of the IMSI value, but is a placeholder (that looks surprising when added to the length byte 89, indicating telecommunication like the ICCID). Table 9-2 shows information on the IMSI and its contents.

Much like the ICCID, the digits within the IMSI represent data to the examiner. The first 3 bytes are the Mobile Country Code (MCC), the next two digits are the Mobile Network Code (MNC), and the remaining digits are the subscriber identification number. The following shows the extracted IMSI using mobile forensic software and the breakdown of the IMSI number. Consider, for example, the IMSI number 310260123456789:

- **310**260123456789 Mobile Country Code
- 310**260**123456789 Mobile Network Code
- 310260**12345678**9 Subscriber identification number

LOCI

The Location Information (LOCI) is an Elementary File under the DF_GSM (DF structure for GSM) that identifies the geographic area *where the device was last successfully powered off*. The last portion of the sentence is critical: The LOCI writes the last tower location to which the device was registered when a successful power off occurred so that the device can access the network quickly upon powering on. If the device's battery is removed, is not powered off correctly, or it is broken prior to powering off, this file may not be available or may be incorrect. If, in fact, the LOCI file contains data, the examiner can use this key to identify the geographic location by contacting the carrier of record with the key information. The LOCI comprises the TMSI (Temporary Mobile Subscriber Identity), LAI (Location Area Information), TMSI Time, and the location update status.

The TMSI, as indicated by its name, is a temporary random ID that is assigned via the VLR (Visitor Locator Register) to the subscriber; the actual IMSI is not sent out via the handset because of possible capture and identification of the mobile subscriber, and the temporary IMSI changes when the device moves to a different VLR. The LAI comprises the MCC (Mobile Country Code), the MNC (Mobile Network Code), and the LAC (Location Area Code). By consulting the web site www.mcc-mnc.com, the examiner can at least identify the country and carrier to contact and obtain possible subscriber information. Table 9-3 shows the identifiable information for the LOCI, and Figure 9-7 shows an example from an actual GSM device.

TABLE 9-3 TS 151 011 Information on the LOCI

File ID	Length (Bytes)	Bytes	Need
6F7E	11	1–4 = TIMSI 5–9 = LAI 10 = TIMSI TIME 11 = Location Update Status	Mandatory

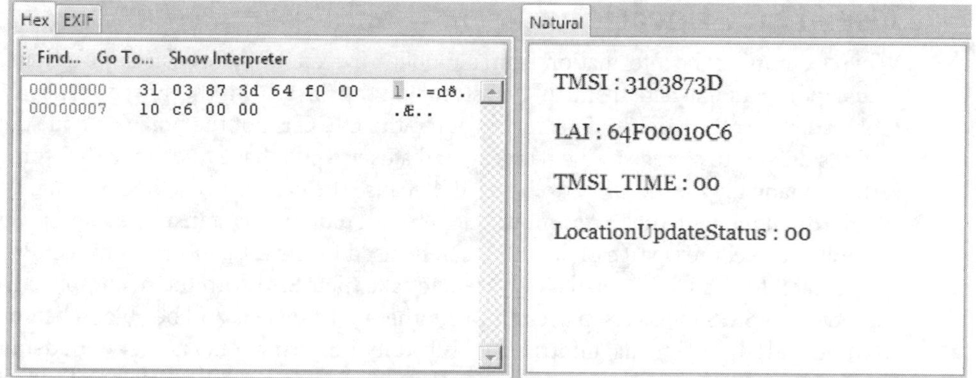

FIGURE 9-7 LOCI and interpreted information from a mobile forensic solution

FPLMN

Forbidden Public Land Mobile Network (FPLMN) is an Elementary File under DF_GSM that identifies networks with which the device carrier does not have a valid agreement to access. In other words, a PLMN (both MCC and MNC) will be written to the FPLMN if the network rejects the location update, because PLMN is not allowed. This Elementary File once had a limit of four records, but with the new UICC specification, it can hold up to *n* records, depending upon the card manufacturer and carrier specifications. When a record is added to the FPLMN Elementary File, that record is placed after the last record; if there are no additional slots, the first record is removed and the new record is added to the last available slot.

In terms of value for the examiner, the FPLMN identifies specific country codes along with the carrier of record, which could also identify a geographic region in which the mobile device was being used or attempted to access. If a user, for example, had stated that he was not in a certain country and admitted to having control of the mobile device, but access was attempted to a forbidden network in the country the user denied being in, an argument could be made that the user was indeed within the country. This information could be based upon the evidence located within the FPLMN Elementary File. Table 9-4 shows the technical information regarding the FPLMN format.

TABLE 9-4 TS 151 011 Information on the FPLMN

File ID	Length (Bytes)	Bytes	Need
6F7B	12	1–3 = PLMN 1 4–6 = PLMN 2 7–9 = PLMN 3 10–12 = PLMN 4	Mandatory

User Data Locations

When examining the information from a mobile device UICC, forensic applications primarily focus upon personal data that could be stored on the SIM. With the storage capacity of today's mobile devices, the storage of personal data to the UICC is not the norm. Mobile device settings default to storage to the handset, and a user would have to change the storage location settings manually for the UICC to be used. Because the capacity of a SIM is finite, as set by standards, along with the mass amount of personal data that is transmitted and received by a mobile device, the storage of data that can be used for investigations is limited. Previously, the portability of a UICC could allow users to take their SIM with them, complete with their contacts and SMS messages, place it into another GSM device, and be able to be up and running with their personal information, subscriber information, and network details. With the movement to world phones that cover the necessary cellular bands globally, there is no need to have multiple devices to cover a particular cellular band using the singular UICC. Because the need for portability is no longer a necessity, carriers and phone manufacturers alike no longer store data to the UICC by default. This does not dismiss the importance of collecting the UICC content, however.

Mobile forensic tools concentrate on several areas to recover this personal data within the UICC, as listed in the following section. The examiner should understand the location, format, and structure of these areas to help validate the recovery of the automated mobile forensic software solution. Again, understanding how an automated tool identifies, converts, and displays mobile device data will satisfy another step in becoming a mobile forensic expert.

SMS

The Short Message Service (SMS) is another Elementary File located on the UICC. It contains several records that define many aspects of the message and service. Either 3GPP TS 23.040 or ETSI 123 040 for UMTS defines these records as messages that either originate from the mobile equipment (ME) or are received from the subscriber's network. The record length cannot be more than 176 bytes, with the first byte being a status of the record and the remaining bytes making up the architecture of the message. Table 9-5 shows the file information obtained from ETSI 123 040 with specific information on the format for EF_SMS files.

The status byte of the record, shown in Table 9-6, will tell the examiner several interesting facts. If the status byte indicates "Unused" and content is still contained within bytes 2–176, the examiner should assume, with great certainty, that the message has been deleted. The ME

TABLE 9-5 TS 151 011 Information on the SMS

File ID	Length (Bytes)	Bytes	Need
6F3C	176	1 = Status Information 2–176 = Remainder	Optional

simply changes the status of the record and does not remove the content. Since the status shows "Unused," the record slot is available and thus can be overwritten with a new message, but until that time the record is available to be recovered by the examiner. The status byte can assist in an investigation if the SMS was alleged to have been sent, but did not have service or had been submitted but rejected by the network and was never delivered. Using the status byte, an examiner can make this determination.

Note It is important that the examiner understand that the recovery of "slack space," or partial SMS messages, from a SIM card is not possible because of the way a record is written to the card. When an SMS message is submitted to be written to a SIM card and an open "unused" slot is identified, the 176-byte record is then written to the SIM. It does not matter if the message occupied only 56 bytes; all 176 bytes will be written to the record, overwriting any record that had previously existed. When is SIM card is written to, it is all or nothing.

TABLE 9-6 Message Status Byte from ETSI TS 131 102 V9.5.0 (2011-01)

Binary Value	Status	Hexadecimal Value
00000000	Unused	x00
00000001	Mobile terminated, read	x01
00000011	Mobile terminated, unread	x03
00000101	Mobile originated, sent to network	x05
00000111	Mobile originated, message to be sent (unsent)	x07
00001101	Status report requested but not (yet) received	x0D
00010101	Status report requested, received, but not stored in EF-SMSR	x15
00011101	Status report requested, received, and stored in EF-SMSR	x1D

Bytes 2–176 make up the content with a set length for the actual message content depending upon how the data is formatted; this is often referred to as the Transport Protocol Data Unit (TPDU). The TPDU contains a variety of data, depending upon whether the message was sent (SMS-SUBMIT) or received (SMS-DELIVER). For an SMS-SUBMIT message, Table 9-7 shows the various types of data stored within the TPDU. For an SMS-DELIVER message, the content differs slightly, as shown in Table 9-8. Each type of content is covered in the following tables with specific comments and explanations for better understanding.

A breakdown, description, and decoding of the TPDU can be found in the following list:

- **Length of SMSC (Short Message Service Center) Information** This is the number of octets (8 bits or 1 byte) that will be used to store the type of number and also the number of the service center. Typically, SMS-SUBMIT messages have the value 00, which indicates the use of the service center number internal to the mobile device. Not all handsets have this value, and if it is missing, it means the SMSC will be obtained from the handset along with the TON/NPI and Service Center Number.
- **Type of Number and Numbering Plan Indicator (TON/NPI)** This single octet indicates the type of number that the preceding telephone number will represent. This byte is representative of the binary number created, with the first bit always 1, and is combined with the TON, which is 3 bits, and the NPI, which is 4 bits. Table 9-9 represents the various combinations and values for TON and NPI values. Once the correct hexadecimal number is located, the number will be converted to a binary number that will be used to decipher the type of number and number plan used in the message.

TABLE 9-7 SMS-SUBMIT Structure from TS 100 901

Type	Description	Need
TP-MTI	TP-Message-Type-Indicator	Mandatory
TP-RD	TP-Reject-Duplicated	Mandatory
TP-VPF	TP-Validity-Period-Format	Mandatory
TP-RP	TP-Reply-Path	Mandatory
TP-UDHI	TP-User-Date-Header-Indicator	Optional
TP-SRR	TP-Status-Report-Request	Optional
TP-MR	TP-Message-Reference	Mandatory
TP-DA	TP-Destination-Address	Mandatory
TP-PID	TP-Protocol-Identifier	Mandatory
TP-DCS	TP-Data-Coding-Scheme	Mandatory
TP-VP	TP-Validity-Period	Optional
TP-UDL	TP-User-Data-Length	Mandatory
TP-UD	TP-User-Data	Optional

For example, a common value is x91, which, when converted to binary, is 1 001 0001 and will indicate that a plus sign (+) is attached to the number in front of the country code. Using Table 9-7, the examiner would be able to confirm that this number is an international number conforming to the ISDN/telephone numbering plan by dropping the first MSB (always 1), decoding the following 3 bits for the TON and the remaining 4 bits for the NPI.

TABLE 9-8 SMS-DELIVER Structure from TS 100 901

Type	Description	Need
TP-MTI	TP-Message-Type-Indicator	Mandatory
TP-MMS	TP-More-Messages-to-Send	Mandatory
TP-RP	TP-Reply-Path	Mandatory
TP-UDHI	TP-User-Date-Header-Indicator	Optional
TP-SRI	TP-Status-Report-Indication	Optional
TP-OA	TP-Originating-Address	Mandatory
TP-PID	TP-Protocol-Identifier	Mandatory
TP-DCS	TP-Data-Coding-Scheme	Mandatory
TP-SCTS	TP-Service-Center-Time-Stamp	Mandatory
TP-UDL	TP-User-Data-Length	Mandatory
TP-UD	TP-User-Data	Optional

TABLE 9-9 Binary Representation of TON/NPI Key of SMS Messages

TON Binary	Interpreted	NPI Binary	Interpreted
000	Unknown	0000	Unknown
001	International number	0001	ISDN/Telephone Numbering Plan
010	National number	0011	Data Numbering Plan
011	Network specific number	0100	Telex Number Plan
100	Subscriber number	0101	Service Center Specific
101	Alphanumeric (7 bit)	0110	Service Center Specific
110	Abbreviated number	1000	National Numbering Plan
111	Reserved	1001	Private Numbering Plan

- **Service Center Number** This value is the representative number of the service center that was used to route the SMS message. This value per ETSI TS 123 040 V12.2.0 (2014-10) is stored in semi-octets in BCD (Binary Coded Decimal) format, as defined in GSM 44.008 and again in ETSI TS 124 008 V11.8.0 (2013-10). This format is also reverse nibble. Often, the numbering does not complete an octet, so an F is added to complete the octet.
- **First Octet of Short Message Transfer Protocol (TP-SM)** This single byte indicates the type of message from the six defined types in ETSI GSM 03.40. This hexadecimal byte should be converted to binary, and the two least significant bits are used to determine the type of the SMS message. Table 9-10 lists the various types of messages that are identified by the two least significant bits (1, 0) in the first octet of the SM-TP message. These bits are referred to as the TP-MTI (Message Type Indicator).
- **Address Length** A single octet represents the length of the actual sender number. This byte will need to be converted to decimal to obtain the number of nibbles that are represented by the telephone number. Unlike the SMSC length, this value will not include the following byte that indicates the TON/NPI.
- **Type of Number and Numbering Plan Indicator (TON/NPI)** Table 9-9 can again be used to determine the number plan type and type of number of the sender.
- **Sender Number** The sender number is again in semi-octets or reverse nibble (BCD) as was the case with the Service Center Number.
- **TP-Protocol-Identifier (TP-PID)** This octet will identify the protocol that has been used for the transmission of the message. For standard ME to SC communication, this value will most likely be 00 as defined by ETSI TS 123 040 V12.2.0 (2014-10).
- **TP-Data Coding Scheme (TP-DCS)** This octet represents the coding that has been used to encode the message. This value will assist the ME in decoding the format once received. As with all other values, this octet, when converted to binary data, can be interpreted to determine the value. In Table 9-11, values are given as represented in 3GPP 3G TS 23.038 V2.0.0 (1999-06). Most often, the value for the TP-DCS will be 00 to indicate that the default 7-bit data code scheme will be used. However, in countries such as China, Korea, Japan, and others that use characters outside the ASCII range, this value

TABLE 9-10 **Binary Representation of TP-SM Byte of SMS Messages, which Indicates the Message Protocol Used**

TP-MTI	Direction	Message Type
0 0	MS → SC	SMS-DELIVER-REPORT
0 0	SC → MS	SMS-DELIVER
0 1	MS → SC	SMS-SUBMIT
0 1	SC → MS	SMS-SUBMIT-REPORT
1 0	MS → SC	SMS-COMMAND
1 0	SC → MS	SMS-STATUS-REPORT

TABLE 9-11 Binary Representation of TP-DCS Byte of SMS Messages, which Indicates the Data Coding Protocol Used

Bits 3 and 2	Translated	Bits 1 and 0	Translated
00	Default alphabet	00	Class 0
01	8 bit data	01	ME - Specific
10	UCS2	10	SIM Specific Message
11	Reserved	11	TE Specific

will be different because UCS2 will most likely be used. An example would be x04 in the TP-DCS section of the SIM record. The x04 in binary would be 01 00, which indicates 8-bit data and class 0 message.

- **TP Service Center Time Stamp (TP-SCTS)** This value is represented by semi-octets and reverse nibble (BCD) in the ordering of Year, Month, Day, Hour, Minute, Second, and Timezone. The Timezone is the number of quarter hours from the local time to GMT time, and the most significant bit of the first octet indicates whether the number is positive or negative GMT. The Timezone is significant because if the ME has knowledge of the local time zone, the ME can display the received time in the local format. The time zone and time are local to the sending entity, which is important for the examiner to understand, especially when time and date are critical to the case.
- **TP User Data Length (TP-UDL)** This integer value, represented in hexadecimal, is the length of data that is contained within the message. This value is also determined by the TP-DCS, or data format, discussed earlier. If the TP-DCS is the default, 7-bit is the length represented by septets (2 bytes) and 8-bit and UCS2 are represented by octets (1 byte). After converting this number into a decimal value, the examiner can identify the length of the message data immediately following as displayed in octets.

The message maximum length set by standards is 140 bytes. If the message is formatted using the 7-bit GSM alphabet, the records shall not exceed 160 characters. However, if the message is formatted using 8-bit, the record content shall not exceed 140 characters. To make matters more confusing, when examining SMS output and UCS2 coding (Unicode) is used in the message content, the message length shall not exceed 70 characters using the 16-bit UCS2 alphabet format. All formats are documented in 3GPP TS 23.038. The various coding formats for the message allow for the transmission and reception of messages in multiple languages and also messages with more than the default 140 characters. The 7-bit or the GSM alphabet as defined by 3GPP TS 23.038 is the default format and is mandatory for network providers, but countries that use languages not supported by the extended ASCII table of the GSM alphabet (China, Korea, Japan) use the UCS2 (16-bit) format. The ME will always default to the 7-bit format, but as soon as a character is entered that is not part of the 7-bit GSM alphabet, the entire message is re-encoded into UCS2.

- **TP-User Data (TP-UD)** The User Data portion of the SMS contains the message in 7-bit, 8-bit, or UCS2 format as specified in the TP-DCS. This data is represented in forensic tools as hexadecimal values.
- **TP-Message Reference (TP-MR)** The single octet is found in sent messages that indicate the integer value of a message reference. This value will typically be x00, but can be a value from 0 to 255.

Both SMS-SUBMIT and SMS-DELIVER use a combination of the items outlined in this section and others outlined in ETSI TS 123 040. Figure 9-8 shows an actual SMS-DELIVER message, and Table 9-12 describes the values and decodes the data in the figure. These illustrations can assist the examiner in locating key artifacts within the SMS message that are typically observed in a UICC file system extraction.

Notice that sometimes characters are within BCD values and must be interpreted as a 0, but in Table 9-13, the extended BCD characters are identified. These can be seen within HEX values throughout SIM records.

Contacts

Contacts on a UICC are referred to as Abbreviated Dialing Numbers (ADN). This Elementary File is located on a SIM application under DF_Telecom and can also be under DF_Phonebook on a USIM application. Before the UMTS and USIM applications, the SIM contained only a single phonebook located under DF_Telecom, where it still is today on the UICC. When the

```
00000000  01 07 91 21 60 13 03 10 f2 04 0b 91
0000000c  21 80 53 33 97 f2 00 00 60 60 71 12
00000018  41 62 8a 1e 57 74 98 0e ca 87 41 e4
00000024  77 da 0d 02 81 86 61 76 da fc 96 bb
00000030  d3 61 90 58 5e 26 03 ff ff ff ff ff
0000003c  ff ff ff ff ff ff ff ff ff ff ff ff
00000048  ff ff ff ff ff ff ff ff ff ff ff ff
00000054  ff ff ff ff ff ff ff ff ff ff ff ff
00000060  ff ff ff ff ff ff ff ff ff ff ff ff
0000006c  ff ff ff ff ff ff ff ff ff ff ff ff
00000078  ff ff ff ff ff ff ff ff ff ff ff ff
00000084  ff ff ff ff ff ff ff ff ff ff ff ff
00000090  ff ff ff ff ff ff ff ff ff ff ff ff
0000009c  ff ff ff ff ff ff ff ff ff ff ff ff
000000a8  ff ff ff ff ff ff ff ff
```

FIGURE 9-8 Actual hexadecimal message from an SMS message

TABLE 9-12 Corresponding Values with Figure 9-8 with Decoded Data for Values Listed

Index Number	Value Description	Decoded Data
1	Status byte	01 = Mobile Terminated, Read
2	Length of SMSC information	7 bytes
3	Type of SMSC	91 = International Format
4	SMSC number	12063130012
5	First octet of SMS-DELIVER message	04 = SMS-DELIVER
6	Length of sender address	0b = 11
7	Type of address of sender number	91 = International Format
8	Sender number	12083533792
9	Protocol identifier	00
10	Data encoding scheme	00 = Default
11	Time stamp	06/17/06 21:14:26
12	Length of user data	1e = 30
13	User data	What ya doin California bred

TABLE 9-13 Extended BCD Values

BCD	Character/Meaning
0	0
9	9
A	*
B	#
D	"Wild" value; this will cause the MMI to prompt the user for a single digit (see GSM 02.07 [3])

USIM application was added to the UICC, two phonebooks were possible. For an examiner, this often led to problems when using a software solution that was unable to obtain both the USIM and SIM applications' stored data. This was typically nontransparent to the examiner and often went unnoticed. Today, mobile forensic solutions support both application phonebooks.

Often these phonebooks coexist and contain duplicate records, but it is entirely possible that the records under DF_Phonebook on the USIM are unique and accessible only by reading the DF_Phonebook on the USIM application. The phonebook located on the USIM application is under the DF_Phonebook, which is under DF_Telecom. This is referred to as the *global phonebook*. Multiple phonebooks are available under the DF_Telecom/DF_Phonebook and can be application specific. This means that a single phonebook under DF_Phonebook can be used by a single application on the mobile device up to 250 record entries. UICCs with the DF_Phonebook can hold thousands of contact names and numbers, and this Dedicated file should be investigated. The contacts located under the USIM and SIM application under DF_Telecom/EF_ADN hold a maximum of 250 records and are duplicated between applications (see Figure 9-9). Contacts can be located in several places within a mobile device's UICC.

Like other data on the UICC, the data within the ADN record is coded in a semi-octet (BCD) format with the possibility of an *alpha identifier*, which is a name associated with the listed phone number. When an alpha identifier is used, the format, as specified by standards in 3GPP TS 23.038, will be 7-bit GSM alphabet, left justified, and all unused bytes will use FF or UCS2 format. The alpha identifier can be 0 to 242 bytes in length, and the rest of the record to include the ADN length, TON/NPI, ADN, Configuration Record, and Extension Record must be 14 bytes.

Much like the SMS record, the ADN will be coded in BCD format, preceded by the length of the ADN and the TON/NPI. The length is much like the SMS embedded Address Length previously discussed. Using Table 9-9, the Type of Number and Numbering Plan Indicator (TON and NPI) can be determined by the examiner before decoding the actual ADN that immediately follows. The ADN, as previously indicated, is coded in semi-octets or BCD format just like the service center and sender number in the SMS records. The balance of the ADN, if larger than 20 characters, will be written to an extension file under EF_EXT1 and is indicated in the last byte of the ADN record. The preceding byte, called the *configuration record* or *capability record*, can indicate whether additional configuration or capabilities are needed for the call and points to a record in the EF_CCP1 file. The complete breakdown of an actual record in an EF_ADN record is shown in Table 9-14.

It is extremely important that the examiner understand the layout and limitations of storage within an ADN record because overflow of data could reside within another file that the

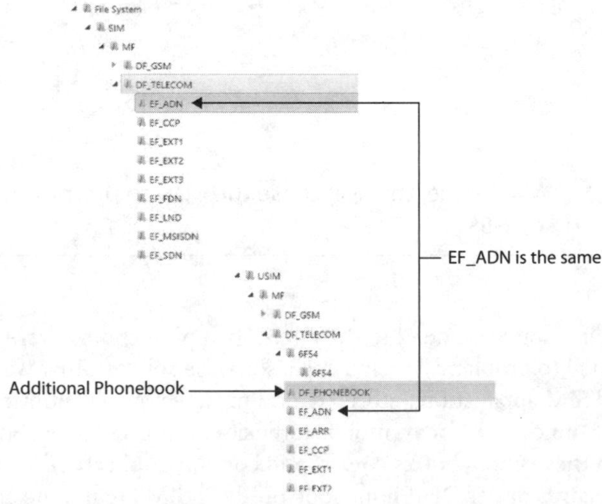

FIGURE 9-9 Both the USIM and SIM applications can hold ADN records; one EF_ADN will be duplicated between the USIM and SIM.

TABLE 9-14 Abbreviated Dialing Number (EF_ADN) Are Contacts that Can Be Found in Both the USIM and SIM Application

File ID	Length (Bytes)	Bytes	Need
4F3A	N+14	1 to n = Alpha identifier	Optional
		n +1 = Length of BCD number	
		n + 2 = TON/NPI	
		n + 3 to n + 12 = Dialing number	
		n + 13 = Capability/Configuration	
		n + 14 = Extension1 record identifier	

forensic software quite possibly will miss. It is also important to examine the UICC to locate data not recoverable or missed by forensic software. For example, if a record from the EF_ADN is deleted, and since EF_ADN does not employ a status byte, the entire record is overwritten with FF when the record is deleted from the SIM. A deleted contact is not recoverable. However, records in the DF_Phonebook do not have to be contiguous, and noncontiguous records could indicate that the record was deleted before another contact could be added to the phonebook. This could be valuable information for the investigation.

Fixed Dialing Numbers

A UICC contains a phonebook that can be set to allow only numbers within the EF_FDN to be dialed from the mobile device. This phonebook, once activated, is protected by CHV (Card Holder Verification) 2, often called PIN 2, which must be entered to access and edit information. By the user disabling the EF_IMSI and EF_LOCI function of the device for any other number, the mobile device cannot call any numbers other than what is included in the fixed dialing list. Of course, emergency numbers can operate without a SIM inserted into a mobile device, so this does not affect emergency services when dialing out. The EF_FDN is located under DF_Telecom in both the SIM and USIM applications.

Companies, and often parents, can restrict a mobile device to allow only specific call-out numbers but still receive incoming calls. At times, this is also used to store a phonebook that is protected by a layer of security. This enables a user to conceal a set of names and numbers and, in essence, creates a secret phonebook. As an investigator, being aware of the location of the EF_FDN is important because no mobile forensic solutions currently check the fixed dialing numbers Elementary File.

The layout of the EF_FDN is exactly the same as that of the EF_ADN with one exception: if the record exceeds the size allotted for the record, the overflow will be stored in EF_EXT2 instead of EF_EXT1 as with EF_ADN records.

Call Logs

A UICC stores only the last numbers dialed (LND) and does not store incoming calls to the ME's SIM memory. Incoming calls would be stored on the device itself. The Elementary File LND is located under DF_Telecom in both the SIM and USIM application. The LND record is similar to the EF_ADN in the storage capacity and data layout. The LND record can store an alpha identifier (name), a byte to identify the length of the phone number, a byte for TON/NPI, and the actual dialing number in BCD format, a configuration/capability byte, and finally the extension byte.

The EF_LND has limited records, depending on the carrier, but typically no more than 10 records can be stored to the UICC. When a new call is made and all records are occupied, the first record is removed and all records then shift up, with the new record taking the last position. Most of today's mobile devices do not store the call history directly to the mobile device, but it is important for an examiner to understand the format, layout, and location of this valuable data should it be populated.

Dialing Number

The dialing number for the mobile device is not necessarily important to the mobile carrier; the carrier relies on the EF_IMSI to identify the mobile user within the network, so a dialing number does not necessarily need to be stored on a UICC. If during an examination the EF_MSISDN is not located on the UICC, this does not indicate that the device was not used or is not in service. As described, the ability for a mobile device to use the cellular network is not dependent on the MSISDN, and only a valid EF_IMSI is needed. However, the EF_MSISDN is located under the DF_Telecom for both SIM and USIM applications on a UICC. The EF_MSISDN can include several records within the file, depending upon the carrier. Multiple EF_MSISDN records allow the user of the UICC to have a phone number for a business, person, fax, or other, with only a single EF_IMSI. This enables the device to be associated to multiple dialing numbers depending on which number was called.

The format structure for the EF_MSISDN and records is the same as that of the EF_ADN and should be used if the records are to be decoded manually. Figure 9-10 shows the EF_MSISDN records and first record of an actual UICC.

The UICC contains a large number of files that can be examined and verified (see Figure 9-11). It is just a matter of how important the UICC file system might be to the examination.

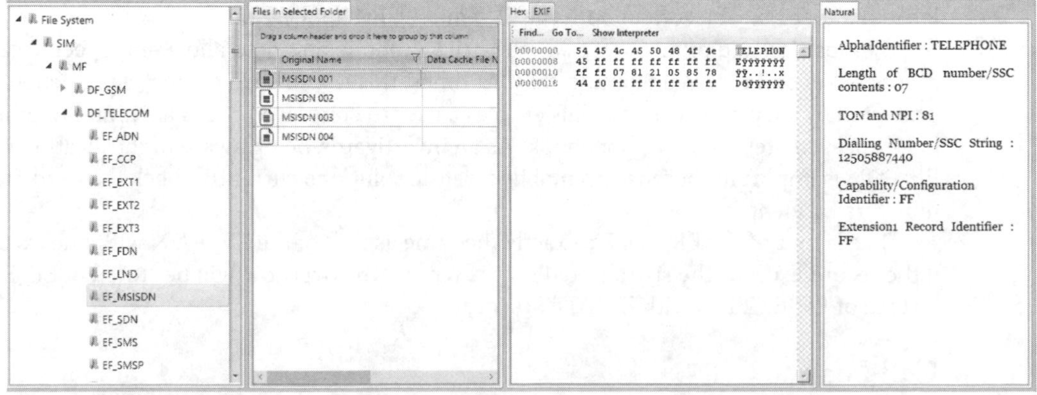

FIGURE 9-10 The MSISDN within the file system, its data, and decoded data

FIGURE 9-11 File system view of a UICC card and the many folders available to the examiner.

Chapter Summary

UICC cards in today's devices might not contain a massive amount of user-related data, such as SMS, contacts, or last numbers dialed. However, the UICC is always needed by a GSM/UMTS when operating on a cellular network.

Even though a UICC is unable to hold data such as videos or other large files, it can hold hundreds of files within the card's file system and applications. Because the UICC must always be inserted while operating on the cellular network, some type of evidence can always be collected—it might be information on last location, networks used, or the vital IMSI needed to crack a case. The UICC should never be neglected in any investigation.

Tip Remember that CDMA devices also must always use a UICC when operating on the GMS/UMTS band.

The UICC data storage methods and structure are clearly documented by standards. This type of documentation can be used to help the examiner understand how to interpret the information contained on the UICC if the forensic software is unable to recover the data or the type of data is not supported.

This chapter introduced the examiner to the decoding of SMS, ADN, LND, IMSI, and ICCID, among other key artifacts. This information will be critical when examining other file system data contained within feature phones and today's smart devices. A lot of the storage formats, such as 7-bit and reverse nibble, are used throughout the industry, and having an understanding will aid the examiner in other decoding exercises within the book and also during actual mobile device investigations.

10 Analyzing Feature Phone, BlackBerry, and Windows Phone Data

In the previous chapter, you were exposed to the advanced analysis of UICC data contained within the file system, which is a small part of the bigger evidence picture. Collecting mobile devices ranging from the feature phones to smart devices involves a connection using supported methods (USB, Bluetooth, JTAG, chip-off), an understanding of supported capabilities of the forensic solution, and a procedure for handling the collected digital evidence. What happens next with the data? Proper analysis of the mobile forensic evidence can uncover information that often makes an ordinary case extraordinary.

Note Analyzing iOS and Android devices are covered in Chapters 11 and 13.

Feature phones are not as prevalent as they used to be, but they occasionally show up in forensic examinations. Typically branded "dumb phones," an inverse to a smart phone, the feature phone can contain information over and above what is collected—or not collected—by a mobile forensic solution. Smart devices, including BlackBerry, Windows Mobile, and Windows Phone devices, can hold the same type of data and files that are stored on a personal computer, but the examination of these devices by most forensic solutions typically captures only a small amount of information. In fact, *most mobile forensic solutions currently used in analysis collect and report only 10 percent of the data.*

The traditionally collected mobile device information is referred to in this book as "tip of the iceberg data." This is generally not the fault of the forensic solution, but the examiner may be to blame because he or she either does not understand that additional data can be accessed or does not have the time to look for it. Either way, an enormous amount of data is missed. With such a wealth of information available within both the logical file system and physical partitions, an examiner must be prepared to get his or her hands dirty.

This chapter is not for those looking for the "Easy" button, but for those who are looking for that needle in the haystack or the smoking gun. This chapter will lead the examiner into the file system of the mobile device, into the areas where the "tip of the iceberg data" has been collected, and beyond. If you're afraid to get your hands dirty with a little hexadecimal digging, this chapter, and mobile device forensics, might not be for you.

Avoiding Tool Hashing Inconsistencies

One big reason for analyzing a device's file system is to confirm or deny a mobile forensic solution's reporting of a hash value. Recall that a hash value is generated by running a mathematical algorithm generally upon a binary file. This hash value can be used as the digital fingerprint for the file. If anything changes within the file, the entire hash value will change, indicating a possible problem with an evidentiary file. Hashes in the mobile forensic solution world can be confusing, however, especially when the same data is collected with two separate software solutions and returns two different hash values. If the information and data are the same, shouldn't the hash values be the same no matter what software is used? In fact, the reality is quite the contrary.

When a mobile forensic solution extracts data from a mobile device, the data is parsed from the file and displayed within the user interface. The examiner can run through the various user data types (such as SMS, contacts, call logs, and MMS), previewing the data. A report can then be created based upon the selected user data. Generally, it is within this report that a hash value is assigned for each selected user data type and prominently displayed alongside the collected data. If an examiner uses a different piece of mobile forensic software to collect the same device, select the same user data types, and create a report, there is an almost 100 percent certainty that if the software supports a hash value function, the hash from the user data type will not match the hash returned by the previously used software. This is not because of corruption of the data by the software solution, but it is determined by what the forensic software is actually hashing and subsequently displaying in the report.

Mobile forensic solutions display a hash within the report dialog after hashing data that was extracted from the actual file; this means that the solution is not extracting data from the original file. In other words, if software A collects the contacts from a mobile device, the contacts are placed into a temporary (or permanent) file and hashed. When software B is used, it also extracts the contacts, writes them to a temporary or permanent file, and then hashes that file. Both software A and B extract the data from the contacts file, transfer the data to their respective files intermediately, and then hash that file. Even if the same software solution conducts the collection of the same mobile device twice, back-to-back, the hash value of the user data types (SMS, MMS, contacts, call logs, and so on) will be different! This is the result of the creating a file on the analysis machine, filling it with the selected user data, and hashing that file. If only 1 bit is different in the file, which could result from simple file type metadata (such as date, time, file type), the entire hash will be different.

Note Understandably, the overall image hash can change upon each collection simply because of system file changes on the device, but the hash of the user type files should never change.

The probability that the hash value will be the same for extracted user data from two extractions is extremely low, and this is why the hash that is created by one software solution should never be used to identify the data fingerprint unless the hash is also the file to which the data was parsed. If an examiner understands that the hash value produced in the report is the hash of the created file (such as a CSV, Excel, or text file) by the mobile forensic software and that any change to the file prior to presentation would change the overall value and could indicate tampering, then the hash has evidentiary value. However, if the hash is used to compare the same data and produced a hash from another software solution, or it is used to testify to the fact that the produced hash is of the actual collected file and not simply the extracted file data, problems in presentation and court could be possible. This, of course, does not pertain to the hash value as reported by the software if the actual physical file has been hashed—only when the hash of the data collected by the software is used.

Hash inconsistencies of reported data in mobile forensic examinations is prevalent with multitool collections, and as such, the examiner should understand that advanced analysis techniques are necessary when multiple tools are used. To circumvent any challenges, the examiner should understand what the hash represents: the file or the extracted data. With this information, the examiner can easily communicate about the method and data the software is representing with the digital fingerprint.

Multiple Tools Often Equal Multiple Hashes

Here's an example of hash inconsistency with a collection conducted on a Motorola V3 device using both Secure View and Cellebrite UFED Classic. This feature phone collection is a simple logical collection, where user data such as SMS, contacts, images, calendar, and call logs are selected for extraction and a report is immediately generated for all the collected data. Both solutions produce HTML reports and display a hash of the captured information above each data type. The hash values for each data type from both software solutions are then compared along with the content. This information is outlined in Table 10-1.

Clearly, the number of each extracted data type matches between solutions, and when the content is examined, all content is identical. What is evident, however, is that the overall hash value shown in the table is not the same. The different hashes, with the same data, drive home the point that a solution's representation of the data by a hash can lead to problems when multiple tools are used on a single device. Understanding why this occurs, as outlined in this section, will assist the examiner in explaining this discrepancy. Individual files, such as images and videos, however, are correctly identified by hashes between both solutions because both solutions hashed the actual file, not the temporary report file into which it is embedded.

TABLE 10-1 List of Collected Data and Hashes from Two Mobile Forensic Solutions

User Data Type	Secure View Number Extracted	Secure View Hash Value	Cellebrite Number Extracted	Cellebrite Hash Value
SMS	11	9f9812c30f011ebb9e506a6b009423d6	Failed	
Contacts	15	7b926b47937770e12610ccb99a7212	15	905151d8dbe2cced352a2d0857c76404
Calendar	4	6779b3ce262c6ccbf8b299379c93dea3	No Support	
Call Logs	16	63987ecdc7bae137fecf6770acb59277	16	C38d019a78108f638c6182b0c41a5d98

Iceberg Theory

An iceberg floats on water because the density of the ice (around 0.92 g/ml) is greater than that of the sea water (1.03 g/ml). Ice is about 90 percent as dense as water, so only 10 percent of the ice is actually above the water's surface. This means that an iceberg's total mass is 90 percent below the surface of the water! What does an iceberg have to do with mobile device forensics? If we compare the total volume of data on a mobile device versus what a mobile forensic tool actually parses and displays to an examiner, the displayed data is what I call the "tip of the iceberg data."

Mobile forensic solutions connect to a mobile device, enable the user to select the items to extract, and then pull the data from the appropriate files. Once complete, the solution will display the collected information and the examiner can then complete a report. The information collected is displayed to the examiner in a parsed format (in a report user interface), but it is actually less than 10 percent of the collected data that the examiner would get if the mobile solution were capable of a file system or physical collection. This fact alone leads credence to the "push-button forensic" aura that mobile forensics produces in the digital forensic circles and propagates the banter that mobile forensics should instead be called "mobile extraction."

The iceberg theory as it relates to a mobile forensic examination is demonstrated in the statistics gathered from an LG VX8300 feature phone and described in the sidebar, "Cellphone-berg."

Cellphone-berg

The LG flip phone was the standard for Verizon in the United States and has since been discontinued, but the statistics produced during the testing of the iceberg theory can be seen across all feature phones. First, the LG VX8300 has 28MB of internal storage. This value represents the storage space for both the firmware of the device and any user data—which considering today's device numbers for internal storage is hard to fathom. The collection of the LG VX8300 produced extracted contacts, call history, SMS, and media—all of which were displayed in the user interface; these capabilities for extraction are generically supported across mobile forensic solutions. The total size of this data was just over 11MB, with most of the space occupied by 61 images and two videos taken with the LG VX8300. The file system containing the files and folders had a total size of 20MB. The images, videos, and other collected user data occupied roughly 55 percent of the file system and were immediately viewable to the examiner. This is the "tip of the iceberg data," the WYSIWYG data commonly regarded as the only data available on the device—so the mobile forensic software says. However, a closer look at the device file system reveals that there are 366 files within the file system, and 65 of these files are the files that produced the WYSIWYG data; what is important to realize is that another 301 files within the file system could potentially hold data that is valuable to the investigation. This is the *WYDSIWYN* (what you don't see is what you need) data and the part of the examination that is often neglected. Out of the 366 files within the file system, only 18 percent are interrogated and examined—quite lazy for an automated process. Within this LG VX8300's file system is the other 82 percent—a mixture of system data and user data. The user data in the file system can be critical, as can the actual files the user data is pulled from during the automated process. An example of this can be expressed by the additional 112 image files that were carved from the file system and unaccounted for in the "tip of the iceberg data" the automated tool collected and displayed within the media view. Also, within the file system are the MMS files that are not automatically parsed out by the mobile forensic solution. See Figure 10-1.

Note *WYSIWYG* (*what you see is what you get*) is a term coined back in the 1970s, when onscreen text in a word processing program (Bravo) looked like what would be output to print. *WYDSIWYN* (*what you don't see is what you need*) is a term I used in a talk on mobile forensics in early 2013.

Each examination, whether it is on a feature phone or a smart device, should be performed by the examiner in a way that extends outside of the automated exam in an attempt to uncover some of the valuable information contained below the surface. This is critical to becoming an expert in mobile forensics—living in the 90 percent below the surface of the mobile device berg.

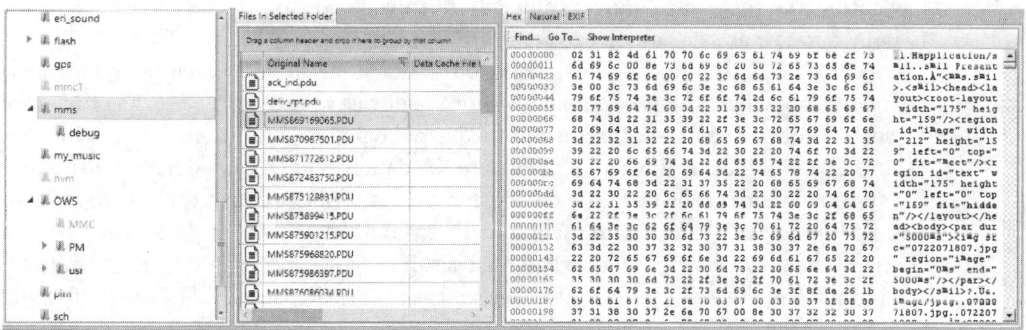

FIGURE 10-1 **MMS folder containing some of the additional files unaccounted for in a "tip of the iceberg data" examination**

Feature Phones

As mentioned, feature phones, or legacy phones, are common even in today's smart device world. Feature phones come with stock apps installed with the firmware of the device, while smart devices can be updated to allow the addition of apps from various online repositories without changing the underlying firmware of the devices. This does not change the fact that a wealth of information can be found within a feature phone file system. A feature phone contains an operating system and file system, where user data is stored and retrievable if the examiner takes the time to investigate.

Culling through the file system of a feature phone can be tedious work because it often represents "uncharted territory." In fact, sorting through the file system of the feature phone is like searching through thousands of papers for the one sheet possibly containing the username and password. Because little documentation exists regarding the format of data and file system structures and the lack of conformity, a feature phone is often more difficult to examine than a smart device. As a result, some mobile forensic examiners may rely on data that an automated tool will extract and present, neglecting the valuable information available within the file system—but this is where the most important data is nested.

Feature phones will continue to be available to users around the world who value price over functionality. Because of this, examiners should be prepared to examine and analyze feature phones at a level that exceeds the data output by a forensic solution.

Feature Phone "Tip of the Iceberg Data"

User data collected automatically by a forensic tool is often the only information an examiner will present in a case; the examiner relies on only this information for the investigation or examination. *User data*, in the context of this section, is data that can be placed into the PIM (personal information manager) category, such as contacts, call logs, SMS, MMS, calendar, and notes. PIM information does not encompass the amount of data that could possibly be stored on a feature phone, but typically it is the only data collected by a mobile forensic solution during many "routine" examinations. These data types are often separated into views for easy navigation and reporting. The examiner should always consult the forensic tool documentation to determine what data can be extracted and parsed.

When a mobile forensic solution presents data, it has already been pulled, parsed, and decoded from a file or files contained within the device's file system. Because the mobile forensic solution then creates a hash of the parsed data, not of the actual file, a thorough examiner should locate the actual file where the data had been pulled from within the device file system and manually examine and hash this data. This hash can then be used to verify a mobile forensic tool's interaction with the file to confirm or deny any allegation that the tool changed the file during extraction and analysis. If the forensic tool does not hash the file in the file system, the examiner can use free tools such as MD5summer (www.md5summer.org) or Bullzip MD5 Calculator (www.bullzip.com/products/md5/info.php) to accomplish the hashing. The hash should then be documented in the examiner's report.

In the following sections, different types of formats for date and time, along with data layouts, will be discussed. Using this information, the examiner can decode files that contain the user data parsed with automated tools to help verify and validate what the automated tool is providing.

Note Not all file systems are accessible on feature phones. These methods apply only to devices from which a file system can be extracted.

Parsing a Feature Phone File System

One of the most important features of any mobile forensic solution is the ability to acquire a feature phone's file system. Even a simple CDMA LG device with only 28MB of storage space can provide a wealth of information should the examiner look into the file system outside of what an automated tool can pull.

Unfortunately, one of the most difficult and time-consuming jobs for an examiner is to look through each and every file and folder for information that might pertain to the case or investigation. There are many different embedded file systems (EFS) formats, and a lot of them are proprietary and specific to manufacturer and carrier. However, CDMA feature phones often contain a similar directory structure because the internal components conform to the Binary Runtime Environment for Wireless (BREW) mobile platform (MP), which is the most widely used application platform in CDMA devices. The BREW MP EFS is documented on the BREW web site (https://developer.brewmp.com/resources/tech-guides/file-system-technology-guide/high-level-architecture/brew-mp-file-system) and outlines the format for the major structures within the EFS. Because Qualcomm chips can be used in both CDMA and GSM devices, understanding the major structures of the BREW MP and what data can be located in these areas can be important in identifying where to look for valuable data.

By comparing the LG file system in Figure 10-2 and the UTStarcom file system in Figure 10-3, you can see that both conform to the BREW MP, and important folders can be readily observed. Accessing the CDMA feature phone EFS is a much easier task than accessing a GSM device EFS because BREW is an open source format developed by Qualcomm. Because of the open API, developers often can obtain file system–level access using the available documentation. GSM feature phones, however, are not as open.

Access to the GSM feature phone EFS is often accomplished only with non-invasive physical access; however, some GSM devices from Nokia allow for file system dumping via

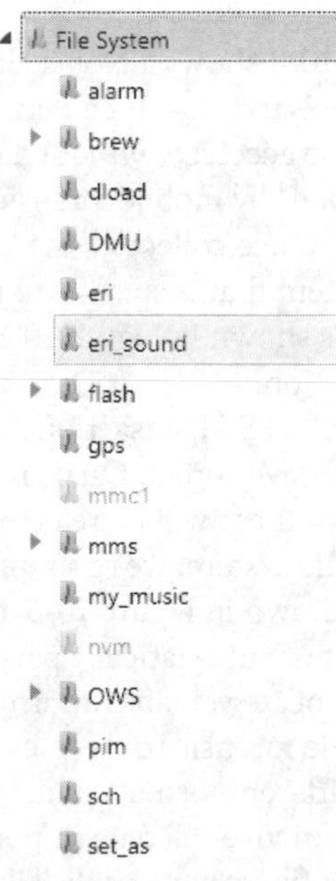

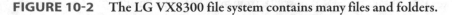

FIGURE 10-2 The LG VX8300 file system contains many files and folders.

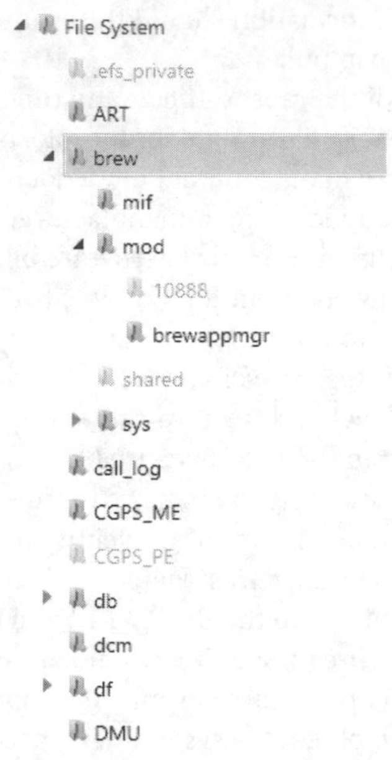

FIGURE 10-3 The UTStarcom feature phone file system also contains many files and folders.

common protocols. Figure 10-4 shows a Nokia GSM file system obtained with MPE+ that was collected from the device and was not a decoded physical binary file. If the GSM feature phone's file system cannot be accessed without a non-invasive physical or invasive collection, the device should be "dumped" by mobile forensic tools (such as Cellebrite UFED, MSAB XRY, or Paraben Device Seizure). Once collected, the binary file can then be decoded. The decoding process rebuilds the file system that is specific to the mobile device "family," the NOR/NAND chip, and underlying EFS, as shown in Figure 10-5, with a Cellebrite decoding of a Samsung non-invasive physical collection.

EFS could be versions of TFS (Transactional File System) for Samsung, Paragon2000 (P2K) and Paragon2005 (P2K05) for Motorola, Qualcomm for LG, or Nokia's proprietary format. (Throughout this book, all of these will be referred to as "EFS" because it is not the intention of this book to rebuild the file system; we're simply navigating and decoding various artifacts.) In the file system example shown in Figure 10-5, the EFS clearly shows an MMS folder with available data, but this was not automatically parsed by any tool. The examiner would now be able to parse manually and locate valuable information once thought nonexistent because it was not parsed by the mobile forensic tool.

Because of the many different formats of data and file systems, it is difficult for any mobile forensic solution to uncover all data important to an investigation. That is where the investigation into the device file system, especially with the feature phone, is most beneficial. The key is to obtain the EFS, if possible, from any feature phone that is to be examined.

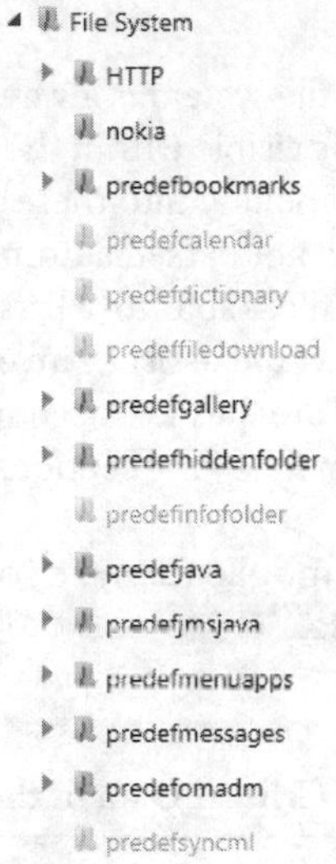

File System
HTTP
nokia
predefbookmarks
predefcalendar
predefdictionary
predeffiledownload
predefgallery
predefhiddenfolder
predefinfofolder
predefjava
predefjmsjava
predefmenuapps
predefmessages
predefomadm
predefsyncml

FIGURE 10-4 Nokia GSM feature phone file system

File Systems
KFAT0
BROWSER
BT
DEFAULT
dir_vfp_temp
dir_vfp_temp
DRM
EMAIL
IM
IMAGES
JAVA
MMS
multimedia
netinfoset
SavePage
SMS
SOUNDS
SUB
SyncML
TEST
USER
VOBJECT
VOICE
WAP
WLAN
TFS4_160.ESS
tfsVersionCode.tfs

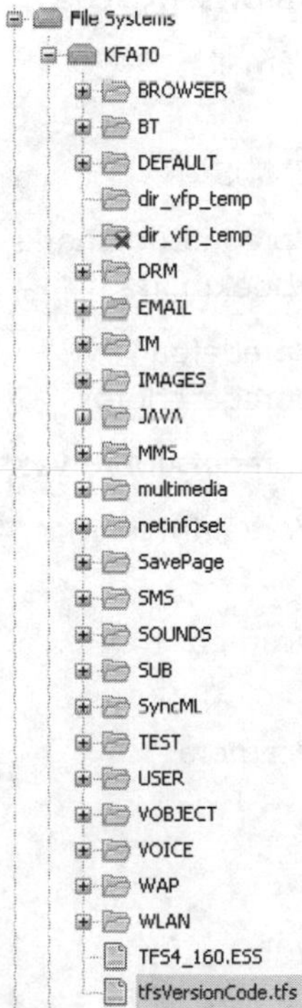

FIGURE 10-5 File system from a binary file obtained with a non-invasive EFS extraction of a Samsung feature phone

Common Layout

Although no specific type of file system is always used within a feature phone, after the data is decoded and a file system is visible within the forensic solution, the examiner can find data in some common locations. Looking into these areas can be critical to obtaining additional information that possibly was not parsed automatically by the tool—or it can help to verify that the tool correctly parsed the file. Table 10-2 lists various folders and files that store information about the user or device that could assist in investigations. Many additional files can also be investigated, and those listed are files I've used in various investigations. Some of the files will be covered in greater detail in following sections.

Tip Remember that the mobile forensic solution must be able to recover the EFS in order to use the table.

TABLE 10-2 Various Locations of Critical Data in the EFS of Feature Phones

Type of Device	Manufacturer	Path	File	Artifact
GSM	Samsung	/Browser/History	.dat	Browser data (NFPKDDAT)
GSM	Samsung	/Browser/Cache	.dcf	Web cache files
GSM	Samsung	/Email	Draft/Inbox/Sent	Browser data (NFPKDDAT)
GSM	Samsung	/MMS	smil files	MMS messages
GSM/CDMA	Nokia	/predefbookmarks /bookmarks	.bak files	User bookmarks
GSM/CDMA	Nokia	/predefgallery /predefphotos	.jpg files	Phone camera storage
GSM/CDMA	Nokia	/predefs40browser	LastURL.bmk	Last visited URL
GSM/CDMA	Nokia	/predefmessages	SMS and MMS	SMS/MMS messages
CDMA	AudioVox	/camera	CameraInfo.dat	Picture names if changed by user
CDMA	AudioVox	/camera	nextphoto.int	Integer of next photo; good to show if one was deleted
CDMA	AudioVox	/db	default_snd.txt	User auto messages
CDMA	AudioVox	/memo	memo_000.pad	User memos
CDMA	AudioVox	/MMS	Various	MMS messages

TABLE 10-2 Various Locations of Critical Data in the EFS of Feature Phones *(Continued)*

Type of Device	Manufacturer	Path	File	Artifact
CDMA	All CDMA devices	/nvm	$SYS.ESN	Electronic serial number
CDMA	AudioVox	/nvm/ch	call_history	Call history file
CDMA	All CDMA devices	/nvm/nvm	nvm_0000	Device serial number, carrier name
CDMA	All CDMA devices	/nvm/nvm	nvm_0002, nvm_minlock, nvm_0000, nvm_002	Name, device lock, subsidy lock
CDMA	AudioVox	/nvm/phbk	phonebook	Device phonebook
CDMA	AudioVox/ Samsung/ others	/nvm/sms	SMS	SMS messages
CDMA	AudioVox	/nvm/smssaved	SMS	Saved SMS messages
CDMA	AudioVox	/VoiceDB/Memos	.qcp	Voice memo files
CDMA	UTStarcom	/db/pb_db	pb_list_table	Copy of contacts
CDMA	UTStarcom	/db/sms_db	sms_inbox_table	Copy of SMS even if SMS deleted
CDMA	LG	/brew/16452/mp	.jpg files	Camera location
CDMA	LG/others	/brew/16452/mf	.3g2 files	Camera location
CDMA	LG/others	/brew/16452/ms	.qcp, .mid files	User recordings
CDMA	LG/Motorola/ others	/brew/mod/4972	Various files db_X	X = Instant Messenger (AOL, MSN, Yahoo!) contacts
CDMA	LG/Motorola// others	/brew/mod/4972	Various files db_X_msg	X = Instant Messenger; stores messages for IM account
CDMA	LG	/pim	Various files	Call history, phonebook

(Continued)

TABLE 10-2 Various Locations of Critical Data in the EFS of Feature Phones *(Continued)*

Type of Device	Manufacturer	Path	File	Artifact
CDMA	Most CDMA	/t9udb	T9udb_eng.dat, T9udb_spa.dat	Dictionary words entered by user for SMS and MMS
CDMA/GSM	Motorola	/motorola/browser /usr	various	Browser data
CDMA	Motorola	/brew/mod/ syncom2	Folders i (inbox), o (outbox), s (saved), d (drafts); each has index folder with mb.idx	Basic SMS/ MMS text
CDMA	Motorola	/brew/mod/ syncom2	Each folder (d, o, i, s) has .att and .env files	Pointers to message and attachments
CDMA	Motorola	/motorola/shared/	Image and video files	Camera location
CDMA	Motorola	/nvm	nvm_security	Device lock
CDMA	Samsung	/cam	Various folders and files	Camera location
CDMA	Samsung	/nvm	dial	Phonebook
CDMA	Samsung	/nvm	dial_tbl	Call history file
CDMA	Samsung	/nvm	schedule	Calendar
CDMA	Samsung	/nvm	T9udb	User dictionary
CDMA	Samsung	/vmemo	.vm files	Voice memo files

File Metadata Cues

Because of the variety of manufacturers and models, all the different files in a feature phone cannot be represented in a single table—unless the table were hundreds of pages long. Some feature phones include more than 4000 different files, most of which are system files, but a tremendous number of these files can hold the "smoking gun." The examiner could search manually through many of the files, but a better approach is to use search terms to locate files that might not be represented by the parsed data extracted by the mobile forensic solution.

To be successful at locating data within the plethora of files in the feature phone file system, the examiner must first understand how to search the files. By using standard text strings and regular expressions, the examiner will be able to locate and examine additional files within the file system (see Figure 10-6, for example). The examiner will not only benefit from the data

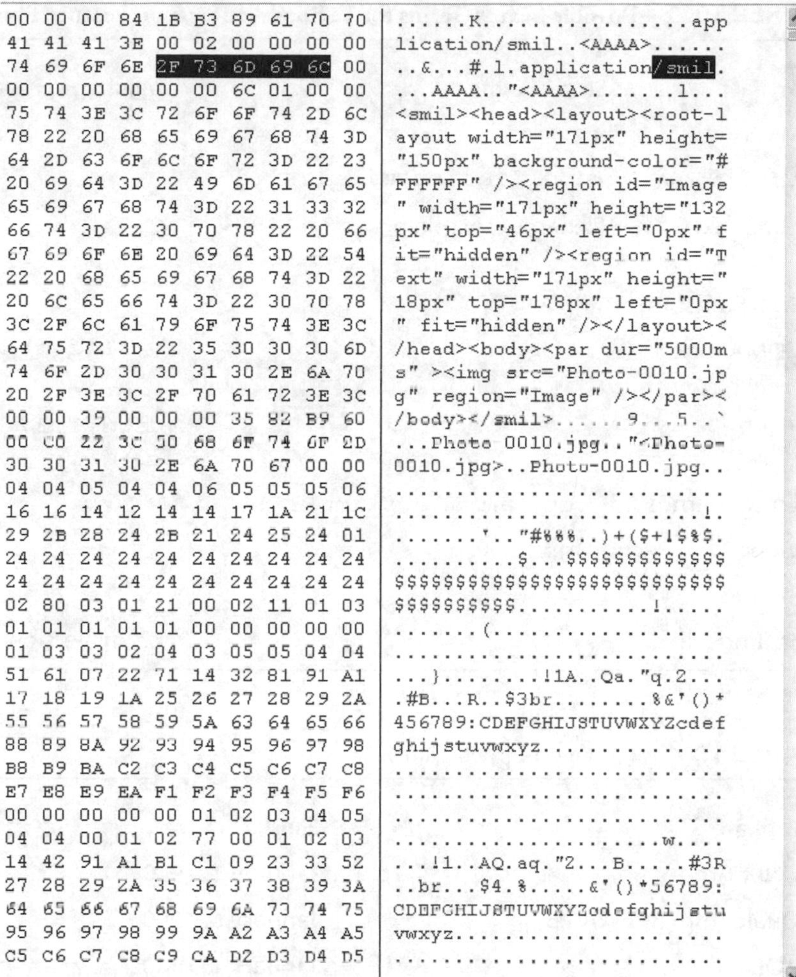

00 00 00 84 1B B3 89 61 70 70
41 41 41 3E 00 02 00 00 00 00
74 69 6F 6E 2F 73 6D 69 6C 00
00 00 00 00 00 00 6C 01 00 00
75 74 3E 3C 72 6F 6F 74 2D 6C
78 22 20 68 65 69 67 68 74 3D
64 2D 63 6F 6C 6F 72 3D 22 23
20 69 64 3D 22 49 6D 61 67 65
65 69 67 68 74 3D 22 31 33 32
66 74 3D 22 30 70 78 22 20 66
67 69 6F 6E 20 69 64 3D 22 54
22 20 68 65 69 67 68 74 3D 22
20 6C 65 66 74 3D 22 30 70 78
3C 2F 6C 61 79 6F 75 74 3E 3C
64 75 72 3D 22 35 30 30 30 6D
74 6F 2D 30 30 31 30 2E 6A 70
20 2F 3E 3C 2F 70 61 72 3E 3C
00 00 39 00 00 00 35 82 B9 60
00 C0 22 3C 50 68 6F 74 6F 2D
30 30 31 30 2E 6A 70 67 00 00
04 04 05 04 04 06 05 05 05 06
16 16 14 12 14 14 17 1A 21 1C
29 2B 28 24 2B 21 24 25 24 01
24 24 24 24 24 24 24 24 24 24
24 24 24 24 24 24 24 24 24 24
02 80 03 01 21 00 02 11 01 03
01 01 01 01 01 00 00 00 00 00
01 03 03 02 04 03 05 05 04 04
51 61 07 22 71 14 32 81 91 A1
17 18 19 1A 25 26 27 28 29 2A
55 56 57 58 59 5A 63 64 65 66
88 89 8A 92 93 94 95 96 97 98
B8 B9 BA C2 C3 C4 C5 C6 C7 C8
E7 E8 E9 EA F1 F2 F3 F4 F5 F6
00 00 00 00 00 01 02 03 04 05
04 04 00 01 02 77 00 01 02 03
14 42 91 A1 B1 C1 09 23 33 52
27 28 29 2A 35 36 37 38 39 3A
64 65 66 67 68 69 6A 73 74 75
95 96 97 98 99 9A A2 A3 A4 A5
C5 C6 C7 C8 C9 CA D2 D3 D4 D5
......K..................app
lication/smil..<AAAA>......
..&...#.1.application/smil.
...AAAA.."<AAAA>.......1...
<smil><head><layout><root-l
ayout width="171px" height=
"150px" background-color="#
FFFFFF" /><region id="Image
" width="171px" height="132
px" top="46px" left="0px" f
it="hidden" /><region id="T
ext" width="171px" height="
18px" top="178px" left="0px
" fit="hidden" /></layout><
/head><body><par dur="5000m
s" ><img src="Photo-0010.jp
g" region="Image" /></par><
/body></smil>......9...5..`
...Photo 0010.jpg.."<Photo-
0010.jpg>..Photo-0010.jpg..
....
.........................!.
.......'.."#%%%..)+($+!$%$.
..........$...$$$$$$$$$$$$$
$$$$$$$$$$$$$$$$$$$$$$$$$$$
$$$$$$$$$$..........!.....
.......(...................
....
...}........!1A..Qa."q.2...
.#B...R..$3br........%&'()*
456789:CDEFGHIJSTUVWXYZcdef
ghijstuvwxyz...............
....
....
....
......................w....
...!1..AQ.aq."2...B.....#3R
..br...$4.%.....&'()*56789:
CDEFGHIJSTUVWXYZcdefghijstu
vwxyz......................
....

FIGURE 10-6 **Using Physical Analyzer to search manually for an MMS message; notice the searched-for string: smil**

recovered, but he or she will gain a better understanding regarding how the mobile forensic solution navigates the feature phone file system. Table 10-3 represents some common search strings that can be used to locate various items within a feature phone file system.

Dates and Times

Dates and times are important for most investigations, and sometimes dates need to be either verified or located. The problem that arises with dates and times within a feature phone are the many different formats available. Depending upon the device, the manufacturer, and even the version of the EFS, the date and time format could be different. Table 10-4 lists the most common date and time types for both GSM and CDMA feature phones along with the epoch that is referenced.

TABLE 10-3 Possible Search Terms for Various Artifacts on Feature Phones

Artifact	Search Terms	Regular Expression
MMS	<smil	
MMS	<applicationsmil_1.smil>	
MMS text content	filename=textplain	
SMS Samsung	DEADBEEF	
CDMA lock codes		\x01\d\d\d\d\x01
IP addresses		\b\d{1,3}\.\d{1,3}\.\d{1,3}\.\d{1,3}\b
Voice memos	.qcp, .amr, .acc, .vm, RIFF	
Videos	.3gp2, .3gp	
Images	.jpg	
Settings files		<?xml version=

TABLE 10-4 Common Epoch Dates

Format	Epoch
UNIX Time	January 1, 1970
Qualcomm BREW/GPS	January 6, 1980
AOL	January 1, 1980

Note The *epoch* is the reference point from which a date and time will start to display.

After a record is located and the examiner manually decodes a date and time, the examiner can look to the table and decide the format. After doing this repeatedly, the examiner will find that decoding becomes easier and will recognize a pattern. Feature phones generally follow a pattern, with the date and time at an offset either from the start of the file or some point within the combined string if multiple records are in a single file. Table 10-5 lists the various date and time formats used by both GSM and CDMA feature phones based upon manufacturer. Most of the date and time formats, along with the epoch, are self-explanatory. The "AOL format," as coined by forensic expert Paul Sanderson, is a represented by 4 bytes, much like UNIX.

TABLE 10-5 Various Date and Time Examples from Feature Phones

Format	Example	Decoded
UNIX time	2E 1A D9 44 (LE)	Aug 8, 2006 23:11
BCD (Binary Coded Decimal)	05 02 19 18 50 26 (YY MM DD HH MM SS)	Feb 19,2005 18:50:26
Qualcomm BREW/GPS	67 D3 5C 33 (LE)	Apr 27,2007 15:04
AOL	2B F0 D6 36 (LE)	Feb 25, 2009 19:04
GSM (BCD reverse nibble)	01 80 71 81 05 30 8A	Aug 17, 2010 18:50:03 (GMT -7)
LG/Samsung	9C 35 6B 7D (LE)	Nov 6, 2006 22:28

Various tools such as DCode and MFI HEX Assistant can help the examiner decode these dates independent of the forensic solution if an embedded HEX interpreter is not included.

The LG/Samsung format needs a little more explanation because the 4-byte values must be converted to a binary number and separated into year, month, day, hour, and minutes:

```
9C 35 6B 7D (LE) converted to binary = 011111010110 1011 00110 10110 011100
                                       \__________/ \__/ \___/ \___/ \____/
                                          Y(2006)   M(11) D(6) H(22)  M(28)
```

Figure 10-7 shows an actual SMS within an LG CDMA phone inbox.dat file with two dates and times outlined. In this particular example, the date and time for the SMS is in Qualcomm BREW format (April 27, 2007 15:04) and BCD format (April 27, 2007 15:03:33), and for this type of file, always 12 bytes from the start of the file using 0-based numbering. Once a format and the offsets are established, parsers can be built to locate and interpret many of these date and time formats. Physical Analyzer, as well as FTK and Oxygen Forensic Analyst, enable the user to search for various formats within the binary files, often converting these formats on the fly. However, the examiner should be aware of the various formats that can be used within a feature phone's file system.

Armed with this information, the examiner can not only verify that the automated tool parsed the data correctly, but when information is located that was not automatically parsed, the examiner can manually decode and present the data. Cellebrite Physical Analyzer decodes many different types of data automatically for the user (see Figure 10-8). However, like all other mobile forensic tools, not all items are located and decoded automatically. Using either Physical Analyzer or Oxygen Forensic Analyst, the examiner can highlight the represented date and time and properly convert that information using a built-in converter. This data can then be bookmarked and recorded for review.

```
sms/inbox049.dat Contents
00000000  C7 00 00 00 50 34 02 C3  DB 74 7D 00 67 D3 5C 33  ....P4...t}.g.\3
00000010  07 04 27 15 03 33 00 00  00 00 00 00 00 00 00 00  ..'..3..........
00000020  00 00 00 00 00 00 00 00  00 00 00 00 00 00 00 00  ................
00000030  00 00 00 00 00 00 00 00  00 00 00 00 00 00 0A 04  ................
00000040  0A 06 03 06 09 01 01 03  05 00 00 00 00 00 00 00  ................
00000050  00 00 00 00 00 00 00 00  00 00 00 00 00 00 00 00  ................
00000060  00 00 00 00 00 00 00 00  00 00 00 00 00 00 00 00  ................
00000070  00 01 00 00 00 00 FF FF  00 00 4C 65 74 20 6D 65  ..........Let me
00000080  20 69 6E 00 00 00 00 00  00 00 00 00 00 00 00 00   in.............
00000090  00 00 00 00 00 03 00 00  00 00 00 00 00 01 09 00  ................
000000A0  00 00 00 00 00 00 00 00  00 00 00 00 00 00 00 00  ................
000000B0  00 00 99 97 A2 0D B9 50  69 DC 00 00 00 00 00 00  .......Pi.......
000000C0  00 00 00 00 00 00 00 00  00 00 00 00 00 00 00 00  ................
000000D0  00 00 00 00 00 00 00 00  00 00 00 00 00 00 00 00  ................
000000E0  00 00 00 00 00 00 00 00  00 00 00 00 00 00 00 00  ................
000000F0  00 00 00 00 00 00 00 00  00 00 00 00 00 00 00 00  ................
00000100  00 00 00 00 00 00 00 00  00 00 00 00 00 00 00 00  ................
00000110  00 00 00 00 00 00 00 00  00 00 00 00 00 00 00 00  ................
```

FIGURE 10-7 An LG file system file from an inbox file; notice two dates and times within a single file, which is indicative of sent and received times for many feature phone files.

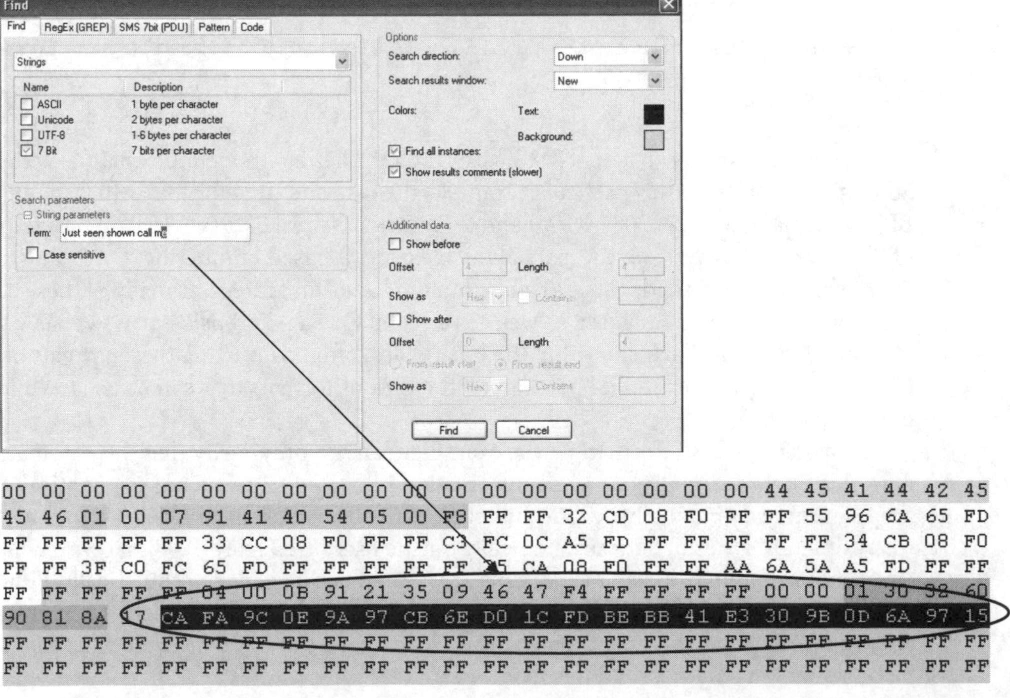

FIGURE 10-8 Using Cellbrite Physical Analyzer, the examiner can search for a string in several formats.

Text Formats

Feature phone mobile data can be difficult to decode. The use of the 7-bit GSM alphabet or UCS-2 (2-byte Universal Character Set, often referred to as PDU, or Protocol Data Unit), use of Unicode, and formatting of phone numbers can cause confusion while deciphering data from feature phones. It also means that data in the mobile device file system cannot always be searched by using a string search.

For SMS messages in the PDU format, the data could be encoded in hexadecimal values, so the examiner must search using a converted string. The string can be converted with a tool such as MFI HEX Assistant, or the mobile forensic solution can automatically convert the string if the feature is supported. Figure 10-9 shows 7-bit data located from a search using MFI HEX Assistant.

Another problem often encountered is when search strings are encoded as Unicode. Some mobile devices store the data as ASCII, but in Unicode, meaning 2 bytes for every character. This means, then, that a standard string search for "dog" would not return a result simply because in the file system, the value is "d.o.g." Because "dog" has a secondary value, here represented by the dot, but actually x00, the search misses the characters. Tools such as Physical Analyzer and FTK enable the user to specify that the search should be in text and Unicode format, which would successfully locate the example term "dog."

For phone numbers, it is important that the examiner remember that numbers can be in reverse nibble (see Figure 10-10) or BCD format. This is also referred to as the "GSM phone number format" by several mobile forensic tools. Tools such as Physical Analyzer enable the examiner to specify the format (GSM phone number) of the data to be searched when entering

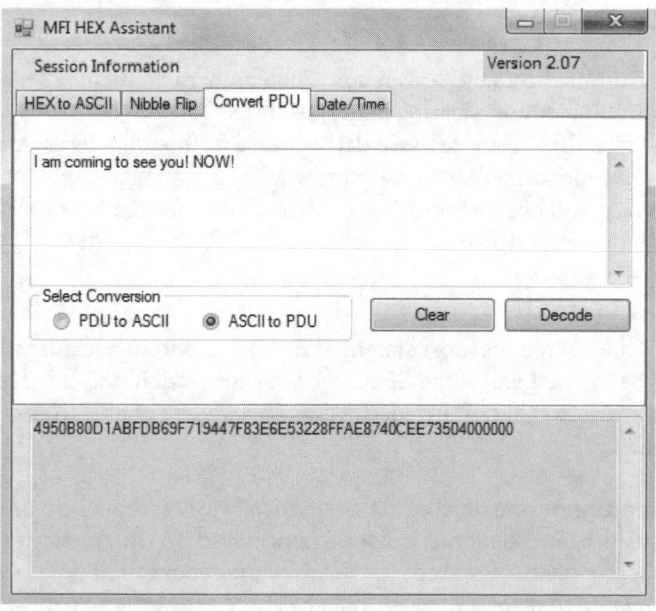

FIGURE 10-9 The search term is entered and 7-bit is selected, which yields a result within the HEX viewer.

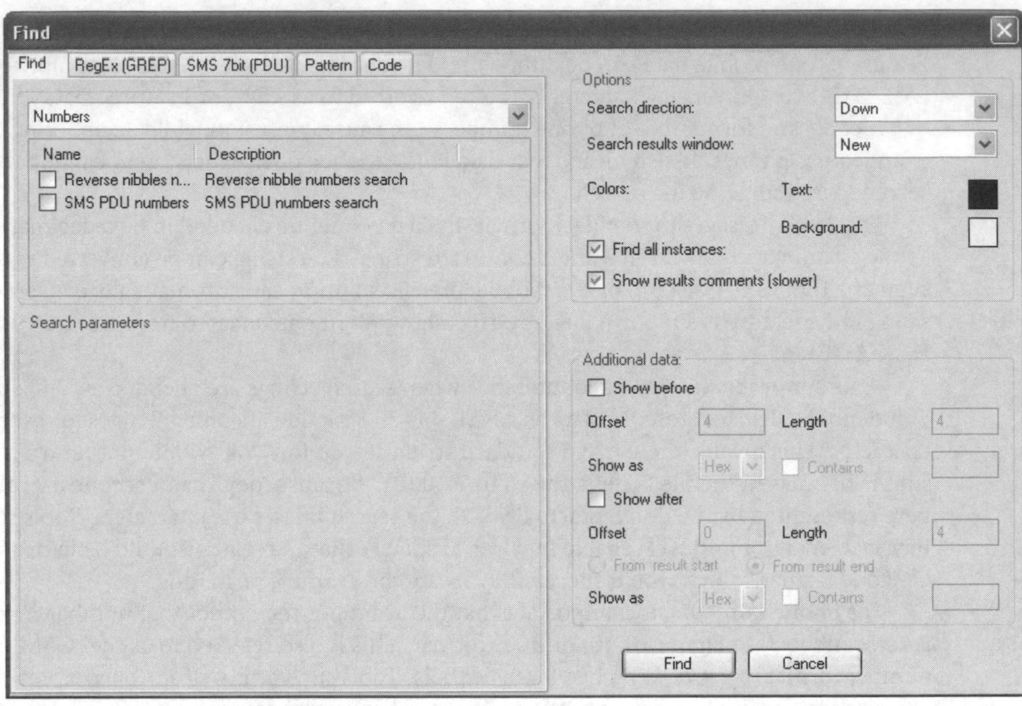

FIGURE 10-10 **Numbers can be stored differently, so searching for numbers in various formats is important.**

the phone number into the search box. The number can then be searched in the various formats simultaneously, yielding better results.

Understanding that text-based data within a feature phone is stored in various formats will help the examiner achieve better success when conducting a search for specific communication. The examiner will be able to convert the string into a format to search both PDU (7-bit) alphabet and standard ASCII strings.

Deleted Data

Deleted data is often the most sought-after artifact within a feature phone file system. Deleted data can be located only if the EFS has been extracted. If only a surface ("tip of the data iceberg") collection has occurred, the examiner will be unable to conduct a search for deleted file artifacts.

Note Feature phone deleted data is typically located outside of the formatted file system, and searches must be conducted on the formatted NAND/NOR binary file. If only a file system is available, the recovery of deleted artifacts on a CDMA or GSM feature phone is unlikely. There are some exceptions, however, such as the Motorola V3 CDMA series, in which the msging folder can store deleted messages, so searching should always be attempted.

BlackBerry Devices

In most situations, forensic examination of a BlackBerry device will involve the examination of a backup produced by either the forensic software or the associated BlackBerry desktop software.

If using a mobile forensic solution, the examiner should recognize that many files within a BlackBerry backup are not automatically parsed by the solution. Mobile forensic tools will import the backup file and parse out the relevant database files into the user interface, often ignoring other files, either because they are not supported or because the data could not be decoded. At this point, the examiner should be competent enough to dive into some of the additional files that are located within the backup file, if needed.

A pre-BB10 BlackBerry device produces a set of database files contained within a single IPD or BBB file, and BB10 devices produce only a BBB file. The difference between the BBB files produced with the BlackBerry desktop software and those of the new BlackBerry Link software is encryption. BlackBerry Link software backups are fully encrypted with credentials independent of any device password. The IPD or BBB file should not be interpreted as the EFS as it existed exactly on the NAND flash within the BlackBerry. If the examiner is assessing the data at a physical level, the information found within the logical backup file should be correlated to what is seen at the flash level. In making this comparison, the examiner can use the logical backup as an aid in locating and sometimes decoding the information within the physical binary image.

BlackBerry desktop software prior to version 7.1x produced IPD files for Windows-created backups, while Mac backups produced a BBB file. With version 7.1x, only BBB files were produced for both Windows and Mac. The difference between the IPD and BBB files is in how the files are constructed. An IPD file is a single file containing numerous tables, representing a resource field and its associated data. The first version of BBB used by the Mac was a compressed zip file that contained an IPD file. Windows, starting with version 7.1x, used BBB files when creating backups. The BBB file was still a compressed file, but the internal resources were now independent files with a .dat extension, a PkgInfo file, and a manifest file (see Figure 10-11). The PkgInfo file contains the version of the BlackBerry Backup Format, and the manifest file contains a listing of all .dat files in their corresponding resource files (see Figure 10-12).

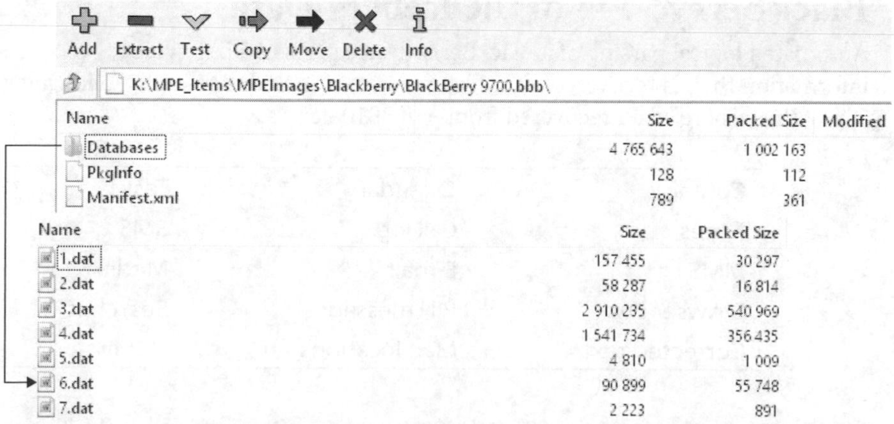

FIGURE 10-11 **The first BBB file that existed outside of a Mac backup comprised a Databases folder with .dat files containing the user databases.**

File Content

Hex | Text | Filtered | Natural


```
<?xml version="1.0" encoding="UTF-8" ?>
- <BlackBerry_Backup>
    <Version>2.0</Version>
    <Client platform="windows" osversion="Microsoft Windows NT 6.1.7601
      Service Pack 1" dtmversion="7.1.0.41" />
  - <SourceDevice pin="2100000A" hwid="4001507">
      <Platform type="BlackBerry" version="3.0.0.159" />
    </SourceDevice>
  - <NessusOSDevice>
    - <Databases>
        <Database uid="1" recordcount="1208">Phone Call
          Logs</Database>
        <Database uid="2" recordcount="608">Phone History</Database>
        <Database uid="3" recordcount="12318">SMS
          Messages</Database>
        <Database uid="4" recordcount="2864">Messages</Database>
        <Database uid="5" recordcount="5">Memos</Database>
        <Database uid="6" recordcount="299">Address Book -
          All</Database>
        <Database uid="7" recordcount="10">Calendar - All</Database>
      </Databases>
    </NessusOSDevice>
</BlackBerry_Backup>
```

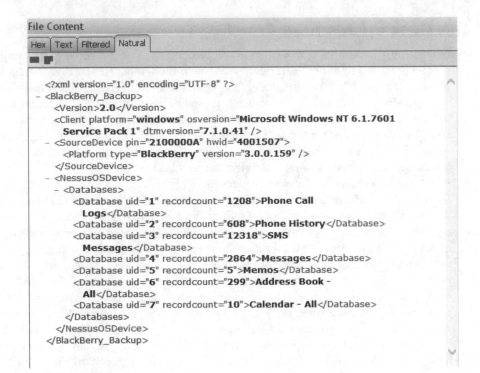

FIGURE 10-12 The manifest file contains the number of records along with the type of data within the .dat file.

BlackBerry devices can also contain a microSD card that includes data such as application files, documents, media, and chat logs.

BlackBerry "Tip of the Iceberg Data"

Automated logical parsing of a BlackBerry device prior to BB10 typically recovers more information than is recovered from feature phones, including e-mail. Following is a list of the "tip of the iceberg" data recovered from pre-BB10 devices:

Contacts	Calendar	Tasks
Notes	Call log	SMS
MMS	E-mail	Media
Browser data	PIN messages	Searches
Corrected text	Map locations	Hot lists

Note Oxygen Forensics and Cellebrite documentation suggest including social media and non-BBM chat application support as typical collection items.

This information is a subset of the available information that exists within the IPD or BBB file produced by a pre-BB10 device. Additional recoverable data is available within the BlackBerry database, but the heavy lifting required to uncover this material often makes it impractical to do so. In general, the material located in the additional databases is deemed of minimal value considering the hours it would take to look through all the records.

Note The BlackBerry device first brought e-mail to the mobile device.

Blackberry Database Breakdown

The standard IPD file contains many records that correspond to the IPD and the first edition BBB file from a Mac backup. The BBB files produced with a Mac are compressed files containing an IPD file (Databases.ipd) and, if the media card is part of the backup, a second file called emmc.zip. Table 10-6 represents the information as detailed by BlackBerry in its Knowledge Base article KB03974. Using this list of databases located within the IPD and BBB, the examiner can manually investigate some of the databases that have been automatically parsed and also those that have not.

TABLE 10-6 Typical Database Files Located Within a BlackBerry IPD Backup

Database	Functionality
Address Book - All	Reflects the total number of contact list entries for multiple contact lists
Address Book - Last Used Hints	Provides information on what phone number or e-mail address was last used to contact a specific contact
Address Book Options	Stores contact list settings
Alarm Options	Stores settings for the alarm application
Alarms	Stores customizations for alarm sounds set by the user
Application Permissions	Stores permissions configured under Options | Security Options | Application Permissions
Attachment Data	Stores attachments that have been viewed on the device
Attachment Data - Calendar	Stores attachments that have been viewed through the calendar application on the device
Attachment Options	Stores user-defined settings for the Attachment Viewer
AutoText/Word Substitution	Contains dictionary for automatic substitution of commonly misspelled words
AutoText Data Version	Contains version of Auto Text Data application
BBGroups	Stores BlackBerry Groups created within the BBM

(Continued)

TABLE 10-6 Typical Database Files Located Within a BlackBerry IPD Backup *(Continued)*

Database	Functionality
BIS Account Data	Stores BlackBerry Internet Service account information that might be used by the Thick Client application in the BlackBerry Internet Service
BlackBerry Messenger	Stores contacts in BBM
Bluetooth Options	Stores settings for Bluetooth technology
Browser Bookmarks	Contains bookmarks for web pages in the browser applications
Browser Channels	Shows browser push service subscribed to by the user, such as weather setup service; lists channels browser is subscribed to, such as weather updates
Browser Data Cache	Holds cached data from the browser
Browser Folders	Enables user to sort bookmarks into various folders
Browser Messages	Contains browser push service notifications
Browser Options	Contains browser setting information
Browser Push Options	Contains push content settings for the BlackBerry browser
Browser Web Address	Contains list of the web addresses that have been typed into the browser
Calendar - All	Contains total number of entries for all calendars (multiple CICAL service records)
Calendar Options	Stores calendar settings
Camera Options	Contains database of settings customization in Options | Camera | Camera Options
Categories	Enables various addresses, appointments, tasks, and memos to be sorted by category
Certificate Options	Contains option list in certificates, whether a user set a certificate to Distrust or Revoke or leaves the default setting when no changes are made
Certificate Summary Data	Contains list of certificates stored on the device (Options | Security Options | Advanced Security Options | Certificates)
Clock Options	Contains customization settings or clock options via Clock | Options
Code Module Group Properties	Stores system software properties for the core system modules

TABLE 10-6 Typical Database Files Located Within a BlackBerry IPD Backup *(Continued)*

Database	Functionality
Compatibility Settings	Contains compatibility mode settings used when the application has been designed for a physical input (non–touch screen) device, where the application expects to receive input events from the keyboard and the trackball
Configuration Channel	Stores configuration information that an administrator may assign using the Configuration Channel feature of BlackBerry Enterprise Server 5.0
Content Store	Stores pictures and other media content in the on-board device memory
CustomWordsCollection	Stores customized words saved to the custom word dictionary
Default Service Selector	Defines the default message service
Device Options	Stores setting changes made within Options on the device; some options have their own database
Diagnostic App Options	Contains test configuration settings in Self Test Application, initiated in Options | Status using the key sequence TEST
DocsToGoCommonPrefs	Contains setting information for the Documents to Go for device application suite
Email Filters - All	Stores settings for filters applied to incoming messages
Email Settings - All	Defines the way messages are sent and received
Enhanced Gmail Plug-in	Stores information used by the Enhanced Gmail plug-in
File Explorer Network Favorites	Stores list of file shares that have been marked as Favorites
File Explorer Network History	Stores list of past network file shares that have been accessed from the device
File Explorer Options	Includes options configured in Explorer, such as Show Hidden, or any new folders created
Firewall Options	Enables or disables the firewall
Folder ID	Determines which folder a message is filed into
Folders	Lists user-created folders in the message list
Full-predictive Options	Stores settings information pertaining to predictive text functionality
Handheld Agent	Contains diagnostic information about the device, including information sent to the BlackBerry Enterprise Server for reporting

(Continued)

TABLE 10-6 Typical Database Files Located Within a BlackBerry IPD Backup *(Continued)*

Database	Functionality
Handheld Configuration	Incoming half of the device agent that sends data from the BlackBerry Enterprise Server to the device
Handheld Key Store	Securely stores encryption keys for encrypted communication and signing
Input Learning Data	Stores list of text that device uses to predict what user is attempting to type
Input Method Switcher Option	Stores selection of input language method when sequence key ALT-ENTER is initiated
Input System Properties	Stores text input and keyboard layout settings specified under Options | Language and Text Input
Key Store Manager	Manages the BlackBerry key store
Key Store Options	Configures options for the BlackBerry key store
LDAP Browser Options	Contains Lightweight Directory Access Protocol (LDAP) browser setting information
Location Based Services	Used mainly for corporate users in a BlackBerry Enterprise Server environment, either for Location Tracking or can be accessed by third-party applications that are developed by BlackBerry MDS Studio
Mailbox Icon Management Options	Stores information regarding inbox settings and delivery of e-mail messages to certain message icons
Map Locations	Stores locations added to Favorites in BlackBerry Maps
Map Settings	Stores configuration settings in BlackBerry Maps | Options
MemoPad Options	Stores MemoPad settings
Memory Cleaner Options	Stores configuration settings in Options | Security Options | Memory Options; set status to Enable
Memos	Contains the memos stored on the device
Message List Options	Defines the way messages are displayed in the messages application
Messages	Contains all the messages on the device
Messenger Options (GoogleTalk)	Contains setting information for Google Talk instant messaging client
Messenger Options (WLM)	Contains setting information for Windows Live Messenger instant messaging client

TABLE 10-6 Typical Database Files Located Within a BlackBerry IPD Backup *(Continued)*

Database	Functionality
Messenger Options (ST)	Contains setting information for IBM Sametime instant messaging client
Messenger Options (OC)	Contains setting information for Microsoft Office Communicator instant messaging client
Messenger Options (Yahoo!)	Contains setting information for Yahoo! Messenger client
MMS Messages	Database that contains a history of sent or received Multimedia Messaging Service (MMS)
MMS Options	Stores MMS settings
Mobile Network Options	Contains information outlining current mobile network settings and configurations
On-Board Device Memory	Database for the on-board device memory that enables the user to store media files, normally in *.cab extension
Options	Stores miscellaneous configuration options
PasswordKeeper	Application that uses Advanced Encryption Standard (AES) technology to store password entries on the device; see KB19098
PasswordKeeper Options	Contains settings configured via Password Keeper | Options
PGP Key Store	Contains the PGP private key and public keys
Phone Call Logs	Logs phone calls made to and from the device
Phone History	Stores information pertaining to phone call history with specific participants (complete history of incoming and outgoing phone calls with selected recipients)
Phone Hotlist	Stores information on the last *x* number of calls placed from the device
Phone Options	Stores phone settings
PIM Folder List - All	Outlines complete list of PIM folders within the associated mailbox; can be set up like a filter—if there are multiple folders, user can filter contact lists based on specific folder
PIN Messages	Stores personal identification number (PIN) messages sent or received
Policy	Stores the IT policy for the device
Profiles	Contains various smart phone alerts, such as a vibration for a new calendar appointment or a tone when a new message arrives

(Continued)

TABLE 10-6 Typical Database Files Located Within a BlackBerry IPD Backup *(Continued)*

Database	Functionality
Profiles Options	Selects the current profile for alerts
Purged Messages	Contains reference for messages deleted from the device
Quick Contacts	Stores telephone numbers in the Speed Dial list
Random Pool	Stores numbers to generate random numbers securely for encryption
Recent Contacts	Stores list of contacts that have recently been contacted (phone or e-mail), such as a quick contact reference tool-tip when creating an e-mail
Recipient Cache	Contains encryption profiles for the people with which the user communicates
RMS Databases	Stores information about registered applications
S/MIME Options	Stores configuration information for Secure Multipurpose Internet Mail Extensions (S/MIME) settings
Saved Email Messages	Contains all saved messages stored on the device
Searches	Stores settings configured in search application
Secure Email Decision Maker	Automatically selects secure e-mail sending method (determined by whether the original sender sent a signed/encrypted e-mail—the device determines whether to send a signed/encrypted/plain text e-mail back)
Service Book	Stores all of the service records that enable the device to access various services
Setup Wizard Options	Contains options configured for personal settings for the device
SheetToGoPrefs	Contains setting information for the Sheet To Go application
SlideshowToGoPrefs	Contains setting information for the Slideshow To Go application
Smart Card Options	Stores saved settings configured for the BlackBerry Smart Card reader
SMS Messages	Contains Short Message Service (SMS) text messages sent to and from the device
Sounds	Contains various notification sounds, such as a vibration for a new calendar appointment or a tone when a new message arrives on the device; for BlackBerry Device Software 5.0
Spell Check Options	Stores settings configured in Options | Spell Check

TABLE 10-6 Typical Database Files Located Within a BlackBerry IPD Backup *(Continued)*

Database	Functionality
SureType Options	Stores SureType keyboard settings specified under Options | Language
Tasks	Lists task items on the device
Tasks Options	Saves settings in Task | Options
Text Messages	Combines total number of SMS text messages received (database in BlackBerry Device Software 6.0)
TCP/IP Options	Stores TCP/IP configuration settings
Theme Settings	Stores settings for icon arrangement on device Home screen
Time Zones	Stores the time zone table
TLS Options	Configures Transport Layer Security settings
Trusted Key Store	Contains the trusted keys for the device
VideoRecorder Options	Saves settings in Video Camera | Options
Voice Activated Dialing Options	Stores settings configured in Options | Voice Dialing
WAP Push Messages	Contains information from Wireless Application Protocol (WAP) push services
WLAN Profiles	Saves Wi-Fi profiles created in Wi-Fi settings
WordToGoPrefs	Contains setting information for the Word To Go application
WTLS Options	Contains settings for Wireless Transport Layer Security

Using Rubus software from CCL Forensics (cclgroupltd.com) or AccessData FTK, the examiner can deconstruct the IPD file (see Figure 10-13). Once this file is deconstructed, the examiner can locate the proper database and decode the underlying data.

For Windows-produced BBB files from BlackBerry Desktop version 7, the databases listed in Table 10-6 do not all exist. The BBB file contains the manifest file that lays out the information within the .dat files. The manifest (Figure 10-14) contains the version of BBDM (dtmversion), the device PIN (SourceDevice PIN), and the databases that have been backed up into the BBB file. Each database listed in the manifest provides the number of records in the file (recordcount) along with the database name. Each .dat file is its own IPD file, which is evident by the file header of each .dat file, Inter@ctive Pager Backup. If a mobile forensic solution does not allow the automated ability to parse one or any of the included .dat files, these files can be manually interrogated to obtain user information. It is important for the examiner to look to the manifest file to determine the data that actually exists within the BBB file. In doing so, he or she has a reasonable expectation of what will and will not be recoverable with the automated software.

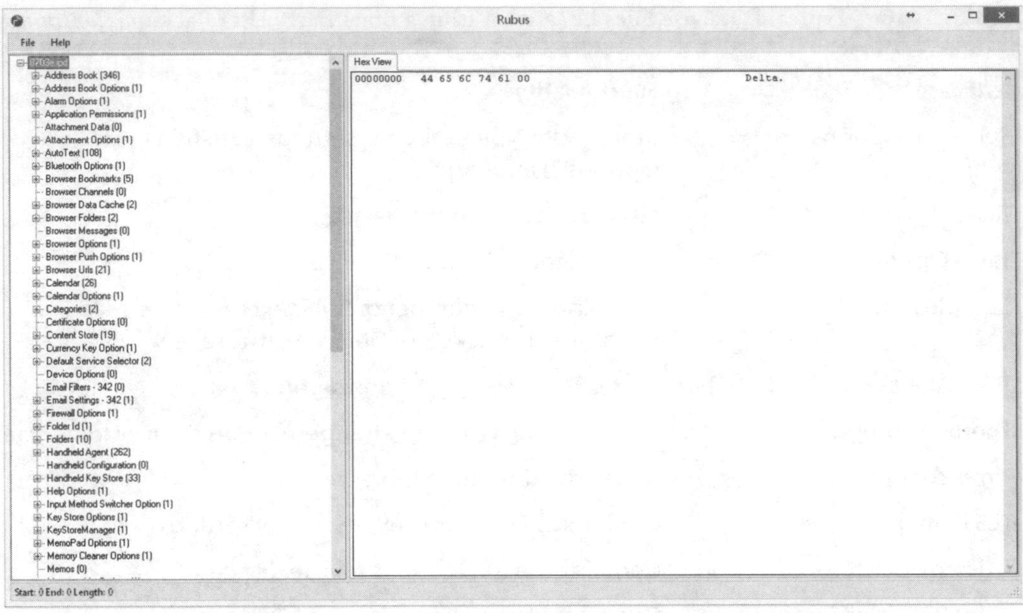

FIGURE 10-13 IPD deconstruction in CCL Rubus

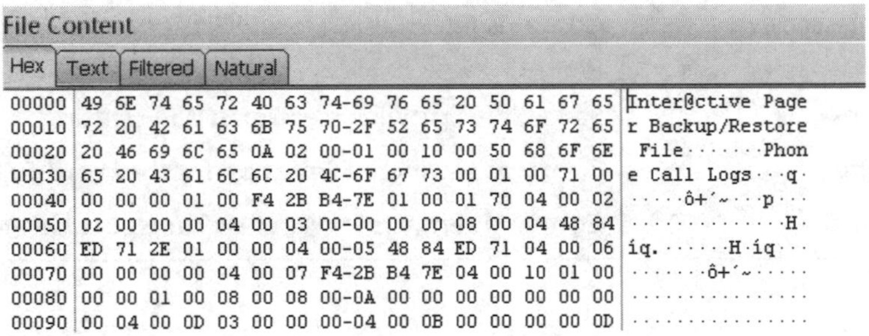

File Content

Hex | Text | Filtered | Natural

```
00000 49 6E 74 65 72 40 63 74-69 76 65 20 50 61 67 65  Inter@ctive Page
00010 72 20 42 61 63 6B 75 70-2F 52 65 73 74 6F 72 65  r Backup/Restore
00020 20 46 69 6C 65 0A 02 00-01 00 10 00 50 68 6F 6E   File······Phon
00030 65 20 43 61 6C 6C 20 4C-6F 67 73 00 01 00 71 00  e Call Logs···q·
00040 00 00 00 01 00 F4 2B B4-7E 01 00 01 70 04 00 02  ·····ô+´~···p···
00050 02 00 00 00 04 00 03 00-00 00 00 08 00 04 48 84  ··············H·
00060 ED 71 2E 01 00 00 04 00-05 48 84 ED 71 04 00 06  íq.······H·íq···
00070 00 00 00 00 04 00 07 F4-2B B4 7E 04 00 10 01 00  ·······ô+´~·····
00080 00 00 01 00 08 00 08 00-0A 00 00 00 00 00 00 00  ················
00090 00 04 00 0D 03 00 00 00-04 00 0B 00 00 00 00 0D  ················
```

FIGURE 10-14 The .dat file header from a BBB file indicating the typical IPD header information

BlackBerry Data Formats and Data Types

As discussed, manual exploration is sometimes necessary—for example, when an automated tool fails to retrieve the necessary data or to verify the validity of the parsed information. Before embarking on a manual exploration, the examiner must be familiar with the various formats BlackBerry uses within the IPD and BBB files. Much like the rest of mobile device forensics, various formats are used throughout the device backups; they are listed in Table 10-7 with information gathered from the *BlackBerry Developers' Journal*, Mike McDonough's IPD Parse (https://sites.google.com/site/ipdparse/home), and Yogesh Khatri's Forensic Blog (swiftforensics.com). Table 10-7 will be further examined and used in the "Manual Decoding" section a bit later.

TABLE 10-7 Data Formats Used for Manual Interpretation Within a BlackBerry Backup File

Artifact	Category	Format	Epoch	Example
Phone Call Log	Date/Time	HEX value little endian 8 bytes	1970/1/1	4A AE 6C 12 2F 01 00 00 2011/04/1 18:56:43 GMT
Phone Call Log	Text	HEX to ASCII		+12085559876
SMS	Date/Time	HEX value little endian 8 bytes	1970/1/1	BC 5C 75 D7 36 01 00 00 2012/04/22 00:30 GMT
SMS	Text	HEX to ASCII		This person called.
Phone History	Date/Time	HEX value little endian 8 bytes	1970/1/1	CC 58 72 E5 36 01 00 00 2012/04/24 17:42 GMT
Phone History	Text	HEX to ASCII		+14547990987
Calendar	Date/Time	HEX value little endian 4 bytes	1900/1/1	74 10 78 03 2010/08/28 19:00 GMT
Calendar	Text	HEX to ASCII		Emik's Birthday
Messages (E-mail)	Date/Time	HEX value little endian 4 bytes	First bytes = Date Second bytes = Time	25 1C D9 61 2010/01/05 12:14 GMT
Messages (E-mail)	Text	HEX to ASCII/ Unicode		Test Message...
PIN Messages	Date/Time	HEX value little endian 4 bytes	First bytes = Date Second bytes = Time	A1 20 21 53 2012/5/1 10:25 GMT

Manual Decoding

BlackBerry uses little endian decoding throughout the IPD and version 2 BBB files but uses two epoch dates. The UNIX epoch of January 1, 1970, is used as the basis for most databases within the BlackBerry backup image, with the exception of Calendar and Tasks, which use January 1, 1900, and E-mail and PIN Messages, which use 1996 as an epoch year. The date and time fields for BlackBerry IPD files are not well documented. A few can be found, but most work comes in to recognizing the various formats and using a tool such as the MFI HEX Assistant or DCode to convert the dates and times. As mentioned, there can be a lot of heavy lifting involved.

Note Many more databases are contained within the IPD and BBB, but using the information in this section can help the examiner in identifying information within many databases not listed.

A better explanation of the dates and times for the data within Table 10-7 is covered next, including data types with specific information and guidance on locating the date and time, along with how to convert the information.

Note Rubus from CCL Forensics and the MFI HEX Assistant were used for this section for IPD files, and FTK and the MFI HEX Assistant were used for v2 BBB files. After loading the IPD or BBB file into the solution of choice, the examiner can view the raw backup.

- **Phone call logs** In Rubus, the second field and the first byte indicate the type (missed-02, outgoing-01, incoming-00), and the fourth field is the date and time (see Figure 10-15). This is an 8-byte value that, when read as a little endian value to obtain a 64-bit integer value, can be assessed as milliseconds from 1970/1/1.

  Note that the value A3BE990A37010000 in LE (little endian) is 000001370A99BEA3. If this is input into the scientific calculator as HEX and then converted to decimal, the value is 1335912677027. This value can then be plugged into fileformat.info/tip/java/date2millis.htm and, upon conversion, the date is displayed (see Figure 10-16).

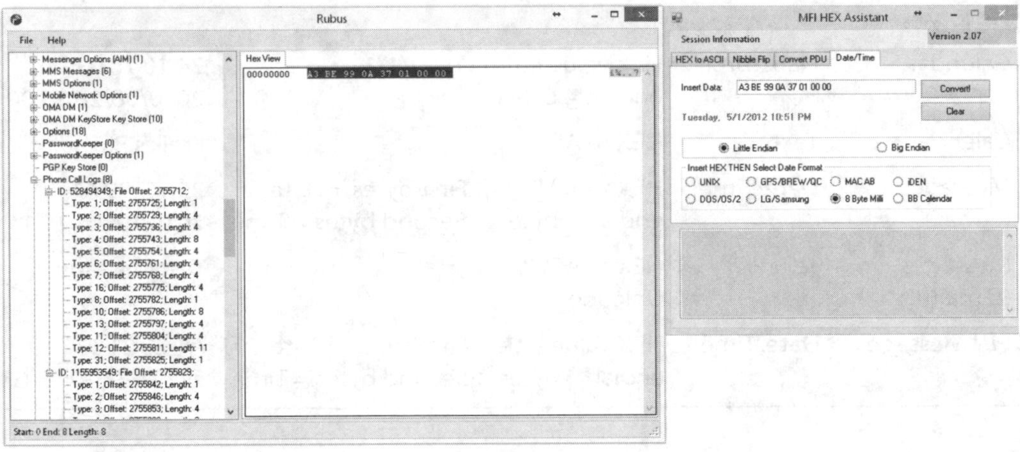

FIGURE 10-15 Call log date and time in the fourth field and converted with the MFI HEX Assistant

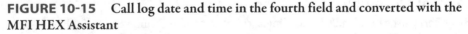

Results	
Input	1335912677027
Input (formatted)	1,335,912,677,027
Date (America/New_York)	Tuesday, May 1, 2012 6:51:17 PM EDT
Date (GMT)	Tuesday, May 1, 2012 10:51:17 PM GMT
Date (short/short format)	5/1/12 6:51 PM

FIGURE 10-16 Use fileformat.info on the Web to convert the HEX value into a readable date.

- **Phone history** In Rubus, the third field is the date and time field and the fourth field is of the type exactly like Phone Call Logs. The 8-byte value can be converted just like phone call logs.
- **SMS messages** In Rubus, the field labeled 11 and the first byte will indicate the direction of the SMS (incoming-01 and outgoing-00), and the field labeled 16 will be the 8-byte date and time in the same format as described for phone call logs.
- **Calendar** In Rubus, the data is located in the field labeled 10 (see Figure 10-17). There are three dates in the Calendar (Start, End, and Reminder) and all dates use 4 bytes that must be converted to little endian to obtain an integer. The integer will represent the number of minutes from 1900/1/1.
- **Messages** E-mail messages were examined within Rubus, and because there are many fields of interest in messages, they are compiled in Table 10-8.

The date and time method for converting the dates is rather intensive. The date and time is a 4-byte value: the first 2 bytes represent the date and the second 2 bytes represent the time. To convert this date and time to a Julian date, the examiner must take the 2 bytes into little endian order: 81 1E becomes 1E 81, and this value must then be converted into a binary number. The binary number 0001111 0100 00001 must be divided up into the most significant (on the left) 7 bits—0001111 represents the days from 1996, the next 4 bits, 0100, represent the month (1–12), and the final 5 bits represent the day (1–31).

```
0001111 0100 00001
\_____/ \__/ \___/
Y(2011) M(4)  D(1)
```

The binary values will be converted to a decimal number to obtain the decoded date. The binary number, as presented, would be 0001111 = 15 (1996 + 15 = 2011), 0100 = 4 (April), 00001 = 1 (1). The date for this message is April 1, 2011.

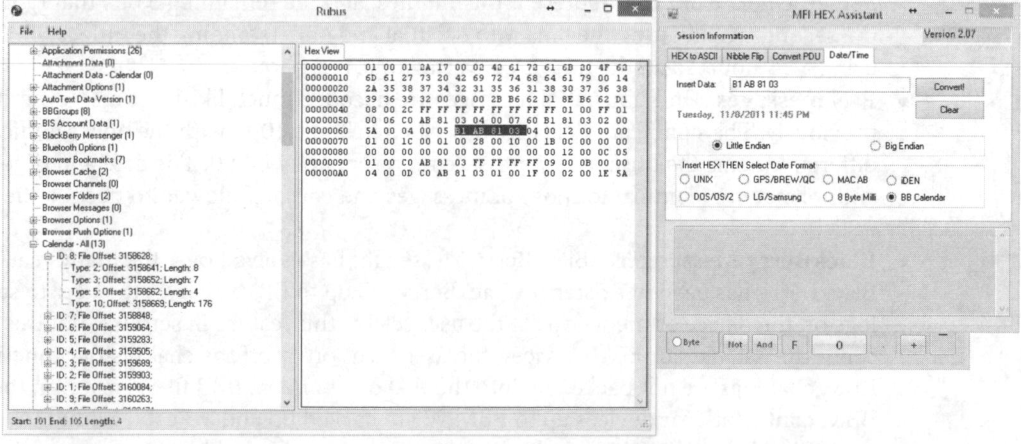

FIGURE 10-17 Calendar date and time format within field 10 using Rubus

TABLE 10-8 E-mail Messages Decoded Using Rubus

Field Number	Type	Location	Format
0	Unread - F2 08 Read - F2 00 Sent - F3 00 Unsent - E3 00	bytes 3–4	
0	Date/Time (three will be found; last time is received/sent)	bytes 29–40	4 byte LE (Date/Time)
1	To		ASCII/Unicode
5	From		ASCII/Unicode
11	Subject		ASCII/Unicode
12	Message if text		ASCII/Unicode
22	Attachments		ASCII/Unicode
24	Message if formatted		HTML

The time is broken down in much the same manner. Here the time is 18 06, and switching to little endian would be 06 18 and the binary representation is 00000 110000 11000.

```
00000 110000 11000
\___/ \____/ \___/
H(0)   M(48) S(24)
```

To decode the time, the examiner, starting at the MSB, will take 5 bits that represent the hour, the next 6 bits that represent the minutes, and the remaining 5 bits that represent the seconds. Converting the binary to decimal and understanding the time is GMT time using a 24-hour clock, the time is converted to 0:48:24 hours.

- **PIN messages** In Rubus, PIN messages are decoded much like messages, described previously. The significant fields are described in Table 10-9, with the only significant difference being the unsent PIN message represented by EB 00. The date and time location and format are identical to those of messages and can be followed to decode the values in field 0.
- **BlackBerry Messenger** BlackBerry Messenger has evolved over the many years BlackBerry has been in existence. BlackBerry OS up to BB10 enables the user to store chat logs on the device or media card if the user selects this feature in settings, but this setting is not the default. For BB10 devices, the user turns on or off the chat history function. BBM chat logs are not backed up into the IPD or v1 and v2 BBB files. However, the BBM contact list for devices up to BBM v7 are backed up and available within the IPD/BBB (Blackberry KB18406), and its format is referenced in Table 10-8, as decoded within Rubus. BBM 7x contacts and settings are synched using the BlackBerry ID and are not stored within a backup file (BlackBerry KB20554).

TABLE 10-9 PIN Message Significant Field with Type and Format

Field Number	Type	Location	Format
2	Contact List (PIN, Status, Name, UID)		ASCII/Unicode
3	BBM User Name		ASCII/Unicode
4	Contact UID		ASCII/Unicode
10	User PIN		ASCII/Unicode
20	User Image (JPG)		Binary

If the user has enabled the option to save BBM message logs, the logs can be recovered in CSV within the content store on the device or on the external media card. The folder containing the BBM data is identified on the device and external card at <home>im\BlackBerry Messenger\<Users PIN>. Within the <history> folder are several CSV files that are uniquely named by the PIN of the user they were communicating with. There is also a <backup> folder that contains the BBM contact list (.con) and backups of the contact list based upon a date (.bak). The chat history CSV file contains the BBM conversation in the following order: date, sender PIN, receiver PIN, message. The date is formatted rather bizarrely, with the first eight most significant digits representing the year, month, and day, and the remaining digits representing the milliseconds from 1970/1/1 and in GMT. This information is shown in Figure 10-18 as parsed using MPE+ and the pythonScripter.

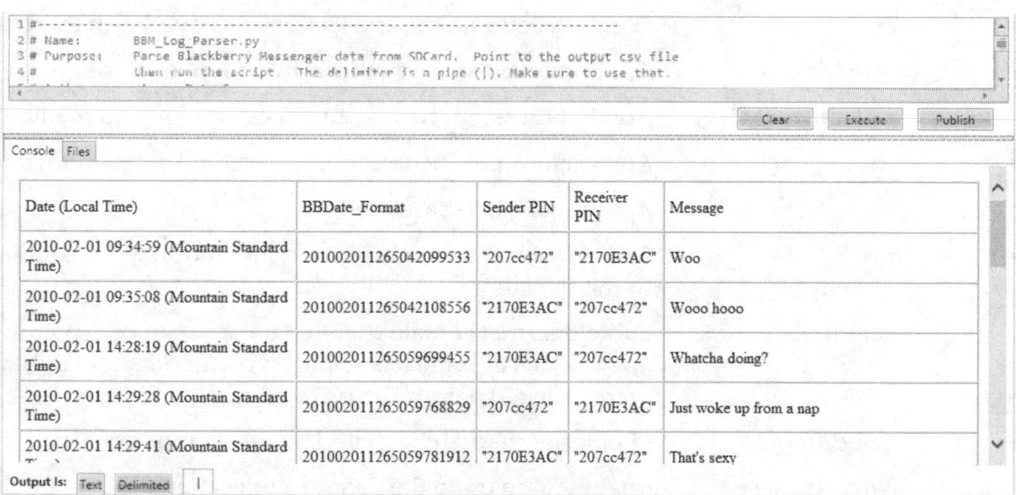

Date (Local Time)	BBDate_Format	Sender PIN	Receiver PIN	Message
2010-02-01 09:34:59 (Mountain Standard Time)	20100201126504209953 3	"207cc472"	"2170E3AC"	Woo
2010-02-01 09:35:08 (Mountain Standard Time)	20100201126504210855 6	"2170E3AC"	"207cc472"	Wooo hooo
2010-02-01 14:28:19 (Mountain Standard Time)	20100201126505969945 5	"2170E3AC"	"207cc472"	Whatcha doing?
2010-02-01 14:29:28 (Mountain Standard Time)	20100201126505976882 9	"207cc472"	"2170E3AC"	Just woke up from a nap
2010-02-01 14:29:41 (Mountain Standard	20100201126505978191 2	"2170E3AC"	"207cc472"	That's sexy

FIGURE 10-18 MPE+ and pythonScripter output from running the BBM parsing script against a backup file produced by a BlackBerry device

If a BBM chat logging service has not been set by the user, the examiner must attempt to obtain a non-invasive or invasive physical collection of the device. With a physical collection, the device's internal system can then be examined, and BBM chat is accessible even if the user has not enabled the logging function from the bbm.db file. The data formats along with the data that was previously stored (device and owner information, contacts [.con/.bak], and chat) within the IPD/BBB and contact database are now contained within the bbm.db file. Within some BlackBerry backup files, another database, BBM Conversations, can be located and is used to enhance the search ability by the BlackBerry device. This database location and file \BBM Conversations\conversations.csv is not included in every backup, and the company that developed BlackBerry Backup Extractor, Reincubate, can parse the CSV file that is formatted much like the CSV backup file as previously discussed.

BlackBerry 10 File System

With BlackBerry 10, many things drastically changed, starting with the operating system, which changed from the BlackBerry Mobile OS (Java MicroEdition-J2ME) to the QNX Neutrino platform. The QNX Neutrino platform is designed to run on several servers concurrently, with only 100,000 lines of code, compared to a single large program such as Linux (9 million lines) or Windows (70 million lines). This is said to improve the operability and reliability of the BlackBerry platform. Table 10-10 outlines the application working areas and repositories an examiner should be familiar with when conducting analysis of BB10 device apps.

TABLE 10-10 BB10 App Working Directory Locations (from https:\\developer.blackberry.com/native/documentation/cascades/device_platform/data_access/file_system.html)

Folder	Description
app	Files installed with the application, packaged with the .bar file
app/native	Application binary and other application resources
app/native/assets	Application assets, such as .qml files, images, and media
data	Application's private data; the application's home directory
db	Application's database files
logs	System logs for an application; stderr and stdout are redirected to this directory
shared	Subfolders that contain shared data grouped by type; an application can write to subfolders of this directory only if the access_shared permission is specified
shared/books	eBook files that can be shared between applications
shared/camera	Images taken using the Camera application that can be shared between applications

TABLE 10-10 BB10 App Working Directory Locations (from https:\\developer.blackberry.com/native/documentation/cascades/device_platform/data_access/file_system.html) *(Continued)*

Folder	Description
shared/documents	Documents that can be shared between applications
shared/downloads	Web browser downloads that can be shared between applications
shared/Dropbox	Files located in the user's Dropbox account
shared/misc	Files that don't belong in any other category and can be shared between applications
shared/music	Music files that can be shared between applications
shared/photos	Photos that can be shared between applications
shared/print	News and print articles that can be shared between applications
shared/videos	Videos that can be shared between applications
shared/voice	Audio recordings that can be shared between applications
sharewith	Files that the application can share with other applications by using the Invocation framework
tmp	The application's temporary working files; application should remove these files regularly—BlackBerry 10 OS may remove these files when the application isn't running

The examination of the BB10 device can occur at different levels. Currently the backup that is produced for the BlackBerry PlayBook is different from the backup from the other BB10 devices. The BBB file from the BlackBerry PlayBook is still a compressed file that can be opened with 7-Zip or WinZip and it contains the same two files (covered previously) included with the v2 BBB (manifest and PkgInfo) file, but it also includes three new .tar files called app.tar, media.tar, and settings.tar that are unencrypted QNX files (see Figure 10-19). All BB10 devices produced after the BlackBerry PlayBook produce the same BBB files with a few exceptions. The associated .tar files are now encrypted with the BlackBerry ID and password, and the manifest file contains the BlackBerry ID associated with each archive type, located in the perimeter type for the archive (for example, Application [app], Media [media], and Settings [settings]). The BlackBerry PlayBook files are unencrypted QNX files, while the rest of the BB10 devices have encrypted QNX files. If the examiner knows the Link password, both Elcomsoft and Oxygen Forensic Analyst enable the backup to be imported and produce an export that contains call logs, applications, phonebook (contacts), messages, and a file system containing the decrypted app, settings, and media folders.

Tip For BlackBerry backups (OS 7 and earlier) that are encrypted, Elcomsoft also enables the bypass of the password using a brute-force attack of plain text passwords.

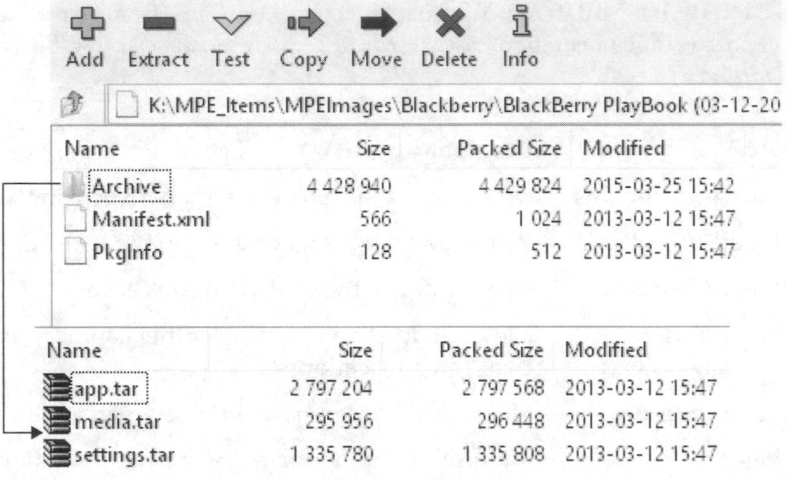

FIGURE 10-19 BBB file from a BlackBerry PlayBook, with the Archive folder instead of the Database folder, as with previous BBB files

Here's another option: If the password is known or the device is not locked, the examiner can plug the BB10 device into a computer and mount the device as a drive. The BB10 will show two drives: One drive will provide access to the internal memory of the BB10 device and anything on the shared path, including books, camera, documents, downloads, Dropbox, miscellaneous music, photos, print, videos, and voice. The other mounted network drive will be the removable storage that will duplicate some of the same folders observed on the mounted internal storage area, but these folders contain unique data. The external SD card should be analyzed for any deleted files using a forensic solution and a built-in file carving utility. This acquisition is conducted using the Media Transfer Protocol (MTP) and was outlined in earlier chapters. This area does not contain PIM data—only files and folders used by applications to store and share data. To obtain PIM data, the examiner must access the logical or physical file system of the BB10 device.

A limited amount of user information is automatically parsed from the backup, even if the examiner is using a forensic solution that can obtain the logical file system or a physical binary image. This means that a lot of manual work is required with IPD and BBB files, but the rewards are worth the effort. With BB10 devices, an incredible amount of information is available to the examiner. These file systems now contain apps with a wealth of information within the SQLite databases. SQLite databases will be covered in Chapter 11, but Table 10-11 represents great locations for finding valuable data within the BB10 device. (This table is not an all-inclusive list, and some areas are not covered here because they were included in Table 10-10.) For date and time artifacts, the time is stored in milliseconds, from 1970/1/1, as is the case with IPD and BBB files.

With a logical file system extraction, the examiner will find user data of value in the settings.tar file, as observed in Figure 10-19. App storage data is located in /accounts/1000/appdata/ in the settings.tar file. In a physical collection, the /accounts/1000/appdata folder is

TABLE 10-11 Artifact Locations for BB10 File System Examinations

Artifact	Path	Considerations	Comments
GEO Location	/accounts/1000/sys /placesservice	Places.db3	Mapping database with latitude and longitude information for device user
User added dictionary	/accounts/1000/sys /input/spell_check	personal_dictionary.wrd	Words added to dictionary by user
Facebook	/accounts/1000/appdata /com.rim.bb.app.facebook	fb-messages.db mall.db friends.db	Messages contain messages and threads; mail contains data on mail interactions with app
WhatsApp	/accounts/1000/appdata /com.whatsapp.WhatsApp	messageStore.db	Call logs and messages
Android PIM	/accounts/1000/appdata /sys.android	databases = autofill.db, browser2.db, webview.db	Many other databases, including contacts, messages, downloads, and more
BBM	/accounts/1000\appdata /sys.bbm	master.db bbgroups.db	Contacts, text messages, calls
Browser	/accounts/1000/appdata /sys.browser	Chrome/Databases.db Chrome/localstorage /local_X.localstorage /webviews/ creditials.db.archived autofill.db Databases.db	Cached WebKit, searches, and usernames
Messages/ SMS/E-mail	/accounts/1000/appdata /sys.pim.messages	unifed.db	Uses table category and UIB Item to match up conversational data from many different types of content
MMS/SMS	/var/db/	messages.db attachments folder	MMS and SMS with links to attachments folder
MediaStore	/accounts/1000/db/	mmlibrary.db	Path information for all media on device internally

(Continued)

TABLE 10-11 Artifact Locations for BB10 File System Examinations *(Continued)*

Artifact	Path	Considerations	Comments
MediaStore	/accounts/1000/db /sdcard_dbcache	<media card serial>.db	Path information for all media on media card even if removed
Media associated to PIM	/accounts/1000/pimdata/	Various folders contacts, messages, events associated to data in /sysdata/db and referenced by number.	Media and messages used by PIM database; messages from SMS and various applications cached here
User usage	/accounts/1000/sysdata /pim/analytics/	analytics.db	Statistics on user (such as e-mails sent, contacts)
PIM storage	/accounts/1000/sysdata /pim/db/	Many SQLite databases	Stores built-in PIM used and cross-linking data for application use of user PIM data
PIM calendar	/accounts/1000/sysdata /pim/db/	1.db	Uses Calendar Event table
PIM contacts	/accounts/1000/sysdata /pim/db/	2.db	Uses Contacts table
PIM unified contacts	/accounts/1000/sysdata /pim/db/	4.db	Data for contacts used in various apps and settings; has deleted field in Unified Contact table
PIM call logs	/accounts/1000/sysdata /pim/db/	8.db	Uses Call Detail table for data; call table has unread attribute
PIM tasks	/accounts/1000/sysdata /pim/db/	22.db	Uses Tasks table

located under root as shown in Figure 10-20. The actual app code will be located in the app file in a logical extraction and the app folder in a physical collection. The examiner can scan the app code for malware or viruses if needed to verify that no malicious apps were installed.

Note There are many similarities between the files found in a BB10 file system and files found in both iOS and Android devices. Figure 10-21 shows a SQLite database, common to both iOS and Android. The investigation into the file types is covered in greater detail in Chapter 12.

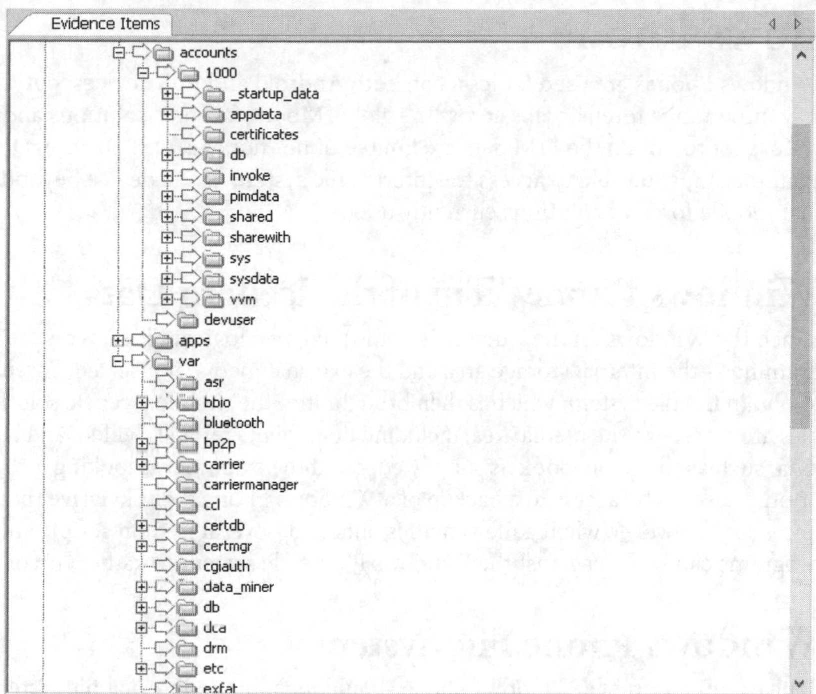

FIGURE 10-20 File system view of the BB10 device from within FTK

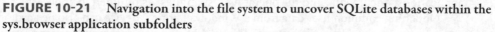

FIGURE 10-21 Navigation into the file system to uncover SQLite databases within the sys.browser application subfolders

Windows Phone

Windows Phones are used far less than both Android and iOS devices, but they do make their way into mobile forensic labs across the globe. Mobile forensic solutions and an automated feature set to obtain the PIM data are limited, if not nonexistent. To access these devices, the examiner must be able to access the internal file system of the device beyond the MTP data that mobile forensic solutions currently offer.

Windows Phone "Tip of the Iceberg Data"

When the Windows Phone 7 device is not locked, two logical file systems are available to the examiner—the internal storage area and the external media, if inserted. Forensic tools use MTP to obtain the file system, which is then brought into the mobile forensic solution. Some user files are stored on the media area, including documents, images, video, and audio. Some PIM data, such as the phonebook, is supported, but if the examiner is looking for messages, call logs, or other user data, access to a backup of a Windows Phone 7 or SkyDrive (now OneDrive) is necessary. However, when a file system is obtained, several Python scripts and EnCase EnScript programs can be run against the Windows Phone file system to gather "tip of the iceberg data."

Windows Phone File System

True examination of a Windows Phone should include the internal file system. Currently, to access valuable user information, the examiner must obtain a physical image, either by non-invasive or invasive methods. Most examiners use JTAG methods for the Windows Phone because it offers a non-invasive method of access to the device without requiring complete disassembly, and many Windows Phone models are supported. A Windows Phone 7 device, depending on the OS version, can be collected with tools such as TouchXperience and Una to obtain a file system–level extraction and registry dump. For Windows Phone 8 devices, most examiners rely on JTAG, but Cellebrite tools currently enable the examiner to ascertain a binary image of select Windows Phone 8 devices as well.

After the images are obtained from the Windows Phone, the examination is much like the BlackBerry examination—extremely labor intensive. Instead of a QNX EFS, the underlying file system is NTFS. For computer forensic examiners, forensic tools that handle Windows Phone file systems more efficiently (such as EnCase, FTK, or X-Ways) can be used.

Because Windows Phone 7 devices were discontinued, and all support by Microsoft was stopped in October 2014 in favor of Windows Phone 8 devices, limited references to Windows Phone 7 is made here, but several tables list important areas for investigation. The file system and artifact locations are different from those of the current Windows Phone 8 device file system, but they resemble the standard Windows desktop file system. Most of the Windows Phone discussion here is devoted to the Windows Phone 8.

Windows Phone 7

The Windows Phone 7 file system resembles the Windows desktop, with locations for applications, documents, and the operating system files, as outlined in Table 10-12.

Obtaining common user data from a Windows Phone 7 device can also be accomplished by navigating to the device file system. Table 10-13 lists some common locations for various

TABLE 10-12 Evidence Folders in Root of Windows Phone 7 File System

Path	Description
\Application Data	Preinstalled applications: Outlook (e-mail), Internet Explorer, and Maps
\Applications	User-installed applications along with the applications' isolated storage
\My Documents	Microsoft documents (Word, Excel), user's videos and music, Downloads folder, Temp Internet files
\Windows	Operating system files

data, and some of the files, such as store.vol, are used within the Windows Phone 8 device and are explained in detail in the following sections.

Most of the file types and formats carried over to the Windows Phone 8, but the path to the file(s) changed. As outlined on the XDA forum (http://forum.xda-developers.com/showthread.php?t=1072796), the store.vol file can be parsed, but the file must be renamed while it's stored on the device because the device operating system continuously has ownership of the file. If the device image is obtained via JTAG or other physical collection, this, of course, would not be the case. The renaming of the store.vol, in an effort to collect and examine data,

TABLE 10-13 Common Artifact Locations Within Windows Phone 7 Device

Artifact	Path	Considerations	Comments
Conversation	\Application Data \Microsoft\Outlook \Stores\DeviceStore \store.vol	Call logs, SMS messages, e-mail subjects	All items that have appeared on the device screen, in chronological order
Contact	\Application Data \Microsoft\Outlook \Stores\DeviceStore \store.vol	Names, e-mail, phone numbers, business addresses	Culmination of records from apps (such as Facebook, Twitter), device contact list
Appointments	\Application Data \Microsoft\Outlook \Stores\DeviceStore \store.vol	Calendar appointments	Information in Unicode, ASCII, dates/times
Attachments	\Application Data \Microsoft\Outlook \Stores\DeviceStore \store.vol	Attachments for various applications	Name of attachment, type of artifact

(Continued)

TABLE 10-13 Common Artifact Locations Within Windows Phone 7 Device *(Continued)*

Artifact	Path	Considerations	Comments
Message	\Application Data \Microsoft\Outlook \Stores\DeviceStore \store.vol	MMS and SMS	Message content, numbers, date and time information
Note	\Application Data \Microsoft\Outlook \Stores\DeviceStore \store.vol	Notes	Notes, content, date and time information
Tasks	\Application Data \Microsoft\Outlook \Stores\DeviceStore \store.vol	Tasks	Tasks, content, date and time information
E-mail	\Application Data \Microsoft\Outlook \Stores\DeviceStore \data\	Outlook client, enables use of IMAP services from Gmail, Exchange, others	Folders include .dat files; .dat files in folder 19 are e-mail messages in HTML format
Internet Explorer	\Application Data \Microsoft\Outlook \Stores\DeviceStore \data\	Various Internet files	TabsStorage.bin lists opened tabs in IE
Apps	\Applications\Data \<app GUID>\Data \IsolatedStore	All app information	Application cache, SQLite databases, other application settings
Location	\Application Data \Location\Cache	Wi-Fi and Cellular location	If user enabled, lists locations for cellular and Wi-Fi
Registry	MainOS Windows \systerm32\config	SAM, SECURITY, SOFTWARE, SYSTEM	Information on typed URLs
Maps	\Application Data\Maps	Map data	If user accessed maps, locations found in MapsSetData.dat

would be necessary only if the examiner were connecting to the device live, via USB, and navigating the file system with Explorer.

Additional information in the store.vol file and other files located within the Windows Phone 7 file system is covered in greater detail in the next section.

Windows Phone 8

To help mitigate the deep dive into the Windows Phone 8 file system, Python scripts composed by Adrian Leong are available (through GitHub at https://github.com/cheeky4n6monkey/4n6-scripts) to help the examiner with the recovery of contacts, call logs, and SMS. These scripts can be run in MPE+, Physical Analyzer, and XRY, to name a few, but the examiner must understand that the scripts are written to be output to a CSV file. If the mobile solution enables the running of Python scripts, the examiner must make sure that the output conforms to the solution, since the output can always be tweaked to fit the examiner's needs. Also, EnCase has an EnScript that was created from Leong's Python scripts at http:\\encase-forensic-blog.guidancesoftware.com/2014/10/encase-and-python-automating-windows.html. Having a file system accessible, as shown in Figure 10-22, will allow an examiner to utilize these powerful parsing scripts.

Table 10-14 outlines the file layout of the Windows Phone 8 data drive, and Table 10-15 shows the various evidence locations within the Windows Phone 8 file system. This is not an exhaustive list, but a starting point for the advanced analysis of the Windows Phone 8 file system.

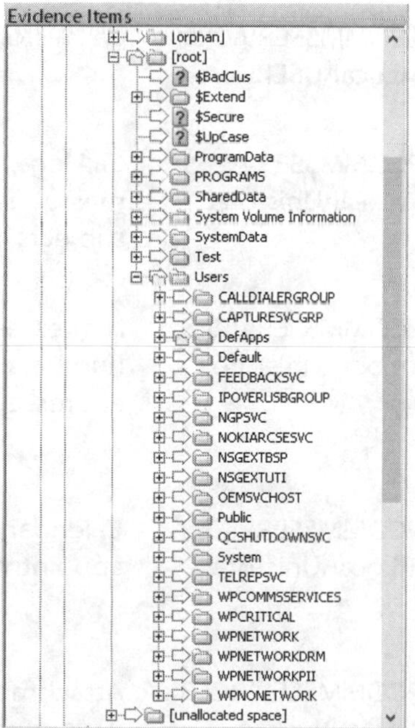

FIGURE 10-22 Internal file system of a Windows Phone 8 device displayed in FTK

TABLE 10-14 Main File Layout for Windows Phone 8 Within the Data Partition

Path	Description
\Programs	Windows Phone Store application code
\Users	Default user account, built-in services, and public data folders
\SystemData	Systemwide files, such as logs and Device Update; data in this folder is not applicable to a particular application
\SharedData	Systemwide shared data, or data shared between multiple applications
\Test	Test code and the data in its subdirectories

TABLE 10-15 Compiled and Known Locations for Critical User Data Within a Windows Phone 8

Artifact	Path	Considerations	Comments
Account Managers	\Users\WPCOMMSSERVICES \APPDATA\Local\BackupVols\	CommsBackup.xml	User login and passwords for various accounts
Call History	\Users\WPCOMMSSERVICES \APPDATA\Local\USERData \Phone	Call history table	Start and stop time, number, resolved contact name
Conversation	\Users\WPCOMMSSERVICES \APPDATA\Local\Unistore \store.vol	Call logs, SMS messages, e-mail subjects	All items that have appeared on the device screen, in chronological order
Contact	\Users\WPCOMMSSERVICES \APPDATA\Local\Unistore \store.vol	Names, e-mail, phone numbers, business addresses	Culmination of records from apps (such as Facebook, Twitter) and device contact list
Appointments	\Users\WPCOMMSSERVICES \APPDATA\Local\Unistore \store.vol	Calendar appointments	Information in Unicode, ASCII date and time information
Attachments	\Users\WPCOMMSSERVICES \APPDATA\Local\Unistore \store.vol	Attachments for various applications	Name of attachment, type of artifact

TABLE 10-15 **Compiled and Known Locations for Critical User Data Within a Windows Phone 8** ***(Continued)***

Artifact	Path	Considerations	Comments
Message	\Users\WPCOMMSSERVICES \APPDATA\Local\Unistore \store.vol	MMS and SMS	Message content, numbers, date and time information
Notes	\Users\WPCOMMSSERVICES \APPDATA\Local\Unistore \store.vol	Notes	Notes, content, date and time information
Tasks	\Users\WPCOMMSSERVICES \APPDATA\Local\Unistore \store.vol	Tasks	Tasks, content, date and time Information
Internet Explorer	\Users\DefApps\APPDATA \INTERNETEXPLORER	Folders for INetCache, INetHistory	XML, HTML, and other files pertaining to Internet usage
Internet Explorer	\SharedData\InternetExplorer \Favorites		URL information for IE cached favorites
Apps	\Users\DefApps\APPDATA \Local\Packages\<GUID>\AC	Location for app certificates and additional security	Installed apps
Apps	\Users\DefApps\APPDATA \Local\Packages\	Location for Microsoft.<appname> apps app	Internet artifacts in INetCache, INetHistory
Apps	\Users\DefApps\APPDATA \<app GUID>\Local	Third-party apps	GUID or app name
Pictures	\Users\Public\Pictures	\Camera Roll \Saved Pictures \Screenshots	Photos from device, saved and shared
Videos	\Users\Public\Videos		Videos from device
Registry	MainOS Windows\systerm32 \config	SAM, SECURITY, SOFTWARE, SYSTEM	Information on typed URLs
App Identify	\PROGRAMS\<PACKAGE GUID>\Install	WMAppManifest.xml	Matches GUID with app name and app capabilities

Windows Phone stores the majority of user data in an Extensible Storage Engine (ESE) database(s). ESE is a sequential storage technology developed by Microsoft that is remarkably different from other storage methods found on any of today's mobile devices. These storage databases contain numerous tables similar to other built-in databases with records and tables (see Figure 10-23). The database allows multiple pieces of transactional data, seemingly unrelated, to be stored in a single repository. A perfect example within the Windows Phone is the store.vol file. This file is located at \Users\WPCOMMSSERVICES\APPDATA\Local \Unistore (see Figure 10-24) and holds transactional data for contacts, messages, activity, conversations, appointments, and others. This method of data storage makes locating key information easy, as long as the information can be viewed. Using applications such as FTK and EnCase, the examiner can view the ESE files and the data contained within them.

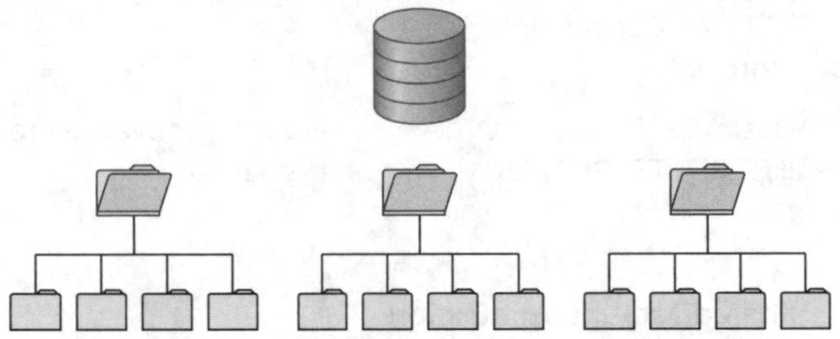

FIGURE 10-23 ESE database structure with the root node on the top

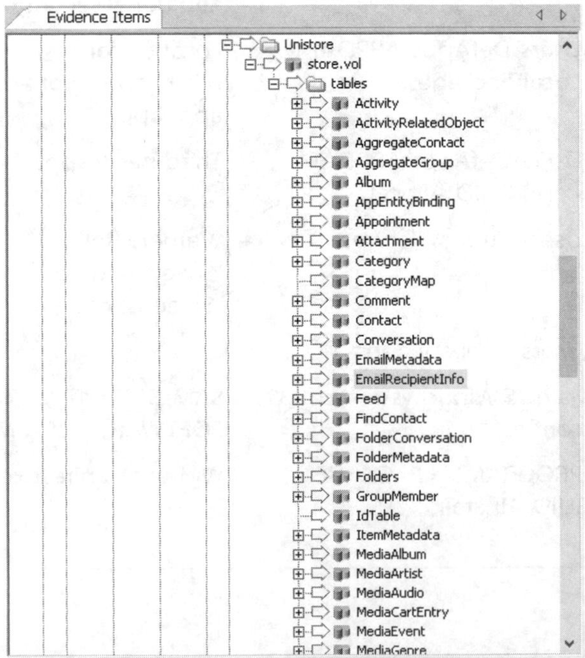

FIGURE 10-24 The store.vol ESE contains a wealth of information for an examiner.

The data for installed apps is located in various subfolders and can be stored in SQLite databases, JSON, XML, and other file types. App data on a Windows Phone can be stored in several locations in the device file system, depending on the way the app was designed to store and share data. Two locations for data storage reside at Users\DefApps\APPDATA\. Microsoft Phone built-in apps such as Facebook and Skype are located in a subfolder at \APPDATA \Local, prefixed with *Microsoft*. Within the \APPDATA\Local folder is also some of the app GUIDs that were located in the root Users\DefApps\APPDATA. Each of the \APPDATA\Local apps includes a subfolder called AC (Application Cache), which contains certificate and crypto key information for any of the apps found in the root of the User\DefApps\APPDATA folder and identified with a GUID. However, some of the apps, such as the Microsoft apps, contain additional folders that pertain to Internet usage. Microsoft added the ability for each app to have its own Internet artifacts, which include its own cache, cookies, and history. These folders are called INetCache (Internet Cache), INetCookies (Internet cookies), and INetHistory (Internet History). These are extremely important, especially the INetCache folder, which can store valuable chat messages when the application uses a web interface; Windows Phone devices cache these conversations in this folder. Also within the app folder system is the Local folder, which contains any data the app wants to persist across restarts, including databases files, settings files, and more. This folder can be found in the app folders in both the DefApps \APPDATA\ and the DefApps\APPDATA\Local folder and can contain valuable evidence.

Many of the app names are GUIDs—the unique identifiers for the product that are declared in the app's WMAppManifest.xml (shown in Figure 10-25). The name of the app can be matched with the GUID by locating the WMAppManifest.xml file located in the \PROGRAMS\<Product GUID>\Install folder. The GUID is much like the naming convention observed in an iTunes backup, and the examiner can obtain additional information along with the actual working name of the application using that file path.

```
  <DefaultLanguage xmlns="" code="en" />
- <Languages xmlns="">
    <Language code="es" />
    <Language code="zh-CN" />
  </Languages>
- <App xmlns="" Title="TextNow" RuntimeType="Silverlight" Version="1.1.0.3" Description="Sample
    description" ProductID="{7769583f-2a8c-48fc-bde9-796970c974d8}" Genre="apps.normal"
    IsBeta="false" Author="Enflick" Publisher="Enflick" PublisherID="{e92c2343-c0db-499d-b210-
    80015cf2c821}">
    <IconPath IsRelative="true" IsResource="false">tile_applist_win8.png</IconPath>
  - <Capabilities>
      <Capability Name="ID_CAP_IDENTITY_DEVICE" />
      <Capability Name="ID_CAP_IDENTITY_USER" />
      <Capability Name="ID_CAP_MICROPHONE" />
      <Capability Name="ID_CAP_NETWORKING" />
      <Capability Name="ID_CAP_PHONEDIALER" />
      <Capability Name="ID_CAP_PUSH_NOTIFICATION" />
      <Capability Name="ID_CAP_SENSORS" />
      <Capability Name="ID_CAP_WEBBROWSERCOMPONENT" />
      <Capability Name="ID_CAP_CONTACTS" />
      <Capability Name="ID_CAP_MEDIALIB_AUDIO" />
      <Capability Name="ID_CAP_MEDIALIB_PHOTO" />
      <Capability Name="ID_CAP_MEDIALIB_PLAYBACK" />
      <Capability Name="ID_CAP_SPEECH_RECOGNITION" />
    </Capabilities>
```

FIGURE 10-25 **Applications have app manifest files that can reveal a lot about an installed application. This example shows a manifest file from TextNow, a popular chatting app.**

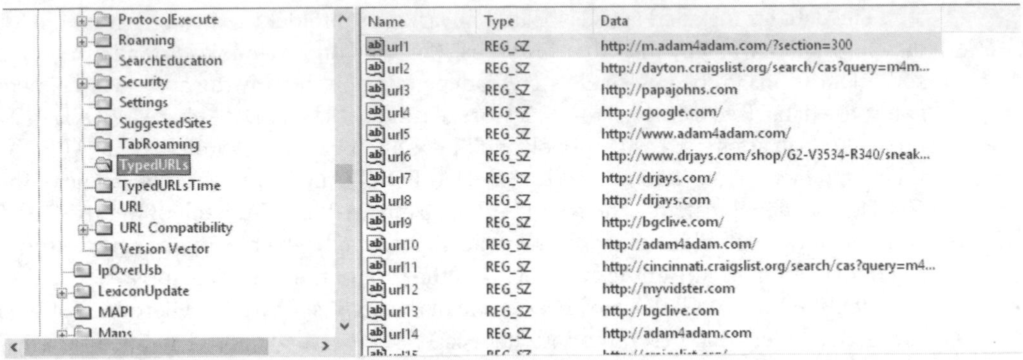

ProtocolExecute
Roaming
SearchEducation
Security
Settings
SuggestedSites
TabRoaming
TypedURLs
TypedURLsTime
URL
URL Compatibility
Version Vector
IpOverUsb
LexiconUpdate
MAPI
Maps

Name	Type	Data
url1	REG_SZ	http://m.adam4adam.com/?section=300
url2	REG_SZ	http://dayton.craigslist.org/search/cas?query=m4m...
url3	REG_SZ	http://papajohns.com
url4	REG_SZ	http://google.com/
url5	REG_SZ	http://www.adam4adam.com/
url6	REG_SZ	http://www.drjays.com/shop/G2-V3534-R340/sneak...
url7	REG_SZ	http://drjays.com/
url8	REG_SZ	http://drjays.com
url9	REG_SZ	http://bgclive.com/
url10	REG_SZ	http://adam4adam.com/
url11	REG_SZ	http://cincinnati.craigslist.org/search/cas?query=m4...
url12	REG_SZ	http://myvidster.com
url13	REG_SZ	http://bgclive.com
url14	REG_SZ	http://adam4adam.com

FIGURE 10-26 Even Windows Phone Registry files are accessible.

Another location in which apps may store data, but which is not recommended by Microsoft, is within the \SharedData path. WhatsApp, for example, stores backup information within the \SharedData\OEM\Public\WhatsApp\Backup path, and a complete backup of the messages and contacts can be recovered from the SQLite database. Also within the \SharedData \Comms folder is both a messaging and unistore folder, among other communication type apps. The unistore folder stores transient data from the store.vol ESE database that is shared among other apps or device functions. The messaging folder contains transient MMS files that are also available to other apps or device functions because of their location within the \SharedData folder. The \SharedData folder can be a good source for evidentiary data because data deleted within an application can be retained in the \SharedData folder. Much like a Windows computer, the Windows Phone also contains a registry. In Figure 10-26 the examiner has full access to the familiar TypedURLs registry key within the Windows Phone Registry.

An examiner must be prepared to analyze the Windows Phone file system in its entirety. Microsoft will continue to advance the device operating system, so continual updating of the various locations of artifacts will be necessary to recover the maximum amount of evidence. As with the BB10 device, an examiner must be diligent and recognize that the examination of these devices is time consuming, but the results can be fantastic.

Chapter Summary

No longer can an examiner rely on "tip of the iceberg data" when conducting an investigation. Even feature phones contain valuable data outside of the normal PIM data. Nevertheless, many examiners believe that data collected using an automated tool includes all the available data, even if the entire file system is extracted! After looking into the file system, most examiners learn that there is life outside of automation when conducting mobile device collections. The examiner must not only recognize that additional data can be recovered, but he or she must also be prepared to interpret the information like a software application would. By understanding the various formats and locations, an examiner can determine whether a deeper analysis of the mobile device file system should be considered. Armed with knowledge of the various formats of data for feature phones, UICC, BlackBerry, and Windows Phone devices, the examiner will be prepared to conduct a thorough file system examination.

BlackBerry 10 and Windows Phone devices present new challenges to the mobile forensic community. The collection of the file system is extremely challenging, and when the internal files and folder structure have never been documented, every examination becomes a research and development exercise. The information contained in this chapter for BB10 and Windows Phone will need to be updated and added to continually as new discoveries are made, artifacts are located, and evidence is uncovered, and another line will be added to the reference tables. The tables provided in this chapter are a starting point in an examiner's journey to uncover even more information from these devices.

As an examiner continues to grow in understanding that the analysis of a mobile device file system is not only for automated tools, the more discoveries within the BB10 and Windows Phone file systems will be made. Hopefully, by using the tables and figures in this chapter, the examiner will be able to start off quickly, showing immediate results for any investigation or case.

11 Advanced iOS Analysis

In 2014, the International Data Corporation (IDC) reported that Android and iOS mobile devices dominated the mobile market worldwide, with Android leading at a 76.6 percent share and Apple at 19.7 percent (www.idc.com/prodserv/smartphone-os-market-share.jsp). That leaves little doubt that these two types of devices also dominate the workload of most mobile device forensic examiners. This chapter deals specifically with the examination of the iOS file structure, which is available with a simple logical extraction or via a backup import created with iTunes.

Automated tools can be used to extract a lot of "tip of the iceberg" iOS device data, which satisfies many investigators. However, considering the total number of files that are available for examination on an iOS device, the number of files analyzed and presented using an automated tool pales in comparison to the number that can be viewed using a logical extraction. The problem lies with the examiner who believes in the "what they see is what they get" theory, who is satisfied with a report created by clicking Print at the end of an automated extraction. However, an iOS device is like no other smart device regarding how data is backed up, and using a simple logical extraction will include more information, such as critical databases, settings, and property lists in the backup—and this type of data is digital gold to the examiner.

Examining actual binary files from which the user data was parsed, along with additional files not traversed by an automated tool, offers the examiner the opportunity to perform a deep analysis of the iOS device's file system. This can include hashing and comparisons, verification and validation, and manual decoding and file carving—to name a few of the possibilities. By having the entire file system available, the examiner can perform a thorough examination without needing to conduct a non-invasive or invasive physical extraction. This chapter outlines the critical file structures and formats that make up the meat of the iOS file system. The goal of this chapter is to encourage the examiner to move away from wholeheartedly trusting an automated tool to conduct an iOS mobile device examination.

TABLE 11-1 Apple Support Technical Specification Links

Device Family	Link to Specification Table
iPhone	http://support.apple.com/specs/#iphone
iPad	http://support.apple.com/specs/#ipad
iPod Touch	http://support.apple.com/specs/#ipodtouch
Apple TV	http://support.apple.com/specs/#appletv

Note With today's iOS devices containing A5 and later chipsets, a non-jailbroken physical collection using a USB is impossible, so a logical collection is the only available method. Because of this physical collection limitation, it is critical that the examiner conduct a logical file system extraction for all iOS mobile devices. Some sources report that a physical collection can be obtained using tools such as Elcomsoft iOS Forensic Toolkit, but this is not entirely accurate. This tool cannot be used to perform a physical partition collection, as it can with A4 chipsets, but simply enables collecting a jailbroken device's internal file system, which all commercial tools can currently do, including UFED Touch, Oxygen Forensic Analyst, and XRY.

This chapter will not discuss the hardware configurations for Apple devices, because many other publications provide information regarding the hardware and internal software versions. By referring to the Apple Developer web site, an examiner can consult the iOS Device Compatibility page to obtain critical information on the internal components and devices. Table 11-1 also shows links to detailed technical specs for various iOS devices.

This chapter will focus on how the examiner can identify the variety of evidence located within the iOS file system, including data that can be used immediately in an investigation and information that will lend credibility to the processes used by automated tools. This information will help the examiner better understand how the extraction processes work and provide information regarding documenting the procedure if the information is needed in court proceedings. The examiner will gain a better working understanding of the iOS device and a greater understanding of how to uncover and process the wealth of information contained within the iOS device file system.

The iOS File System

Apple mobile devices share some of the OS X foundation, but they use a different framework, which means OS X applications will not run on iOS. Both are based on the UNIX file system, and although the structures of the file systems are similar between iOS and OS X, there are differences in the way each stores apps and user data. In an iOS mobile device, apps interact with the file system. The interactions are limited ("sandboxed") by design, so each has a container or a number of containers with specific roles (containers include the App Bundle, App Storage, and iCloud Data, as shown in Figure 11-1). iOS and OS X devices both use a type

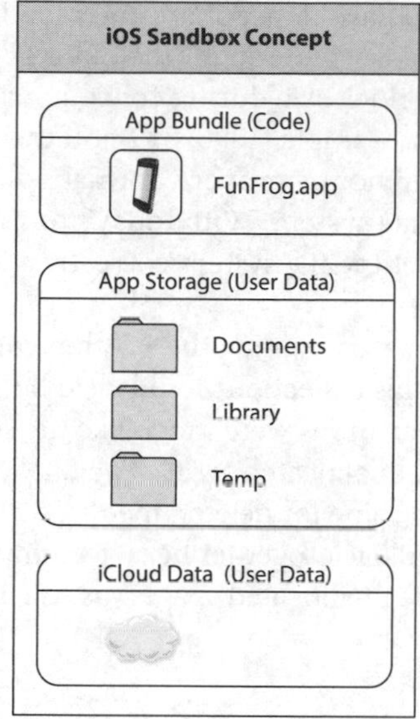

FIGURE 11-1 The containers of the iOS sandbox

of hierarchical file system (HFS). An iOS device uses HFSX | HFS+ (Mac OS Extended), and OS X computers use HFS+. Apple indicates that the only difference between HFS+ and HFSX is that the latter contains case-sensitive filenames, which is commonly observed in iOS devices.

When mobile forensic tools were first used to conduct non-invasive physical collections of iPhone devices, these solutions had to interpret the predicted binary HFS/HFSX file system. Early on, the forensic tools could interpret HFS+ file systems, but when the forensic tools looked for the telltale H+ around the 0x400 offset of the disk image, the process failed. Because the HFS/HFSX file system contains *HX* (Figure 11-2), the examiner had to change the *X* to a + in order for common computer forensic tools to mount the file system properly.

```
000003b0 00 00 00 00 00 00 00 00-00 00 00 00 00 00 00 00 ................
000003c0 00 00 00 00 00 00 00 00-00 00 00 00 00 00 00 00 ................
000003d0 00 00 00 00 00 00 00 00-00 00 00 00 00 00 00 00 ................
000003e0 00 00 00 00 00 00 00 00-00 00 00 00 00 00 00 00 ................
000003f0 00 00 00 00 00 00 00 00-00 00 00 00 00 00 00 00 ................
00000400 48 58 00 05 00 00 01 00-31 30 2E 30 00 00 00 00 HX······10.0····
00000410 C6 3B A3 A0 C6 61 E6 47-00 00 00 00 C6 3C 06 10 Æ;£ ÆaæG····Æ<··
00000420 00 00 2F F4 00 00 0E 6C-00 00 10 00 00 01 F4 00 ··/ô···l······ô·
00000430 00 00 39 F8 00 00 B4 AE-00 01 00 00 00 01 00 00 ··9ø··´®········
00000440 00 00 3F 18 00 00 43 85-00 00 00 00 00 00 00 01 ··?···C·········
00000450 00 00 05 9A 00 00 00 00-00 00 02 00 00 00 00 00 ················
00000460 00 00 00 00 00 00 05 9A-BB E6 43 0C 8D F3 53 09 ·······»æC··óS·
00000470 00 00 00 00 00 00 40 00-00 00 40 00 00 00 00 04 ······@···@·····
```

FIGURE 11-2 The *HX* marker is highlighted, indicating the HFS/HFSX format. The *X* had to be changed to a + during the early years of examining iPhones.

The software would also have to negotiate and rebuild the file system from the raw disk image. As a result, to display and mount the directory structure properly, the solutions had to interpret the correct block size during collection and later decoding, which progresses in sizes of 512 bytes (for example, 4096, 8192). If the block size was not interpreted, the directory structure could not be properly formatted—which of course meant the examiner couldn't work with the file system. With today's tools, however, this is no longer an issue, because they all interpret the file system correctly and structure and display it properly to the examiner.

Devices prior to those containing the A5 chip could undergo a non-invasive collection of the entire raw disk. This collection would yield both the system and user partitions within the iOS device. These partitions were much like the standard hard drive, with a directory structure, file slack, and unallocated areas. The unallocated space, or free area, within the iOS partition was a gold mine for deleted media, including images and videos. Granted, the videos had to be stitched back together because they were stored as separate image files, but recovering data from the unallocated space was still a dream come true with iOS devices, as shown in Figure 11-3.

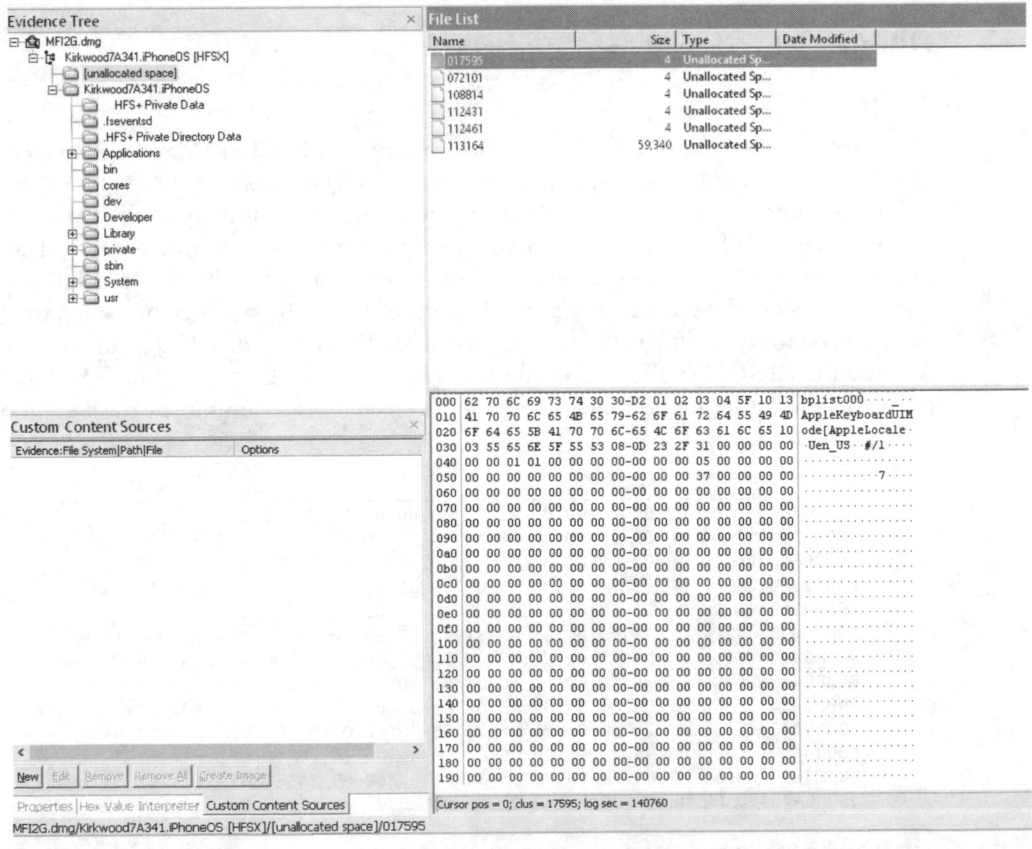

FIGURE 11-3 **An iPhone raw disk image with unencrypted unallocated space containing many deleted files**

This all ended with iOS 5, however, when Apple changed the way data was encrypted on disk along with data protection class keys and a file system key. With iOS 5, examiners and software developers alike were required to obtain the keybag and keys to decrypt the extracted user partition at the file level based upon file permissions to rebuild and ultimately analyze the extracted partition. Software vendors that had previously supported a non-physical collection of iOS devices quickly created modified versions of Jean Sigwald's code (https://code.google.com/p/iphone-dataprotection) that was in the wild. Soon user data was again visible to the examiner, but unfortunately the key needed for unallocated space was not available. As a result, when the unallocated space was extracted, it remained encrypted. The files are encrypted at the file level, and without having a valid file path and key and data protection key, the files cannot be decrypted.

Since then, new techniques have provided some benefits. For example, an article presented by Aaron Burghardt and Adam J. Feldman in 2008 (www.dfrws.org/2008/proceedings/p76-burghardt.pdf) discussed using the journal file within a Mac OS partition to locate and identify catalog file entries for deleted files, with limited results. This technique was extended by Jean-Baptiste Bédrune and Jean Sigwald within the iphone-dataprotection code on the google.com code repository using a Python script for iOS devices. As indicated by Sigwald, and also from personal experience, the journal file is extremely small, and only a small number of files can be recovered. To this day, this limitation means that the unallocated space is generally safe from an examiner's data carving tools.

When devices containing the A5 chip (iPad 2 was first, followed by the iPhone 4S) first hit the market, examiners realized they had a problem. Placing the devices into Device Firmware Update (DFU) mode still worked, but every attempt to use the same function with an automated tool no longer allowed for a collection. The iOS device, while still in DFU mode, did not accept the custom RAM disk, and examiners were blocked from acquiring the iOS device using this non-invasive physical technique. Although devices without the dreaded A5 chip were still being sold and updated, forensic software vendors continually had to explain to their customers that a non-invasive approach was not possible unless the device was jailbroken. This dashed the hopes and dreams of a lot of examiners, for now they thought all had been lost: the iOS device—the most widely sold mobile device—was inaccessible to a forensic examiner. This mentality stormed through the community, and it is still a belief held by many examiners. However, this could not be further from the truth.

In iOS 4, Apple introduced a feature that enables the user to encrypt the backup produced by iTunes within the app's settings. This setting had to be initiated within iTunes by the user checking the box to encrypt the iOS device backup and entering a password for the backup and subsequent restore to that device. This password would then be used to encrypt the backup, instead of using the hardware key of the iOS device. Using this method, the iTunes backup password is stored within the iOS device keychain database, and the backup keybag is encrypted with the backup password. Because the backup keybag is accessible within the backup, it is possible to decrypt the backup without involving the iOS device itself.

The encryption of the backup processes poses a problem to the mobile forensic examiner on several fronts. One, the encryption of the backup is not a setting that a user can set or disable on the actual iOS device, so an examiner cannot turn off the encryption on the device itself. Two, this setting is not on by default, but if a user checked the box and secured the backup with a password, the connected iOS device would then produce an encrypted backup when the Apple Mobile Backup service was initiated. This second condition posed another problem for the mobile forensic community when dealing with iOS devices. Because mobile forensic tools used the Apple Mobile Backup service to initiate a backup to the forensic computer, an encrypted backup was of no use. This road block was averted by Sigwald, who produced open source code that effectively decrypted the backup with the known password, again putting mobile forensic solutions back in business—so long as the examiner has the iTunes password that was used by the device owner. With that password, the mobile forensic solution would decrypt the backup and analyze the data for the user. There was still a potential problem, however: What if the examiner did not know the iTunes password or the owner would not give it up?

The inability of the examiner to conduct a proper collection of an Apple device if backup encryption was turned on was a serious threat to forensic examinations. The Apple hacking community had the same problem, so they trudged on in an effort to discover other methods of accessing an iOS device. Several groups began to publish open source tools that would allow not only a backup of the iOS device using iTunes, but also using the Apple File Connection (AFC) protocol used by iTunes to move files on and off and for device-level communication. Because iTunes is given access only to specific portions of the device (jailed environment), AFC is limited only to the media area. However, a jailbroken device, as the community discovered, can have all files available using the AFC protocol/backup service. The service was altered and installed to a jailbroken device, and AFC2 was born, which enabled access to the complete file system of the iOS device.

This method, however, was not observed by the forensic community as viable because of the implications often imposed by a jailbreak. However, further research into the mobile device soon brought to light additional services such as com.apple.mobile.house_arrest and com.apple.mobile.file_relay. These services, primarily the file_relay service, had been developed by Apple as an internal testing mechanism for file transfer, but they had been a part of libimobiledevice code since 2009. This was not just any file transfer, but the transfer of user data–laden files, without the need for an iTunes connection. The type of data depends on the iOS version, but an iTunes backup was not invoked, and since Apple Mobile Backup was not initiated, the backup encryption was not triggered and any data transferred from the device would not be encrypted.

The house_arrest service enables access to the application folder and its contents. Mobile forensic solutions jumped on this new ability and began to incorporate this feature into their products. Examiners could then conduct a mobile device forensic exam on an iOS device even if the iTunes password was not known. Examiners were able to extract personal information manager (PIM) data and app data from these devices in a fully decrypted format. Mobile forensic vendors were back in business. Then, in 2015, an ex-employee of a mobile forensic company "outed" Apple on this "security flaw" and published how forensic companies were exploiting this "backdoor" and exposing customers' personal data. This self-serving revelation of a function already known by many researchers, and not new information by any stretch, effectively closed the door for law enforcement, enterprise, and corporate investigators if the file_relay service was going to be used to recover user data.

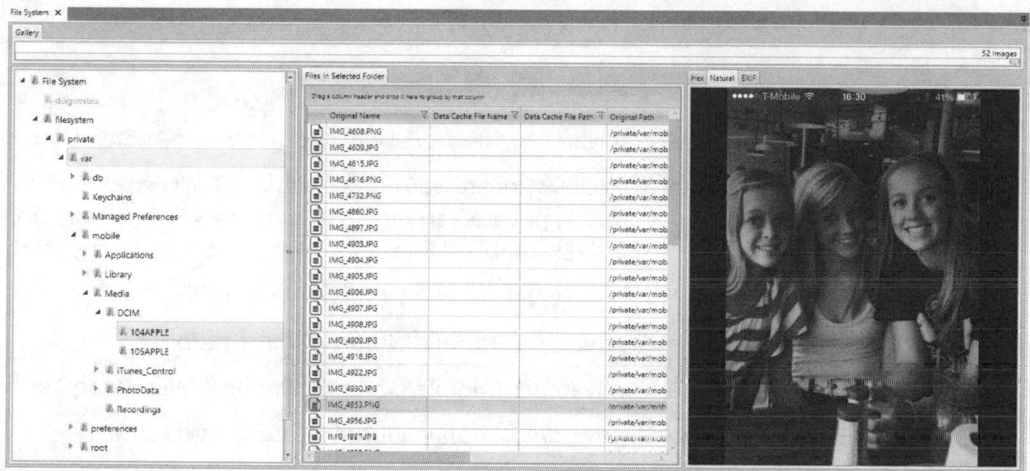

FIGURE 11-4 iOS logical file system view; many files and folders are still available for an examiner to analyze.

Apple followed suit and released iOS 8, closing the door on the retrieval of PIM user data by any means other than using the built-in Mobile Backup function and limited the additional services. All iOS devices below OS version 8 still allow for connections to both the house_arrest and file_relay services even if the iTunes password is not known.

Tip A mobile forensic software solution must use the file_relay service to achieve a more robust file system collection, and not all mobile forensic software has this ability. The examiner should check with the software vendor before assuming that the software is capable of this function. UFED Physical Analyzer and Oxygen Forensic Detective and Analyst both support this feature.

The logical collection of an iOS device without access to the additional services still contains an extraordinary amount of information. Examiners must be diligent in the recovery and discovery of the many files available within the iOS file system, as shown in Figure 11-4.

iOS "Tip of the Iceberg Data"

The type of data collected by mobile forensic solutions from an iOS device is comparable to that collected on the majority of devices. There are, of course, small exceptions among solutions, but the collected data listed in Table 11-2, if available on the device, is always a part of a mobile forensic collection barring a locked device, encrypted backup, or other impedance. The information in Table 11-2 can be used to identify the type of data and where the physical files are located so that further investigation can be conducted within the extracted file system when needed. Further investigation into the database files and other associated files can uncover usernames, passwords, and even deleted data.

TABLE 11-2 "Tip of the Iceberg Data" Commonly Collected by Automated Tools

User Data	File Type	Path in File system
Contacts	SQLite database	private/var/mobile/Library/AddressBook/Addressbook.sqlitedb
Call logs	SQLite database	(<iOS 7) private/var/mobile/Library/CallHistory/CallHistory.db (iOS 7) private/var/wireless/CallHistory/call_history.db (iOS 8x) mobile/Library/CallHistoryDB/CallHistory.storedata
SMS	SQLite database	private/var/mobile/Library/SMS/sms.db
MMS	SQLite database	private/var/mobile/Library/SMS/sms.db
Calendar	SQLite database	private/var/mobile/Library/Calendar/Calendar.sqlitedb
Notes	SQLite database	private/var/mobile/Library/Notes/notes.sqlite
Images	Individual .jpg files named IMG_<Sequence #>	private/var/ mobile/Media/DCIM/1XXAPPLE
Videos	Individual .mov files named IMG_<Sequence #>	private/var/ mobile/Media/DCIM/1XXAPPLE
Browser bookmarks	SQLite database	private/var/ mobile/Library/Safari/Bookmarks.db

The examiner should soon recognize that Table 11-2 contains only surface-level data; a wealth of additional data is contained within the file system. The next section discusses the file system arrangement, with major file and folder locations in a typical iOS file system.

Tip

With the introduction of iOS 8, devices that contained migrated data from iOS 7 now had two database files in two different locations: the call_history.db for iOS 7 was stored at private/var/wireless/CallHistory, and CallHistory.storedata for iOS 8x was now at mobile/Library/CallHistoryDB. Examiners should be aware that some tools do not obtain both databases. The call_history.db can contain historical calls before migration of the data and some duplicated calls also found in the iOS 8 CallHistory.storedata database. Because of this, the examiner should complete a manual inspection of these databases.

File System Structure

An iOS file system obtained by both open source and commercial mobile forensic tools primarily relies on the Apple Mobile Backup function. Because of this, the output by tools and interpretation of the file system is similar across the board. This section represents the major "landmarks" that an examiner may see within the collected files and folders, along with some additional folders that might be discovered if the file_relay and house_arrest functions are used by the forensic software solution.

App Data

Figure 11-1 showed the sandbox concept and partitions. This storage method helps the examiner realize that app data that is of value is contained within the Documents, Library, and Temp folders within the App Storage area. Table 11-3 outlines evidence locations based on the storage of user data and app data. These folders are stored directly under the main application folder within the iOS device file system. The application folder for iOS is located at /private/var/mobile/Applications, and the folder for iOS 8x is at /private/var/mobile/Containers/Data/Application. This table can help steer the examiner to the most likely location for digital artifacts within the application folders. Note that the application name within a raw iOS file system is a globally unique identifier (GUID), and that the GUID can change upon application updates, so the examiner should not rely on the GUID to identify a specific application. Most mobile forensic software titles will translate the GUID to the bundle identifier if the manifest is used and available.

Note Apple development insists that developers use the reverse DNS format for apps: the web site extension (.com, .net, .tv, .info, .co.uk, and so on), followed by the web site name, ending with the application name (such as com.oxygen.oxyagent). Tying an application to its bundle identifier is often as easy as looking into the manifest property list located at private/var/root/Library/Caches/Backup/.

The Documents folder within the app file system structure contains, as mentioned in Table 11-3, the user-facing data, which is available to the user via the app. Here the examiner will find SQLite databases the app developer used for persistence, along with folders containing stored files. The Documents folder and its subdirectories store data that the user of the device can add, delete, and alter via the app. It can also contain additional custom folders for the storage of images, configuration settings, and SQLite files. The storage file for the app does not have to be a SQLite database and can be proprietary binary files whose format depends on the app developer's preference for storage, but the method must conform to the Apple SDK. The Documents folder can also contain property lists, XML, text files, and more. Analysis of custom binary files, text files, or property lists may involve building a custom parser, since most mobile forensic solutions cannot account for every file type within an iOS system. The examiner should understand as well that there are limitations with the folder availability, file availability, and file-level encryption—that is, this folder and associated files are not always available.

TABLE 11-3 Major Landmarks Within the App File and Folder Structure Important for an Investigator

Folder	Data Description
Documents	This folder contains user-generated content, where a developer would place data that can be accessible and exposed to the app user and data that the app cannot re-create. Often contains the SQLite databases used and available to the user along with Plist files detailing user settings.
Documents/Inbox	This folder is used often by app developers to enable the app to access files that the app opened from outside requests. An example would be a mail application that places e-mail attachments into the directory. The app can read and delete the files, but cannot create or edit files within this directory. This folder is backed up by iTunes if used.
Library	The app uses this top-level directory to store data that it does not want to expose to the user; it is not advisable to store user data here that can be directly interacted upon by the user. This folder uses a subdirectory structure, and the app developer can create custom folders. Any folder with the exception of the Caches subdirectory is backed up by iTunes.
Library/Application Support	This folder contains subfolders and files used by the app for function support. This is where the examiner can find advertisement support, database files supporting features, and additional app settings. This area should be examined, especially with browsers and apps not using SQLite databases. Chrome for iOS, for example, stores bookmarks, history, and other information within the Application Support/Google/Chrome/ Default folder.
Library/Caches	The Caches folder is often a gold mine. The folder is obtained either via the house_arrest or file_relay service on a jailbroken device. This folder is not available in an iTunes backup. The folder is described later in the "App Caches" section of this chapter.
Library/Cookies	This subfolder contains the Cookies.binarycookies file, which stores the persistent session cookies used by the app. This file is discussed later in this section.
Library/Preferences	This subfolder contains the application preferences. For example, mobile Safari contains all the search strings within the com.apple.mobilesafari .plist file. Other property lists in this folder provide user login details and application details.
tmp	This is temporary storage for the app. This data seldom persists unless the app developer is not purging the data, which is generally not the case. However, if the app is still running in the background when an examiner completes a collection, temporary data could be available, including media, text, and settings files. If available, the examiner should investigate.

In iOS 5 and earlier versions, the app developer was not allowed to exclude folders from the backup, but this limitation was lifted in iOS 5.1 and has continued to the current iOS version. The app developer can use NSURLIsExcludedFromBackup or kCFURLIsExcludedFromBackupKey file system properties to exclude files or directories from backups. This can be extended to system-defined directories, but doing this is not recommended by Apple. However, the examiner will recognize that some apps do not have a Documents folder, or they may have the Documents folder but do not use SQLite databases or other user-defined data. This would indicate that the app developer used the exclusion property, and reliance on the Caches folder will be critical.

The /Library/Cookies folder contains the Cookies.binarycookies file that stores cookies for the particular app; a similar folder is found in most app file systems. A cookie is used to identify the user on a particular web site or web server. Cookies are of particular interest to the examiner because they can show that the user of the iOS device accessed particular web sites using that app. The /Cookies folder can also hold a second Cookies.binarycookies file that is appended with a `-corrupt` flag. The `-corrupt` flag is rumored to be a failed authentication or corrupted file and is marked as such, so a new file is created. The Cookies .binarycookies file and the file marked `-corrupt` both can be decoded using some helpful Python scripts.

A script from satishb3 (www.securitylearn.net) was used as the basis to create the code that follows to operate with Python 3. It has been modified to decode, parse, and output to a file called CookieMonster.csv. The examiner can view the decoded data within a text reader or spreadsheet application. To run the script, the examiner can use any forensic solution that incorporates a Python scripting tool or an open source tool such as PyScripter. The examiner must have Python 3 installed to run the script and will use Cookies.binarycookies as the argument. Information and descriptions are incorporated throughout the following code.

We start by importing the needed Python modules that will be used in the script:

```
import sys
from struct import unpack
from io import BytesIO
from time import strftime, gmtime
import csv
```

This will be the file the script will parse. The `sys_argv`, shown next, is the file following the name of the script if the script is run from the command line or a system argument variable (for example, `mypythonprogram.py Cookies.binarycookies`, where `Cookies.binarycookies` is the `sys_argv`).

```
FilePath= sys.argv[1]

try:
      binary_file=open(FilePath,'rb')

except IOError as e:
      print ('File Not Found :'+ FilePath)
      sys.exit(0)
```

This portion of the code will look at the header of the file for `'cook'` to determine whether it is a valid cookie file per this script:

```
file_header=binary_file.read(4)
file_header=file_header.decode()

if str(file_header)!='cook':
        print ("Not a Cookies.binarycookies file")
        sys.exit(0)
```

Next, the script begins to read through the file to determine the number of pages (cookies) that will exist in the binary file and reports them back to the script as a variable to be used later. Once the pages are determined, the script will know how many cookies are within the file.

```
num_pages=unpack('>i',binary_file.read(4))[0]
page_sizes=[]
for np in range(num_pages):
        page_sizes.append(unpack('>i',binary_file.read(4))[0])
pages=[]
for ps in page_sizes:
        pages.append(binary_file.read(ps))
```

Next, the conversions of each page (cookie) occurs. The cookie name, creation date, expiry date, and domain the cookie is from are all decoded and extracted from the binary page:

```
for page in pages:

     page=BytesIO(page)
     page.read(4)
     num_cookies=unpack('<i',page.read(4))[0]
     cookie_offsets=[]
     for nc in range(num_cookies):
     cookie_offsets.append(unpack('<i',page.read(4))[0])

     page.read(4)
     cookie=b''

     for offset in cookie_offsets:
               page.seek(offset)
               cookiesize=unpack('<i',page.read(4))[0]
               cookie=BytesIO(page.read(cookiesize))
               cookie.read(4)

flags=unpack('<i',cookie.read(4))[0]
cookie_flags=''
               if flags==0:
                    cookie_flags=''
```

```
        elif flags==1:
            cookie_flags='Secure'
        elif flags==4:
            cookie_flags='HttpOnly'
        elif flags==5:
            cookie_flags='Secure; HttpOnly'
        else:
            cookie_flags='Unknown'

        cookie.read(4)

        urloffset=unpack('<i',cookie.read(4))[0]
        nameoffset=unpack('<i',cookie.read(4))[0]
        pathoffset=unpack('<i',cookie.read(4))[0]
        valueoffset=unpack('<i',cookie.read(4))[0]
        endofcookie=cookie.read(8)
```

Dates listed are MAC times with an epoch of January 1, 2001, so an adjustment is made. The date depends upon the application examined, so this value should be analyzed upon output.

```
        expiry_date_epoch= unpack('<d',cookie.read(8))[0]+978307200
        expiry_date=strftime("%a, %d %b %Y ",gmtime(expiry_date_epoch))[:-1]
        create_date_epoch=unpack('<d',cookie.read(8))[0]+978307200
        create_date=strftime("%a, %d %b %Y ",gmtime(create_date_epoch))[:-1]
```

The data from each page is systematically extracted, starting with the URL, then the name, the path, and finally the actual cookie value:

```
        cookie.seek(urloffset-4)
        url=b''
        u=cookie.read(1)

        while unpack('<b',u)[0]!=0:
            url=url+bytes(u)
            u=cookie.read(1)
        url=url.decode('utf-8')

        cookie.seek(nameoffset-4)
        name=b''
        n=cookie.read(1)
        while unpack('<b',n)[0]!=0:
            name=name+bytes(n)
            n=cookie.read(1)
        name=name.decode()

        cookie.seek(pathoffset-4)
        path=b''
        pa=cookie.read(1)
```

```
while unpack('<b',pa)[0]!=0:
    path=path+bytes(pa)
    pa=cookie.read(1)
path=path.decode()

cookie.seek(valueoffset-4)
value=b''
va=cookie.read(1)
while unpack('<b',va)[0]!=0:
    value=value+bytes(va)
    va=cookie.read(1)
value=value.decode()
```

The CookieMonster.csv file is created at the location shown in the following code listing. The information is systematically written to the open file that loops until the final page (cookie) has been located and printed, and the dates obtained are also added to the string. The file is then closed along with the Cookies.binarycookies file.

```
            f = open('C:\\CookieMonster.csv', 'a')
            f.writelines ('Cookie= {0};Value= {1};Domain= {2};Path= {3};
Created= {4}; Expires= {5} \n\n'.format(name,value,url,path,create_date,expiry_date))
f.close()
binary_file.close()
```

Once the process completes, the examiner can retrieve the file from the location specified within the code; here it is at C:\. This script output as shown in Figure 11-5 includes some valuable data for the examiner, especially if web history is of interest in an investigation.

The /Library/Preferences folder is included in just about all app directory structures and contains the settings specific to the user and the app. The property list to examine is the Plist file assigned to the bundle ID (for example, com.google.Drive.plist, com.skype.skype.plist, as shown in Figure 11-6). This plist file will often contain the user login name, last settings, last searches, date of last use, and other settings that could be critical to an examination. Settings files for many of the apps are also located in the Caches folder.

```
Cookie= __utmb; Value= 79739147; Domain= .maltandvine.com; Path= /; Created= Sun, 06 Oct 2013; Expires = Sun, 06 Oct 2013

Cookie= __utmz; Value= 79739147.1381019391.1.1.utmccn=(direct)|utmcsr=(direct)|utmcmd=(none); Domain= .maltandvine.com; Path= /; Created= Sun, 06 Oct 2013; Expires = Sun, 06 Apr 2014

Cookie= A3; Value= +XbXfAwS02Kd00000; Domain= .serving-sys.com; Path= /; Created= Sat, 05 Oct 2013; Expires = Fri, 03 Jan 2014

Cookie= u2; Value= 701d7605-6970-4af1-ac4e-6251e2f7e82e3VL02g; Domain= .serving-sys.com; Path= /; Created= Sat, 05 Oct 2013; Expires = Fri, 03 Jan 2014

Cookie= qntcst; Value= D; Domain= m.yelp.com; Path= /; Created= Sun, 06 Oct 2013; Expires = Sun, 06 Oct 2013

Cookie= __utma; Value= 25995189.1461873737.1382294402.1382294402.1382294402.1; Domain= .youngs.co.uk; Path= /; Created= Sun, 20 Oct 2013; Expires = Tue, 20 Oct 2015

Cookie= __utmb; Value= 25995189.2.10.1382294402; Domain= .youngs.co.uk; Path= /; Created= Sun, 20 Oct 2013; Expires = Sun, 20 Oct 2013

Cookie= __utmz; Value= 25995189.1382294402.1.1.utmcsr=(direct)|utmccn=(direct)|utmcmd=(none); Domain= .youngs.co.uk; Path= /; Created= Sun, 20 Oct 2013; Expires = Mon, 21 Apr 2014

Cookie= mc; Value= 5250b5fb-6e111-c8995-5dc53; Domain= .quantserve.com; Path= /; Created= Sun, 06 Oct 2013; Expires = Tue, 07 Apr 2015

Cookie= api_s; Value= 6WSqwIDm1biOMPXBNZ1fLz-sWFKLUrRb; Domain= auto-api.yelp.com; Path= /; Created= Wed, 08 May 2013; Expires = Tue, 03 May 2033

Cookie= api_ss; Value= Z1o6RyYevnfxaBOhVuYB5am9PitiOrGq; Domain= auto-api.yelp.com; Path= /; Created= Wed, 08 May 2013; Expires = Tue, 03 May 2033

Cookie= UID; Value= a6b9aca-184.51.159.188-1381021179; Domain= .scorecardresearch.com; Path= /; Created= Sun, 06 Oct 2013; Expires = Sat, 26 Sep 2015

Cookie= UIDR; Value= 1381021179; Domain= .scorecardresearch.com; Path= /; Created= Sun, 06 Oct 2013; Expires = Sat, 26 Sep 2015
```

FIGURE 11-5 Output and review of the file created by running the script against the cookies file from com.yelp.yelpiphone

Hex | Natural | EXIF

A8F70AB	*Number*	1255696820
A811AE1	*Number*	1255622585
66F2079	*Number*	1303524682
LocationManagerCountryCode	*String*	US
lastVersionCheckTimeStamp	*Number*	366984650.62460601
BubbleDial	*Boolean*	True
LastCalledNumberKey	*String*	+12084842338
SkypePrefsDefaultContactGroup	*String*	CONTACT_GROUP_ALL_BUDDIES
SkypePrefsPresence	*Number*	3
LastPhoneNumberString	*String*	+12084842338
kShowTechCallInfoDefaultsKey	*Boolean*	False
SkypeUserCountryCode	*String*	US
SkypePrefsPersonalInfoAlertShownToAccounts	*Array*	*(1 values)*
[0]	*String*	mfi_trainer
BITUpdateDateOfVersionInstallation	*Number*	415643874.492006
WebKitAllowMultiElementImplicitFormSubmissionPreferenceKey	*Boolean*	False
PostCallReporterLastSkypeCallDate	*Date (GMT)*	2011-09-23T21:07:50Z
SkypePrefsLastLoggedInFullName	*String*	Lee Reiber
HasReportedToAdMobDefault	*Boolean*	True
adSecondTimeUser	*Number*	1
SkypePrefsAccountStayOnline	*Number*	-1
SkypePrefsForcedUpdateVersion	*String*	1.0.0.0
BITUpdateDateOfLastCheck	*Date (GMT)*	0000-12-30T00:00:00Z
SkypePrefsLastAttemptedLoginWasViaSkypeAccount	*Boolean*	True
PreviousSkypePrefsAccountStayOnline	*Number*	-1
3GTrialActive-FirstLaunchInfoDisplayed	*Boolean*	True

FIGURE 11-6 A plist file for com.skype.skype.plist showing critical information on last calls, last login, and more

The examiner could also encounter the /Library/WebKit folder or SQLite databases with the .localstorage extension. These files and the WebKit folder use the WebKit framework, which enables an application to use a built-in browser to display web content. In doing this, the app will cache the entire database that is used for that particular instance or site visited using the app. If the app uses an internal browser, when the app launches the browser and navigates to a site such as Hootsuite, for example, the app will then cache the mobile web site's browser settings and/or local data for that site (see Figure 11-7). The site name is part of the filename along with the extension .localstorage. Full web pages, searches, and other useful data can be located within the WebKit folder and also the .localstorage files.

Note The WebKit folder is still available within the main /private/var/mobile/Library folder for iOS, but it is seldom populated because most applications now house the WebKit folder within their app folder structure. A lot of apps have a WebKit folder in the app directory structure but store the .localstorage files within the Caches folder in the app /Library folder.

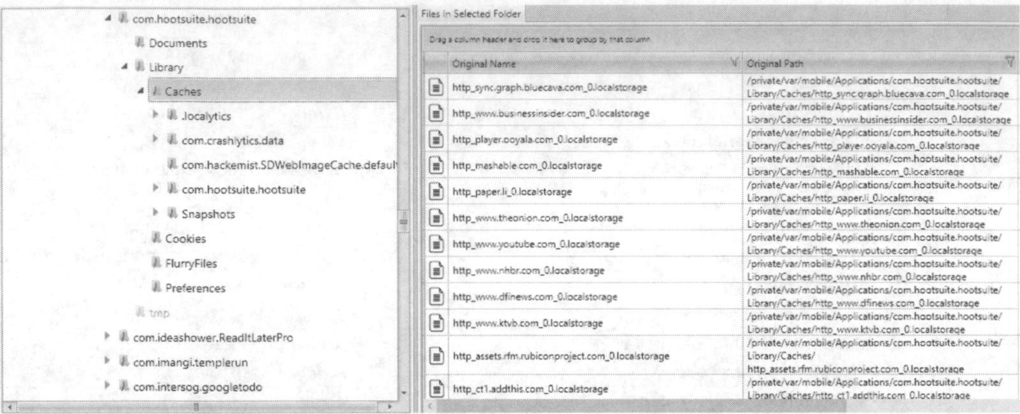

FIGURE 11-7 Hootsuite, a social media application, uses WebKit functionality to offer the user a built-in web browser that caches data from each site within its directory structure.

Installed Apps

An examiner may often be curious as to whether an app had been installed and later removed from an iOS device. The Launch Services Daemon Identifiers file com.apple.lsdidentifiers.plist located at private/var/db/lsd/ indicates applications that have been installed on the device and launched by the LSD service and provides the actual vendor ID GUID assigned to the app(s). (Note that this vendor ID is not the product GUID that would be found in the manifest file or the /Library/Application folder.) Comparing the list of apps in the com.apple.lsdidentifiers.plist to that in the Manifest.plist file and iOS file system, the examiner can determine whether the app once existed and has since been removed. (This has been verified in several tests in which an application has been installed, run, and subsequently deleted. Upon analyzing the backup, the bundle ID was still visible within the com.apple.lsdidentifiers.plist file but was no longer referenced within the file system or Manifest.plist.)

App Caches

An app on the iOS device, like any other program, uses an area on disk to store volatile and temporary data. As described earlier, app development dictates that data that should not be available to the user be stored in the /Library folder and its subdirectories. The Caches folder is one of those subdirectories in which the app stores volatile data (such as web sites, media from web sites, and site-specific settings), and it is typically visible within the application only during the session. The folder can have children files in the root of the folder, but it can also store additional subfolders and files that are used by the app. The folders and files under the Caches folder are up to the app developer to create; Apple does give some direction and guidance regarding iCloud (https://developer.apple.com/icloud/documentation/data-storage/index.html)—but again, this is ultimately determined by the developer. There are some consistencies within the Caches folder that can steer the examiner, however, and within these files and folders is a wealth of information waiting to be recovered.

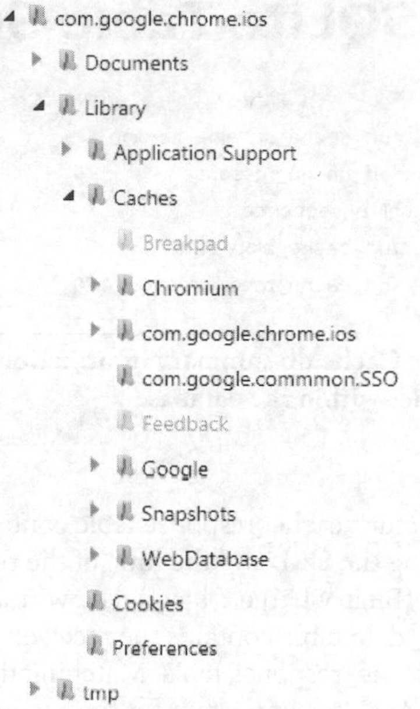

- com.google.chrome.ios
  - Documents
  - Library
    - Application Support
    - Caches
      - Breakpad
      - Chromium
      - com.google.chrome.ios
      - com.google.commmon.SSO
      - Feedback
      - Google
      - Snapshots
      - WebDatabase
    - Cookies
    - Preferences
  - tmp

FIGURE 11-8 The Caches folder expanded for com.google.chrome.ios

The Caches folder is located under the Library folder, which is a subfolder of the application main folder (see Figure 11-8). (The examiner should not confuse this with the Caches folder found under /private/var/mobile/Library.) Because the Caches folder is not contained within an iOS standard iTunes backup, the mobile forensic solution must use the house_arrest and file_relay services for recovery and collection. If the Caches folder is not visible after the extraction, the examiner should consider attempting with a secondary tool to ensure that this important data is recovered.

Within the Caches folder, an app can store many custom folders, but apps also have some commonalities, as discussed in the following sections.

Bundle ID Folder

A good place to start will be looking for a folder that is named after the bundle ID (com.<company><app name>). This does not necessarily have to be the same bundle ID that describes the app, but this is usually the case. Additional folders can also be in a bundle ID format—these are apps within the app, used by the main app and often advertising caches for images and other web details, analytics, and app crash details. The subfolder of importance will typically be the one with the bundle ID that is consistent with that of the actual app.

Once the examiner locates that bundle ID folder, a Cache.db and sometimes an ApplicationCache.db will be available within it. The Cache.db file can also be located in another subfolder within the parent folder and typically contains five tables, with three of particular significance: cfurl_cache_response, cfurl_cache_blob_data, and cfurl_cache_receiver_data (Figure 11-9). The file represents the data that the app has received from an outside source (such as the server or the Internet) and holds in cache for speed of loading,

SQLite Table Summary

Table	Row Count
cfurl_cache_schema_version	1
cfurl_cache_response	70
sqlite_sequence	1
cfurl_cache_blob_data	70
cfurl_cache_receiver_data	70

FIGURE 11-9 The Cache.db summary information showing that 70 records are still available in three tables within the database

if needed again. The cfurl_cache_response table contains the data that was requested and the response, including the URL and the time of the request. The cfurl_cache_blob_data table contains BLOB (Binary Large Object) data with the response from the server. The cfurl_cache_receiver_data table contains the received data from the server in response to the server via the cfurl_cache_response table. Matching these tables can yield information that is not stored anywhere else. It is important for the examiner to pay attention to the isDataOnFs field within the cfurl_cache_response table. If the table contains a *1*, then the data is stored within another folder on the iOS device within the Caches folder. A BLOB of 4096 bytes or larger will be stored locally and assigned a GUID, and all other files will be stored within the database and represented by a *0*. The files and the locations that are cached locally are covered in the next section.

Note It is extremely important that the examiner remember that the Cache.db file will be in the root of the bundle ID, but the structure may not conform to the schema described. App developers can, and many do, create schemas that will suit their particular applications, especially if the app does not use external servers or Internet resources.

The Caches folder also contains a subfolder used to store file data, including JPEGs, GIFs, PNGs, HTML files, JSON files, and others. This folder, fsCachedData, is located under the bundle ID and is used to store files identified in the cfurl_cache_response table by a TRUE (1) Boolean value in the isDataOnFs field. Instagram, for example, a widely used photo app, prescribes storing information locally, without a database, and this information is available in the fsCachedData folder. The files contained in the folder are directly referenced in the cfurl_cache_receiver_data table within the Cache.db file, as shown in Figure 11-10. The files within the Instagram fsCachedData folder range from MOV to JPEG, GIF, and HTML files. If the examiner matches the information contained within this table against the cfurl_cache_response table, he or she has all of the files that are referenced along with a timetable of the event, as shown in Figure 11-11. This can provide an incredible amount of information for any investigation when dealing with applications that do not have a main database. In fact, this might be the only data that can be recovered!

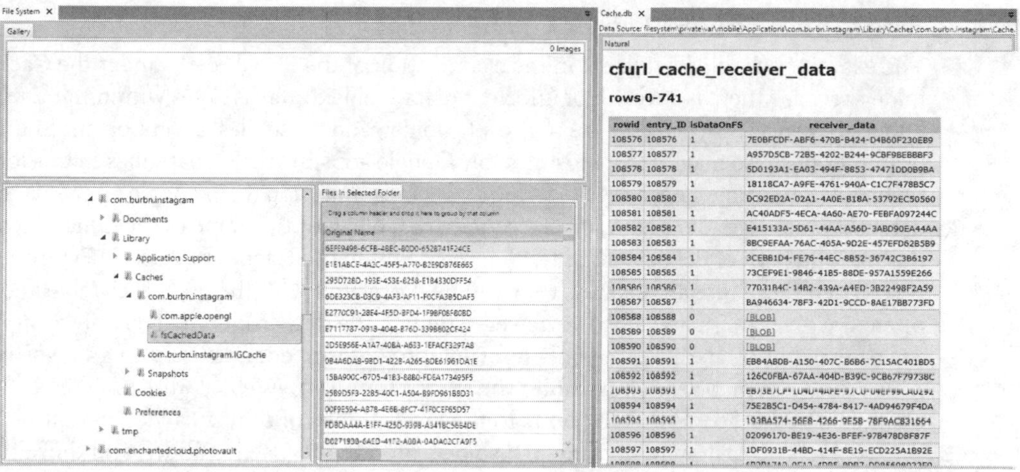

FIGURE 11-10 The fsCachedData folder in Instagram gives the investigator a folder full of GUID named files that can be matched to the GUID within the cfurl_cache_receiver_data table.

time_stamp	request_key	isDataOnFS	receiver_data
2013-11-19 23:29:00	http://distilleryimage4.ak.instagram.com/89af35b8515211e380770e881b7f4bd6_5.jpg	0	
2013-11-19 23:29:00	http://distilleryimage7.ak.instagram.com/8219468250de11e3b9f2120cbb90aa70_5.jpg	0	
2013-11-19 23:29:00	http://images.ak.instagram.com/profiles/profile_190044284_75sq_1378535306.jpg	0	
2013-11-19 23:29:00	http://distilleryimage10.ak.instagram.com/a270f9bc50e211e3b554122b944cbca2_5.jpg	0	
2013-11-19 23:29:00	http://images.ak.instagram.com/profiles/profile_175182644_75sq_1384238214.jpg	0	
2013-11-19 23:29:00	http://distilleryimage11.ak.instagram.com/5059f9f2515611e382a412f3be713f7b_5.jpg	0	
2013-11-19 23:29:00	http://images.ak.instagram.com/profiles/profile_5394138_75sq_1320534656.jpg	0	
2013-11-19 23:29:00	http://distilleryimage8.ak.instagram.com/15735a3a516b11e38c480ea056cf7464_5.jpg	0	
2013-11-19 23:29:00	http://distilleryimage10.ak.instagram.com/6d5467d0517011e381b312310118f31f_5.jpg	0	
2013-11-19 23:29:00	http://distilleryimage0.ak.instagram.com/cc4c0fa2510d11e3a2d012d2e25a0010_5.jpg	0	
2013-11-19 23:29:00	http://images.ak.instagram.com/profiles/profile_144264636_75sq_1384301096.jpg	0	
2013-11-19 23:29:00	http://distilleryimage3.ak.instagram.com/f34139e250ce11e380a30e9a0402a7de_5.jpg	0	
2013-11-19 23:29:00	http://distilleryimage1.ak.instagram.com/a023aa0050cf11e3aa1d12fe49d61113_5.jpg	0	
2013-11-19 23:29:00	http://distilleryimage10.ak.instagram.com/0e0cc4ac50d011e387f70ea2ccaa61ad_5.jpg	0	
2013-11-19 23:29:00	http://distilleryimage7.ak.instagram.com/f1a03c5450d411e3ba74128f0696eb74_5.jpg	0	
2013-11-19 23:29:00	http://distilleryimage9.ak.instagram.com/c62f6302511911e390490e5bf30b73cc_5.jpg	0	
2013-11-19 23:29:00	http://distilleryimage2.ak.instagram.com/09f00516512311e3849f0a3c3a25f78e_5.jpg	0	
2013-11-19 23:29:00	http://distilleryimage4.ak.instagram.com/e8a90fc8516e11e39c500ee695acc826_5.jpg	0	
2013-11-19 23:29:00	http://distilleryimage3.ak.instagram.com/c17aaa064fe811e3b90d121d6df4beab_5.jpg	0	
2013-11-19 23:29:00	http://distilleryimage4.ak.instagram.com/7fbdfd98516911e3b76e126830c1a143_5.jpg	0	
2013-11-19 23:29:00	http://distilleryimage0.ak.instagram.com/e7e3a930516a11e385be122f6f4f6846_5.jpg	0	
2013-11-19 23:29:00	http://distilleryimage6.ak.instagram.com/fa35bae0516c11e385ae12776198573d_5.jpg	0	
2013-11-19 23:29:00	http://distilleryimage4.ak.instagram.com/3c2dd7b0516e11e3ac801282e89d384a_5.jpg	0	
2013-11-19 23:29:00	http://distilleryimage9.ak.instagram.com/0f4ffc92516d11e3adc2123587d614a2_5.jpg	0	
2013-11-19 23:29:00	http://distilleryimage0.ak.instagram.com/027115c4510d11e3967112004400065e_5.jpg	0	
2013-11-19 23:29:00	http://distilleryimage11.ak.instagram.com/876871fc516b11e3805212f9dfc57889_5.jpg	0	
2013-11-19 23:29:00	http://distilleryimage3.ak.instagram.com/32e513c2516d11e3b4cb0a0d88bf3520_5.jpg	0	
2013-11-19 23:29:00	http://distilleryimage9.ak.instagram.com/6c31526c516d11e3be2f126b6b44507b_5.jpg	0	
2013-11-19 23:29:00	http://images.ak.instagram.com/profiles/profile_200749890_75sq_1376258947.jpg	0	
2013-11-19 23:29:00	http://distilleryimage10.ak.instagram.com/6835224c512711e39889127781d381c8_5.jpg	0	
2013-11-19 23:29:00	http://distilleryimage9.ak.instagram.com/424564a0512e11e3b90d121d6df4beab_5.jpg	0	
2013-11-19 23:29:00	http://distilleryimage1.ak.instagram.com/4c0ed004513611e3919e124f792e77d9_5.jpg	0	
2013-11-19 23:29:00	http://distilleryimage9.ak.instagram.com/761fca1e513711e3867f0ef52b0b4d48_5.jpg	0	
2013-11-19 23:29:00	http://distilleryimage3.ak.instagram.com/6fee4f72516d11e3bd3412f37c1fe9df_5.jpg	0	
2013-11-19 23:29:00	http://images.ak.instagram.com/profiles/profile_187127093_75sq_1384758276.jpg	0	

FIGURE 11-11 When a SQL query is built to JOIN the cfurl_cache_response table and cfurl_cache_receiver_data, table files and binary data can be viewed.

Additional Folders Under Caches

The examiner should be diligent in the examination of the files directly under the Caches folder because there is a wealth of information available. Database files within the Caches folder are generally located in the root of the folder, and these files are important to the examiner because many apps, most notably Google apps, store database files in this location. One very important database to look for under the Gmail app (com.google.Gmail) is the database Databases.db. This database contains a table with the name of the Gmail account and the size and path of the database file, all located within the Caches folder (see Figure 11-12).

When these files are located, they can be correlated with the databases table and opened within a SQLite database viewer. Granted, the data from Gmail is only a snippet of the e-mail, but often this is the only information that is needed to assist in an investigation. This type of format clearly resembles the methods used by WebKit, discussed earlier in the chapter. The Databases.db file points to the local storage of offline cached e-mail.

Numerous custom folders could also be stored in the Caches folder, and those that appear consistently are covered in this section. If an app is heavy into image display, either via online sources or server, folders typically named Media, ImageCache, or another derivative of "image" are often visible (see the LinkedIn example in Figure 11-13). These folders contain GUIDs that are referenced within a database within the main Caches folder.

Also within the Caches folder is a Snapshots folder that contains another identical bundle ID equal to the main app bundle ID. Within this folder are the PNG files that have been saved to represent the app in different perspectives when the app was moved to the background.

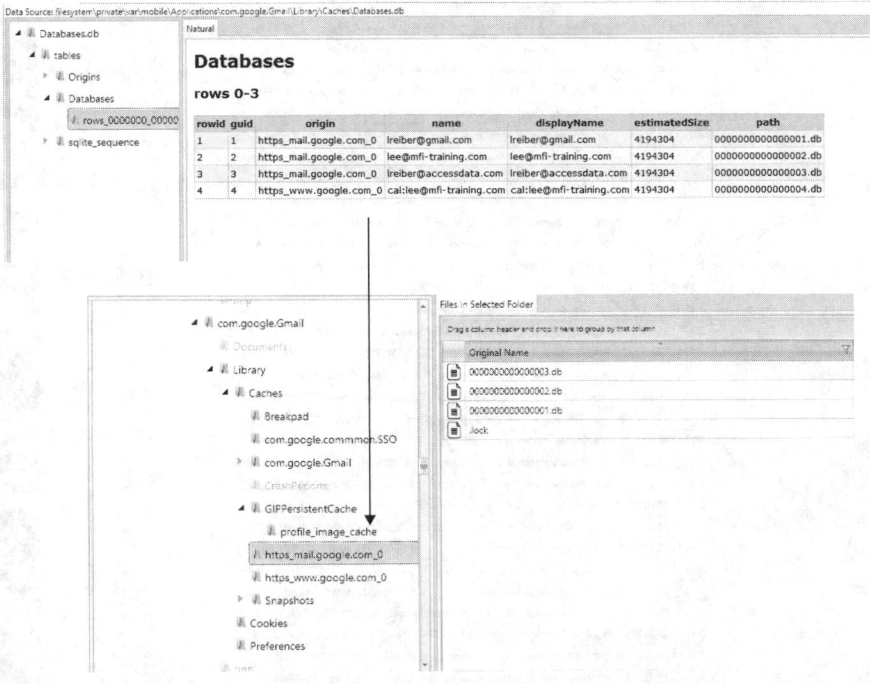

FIGURE 11-12 **Gmail Databases.db file pointing to the location of associated databases that store the user's e-mail and other data**

FIGURE 11-13 **The LinkedIn app contains an ImageCache folder that stores images much like an examiner would expect in a temporary Internet folder.**

When an iOS app is minimized, it is animated by first taking a screen capture of the currently active screen, creating a PNG, and shrinking the PNG file. The iOS saves this PNG file to the Snapshots folder.

A PNG file is created for each of the app's orientations (such as landscape, vertical, inverted) when the app was minimized. Multiple PNG files can be found in this folder with an actual snapshot of data that might not be recoverable anywhere else on the device. Examiners have recovered e-mail, text messages, conversations, and more that the user had permanently deleted, but the snapshots remained, lending critical evidence to the case.

Additional File System Locations

App files are important to every forensic examination, but settings files and additional database files will also aid an examiner in analyzing an iOS device. These files are available within the file system using a standard logical collection unless otherwise noted. How these files are viewed is determined by the file type. This section discusses several main locations within the iOS file system that the examiner can quickly review for information. Some of the folder locations shown in Table 11-4 have already been covered and are mentioned; however, some of the paths contain several files and folders that are of particular significance to an examiner and are covered in detail.

Within the private/var/mobile/Library folder is not only the "tip of the iceberg data" contained within databases, but other significant databases in which an examiner may locate additional information:

- **/Library/Accounts/Accouts3.sqlite** This folder has usernames of application accounts including date and time information.
- **/Library/Caches** This folder used to contain vast numbers of property lists and files that were cached by Apple Services, and it may be available if advanced services such as file_relay can be run; with a standard iTunes backup, the folder is not accessible with most forensic tools. If the device has been jailbroken, this folder will be available with cached data and should be examined by the investigator.

TABLE 11-4 iOS File System Parent Landmarks for Significant Evidentiary Files

Folder	Data Description
private/var/mobile/	Contains /Application, /Library, and /Media folders. iOS 8x includes an additional /Containers folder.
private/var/preferences/SystemConfiguration	Contains the main user configuration files for Apple apps and services; these files are discussed in this chapter.
private/var/root/Library/Caches/Backup	Stores the Manifest.mbdb and Manifest.plist files that indicate the files and folders that will be backed up using iTunes.
private/var/root/Library/Caches/locationd	Contains the consolidated.db, which includes geofence information, but with new devices there is generally limited information. The clients.plist contains every application that has used GPS location services and whether the app is authorized.
private/var/root/Library/Preferences	Contains many property lists that pertain to backups and phone services. This should not be confused with the app-level /Library /Preferences. Important Plist files are outlined in a separate section.
private/var/wireless/Library	Contains /CallHistory, /Databases, and /Preferences. The /CallHistory subfolder stores historic and current data in a database, call_ history.db, that is a leftover from iOS 7 and is visible only on an iOS 8x device if it has been restored with iOS 7 data.

- **/Library/Calendar/Extras.db** This folder contains current alarms and those that had been set but are no longer used on the device.
- **/Library/ConfigurationProfiles/ProfileTruth.plist** This folder contains a key, forceEncrpytedBackup, that indicates whether the backup will be encrypted when calling an iTunes backup.
- **/Library/Keyboard/** This folder contains any keyboard that the device has been set to use and its associated cache. The keyboard cache is identified as <language of keyboard>-dynamic-text.dat. This text file includes everything the user has typed in areas identified as "text fields." This recording takes place to assist with the iOS device's ability to auto-correct, which allows words to be suggested as the user types. If an app has a field marked "secure," the data that is typed into that field will not be populated in the dynamic-text.dat file. Secure fields typically include passwords, credit card numbers, and other personal data.

- **/Library/Mail/Recents.db** This database file contains recent e-mail and SMS addresses that include name, e-mail address, and phone number along with the dates accessed and the last date accessed. This database is a gold mine for an examiner because the file grows indefinitely, and if a user deletes a contact, the information in Recents.db remains, regardless of the deletion.
- **/Library/MobileBluetooth/com.apple.MobileBluetooth.ledevices.paired.db** This database file is found only within iOS 8x devices and contains the devices that have been paired with the iOS device.
- **/Library/Maps/Bookmarks.plist** This binary Plist contains bookmarks the user has added to the internal iOS mapping app. This file for iOS 8 is located within the /Containers/Application folder and is no longer stored in the /Library/Maps location.
- **/Library/Maps/Directions.mapsdata** This proprietary file can be read as text to gather the start point and destination when using the internal iOS mapping app. This file for iOS 8 is located within the /Containers/Application folder and is no longer stored in the /Library/Maps location.
- **/Library/Maps/FailedSearches.mapsdata** This proprietary file can be read as text to gather searches conducted using the internal app for iOS or an app that uses the internal app. An example is Yelp: If Yelp uses the internal iOS map, any searches in Yelp that failed to find a location could be stored here, as shown in Figure 11-14. This file for iOS 8 is located within the /Containers/Application folder and is no longer stored in the /Library /Maps location.
- **/Library/Maps/History.mapsdata** This proprietary file can be read as text to gather a history of routes used within the internal iOS Maps app. This file also contains data from apps that use the Maps program within the app. If a user used Yelp to locate a restaurant, for example, then information about the restaurant, the directions, and even reviews would be located within this file. This file for iOS 8 is located within the /Containers /Application folder and is no longer stored in the /Library/Maps location.
- **/Library/Maps/SearchResults.mapsdata** This proprietary file lists the searches conducted within the internal iOS Maps app and also any app that uses the Maps app within the app. This file for iOS 8 is located within the /Containers/Application folder and is no longer stored in the /Library/Maps location.


```
..yelp_RestaurantsPriceRan
ge2..yelp_RestaurantsReser
vations..yelp_GoodForKids.
.yelp_RestaurantsDelivery.
.yelp_natural_category_1..
yelp_natural_category_2..Đ
..Ú..Heroes parkâ..USê...è
®!1.ËE@..Ø÷.q.]Àò..en-US..
.¡....¾Ö5<@©.....vQ6@±.ìØà
¼...Ah.RØ.RÕ.RĐ.*.Sweeter
side2$)É.Í.´¾E@laà!.`.\À9m
Â.¼jÀE@AþX"...\À@.H.b...ÆÞ
..êç v...ð°ÿ±×·..p.x.....¨.
```


FIGURE 11-14 **A search for "Heroes park" did not find the location and was deposited into the FailedSearches file.**

The Preferences folder contains many property list files. Only a small number have proved to hold valuable information for many examiners and are listed here:

- **/Library/Preferences/com.apple.conference.plist** This property list identifies the FaceTime settings for the device.
- **/Library/Preferences/com.apple.conference.history.plist** This property gives the history for the user's FaceTime account, indicating the ID or e-mail of the user and whether a FaceTime message was sent to the user. This is great information for an examiner.
- **/Library/Preferences/com.apple.identityservices.idstatuscache.plist** This property list can also be a gold mine of information for deleted messages in FaceTime, iMessage, or e-mail. Identity services confirm the validity of a user's credentials as it travels across the ESS (Enterprise Shared Services) of Apple. So within this file are phone numbers and e-mail addresses along with a UNIX date of the lookup for clear credentials. Content is not included, but simply having the metadata of the occurrence is enough.
- **/Library/Preferences/com.apple.ids.service.com.apple.ess.plist** This file holds the accounts capable of authenticating on the Apple ESS and includes the AppleID, VettedAliases, Aliases, and LoginAs information. This key contains phone numbers and e-mail addresses of the device user.
- **/Library/Preferences/com.apple.ids.service.com.apple.madrid.plist** This is the identity services property list for iMessage. It contains e-mail addresses and phone numbers that have been used and are currently being used to access the ESS, along with the user's Apple ID.
- **/Library/Preferences/com.apple.imservice.FaceTime.plist** This file identifies the credentials used for FaceTime.
- **/Library/Preferences/com.apple.imservice.iMessage.plist** This file identifies the credentials used for iMessage.
- **/Library/Preferences/com.apple.locationd.plist** This file identifies the apps that have been accessed and are currently using location-based services.
- **/Library/Preferences/com.apple.madrid.plist** This file can be used to determine whether the user has ReadReceiptsEnabled set to on or off, which, when set to on, indicates whether the receiver of the iMessage has read the message or not.
- **/Library/Preferences/com.apple.Maps.plist** This file identifies the last map location searched for by longitude and latitude and the last viewed credentials used for iMessage.
- **/Library/Preferences/com.apple.MobileBluetooth.devices.plist** This file identifies the paired Bluetooth devices along with the MAC address and the LastSeenTime, indicating when the device was last observed by the iOS device.
- **/Library/Preferences/com.apple.MobileBluetooth.ledevices.plist** This file is another Bluetooth listing of identified Bluetooth Low Energy (BLE) devices that have been observed by the device. This settings file can be used by third-party apps that use BLE functions and are not compatible with classic Bluetooth protocols. A random MAC address is created, and a LastSeenTime indicates when the object was last observed by the iOS device.
- **/Library/Preferences/com.apple.mobileipod.plist** This file identifies the music and, more importantly, the last media item played on the iOS device.

- **/Library/Preferences/com.apple.mobilephone.plist** This file identifies the last phone number that was displayed on the dialer screen. This will be visible even if the phone call was not initiated or completed. This file also contains a key called AddressBookLastDialedUid to assist with associating an Address Book entry.
- **/Library/Preferences/com.apple.mobilephone.settings.plist** This file identifies the call-forwarding number, if one is enabled, and other general settings.
- **/Library/Preferences/com.apple.mobilephone.speeddial.plist** This file identifies favorites from the contact list.
- **/Library/SpringBoard/IconState.plist** This property list lays out the icons and folders for the apps that are currently displayed to the user on the iOS device (see Figure 11-15). Several keys within the property list can be important to the examiner. The key button bar is found at the top of the list and identifies the apps that are located along the bottom of the main screen and accessible from any page on the iOS device. The key listType identifies a folder, and directly above is displayName, which identifies the name of the folder. The apps contained in the folder are directly above the displayName, starting with [0] and identified by the array number until reaching the displayName key.
- **/Library/TCC/TCC.db** This database file identifies the apps on the iOS device (such as microphone, photos, Contacts, Calendar, Twitter) and indicates to which services they have access. This can help the examiner identify rogue apps that might be attempting to gain elevated privileges.
- **/Library/Voicemail/voicemail.db** This database file identifies the voicemail date, sender, duration, and even when voicemail was deleted. Also within the /Library /Voicemail/ folder are the .amr files that contain the actual messages that are identified by the rowid in the database. Voicemails that are deleted can be recovered in this folder.

[0]	*Array*	*(9 values)*
[0]	*String*	com.apple.webapp C9937477D203475F9DDC9855D20915F3
[1]	*String*	com.beejive.BeejiveIM
[2]	*String*	com.linkedin.LinkedIn
[3]	*String*	com.osfoora
[4]	*String*	org.wordpress
[5]	*String*	com.hootsuite.hootsuite
[6]	*String*	com.google.GooglePlus
[7]	*String*	com.google.hangouts
[8]	*String*	com.facebook.Facebook
[1]	*Array*	*(3 values)*
[0]	*String*	net.whatsapp.WhatsApp
[1]	*String*	com.vine.iphone
[2]	*String*	com.toyopagroup.picaboo
displayName	*String*	Social
listType	*String*	folder

FIGURE 11-15 Within the IconState.plist are the folders the user has created. Here a Social folder was created, and the icons directly above are the apps contained within this folder.

Photo Stream, SMS, and Maps all have separate Plist files in the /Library /Preferences/ folder and are prefixed by the com.apple.ids.service.com.apple file. These all contain information for proper authentication to the ESS.

Within the private/var/mobile/Media folder are pictures and videos, but this folder also is a storage place for additional files that may be of forensic significance:

- **/Media/Recordings/Recordings.db** This database file identifies voice recordings made with the iOS device along with the date and duration of the recording. The recordings themselves are also stored in the /Media/Recordings/ folder with an .m4a extension.
- **/Media/PhotoData/Thumbnails** This folder contains the thumbnail files of the images located in the DCIM folder and also can contain pictures that have been deleted. Not many tools can interpret the .thmb extension. These files are raw uncompressed images but can be viewed with an inexpensive application called iThmb Converter (www.ithmbconverter .com/en/download/).

Within the private/var folder is a preferences subfolder that contains additional iOS preference and network information. Here are some files that should be of interest to every examiner:

- **/preferences/SystemConfiguration/com.apple.network.identification.plist** This property list contains the IP addresses used and assigned to the iOS device when communicating on both the cellular WAN and Wi-Fi. This file also lists the domain and IP addresses of the router, along with a timestamp of each event (see Figure 11-16).

[87]	*Dictionary*	*(4 values)*
Signature	*String*	IPv4.Router=10.0.0.4;IPv4.RouterHardwareAddress=00:25:90:39:4f:11
Timestamp	*Date (GMT)*	2012-06-21T15:33:00Z
Services	*Array*	*(1 values)*
[0]	*Dictionary*	*(3 values)*
IPv4	*Dictionary*	*(6 values)*
Addresses	*Array*	*(1 values)*
[0]	*String*	10.0.7.154
Router	*String*	10.0.0.4
SubnetMasks	*Array*	*(1 values)*
[0]	*String*	255.255.248.0
ARPResolvedHardwareAddress	*String*	00:25:90:39:4f:11
InterfaceName	*String*	en0
ARPResolvedIPAddress	*String*	10.0.0.4
DNS	*Dictionary*	*(2 values)*
ServerAddresses	*Array*	*(2 values)*
[0]	*String*	10.0.0.4
[1]	*String*	10.0.0.4
DomainName	*String*	portal.armanidubai.com
ServiceID	*String*	31128721-00AD-415C-9458-37557F3C6E47
Identifier	*String*	IPv4.Router=10.0.0.4;IPv4.RouterHardwareAddress=00:25:90:39:4f:11

FIGURE 11-16 Information on the domain to which the device is connected, as well as IP addresses assigned, are available within com.apple.network.identification.plist.

- **/preferences/SystemConfiguration/com.apple.wifi.plist** This property list contains the Wi-Fi addresses to which the iOS device has connected when auto-joined, plus the name of the access point, the MAC address, and the type of security for the access point.
- **/preferences/SystemConfiguration/preferences.plist** This property file lists various configuration preferences for communication, but also identifies the device name under the HostName and ComputerName keys.

Within the private/var/wireless folder is the CallHistory folder, where iOS 7 call data is located, but other subfolders also contain information that can help to identify not only app usage, but also the exchange and substitution of subscriber information.

- **/wireless/Databases/CellularUsage.db** This database file contains a subscriber_info table within the database that lists the subscriber ID (IMSI), the subscriber MDN (dialing number), and the last update date. The update date is when that IMSI and MDN were last used. This table also contains all SIM cards inserted and used within the device (see Figure 11-17). This is incredible information when attempting to determine subscriber information.
- **/wireless/Databases/DataUsage.db** This database file contains two significant tables within the database: LiveUsage and Process. These tables contain the app name (bundle name), the process associated with the app, timestamps of usage, and the data coming in and out via the WAN. When these tables are put together using the foreign key OPT, the SQL query shows the activity of the app and its process (see Figure 11-18). This table can help the examiner determine whether a subject was using an app at the time of an event.
- **/wireless/Preferences/com.apple.commcenter.plist** This property list identifies the ICCID along with the phone number assigned to the device.

Using these locations, the examiner will be searching in the *what you don't see is what you need* area. Expert examiners will conduct this type of analysis and examination of mobile device data from an iOS device. Treating an iOS device as a small computing platform by examining, researching, and testing each file and location in an effort to uncover the meaning behind the data is a necessity.

subscriber_info

rows 0-2

rowid	ROWID	subscriber_id	subscriber_mdn	tag	last_update_time
3	3	8901260262813737899	+12088413400	3	418438568.032524
4	4	8944302111721732512	+447946725618	4	406312370.397823
5	5	8901260131580880713		5	406328521.006663

FIGURE 11-17 **The subscriber_info table in the CellularUsage.db, which shows that multiple SIM cards have been used in this iOS device**

ZTIMESTAMP1	ZWWANIN	ZWWANOUT	ZBUNDLENAME	ZPROCNAME
03-03-2014 01:20:03	164.0	132.0	com.apple.mobilesafari	com.apple.Safari.SocialHelper/com.apple.mobilesafari
09-18-2013 16:56:18	250.0	130.0	com.facebook.Messenger	Messenger/com.facebook.Messenger
09-27-2013 11:57:37	250.0	130.0	com.apple.datausage.softwareupdate	softwareupdateservicesd/com.apple.datausage.softwareupdate
03-09-2014 00:11:12	250.0	130.0	com.apple.MobileStore	itunesstored/com.apple.MobileStore
01-20-2014 15:07:34	250.0	130.0	me.attachments.iphoneapp	attachments.me/me.attachments.iphoneapp
03-03-2014 01:20:03	250.0	130.0	com.apple.mobilesafari	com.apple.Safari.SocialHelper/com.apple.mobilesafari
10-24-2013 06:24:35	103217.0	48624.0	com.apple.podcasts	Podcasts/com.apple.podcasts
09-27-2013 11:57:37	21534.0	11967.0	None	com.apple.MobileSoftwareUpdate.UpdateBrainService
10-12-2013 18:47:38	21534.0	11967.0	com.winzip.wzstd	WinZip Standard/com.winzip.wzstd
10-29-2013 18:28:04	21534.0	11967.0	com.eurosmartz.mobile.printmore	Print n Share/com.eurosmartz.mobile.printmore
04-05-2014 21:37:31	21534.0	11967.0	com.locometric.RoomScan	RoomScan/com.locometric.RoomScan
04-06-2014 18:28:47	177164.0	42632.0	com.apple.datausage.gamecenter	gamed/com.apple.datausage.gamecenter
10-05-2013 16:05:35	177164.0	42632.0	com.cloudmosa.PuffinFree	Puffin Free/com.cloudmosa.PuffinFree
01-19-2014 12:41:15	177164.0	42632.0	com.mobilityapps.gategurufull	GateGuru/com.mobilityapps.gategurufull
02-18-2014 10:43:56	177164.0	42632.0	com.webex.meeting	WebEx/com.webex.meeting
04-03-2014 05:45:40	177164.0	42632.0	com.apnews.mobilenews	AdSheet/com.apnews.mobilenews
04-06-2014 18:28:47	6186555.0	21637.0	com.apple.datausage.gamecenter	gamed/com.apple.datausage.gamecenter
10-05-2013 16:05:35	6186555.0	21637.0	com.cloudmosa.PuffinFree	Puffin Free/com.cloudmosa.PuffinFree
01-19-2014 12:41:15	6186555.0	21637.0	com.mobilityapps.gategurufull	GateGuru/com.mobilityapps.gategurufull
02-18-2014 10:43:56	6186555.0	21637.0	com.webex.meeting	WebEx/com.webex.meeting
04-03-2014 05:45:40	6186555.0	21637.0	com.apnews.mobilenews	AdSheet/com.apnews.mobilenews

FIGURE 11-18 Running a query on the DataUsage.db clearly shows critical information is available within this database file.

iOS Evidentiary File Types

The examiner should understand the way and in what types of files the data is stored. So far, this chapter has dealt with the location of artifacts; it now shifts to discuss the types of files that are commonly found within the iOS file system.

SQLite databases are the primary source of storage for apps and understandably a primary source of evidence for the examiner. User data types such as SMS, MMS, Contacts, Call Logs, Calendars, Notes, and Browser History all discussed as "tip of the iceberg data" come from SQLite databases. Just because an automated tool pulls the information from the SQLite database does not necessarily mean that *all* the data has been collected from that particular database. To add to that statement, *all* data may have been collected, but it could be translated or decoded incorrectly. And what about the data contained within the many apps on the iOS device? The examiner was exposed to the various database locations and also cache areas that hold SQLite databases. These, too, will be a wealth of information, so gaining an understanding of these files is necessary.

Property list, or Plist, files are also within the iOS file system; these are used to store app settings, device settings, and user-specific settings. Next to SQLite databases, these files are the second-most observed and examined file for the mobile forensic examiner. Plist files come in two forms—binary and XML. Both file types are covered in this section to help the examiner learn to interpret and view these files using several different tools.

Several other file types are not as prevalent within the iOS file system, but these will also be covered to give the examiner an idea as to what is generally stored and what can be recovered to assist in an examination. Gaining knowledge about what these files can yield to an examination will help the examiner understand how these files store data and how to recover their hidden treasures.

SQLite Databases

According to SQLite.org, SQLite is the most widely deployed SQL database engine in the world. SQLite is used not only in iOS devices, but also in Android devices, Windows Phone, and BlackBerry 10 devices, and in both Windows and Mac desktop applications. Many desktop applications use SQLite because of its simplistic deployment and use, and this is the case within mobile apps as well. SQLite does not need a client–server relationship like SQL, nor does it have to be installed. All tables, views, and other associated methods are included in a single file within a compact library. SQLite is a public-domain software library that is well documented and free for both commercial and private use.

The current build of SQLite, as of this writing, is 3.8.9, and, because of its forensic implications, an examiner should become familiar with the structure of this common file type. A surface-level explanation of the SQLite file type is outlined here with the major structural pieces defined.

Note Many SQLite database browsers will enable the examiner to view the contents of a SQLite database, so this section is not intended to inform the examiner on how to create a tool, decode, and visually display a SQLite database. The intention is to help the examiner understand the structure and to "see" that data will not be displayed within a SQLite database viewer if it is no longer referenced (that is, deleted). Many SQLite documents and books cover the structure, ideology, and methods, and the examiner can supplement the introduction and overview of this section by consulting those documents.

This section is intended to arm the forensic examiner with the information needed to recover valuable "hidden" data from these files and to help the examiner understand why, where, and how this can be accomplished. The recovery of data from the logical structure of tables and rows will be covered in Chapter 12.

A SQLite database is like a file that stores many records. SQLite.org defines the SQLite file as the "main database file." SQLite is *transactional*, which means that it stores data within a second file called a *rollback journal*; in other words, if transactions on the database are not completed properly, they are able to be rolled back. If the SQLite file is in write-ahead log (WAL) mode, transactions will be stored in the associated WAL file (covered in detail in the next section). In the main database file, the records are stored in pages. The page size is determined by the 2-byte big-endian integer located at an offset 16 bytes from the start of the main database file. The page size is based on a power of 2 and is between 512 and 65,536 bytes.

The first 100 bytes of the database file is the file header, which is divided up into fields: the first 16 bytes contain SQLite format 3, followed by the 2 bytes for the page size at offset 16.

TABLE 11-5 SQLite Database Header Details as Outlined on SQLite.org

Offset	Size (Bytes)	Description
0	16	The header string: `"SQLite format 3\00"`.
16	2	The database page size in bytes.
18	1	File format: 1 for legacy journal and 2 for WAL.
19	1	File format: 1 for legacy journal and 2 for WAL.
28	4	Size of the database file in pages.
32	4	Page of the first freelist trunk page.
36	4	Total number of freelist pages.
52	4	Page number of largest root B-tree page when in auto-vacuum or incremental vacuum. If 0, auto-vacuum is not enabled and the examiner can use only the freefile table, and parent/child tables cannot be mapped to a pointer map.
56	4	Text encoding used: UTF-8 = 1, UTF-16le =2, UTF-16be=3.
64	4	If any number other than 0 is used, incremental-vacuum mode is enabled.
96	4	SQLite version number.

These values in the header are all stored in big-endian format. The maximum page number is 2,147,483,646 and the minimum is one 512-byte page starting at page 1. The maximum database size could be around 140 terabytes if the maximum number of pages each held the maximum number of bytes! Table 11-5 shows the database header formats most critical to the examiner, which are visually represented in Figure 11-19.

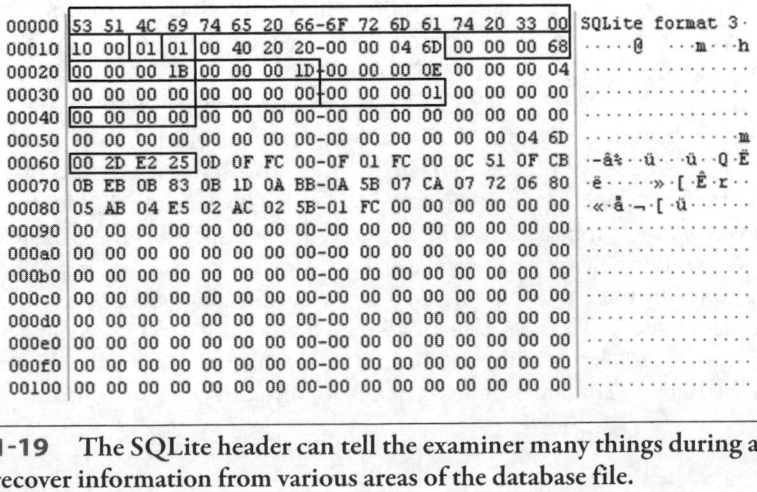

```
00000 53 51 4C 69 74 65 20 66-6F 72 6D 61 74 20 33 00 SQLite format 3·
00010 10 00 01 01 00 40 20 20-00 00 04 6D 00 00 00 68 ····@ ···m···h
00020 00 00 00 1B 00 00 00 1D-00 00 00 0E 00 00 00 04 ················
00030 00 00 00 00 00 00 00 00-00 00 00 01 00 00 00 00 ················
00040 00 00 00 00 00 00 00 00-00 00 00 00 00 00 00 00 ················
00050 00 00 00 00 00 00 00 00-00 00 00 00 00 00 04 6D ···············m
00060 00 2D E2 25 0D 0F FC 00-0F 01 FC 00 0C 51 0F CB ·-â%··ü···ü··Q·Ë
00070 0B EB 0B 83 0B 1D 0A BB-0A 5B 07 CA 07 72 06 80 ·ë·····»·[·Ê·r··
00080 05 AB 04 E5 02 AC 02 5B-01 FC 00 00 00 00 00 00 ·«·å·¬·[·ü······
00090 00 00 00 00 00 00 00 00-00 00 00 00 00 00 00 00 ················
000a0 00 00 00 00 00 00 00 00-00 00 00 00 00 00 00 00 ················
000b0 00 00 00 00 00 00 00 00-00 00 00 00 00 00 00 00 ················
000c0 00 00 00 00 00 00 00 00-00 00 00 00 00 00 00 00 ················
000d0 00 00 00 00 00 00 00 00-00 00 00 00 00 00 00 00 ················
000e0 00 00 00 00 00 00 00 00-00 00 00 00 00 00 00 00 ················
000f0 00 00 00 00 00 00 00 00-00 00 00 00 00 00 00 00 ················
00100 00 00 00 00 00 00 00 00-00 00 00 00 00 00 00 00 ················
```

FIGURE 11-19 The SQLite header can tell the examiner many things during a manual attempt to recover information from various areas of the database file.

TABLE 11-6 SQLite Page Types and Descriptions

Type	Description
Index B-Tree internal node	Also called a root page; can point to the other internal pages using keys, are always first, and are not moved during auto-vacuum or incremental vacuums. Byte 0 = *x02*
B-Tree Table internal node	Pages pointed to and from the root page, but also point to a leaf page. Byte 0 = *x05*
Index B-Tree leaf node	Pages that store keys but no data. Byte 0 = *x0A*
B-Tree Table leaf node	Pages that store the user data; cannot point to another leaf page, but if additional data exceeds the page size, an overflow page is used. Byte 0 = *x0D*
Overflow page	This page stores data from the leaf node that has exceeded the page size and can point to another overflow page as indicated in the first 4 bytes of the header. If 0, it is the last page. This can be referred to as spillover data. BLOB data frequently requires overflow pages, and each overflow page stores exactly one record.
Freelist page	Page of the first freelist trunk page.
Pointer map page	Total number of freelist pages.

A SQLite database contains several types of pages, outlined in Table 11-6. B-tree parent pages within a database point to their children, but the reverse relationship is not the same. Children can point to an overflow page, which can then point to another overflow page, and so on, but they cannot point back to their parent. Understanding the various table types can help the examiner identify the location and identity of pages that may contain freefile pages, which could ultimately hold deleted data. Using the freefile list to identify the location of the various freefile pages can help the examiner uncover substantial records not otherwise collected by most mobile forensic tools.

The page header in the SQLite database file can be examined to assist in identifying the type of page, the first free block on the page, the number of cells on the page, and much more information. The page header comprises 8 bytes for leaf pages and 12 bytes for interior pages in big-endian format. The fields for the header are outlined in Table 11-7. (Table 11-6 identifies the type of pages along with the first byte that identifies the page type.)

Using the file type along with the storage areas, the examiner can identify the contents within the page and uncover data that might not be referenced by the database active index. This will be evident as the examiner becomes more familiar with the freelist and free pages within the SQLite database.

TABLE 11-7 Page Header Format as Described in SQLite.org Documentation

Offset	Size Bytes	Description
0	1	The type of page as listed in Table 11-6, represented by the first byte
1	2	Two-byte integer is the start of the first free block, zero if there are no free blocks
3	2	Two-byte integer giving the number of cells on the page
5	2	Start of the cell content area; 0 value is interpreted as 65,536 bytes
7	1	Number of fragmented free bytes in the cell content area
8	4	This value appears only in the header of interior tree pages and is the page number of the rightmost pointer (map)

The freelist, or free page list, is a list of the unused pages within a database (see Figure 11-20). However, if the offset 32 (number of freelist pages) 4-byte value is *0*, then the freelist does not contain any unused pages within the database. This freelist and the subsequent free pages can be important to an investigator. The free pages are not active and are where the database stores the data that is no longer referenced within the SQLite table. An examiner may understand this as deleted data. Information the user of the app has chosen to delete is removed from the table references and moved to the free pages within the freelist area. Freelist pages can either be trunk pages or leaf pages. The freelist file header, as dissected in Table 11-8, points to a trunk page, which can then point to multiple leaf pages. When a SQLite page becomes inactive, it is added to the freelist and will not be released to the database file system. When information is added to the database by the user, the database will take free pages from the freelist to store the data, and the table becomes active and no longer referenced in the freefile index. If the list is empty, the database will obtain new pages and then add them to the database file.

The examiner should also understand both the auto-vacuum and the pointer map of the SQLite database. *Auto-vacuum* is the ability of a SQLite database to stay small. Auto-vacuum is not the same as vacuum in SQLite; *vacuum* cleans the main database by copying

TABLE 11-8 Freelist Header Breakdown to Assist When Locating Inactive Pages

Offset	Bytes	Description
0	4	Integer is the page number of the next freelist trunk page, or *0* if this is the last freelist trunk
4	4	Integer that is the number of leaf page pointers to follow
8	4	Subsequent integers are page locations for free pages that will follow the number of leaf page pointers specified in bytes 4–7

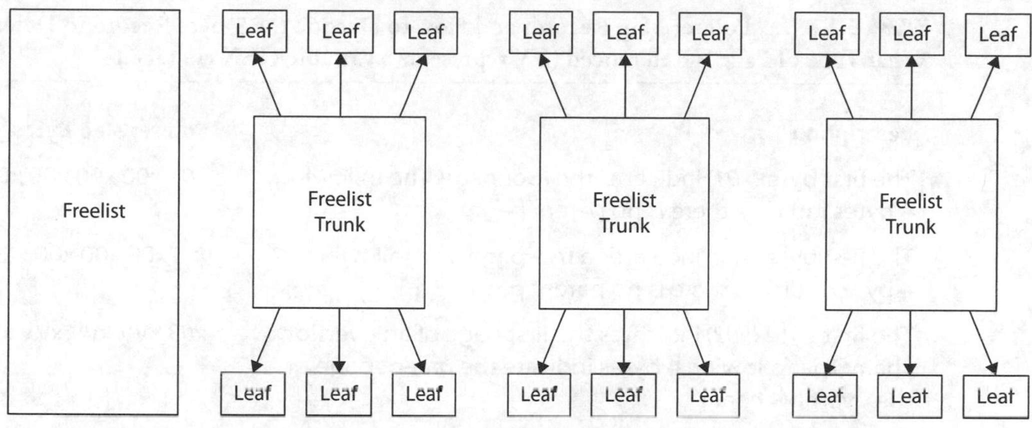

FIGURE 11-20 The freelist is an index to trunk files that point to leaves where the data is stored.

the contents to a temporary file and then reloading the file from the copy; this action removes deleted data (free pages) and completely cleans the database structure. Auto-vacuum does not eliminate the free pages; it moves them. This is very crucial information to an examiner regarding the recovery of deleted data from a SQLite database. However, to understand how the database locates information within the table and moves information around, the examiner should also understand the pointer map (ptrmap) pages.

The *pointer map* and pages are inserted into the SQLite database to assist with the efficiency of both the auto- and incremental vacuum processes. The pointer map is not available within the SQLite database if the auto-vacuum or incremental vacuum are not enabled. This can be determined by looking at offset 52: if this is *0*, then auto-vacuum or incremental vacuum has not been set. When the database moves a page, the pointer is updated. The pointer map is also a lookup table that can be used to find the parent of the child leaf—something that is not contained within the actual child leaf. Within the pointer map, each pointer is made up of 5 bytes that represent the type of page and the related parent. The pointers are in order starting at page 3 and progress to the number of pages. Each pointer represents one page within the database file. The size of the pointer map in bytes can be obtained using the following formula:

$$(2 - \text{number of pages}) \times 5 = \text{number of bytes}$$

The pointer map is confined to the page size outlined by the SQLite database, as identified by byte 16 in the database header; any pointers that exceed page size/5 will be assigned to another pointer map page.

Tip

If an examiner had a database file with a page size of 1024 bytes per page, the total number of pages that could be referenced within a pointer map page would be 1024/5 = 204 page references maximum. Because the first and second pages are not counted (database header and pointer map), if a new page is needed, a new pointer map page will be created and the new page (206) will be referenced.

TABLE 11-9 Pointer Map Records and How to Decode the 5-byte Record to Determine What Type of Page Is Referenced (VV represents a variable HEX character)

Description	Pointer Map Bytes
The first byte (*x01*) indicates the root page. The following 4 bytes indicate there is no parent page.	*x01* x00 x00 x00 x00
The first byte (*x02*) indicates a free page. The following 4 bytes indicate there is no parent page.	*x02*x00 x00 x00 x00
The first byte (*x03*) indicates the first page of an overflow chain. The following 4 bytes indicate the parent page of the overflow chain.	*x03* xVV xVV xVV xVV
The first byte (*x04*) indicates it is not the first page in an overflow chain. The following 4 bytes indicate the parent overflow chain.	*x04* xVV xVV xVV xVV
The first byte (*x05*) indicates a page that is part of a table or index but not an overflow page or root page. The following 4 bytes indicate the parent page of the parent tree node.	*x05* xVV xVV xVV xVV

To help with decoding the pointer map, Table 11-9 outlines the significant bytes and defines the meanings. The pointer map can be important to the examiner when attempting to identify the parent of a deleted record when coupling the information obtained from the freelist and associated free pages.

Uncovering Inactive SQLite Data via Freelists

As mentioned, inactive data within the SQLite database can be recovered using the database header, the freelist, and then the associated pages. In this section, the previously covered material will be put to the test to uncover deleted data from an sms.db from an iOS device. This technique can be used on any SQLite database the examiner may encounter.

First, we open the SQLite database within FTK Imager and examine it within the HEX viewer. (FTK Imager is a free tool from AccessData.) Figure 11-21 shows the database file, and highlighted is the size of the page in bytes (4096), the freelist page number (1310), and the number of free pages available (6234).

```
0000000 53 51 4C 69 74 65 20 66-6F 72 6D 61 74 20 33 00 SQLite format 3·
0000010 10 00 02 02 00 40 20 20-00 04 61 62 00 00 1D BE ·····@ ··ab···¾
0000020 00 00 05 1E 00 00 18 5A-00 00 07 04 00 00 00 04 ·······Z········
0000030 00 00 00 00 00 00 00 1C-00 00 00 01 00 00 00 00 ················
0000040 00 00 00 01 00 00 00 00-00 00 00 00 00 00 00 00 ················
0000050 00 00 00 00 00 00 00 00-00 00 00 00 00 04 61 62 ··············ab
0000060 00 2D E2 25 05 00 00 00-01 0F FB 00 00 00 00 1E ·-â%·····û·····
0000070 0F FB 0E EE 0A 6C 08 FA-0A 43 07 59 08 C5 06 37 ·û·î·l·ú·C·Y·Å·7
0000080 07 2C 06 FF 04 D9 05 E8-03 B3 04 98 02 7F 03 70 ·,·ÿ·Ù·è·³·····p
0000090 02 32 01 BC 01 4A 00 E7-00 00 00 00 00 00 00 00 ·2·¼·J·ç········
00000a0 00 00 00 00 00 00 00 00-00 00 00 00 00 00 00 00 ················
```

FIGURE 11-21 The page size, the freelist page number, and the number of pages within the sms.db database file from an iOS device

Next, we navigate to the freelist area. The formula subtracts 1 from the freelist page number from the freelist (to take into account the database header that always holds the first page). The size of the page is then multiplied by the bytes to obtain the offset within the sms.db for the freelist (see Figure 11-22):

$$(1310 - 1) \times 4096 = 5361664$$

As outlined in Table 11-8, the freelist's first 4 bytes identify whether there is another freelist trunk. If this value is equal to *0*, then this is the last freelist or the last freelist trunk. In this example, the first 4 bytes (x00 x00 x14 x38) equals integer 5176, indicating the page size of the next freelist trunk page:

$$(5176 - 1) \times 4096 = 21196800$$

However, the first freelist should be examined.

The second set of bytes after the freelist trunk list pointer, starting at offset 4, indicates the number of pages referenced within this freelist. This value (x00 x00 x00 x83) in the example equals integer 131, indicating there are 131 pages within this freelist. The rest of the 4-byte values starting at offset 8 within the freelist page represent the location of the leaf pages. These are the pages that represent the inactive data within the database file.

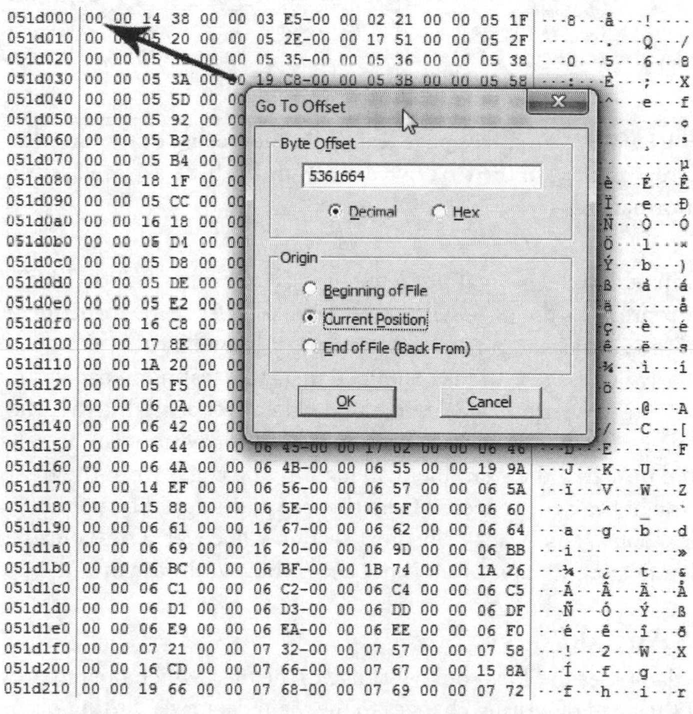

FIGURE 11-22 **The location of the freelist is obtained by using the Go To Offset in FTK Imager.**

```
1426000 0D 09 ED 00 04 06 CD 00-06 CD 08 6D 0B 68 0D B5  ··í···Í··Í·m·h·µ
1426010 0D B5 0D B5 0D B5 0D CC-0E 93 00 00 00 00 00 00  ·µ·µ·µ·Ì········
1426020 00 00 00 00 00 82 76 82-F7 10 28 00 55 43 08 00  ······v·÷·(·UC··
1426030 02 00 00 83 20 01 08 1D-29 55 08 04 04 08 09 09  ····  ···)U·····
1426040 08 08 08 08 08 82 76 82-F7 10 28 00 55 43 08 00  ······v·÷·(·UC··
1426050 02 00 00 83 20 01 08 1D-29 55 08 04 04 08 09 09  ····  ···)U·····
1426060 08 08 08 08 08 08 09 08-08 08 08 08 08 08 08 00  ················
1426070 09 08 45 37 46 41 39 44-46 37 2D 45 41 45 45 2D  ··E7FA9DF7-EAEE-
1426080 34 32 45 38 2D 41 37 30-32 2D 46 31 37 34 34 38  42E8-A702-F17448
1426090 44 37 45 30 46 35 59 6F-75 72 20 77 65 6C 63 6F  D7E0F5Your welco
14260a0 6D 65 2E 20 53 6F 72 72-79 20 73 6F 20 6C 61 74  me. Sorry so lat
14260b0 65 01 E0 04 0B 73 74 72-65 61 6D 74 79 70 65 64  e·à··streamtyped
14260c0 81 E8 03 84 01 40 84 84-84 12 4E 53 41 74 74 72  ·è···@····NSAttr
14260d0 69 62 75 74 65 64 53 74-72 69 6E 67 00 84 84 08  ibutedString····
14260e0 4E 53 4F 62 6A 65 63 74-00 85 92 84 84 84 08 4E  NSObject·······N
14260f0 53 53 74 72 69 6E 67 01-94 84 01 2B 1B 59 6F 75  SString····+·You
1426100 72 20 77 65 6C 63 6F 6D-65 2E 20 53 6F 72 72 79  r welcome. Sorry
1426110 20 73 6F 20 6C 61 74 65-86 84 02 69 49 01 1B 92   so late··iI···
1426120 84 84 84 0C 4E 53 44 69-63 74 69 6F 6E 61 72 79  ····NSDictionary
1426130 00 94 84 01 69 01 92 84-96 96 1D 5F 5F 6B 49 4D  ····i·······__kIM
1426140 4D 65 73 73 61 67 65 50-61 72 74 41 74 74 72 69  MessagePartAttri
1426150 62 75 74 65 4E 61 6D 65-86 92 84 84 84 08 4E 53  buteName······NS
1426160 4E 75 6D 62 65 72 00 84-84 07 4E 53 56 61 6C 75  Number····NSValu
1426170 65 00 94 84 01 2A 84 99-99 00 86 86 86 0A 69 4D  e····*········iM
1426180 65 73 73 61 67 65 70 3A-2B 31 32 30 38 38 34 31  essagep:+1208841
1426190 33 34 30 30 36 39 39 30-30 42 41 36 2D 33 30 30  340069900BA6-300
14261a0 42 2D 34 32 33 41 2D 42-38 35 35 2D 83 61 82 F8  B-423A-B855-·a·ø
14261b0 2E 29 00 55 81 13 08 00-01 00 00 84 50 01 08 13  .)·U········P···
14261c0 11 55 08 04 08 08 08 09-08 09 08 08 08 08 08 08  ·U··············
14261d0 09 08 08 08 08 08 08 00-09 08 46 35 30 39 34 31  ··········F50941
14261e0 45 37 2D 37 32 31 39 2D-34 42 34 36 2D 41 42 37  E7-7219-4B46-AB7
14261f0 37 2D 36 30 45 36 32 37-44 39 34 34 38 46 48 6F  7-60E627D9448FHo
1426200 70 65 20 79 6F 75 20 68-61 64 20 61 20 67 72 65  pe you had a gre
1426210 61 74 20 62 20 64 61 79-2E 20 4D 61 79 62 65 20  at b day. Maybe
1426220 77 65 20 73 68 6F 75 6C-64 20 67 65 74 20 74 6F  we should get to
1426230 67 65 74 68 65 72 20 73-6F 6D 65 74 69 6D 65 3F  gether sometime?
```

FIGURE 11-23 First free page leaf list in the freelist of the sms.db. This is a table leaf node as represented in the first byte (*x0D*), and Table 11-7 can assist in obtaining additional page information.

In this example, navigating to the first listed leaf (x00 x00 x14 x27) with an integer value of 5159 represents the page within the database. Using the same formula, (5159 – 1) × 4096 = 21127168, and navigating to this location, it is evident that the page contains text messages, particularly iMessages, and is contained in a table leaf node page as indicated by the first byte (*x0D*) (see Figure 11-23). Some of the data is repeated within the free pages, but this is extremely useful for any investigation. This information can be collected, searched, and extracted now that the examiner can identify the pages from the freelist pages.

Some of the data collected from the free pages could be void of metadata (such as phone numbers, dates, and times). The next section will cover write-ahead logs, which can also hold significant data that often is not accessible within the original database.

Write-Ahead Logs

SQLite databases use files somewhat like cache files, which operate in a way similar to journal files, but instead of writing changes to the main database, writing occurs to a separate file. Beginning with SQLite version 3.7.0, the write-ahead log (WAL file) became supported as a new transaction control mechanism. All data that has yet to be committed, new data and altered data, is saved to the WAL instead of directly to the main SQLite database if the main database is in WAL mode. What is also extremely interesting about WAL files is that the database engine will reference an altered page within the WAL and ignore that page in the main database until a checkpoint operation occurs.

A SQLite database can use either a journal file or a WAL file, but it cannot use both concurrently. A WAL file must be located in the same folder as the main database file in order to operate properly. If a WAL file is removed, or if a database is removed and subsequent queries are run against the database without an associated WAL file, a WAL file will be created to support the database. The SQLite database transactions will COMMIT when a WAL *frame* is written that contains a COMMIT marker. A WAL will generally contain multiple transactions. When a COMMIT occurs, the information that is unique and has yet to be written to the main database gets committed, and any data that is non-unique or inactive remains within the WAL file. The WAL file can assist with corruption and failure of the main database, and if this occurs, the WAL file can then rebuild the main database with the data contained within the WAL. As mentioned, the WAL does not have to exist within the logical file system, and these files are not recovered with a standard Apple Mobile Backup (such as iTunes). The recovery of these files is available only by using a mobile solution capable of conducting a more advanced collection using the file_relay service.

The main database the WAL file supports can be easily recognized because it shares the database name. The WAL file often is much larger than the database itself (see Figure 11-24) and quite often contains duplicate data along with unique data from the main database. This is primarily due to the main database leaving the WAL file even upon issuing a checkpoint. The WAL file just continues to grow.

The WAL file is not used just as a backup, but as a storage location for data prior to the data reaching the main database. All changes to the database are recorded to the WAL file by use of *frames*, recordings of the changed content from a single page within the main database file. Data is written back to the main database in what is called a *checkpoint* operation. During this operation, the data within the WAL file is not removed, but it is marked as inactive and can be overwritten if a new frame or frames are introduced to the WAL.

The WAL file has a unique file header, as shown in Figure 11-24, along with unique frame headers with the file itself. The mapping of each is outlined within Tables 11-10 and 11-11. Using this information can help the examiner identify the size and characteristics of each page within the file. Like the main SQLite database the WAL represents, the WAL header can describe much about the contents of the contained file, and using the header map, the investigator can traverse the file to identify data that may have been committed or that has not been committed to the main database file.

Original Name	Size (KB)
ApplicationCache.db	6624
Cache.db	4
Cache.db-shm	32
Cache.db-wal	2398

FIGURE 11-24 Often the WAL file is much larger than the main database since it caches data from many instances of the database runs with the *frames*. In this instance, the Cache .db WAL file is almost 600 times larger than the main database!

TABLE 11-10 The WAL Header Format as Outlined on SQLite.org

Offset	Bytes	Description
0	4	Identity of the WAL file commonly referred to as the "magic number." Using this can help located deleted WAL files. It will be either x37 x7F x06 x82 or x37 x7F x06 x83.
4	4	File format version.
8	4	The page size of the database.
12	4	Checkpoint sequence number.
16	4	Salt-1: This is an integer that increments with each checkpoint. It can be used to determine the order of pages if there are duplicates within the WAL. Newer pages have larger values, and if the Salt-1 is the same, the page that is positioned closest to end of file is the newest version.
20	4	Salt-2: This will be a different random number for each checkpoint.
24	4	Checksum-1: First part of a checksum on the first 24 bytes of the header.
28	4	Checksum-1: Second part of the checksum on the first 24 bytes of the header.

TABLE 11-11 The Frame Header Format as Outlined by SQLite.org

Offset	Bytes	Description
0	4	Page number of the record.
4	4	For committed records, the size of the database file in pages after the commit. All other records will be 0.
8	4	Salt-1 that is copied from the WAL header.
12	4	Salt-2 that is copied from the WAL header.
16	4	Checksum-1: Cumulative checksum up to and including this page.
20	4	Checksum-1: Second half of the cumulative checksum.

To traverse the WAL, the examiner must first obtain the page size from the 4 bytes staring at offset 8. Once the page size is obtained, the examiner should navigate to offset 32, which is the start of the first frame. The examiner can then navigate using the following formula:

$$(P + 24 = F)$$

where P equals the page size and F is the resulting frame offset. The *24* is added to the solution to take into account that the examiner will be starting from the beginning of the frame header. If the examiner starts at the actual start of the page, the offset would be equal to the page size. Each page, with the exception of a root table, will contain the page identifiers listed in Table 11-6. The root table is easily identified with the database header SQLite format 3.

Committed data that still resides within the frames, as shown in Figure 11-25, can also be historical data that was once removed by the user and is no longer listed in the main database. This is another place the examiner should traverse when looking for information that may have not been added to the main database at the time of the collection. In addition, data that has been removed from the main database but still resides in the WAL file can be located. Using the information in the file header, additional pages can be located and the contents of the entire WAL file can be mapped, as shown in Figure 11-26.

The WAL file cannot be viewed in a standard database viewer for various reasons, including the fact that the WAL file does not have a SQLite file header at the correct offset, there are multiple SQLite headers, and it contains incomplete and sometimes unintelligible bytes for a database viewer. Also, if the WAL file exists in a folder outside of a forensic

```
000000 37 7F 06 82 00 2D E2 18-00 00 10 00 00 00 00 00 7····-å·········
000010 73 3B 62 BA 28 6D CA 6E-8F 49 3E 86 B5 FB 83 53 s;b°(mÊn·I>·µû·S
000020 00 00 00 01 00 00 00 01-73 3B 62 BA 28 6D CA 6E ········s;b°(mÊn
000030 41 D8 A5 1C A7 27 51 6D-53 51 4C 69 74 65 20 66 AØ¥·§'QmSQLite f
000040 6F 72 6D 61 74 20 33 00-10 00 02 02 00 40 20 20 ormat 3·····@
000050 00 00 00 03 00 00 00 01-00 00 00 00 00 00 00 00 ················
000060 00 00 00 00 00 00 00 00-00 00 00 00 00 00 00 01 ················
000070 00 00 00 00 00 00 00 00-00 00 01 00 00 00 00 00 ················
000080 00 00 00 00 00 00 00 00-00 00 00 00 00 00 00 00 ················
000090 00 00 00 00 00 00 00 03-00 2D E2 25 0D 00 00 00 ·········-â%····
0000a0 00 10 00 00 00 00 00 00-00 00 00 00 00 00 00 00 ················
```

FIGURE 11-25 The header of a WAL file from a Cache.db file, with the magic number, file version, and database page size. Also, the first frame is visible.

```
000fb0 00 00 00 00 00 00 00 00-00 00 00 00 00 00 00 00 ················
000fc0 00 00 00 00 00 00 00 00-00 00 00 00 00 00 00 00 ················
000fd0 00 00 00 00 00 00 00 00-00 00 00 00 00 00 00 00 ················
000fe0 00 00 00 00 00 00 00 00-00 00 00 00 00 00 00 00 ················
000ff0 00 00 00 00 00 00 00 00-00 00 00 00 00 00 00 00 ················
001000 00 00 00 00 00 00 00 00-00 00 00 00 00 00 00 00 ················
001010 00 00 00 00 00 00 00 00-00 00 00 00 00 00 00 00 ················
001020 00 00 00 00 00 00 00 00-00 00 00 00 00 00 00 00 ················
001030 00 00 00 00 00 00 00 00-00 00 00 01 00 00 00 01 ················
001040 73 3B 62 BA 28 6D CA 6E-AF 5C F1 0A 31 1D F0 DF s;b°(mÊn¯\ñ·1·ðß
001050 53 51 4C 69 74 65 20 66-6F 72 6D 61 74 20 33 00 SQLite format 3·
001060 10 00 02 02 00 40 20 20-00 00 00 03 00 00 00 01 ·····@  ········
001070 00 00 00 00 00 00 00 00-00 00 00 00 00 00 00 00 ················
001080 00 00 00 00 00 00 00 01-00 00 00 00 00 00 00 00 ················
001090 00 00 00 01 00 00 00 00-00 00 00 00 00 00 00 00 ················
0010a0 00 00 00 00 00 00 00 00-00 00 00 00 00 00 00 03 ················
0010b0 00 2D E2 25 0D 00 00 00-00 10 00 00 00 00 00 00 ·-â%············
0010c0 00 00 00 00 00 00 00 00-00 00 00 00 00 00 00 00 ················
```

FIGURE 11-26 Traversing 4096 bytes as indicated in the header for the page size, the next frame is located within the WAL.

solution's reach—say, within a logical folder on a desktop computer with its main database file—problems could immediately be recognized. The WAL file will vanish if any SQLite statement is conducted on the main SQLite database, and the main database will *grow*! The growth results from the addition of data from the WAL to the main database for records that are marked to be committed. Because the WAL can support concurrent-write transactions, new log records and appended log records are occurring. Because of this, the marked frame within the WAL is referenced only for a unique transaction so that any newly appended data to the WAL that may also be occurring on another thread is ignored. The problem arises when running a query on a main database with the WAL file available: A single transaction referencing a single marked frame can omit other data within the WAL file, leaving the examiner believing that all data within the WAL is now moved to the main database. This is not always the case, however, because frames that are not marked to be committed could be discarded. Also, the WAL file can grow exponentially, and because of this growth will be checkpointed. SQLite by default sets this threshold at 1000 pages, but this can be changed by the app designer using SQLite commands. Also, the WAL file uses a Shared Memory file that is located within the same directory as the WAL file, with the same name as the main database and the .shm extension. This file is used by the WAL file as an index. Because multiple processes are accessing the database concurrently, the SHM file is used to keep track of these transactions. The SHM file is joined to the WAL file, and when the WAL is created, the SHM is created; when the WAL is deleted, the SHM is also deleted. The SHM file contains no persistent data and is not generally of value to an investigation.

An examiner should make sure the solution that will be used to examine SQLite databases does not taint the database with the contents from the WAL file so a pristine snapshot-in-time image of the main database is maintained. However, the examiner must also conduct a secondary examination of the contents of the WAL file and, if available, commit the contents to the database and then find the delta information from the main database and subsequent query. The secondary examinations should always be on copies of the evidentiary files obtained from the original evidence.

A perfect example of the changes that can occur with a database file can be observed in the following figures. A Cache.db file was exported from the com.google.GooglePlus app within an iPhone 5 file system. The Cache.db file was 4KB in size, and a table schema had not been created for the SQLite database. The SQLite header was in place, but a table had not been built. Figure 11-27 shows what the database revealed in a SQLite database view—nothing. Table Schema is empty, so there are no records.

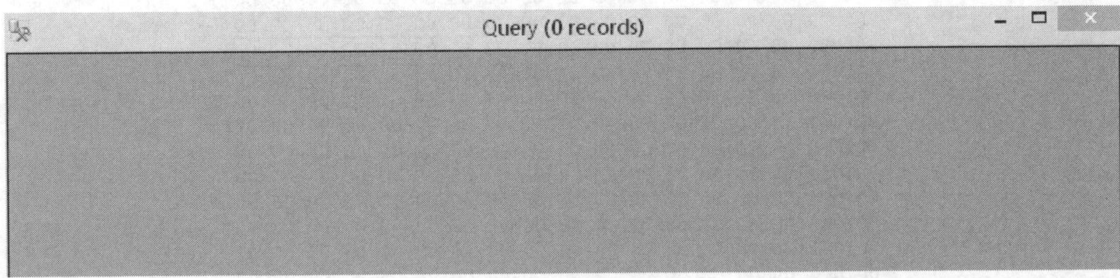

FIGURE 11-27 A query of the Cache.db file from com.google.GooglePlus did not reveal any records.

Query (2 records)

	isDataOnFS	receiver_data	request_key	datetime(cfurl_cach 'unixepoch')
	1		https://www.googleapis.com/batch	
▶	0		https://lh6.googleusercontent.com/-DvQRZZX7E60/AAAAAAAAAAI/AAAAAAAAAAA/fZ5GbqpT60Q/s200-c/photo.jpg	

FIGURE 11-28 A query of the Cache.db file with the associated Cache.wal file revealed records that had not been committed and are now visible.

The main database, Cache.db, as well as the Cache.wal file, were exported into a directory, and tables became available (Figure 11-28). A query of several of the tables and their rows revealed two records, both of which had BLOB data and user data, important to the examiner.

Note The Cache.db file grew from 4KB to 52KB, but the original Cache.wal file within the forensic solution indicated its size was 1248KB. Further investigation of the Cache.wal file using the methods outlined in this section revealed that a single page had been created 11 times within the WAL file, contributing to the size of the original.

The investigation of write-ahead logs can be just as important as examining the freelist and free pages within the main database. These files can reveal information that is not readily available within any mobile forensic solution. Some pages within the WAL file had not been added to the main database file, and some pages that had been marked inactive (deleted), upon checkpoint, could be resolved to the main database and also removed. The examination of the delta between these two files could be eye opening if done correctly.

Property Lists

Property lists, or Plists, are used in Mac OS and iOS devices; these filenames have the .plist extension, although the extension is not always used with files in the iOS system. Plists store Apple configuration files and settings, application configuration files and settings, storage of history events for apps, and information that is to be stored temporarily. They are sometimes compared to the Registry within a Windows operating system. Apple describes a Plist as a structured data representation to store, organize, and access standard types of data. Furthermore, data can be expressed within a Plist, but only certain types of data can be within a Plist: *containers* and *single values* (often called standard types). Both containers and single values are assigned to a key, which contains a value or values depending on whether the data is a container or a single value. A Plist container and single value are represented by the name of the key value in brackets <KeyOrValueName> and ending with a closing bracket </KeyOrValueName>. The only exception to this is the Boolean values that contain only the closing bracket at the end of the value: <true/> or <false/>.

Collections within a Plist are either a dictionary or an array. A *dictionary* (Figure 11-29) contains key–value pairs. An entire single Plist in actuality is a single dictionary and is often represented as the root node. The value can be obtained outside of the Plist by a reference

```
<key>System</key>
<dict>
    <key>Network</key>
    <dict>
        <key>HostNames</key>
        <dict>
            <key>LocalHostName</key>
            <string>MFIServer</string>
        </dict>
    </dict>
    <key>System</key>
    <dict>
        <key>ComputerName</key>
        <string>MFIServer</string>
        <key>ComputerNameEncoding</key>
        <integer>134217984</integer>
        <key>HostName</key>
        <string>MFIServer</string>
    </dict>
</dict>
```

FIGURE 11-29 A dictionary contains values and keys and can also contain other dictionaries, arrays, or single independent objects.

to the dictionary and key that is assigned to the value. An *array* (Figure 11-30) is a collection of values that are indexed and can be referenced to by a single key outside of the Plist with an associated index or ordinal value (that is, name [0], name [1], name [2]). Array objects are contained within the single container and can be single values and dictionaries.

Both arrays and dictionaries can be contained within each other. An array can be a part of a dictionary and dictionaries can be a part of an array. The examiner should understand that a collection and an array are not independent storage methods, but methods that store a list of common data in different ways to be easily referenced.

```
<?xml version="1.0" encoding="UTF-8"?>
<!DOCTYPE plist PUBLIC "-//Apple//DTD PLIST 1.0//EN" "http://www.apple.com/DTDs/PropertyList-1.0.dtd">
<plist version="1.0">
<dict>
    <key>WARNING</key>
    <string>Do not edit this file by hand. It must remain in sorted-by-date order.</string>
    <key>wake</key>
    <array>
        <dict>
            <key>eventtype</key>
            <string>wake</string>
            <key>scheduledby</key>
            <string>com.apple.persistentconnection[apsd,60,0xd62fd50,com.apple.apsd(push.apple.com)]</string>
            <key>time</key>
            <date>2012-09-20T18:13:45Z</date>
        </dict>
        <dict>
            <key>eventtype</key>
            <string>wake</string>
            <key>scheduledby</key>
            <string>com.apple.persistentconnection[imagent,48,0x14b960,com.apple.imagent.peer-purge-timer]</string>
            <key>time</key>
            <date>2012-09-20T18:16:15Z</date>
        </dict>
        <dict>
            <key>eventtype</key>
            <string>wake</string>
            <key>scheduledby</key>
            <string>com.apple.persistentconnection[locationd,28,0x6aa100,FenceDownloadTimer]</string>
            <key>time</key>
            <date>2012-09-20T18:30:45Z</date>
        </dict>
```

FIGURE 11-30 An array is identified by a key and can contain multiple dictionaries or other single independent objects.

> **Note** If order index matters to the values and a change to the order index will alter the results, an array should be used. A dictionary can represent a list of items, where the addition or removal of data does not change the overall value since ordering is not a concern.

Plist data also contains single values, or standard values. Single values can be independent or contained within an array or dictionary. These values must be of the following types as defined by Apple: string <string>, data <data>, date <date>, number <integer>, number <real>, or Boolean <true/> or <false/>. This data can be found within arrays, dictionaries, and the root node. These values are always referenced by a key–value pair unless they are contained within an array. If they are within an array as shown in Figure 11-31, the key is defined by the array, which then will have one or more values, each indexed. Tools such as Windows Plist Editor can make it easy to view a Plist that contains many different types and data (see Figure 11-32).

```
<key>RATES</key>
<array>
    <integer>1</integer>
    <integer>2</integer>
    <integer>5</integer>
    <integer>11</integer>
    <integer>18</integer>
    <integer>24</integer>
    <integer>36</integer>
    <integer>54</integer>
    <integer>6</integer>
    <integer>9</integer>
    <integer>12</integer>
    <integer>48</integer>
</array>
```

FIGURE 11-31 An example of an array holding several values all related and indexed to the RATES key

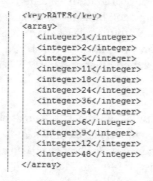

Key	Type	Value
⊟ Root	dict	
AllowEnable	boolean	true
⊟ Custom network settings	dict	
LETSPLAYFREE	string	DADC8922-E644-43FF-9EA3-758687C6B5
DisassociationInterval	real	1800
DriverLoggingFile	string	/Library/Logs/wifi_driver.log
Fallback Preference	integer	2
JoinMode	string	Automatic
⊞ List of known networks	array	
LoggingEnabled	boolean	true
LoggingFile	string	/Library/Logs/wifi.log
SignalStrengthThreshold	integer	10
Version	integer	2
IpasEnable	boolean	true
mStageAutoJoin	boolean	true

FIGURE 11-32 A list view showing the many standard values both within the root and in a dictionary using the Windows Plist Editor

Note Apple recommends the use of property lists for the storage of a small amount of persistent information. If large objects are required to persist, however, property lists should not be used, and other alternatives, such as SQLite databases or other archiving files, should be used instead.

Obtaining information from the Plist files within an iOS system is often automated by mobile forensic software, such as AccessData MPE+ and Oxygen Forensic Detective and Analyst, but the examiner should be extremely cautious with the displayed results. Some tools, such as MPE+, do not display the binary data within the rendered natural view. The examiner must view this data outside and independent of most forensic tools. To do that, he or she can use the free Property List Editor for Macs, available from the Apple Developers site, and for Windows, the Plist Editor Pro is available from www.icopybot.com/. Both tools enable the examiner to navigate XML and binary Plist files obtained from an iOS device. Using these tools can help the examiner recover data more easily than using some of the mobile forensic solutions currently available.

Property lists can be stored in three different formats: text XML, binary, or ASCII. ASCII format is seldom seen because it was used in the OpenStep framework, which Cocoa is derived from. With the release of OS X, ASCII property lists became obsolete, likely because of their read-only format. The ASCII property list storage method will not be covered in this chapter. Both text and binary property lists are covered in the following sections.

Text XML

A text XML property list is readable within an application such as Notepad or TextEdit natively, without conversion. As an examiner moves through an iOS file system, a text XML file is easily recognized by the header viewable in a HEX editor, as shown in Figure 11-33. The term "XML property list" is often used to describe the Plist file, when in actuality XML is a storage format, not a type of Plist. Note that a binary Plist does not use XML but can be easily converted to XML to show the converted binary representation of the data in XML format!

Text XML property lists can be viewed and edited, and they are far more portable than a binary Plist. However, when only a small amount of data is stored, a text XML property list can be much better for reads and writes. The inverse would be true: if the persistent data is required to be large, the text XML format would not be the best choice. To the examiner,

```
<?xml version="1.0" encoding="UTF-
8"?>.<!DOCTYPE plist PUBLIC "-//Ap
ple//DTD PLIST 1.0//EN" "http://ww
w.apple.com/DTDs/PropertyList-1.0.
dtd">.<plist version="1.0">.<dict>
```

FIGURE 11-33 The header of a text XML Plist is easily recognized within a HEX editor.

this means a text XML Plist will contain generally <strings>, <integers>, <real>, <date>, and Boolean <true/> or <false/>. Data <data> values are generally not used within a text XML property list. The examiner should look into the text XML file for app settings and, most importantly, the device settings as listed in the "Additional File System Locations" section earlier in this chapter.

Binary

Binary formatted property lists are the most prevalent type used within the iOS file system, and binary is now the default format for preference files. This was not always the case, as earlier versions of iOS used the standard text XML format. This change occurred primarily because of the need to store more <data> within the Plist. Apple recommends using a binary property list format when data size is important. The size will negatively affect performance and speed of reads and writes if this information is stored within a text-based property list. The binary format of the property list has a common header, bplist00, which represents a binary Plist. An example of the header is shown in Figure 11-34 within the com.apple.wifi.plist.

Although binary Plist files are better suited to hold <data> for faster read and write speeds, data values for binary Plists are generally stored as Base64 values because most developers, including Apple developers, seem to prefer using Base64 for its compactness and lack of "plain textedness," which is better for security (through obscurity). Some Plists using Base64 encode small files, strings, and even XML and binary Plists within a <data> key of a property list! Base64 is a function that allows binary data to be transferred over media,


```
00000 62 70 6C 69 73 74 30 30-DD 00 01 00 02 00 03 00 bplist00Ý·······
00010 04 00 05 00 06 00 07 00-08 00 09 00 0A 00 0B 00 ················
00020 0C 00 0D 00 0E 00 0F 00-10 00 11 00 0E 00 15 1C ················
00030 C5 00 3F 1C C6 00 0E 00-0E 12 27 00 3F 5E 4C 6F Å·?·Æ·····'·?^Lo
00040 67 67 69 6E 67 45 6E 61-62 6C 65 64 5B 4C 6F 67 ggingEnabled[Log
00050 67 69 6E 67 46 69 6C 65-5F 10 11 44 72 69 76 65 gingFile_··Drive
00060 72 4C 6F 67 67 69 6E 67-46 69 6C 65 5F 10 17 43 rLoggingFile_··C
00070 75 73 74 6F 6D 20 6E 65-74 77 6F 72 6B 20 73 65 ustom network se
00080 74 74 69 6E 67 73 5B 41-6C 6C 6F 77 45 6E 61 62 ttings[AllowEnab
00090 6C 65 5F 10 16 4C 69 73-74 20 6F 66 20 6B 6E 6F le_··List of kno
000a0 77 6E 20 6E 65 74 77 6F-72 6B 73 58 4A 6F 69 6E wn networksXJoin
000b0 4D 6F 64 65 57 56 65 72-73 69 6F 6E 5F 10 16 44 ModeWVersion_··D
000c0 69 73 61 73 73 6F 63 69-61 74 69 6F 6E 49 6E 74 isassociationInt
000d0 65 72 76 61 6C 5A 6C 70-61 73 45 6E 61 62 6C 65 ervalZlpasEnable
000e0 5E 6D 53 74 61 67 65 41-75 74 6F 4A 6F 69 6E 5F ^mStageAutoJoin_
000f0 10 17 53 69 67 6E 61 6C-53 74 72 65 6E 67 74 68 ··SignalStrength
00100 54 68 72 65 73 68 6F 6C-64 5F 10 13 46 61 6C 6C Threshold_··Fall
00110 62 61 63 6B 20 50 72 65-66 65 72 65 6E 63 65 09 back Preference·
00120 5F 10 16 2F 4C 69 62 72-61 72 79 2F 4C 6F 67 73 _··/Library/Logs
00130 2F 77 69 66 69 2E 6C 6F-67 5F 10 1D 2F 4C 69 62 /wifi.log_··/Lib
00140 72 61 72 79 2F 4C 6F 67-73 2F 77 69 66 69 5F 64 rary/Logs/wifi_d
00150 72 69 76 65 72 2E 6C 6F-67 D1 00 12 00 13 5C 4C river.logÑ····\L
00160 45 54 53 50 4C 41 59 46-52 45 45 5F 10 24 44 41 ETSPLAYFREE_·$DA
00170 44 43 38 39 32 32 2D 45-36 34 34 2D 34 33 46 46 DC8922-E644-43FF
00180 2D 39 45 41 33 2D 37 35-38 36 38 37 43 36 42 35 -9EA3-758687C6B5
```


FIGURE 11-34 Binary Plist file header represented starting at offset 0

allowing only printable characters. Base64's need was generated when binary content was required to be attached to e-mails. Items such as media and files are converted to Base64 and attached per the Internet Engineering Task Force RFC 4648 Standards track from October 2006. Base64 uses values from the US-ASCII characters table (26 [a–z], 26 [A–Z], 10 [0–9]), and to round out the extra two characters for an even 64, both + and / are included. Often, the examiner will see an equal sign (=) also used within the Base64 value. This character is used for padding purposes if there are fewer than 24 characters; if the number of bits in the input stream is not a multiple of 24, padding is needed to make up the remaining bits. The extra character is not part of the encoded data, per se, but to decode the Base64 value, the padding value (=) will be needed.

Some forensic tools such as FTK and EnCase will decode the Base64 values when they are located within a Plist file, but if the tool is unable to decode them, other online services and portable tools can assist with the decoding (Figure 11-35).

Investigation and understanding of property lists and their role throughout the iOS device can be profitable for the examiner, most importantly during the documentation and testimony phase.

Miscellaneous iOS Files

iOS supports not only SQLite databases and property lists, but also uses other standard files types such as text, XML, JSON, and some other proprietary files. Also, encryption has become available for individual files that pose a problem to the investigation at the file level. Nevertheless, additional files should also be investigated within an iOS file system.

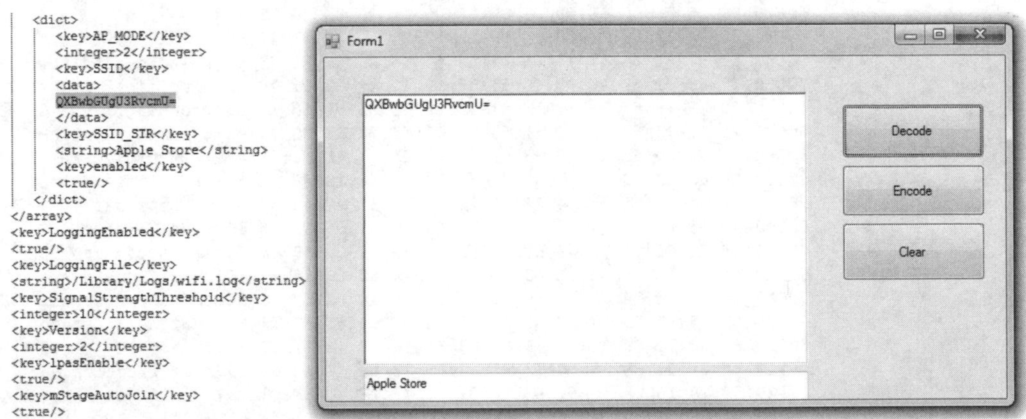

FIGURE 11-35 Binary Plist com.apple.wifi.plist encodes the SSID values as Base64, which are easily decoded to show the string value.

Log Files

Log files within an iOS file system do not hold much user data, but they can lend an overview of the device operation. Some of the files and their definitions are listed here:

- **/diagnostics/device_info.txt** This file is located just off the root of the device file system and contains many items of interest about the device, including the phone number, serial number, phone type, the MEID or IMEI, and many more user-specific and phone-specific details. This folder is obtained only with a diagnostic collection using advanced services. *This file is not generally available on an iOS 8 device collection.*
- **private/Library/Logs/lockdown.log** This text file shows all of the connections attempted and made to pair with the iOS device. The examiner can use this to observe connections and pairing of the device along with the dates. *This file is located at private /var/logs in iOS 8 and is available with a jailbroken device.*
- **private/Library/Logs/lockdown_service.log** This interesting text file shows the services that are accessed when the device is paired. This file shows the services that the mobile forensic solution would access on the device. This information could be important to help an examiner understand how certain files where obtained, while others were not. *This file is located at private/var/logs in iOS 8 and available with a jailbroken device.*

JSON

The JSON (JavaScript Object Notation) format is an open standard and uses readable text to transmit data. Much like a dictionary, JSON uses a key–value pair to store data. JSON can be used on any platform, which makes it suitable for use within an iOS device. JSON is based on standards from RFC 7159 and is used in apps within the iOS file system as a substitute for a SQLite database. Both Instagram and Facebook apps use JSON: Instagram uses a JSON file to identify media and associated text, and Facebook embeds JSON strings within fields in the main database file. Since JSON was developed for server-to-browser communication without plug-ins, it makes sense that JSON is used in these applications. Note, too, that web servers such as Google, Yahoo!, and Twitter also return JSON-formatted strings. Typically JSON will not hold media streams, but it will include the string to a local or remote URL that can be called to display the media.

JSON files, like the property list, can contain numbers, strings, Boolean values, arrays, objects (such as a dictionary of an unordered set of name–value pairs), and nulls. The object value, much like the dictionary within a Plist, is the most widely used type of variable within the JSON file. The object can hold any other type of variable available in the JSON open source format and is being used more widely within apps in the iOS file system.

To recognize the JSON format, the examiner should look for the use of the curly brackets ({ and }) starting and ending the file, brackets ([and]) enclosing data strings, and colons (:) separating names from values. The following example is a return from a server when the weather for the state of Idaho in the United States was requested:


```
{
    "coord": {
        "lon": -116.19,
        "lat": 43.61
    },
    "sys": {
        "message": 0.0211,
        "country": "United States of America",
        "sunrise": 1429793285,
        "sunset": 1429843074
    },
    "weather": [{
        "id": 800,
        "main": "Clear",
        "description": "sky is clear",
        "icon": "02d"
    }],
    "base": "stations",
    "main": {
        "temp": 289.49,
        "temp_min": 289.49,
        "temp_max": 289.49,
        "pressure": 907.98,
        "sea_level": 1019.4,
        "grnd_level": 907.98,
        "humidity": 27
    },
    "wind": {
        "speed": 2.23,
        "deg": 294.007
    },
    "clouds": {
        "all": 8
    },
    "dt": 1429826138,
    "id": 5586437,
    "name": "",
    "cod": 200
}
```

If the data in the JSON is analyzed, the examiner will see several objects defined: cord, sys, weather, base, main, wind, clouds, dt, id, name, and cod. Values are associated with each object, which can be strings, arrays, numbers, other objects, and, of course, Boolean values. The file can be more easily read using a free viewer called Notepad ++ and a free JSON Viewer plug-in, as shown in Figures 11-36 and 11-37.

JSON files can hold valuable information within iOS devices. An examiner should be familiar with the location and subsequent analysis of these files.

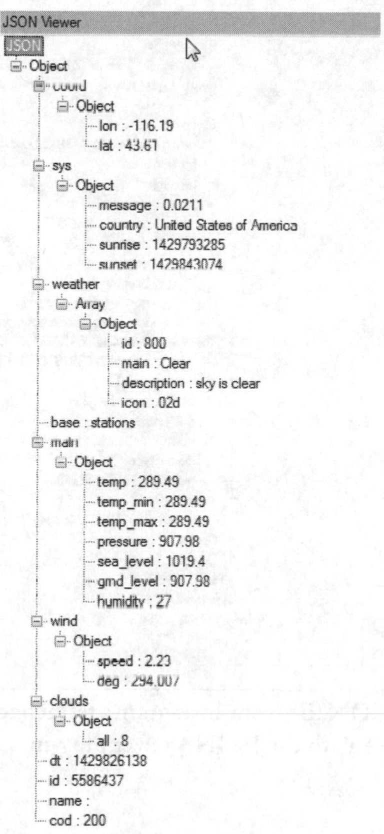

FIGURE 11-36 JSON file from the sample weather from the Idaho example when viewed in Notepad ++

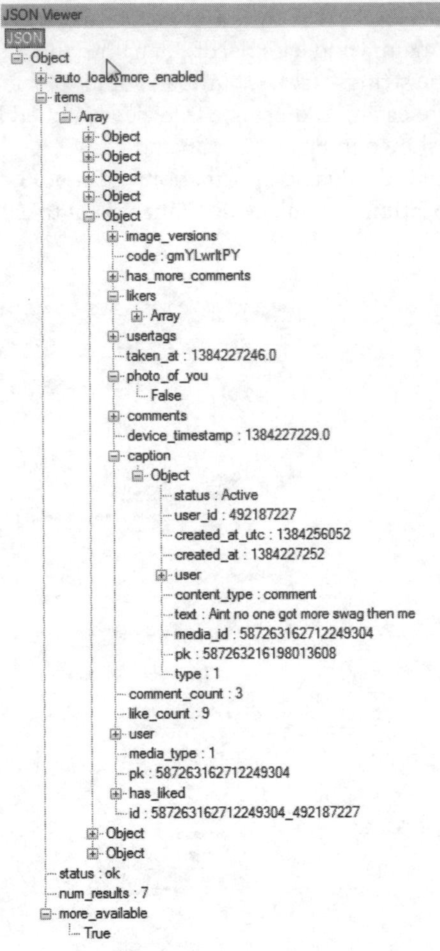

FIGURE 11-37 **JSON file from Instagram's fsCachedData folder decoded into a readable format in Notepad ++ with the JSON Viewer plug-in**

Chapter Summary

The iOS file system contains thousands of files that are examined by automated tools. With the examiner's ability to obtain the file system of an iOS device using iTunes backups, many files are already available. Special services such as file_relay and house_arrest enable some automated tools to obtain files and folders that simple iTunes backups fail to provide. Apple has disabled the file_relay service in iOS 8 devices, so files that could have been recovered in previous iOS versions are no longer available. This does not, however, mean the examiner should not navigate and search the file system.

Files such as SQLite databases contain valuable data, and free pages can be recovered with little effort. Free page data includes data no longer referenced, often referred to as inactive pages, within an active database. Within the freelist, an examiner can navigate the page and identify these inactive pages—often recovering valuable deleted data. Often the default in SQLite version 3.7x database files, the write-ahead log holds valuable data that enters the WAL file prior to entering the main database. Automated tools often miss the most recent data in the main database, but this data is still within the WAL file. Using the knowledge and suggestions in this chapter, the examiner can recover and display this information, leading to results far superior to those most automated forensic tools provide. Because a WAL file can also contain frames that are marked inactive, deleted data can also be recovered, often identified by automated tools as undeleted. Having the skills to determine where the data actually resides within the main database or WAL file is critical to the examiner.

iOS devices contain many other files, including property lists, or Plist files, which are generally either text XML or binary files. The Plist files within an iOS device include great information detailing settings, configurations, user data, and passwords. Many forensic tools support these files natively, but some do not. The examiner should be sure to identify the support of Plist files by the mobile forensic solution and whether or not the viewer within the solution displays all of the information. Some tools will show that there is binary data within a key, but they will not display this data, such as AccessData MPE+ and FTK. The examiner should use tools such as the Property List Editor for Macs and Plist Editor Pro for Windows to dive into the property lists from iOS devices. Both of these tools allow the examiner to rummage through both text- and binary-based property lists, showing binary data within keys and more. Many other text files and settings files can be found within the file system of an iOS device that can show not only device information and diagnostics, but also user information that can be important for any investigation.

The examiner can use the tables within this chapter to help develop a course of action. Using the information on file location and file types can help the examiner peel the many layers of the iOS onion, exposing the many artifacts often overlooked by automated solutions.

12 Querying SQLite and Taming the Forensic Snake

Chapter 11 covered the various files within the iOS file system, and Chapter 13 will deal with files within the Android file system. This chapter introduces the methods for scraping, carving, infiltrating, and exposing the maximum amount of data from iOS and Android mobile devices—or any device with which the examiner has access to files and folders. With repetition, practice, and desire, an examiner can uncover, dissect, and parse critical data that an automated tool can miss.

In this chapter, SQLite database parsing will be demystified to offer the examiner a better understanding of how automated tools pull data from these files. It includes instructions on creating queries within apps that may (or may not) be supported by an automated tool that may be missing critical data or data types. SQLite database files are the primary source for today's smart devices, including iOS, Android, Windows Phone, and BlackBerry 10 devices. These files, along with their cache files, contain an enormous amount of evidence. Because of the many devices supporting this file type, the treasure trove of information about SQLite provided in this chapter can be helpful for the examiner involved in any smart device collections that involve these files.

Thousands of files are contained within a smart device file system, and the examiner should by now recognize that automated tools cannot support every file type, dissecting each file and displaying its contents. Because of this impossibility, the examiner should be versed in how to obtain that information without having to document the contents of the file manually by photographing the mobile device or printing the screen containing the data. Instead, the examiner can automate the process by creating custom-built SQL queries or custom-built code using Python, a free open source scripting language that is making its way into many forensic tools.

Python enables an examiner to build file parsers, file identifiers, file searchers, and much more, removing the bottleneck that can be created by the process of software design, from implementation to release. An examiner can now create, in sometimes eight lines of code, support for a file type within an app that would have taken a software company two months to release to the public.

Technological power must shift back to the examiner because of tech growth volatility. A software company releases fixes and updates to apps that have been updated three times prior to the solution's support release. Essentially, a forensic solution's release is built on a previous version of an app and as such can be completely useless to the examiner. Given the tools and information, the examiner can supplement the automated tools to fill the gap between solution release and app proliferation. This is how a mobile forensic expert is born.

Querying of the SQLite Database

Probably the most important tool for an examiner is his or her ability to analyze a SQLite database. Of course, there are automated tools that will query and recover information from these file types, but what if the data is not retrieved, it is in an improper format, or the particular app database is not directly supported? With the millions of available apps for iOS, Android, Windows Phone, and BlackBerry 10 devices, an examiner needs to have advanced skills to open the associated SQLite databases, examine the contents, and create queries to recover the needed data.

Many tools are available for both Windows and Mac devices that can enable an examiner to view the contents of SQLite files and extract targeted information to produce data for any investigation. An examiner's reliance on an automated tool to recover app data consistently will be short lived, however—not because the automated tools are not up to par, but because the forensic software companies are aiming their products at moving targets. Apps can be updated weekly or monthly, so keeping up with the database schema changes, data value formats, and addition of functionality is an almost impossible task. To combat that, the examiner must be able to traverse the SQLite database and build queries to stay current with even the "zero-day" apps.

What Is a SQL Query?

SQLite, as mentioned earlier in the chapter, is a structured language and, as such, SQLite understands most of the standard SQL queries and uses a few of its own. Communicating with a SQLite database is completed by formulating a structured query using a properly formatted statement. Several types of queries can be used to create, delete, and alter tables (these will not be covered in this book because for forensic investigations, they will not be needed). An examiner querying SQLite databases should be aware of several basic statements shown in Table 12-1 that are often used "under the hood" of forensic software. Other statements not covered in this book can be found at SQLite.org.

If an investigation of the SQLite database will occur outside of the forensic environment, the examiner should use a compiled SQL browser because of communication requirements with the SQLite database. Windows does not natively communicate with a SQLite database unless the SQLite engine is installed, available, and used for communication; using a compiled application, either portable or installed, will be much easier. (Alas, if the examiner wants to communicate at the command prompt with the database, that is also easily done—but is not covered in this book—and the sqlite3 library is needed.)

TABLE 12-1 SQL Syntax for the Investigation of App Data Within SQLite Databases

Statement	Description
SELECT	Used to query the database. A SELECT statement does not make any changes to the database, and the result is 0 or more rows of data.
FROM	Used to direct the SELECT statement to the location the data should be queried FROM.
INNER JOIN	The default JOIN used in SQL, which will select records only from the database tables that have matching values.
LEFT OUTER JOIN	The only OUTER JOIN that can be used in SQLite, which returns ALL records from the table on the left of the JOIN statement, plus the matched records from the table on the right of the JOIN statement. OUTER can be omitted from the statement. However, SQLite will ignore the LEFT JOIN statement if ON or USING is used instead of WHERE and treat it like an INNER JOIN.
WHERE	This condition is used to specify whether an expression or column in a table has a relationship with another column or expression. The standard operands can be used (=, >, >=, <, <=). WHERE shows relationships between tables and columns, particularly an index, and is also used to filter data.
ON	This condition executes ON the JOIN statement and indicates how the JOIN should be performed, unlike WHERE, which is a filter of the collected data from the table.

Note Of course, prior to communicating with the SQLite database, the sqlite3 library (www.sqlite.org/download.html) must be available or used by any software the examiner will use to complete the navigation of the database. Literally hundreds of SQLite browsers are available on the SQLite.org site (www.sqlite.org/cvstrac/wiki?p=ManagementTools).

The examiner should become familiar with the SQLite database by using a database browser such as DB Browser for SQLite (http://sqlitebrowser.org/), which supports Windows, Mac, and Linux. This software will allow for navigating, viewing, query building and saving, and exporting the executed query data. The following section outlines the examination of a database file within DB Browser for SQLite in an effort to convey the usefulness of the tool.

Caution DB Browser for SQLite can alter, create, delete, add, and modify the SQLite database with features included within the product. Examiners should work only on a copy of the evidence file and learn about the feature set by reading the application documentation before using it.

Looking into a database after being exposed to the interworkings and file metadata, an examiner should be able to understand the information displayed by the automated tool. As you examine the figures in this chapter, you will see that the information identified within the DB Browser GUI includes the kind of journaling used and the size of the page in bytes, as shown in the Edit Pragmas tab in Figure 12-1. If necessary, the examiner could find this information manually, now armed with the knowledge of its location in the database file.

While using a database viewer, the examiner can view tables and rows as a hierarchy and concentrate on identifying the relationships between the tables as defined in the schema. SQLite databases within apps will include some information in one table, more in another, and sometimes even more in a third. Being able to locate these relationships are important to the examiner, and using a GUI to identify *keys* within a database can assist when these tables need to be joined in an effort to merge the tables using their relationships. Keys define the relationships within a database, and using a key within a query will allow the JOIN to be successful and show all the related data. There are two types of keys: *primary keys* and *foreign keys*.

Primary keys are unique and singular, and only one can be assigned within a single table, although the table is not required to have a primary key. The primary key is generally an integer primary key and can often contain an empty column (NULL) if the table does not contain a ROWID (rowid). Most SQLite databases will use ROWID (rowid) or a derivative of ROWID to indicate the primary key. Within a database viewer, the primary key is often shown graphically as a key next to the table. The primary key is used by the database to create tables and to make updates and other changes to the database to ensure that information is not overwritten.

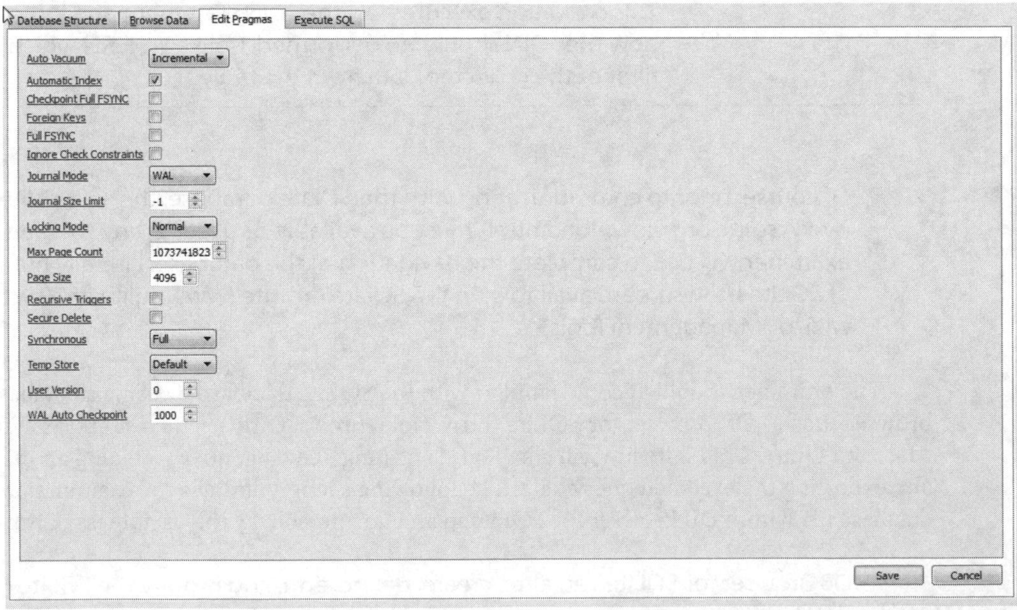

FIGURE 12-1 **The Edit Pragmas tab, where you can see and edit information about the database**

Tip To maintain uniqueness, an examiner should look at the ROWID in iOS databases. A gap in the ROWID indicates that a row has been deleted, because the ROWID is never duplicated, to maintain uniqueness within the table.

Foreign keys, on the other hand, are references that show the relationship *between* tables. You can observe this relationship when a value in the parent table is equal to a value in the associated child table. You can also identify a foreign key within a SQLite database table if a column contains one or more NULL values, which indicates that the column is a foreign key per SQLite standards (this will also be reported by database viewers). The examiner will use the related values between existing parent and child tables to build JOINs within a SQL query.

When constructing and viewing app databases, the examiner should pay special attention to foreign keys by first checking the tables and verifying the relationships prior to creating a SQL query. This information is available in the Database Structure tab, shown in Figure 12-2. Some keys may be related to other tables, and on many occasions, a field (column) is not identified as a key but can be used as such to create stellar results.

BLOB (Binary Large Object) data is used in many SQLite databases to store binary data representing large objects (such as images and files) not to exceed 65,535 bytes. Typically, the BLOB data will be displayed as thumbnails of images, small video clips, or text. Having a tool to look at the BLOB data (Figure 12-3) can be extremely important, since most mobile forensic solutions do not resolve the BLOB data. If binary files are too large to be stored efficiently within the database, they will be stored to disk and then referenced within the BLOB data.

Database Structure | Browse Data | Edit Pragmas | Execute SQL

Create Table | Modify Table | Delete Table

Name	Type	Schema
Tables (5)		
cfurl_cache_blob_data		CREATE TABLE cfurl_cache_blob_data(entry_ID INTEGER PRIMARY KEY, response_object BLOB, request_object BLOB,
cfurl_cache_receiver_data		CREATE TABLE cfurl_cache_receiver_data(entry_ID INTEGER PRIMARY KEY, isDataOnFS INTEGER, receiver_data BLOB)
entry_ID	INTEGER	\`entry_ID\` INTEGER
isDataOnFS	INTEGER	\`isDataOnFS\` INTEGER
receiver_data	BLOB	\`receiver_data\` BLOB
cfurl_cache_response		CREATE TABLE cfurl_cache_response(entry_ID INTEGER PRIMARY KEY AUTOINCREMENT UNIQUE,
entry_ID	INTEGER	\`entry_ID\` INTEGER PRIMARY KEY AUTOINCREMENT UNIQUE
version	INTEGER	\`version\` INTEGER
hash_value	INTEGER	\`hash_value\` INTEGER
storage_policy	INTEGER	\`storage_policy\` INTEGER
request_key	TEXT	\`request_key\` TEXT UNIQUE
time_stamp	TEXT	\`time_stamp\` TEXT NOT NULL DEFAULT CURRENT_TIMESTAMP
partition	TEXT	\`partition\` TEXT
cfurl_cache_schema_version		CREATE TABLE cfurl_cache_schema_version(schema_version INTEGER)
sqlite_sequence		CREATE TABLE sqlite_sequence(name,seq)
Indices (6)		
proto_props_index		CREATE INDEX proto_props_index ON cfurl_cache_blob_data(entry_ID)
receiver_data_index		CREATE INDEX receiver_data_index ON cfurl_cache_receiver_data(entry_ID)
request_key_index		CREATE INDEX request_key_index ON cfurl_cache_response(request_key)
sqlite_autoindex_cfurl_cache_response_1		
sqlite_autoindex_cfurl_cache_response_2		
time_stamp_index		CREATE INDEX time_stamp_index ON cfurl_cache_response(time_stamp)
Views (0)		
Triggers (0)		

FIGURE 12-2 Once the database is imported into the application, the Database Structure tab shows the tables and keys associated with a column; these are important for joining tables.

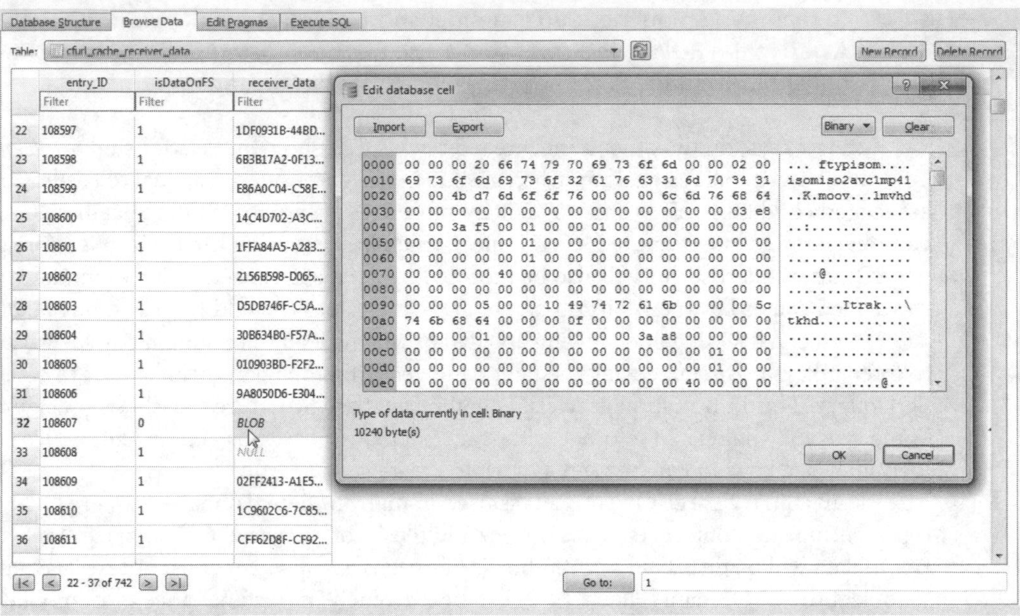

FIGURE 12-3 Looking into the table cfurl_cache_receiver_data, the examiner can click any record labeled BLOB and the data will be exposed in a separate window, as shown with a video file that can be exported and viewed within a native viewer.

The examiner should carefully examine BLOB data, because this might be the only location of important images, videos, or text from the mobile device.

Once an examiner has located the tables and significant columns within the table, any associated foreign keys between tables and child tables should be ascertained. A SQL query should then be created outlining the significant tables and their rows, the related table columns (foreign key), and either a reference or filter. The SQL statement can then be executed on the database. The SQLite engine will parse the database based upon the built statement and produce the results. As shown in Figure 12-4, the examiner can manually input, paste, or load a saved SQL statement into the Execute SQL tab to execute the script.

Using a GUI to navigate a SQLite database, an examiner can uncover much more information than is available by relying on a software engineer to decide what is important in a SQLite database. No automated tool supports the many cache.db files within an iOS device, and as shown in the example, a lot of additional information gathered using a SQL query can assist any mobile forensic examination.

Building a Simple SQL Query

Building a query is not the most difficult thing to do, but some examiners believe it may not be the best use of their time. For those examiners, there are automated tools that build SQL

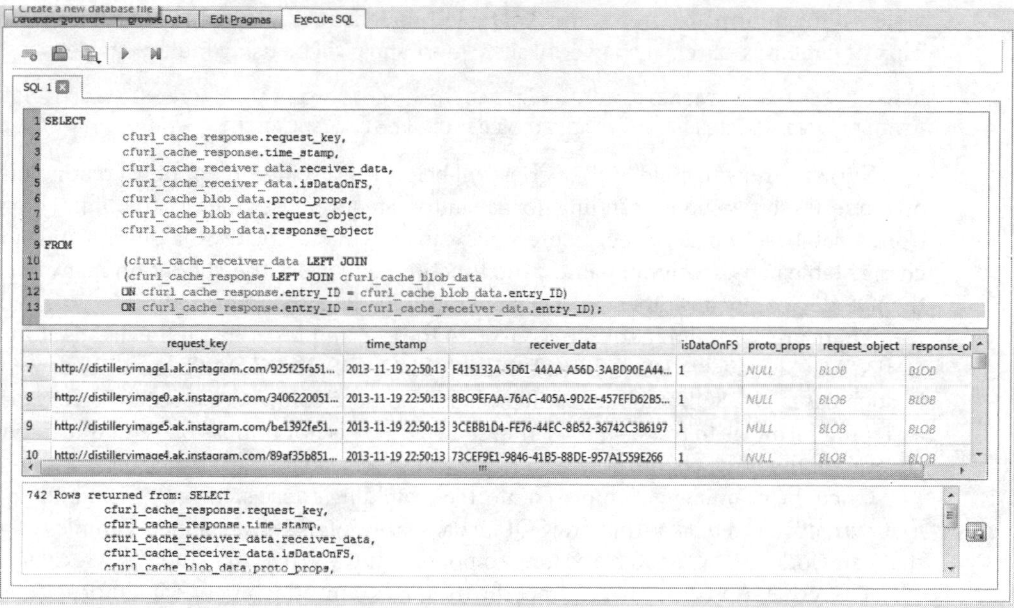

FIGURE 12-4 Results of the executed SQL statement

queries with just a few clicks of the mouse. Others will appreciate some basic queries covered within this section to help them understand the compilation and execution of a statement on a database.

The easiest queries can be formulated using some of the following examples. Note that data shown within brackets (< >) are variables the examiner would fill in with a unique name from the database being examined.

The first query starts with a `SELECT` and asks the database to retrieve ALL (`*`) of the rows from a table the examiner specifies after the `FROM` statement:

```
SELECT * FROM <TABLENAME>;
```

The next query asks for four columns within the table. The data from the four columns will be retrieved and displayed:

```
SELECT <column1>,<column2>,<column3>,<column4> FROM <TABLENAME>;
```

The next query will obtain all the records from a single table, but will show the matching records only if column 4 contains the string `Lee`. This query can help the examiner search for records with a column and return only data that contains that record.

```
SELECT * FROM <TABLENAME> WHERE <column4> = 'Lee';
```

The next query will obtain records from two different tables within the same database and combine the results. The statement requests the data from columns 1 and 2 in both table 1 and table 2 if the information in column 3 of table 1 matches the information in column 4 in table 2. This statement is extremely powerful since most apps will be using multiple tables.

```
SELECT <column1.TABLE1>,<column2.TABLE1>,<column1.TABLE2>,<column2.TABLE2> FROM
<TABLENAME1> INNER JOIN <TABLENAME2> ON <column3.TABLE1> = <column4.TABLE2> ;
```

Knowing how to build SQL queries will help the examiner in not only creating his or her own queries, but in understanding how an automated tool uses queries to obtain information from a database. Furthermore, an examiner can save the template SQL queries and simply change table names, column names, and functions and reuse the queries on many apps within the iOS device and any other media where a SQLite database is located.

There are some limitations, of course, to these examples. What if the data is stored in UNIX, MICROSECONDS, WEBKIT, MILLISECONDS, MAC DATE, or other date formats? In such cases, the SQL statement will probably be more complex, especially if the examiner is assigning formulas to rows—but writing such a query is not impossible, and more about this is covered in the next section.

Once the examiner gets more comfortable building queries, he or she can build queries that extract selected data from any SQLite database. Following are some examples of queries that can work with iOS databases for two popular apps, WhatsApp and Kik Messenger.

The WhatsApp query will extract the messages, any attachment data information, and associated metadata and match it with the username of the sender.

```
SELECT
      ZWAMESSAGE.ZFROMJID,
      ZWAMESSAGE.ZPUSHNAME,
      ZWAMESSAGE.ZTEXT,
      ZWAMESSAGE.ZISFROMME,
      ZWAMESSAGE.ZTOJID,
      ZWAMEDIAITEM.ZMEDIAURL,
      ZWAMEDIAITEM.ZMEDIALOCALPATH
FROM
      ( ZWAMESSAGE LEFT JOIN ZWAMEDIAITEM
      ON ZWAMEDIAITEM.Z_PK = ZWAMESSAGE.Z_PK);
```

The next query for Kik Messenger will extract valuable message data, convert date and time information, and match the associated data with the username of the sender:

```
SELECT
      datetime(ZKIKMESSAGE.ZTIMESTAMP + 978307200, 'unixepoch'),
      datetime(ZKIKMESSAGE.ZRECEIVEDTIMESTAMP + 978307200, 'unixepoch'),
      ZKIKMESSAGE.ZBODY,
      ZKIKUSER.ZDISPLAYNAME,
      ZKIKUSER.ZEMAIL,
      ZKIKUSER.ZFIRSTNAME,
      ZKIKUSER.ZLASTNAME
FROM
      (ZKIKUSER INNER JOIN ZKIKMESSAGE
      ON ZKIKMESSAGE.ZUSER = ZKIKUSER.Z_PK);
```

Automating Query Building

An examiner can manually build queries within many SQL database browsers. As mentioned, time is sometimes against many examiners as they perform forensic examinations; they might not have the time to learn, dive into, or formulate their own queries. These examiners tend to rely on automated tools to extract data from SQLite databases or apps that come their way. There are just too many apps in the world today—with no end in sight—to rely on commercial tools. For these examiners, and even those who feel comfortable writing queries, there are automated query building tools available within many mobile forensic tools and in standalone products.

For example, AccessData includes the SQLBuilder within MPE+ that enables an examiner to build queries based upon the selection of the table and then the rows. Using SQLBuilder, the examiner can assign a data format (such as a String, Date/Time, Duration) and create a SQL query without having to write a single line of SQL code. MPE+ SQLBuilder is limited, however, in that it allows for the joining of only two tables.

Paul Sanderson, from Sanderson Forensics, created a tool called Forensic ToolKit for SQLite, which is similar to SQLBuilder. It also enables browsing, write-ahead-log reviewing, and SQLite navigation. This tool can be used to verify information discussed within this chapter, such as exploration of pages, frames, and byte-level information with a built-in HEX view.

A third tool that automates query building is SQLQuery Builder (Figure 12-5). Using this tool, the examiner drags and drops, double-clicks, and joins tables by dragging the parent table to the child table to form the relationship. Columns can be added to the query or entire tables by simply moving them into the query build frame. There is no limit on the foreign keys that can be joined between multiple tables within a single database, and, when completed, the SQL query can be executed and results reported.

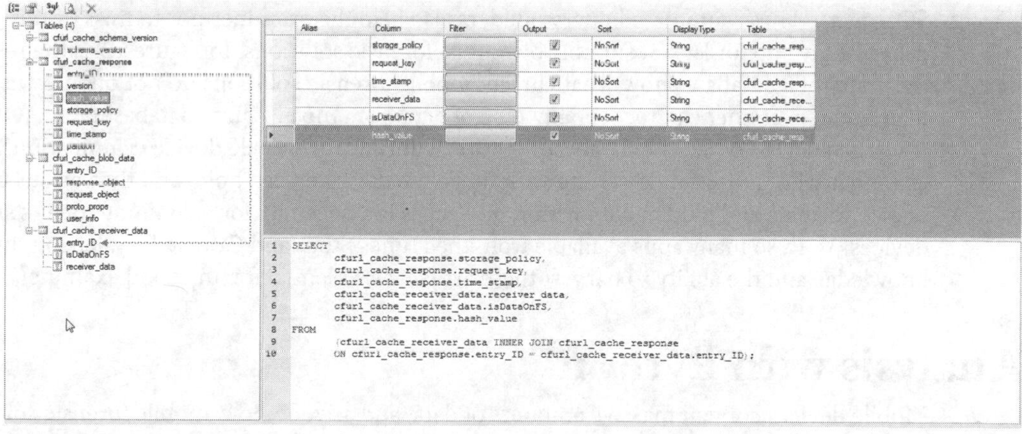

FIGURE 12-5 **A complex query between two tables with multiple rows using a foreign key can be completed in a short time using automated query builders such as SQLQuery Builder.**

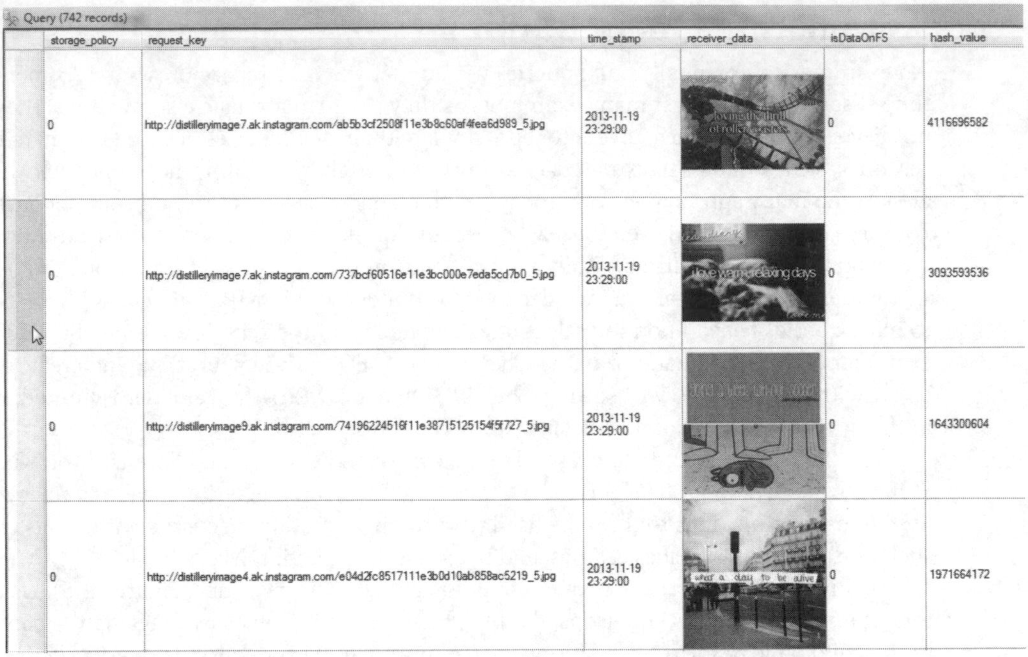

Query (742 records)

storage_policy	request_key	time_stamp	receiver_data	isDataOnFS	hash_value
0	http://distilleryimage7.ak.instagram.com/ab5b3cf2508f11e3b8c60af4fea6d989_5.jpg	2013-11-19 23:29:00		0	4116696582
0	http://distilleryimage7.ak.instagram.com/737bcf60516e11e3bc000e7eda5cd7b0_5.jpg	2013-11-19 23:29:00		0	3093593536
0	http://distilleryimage9.ak.instagram.com/74196224516f11e38715125154f5f727_5.jpg	2013-11-19 23:29:00		0	1643300604
0	http://distilleryimage4.ak.instagram.com/e04d2fc8517111e3b0d10ab858ac5219_5.jpg	2013-11-19 23:29:00		0	1971664172

FIGURE 12-6 Results of a SQL query

These tools will assist the examiner who does not have the time to create his or her own queries, but they also help the examiner gain a better understanding of what it takes to create a SQL query. These automated query builders also help the examiner not to miss or misidentify data—or give up for lack of support by mobile forensic solutions. In Figure 12-6, the results of the query of a database show what current mobile forensic solutions do not offer: by using SQL queries, an examiner can recover any type of data from most SQLite databases.

The analysis of SQLite databases is critical during any mobile device examination. An examiner who understands SQLite structures, the data they can hold, and the various types of data formats and hidden data within free pages is a necessity for examining today's smart devices. With so many apps available from the iTunes Store and Google Play, having this knowledge and the ability to harvest these artifacts is essential for any good examiner.

Analysis with Python

Mobile devices contain massive amounts of data, and as you know, mobile forensic solutions cannot extract every app's data or parse every file for its data. For an examiner to be successful and eliminate such obstacles, he or she will have to think outside of the box, forget about the limitations imposed by a software solution, and start thinking of ways to parse the information from these valuable files. A mobile forensic examiner today must believe that *in order to be prepared for tomorrow, you have to think about tomorrow today.*

In the early days of mobile forensic examination, data on mobile device file systems was usually parsed manually. Most early forensic examiner training focused on extracting, manually locating the data, converting it into a readable format, and finally making the data presentable for court. As device storage grew, these tasks became extremely time consuming, often taking weeks for a first-generation iPhone. Forensic solution providers struggled to release updates to their software to deal with the growing number of smart devices. To make the best use of their limited time, examiners needed a way to automate the repetitive task of manually parsing data that was not supported by mobile forensic solutions.

Enter Python, the most widely used scripting language in mobile forensics today. Using Python, examiners can create individual "programs" to act upon a file, folder, image, or really anything stored on a mobile device. Python scripts act as parsers to complete the task the examiner previously undertook manually.

Python was created in 1989 by Guido von Rossum, who also helped create the ABC language, a precursor to Python. Python also has roots in the C programming language. It was targeted at nonprofessional programmers with its ease of readability, many supported functions, modules, and cost. Python is 100 percent free, and because of its many contributors, it has a large repository of modules for building powerful scripts with little effort. Python is currently at version 3.4.x and 2.7.x, which are available on the python.org web site. The most popular version of Python is still version 2.7, and most available scripts in the community are written for that version. Version 2.7 does not contain many of the new modules introduced in Python 3, however, which makes Python 2.7 and 3.x not cross-compatible; modules are version specific, and running a 2.7 script against a 3.x interpreter will fail. In the following section and all included examples, Python 3.x is used.

Note If the examiner is looking to keep current with modules and support, using Python 3.x is recommended. If a software solution has built-in Python support, such as MPE+ or Physical Analyzer, it is important to read the documentation to determine what version of Python the solution supports. Because Python 2.7 and 3.x are not 100 percent compatible, understanding the version of Python supported by the tool is important.

Python can be used in forensics to recover volatile memory from mobile devices, recover files, decrypt files, parse strings and dates from a file, recover passcodes from a binary image, pull exchangeable image file format (EXIF) data from photos taken with the device camera, and so much more. The things a Python script can do are limited only by the examiner's imagination. If an examiner becomes familiar with the creation and execution of a Python script, the limitation of forensic tools will be negligible and the script will be invaluable.

This section is not intended to teach every aspect of Python, but to introduce the concept of using scripts to automate processes and supplement the mobile forensic solutions available. If you are looking for additional information on learning Python, the python.org web site offers guides for both nonprogrammers and programmers and is a wealth of information.

Tip Python binaries can be downloaded from www.python.org/downloads. To use Python, the interpreter must be installed prior to running a script. However, if scripts are being created to be used within a forensic tool such as MPE+ or Physical Analyzer, the interpreter does not need to be installed. Both forensic solutions have built-in interpreters and have installed their respective Python bundles.

Python Terminology

An examiner will hear many terms when getting involved with a programming language. These terms describe actions and data types and are also important to know while creating statements within the code. Of course, all terms used in Python cannot be included within this section, but terms that are commonly seen, heard, and used are included here. These terms will be used throughout the section to create scripts that complete tasks the examiner can immediately use in a mobile forensic examination.

Functionality Terms

Python's syntax can explain the code in comments, load common libraries, and commence and end the executed code. Common syntax that anyone conducting mobile forensic exams using Python should understand are listed here:

- **Comments** Python and any other programming language can become difficult to read, especially when the code contains many lines. To help with readability, an author can annotate the code with comments to assist with the interpretation. A statement is not processed by the interpreter as long as the comment annotation (#) precedes the comment.

```
# This is to instruct the reader the code below prints "Mobile Forensics Rocks!"
print('Mobile Forensics Rocks')
```

- **Expressions** When values, variables, and operators are combined, an expression is formed.

```
x = 11
x + 6
lastname = 'Reiber'
```

- **Operators** Symbols are used to represent some type of computation in an expression. Examples of operators are addition (+) subtraction (–), multiplication (×), and division (/) operators.
- **Statements** In Python or any other programming language, a statement is a unit of code that can be executed. A statement can comprise a single word, multiple words, a single line, or many lines.
- **Variables** All programming languages, including Python, use a name to represent a value. This value can be assigned a name, and the name can be used to refer to the value throughout the script. In this example, `x` and `lastname` are both variables: `x` holds the integer 11 and `lastname` holds the string `'Reiber'`.

```
x = 11
x + 6
lastname = 'Reiber'
```

- **Values** Values are the represented data within a variable and the data with which a script is working. Data is represented by values, and values are represented as a type.

Data Types

The data type or value will tell Python how the data is to be handled and how expressions should be evaluated. Python is different from some other popular programming languages, because the type of value or variable does not have to be declared; Python just knows. In some languages, such as C#, a variable must be declared and a type assigned prior to use, as shown in this C# example:

```
string lastname = 'Reiber';
```

The Python equivalent does not have to declare the type; the interpreter knows the value is a string because of the quotation marks:

```
lastname = 'Reiber'
```

Python's data types are listed here with some examples:

- **Boolean** A Boolean value is either a true or false value. A Boolean is used to make a decision. The Python interpreter evaluates a statement, determines the Boolean value of the statement, and then acts as instructed in the code depending on whether the statement is true or false.

  ```
  11==11
  ```

  This is true (the == tests for equality).

  ```
  11==1
  ```

  This is false.

  ```
  11!=11
  ```

  This is false (the != tests for inequality).

  ```
  11!=1
  ```

  This is true.

- **String** A string is text that contains characters—numbers, letters, spaces, and anything else as long as it is surrounded by double (`"string"`) or single (`'string'`) quotation marks.

  ```
  print ('Python can be good for forensics')
  ```

- **Integer** Numbers without a decimal point are integers. Integers are recognized by Python in a statement because they are not surrounded by quotation marks.
- **Float** Numbers with a decimal point are integers. Floats are also recognized by Python in a statement because they are not surrounded by quotation marks.
- **List** Lists are represented to Python enclosed within brackets: `[ ]`. A list is used in Python when ordering is important and an index is needed to represent a store of data that can include any Python type. The index within a list always starts at 0, so the first value in a list would be referenced by `[0]`.

  ```
  phone_list = ['android', 'iOS', 'WindowsPhone', 11, 9518, 'BlackBerry']
  print (phone_list[2])
  ```

The result would be

```
'WindowsPhone'
```

- **Dictionary** Much like lists, dictionaries store multiple types of data within a single listing, but instead of using ordering by an index like a list, a dictionary uses a key–value pairing system. Dictionaries are represented in Python using braces: { }. Each key can have only one value, but multiple keys can store the same value. The key and value within a dictionary are separated using a colon (:), and values can be accessed with the key.

```
addressbook = {'firstname': 'Bob', 'lastname':'Smith','street': '104 S     Overland']
print (addressbook.get('street'))
```

The result would be

```
'104 S Overland'
```

Additional Terms

Additionally, Python provides ways to create arguments, import common or created libraries, assign parameters, and create functions to run methods within a single script:

- **Argument** An argument is the value (or values) that is passed to a function. The two types of arguments are a keyword (kwargs) and positional argument (args). A keyword argument contains an identifier, whereas a positional argument does not.

```
def my_name(firstname, lastname='reiber'):
       print ('My name is {} {}').format(firstname,lastname)
```

In this example, `firstname` is an args and `lastname` is the kwarg.
Another argument commonly used within Python is a system-specific function/parameter, which allows command-line arguments to be used with a Python script called `sys.argv`. To use `sys.argv`, the `argv` module must be imported from the Python `sys` module into the script. Once this module is imported, the script can assign a variable that will be used as the command-line argument. The first `argv` will always be the script name and can be referenced as `argv[0]`; subsequent command-line arguments then follow.

```
from sys import argv

script, directory = argv
```

The first line imports the module `argv` from the module `sys`, and the second line holds two variables, `script` and `directory`; both are assigned the `argv` argument. The `directory` value can then be used in the script after the value is obtained at the command line when the script is executed (that is, `my_script.py C:\Path\To\Directory`).

- **Parameter** A parameter value is contained within the parentheses of a function and defines which types of arguments are accepted by the function.

- **modules** Modules are separate, precomposed scripts that can be imported by another script to use the module's function. Using modules expands the functions of a script without having to recode many lines since they are already composed within the imported module.
- **import** This statement is generally accompanied by a value telling the Python interpreter what module should be loaded into memory.

```
import sys
import os
```

  This import statement imports the standard Python system module and OS module, making that code available to the script that is being composed.
- **def** These three letters represent *define* and are often included within Python code to define a function. A *function* is a block of reusable code that performs a single action and is often requested multiple times within a Python script, where writing the code block over and over would be inefficient. A statement within the code can call the defined function using the function name followed by parentheses. The parentheses often contain a variable that represents an input parameter or argument. Using functions is highly recommended when repetitive tasks are required.

```
def create_and_check_path(tmpDir):

#Check first to see if there is this path

    if not os.path.exists(tmpDir):

#If not will create the directory

        os.makedirs(tmpDir)
```

  Here's how to call the function and perform the creation of a directory if one does not exist:

```
   tmpDir = "C:\Temp\Test"

    #run function to check to see if path is there
    create_and_check_path(tmpDir)
```

  The function `create_and_check_path( )` is called, and the variable `tmpDir` is passed and used within the function to see if this path exists and, if not, to create the path.

Python Rules

When creating a Python script, you must follow some rules, which allow the interpreter to make sense of the script, understand what blocks of code work with others, and know how the script should progress. These rules are based upon the Python Enhancement Proposals (PEPs) within the Python Developer's Guide (www.python.org/dev/). The information in this section does not cover every rule that is suggested in the PEPs, but it represents the most frequent issues examiners might encounter when creating or running Python scripts.

- **Indentation** Python defines blocks of code using indentation—exactly four spaces should be used per indention level. Indenting a statement four spaces tells the interpreter that it belongs with the statement immediately preceding it. Using indentation levels enables blocks of code to work either together or independently, depending on the function the block of code is providing. Mixing tabs and spaces within a script will often create interpreter errors; spaces are the preferred indentation method. Colons are also used to declare that the following line will be the start of an indented block. Colons are not entirely needed within the code to declare an indentation is coming, but their use is widely accepted to help with the readability of the code, and if an editor uses syntax highlighting, it keys off the colon to identify syntax problems. Here's an example:

```
if foo:
    if bar:
        x = 518
        y = 911
else:
    x=11
```

  The preceding code shows the colon in the first line, which indicates the next line will be indented four spaces. The second line is indented, which indicates that it is a part of the block started in the first line. This line also has a colon, which indicates that the following line will be indented. The next line, `x = 518`, is indented to indicate it is a part of the block immediately preceding `if bar:` and tells the interpreter the statements at this level, which also include `y = 911`, will be evaluated as part of the `if bar:` statement block. The code continues with a *dedent* (the opposite of indent) and the `else:` statement. The dedent indicates to the interpreter that this statement is at the same level of the `if foo:` statement and will be evaluated along with the `if foo:` statement. If the `else:` statement is true, the following statement will be evaluated because the interpreter recognizes the indent and associates `x = 11` with the `else:` statement.
- **Line length** Python documentation recommends that a single line be limited to 79 characters.
- **Imports** Python rules state that import statements will always be placed at the top of the file and on separate lines, as shown earlier in the section "Additional Terms."
- **String quotes** Python allows either double or single quotation marks, which should be mixed only when a literal quote must be added to the string.
- **String formatting** Python allows two methods of formatting strings using placeholders instead of using the variable within the string. This method is much like creating a template and filling the placeholders with variable data assigned at runtime. This is often referred to as *string interpolation*. The variables are located at the end of the statement, and the placement of the variables into the statement string is dictated by the placement in the list. One method uses braces ({ }), whereas the other method uses the percent sign (`%`). The `%` is currently depreciated in Python 3.x, but because it is frequently used in Python 2.7x, it is important that the examiner understand its use within a Python statement. The difference between the two methods is that if the examiner uses the { } string formatting technique, he or she must use the .format `()` method within the statement; if the examiner uses the `%` string formatting, he or she does not use the .format `()` method.

The following would be used and observed in Python 2.7x and older versions:

```
#This line prints to console the files written to the directory

  print 'Done! %s was copied to %s successfully!'%(filename,dirname)
```

The following example would be used and observed in Python in version 3.x:

```
#This line prints to console the files written to the directory

  print('Done! {} was copied to {} successfully!'.
format(filename,dirname))
```

When using this technique, if the placeholder contains an integer (such as {0} or{1}), the integer within the braces identifies the variable that will be used at that position. If there is no integer, as in the example, the placement in the string indicates the ordinal position within the list.

- **print** A big change from 2.7x and 3.x versions of Python is the use of parentheses for print statements. To print in Python 3.x, the examiner must enclose the information that is to be printed in parentheses. When converting any 2.7 scripts to 3.x scripts, this change will be the most frequently encountered. An example of the print statement is in the preceding string formatting example.

Using Python Scripts

As indicated earlier in the chapter, Python can be used within every forensic examination to complete various tasks that automated tools cannot do. Much like using SQL queries, Python scripts enable an examiner to dive deeper within mobile device file systems, uncovering data and formatting that data into readable output. Python scripts can be built to search for files; to search for strings; to carve data from binary files and file systems; to pull out laser-focused data from files such as EXIF, IP addresses, or names; and even to convert data into a readable format. As mentioned, Python scripting can enable an examiner to do just about anything with the data; the only limitation will be imposed by the examiner's imagination.

The following sections contain code examples that the examiner can use in forensic situations. These scripts can be copied, modified, or used as is. Included within the code snippets are comments that explain the code to aid in understanding or to enable the examiner to make adjustments when needed.

EXIF

Exchangeable image file format (EXIF) can be important for any investigation. Several tools will parse EXIF data from photographs and display it, including Physical Analyzer, XRY, and MPE+, and enable the reporting of such—but what if the examiner simply wants to extract the location information from all the images within a directory without having to look at each one within a directory? A customized script is the answer. Using the script located here and the directory to be searched as the argument, the examiner can run this code as a Python file at the command linc or within an interpreter against a directory containing photos. The output data will contain the latitude and longitude along with the name of the file from which it was obtained.

```
# import all needed modules

import os
import sys
from sys import argv
from PIL import Image
from PIL.ExifTags import TAGS, GPSTAGS

#Returns a dictionary from the exif data of an PIL Image item. Also converts the GPS Tags
def get_exif(image):

    exif_data = {}
    info = image._getexif()
    if info:
        for tag, value in info.items():
            decoded = TAGS.get(tag, tag)
            if decoded == "GPSInfo":
                gps_data = {}
                for gps_tag in value:
                    sub_decoded = GPSTAGS.get(gps_tag, gps_tag)
                    gps_data[sub_decoded] = value[gps_tag]

                exif_data[decoded] = gps_data
            else:
                exif_data[decoded] = value

    return exif_data
#function to convert the GPS coordinates stored in the EXIF to degree

def convert_to_degrees(value):
    deg_num, deg_denom = value[0]
    d = float(deg_num) / float(deg_denom)

    min_num, min_denom = value[1]
    m = float(min_num) / float(min_denom)

    sec_num, sec_denom = value[1]
    s = float(sec_num) / float(sec_denom)

    return d + (m / 60.0) + (s / 3600.0)
#Returns the latitude and longitude, if available, from the get_exif_data function
def get_lat_lon(exif_data):

    lat = None
    lon = None
```

```
    if "GPSInfo" in exif_data:  #Check for tag
        gps_info = exif_data["GPSInfo"]

        gps_latitude = gps_info.get("GPSLatitude")   #Check for tag
        gps_latitude_ref = gps_info.get('GPSLatitudeRef')  #Check for tag
        gps_longitude = gps_info.get('GPSLongitude')  #Check for tag
        gps_longitude_ref = gps_info.get('GPSLongitudeRef')  #Check for tag
        if gps_latitude and gps_latitude_ref and gps_longitude andgps_longitude_ref:
            lat = convert_to_degrees(gps_latitude)
            if gps_latitude_ref != "N":
                lat *= -1

            lon = convert_to_degrees(gps_longitude)
            if gps_longitude ref != "E":
                lon *= -1

    return lat, lon

def processDirectories(directory):



    for root, dirs, files in os.walk(directory):

        for file in files:
            try:  #This tests to see if valid image file
                fname = Image.open(os.path.join(root, file))
                exif_data = get_exif(fname)



                items = get_lat_lon(exif_data)
                e=items
                #','.join(str(i) for i in items)
                print (','.join(str(i) for i in e)+ "," + file)


            except IOError:  #This is raised if NOT image file

                print ('+++++ This is not an image file: ',file)

if __name__ == '__main__':   #Entry point for script

    script, directory = argv  #Assign the variable dictionary the argument
    processDirectories(directory)  #Send argument to the directory function
```

Searching for Files

Examiners may want to search through a file system within a mobile device and identify and output certain files, or at least obtain their names and locations. This would be much like filtering the files by extension in an effort to find important files quickly. Why not write a Python script?

> **Tip** The file extension is important; if the file extension is changed to hide the real file type, this script will not locate the file. However, a simple MIME type script could easily be created with this script to identify the file by its header, which would identify the file even if the user changed the extension.

```
# import all needed modules
import os
from sys import argv
import shutil

#function to walk directory and copy files to tmp location

def processDirectories(directory):

    for root, subdirs, files in os.walk(directory):
            for file in files:

                #Here you can specify ANY file extensions
                if os.path.splitext(file)[1].lower() in ('.db', '.png', '.html'):

     #This will copy out all files with their metadata using copy2
                     shutil.copy2(os.path.join(root, file), os.path.join(tmpDir,file))

   #This line prints to console the files written to the directory
    print('Task Done!, All files were copied to ' +tmpDir +' successfully!')

def create_and_check_path(tmpDir):

#Check first to see if there is this path
    if not os.path.exists(tmpDir):

#If not will create the directory
        os.makedirs(tmpDir)

if __name__ == '__main__':   #Entry point for script
    script,directory = argv

#Use this path as a place you are going to move found files to: You can add any path here

    tmpDir = "C:\Temp\Test"
```

```
#run function to check to see if path is there
create_and_check_path(tmpDir)

#Send argument to the directory function
processDirectories(directory)
```

Hashing a Directory of Files

As you'll recall, obtaining hashes for files is important for verification, validation, and overall case success. Many mobile forensic solutions provide hashes for media only and another for created reports. The examiner can create a hashing script that will enable him or her to hash an entire file system and output that list of data to a CSV. When access to a file system is available, examiners can process and list all files using this script:

```
# import all needed modules
import os
import hashlib
from sys import argv
import datetime


def processDirectories(directory):

    global ProcessCount
    global ErrorCount

    ProcessCount = 0
    ErrorCount = 0

    for root, dirs, files in os.walk(directory):

        for file in files:
            fname = os.path.join(root, file)
            result = hashFile(fname, file)
            if result is True:
             ProcessCount += 1
        else:
            ErrorCount += 1

def hashFile(theFile, simpleName):

    # Is the path is valid
        if os.path.exists(theFile):

              #Verify that the file is real
```

```
if os.path.isfile(theFile):

    try:

    # any errors will be processed in the exception clause

        fp = open(theFile, 'rb')
        fData = fp.read()
        fp.close()

     # stats will get the file information
     # we did not include dates
     # and times will be when copied to local disk.

        theFileStats =  os.stat(theFile)
        (mode, ino, dev, nlink, uid, gid, size, atime,
        mtime, ctime) = os.stat(theFile)

        hashType = 'MD5'
        SHAtype = 'SHA256'

    # Create the hash objects
        hash = hashlib.md5()
        hash256 = hashlib.sha256()

    #  hash the contents obtain from the file
        hash.update(fData)
        hash256.update(fData)

    # extract the hexidecimal version of the hash
        hexMD5 = hash.hexdigest()
        hexSHA = hash256.hexdigest()

    # convert the hex string to upper case
        hexMD5 = hexMD5.upper()
        hexSHA = hexSHA.upper()

    # Print the results
        print ('Filename: {} , Hashtype: {} , {} ,
                Hashtype: {}, {},size: {}.format(
                os.path.basename(theFile), hashType,
                hexMD5, SHAtype, hexSHA, size))
```

```
                except IOError:
                # An exception occured when processing the file
                    print (theFile + ' File Processing Error')


if __name__ == '__main__':

    script, directory = argv
    processDirectories(directory)
```

Using Regular Expressions

Searching across a data set to locate strings and other values can often provide the "smoking gun"; however, most mobile forensic tools do not enable searching across data sets, and if a tool does support searching, it can be limited by what can be searched and how a search can be performed. By creating a Python script, the examiner can create regular expressions for things like credit card numbers, Social Security numbers, name formats, IP addresses, and more. These regular expressions can be controlled within the script to turn on and off what regular expressions will be used. An examiner can also add to the list in the following example when needed. Python is very versatile.

```
# import all needed modules
import os
import glob
from sys import argv
import shutil
import re

#function to walk directory and copy files to tmp location

def processDirectories(directory):

    for root, subdirs, files in os.walk(directory):
            for file in files:

                f = os.path.join(root, file)
                f = open(f, 'rb' )
                file_contents = str(f.read())

                #You can place any string here to look for

                #SocialSecurity ("^\d{3}-\d{2}-\d{4}$")
                #Website
                #("(http://|)(www\.)?([^\.]+)\.(\w{2}|(com|net|¬
                            org|edu|int|mil|gov|arpa|biz|aero|name|coop|info|pro|¬
                            museum))$")
```

```
                #Latitude/Longitude
                #("^[-+]?([1-8]?\d(\.\d+)?|90(\.0+)?),\s*[-+]?(180(\.0+)?|((1[0-
                        7]\d)|([1-9]?\d))(\.\d+)?)$")
#IP Addresses
                #("\b\d{1,3}\.\d{1,3}\.\d{1,3}\.\d{1,3}\b")

                # ********** Paste or Enter your regular expression below

                rxo = re.compile("(?:\d{1,3}\.){3}\d{1,3}")

                #If the string is located it will print out to the console the
                # offset, hit and the filename

                pos = 0
                while 1:
                    evid_hits = rxo.search(file_contents, pos)
                    if not evid_hits: break
                    #for found in evid_hits:
                    print ('Offset: %4s: 4%s filename: 2%s' %
                              (evid_hits.start(), evid_hits.group(),file))
                    pos = evid_hits.end()
                f.close()

if __name__ == '__main__':   #Entry point for script
    script,directory = argv

    #Send argument to the directory function
    processDirectories(directory)
```

Chapter Summary

Building SQLite queries to supplement an automated tool's poor support, or even lack of support, for extracting information from an app is a necessity for today's mobile device investigations. Queries can be built using many free tools along with commercial tools such as the SQLQuery Builder and SQLite Toolkit with little knowledge of SQLite structures and statement building. However, the examiner must understand the `SELECT` command and various others, such as `JOIN`, `ON`, and `WHERE`, even when using an automated query builder. This knowledge will help the examiner explain what the commercial mobile forensic tools are doing when extracting information. Understanding what is "under the hood" will help an examiner build superior queries that extract much more information, surpassing even the most expensive mobile forensic solutions. The information in this chapter showed that data is available and within the examiner's grasp—just build a query and extract it!

SQLite queries cannot be built for files that are not SQLite files, but there are thousands of these types of files within a mobile device. Armed with the power of Python, no file is safe from an examiner's custom Python scripts. Building Python scripts from scratch may seem intimidating, but many online resources can be consulted to help an examiner write scripts. In this chapter, the examiner was exposed to the surface-level scripting needs and rules, along with terminology frequently used to build simple, quick, and effective scripts for mobile device file interrogation. By using this information, an examiner gains the basic skills to complete several tasks using Python. An examiner should be able to take an already built Python script and modify it as needed to complete a specific task. In addition, an examiner should be able to create small scripts using the various statements, variables, expressions, and operands in the Python language. The take-away is the realization that these tools and methods enable an examiner to parse information from any file, any file system, and any mobile device image using custom-built Python scripts. The sky is the limit, and the options are unlimited for an examiner who has the desire and aptitude to learn.

13 Advanced Android Analysis

Android devices are the most widely used smart devices globally. In fact, several web sites (including Android Authority and CNET) report that more than 1 billion Android devices were sold globally in 2014, comprising about 81 percent of all smart phones sold that year (www.androidauthority.com/one-billion-android-phones-2014-583506/). And some research firms forecast that the Android OS will retain that market share of smart phone sales for the next few years (www.businessinsider.com). Consumers can purchase any of the approximately 12,000 Android devices available, including smart phones and tablets. Luckily for the mobile examiner, these devices all have similar file system structures.

This chapter is dedicated to the deconstruction and analysis of the many files stored within the Android file system. As with a logical analysis of Android devices, in order for an examiner to perform an advanced analysis, a file system must be available. Such an analysis can be accomplished using a backup of the device, a noninvasive rooting technique, acquisition via JTAG (Joint Test Action Group), or a chip-off procedure. An examiner can also obtain some app and file system files using the Media Transfer Protocol (MTP) method discussed in Chapter 8, which will obtain the internal storage area along with external media.

As with iOS devices, there is, of course, the "tip of the iceberg data," but that information pales in comparison to the app data, file system cache files, and user storage files that can be found intertwined within the Android file system. Using SQLite queries and Python scripting, as discussed in Chapter 12, the examiner can analyze artifacts that an automated tool is incapable of parsing. Deep analysis of the Android file system should be attempted with each examination. This chapter lists common storage areas, such as SMS, contacts, MMS, and call logs, along with files that are found within most Android file systems. Tables and lists of additional file locations are also revealed throughout the chapter.

As discussed in Chapter 11 with regard to iOS advanced analysis, freefile lists and the write-ahead log (WAL) are also present within an Android device, and this data will be extremely helpful during many examinations. Android malware can also pose a significant problem for the Android operating system, and malware can infiltrate many of the apps from Google or any other Android app repository. An examiner must investigate the possibility of malware within the apps on an Android device, which can add complexity to any Android investigation.

The examination of an Android device should never be limited simply to obtaining a logical collection using a mobile forensic solution's application package (APK) file. Using the correct processes, procedures, and methodologies can yield a monumental amount of investigatory data in any Android mobile forensic examination.

Android Device Information

Android device manufacturers include LG, Samsung, Motorola, ZTE, and others, but it is the underlying file system that is of importance to an examiner, not the manufacturer. The file system is formulated by the Android OS and the version used by the actual device. One Android device might look like an apple while another looks like a banana—but the examiner should understand that the data under the hood, including the file system look and feel, is almost identical in all of them. Granted, an Android device's firmware can make a difference—so Samsung might include some files that Motorola does not, and LG might include some files not found in a ZTE device. The point is that an Android device might look different on the outside, but the underlying file system is remarkably similar.

Examiners should refer to the device examination by operating system type instead of by simply stating they are examining a Samsung Galaxy device. With more than 60 Samsung Galaxy devices on the market, referring to the operating system version first will help solidify the file system variations, since even two of the same Samsung Galaxy devices can be using two different versions of the OS, depending on the carrier. Documenting the OS version can also assist the examiner when analyzing a similar device, because often file system location and other data remain consistent.

The different methods used to obtain the information should not matter so long as a file system is available. The location of data within the file system will not change, whether the image is obtained from a binary dump, backup, or JTAG. The information in this chapter should be used as a map to point the examiner toward the various pots of gold within the Android file system.

Partitions

When an examiner is completing a non-invasive or invasive physical collection of an Android device, he or she can find many partitions within the file system. Some practitioners state that there are six partitions, but from personal experience, I know that there is too much variation among devices to estimate the number of partitions an examiner may encounter—I have encountered four, eight, and even twelve partitions.

Partitioning in Windows creates independent areas on disk, assigns a drive letter, decides where an operating system can be loaded if active, and determines where files can be stored or designated as a program directory. Android devices, however, do not use drive letters, but instead use *mount points*, directories under the root directory (/) that contain the data from each partition. All partitions are within the internal storage of the Android device but are logically separated (see Figure 13-1). The Android system sees partitions as separate, independent media, even though they are mounted in a single logical location under root. This root location is in fact a virtual pointer to the actual location of the data in flash media, and this is evident when you look at a JTAG binary dump or chip-off, where many folders are located under root and contain various file system files and folders.

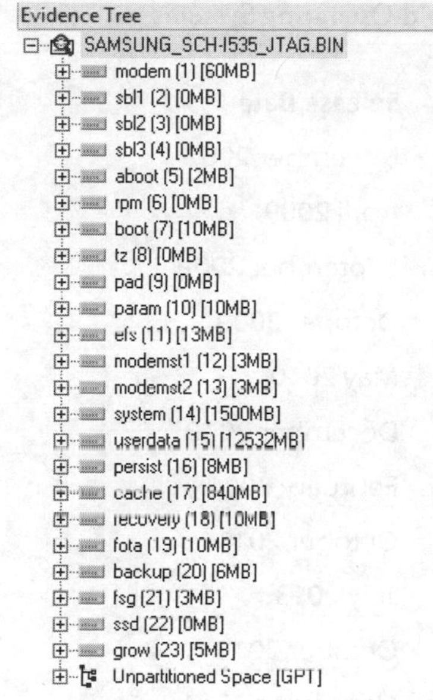

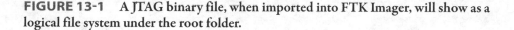

FIGURE 13-1 A JTAG binary file, when imported into FTK Imager, will show as a logical file system under the root folder.

Depending upon the Android's operating system version, an examiner can encounter various options. For example, prior to Honeycomb (version 3.0), the sdcard0 partition would be accessible within the partition table and was often included in a collection by use of a *symlink* (symbolic link) to /mnt/sdcard, the mount point for the media card. However, on device versions later than Gingerbread (version 2.3), the examiner may see another "external media card" that may actually be the internal media card. Because some devices can contain both internal and external media, an examiner should always examine both the sdcard and ext_sd (sdcard2, sd, external_sd) partitions. In addition, some other partitions reside only within certain device families. Table 13-1 shows the Android OS version number, release date, and common name.

For example, Samsung Android devices have a data partition within their file systems called dbdata. With the Samsung Galaxy series, the devices not only kept the legacy dbdata partition but conformed to the other Android operating systems and also included a userdata partition. Samsung devices are the only devices in which the user data is split between the dbdata and userdata partitions, which is observed primarily in Samsung S Series Galaxy devices running Froyo and Gingerbread (2.2 and 2.3) versions of Android. An examiner should know whether both of the partitions are available or the singular dbdata partition is available. When data is split between these two partitions, the personal information manager (PIM) data and "tip of the iceberg data," along with their respective databases, are generally stored in the dbdata partition, and app data, phone settings, and configurations are stored on the userdata partition. If the examiner's solution does not allow for simultaneous importing of both partitions, these locations will have to be individually analyzed to recover valuable user data.

TABLE 13-1 Android Operating Systems

OS Version	Release Date	Common Name
1.0	November 2007	Beta
1.5	April 2009	Cupcake
1.6	September 2009	Donut
2.0	October 2009	Eclair
2.2	May 2010	Froyo
2.3.x	December 2010	Gingerbread
3.0	February 2011	Honeycomb (tablet only)
4.0–4.2.x	October 2011	Ice Cream Sandwich
4.3	July 2013	Jellybean
4.4	October 2013	KitKat
5.0	November 2014	Lollipop (Android L)

When examining an Android device, the examiner usually will be looking through the userdata partition for critical artifacts, but the cache partition often contains valuable data as well. The various file system types, along with paths to various files, will be covered in the following section; Table 13-2 shows various memory partitions and descriptions that might be encountered. Note that this list is not all inclusive but represents partitions commonly encountered.

The File System

The various Android file system types were referenced in Chapter 6 and range from the first Android devices using YAFFS (Yet Another Flash File System) or YAFFS2, to Robust File System (RFS), to the EXT (Extended File System) variants, and F2FS (Flash-Friendly File System) developed by Samsung. If the device utilizes an internal or external media card, various File Allocation Table (FAT) file system formats could be used. These various file systems are currently interpreted by most mobile forensic tools, with the differences in file systems generally being the size of the storage blocks on the flash, journaling, read/write speed, and minimum/maximum file sizes. The newer the device OS version, the larger the block size typically. Today's mobile forensic tools can distinguish and mount these file systems without a problem, displaying a file system to the examiner that can be navigated and parsed. It was typical in the earlier years of Android analysis for the examiner to use Linux tools and command-line tools within Windows to format these file systems and view them properly. That, fortunately, is no longer the case. What this means to the examiner is that the examination and analysis can occur immediately, requiring little work to maintain or rebuild the Android file system's integrity—so the examiner can concentrate on the analysis.

TABLE 13-2 Partitions Encountered Within an Android Mobile Device

Partition Name	Description
boot	RAMDisk, kernel
cache	App and OS cache area: may include artifacts
data	User data, settings, applications, and third-party apps for some Samsung devices; can be represented as userdata as well
dbdata	User data, settings, and some stock applications and settings (Samsung)
emmc	Internal media card
misc	System feature settings; used by the device for configuration and hardware settings
modem	Firmware for modem; hardware dependent
radio	Firmware for radio, cellular, GPS, data connection, and Bluetooth; hardware dependent
recovery	Device stock recovery image often used as alternative boot partition by mobile forensic tools; no user data here unless hidden by user
sdcard	Internal or external media card; for some phones, other partitions could be sd, emmc, and so on, depending on device type and whether internal or external to the device
system	Operating system and settings, built-in application settings
userdata	User data, settings, applications and third-party apps for some Samsung devices; can also be represented as data
wimax	Firmware for WiMAX; hardware dependent

The userdata partition not only contains the user data storage areas but also app information, app configuration files, uncompiled app code, and virtual sandboxed compiled code. With the exceptions mentioned with the dbdata partition, on some Samsung Android devices, the examiner will find a gold mine of information within this area. Not only are user files and app data available, but the actual app code is within the examiner's reach. With the app code, an examiner can also look for malware instances—something a standard logical collection and analysis cannot offer. The cache partition (Figure 13-2) can contain /backup, /lost+found, and /recovery folders. The /backup folder often contains Android app packages with stored temporary data and can yield good artifacts. The /lost+found folder will contain files that had been recovered as a result of file-system corruption and should also be examined. Finally, the /recovery folder holds log files listing the recovery operations of the mobile device.

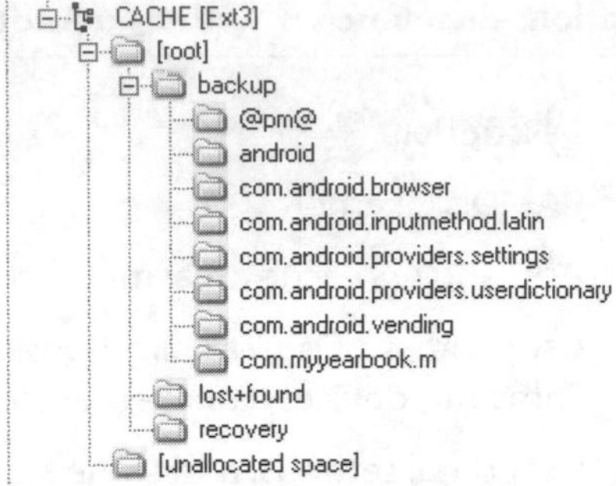

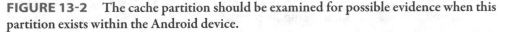

FIGURE 13-2 The cache partition should be examined for possible evidence when this partition exists within the Android device.

Android dbdata and userdata partitions extracted from a Samsung SCH-I500 running version 2.2.3 are shown in Figures 13-3 and 13-4. There are obvious differences between the two partitions in the number of folders and files stored. Within the userdata partition is the majority of user data within an Android file system, including valuable app data and system configuration files; the dbdata partition contains valuable user data in the lone /databases directory. The separation of user data between partitions is not typical, and generally the examiner will concentrate on artifact hunting within the userdata partition and media storage (such as sdcard, emmc, sd) partitions within the Android device output. Outlined in Table 13-3 are good locations for an examiner to investigate when conducting an advanced analysis of an Android's userdata file system.

Unallocated space can be observed within each Android partition. This area typically is unstructured because software is unable to build a file view. Generally, an examiner must use data carving tools to parse through the many blocks of data within this area. Many mobile forensic tools contain some type of data carving tool, but any data carving conducted by a forensic tool should allow for custom file type searching along with typical file types (such as jpeg, .html, .pdf, .doc). FTK, EnCase, and Scalpel are recommended. The carving of unallocated space, when available, should occur because many images, videos, database files, text strings, and other evidentiary files can be recovered from this space. (This luxury of unallocated space is not available for iOS, as discussed in Chapter 11.) Of course, if the file

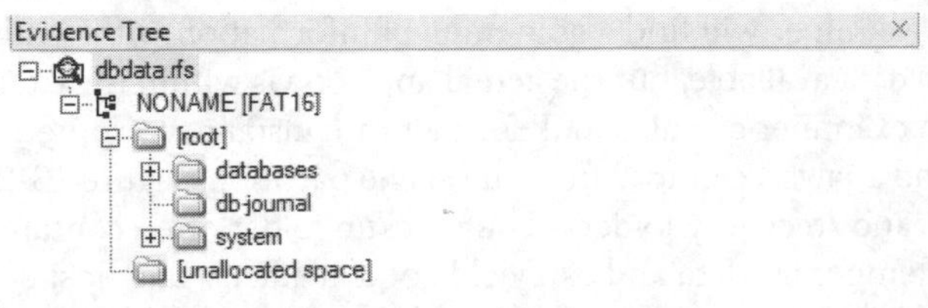

FIGURE 13-3 The dbdata partition in some Samsung Android devices can contain valuable data within the databases folder.

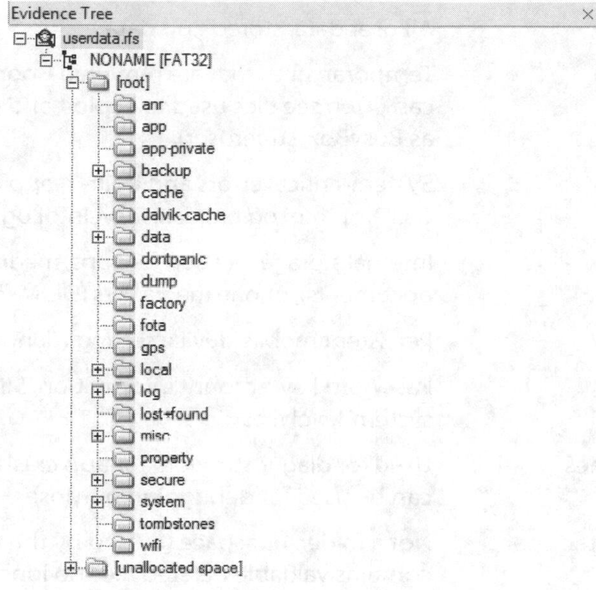

FIGURE 13-4 The userdata (data) partition is much more robust and is found with the dbdata in some Samsung Androids, but is generally by itself.

TABLE 13-3 Android Partitions Compiled to Show the Major Landmarks Within the userdata, dbdata, sdcard, and emmc Partitions

Folder (data partition)	Data Description
anr	(App Not Responding) Debug and threading information, including dates and times for app execution.
app	Android application package files (APK).
app-private	Apps marked as private by the developer for copy protection. Beginning with Android 4.4, an app can have an app-private folder within its own file system, depreciating this folder from use for an app storage or APK file.
backup	File metadata, settings, and other user data marked to be backed up using enterprise, Google, or other backup services.
clipboard	Any data copied and pasted into an app; Samsung devices generally.
davlik-cache	DEX (Dalvik Executable) files for APK files installed on the system. Third-party apps are prefixed with *data@*, system files are prefixed with *system@*.

(Continued)

data	All user data, stored app data.
local/tmp	Temporary files that are removed upon restart. An examiner can often see files used to exploit and obtain root access (such as BusyBox, superuser).
log	System-critical errors and built-in app errors (such as CallDropInfoLog.txt, CallNosvcInfoLog.txt).
media	Internal storage location for apps, media files (images, videos, documents), phone media files (DCIM folder), and phone settings.
property	Persistent mobile device settings (language, country, time zone).
system	Password key, account information, SIM information, and other system-level files
tombstones	Used for diagnostic work for app crashes; contains log files that can be used for debugging purposes.
[unallocated space]	Not a folder, but space unused by the Android system; also contains valuable deleted files no longer used by the system and user apps.
Folder (sdcard/ emmc partition)	
Android/data	App file storage area for third-party apps storing data to the removable media.
DCIM	Thumbnail and camera data.
download	Device storage for downloads from apps, if specified, on the device.
Pictures	Apps storage for editors, apps.
ScreenCapture	Screen shots produced on the Android.
Various app folders	Apps can store data within the root of the media and produce folders to hold media files.
Folder (dbdata partition)	
databases	Storage for user system-level apps.
databases/system	Storage for all installed apps with permissions along with installation paths.

system of an Android device has been encrypted, recovery is much more difficult and sometimes impossible.

Android devices use an encryption based on dm-crypt, which works at the block device layer and can encrypt the device and removable media. This is not a file-level encryption but a full-disk encryption, which differs from iOS encryption. Full-disk encryption on an Android applies only to the user partition (/data), not the entire system. This means that the system partition containing the OS is unencrypted, and often the way in which decryption techniques exploit the OS is via the system partition. The encryption is only as good as the password in place, since the algorithm is based on the complexity of the password or phrase. Some methods exploit devices with unlocked bootloaders, replace the system OS partition, and attempt to capture a user entering a password with a keylogger. Others, such as Santoku Linux, tested up to Android 4.0, brute-force the password or phrase and then use the information to decrypt the user data.

Note The caveat to all of these tools is an unlocked bootloader because using these methods on a locked bootloader can lead to all data on the user partition being wiped.

Also, open source tools such as hashkill can break the passcode or phrase in versions up to Android 4.4, even when another encryption password is used along with the lock PIN or password. Android L (5.x) changed the encryption to rely not only on the PIN or passcode, but also a secondary salt; thus, the currently available methods will not work. Android 5.x devices come out of the box with decryption turned on, but without a password, and using the randomly generated keys shipped with the device, the user data is available when the device is turned on. If the user does not enter a password, the device will still be locked and data will be accessible with forensic tools. Continuous advancements in the Android development community will bring a solution to the collection of these devices soon.

A logical examination of the Android device does not allow access to the device file system, since the methods employed by software solutions simply use an installed APK file to run code to query known databases. If the database has a permission level appropriate for communication with another app, the data can be extracted. As mentioned, access to the internal and external media partitions is accessible with MTP tools and will allow for the collection of this data and give the examiner a file system–like experience—often containing many app storage areas—but access to the /data area of the device is not available unless root access is granted. If an examiner must conduct an advanced analysis of an Android device, the tool or method must either gain root or access via JTAG or chip-off. Some access to app data can be obtained using the built-in backup function within Android versions 4.x and later, but again this is only a portion of the data from the Android user data partition.

Predominate Android File Types

Android devices contain a multitude of file types, ranging from APK, DEX, LOG, SO, ASEC, DB, and JSON, to XML and TXT files. Also included are WAL files and journal files for SQLite databases—significantly more journal files than are found within the iOS file system. As an examiner, the types of files that will be used in artifact investigations will be SQLite and XML files. APK and DEX files can be used for malware investigations, as discussed later in the chapter in the section "Android App Files and Malware."

SQLite databases contain significant information, and an investigator would be remiss if he or she did not conduct a comprehensive analysis of these files. Android SQLite databases are no different from those of iOS and can be examined in much the same way. SQLite databases

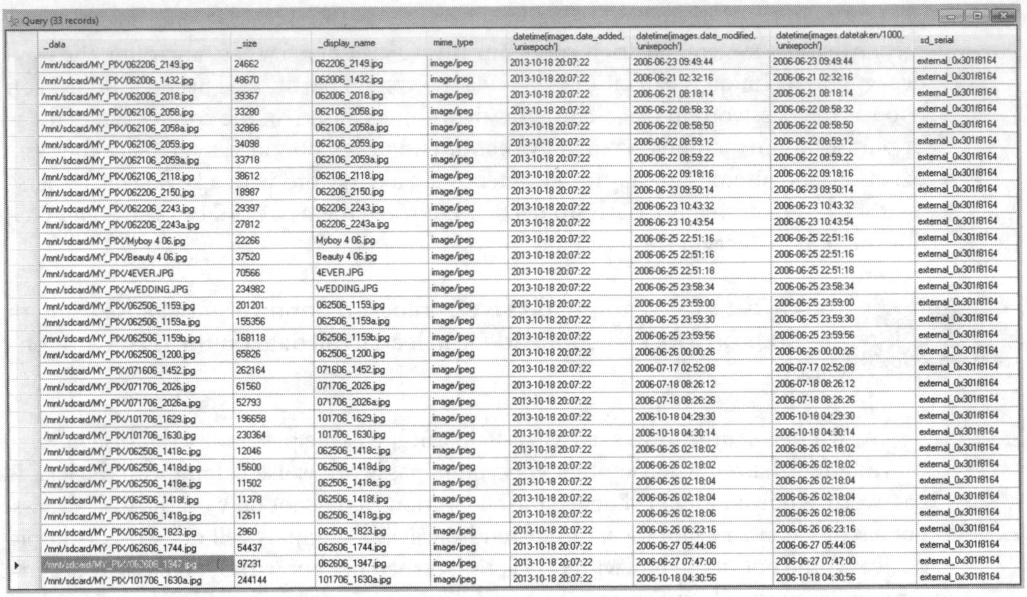

Query (33 records)

_data	_size	_display_name	mime_type	datetime(images.date_added, 'unixepoch')	datetime(images.date_modified, 'unixepoch')	datetime(images.datetaken/1000, 'unixepoch')	sd_serial
/mnt/sdcard/MY_PIX/062206_2149.jpg	24662	062206_2149.jpg	image/jpeg	2013-10-18 20:07:22	2006-06-23 09:49:44	2006-06-23 09:49:44	external_0x301f8164
/mnt/sdcard/MY_PIX/062006_1432.jpg	48670	062006_1432.jpg	image/jpeg	2013-10-18 20:07:22	2006-06-21 02:32:16	2006-06-21 02:32:16	external_0x301f8164
/mnt/sdcard/MY_PIX/062006_2018.jpg	39367	062006_2018.jpg	image/jpeg	2013-10-18 20:07:22	2006-06-21 08:18:14	2006-06-21 08:18:14	external_0x301f8164
/mnt/sdcard/MY_PIX/062106_2058.jpg	33280	062106_2058.jpg	image/jpeg	2013-10-18 20:07:22	2006-06-22 08:58:32	2006-06-22 08:58:32	external_0x301f8164
/mnt/sdcard/MY_PIX/062106_2058a.jpg	32866	062106_2058a.jpg	image/jpeg	2013-10-18 20:07:22	2006-06-22 08:58:50	2006-06-22 08:58:50	external_0x301f8164
/mnt/sdcard/MY_PIX/062106_2059.jpg	34098	062106_2059.jpg	image/jpeg	2013-10-18 20:07:22	2006-06-22 08:59:12	2006-06-22 08:59:12	external_0x301f8164
/mnt/sdcard/MY_PIX/062106_2059a.jpg	33718	062106_2059a.jpg	image/jpeg	2013-10-18 20:07:22	2006-06-22 08:59:22	2006-06-22 08:59:22	external_0x301f8164
/mnt/sdcard/MY_PIX/062106_2118.jpg	38612	062106_2118.jpg	image/jpeg	2013-10-18 20:07:22	2006-06-22 09:18:16	2006-06-22 09:18:16	external_0x301f8164
/mnt/sdcard/MY_PIX/062206_2150.jpg	18987	062206_2150.jpg	image/jpeg	2013-10-18 20:07:22	2006-06-23 09:50:14	2006-06-23 09:50:14	external_0x301f8164
/mnt/sdcard/MY_PIX/062206_2243.jpg	29397	062206_2243.jpg	image/jpeg	2013-10-18 20:07:22	2006-06-23 10:43:32	2006-06-23 10:43:32	external_0x301f8164
/mnt/sdcard/MY_PIX/062206_2243a.jpg	27812	062206_2243a.jpg	image/jpeg	2013-10-18 20:07:22	2006-06-23 10:43:54	2006-06-23 10:43:54	external_0x301f8164
/mnt/sdcard/MY_PIX/Myboy 4 06.jpg	22266	Myboy 4 06.jpg	image/jpeg	2013-10-18 20:07:22	2006-06-25 22:51:16	2006-06-25 22:51:16	external_0x301f8164
/mnt/sdcard/MY_PIX/Beauty 4 06.jpg	37520	Beauty 4 06.jpg	image/jpeg	2013-10-18 20:07:22	2006-06-25 22:51:16	2006-06-25 22:51:16	external_0x301f8164
/mnt/sdcard/MY_PIX/4EVER.JPG	70566	4EVER.JPG	image/jpeg	2013-10-18 20:07:22	2006-06-25 22:51:18	2006-06-25 22:51:18	external_0x301f8164
/mnt/sdcard/MY_PIX/WEDDING.JPG	234982	WEDDING.JPG	image/jpeg	2013-10-18 20:07:22	2006-06-25 23:58:34	2006-06-25 23:58:34	external_0x301f8164
/mnt/sdcard/MY_PIX/062506_1159.jpg	201201	062506_1159.jpg	image/jpeg	2013-10-18 20:07:22	2006-06-25 23:59:00	2006-06-25 23:59:00	external_0x301f8164
/mnt/sdcard/MY_PIX/062506_1159a.jpg	155356	062506_1159a.jpg	image/jpeg	2013-10-18 20:07:22	2006-06-25 23:59:30	2006-06-25 23:59:30	external_0x301f8164
/mnt/sdcard/MY_PIX/062506_1159b.jpg	168118	062506_1159b.jpg	image/jpeg	2013-10-18 20:07:22	2006-06-25 23:59:56	2006-06-25 23:59:56	external_0x301f8164
/mnt/sdcard/MY_PIX/062506_1200.jpg	65826	062506_1200.jpg	image/jpeg	2013-10-18 20:07:22	2006-06-26 00:00:26	2006-06-26 00:00:26	external_0x301f8164
/mnt/sdcard/MY_PIX/071606_1452.jpg	262164	071606_1452.jpg	image/jpeg	2013-10-18 20:07:22	2006-07-17 02:52:08	2006-07-17 02:52:08	external_0x301f8164
/mnt/sdcard/MY_PIX/071706_2026.jpg	61560	071706_2026.jpg	image/jpeg	2013-10-18 20:07:22	2006-07-18 08:26:12	2006-07-18 08:26:12	external_0x301f8164
/mnt/sdcard/MY_PIX/071706_2026a.jpg	52793	071706_2026a.jpg	image/jpeg	2013-10-18 20:07:22	2006-07-18 08:26:26	2006-07-18 08:26:26	external_0x301f8164
/mnt/sdcard/MY_PIX/101706_1629.jpg	196658	101706_1629.jpg	image/jpeg	2013-10-18 20:07:22	2006-10-18 04:29:30	2006-10-18 04:29:30	external_0x301f8164
/mnt/sdcard/MY_PIX/101706_1630.jpg	230364	101706_1630.jpg	image/jpeg	2013-10-18 20:07:22	2006-10-18 04:30:14	2006-10-18 04:30:14	external_0x301f8164
/mnt/sdcard/MY_PIX/062506_1418c.jpg	12046	062506_1418c.jpg	image/jpeg	2013-10-18 20:07:22	2006-06-26 02:18:02	2006-06-26 02:18:02	external_0x301f8164
/mnt/sdcard/MY_PIX/062506_1418d.jpg	15600	062506_1418d.jpg	image/jpeg	2013-10-18 20:07:22	2006-06-26 02:18:02	2006-06-26 02:18:02	external_0x301f8164
/mnt/sdcard/MY_PIX/062506_1418e.jpg	11502	062506_1418e.jpg	image/jpeg	2013-10-18 20:07:22	2006-06-26 02:18:04	2006-06-26 02:18:04	external_0x301f8164
/mnt/sdcard/MY_PIX/062506_1418f.jpg	11378	062506_1418f.jpg	image/jpeg	2013-10-18 20:07:22	2006-06-26 02:18:04	2006-06-26 02:18:04	external_0x301f8164
/mnt/sdcard/MY_PIX/062506_1418g.jpg	12611	062506_1418g.jpg	image/jpeg	2013-10-18 20:07:22	2006-06-26 02:18:06	2006-06-26 02:18:06	external_0x301f8164
/mnt/sdcard/MY_PIX/062506_1823.jpg	2960	062506_1823.jpg	image/jpeg	2013-10-18 20:07:22	2006-06-26 06:23:16	2006-06-26 06:23:16	external_0x301f8164
/mnt/sdcard/MY_PIX/062606_1744.jpg	54437	062606_1744.jpg	image/jpeg	2013-10-18 20:07:22	2006-06-27 05:44:06	2006-06-27 05:44:06	external_0x301f8164
/mnt/sdcard/MY_PIX/062606_1947.jpg	97231	062606_1947.jpg	image/jpeg	2013-10-18 20:07:22	2006-06-27 07:47:00	2006-06-27 07:47:00	external_0x301f8164
/mnt/sdcard/MY_PIX/101706_1630a.jpg	244144	101706_1630a.jpg	image/jpeg	2013-10-18 20:07:22	2006-10-18 04:30:56	2006-10-18 04:30:56	external_0x301f8164

FIGURE 13-5 Collecting SQLite information manually parsed from apps that are not supported by any automated tool is a necessity with Android devices, such as the MediaStore database from com.android.providers.media.

contain tables and fields with user preferences, data, and any persistent data the user and app needs stored for later use. Hundreds of thousands of apps are available for installation on any Android device, and mobile forensic solutions cover only 0.01 percent of the available applications. Of those supported apps, automatic parsing of data is often flawed. Because apps can change upon each update, a mobile solution is often outdated at release, so these solutions are always at a technological disadvantage. An examiner who can parse apps manually will always have the upper hand on these advances. Figure 13-5 shows an example of parsed data from a SQLite database.

XML (EXtensible Markup Language) is used extensively within the Android file system for settings, passwords, application protocols, network data sharing, and other preferences. The most significant XML files are located in the shared_pref folder within the app folders (see Figure 13-6). XML is a file type that uses `<?xml version="1.0" encoding="utf-8"?>` as a header, with a set of rules for encoding documents in machine-readable form. As discussed in Chapter 12, XML can be cleanly parsed using Python scripts to decode and display the key and values listed within the file.

Other file types within the Android file system include text files, log files, APKs, and DEX files, as discussed in the following sections.

```xml
<?xml version="1.0" encoding="utf-8" standalone="yes" ?>
- <map>
    <boolean name="accept_cookies" value="true" />
    <int name="double_tap_zoom" value="5" />
    <string name="bbp_group_state">{}</string>
    <boolean name="enable_javascript" value="true" />
    <boolean name="show_security_warnings" value="true" />
    <string name="notification_state">ON</string>
    <boolean name="enable_hardware_accel_skia" value="false" />
    <string name="default_text_encoding">AutoDetect</string>
    <long name="last_recovered" value="1402691823889" />
    <string name="link_prefetch_when">WIFI_ONLY</string>
    <string name="default_zoom">MEDIUM</string>
    <string name="preload_when">WIFI_ONLY</string>
    <boolean name="remember_passwords" value="false" />
    <boolean name="reset_default_preferences" value="false" />
    <boolean name="debug_menu" value="false" />
    <string name="colors">colorize3</string>
    <boolean name="load_page" value="true" />
    <boolean name="block_popup_windows" value="true" />
    <string name="download_default_storage">MEMORY_CARD</string>
    <string name="search_engine">google</string>
    <long name="last_autologin_time" value="1375045949282" />
    <boolean name="load_images" value="false" />
    <boolean name="privacy_clear_geolocation_access" value="false" />
    <int name="text_zoom" value="10" />
    <boolean name="enable_geolocation" value="true" />
    <null name="keep_download_default_storage" />
    <boolean name="save_formdata" value="true" />
    <string name="plugin_state">ON</string>
    <string name="last_read_allow_geolocation_origins">http://www.google.co.uk http://www.google.com</string>
    <boolean name="autofill_enabled" value="true" />
    <string name="factoryreset_url">http://search-results.mobi/?
      sourceid=6&app=YKbThEQe8tE26gy4mmcniwE3KP1JpiEjMK2Lt2pPRwzrt0KoZN9IeKY0HeNcBEagpx4ot1OOLDvCtJ5
      2FOS1foP%2BdabOrYaVXUd3</string>
    <boolean name="last_paused" value="true" />
  </map>
```


FIGURE 13-6 XML files found within an app's shared_pref folder can be used by an examiner to obtain critical investigation data.

Artifacts

Much like iOS, an Android device is full of digital gold if the file system is obtainable. Hundreds of SQLite databases, XML files, text files, media files, and more are stored within the user data area of the device. A logical extraction of an Android device still yields some great data, but the information has no "meat"—in other words, the information displayed is simply a query of the appropriate database, and the data is rendered to the examiner within the user interface. What about the files this data came from? These files contain valuable fields that might not have been queried by the mobile forensic solution's APK file but can be accessed if the file is obtained. Also, deleted data within the database free pages can be recovered, as discussed in Chapter 11 with iOS, along with the WAL files that are used. This "tip of the iceberg data" and its locations are listed in Table 13-4 (in the next section) to assist the examiner in recovering the data that cannot be recovered with a logical collection.

Additional files such as system files, log files, and user settings within the Android file system are also available and can reveal many things about the device, including the OS version, mobile device specifics, user information, and other items pertinent to mobile devices use. By relying on a standard logical Android collection, the examiner is limiting his or her examination to a very small percentage of the available data within the mobile device.

"Tip of the Iceberg Data"

The mobile forensic solutions used by the examiner often collect significant data from an Android device. This data is *active* data from the databases within the user data and typically includes data from contacts, call logs, SMS, MMS, media, browser, Wi-Fi, and a few others. This is the "tip of the iceberg data," with the bulk of the information residing "underwater," however—even more so than with iOS. Because an Android logical extraction queries only the active data, the inactive or free page data or any other field not queried will not be collected. At least with iOS, an examiner would have access to the database the mobile solution queried to obtain the data presented in the user interface—but with Android, not so much.

However, using advanced collection methods, the examiner can collect the entire file system, including database files and others, for advanced analysis. Table 13-4 represents the typical data that is extracted using a mobile solution's APK file. Using the associated paths, the examiner can investigate the various database files for additional information. Also, information logically obtained by the mobile forensic solution can be verified and validated to ensure that dates and times are accurate along with any missing fields from the reported data. An examiner can pull additional information from these locations that the logical collection missed.

TABLE 13-4 Standard "Tip of the Iceberg" Android Data, with Database Locations for Additional Analysis when Needed and Validation on Automated Parsing by Forensic Tools

Artifact	Path and Description
Bluetooth devices	/data/com.android.bluetooth/btopp.db
Browser bookmarks	/data/com.android.browser/browser.db Or if dbdata exists, /dbdata/databases/com.android.browser/browser.db Bookmarks table in browser.db and bookmark = 1
Browser history	/data/com.android.browser/browser.db Or if dbdata exists, /dbdata/databases/com.android.browser/browser.db Bookmarks table in browser.db and bookmark = 0
Browser searches	/data/com.android.browser/browser.db Or if dbdata exists, /dbdata/databases/com.android.browser/browser.db Searches table in browser.db

Call history	/data/com.android.providers.contacts/contacts2.db **Motorola:** /data/com.motorola.blur.providers.contacts/contacts2.db Calls table in contacts2.db **Samsung:** /data/com.sec.android.provider.logsprovider/logs.db Or if dbdata exists, /dbdata/databases/com.sec.android.provider.logsprovider/logs.db Calls in log table and logtype = 100
Contacts	/data/com.android.providers.contacts/contacts2.db Or if dbdata exists, /dbdata/databases/com.android.providers.contacts/contacts2.db
Media (images, video, audio)	/data/com.android.providers.media/external.db or if dbdata exists /dbdata/databases/com.android.providers.media/external.db This is the mediastore that is used to determine the location of media files cached and used by forensic tools to location media on the device.
MMS	/data/com.android.providers.telephony/mmssms.db Or if dbdata exists, /dbdata/databases/com.android.providers.telephony/mmssms.db MMS in PDU table
SMS	/data/com.android.providers.telephony/mmssms.db Or if dbdata exists, /dbdata/databases/com.android.providers.telephony/mmssms.db SMS in SMS table
Installed apps	/system/packages.list—text file no permission listings /system/packages.xml—XML file with app permissions
Wi-Fi hotspots	/misc/wifi/wpa_supplicant.conf /wifi/bcm_supp.conf

Additional File System Locations

A common mistake made by many examiners is to begin the investigation immediately by going to the app area. Although the app area is a fruitful place and often mesmerizes even the most seasoned examiners, a better idea is to venture into many other areas within the Android file system.

Device configuration files, installed application accounts and device accounts, user settings, device details, and often password information can be gleaned from outside of the app

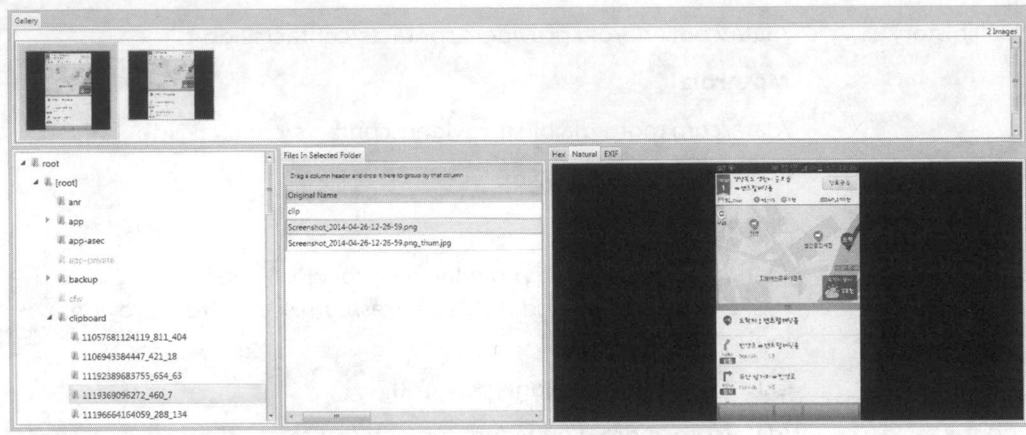

FIGURE 13-7 **A clip file along with the associated image files**

data folder. Needless to say, the actual APK file and the compiled DEX files can be obtained in a file system–level extraction. With the actual files, static malware analysis of the code within the APK and DEX files often helps determine whether malicious code is present. The following section will outline some of the more plentiful areas for gathering system information. All of the root directory information and path data is located in Table 13-3 earlier in this chapter.

Clipboard Information

The path /clipboard/ is generally found only within a Samsung Android device and contains various folders, each identified with a unique number. Pure Android systems store clipboard data in RAM by the Clipboard service. However, each folder holds a file called *clip* (see Figure 13-7). The clip file header holds a value, `android.sec.clipboard.list.ClipboardData`*`<type of data>`* and the end of the header is `xpt`*X* (X = a variable value that changes depending upon the clip file). If the *`<type of data>`* is `text`, the clipboard content will be a text string; if it's `HTML`, it's a web page; if `Bitmap`, it's an image file. If a bitmap is indicated within the header, the image files will be in the same folder as the clip file. If text or HTML, the data immediately follows the header.

Log Files

In Samsung devices, services report errors and then log these errors within the log folder for exceptions within an app or device service. An examiner can find significant information in this folder and associated text files. Some text files of interest are listed here:

- **/log/CallDropInfoLog.txt** Listing of failed calls along with the dates and times of the dropped calls. The date is in the format YYYY.MM.DD HH:MM:SS.
- **/log/CallNosvcInfoLog.txt** Listing of calls that were attempted when the device did not have service. The date is in the format YYYY.MM.DD HH:MM:SS.

- **/log/dumpstate_app_error_x.txt.gz** If more than one dumpstate file is within the folder, the *x* will be an ordinal number. This file is a compressed folder created when an app crashes with an uncaught runtime exception. Tools such as 7-Zip can be used to access dumpstate files. Android versions up to 4.4.2 can contain significant user logins, settings, and more. The dumpstate file captures the state of the device at the time of the app failure, often producing data that cannot be found anywhere on the device. Android 4.4.4 patched some of these vulnerabilities. The following illustration shows a log file produced within an Android 2.3 Samsung SGH-I727 device. It clearly indicates an incoming message alert from a phone number that was critical to an investigation, since the date and time were also logged.

```
[1084109088,com.android.mms/.transaction.MessagingNotificationAlert,6068]08-25 14:42:59.281   308   486 I notification_cancel
content_query_sample: [content://com.android.contacts/data,raw_contact_id,data1='+18018227746',,136,,28]08-25 14:42:59.321
4004961172862388177,7624391]08-25 14:42:59.381   308 18845 I notification_cancel: [com.android.phone,7,0]08-25 14:42:59.451
```

- **/log/dumpstate_app_anr_x.txt.gz** If more than one dumpstate file is within the folder, the *x* will be an ordinal number. This file is a compressed folder that is created when an app receives an App Not Responding (ANR) event. A message to the user of the device is generated, indicating that the app is not responding and the log will be created. This file can be opened with tools such as 7-Zip. By using regular expressions formatted for e-mail, there is a possibility that data can be recovered. Android 4.4.4 patched some of these vulnerabilities.
- **/log/dumpstate_app_native_x.txt.gz** If more than one dumpstate file is within the folder, the *x* will be an ordinal number. This file is a compressed folder that is created when an app error occurs during a process. This error does not cause an exception and subsequent crash, and the user is not notified because this process is moved into the background services. This file can be opened with tools such as 7-Zip. By using search terms such as *contentView*, *contentText,* and *tickerText,* an examiner can find relevant data within some Samsung device log files. Android 4.4.4 patched some of these vulnerabilities.

System Configuration

Settings that persist over restarts on an Android device can be stored within the /property folder and can assist an examiner in determining user and device settings. These files are all prefixed with *persist* and then the <data description>.

- **/property/persist.radio.cdma.mdn** This setting within a CDMA device, if available, will show the device's mobile dialing number (MDN), the device phone number.
- **/property/persist.service.adb.enable** This setting indicates whether or not Android Debug Bridge (ADB) is enabled on the device. This is a Boolean value; 0 is false and 1 is true. This will generally be 1 if the device was collected using mobile forensic tools, so the state will not determine whether the user had enabled ADB. However, if the examiner uses JTAG or chip-off techniques, this value will be indicative of the user's actions.
- **/property/persist.sys.country** This setting indicates the country in which the device service is registered, which may or may not indicate where the device was last or is currently located. This will be a two-character representation such as US, KR, or UK.

- **/property/persist.sys.language** This setting indicates the language the device is currently set to display and use, represented by two characters; these identify the culture code used by the device for letters, numbers, signs, and so on.
- **/property/persist.sys.timezone** This setting is the last system time zone update to the device. Since most mobile devices update their time zone, this value will represent the last time zone location of the device. This can be obtained via a cellular or Wi-FI connection, so an examiner must be sure to isolate the device because this value could update if the device connects to another network.
- **/property/persist.usb.config** This value indicates what services will be enabled when the device is plugged into a computer. Some examples:
    - **mtp** Only MTP will be available.
    - **mtp, adb** Both services will be active when the device is plugged in. This will be seen frequently if the examiner is using mobile forensic tools that root the device, and a true value will generally be available only with a JTAG or chip-off collection.
- **/property/persist.mot.encrypt.mmc** This Boolean value is present only in a Motorola Android and indicates whether or not the external media card will be encrypted.

Usage and Logs

The /system folder contains a wealth of information for the examiner, including more settings and storage files for Android system functions, account information, security information, and app listings.

- **/system/accounts.db** This SQLite database lists all of the accounts that are used on the Android device. The app username and password can be located in this file. As of version 2.3, the password value is no longer plain text but a base64 encrypted value. For an examiner, this can be valuable information for identifying usernames for specific Android accounts.
- **/system/dmappmgr.db** This is a fantastic SQLite database (Figure 13-8) for an examiner to determine apps that are frequently used and apps that had at one time been installed on the device and are no longer there, including the last time the app was launched. For an examiner, being able to determine app usage and services used can be critical to an investigation.
- **/system/gesture.key** This file contains the SHA-1 value of the device gesture lock if it was used. The gesture.key file is a hash of the pattern in a byte array. Many online sources can be used to obtain the gesture coordinates from the SHA-1 hash, but this is not really necessary for an analysis of the file system. If the examiner wanted to examine the device powered on and navigate the user interface, he or she could replace the gesture.key with a hash that has been generated in another Android device and use that file instead of the original. The examiner can then enter the created gesture to unlock the device.
- **/system/packages.list** This text file identifies the app location and app that is currently on the Android device.
- **/system/packages.xml** This XML file identifies the app location and app that is currently on the Android device and the app permissions.
- **/system/password.key** This file contains the salted SHA-1/MD5 calculation concatenated. The salt is located in the settings.db secure table under the key

Query (379 records)

_id	pkgname	datetime(ApplicationControl.lastpaus 'unixepoch')	datetime(ApplicationControl.applastservices 'unixepoch')	datetime(ApplicationControl.applastservicestoptime/ 'unixepoch')	totalusagetime	launchcount	datetime(ApplicationControl.lastlaunchtime/ 'unixepoch')
1	com.google.android.gsf	2012-12-13 15:30:42	2014-05-15 21:41:20	2014-05-16 01:30:23		58	2012-12-13 15:30:42
2	com.google.android.setupwizard	2012-01-01 00:01:01				2	2012-01-01 00:01:01
3	com.osp.app.signin	2013-12-12 04:38:47	2014-05-15 21:41:39	2014-05-16 01:30:23		23	2013-12-12 04:38:44
4	com.android.settings	2014-05-16 00:19:16	2014-05-15 20:39:25	2014-05-15 21:36:32		992	2014-05-16 00:19:11
5	com.google.android.gsf.login	2013-10-09 01:35:07				15	2013-10-09 01:34:55
6	com.android.contacts	2014-05-14 21:47:34	2014-05-15 21:41:17	2014-05-16 01:30:22		7210	2014-05-14 21:47:27
7	com.sec.android.app.launcher	2014-05-16 01:30:21				152877	2014-05-16 00:19:16
8	com.android.phone	2014-05-14 16:20:00				7003	2014-05-14 16:20:00
9	com.sec.android.app.SecSetupWizard	2012-01-01 00:01:01				8	2012-01-01 00:00:58
10	com.google.android.location	2012-09-13 07:26:01	2014-05-15 21:41:00	2014-05-16 01:30:22		2	2012-09-13 07:25:58
11	com.skt.skaf.Z0000SLOAD		2013-08-04 11:46:42	2013-08-05 09:51:00			
12	com.sec.phone		2014-05-15 21:41:17	2014-05-16 01:30:22			
13	com.sec.pcw		2014-05-15 21:41:17	2014-05-16 01:30:23			
14	com.sec.android.fotaclient	2012-12-16 09:37:20	2014-05-15 21:41:20	2014-05-16 01:30:22		2	2012-12-16 09:37:05
15	com.google.android.partnersetup		2014-05-15 21:41:20	2014-05-16 01:30:22			
16	com.skt.iwlan		2014-05-15 21:41:21	2014-05-16 01:30:22			
17	com.sec.android.providers.downloads		2014-05-15 21:41:28	2014-05-16 01:30:23			
18	com.android.exchange		2014-05-15 21:41:25	2014-05-16 01:30:23			
19	com.android.systemui	2014-04-13 23:55:54	2014-05-15 21:40:57	2014-05-16 01:30:23		6	2014-04-13 23:55:54
20	com.android.providers.calendar		2014-05-16 00:19:05	2014-05-16 00:27:44			
21	com.vlingo.midas	2012-12-18 06:30:53	2014-05-15 21:41:22	2014-05-16 01:30:22		35	2012-12-18 06:30:35
22	com.google.android.gm	2014-05-14 06:37:55	2014-05-15 21:41:39	2014-05-16 01:30:23		2167	2014-05-14 06:37:43
23	com.google.android.talk	2013-12-08 03:25:21	2014-05-15 21:41:29	2014-05-16 01:30:22		8	2013-12-08 03:25:16
24	com.amldm		2014-05-15 21:41:30	2014-05-16 01:30:23			
25	com.android.email	2014-05-13 05:19:30	2014-05-15 21:41:25	2014-05-16 01:30:23		1536	2014-05-13 05:19:21
26	com.sec.chaton	2012-09-23 15:02:07	2014-05-15 21:42:02	2014-05-16 01:30:22		3	2012-09-23 15:02:00
27	com.broadcom.bms		2012-12-13 15:30:41	2012-12-16 08:58:12			
28	com.sec.android.app.factorymode		2014-05-14 03:03:37	2014-05-15 21:36:31			
29	com.tms	2013-05-01 00:50:39	2012-09-10 16:11:28	2012-09-13 00:05:40		18	2013-05-01 00:50:35
30	com.android.ahnmobilesecurity	2012-10-27 13:34:13	2014-05-15 21:41:29	2014-05-16 01:30:23		4	2012-10-27 13:33:37
31	com.android.mms	2014-05-15 08:16:23	2014-05-15 21:41:08	2014-05-16 01:30:22		4658	2014-05-15 08:16:18
32	com.sec.dsm.system	2012-09-22 09:40:42	2014-05-15 21:41:20	2014-05-16 01:30:23		2	2012-09-22 09:40:25
33	com.android.providers.media	2014-02-02 13:11:03	2014-05-15 22:27:18	2014-05-16 01:30:23		18	2014-02-02 13:10:18
34	com.skt.skaf.OA00018282		2014-05-15 21:41:45	2014-05-16 01:30:23			
35	com.android.providers.downloads		2014-05-15 21:41:00	2014-05-16 01:30:23			
36	com.iloen.melon	2012-12-28 07:00:09	2013-08-05 22:46:21	2013-08-10 13:43:02		4	2012-12-28 06:59:52
37	com.samsung.map		2014-05-15 21:41:19	2014-05-16 01:30:23			
38	com.google.android.syncadapters.contacts		2014-05-15 21:41:20	2014-05-16 01:30:23			
39	com.sec.android.app.music	2014-05-13 05:10:33	2014-05-10 00:19:36	2014-05-13 07:11:44		1134	2014-05-13 05:10:26

FIGURE 13-8 Actual dmappmgr.db from Samsung Android device showing the 379 app records outlining the app name, number of launches, and critical date and time information

lockscreen.password_salt within the /data/com.android.providers.settings folder. Again, if the examiner is looking at this file, access has already been made, and accessing the device via the UI is probably unnecessary. If it is necessary, the examiner can use the salt and the hash with a tool such as Hashkill.

- **/system/SimCard.dat** This text file lists the previous and current SIM operator, SIMSerialNumber, PhoneNumber, CurrentSIMCountry, SIMOperator, SIMOperatorName, CurrentSIMSerialNumber, and SimChangeTime, which is encoded in milliseconds. For an examiner, this can be a location to obtain the SIM information of previous UICC cards inserted and the current UICC, even if the UICC is not in the device at the time of collection.
- **/system/sync/accounts.xml** Android devices enable the user to sync all data across accounts. For an examiner, this can create recoverable evidence because the account usernames for apps are listed in this file. The examiner can link the username to the associated app using the information found in the accounts.xml file.
- **/system/usagestats/usage - <*date*>** These files can assist the examiner when looking for apps on a particular date. The text file is named *usage - <YYYYMMDD>* and is a Unicode binary file.

Wi-Fi Information

Wi-Fi information can be critical for many investigations. The data located within the /misc/wifi folder is recoverable and contains Wi-Fi and hotspot information. This data often shows the SSID and configuration settings.

- **/misc/wifi/wpa_supplicant.conf or /wifi/bcm_supp.conf** With logical extractions using an APK, the Wi-Fi information is collected, often without passwords. By navigating to the location within the file system, the examiner can locate each Wi-Fi spot to which the device was connected, along with the SSID and password. This information is stored within a dictionary and is readable in a text editor (see Figure 13-9).
- **/misc/wifi/hostapd.conf** If the device was set as a hotspot, the information in this file will identify the SSID that was transmitted by the device and the hash of the password.
- **/misc/wifi/softap.conf** The SSID of the hotspot and password configuration.

```
network={
     ssid="38000BD-302"
     psk="3800obd302"
     priority=1
}

network={
     ssid="timeoutboise"
     key_mgmt=NONE
     priority=2
}

network={
     ssid="807Wind"
     psk="807windemere"
     key_mgmt=WPA-PSK
     priority=3
}

network={
     ssid="BWLasVegasWest"
     key_mgmt=NONE
     priority=4
}

network={
     ssid="NewRoyalPlaya"
     key_mgmt=NONE
     priority=12
}

network={
     ssid="NewRoyalPlaya388"
     key_mgmt=NONE
     priority=13
}

```

FIGURE 13-9 Information from the wpa_supplicant.conf file is clearly readable within a text editor and contains access point names and passwords.

/data Folder

The primary source for examiner gold is the /data folder. This folder contains not only the stock Android apps such as e-mail, contacts, call logs, SMS, and MMS, but device-specific apps, which may be found only on Samsung devices. This folder will also contain third-party apps and content. Unlike iOS, which had a distinct folder for iOS stock apps and another for third-party apps, the Android does not make that distinction. All apps and even some Android settings files are located within the /data folder. As referenced previously in Table 13-4, some Samsung devices also use a dbdata partition to store this same data, and references within this section will indicate this distinction. This section covers Android settings locations, stock Android apps, some Samsung-specific databases, and third-party apps.

Like iOS, Android will prescribe to the reverse-DNS naming scheme for the apps located in this folder using the top-level domain (such as com, net, kr, org), the domain, and then the app name as the package name (pkg). Some apps use subdomains as well. For example, Samsung uses com.sec to prefix its stock applications (*sec* stands for Samsung Electrical Company).

The app folders have a hierarchy much like that of iOS. Android development API and SDK guidelines direct developers on how an app should store data, but like iOS, an app can create folders and store data in these folders if it must persist. Android does indicate that some folders must be used for certain circumstances, and these folders and the other common folders are outlined in Table 13-5.

Stock Android Folders

Android devices usually contain these folders within the /data folder. Android has two levels of locations that store data—one level uses com.android.providers.<*name of app*> and the other uses com.android.<*name of app*>. The com.android.providers apps use the android.providers class, which allows other apps to access the content providers within the apps that are using

TABLE 13-5 App Folder Common Directories and Associated Content

Folder	Description
/cache	Temporary data for the Android application. This folder can have many subfolders organized according to the type of files within the folder (such as audio, image, upload).
/databases	One or more SQLite databases to support the main app and significant data for the examiner.
/files	App files that do not belong within the database or are referenced from the database. An app developer can use this area for many different file types.
/lib	Library files for the app. These files are generally .so files, which are library files for Linux and used by the app to perform functions.
shared_prefs	Settings that can be accessible by other apps and the mobile device. These files are often XML files that can contain valuable information for an examiner.

this class. These apps are generally those with contacts, images, calendar, and SMS. An examiner should recognize all of these items using this class since most of them are artifacts that can be extracted using a logical collection. Because mobile forensic solutions use an APK file to access the content stores within an Android device, the accessible data types must conform to the classes allowed by Android. The standard com.android apps are stock Android apps that ship with the OS; they do not generally allow com.android.provider type control and are infrequently used. A few stock com.android apps contain data, such as com.android .browser, but typically these apps are void of user data. The following stock Android folders are the places an examiner will likely uncover valuable data on each Android investigation:

- **/data/com.android.browser/databases/browser2.db** This is the SQLite database of the built-in Android browser that contains tables for bookmarks, history, and user searches. This area should be investigated even if the mobile solution parses this data, because some columns are not reported by automated solutions.
- **/dbdata/databases/com.android.browser/databases/browser.db** Same as the previous entry, but this location can be found within some Samsung devices, particularly the Samsung Galaxy S series.
- **/data/com.android.browser/databases/autofill.db** This SQLite database stores user saved information such as name and address information to be filled into forms stored within the browser history.
- **/data/com.android.browser/app-databases/Databases.db** This SQLite database stores the app and path information for apps using the Android web browser via WebKit functions. The mobile web app database will be stored within the app-databases folder identified within the Databases.db and can be explored to uncover use of that mobile web app.
- **/dbdata/databases/com.android.browser/app-databases/Databases.db** Same as the previous entry, but this location can be found within some Samsung devices, particularly the Samsung Galaxy S series.
- **/data/com.android.browser/app-geolocation/CachedGeoposition.db** This SQLite database stores the app geolocation information if the user enables this feature when asked within the browser. This is typically seen within WebKit apps such as Yelp, Walmart, Google, and many others. This file will show the date and time, in milliseconds, when the location was requested.
- **/dbdata/databases/com.android.browser/app-geolocation/CachedGeoposition.db** Same as the previous entry, but this location can be found within some Samsung devices, particularly the Samsung Galaxy S series.
- **/data/com.android.email/databases/EmailProvider.db** This SQLite database stores the built-in Android e-mail client data for the user. The primary tables are Message, Attachment, and EmailAddressCache. The secondary database located in this same folder is called EmailProviderBody.db, and it contains the actual content of the entire e-mail message JOINed using the messageKey in the body table. Of course, if a user uses another app for e-mail, these databases could hold limited information.
- **/data/com.android.email/cache/** This folder can store many files that were embedded into the sent e-mails, including pictures, HTML banners, and much more. An examiner can find many artifacts in the cache area that have been deleted from e-mail or other file locations on the device.

- **/data/com.android.phone/databases/** This folder can contain several SQLite databases, including autoreject.db, callreminder.db, and rejectmessage.db, if the user has set them up to handle certain phone tasks. These databases will not be created unless the user has set them up. The database names identify the action and subsequent storage of that data. Autoreject stores numbers the user has identified to be rejected when receiving a call, callreminder will notify the user of a call, and rejectmessage enables the user to send a customized message on rejection of calls.
- **/data/com.android.vending/databases/localappstate.db** This database stores installed apps and the installation date along with the username associated with the app.
- **/data/com.android.vending/databases/suggestions.db** This database stores search terms used by the device user when searching for Android apps to purchase.
- **/data/com.android.providers.download/databases/downloads.db** Android devices have always controlled the information that is downloaded from the Internet independently of the app using class DownloadManager. Apps use this class when a file is downloaded to the device, and the information related to the download is stored within this database. This includes downloaded e-mail attachments, downloaded web content, and much more. If the file no longer exists on the mobile device, the metadata can possibly still be recovered from this database to indicate that it was, in fact, downloaded to the device.
- **dbdata/databases/com.android.providers.download/downloads.db** Same as the previous entry, but this location can be found within some Samsung devices, particularly the Samsung Galaxy S series.
- **/data/com.android.providers.media/databases/external<*variable*>.db** Android devices use another class called MediaStore, which caches all media on the internal device and external media. The media can include images, videos, audio, and even files. This database holds any data within the storage areas that does not contain a file named .nomedia. If the .nomedia file is encountered, the MediaScanner will not search that folder, and the information will not be cached in the external.db file. The <*variable*> listed in the path can be seen in some Android devices—it is the actual serial number of the SD card that was inserted. Some Android device's com.android.providers.media folder can contain multiple external.db files because multiple external SD cards were inserted, and subsequently the MediaScanner scanned and documented the data from each, storing the data in independent files. The external.db SQLite database contains many tables, but the most important is the files table, which contains all the files that have been scanned, including dates/times, paths, geolocation, and size, and what app the file is associated with—to name a few. An examiner can gather critical information on the files within the Android mobile device with associated metadata.
- **/data/com.android.providers.media/databases/internal.db** The internal.db file stores media paths to Android built-in system needs. The information found in the internal.db is generally of no use to an examiner because the information is system-based, not user-based, data.
- **/dbdata/databases/com.android.providers.media/** Same as the previous entry, but this location can be found within some Samsung devices, particularly the Samsung Galaxy S series.
- **/data/com.android.providers.settings/databases/settings.db** The settings.db file is used by the device to persist all of the user's settings within a SQLite database. The tables

of interest within the database are the system and secure tables. The system table identifies the setup of the mobile device, including the location of service prior to collection within the aw_daemin_service_key_city_name key and also whether the device was in hands-free mode using the driving_mode_on key. Both of these keys can provide critical information for an examiner, and the settings of the device at the time of collection can be found within this database.

- **/dbdata/databases/com.android.providers.settings/settings.db** Same as the previous entry, but this location can be found within some Samsung devices, particularly the Samsung Galaxy S series.
- **/data/com.android.providers.telephony/optable.db** This database is used to store the carriers on which the mobile device has operated and lists the carrier name and the public land mobile network (PLMN) identifier within the operator table.
- **/data/com.android.providers.telephony/databases/mmssms.db** This database stores all the MMS and SMS messages. The MMS information is stored within the pdu table, and attachments and content can be associated with the parts table. SMS uses the sms table, and several other significant tables reside within this database, including words and words_content, which both store text-based data that can prove valuable for an examiner. The words table is used by the sms and pdu tables to store searchable, indexed data for a mobile device, and the words_content table is used by the pdu table to store indexed, searchable text-based data for a mobile device. Because the pdu table uses both the words and words_content table, some data can be duplicated, but it can be filtered by using the foreign key in both tables. If the MMS or SMS session does not use a delete function, the information that is within the words and words_content may remain and can be harvested by the examiner even if the original SMS or MMS is deleted.
- **/data/com.android.providers.telephony/app-parts/** This folder contains the attached files to MMS messages and is referenced in the mmssms.db parts table.
- **/dbdata/databases/com.android.providers.telephony/mmssms.db** Same as the previous entry, but this location is within some Samsung family devices, particularly the Samsung Galaxy S series.

Google Stock Apps

Because Google is Android and Android is Google, it should be no surprise to any examiner that most Android devices are populated with stock apps from Google. The following outlines some of these applications and where an examiner may find additional artifacts while examining the Android file system:

- **/data/com.google.android.apps.maps/databases/gmm_myplaces.db** This database contains saved places or Google Maps favorites. The information is stored within the sync_item table and lists the latitude and longitude, timestamp, and the sync_item as a BLOB file, which is the location name along with the HTTP data to maps.google.com.
- **/data/com.google.android.apps.maps/databases/gmm_strorage.db** This database is the storage location for the turn-by-turn instructions for each route entered in the Google Maps app. The information is stored in the gmm_storage_table in the data field. The data field is BLOB data and, when viewed, it gives the examiner a view of the directions

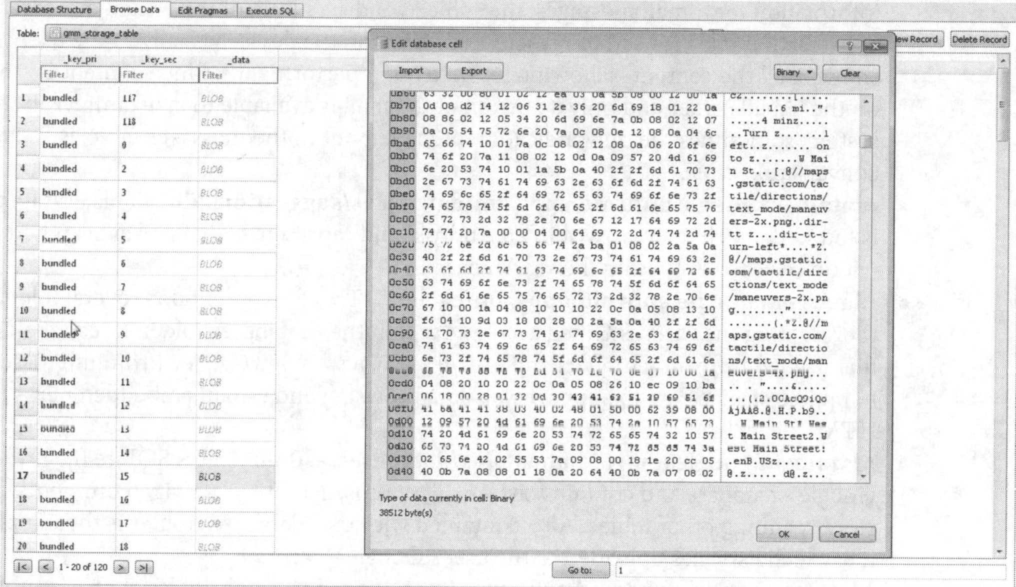

FIGURE 13-10 BLOB data within the gmm_storage_table

followed by the user to a destination—the location name along with the HTTP data to maps.google.com. Figure 13-10 shows BLOB data within the gmm_storage_table that can assist an examiner when using mapping data in a case.

- **/data/com.google.android.apps.maps/databases/search_history.db** This database records the searched locations within the Google Map app, storing the latitude and longitude along with a timestamp. This data is in the suggestions table in the SQLite database.
- **/data/com.google.android.apps.maps/app_da_speech/** This folder stores the voice WAV files for the directions given.
- **/data/com.google.android.apps.maps/cache/http/** This folder stores cached data in the form of GUID named files. Generally two related files with the same GUID are differentiated by a *0* or *1*; *0* ending files are the description of the associated file ending in *1*. This can be helpful for an examiner, since some streetview JPGs are stored in this location when a user requests that view of a location.
- **/data/com.google.android.apps.maps/shared_prefs/settings_preferences.xml** This XML file contains values Google Maps is using. One key, current_account_name, lists the registered account name for Google Maps. This information can be used to obtain court-ordered information on geolocation data that's not stored on the mobile device but might be stored on the user's account.
- **/data/com.google.android.apps.gm/databases/mailstore.<*username*>.db** This Google app store is for Gmail. Each mailbox is prefixed by *mailstore* and then the Gmail e-mail address. The SQLite database contains several tables, including messages, attachments, and conversations. The messages table contains the date and time

information for e-mail messages, the subject, and a snippet of the e-mail message. The conversation table is used to present the e-mail on the device visually to the user without showing all the content—allowing for better app performance. Since content is stored on the Gmail server and only a portion of the mail is available to an examiner in the file system, sometimes the only indication of mail, if not in the messages table, is cached in the conversation table.

- **/data/com.google.android.apps.gm/databases/suggestions.db** This SQLite database is found throughout apps within an Android and represents what a user searched for within the app itself using the search bar.
- **/data/com.google.android.apps.gm/cache/** This folder contains several folders representing the various Gmail accounts within the /databases folder. In each folder are files cached from attachments and e-mail. Also, a webViewCacheChromium folder stores temporary cache data to support web data browsing and e-mail embedded items using HTML pages.
- **/data/com.google.android.apps.plus/databases/es0.db** This SQLite file is the main Google+ database and contains circles, all_photos, activities, activity_comments, and stories, among other tables. Also contained with the /databases folder is the iu.upload.db file, which lists files uploaded to the user's Google+ account.
- **/data/com.google.android.apps.plus/cache/media/** This folder contains subfolders referenced by both the es0.db and iu.upload.db file. Each folder has numerous media files. Using a data carver in this folder system will yield many media items an examiner may need in an investigation.
- **/data/com.google.android.apps.plus/shared_prefs/accounts.xml** This XML file contains the account information for the Google+ account.
- **/data/com.google.android.googlequicksearchbox/databases/icingcorpora.db** This SQLite file is used to store indexed applications, contacts, e-mails, phone calls, and postal codes. Within the database, the tables to view are applications, contacts, emails, phones, and postals. These tables list values that are most prevalent for that type based upon the score field. The value ranges from 1 to *n*. The highest *n*-valued item in the score column for each type will show first when the user begins to type into the Google Search box within each category (such as contacts, call log, e-mail, application). The score is typically based upon frequency of use per each category. An examiner can use this intelligence to determine most frequently contacted and used data within the device.
- **/data/com.google.android.googlequicksearchbox/cache/http/** Like all other HTTP folders within the cache, GUIDs are stored in this location. This folder stores cached data in the form of GUID named files. There are generally two related files with the same GUID differentiated by a *0* or *1*; *0* ending files are the description of the associated file ending in number *1*. This information can be helpful for an examiner because voice searches, Internet searches, and typed searches using the Google Quick Search box are stored along with the data that was returned to the user (see Figure 13-11). The search, stored in the GUID with an appended *0*, contains date and time information for both the search and return of data along with the content type description.
- **/dbdata/databases/com.google.android.googlequicksearchbox/qsb-history.db** This SQLite file is found in some Samsung Galaxy S series devices and contains the history of the searches used in the Google Quick Search box. This database has been

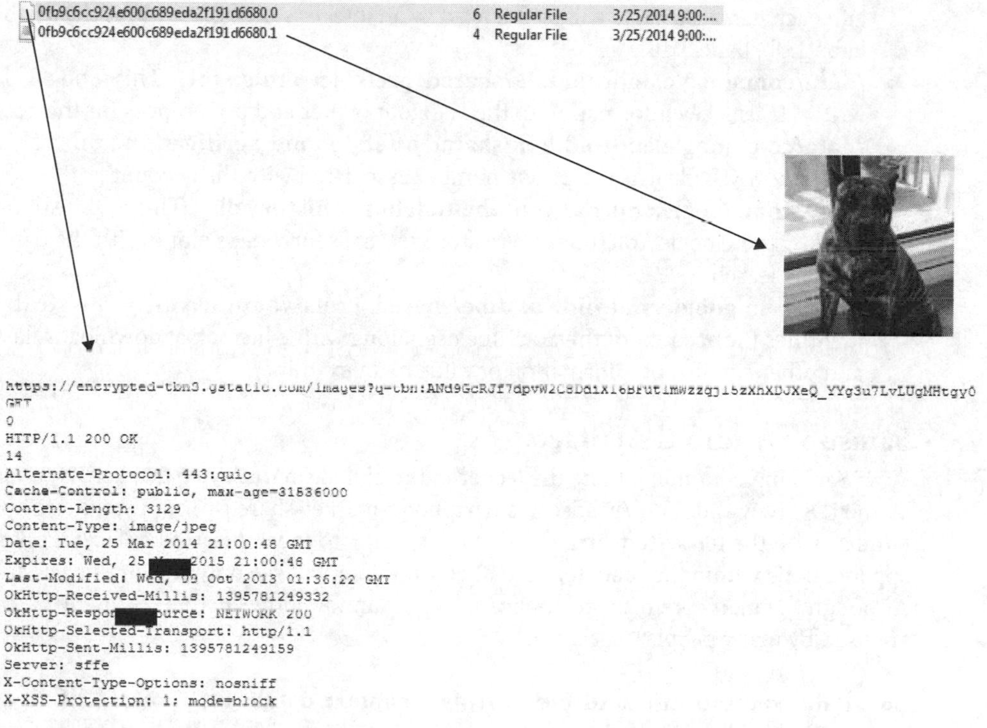

FIGURE 13-11 The file in the search describes what was searched for with the associated result displayed.

deprecated, but the table history contains the query used and the date and time. Another database in the same directory, qsb-log.db, can be used to log web clicks used in a search. This information is obtainable within the clicklog table.

- **/data/com.google.android.gsf/databases/subscriberfeeds.db** This app is the Google Services Framework, and this SQLite database contains the Google accounts that are subscribed to, along with the user's e-mail address.
- **/data/com.google.android.gsf/databases/talk.db** This SQLite database contains the Google Talk settings such as account and contacts within the app.
- **/data/com.google.android.street/cache/** This folder contains streetview images from a Google Maps instance. The images are all prefixed by *tile_* and then ordered by a three-digit number. The examiner can use these tiles to obtain images that the user of the device accessed while using the streeview function in Google Maps.
- **/data/com.google.android.talk/databases/message_store.db** This SQLite database contains the Google Hangouts messages within the messages table.
- **/data/com.google.android.talk/databases/babel.db** This SQLite database is the conversation database for active conversations, participant names, messages, and

information about the Google Hangout event. There can be multiple babel.db databases, and each database name will be followed by an integer starting with *0* (such as babel0.db, babel1.db, babel3.db).

- **/data/com.google.android.talk/shared_prefs/accounts.xml** This Google Hangout XML file lists key information to the Hangout owner and preferences for the account.
- **/data/com.google.android.talk/shared_prefs/phone_verification.xml** This Google Hangout XML file lists the phone number associated with the account.
- **/data/com.google.android.youtube/databases/history.db** This SQLite database is used by the Google YouTube app to store searches for videos along with the date and time of each search.
- **/data/com.google.android.youtube/shared_prefs/youtube.xml** This XML file identifies the account of the YouTube user along with a history of downloads, last login, and other significant information of value to an examiner.

Samsung Android Artifacts

With Samsung continuing to be the leader in the global smart device market, as reported by the IDC (www.idc.com/prodserv/smartphone-market-share.jsp), an examiner should be familiar with the file system artifacts that are specific to these Android devices. Following are app locations within the /data folder that an examiner will see only within the Samsung device. Although the many preinstalled applications may annoy some customers, many of these apps are used by many people.

- **/data/com.samsung.android.providers.context/databases/ContextDB.db** This SQLite database can help an examiner determine whether an application was running or had been launched around the time of an incident. The app's internal services are exposed, showing the service that was launched as part of the app, to identify messages, notifications, and conversations. By using the app_usage table and fields package_name, class_name, and app_usage_last_access_time (in milliseconds), an examiner can gain interesting intelligence for a timeline. A similar location for the device can also be found at /system/dmappmgr.db and the ApplicationControl table. In Figure 13-12, a parsed ContextDB.db file using the SQLQuery Builder application shows a considerable amount of information that can quickly be placed into a timeline.
- **/data/com.sec.android.app.clockpackage/worldclock.db** This SQLite database contains all of the set clocks the user has added to the clock app. The examiner can use the worldclock table within this database to view any city that has been added to the wordclock view.
- **/data/com.sec.android.app.clockpackage/alarm.db** This SQLite database contains all of the set alarms the user has added to the clock app. This table alarm contains the date and times of alarm creation, the alert time, and the name of the alarm.
- **/data/com.sec.android.im/databases/taConvDB.db** This SQLite database contains conversations and messages tables that can be used to recover the user's instant messages, as long as the user is using the Samsung instant messaging platform.

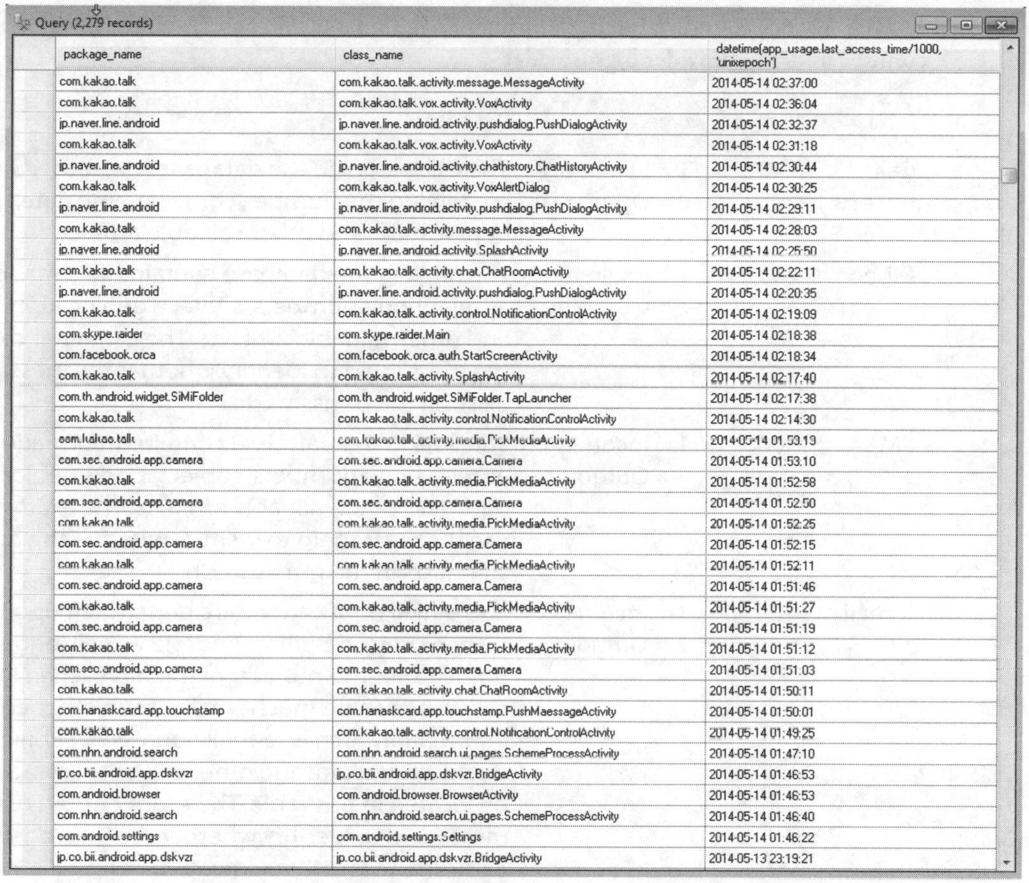

Query (2,279 records)

package_name	class_name	datetime(app_usage.last_access_time/1000, 'unixepoch')
com.kakao.talk	com.kakao.talk.activity.message.MessageActivity	2014-05-14 02:37:00
com.kakao.talk	com.kakao.talk.vox.activity.VoxActivity	2014-05-14 02:36:04
jp.naver.line.android	jp.naver.line.android.activity.pushdialog.PushDialogActivity	2014-05-14 02:32:37
com.kakao.talk	com.kakao.talk.vox.activity.VoxActivity	2014-05-14 02:31:18
jp.naver.line.android	jp.naver.line.android.activity.chathistory.ChatHistoryActivity	2014-05-14 02:30:44
com.kakao.talk	com.kakao.talk.vox.activity.VoxAlertDialog	2014-05-14 02:30:25
jp.naver.line.android	jp.naver.line.android.activity.pushdialog.PushDialogActivity	2014-05-14 02:29:11
com.kakao.talk	com.kakao.talk.activity.message.MessageActivity	2014-05-14 02:28:03
jp.naver.line.android	jp.naver.line.android.activity.SplashActivity	2014-05-14 02:25:50
com.kakao.talk	com.kakao.talk.activity.chat.ChatRoomActivity	2014-05-14 02:22:11
jp.naver.line.android	jp.naver.line.android.activity.pushdialog.PushDialogActivity	2014-05-14 02:20:35
com.kakao.talk	com.kakao.talk.activity.control.NotificationControlActivity	2014-05-14 02:19:09
com.skype.raider	com.skype.raider.Main	2014-05-14 02:18:38
com.facebook.orca	com.facebook.orca.auth.StartScreenActivity	2014-05-14 02:18:34
com.kakao.talk	com.kakao.talk.activity.SplashActivity	2014-05-14 02:17:40
com.th.android.widget.SiMiFolder	com.th.android.widget.SiMiFolder.TapLauncher	2014-05-14 02:17:38
com.kakao.talk	com.kakao.talk.activity.control.NotificationControlActivity	2014-05-14 02:14:30
com.kakao.talk	com.kakao.talk.activity.media.PickMediaActivity	2014-05-14 01:53:19
com.sec.android.app.camera	com.sec.android.app.camera.Camera	2014-05-14 01:53:10
com.kakao.talk	com.kakao.talk.activity.media.PickMediaActivity	2014-05-14 01:52:58
com.sec.android.app.camera	com.sec.android.app.camera.Camera	2014-05-14 01:52:50
com.kakao.talk	com.kakao.talk.activity.media.PickMediaActivity	2014-05-14 01:52:25
com.sec.android.app.camera	com.sec.android.app.camera.Camera	2014-05-14 01:52:15
com.kakao.talk	com.kakao.talk.activity.media.PickMediaActivity	2014-05-14 01:52:11
com.sec.android.app.camera	com.sec.android.app.camera.Camera	2014-05-14 01:51:46
com.kakao.talk	com.kakao.talk.activity.media.PickMediaActivity	2014-05-14 01:51:27
com.sec.android.app.camera	com.sec.android.app.camera.Camera	2014-05-14 01:51:19
com.kakao.talk	com.kakao.talk.activity.media.PickMediaActivity	2014-05-14 01:51:12
com.sec.android.app.camera	com.sec.android.app.camera.Camera	2014-05-14 01:51:03
com.kakao.talk	com.kakao.talk.activity.chat.ChatRoomActivity	2014-05-14 01:50:11
com.hanaskcard.app.touchstamp	com.hanaskcard.app.touchstamp.PushMaessageActivity	2014-05-14 01:50:01
com.kakao.talk	com.kakao.talk.activity.control.NotificationControlActivity	2014-05-14 01:49:25
com.nhn.android.search	com.nhn.android.search.ui.pages.SchemeProcessActivity	2014-05-14 01:47:10
jp.co.bii.android.app.dskvzr	jp.co.bii.android.app.dskvzr.BridgeActivity	2014-05-14 01:46:53
com.android.browser	com.android.browser.BrowserActivity	2014-05-14 01:46:53
com.nhn.android.search	com.nhn.android.search.ui.pages.SchemeProcessActivity	2014-05-14 01:46:40
com.android.settings	com.android.settings.Settings	2014-05-14 01:46:22
jp.co.bii.android.app.dskvzr	jp.co.bii.android.app.dskvzr.BridgeActivity	2014-05-13 23:19:21

FIGURE 13-12 A parsed ContextDB.db file using the SQLQuery Builder application

- **/data/com.sec.android.provider.logsprovider/databases/logs.db** This SQLite database is a goldmine of information. This file stores information that has been displayed on the Samsung device, such as notifications from e-mail, MMS, SMS, and calls. To detail the contents, the database file stores call logs, message snippets (SMS/MMS), and e-mail snippets along with their associated metadata. If a message has been deleted from the main SMS, call log, message, or e-mail, the data remains within this log. Experience has shown that even if the user has reset the messages within the device, data can still be recovered from logs.db. Table 13-6 lists some of the information available from this telltale Samsung database with logtype and type coming from the logs table in logs.db.
- **/data/com.sec.android.provider.smemo/databases/pen_memo.db** This SQLite database stores data from the Memo app, including voice, pictures, and text. The

TABLE 13-6 logs.db from the Samsung Logging Function and Database Located at com.sec.android.provider.logsprovider

Data	logtype	type	Description
Call history	100	1 = Incoming 2 = Outgoing	The call history in the database is verbose, containing the number, contact name date, geolocation, and other valuable artifacts.
MMS	200	1 = Incoming 2 = Outgoing	The MMS in the database contains information such as telephone numbers, subject, geolocation data, and other valuable artifacts. The examiner can use the messageid to identify whether the message still exists in the mmssms.db.
SMS	300	1 = Incoming 2 = Outgoing	The SMS in the database contains information such as telephone numbers, subject, body, geolocation data, and other valuable artifacts. The examiner can use the messageid to identify whether the message still exists in the mmssms.db.
E-mail	400	1 = Incoming 2 = Outgoing	The e-mail notifications are dependent upon user settings for the built-in Android e-mail logged by this feature. The number of e-mails cached in this database can be much smaller than other artifacts. Information such as e-mail addresses, subject, body, geolocation data, and other valuable artifacts may be located in this table. The examiner can use the messageid to identify whether the message still exists in the EmailProvider.db.

information is located in the table PenMemo within several fields, including CreateDate, Date, Content, Text, Text_sub, Drawing, and Thumb.

- **/data/com.sec.android.provider.downloads/databases/sisodownloads.db** This SQLite database is comparable to the com.android.providers.downloads database. This is a good database for an examiner to investigate because media downloaded from web sites can be located here.
- **/data/com.sec.android.socialhub/databases/UniboxProvider.db** This SQLite database contains accounts and messages tables that can be used to match accounts for social media, instant messaging, text messaging, and e-mail notifications with the messages themselves. If the user has enabled this feature, this database can contain current and historical data.
- **/data/com.seven.Z7/databases/email.db** This SQLite database contains more data from the social hub addition to the Samsung line. It can store e-mail addresses, passwords, and e-mail content. Also, associated accounts and their instant message data can be stored here.

Third-Party Apps

Unlike iOS devices, third-party applications are stored in the same /data folder along with all of the other stock, phone, and often carrier apps. The third-party apps use the domain name format previously outlined.

Note There are more than 1.5 million Android apps available on the Google Play site, and documenting each and every app naming convention would take hundreds of pages. An examiner should understand that the layout of the folders within each app and the databases used to store the artifacts will be generally similar to what is outlined in Table 13-5. App designers can build their own app folder structures, and one of the difficult things for the automatic parsing of the apps within an Android, or any smart device, is that folder structure and database naming can change with an app update.

Third-party apps generally store the temporary data within the /cache folder, which can also include additional folders, such as webViewCacheChromium. This folder contains data that was displayed to the user using the app. Files of interest will be prefixed with an *f_* and then a number. The *f* stands for files, and the files used by the web view in the app are listed. The /databases folder contains the databases for the app, along with another database called webview.db that stores form information and user information to be used within a web view in the app. This database can hold passwords, usernames, and other data important to an examiner. Although Android development clearly encourages developers to use the correct controls of this class, WebViewDatabase, this database still should be queried. Apps also use the shared_prefs folder within the app structure, which contains XML files that outline the preferences for the app, including usernames and passwords. Because some apps do not store data on the mobile device for security concerns, the app simply uses a built-in browser to interface with a secure server, but often automated login information is located within the shared_prefs folder. This location should also be examined when conducting an examination of third-party apps.

Most Android apps use SQLite databases, and as outlined in Chapter 12, building a SQL query to support an application, along with recovering free pages and WAL data, should be conducted on any app important to the examination. Even in today's most popular games, users can chat with each other, often adding to an examiner's investigation, as shown in Figure 13-13.

File Interrogation

Every file mentioned in this chapter and any other file within the Android file system can be parsed to recover every bit of data within that particular file. The attack surface within the Android is limitless for an examiner with the right tools and, more importantly, the drive to succeed. The SQLite database queries along with Python scripting can enable an examiner to interrogate most of the files within the Android file system. With the primary file for storage being SQLite databases and the primary file type for settings and preferences being XML,

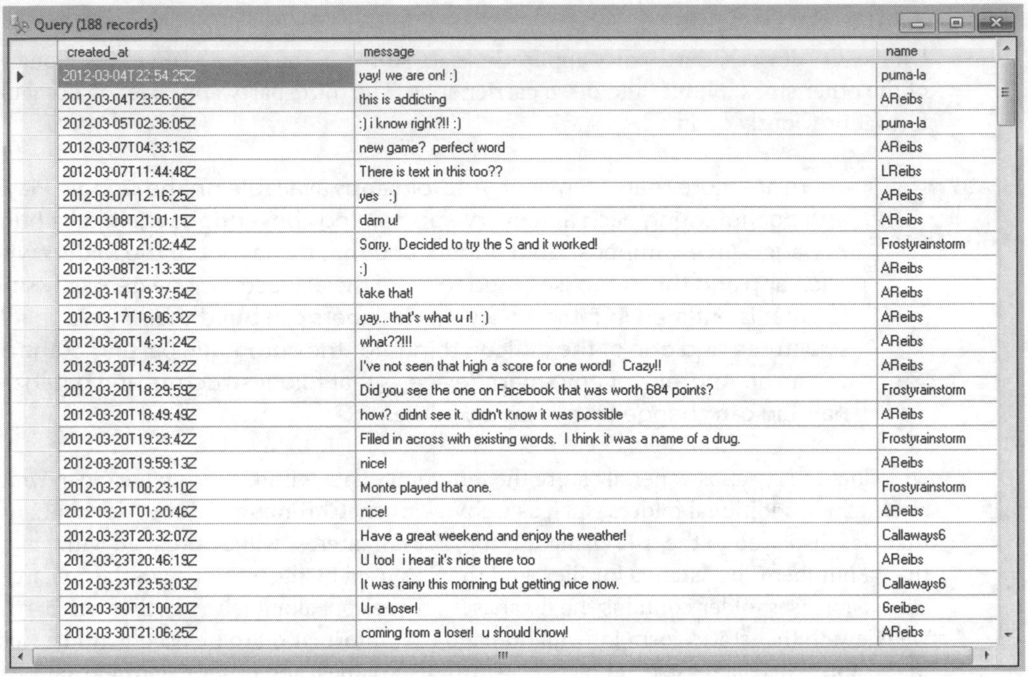

Query (188 records)

created_at	message	name
2012-03-04T22:54:25Z	yay! we are on! :)	puma-la
2012-03-04T23:26:06Z	this is addicting	AReibs
2012-03-05T02:36:05Z	:) i know right?!! :)	puma-la
2012-03-07T04:33:16Z	new game? perfect word	AReibs
2012-03-07T11:44:48Z	There is text in this too??	LReibs
2012-03-07T12:16:25Z	yes :)	AReibs
2012-03-08T21:01:15Z	darn u!	AReibs
2012-03-08T21:02:44Z	Sorry. Decided to try the S and it worked!	Frostyrainstorm
2012-03-08T21:13:30Z	:)	AReibs
2012-03-14T19:37:54Z	take that!	AReibs
2012-03-17T16:06:32Z	yay...that's what u r! :)	AReibs
2012-03-20T14:31:24Z	what??!!!	AReibs
2012-03-20T14:34:22Z	I've not seen that high a score for one word! Crazy!!	AReibs
2012-03-20T18:29:59Z	Did you see the one on Facebook that was worth 684 points?	Frostyrainstorm
2012-03-20T18:49:49Z	how? didnt see it. didn't know it was possible	AReibs
2012-03-20T19:23:42Z	Filled in across with existing words. I think it was a name of a drug.	Frostyrainstorm
2012-03-20T19:59:13Z	nice!	AReibs
2012-03-21T00:23:10Z	Monte played that one.	Frostyrainstorm
2012-03-21T01:20:46Z	nice!	AReibs
2012-03-23T20:32:07Z	Have a great weekend and enjoy the weather!	Callaways6
2012-03-23T20:46:19Z	U too! i hear it's nice there too	AReibs
2012-03-23T23:53:03Z	It was rainy this morning but getting nice now.	Callaways6
2012-03-30T21:00:20Z	Ur a loser!	6reibec
2012-03-30T21:06:25Z	coming from a loser! u should know!	AReibs

FIGURE 13-13 **Here, /data/com.zynga.words/WordsFramework is queried for its internal messaging with more than 100 messages returned.**

the examiner already has a leg up, since the parsing of both of these file types were covered previously.

Android non-invasive or invasive physical recovery of the partitions also enables the examiner to carve the unallocated space on both the cache and userdata partitions. The unallocated space within the Android device can hold media files, SQLite databases, XML, HTML, deleted MMS media, and other settings that are no longer active within the file system. Using a forensic tool to carve the unallocated space for these particular file types should be attempted by the examiner prior to the conclusion of the examination. Hundreds and possibly thousands of additional files can be recovered. In Figure 13-14, hundreds of images deleted from MMS along with HTML files were recovered using data carving techniques with MPE+.

SQLite, XML files, and any other file within the file system of an Android should be examined. Some examples of parsing of files using Python parsing are covered next with files that have been recovered from an Android device. The creation of SQL queries for Android databases was covered in Chapter 12.

Scripts

Often an examiner will need to locate the operating system information from an Android device. This information is often difficult to find within the different files of the file system.

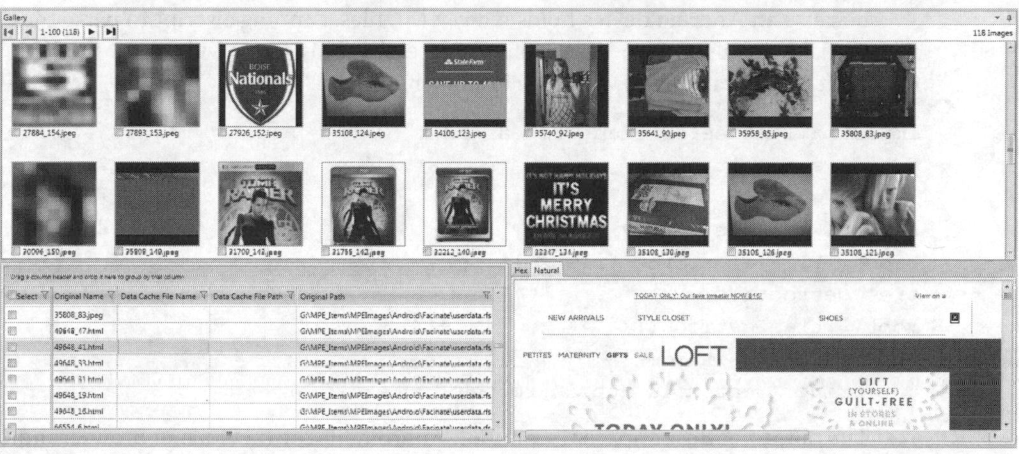

FIGURE 13-14 Many forensic tools support the data carving functionality.

If the examiner's mobile forensic tool does not recover this information automatically, the examiner can create a simple script to run against the file located in the userdata partition at /log/recovery_log.txt to search and list only the operating system information.

```
import re
from sys import argv
script,f = argv
fstuff = open(f,'r')

for line in fstuff:
    if re.match("(.*)ro.build(.*)", line):
        print (line,)
```

An abbreviated output from running the script against recovery_log.txt displays the required operating system information:

```
ro.build.id=JZO54K
ro.build.display.id=JZO54K.E210SKSJLL5
ro.build.version.incremental=E210SKSJLL5
ro.build.version.sdk=16
ro.build.version.codename=REL
ro.build.version.release=4.1.2
ro.build.date=Tue Dec 11 10:47:12 KST 2012
ro.build.date.utc=1355190432
ro.build.type=user
ro.build.user=se.infra
ro.build.host=SEP-129
```

Because an Android device holds many XML files, running a script to parse these XML files to make them more readable is often a necessity. This script will output the XML into a form that can be easily read within an examiner's report:

```
import xml.etree.cElementTree as ET
from sys import argv

script, xmlfile = argv
tree = ET.ElementTree(file=xmlfile)
tree.getroot()
root = tree.getroot()
for rootchild in root:
    print (rootchild.attrib,rootchild.text)
```

The output of this script for a common Android file for the built-in browser indicates last search times and the web search engine located at /data/com.google.android .googlequicksearchbox/SearchSettings.xml. The script could be further refined to translate the date and time information as well.

```
{'name': 'psuggest_available', 'value': 'false'} None
{'name': 'search_domain'} .google.com
{'name': 'next_voice_search_hint', 'value': '3'} None
{'name': 'search_history', 'value': 'true'} None
{'name': 'search_domain_apply_time', 'value': '1387471182477'} None
{'name': 'search_domain_country_code'} US
{'name': 'num_visible_suggestion_slots_2', 'value': '4'} None
{'name': 'voice_search_version', 'value': '211'} None
{'name': 'num_visible_suggestion_slots_1', 'value': '4'} None
{'name': 'first_voice_search_hint_time', 'value': '1358826686102'} None
```

Applying scripting to an Android examination, along with building SQL queries, can have an enormous impact on the outcome of an investigation. By using these types of techniques, an examiner will be sure to uncover the maximum amount of data from these treasure troves.

Android App Files and Malware

Android apps are created and installed to a device in the form of an APK file. APK files are compressed binary files containing DEX files, resource files (.arsc), uncompiled resources, and the AndroidManifest.xml file. These files and folders make up the app much like a Windows MSI or Mac .dmg file. The APK is installed to the device and stored in the /app folder within the Android file system for non-system apps; system apps are stored in the system partition. If an app is installed to the sdcard partition, the contents are generally encrypted and stored in a /sdcard/.android secure directory. The filenames have an *asec* extension instead of *apk*. If the device has decrypted these apps from the SD card, they will be stored at /data/app-asec and can be examined. The /dalvik-cache folder stores the installed app code for execution within the Dalvik VM instance when the app is called to run.

The important aspect of these two areas for an examiner concerns malware. Malware on an Android device is far more likely to occur than on any other smart device on the planet. Kaspersky Labs reports that more than 97 percent of mobile malware they detected was from the Android platform. There are various reasons for the malware infiltration on the mobile device, but it typically comes down to monetary gain for the group infecting devices. From SMS for a service to ransomware, an Android device can be susceptible. An examiner must be prepared for malware being involved on an Android device and understand the consequences.

Computer forensic examiners are trained to scan computer digital repositories for known malicious applications, viruses, keyloggers, and other similar files to disprove or prove malware added to, deleted from, or modifying the data being examined. Mobile device examiners do not show this same diligence, however, which could possibly discredit any data that might be recovered from an Android device. Android malware is already outpacing Windows for malware infections, and what took Windows 14 years to achieve with infections, Android has overtaken in only 3. An examiner should be ready to complete an examination of malware on a mobile device, particularly an Android device.

Cellebrite offers a malware scanner within its mobile forensic software that uses Bitdefender to locate malware signatures. An examiner should realize, however, that a signature-based examination is the lowest form of malware analysis because a signature is based upon a known hash. This known hash is placed into a blacklist and uploaded to a signature repository to be used against the app. Because an app can change daily after being morphed into an illegitimate form of a legitimate app, or because a zero-day app can drop at any moment, using signature-based analysis could miss valid malware. (This is not to say that the examiner should not perform an analysis of an Android device with a signature-based tool. Anything is better than nothing, and as long as the signatures are current, the analysis would be comparative to a computer's virus/malware scanner.) Malware companies base the signatures upon the DEX file within the /davlik-cache folder. However, there are instances where malware has injected or patched a legitimate app's DEX file within the davlik-cache, thus evading malware signature-based analysis.

Malware installed on an Android device can cause problems for an examiner, most importantly during the court testimony stage. Malware software can be used to gather information, disrupt service, connect to premium services, and even enable remote access to a device. Malware to disrupt can cause the device to be inoperable, cause redirects to web sites, install ransomware, and result in other problems. The following list shows several types of malware and how they work:

- **Ransomware** After locking the device, the user is shown a screen indicating that illegal material has been found on the device by the authorities and it will not be unlocked until a fine has been paid.
- **Premium services** These apps redirect phone and messaging services to a pay-per-use service to add phone charges. They collect money for every message sent and charge it to the carrier and then to the user's account.
- **Spyware** Spyware can turn on and monitor microphones, cameras, messages, keystrokes, and other data from a mobile device. This type of malware is often sold as a legitimate "monitoring" app. The information gathered is sent from the device to a server under control of the criminal.

- **Trojan** This was the most prevalent type of malware at one time, with designers injecting malicious code into legitimate apps. Google Play at the time failed to identify this malware, and many unsuspecting users downloaded what they thought was the original app. For example, Svpeng, a Russian Trojan, affected Androids by asking for credit card information each time the user visited Google Play. The data was then sent directly to a server, and credit card details were sold. The Google Play store now uses "Bouncer" to scan the app for malicious code or changes—eliminating some of the risk.
- **Data miner** This app steals data from the device, including contacts and phone information. Often, the malware will steal contacts and extort money from the user—saying an image they have will be sent to all of the user's contacts. Also, phone details such as IMEIs are stolen to sell to others to clone onto blacklisted handsets.
- **Adware** Messages from apps that should not be advising the user that "Your phone is slow," "You have been infected," or "Your device is being tracked," is a sign of adware, a prevalent malware type.
- **Downloader** This app directs users to additional downloads that appear to be content—such as PDF, JPG, and so on—but are additional malware apps, often Trojans.
- **Browser hijacker** These apps use WebView and not the Android internal browser to redirect and incur browser drive-by hacks, often infecting the device without the user even doing anything on the web page.
- **BotNet** Like computer systems, mobile devices are subject to malware packages that turn the device into a zombie. The command and control (C&C) servers are connected, and the device becomes a part of a network of devices that often distribute more malware.

Malware actions might include modifying the permissions for an Internet game to read the contacts, SMS, or other phone details to transmit that data to another server, or using the details to send messages and even clone the serial number to another device.

Analysis Levels

Three levels of malware analyses—permissions, static, and dynamic—are used to root out malware and determine the legitimacy of the app and its intentions. Permissions is the first level of malware detection and analysis. Static analysis is the second level of malware detection, and dynamic analysis is the third and top-level analysis type.

Permissions Analysis

Android apps list permissions (Figure 13-15) that must be granted to the app to enable it to function as the developer intended. The user typically sees these permissions prior to installing the APK file on the device, and they can also be viewed by navigating to app settings. Permissions for all APK files can also be viewed on the Google Play Store. The permissions granted to an Android app can assist the examiner as to the app's intentions. Table 13-7 lists Android permissions and their descriptions, including ways in which malware can affect the permission.

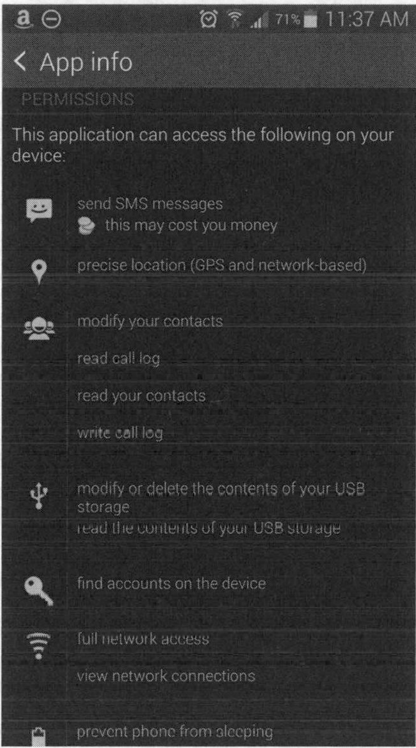

FIGURE 13-15 App permissions

Tip Permissions for all apps on a device can also be examined within the /system/packages.xml if this file can be accessed.

An app cannot access parts of the mobile device or provider apps if permission has not been granted. Most Android users do not understand the implications of accepting all permissions requested by the app and choose to accept all—granting dangerous access to malicious apps. Obviously this is a security concern for the user, but how about the examiner? As an examiner, these permissions should be investigated on apps that are primary evidence within the investigation. An examiner should unequivocally explain the intentions of that app, the expected outcome of using the app, and the evidence it produced. This perceptive investigation of the app's behavior will solidify the stance of the investigation and evidence recovered.

Static Analysis

Static analysis is a more in-depth analysis of any app that the examiner believes to be malware, based upon a permission or signature alert. A static analysis allows an examiner to look into the app code in a controlled environment—to look for "hooks" that might indicate malware, identify calls or posts to a third-party server, or recognize other anomalies within the app.

TABLE 13-7 Android Permissions and Descriptions (from Lost Packet Software, http://alostpacket.com)

Permission	Description
Make phone calls	Moderate to high importance. Used by VoIP apps. Malware could dial paid services to route calls.
Modify contacts, read call log, read contacts, write call log	Moderate to high importance. Many legitimate apps use this permission. Malware could capture device contacts and other phone call–related functions.
Send SMS messages	Moderate to high importance. Used by many apps to post results, invite others to games, and more. Malware could use paid services to send messages.
Storage—modify/delete SD card contents	Investigate this permission. Many apps must be granted this permission for storage, and there are many legitimate uses for this permission. Allow an app to read, write, and delete anything stored on the device media card. Control is granted to the entire SD card and generally not just the area the app controls.
Modify calendar data, write calendar data, read calendar data	Moderate to high importance. Malware could capture the device calendar information, and if the app is not used for calendar functions, this should be investigated.
Phone call—read phone state and identity	Moderate to high importance. Many apps use this permission to function if another phone function is needed. The IMEI, IMSI, and a 64-bit unique ID that Google provides for your phone is accessible using the same permission.
Precise location—network and GPS	Can be high importance if the app is not one of the previously listed types and location is not needed for the app to function correctly. Many apps use this function for restaurant directories, location finders, mapping applications, health apps, and many others. Malware could use permission to track the device.
Create Bluetooth connection	Investigate this permission. Since data can be transferred via Bluetooth, determine how the app uses it.
Full Internet access	Investigate this permission. Many apps ask for this permission but do not need this access. Determine whether the app really needs this type of permission to operate correctly—if so, determine what is being transferred. Most apps need this permission enabled because of ads, offsite storage of statistics and settings, and data storage to the Cloud. Malware can transfer data from the device to a third-party server using this permission.
View network state, view Wi-Fi state	Allows an application to determine whether the device is connected to the Internet via cellular or Wi-Fi.
Prevent phone from sleeping	Because of background processing, an app may need to maintain availability, so the device must not sleep.

Modify global system settings	Allows an app to interact with and change any settings within the General | Settings area of the device.
Read sync settings	Many Google apps or apps that interact with these services use this permission to detect these settings.
Write Access Point name settings	If this setting is requested by an app other than a telco, it could be important. Some prepaid devices use other large carriers' networks and in doing so must set up the APN settings. Allows the app to change these to route data services.
Automatically start at boot	Allows the app to start with each boot. Could be important if this is not a system type app and is labeled as a game. Understand the app type and need to help determine the intention.
Restart other applications	Allows an app to control another app by stopping the app and then allowing it to be restarted.
Retrieve running applications	Allows an app to determine the running apps. Examine the app to see if it interacts with other apps on the device and to determine whether this permission is legitimate.
Set preferred applications	Allows the app to set the preferred apps to be used for MMS, SMS, e-mail, and other communication apps. Can be used by malware to hijack a function, similar to a toolbar injection with a computer browser.
Take pictures	Used by picture-taking apps. Malware could use this function to take pictures secretly with the device camera. If the app is a game with no function other than playing a game, this could be of importance.
Discover known accounts	Allows the app to discover the accounts on the device. Does not provide credential information, however.

Several tools are available to assist an examiner in the static analysis of Android apps; this type of examination is not automated and can be time consuming, but it is often a necessity.

Note In 2012, as part of course development for a malware analysis course, I created content and a virtual machine to enable students and attendees to analyze actual malware, both statically and dynamically. The virtual machine was created using Linux Ubuntu as the OS with Eclipse, Wireshark, Androguard, and APKInspector installed. Eclipse was used for live active analysis using logcat and threading; APKInspector was used for the disassembly and analysis of the APK and DEX code; Androguard was used for disassembly of APK, ODEX, and DEX files; and Wireshark was used for active communication protocols. The benefit of using these tools was easy: they all are open source and freeware, and they allow for the investigation of malware within a virtual sandbox—the Ubuntu VM. The course introduction was given to a group at a High Tech Crime Investigators Association conference, which spawned several other virtual appliances for this type of analysis, using the same setup and tools.

For static analysis, APKInspector, an appliance built with Python, can be used to look for values that would be typical for a malicious app, but some of these permissions can be found in legitimate apps, too. The total number of "hooks" the examiner uncovers will determine the threat score of the identified app. Table 13-8 represents some of the more common requests found in malicious apps. Using APKInspector, the examiner can search for these terms to determine whether the app is using processes and commands that should not be a part of the app's functioning.

To launch APKInspector, Python must first be installed within the Linux instance. Then, from the Ubuntu Linux terminal, type **python StartQT.py** from within the APKInspector

TABLE 13-8 Common Commands Observed Within the Codebase of Malicious Applications

Permission	Description
`chmod`	Change mode: This UNIX command changes permissions for files or directories. An app that changes a file directory from read-only to read-write and executes privileges using `chmod 777` could indicate a malicious app. Search for `chmod` within the app code.
`chown`	Change owner: This UNIX command changes the ownership of a file. If root is "owned," the device can be compromised.
`root`	In conjunction with other terms, any app requiring root privileges will undoubtedly be malicious.
`rmmod`	This process attempts to remove a module from the kernel and should be interpreted as malicious when found.
`link`	This command/process attempts to link an existing file with another file, often creating a new file with additional content; can enable data to be injected into another file.
`unlink`	Deletes filenames outside of the app.
`symlink`	Symbolic link: Directs a link to a legitimate app to a newly installed malicious app.
`open`	Common in many apps, but this should be evaluated by the examiner to determine what files are being opened.
`ifconfig`	Configures or changes configuration of a network resource. This command can redirect output to another network address.
`mount`	Can be used to mount a file system as read-write, allowing access to a file system that should always be read-only.
`HttpPost`, `HttpRequest`, `Http`	HTTP commands used to post, get, and respond to information sent to or from a third-party server. Should be closely monitored to find out what data is posted and received and to where.
Permission-based terms	These terms can be standard for many apps, but can be used when searching an app that may not identify these permissions in the AndroidManifest .XML: `getDeviceId`, `getSimSerialNumber`, `getSubscriberId`, `sendToHost`, `sendToPort`.

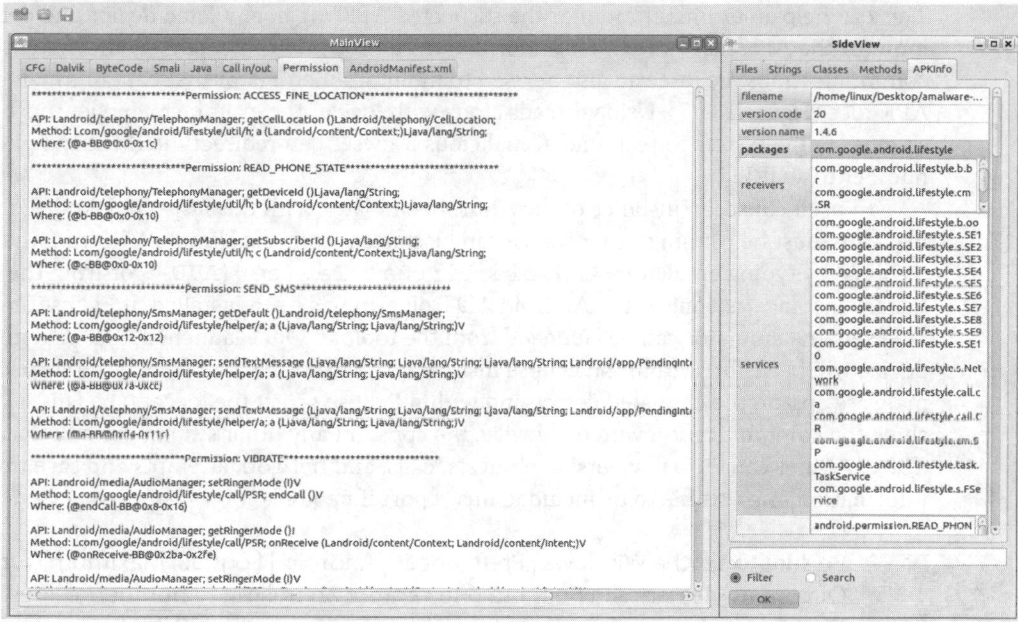

FIGURE 13-16 **APKInspector can be a good static analysis tool that shows permissions, calls, and even code.**

directory. The APKInspector UI will open, where the examiner can select to open an APK file by clicking the open folder (blue folder with a plus sign). Using the interface SideView in conjunction with the MainView (Figure 13-16), an examiner can view permissions, code, and calls made in and out, along with the DEX-translated code information. The examiner can view the actual code to determine exactly how the app is functioning, any classes used, and any malicious code calls if they have been identified. Sometimes the examiner can find information that can be used to track the malware developer when comments (`// This is a comment`) are included within the code. APKInspector is not an automated tool, but it can help an examiner conduct a thorough static analysis of Android apps in an attempt to identify known malware "hooks." However, a dynamic analysis must also be run to understand the malware and any malicious intent completely.

Dynamic Analysis

Dynamic analysis of an Android app can also be accomplished within a Linux Ubuntu virtual machine using an Android emulator and Wireshark, plus an emulator instance with Eclipse. Conducting a dynamic analysis of an Android app enables the examiner to monitor the app as it is running within the Android emulator, to watch the way the app works and monitor the output and input when the app is running certain processes.

Using Eclipse, the examiner can select the app within the interface and monitor the threads, as well as use logcat to monitor the device and app functions. Eclipse can also be used to monitor and debug the app APK while running in the instance of Eclipse, if needed.

This can help an examiner monitor the suspected APK on an emulated device and debug/monitor the APK files as well. This information can show HTTP attempts and system communications. Eclipse can also be used to monitor an emulator that contains malicious APK files (Figure 13-17). Using threads along with logcat, the examiner can view occurring changes in the system in real time. A malicious browser can redirect the IMEI and phone number to a URL.

To use Eclipse, an instance of the Android emulator with the suspected Android malware must be running. An instance can be started from the Ubuntu VM from the terminal by typing emulator `<Android Virtual Device (AVD)>` or from the Eclipse instance, as long as the Android ADT plug-in has been installed. If Eclipse and ADT are used, the emulator can be launched from the toolbar. Once launched, the emulated device will be visible within the Eclipse instance. The examiner can launch the suspected malware app on the emulated device and within Eclipse select the logcat tab. This will show the communication with the device, the app, and any other system communication. The examiner can view any outside requests, calls, and network attempts and save this information to a text file to be included in a report if needed.

Tip **Be sure to set the Windows | Preferences | Android | LogCat | Maximum Number Of LogCat Messages In Buffer to 0 to capture an unlimited number of lines, and then restart Eclipse. If this is not set, the default is only 5000 lines.**

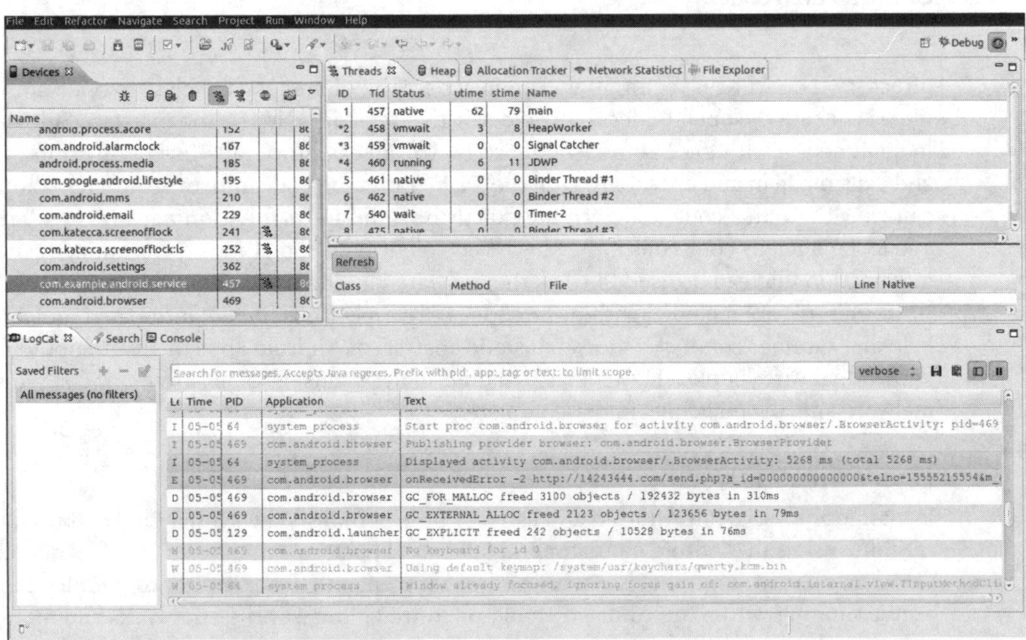

FIGURE 13-17 **Monitoring malicious files in Eclipse**

Data from Wireshark can also be analyzed to determine whether any data was sent or received from an outside source using TCP. If information is transferred or received, the examiner can determine whether this data is reasonable and whether the data is being transmitted or received from the correct server for the app or is going to a third-party location not specified by the app documentation. If the latter is the case, the examiner should analyze exposure to the device along with any received information from the third-party server. This analysis can often refute allegations that an app downloaded material automatically, without the user's knowledge, or that the app installed another unknown app that caused the evidence to appear on the device. This analysis can also help to determine a security breach and what type of data was lost.

Note Conducting a dynamic analysis using Wireshark is a good alternative. This is a basic introduction to its use; other resources are dedicated to using Wireshark with advanced methods that are not covered in this section. An examiner should at least comprehend that there are methods for the dynamic analysis of Android apps using Wireshark.

To use Wireshark, an examiner should create a TCP dump file when launching an emulator instance. This dump file will contain the recorded network traffic between the emulated device and the outside network. While running a suspected app, the examiner can observe any anomalies with the app and its communication with the network. These anomalies can include sending data, receiving data, and connecting to unknown IP addresses and servers. The examiner can run the following command from the terminal within the Linux virtual machine to start an instance of Wireshark's TCP recording on an instance of the Android emulator:

```
> emulator -tcpdump <name of capture file .cap> <Android Virtual Device (AVD)>
```

The app or apps can then be launched and the information can be examined to determine whether TCP/HTTP traffic has malicious intent. A capture file is then created, and this file will be imported into Wireshark and analyzed for any TCP or HTTP traffic.

Using advanced tools to combat the allegations of malware within an Android examination can be complicated, as shown in Figure 13-18, but an examiner must be prepared to conduct this type of analysis should these allegations be raised.

Note Commercial tools from AppSec Labs and NowSecure also use a Linux Ubuntu VM and include various tools, many of which have been discussed in this section. AppSec Labs' AppUse VM includes a dashboard that directs the examiner to certain functions within the VM and is used primarily for penetration testing, but it can also be used to analyze malware from mobile devices.

Chapter Summary

By obtaining the file system from an Android device using ADB backup, non-invasive, or invasive physical partition recovery techniques, an examiner can uncover artifacts that could prove critical to any investigation. If partition information cannot be recovered, the

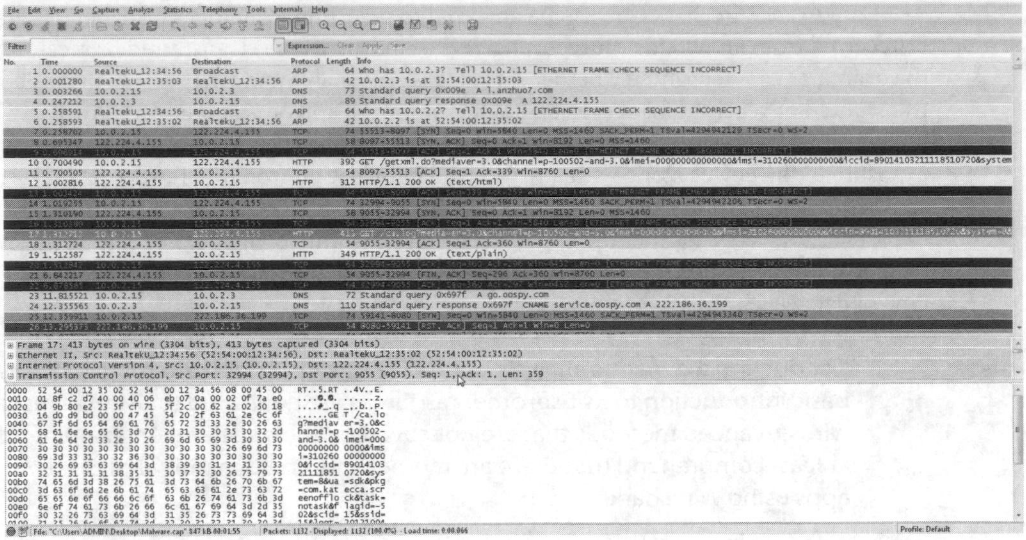

FIGURE 13-18 Advanced tools can produce complicated results.

examiner still has an opportunity to recover data from the device's internal or external media areas using MTP. App data, file settings, and persistent user data can be recovered from this area as well. Not all is lost if the partition-level file system data is not available; many users, and app developers, store data to the media area of the device, so as long as the device is unlocked or the examiner can access the device by circumventing the security, data can still be recovered.

Automating the recovery of Android artifacts is a difficult proposition for any software development team. Staying ahead of the ever-changing app and mobile device technology wave can be extremely difficult. When an examiner uses techniques discussed in this chapter and the two previous chapters in conjunction with the mobile forensic automated solution, a mind-boggling amount of data will be recovered. By using the scripting and query principles, even on databases and files already parsed by an automated tool, the examiner can be sure that recovered data is valid and properly recovered. The search for artifacts within an Android device should extend far below the surface of the "iceberg" to uncover the many files discussed in this chapter—from user settings to application data, this critical information is at the examiner's fingertips.

In addition, "tip of the iceberg data," such as SMS, MMS, call logs, and contacts, can be examined to uncover additional information that the automated tool neglected to report using a standard logical collection. By examining the SQLite databases, an examiner can look into the free pages, write-ahead-logs, and the databases themselves to bring missing data to the surface.

Malware is a problem with mobile device forensics, and the examiner, as part of normal procedures, should make sure to scan and report any anomalies. This procedure comes from many years of court proceedings and reports that malware, Trojans, or viruses can install applications, download inappropriate images and videos, and modify the system somehow without the user's knowledge. With a mobile device's ability to extend itself into the Internet and network, along with the massive onslaught of Android malware, this type of issue is important to a court procedure. An examiner must take steps to scan the device's contents when possible to cover this critical examination gap within the current Android investigations.

14 Presenting the Data as a Mobile Forensics Expert

Making a case after collecting a significant amount of data from a mobile device examination is only as good as the documentation. If the entire process, from seizure to data analysis, is not properly documented or explained in a way that's appropriate for the audience, then a comprehensive and proper exam is often pointless.

Documentation is an examiner's most important tool, especially when many different exhibits, methods, or custodians are involved. Without proper documentation, an examiner will be relying on memory or only the extracted and analyzed data. Recalling details from even a day prior is often difficult for most, let alone recalling every detail from the start of a process that may have taken weeks or even months to complete. An examiner must take detailed notes during the entire process. Notetaking at the onset and throughout the entire process is mandatory.

Before beginning the formal documentation process, an examiner should be aware of who will be reading the documentation. Often, if the evidence seems too complex or technical, the intended audience will not comprehend the message, and if they cannot comprehend the message, the examiner's work will be pointless, no matter how significant the data. An examiner often neglects the technicality of what he or she has accomplished and regurgitates this technical journey in the documentation, without considering the audience. When the documentation presentation is too technical and is too difficult for the readers or listeners, the information provided may be dismissed. The examiner must find a way to express the details of the examination in a format and using terms that help the audience understand the gravity of the evidence.

An examiner should also be mindful of the data that *should* be a part of the completed report. Some examiners simply dump all the information into a document, place the information on a storage device, and hand it over to the requester/audience. But this often creates additional work for the requester/audience, because the examiner has confused details of the examination with what was actually requested. The documentation should be concise and to the point, but an examiner should always be able to elaborate, if requested, with additional information.

The journey to becoming a mobile forensic expert is long, and it is often misconstrued as gathering certifications, awards, and endorsements. But this is not the true path. Becoming a mobile forensic expert comes from a desire to find the truth within the data. In finding this truth, the examiner must follow processes and procedures, constantly research new technologies, meticulously document the process, and, most important, understand and supplement what the automated solutions are doing to recover mobile device data. The road to becoming an expert is paved with examiners who think mastering mobile forensic tools and achieving certifications are all it takes to get there. By this point, however, every examiner reading this book should recognize that this statement could not be further from the truth.

There is a difference between an expert in the field and an expert who has been qualified as an expert. The examiner should recognize the distinction between individuals who classify themselves as experts in the field by experience and accolades and those who give qualified expert testimony. One is not better than the other, but the examiner must understand the difference. One aspect of being a qualified expert witness requires that the following criteria be met and decided upon by the court—and no one else. In the Federal Rules of Evidence, "Rule 702. Testimony by Expert Witnesses" (www.law.cornell.edu/rules/fre/rule_702) specifically states that expert opinions may be admissible if

- **(a)** the expert's scientific, technical, or other specialized knowledge will help the trier of fact to understand the evidence or to determine a fact in issue;
- **(b)** the testimony is based on sufficient facts or data;
- **(c)** the testimony is the product of reliable principles and methods; and
- **(d)** the expert has reliably applied the principles and methods to the facts of the case.

Even if Rule 702 is not followed, most states and many nations adhere to this philosophy, with similar requirements. Courts require that the witness be competent on the subject and know the underlying methods and procedures used in the examination and relied upon as a basis on the opinion.

Presenting the Data

When presenting the data, examiners must consider several factors that are generally based on the audience or individual requesting the work. The format should be established at the onset of the examination so that the examiner can tailor the examination to meet the requirements of the requestor. Determining the presentation format up front saves the examiner time and resources. Failing to comprehend how the data should be formatted from the beginning can result in the examiner following the wrong path, which can result in an exorbitant amount of time and sometimes money to remedy.

An examiner should also understand the target of the examination at the start. The investigation of the mobile device data should provide insight into the investigation, with not only the "tip of the iceberg data," but also a massive amount of relevant data located within the device file system. An examiner should be able to target specific apps for investigation according to the requirements of the investigation, but he or she should also not dismiss any other relevant data uncovered during the investigation.

The relevance of the collected data is determined by the presentation of what data was collected and how. For example, merely stating that a message was sent from Google Voice to another device that received it via an SMS is often not enough—the data should correlate the sent message in the Google Voice app with the data from the receiving device's SMS message container, relating the date/time, time zone, content, and user ID to the relevant factors of the investigation. Furthermore, the examiner must detail and document SMS messages, which can be sent from third-party apps to other mobile devices. Using apps for messaging instead of the carrier SMS conduit occurs frequently. Consequently, the sender using Google Voice can evade a mobile solution's ability to recover a message from the standard SMS messaging because it was sent from a third-party app. Including this type of information within the presentation documentation is critical, especially for data that is significant to the outcome of the case. Outlining the importance of the data as it pertains to the overall case, using common language and including lots of information, is critical.

Unfortunately, however, use of the many available mobile forensic solutions can lead to confusion when it comes to documentation—not only because of the number of varying reporting formats, but also because of several different aspects of the documentation. An examiner may complete the processing of the mobile device, select to output the data into a report format, and move on to the next piece of mobile forensic software. The data is processed in the secondary software, or the device is collected again and another report is generated. This secondary report may contain additional data that the first solution did not contain, but it may also duplicate data included in the first software's report. The problem is not in the employment of multiple tools within an examination, but the improper presentation of this material.

No matter whether one or multiple tools are used in a mobile forensic investigation, one report should outline the complete seizure, collection, and analysis, and any reports created by the mobile forensic tools should be used to supplement the main document because they often do not contain enough detail or commentary.

I can recall several instances when a Cellebrite report comprising thousands of pages was entered as evidence. Legal teams pored over the pages, searching for germane data, with absolutely no idea how the information was obtained, where it was obtained from, or what the data actually meant to the investigation. This issue is not limited to Cellebrite, because practically all mobile forensic solutions ordinarily output generated data compiled by the automated methods that place no value on the process by which it was collected or the requirements of the overall case—that is left up to the examiner. Unfortunately, many examiners do not add information to the solution's automatically created report. But without including important details in the presentation, the audience may find it difficult or impossible to comprehend the meaning behind the data hidden within the many pages. *An expert is not defined by the number of pages generated by an automated tool, but by the explanation of the content that is presented with the supporting tool's output.*

The Importance of Taking Notes

The entire process, from seizure to analysis, should be documented in chronological order in the examiner's notes. The date and time of each function should accompany any details of the event, along with all observations. Using these detailed notes, an examiner can paint a picture of the event precisely how it occurred. An examiner may attempt to recall the entire event during the final documentation phase, but in doing this, he or she may leave out many forgotten but valuable details.

Guessing and filling in the blanks of an examination is never the right choice. By documenting every detail at every step, the examiner will be sure to include even the minutest detail in the final report. Suppose, for example, that an examiner "always" places a device in airplane mode as soon as a device is seized, and he never documents this process because it's always the same. He always writes the report and adds this detail at the end of the examination. However, on this particular case, he's not entirely sure he remembered to place the device in airplane mode because he was interrupted by an important phone call just as he collected the device. Still, because he believes he always follows the same procedures, he writes the report assuming that he followed his usual routine. Another examiner is called to validate the findings of the first examiner and happens to look into the settings file. He or she determines that the mobile device was *not* put in airplane mode at the time of seizure. The entire first examination is discredited and deemed unusable.

Instead of guessing, the examiner can create a Chronology log. This log is a detailed grid similar to Table 14-1, which can be filled out to include the various tasks with clear details for

TABLE 14-1 Sample Examiner's Notes Table Used to Document Every Detail of the Investigation, from Reception to Reporting

Date	Time	Task	Description	Comments
3/3/15	900	Reception	Det. Smith requested an analysis of a mobile device	Device was obtained from the property room and transported to lab. Det. Smith completed processing request form.
3/3/15	945	Open evidence	Mobile device and SIM	Photographed, sealed, and then when the bag was opened—mobile device was off.
3/2/15	1015	Document	UICC and mobile device	Gathered mobile device information and UICC information using photographs.
3/3/15	1100	Collection	SIM	UICC was photographed and collected using USIM Detective. File system and PIN data recovered.
3/3/15	1130	Isolation	Mobile device	Mobile device was isolated from cellular by its lack of UICC. Network was isolated after pressing power button and selecting Airplane Mode while in Faraday box. Device was unlocked.
3/3/15	1300	Collection	Mobile device	Device was collected using non-invasive means physically using UFED. Binary file was produced of the userdata partition.
3/4/15	900	Collection	Mobile device	Device was collected logically using UFED. SMS, MMS, Calls, Contacts.

later recall. This is similar to a log of the events, and it will help the examiner immensely when recalling each task and resolution when later writing a report.

When completing any notes of the event, the examiner must understand that any documentation produced as part of the investigation is *discoverable*. In other words, the examiner's notes can be requested as part of the proceedings if he or she was not acting as a consulting expert based upon Federal Rule of Evidence 502 and Federal Rule of Civil Procedures 26(b)(A). If the examiner is acting as a consulting expert and will not be testifying, but is advising counsel, his or her notes are a work product and protected under attorney-client privilege. With that being said, the information contained within the examiner's notes should be free from generalizations and opinions and should simply state the facts. The only facts that should be included in the examiner's notes are the procedures taken and the outcomes of completing the procedures. Listing opinions, comments, or even doodles in the margin could result in considerable hurdles during the court proceedings, particularly if the court requests these documents. The notes should be used for an examiner's recollection of the entire process, and they serve as a guide as the examiner creates the final presentation of evidence.

The Audience

The *audience* is any person or group of people who will be exposed to the investigational report created by the examiner. The audience could be the examiner's supervisor, human resources, a company CEO, an attorney, a jury, a judge, or any other entity coming into contact with this compiled information. Knowing who will be exposed to the produced documentation can help guide the examiner during the final documentation phase. The presentation of the materials should be compiled in a form that caters to each group or individual person mentioned, but it should also contain information as it relates to the specific audience that requested the report. For example, a report created for the CEO of a company might contain sensitive information that is not appropriate for an employee of the company. This does not mean the examiner should permanently omit data, but he or she should be selective in providing the information needed and requested for that particular audience member. When the examiner creates reports using automated tools, this can be difficult unless some sort of filtering is available. This is an important reason why an automated report should supplement the main documentation: the primary document will contain information specific to the request, outlining the details of the collection and analysis of the scoped data, and the supplemental solution report can be used in a redacted form. Of course, if the requesting party would like to see the information originally omitted, that would not be a problem because a full collection would have already been completed and a more verbose report created.

Note A full collection should always be completed unless a full collection exceeds the scope of the request or warrant. In those limited cases, only a portion of the information will be available, as outlined by the requestor or warrant. If additional information is requested outside of scope, an examiner should follow proper procedures in obtaining the right to gather this additional information from the device.

Knowing the audience and creating a pointed report that details the information specific to the audience will resonate more than producing a generic solution report containing all data.

Having regard for the viewer and targeting the report based upon his or her request will often mean little follow-up work by the examiner. By giving the audience member the data that was specifically requested, in a form detailing the examination, analysis, and findings, the examiner will satisfy the requirements set forth by the audience. Delivering a 1000-page report that requires the reader to decipher technical details can result in many questions and more work for an examiner after the fact. If an examiner bases the presentation on the audience, outlining and detailing the data to fit the request, he or she is sure to meet the needs of the request.

Format of the Examiner's Presentation

In addition to knowing who the report's audience is, an examiner should know the type of format that is required for the report. The format can be dictated by the working standard operating procedure (SOP) by the company or agency sponsoring the collection and analysis. Most automated tools' reporting systems output reports as Microsoft Word documents, PDFs, HTML documents, CSV documents, and sometimes XML. Because the output produced by these tools will be used to supplement the main document, the format of this report often is not as important to the audience as the main document's format. However, if the audience has requested the solutions output in a format such as CSV or XML for specific reasons, such as to import it into intelligence software such as i2 Analyst's Notebook, the type of supplemental documents provided does significantly matter. This formatting information should be discussed and settled prior to beginning the collection and analysis of the mobile device evidence.

The main document may be created in a word processor such as Microsoft Word or Apple's Pages and then saved and printed as a PDF. Some agencies and companies have internal word processing applications specific to their business; these are completely acceptable to use since most will output to a PDF. A PDF is important for final documentation, because the content within the PDF remains read-only. Of course, if the company or agency format is different based upon an SOP, the SOP should be followed so long as the final output cannot be modified. Some agencies and companies use HTML for their reporting to organize and display their findings. This method can be used as well, but a main report should always be included as a PDF, and the HTML format should be used for navigation purposes only.

Note **It used to be common practice to use HTML with an auto-run function, but because modern operating systems allow this function to be disabled, using this methodology is not advised.**

Whatever the format of the completed report and supplemental data, the examiner should organize the information using the following guidelines:

- All information should be placed on storage media (such as CD, DVD, flash drive).
- The information should be categorized within a README file in the root of the storage media that outlines the contents. An example is shown here:

```
Case #12345  Examination of Mobile Device 1234, 1238, 1123
DVD Contents
README.txt - This file
```

```
Case12345-MDF.PDF - The main report containing case details, findings
and conclusions
Supplemental Docs - Folder containing output reports from UFED, MPE+
and XRY
Evidence - Folder containing native files exported from mobile forensic
solutions organized in separate folders Images, Audio, Video, Docs,
Misc
```

- If the examiner will be using HTML pages, the main index.html and associated files should be placed into a separate folder named HTML Report and listed in the README .txt file with instructions on its operation.
- If the examiner has placed media files within the evidence folder, the audience might need special software to view the material (such as .mov, .mp4, .qcp files). The viewing software should be included in a folder called MISC Software and its use and need described in the README.txt file.

When the information is organized by the examiner, the audience is less likely to request an explanation or require assistance from the examiner when viewing the results. Making information clear and concise will save the examiner from unnecessary requests, saving time for both the audience and the examiner.

Why Being Technical Is Not Always Best

When documenting the process, procedures, and analysis, the examiner should remember to write in a way that the audience will understand. Often, forensic examiners will create a document that contains information that only another examiner will understand, but this defeats the purpose of the report. An examiner should think in terms of customer satisfaction when creating the main document and any supplementary documents; all should be written and compiled so that a person with absolutely no forensic background or technical experience can visualize and comprehend the contents.

Tip **If the client requests that the examiner create a PowerPoint presentation to explain his or her report, this is a clue that the information contained in the report does not paint an understandable picture of the procedure and data.**

Examiners must understand that the report's audience may have an entirely different perspective regarding the data. Using jargon and acronyms known only to mobile forensic examiners can confuse and frustrate a reader who is not versed in these terms. A report can be quickly dismissed if it is simply a well-written document that only the examiner understands. Some examiners go the opposite route, "dumbing down" the content. This has the same effect on readers, who realize the author is "talking down" to them. The most frequently requested change clients make when receiving an examiner's final report is to explain the technical jargon used in the document. The examiner is challenged to find middle ground to discuss technical aspects, procedures, analyses, and conclusions in simple terms, but not so simple as to demean the readers.

An examiner may find that using analogies can help in documenting the technical aspects of the device analysis. By using every day, real-life examples, an examiner can describe a technical procedure within the document or during testimony by comparing the information to something more familiar. For example, if the examiner includes information about unallocated space, he or she might compare it to a shelf in the public library. The user goes to the catalog system, looks up a book by the author or title, and is directed to a shelf where the book is located. However, not all books are referenced in the catalog system—perhaps they have been removed to discard—yet they still exist on a shelf somewhere in the library. The books may still be read, and they still physically exist, but they cannot be found using the catalog. Unallocated space is like the shelf where the discarded books are stored, and the information stored here is similar to the discarded books. This storage space contains deleted files, file remnants, and empty space. Because the files within the unallocated space are not referenced within a file table (catalog), an examiner must search to find each file within this space.

"Tech speak" is best left to conversations with other forensic examiners, but sometimes technical terms and concepts must be included in a forensics report. In this case, the document should contain a list of terms used in the document and simple definitions. The definitions should explain the concept in an appropriate way so that the audience will understand. An examiner can then reuse a definition document for each examination as needed.

By creating a nontechnical document that caters to the intended audience, describes the processes and procedures, and supports the conclusion based upon the evidence, additional explanations to the content are seldom needed. An examiner should strive to produce a concise, detailed document that can stand on its own without additional explanation or commentary.

What Data to Include in the Report

The content of an investigatory report should be consistent and structured so that the examiner can use a similar format for each mobile device investigation report. When an examiner creates a report using boilerplate language and format, he or she can use the same configuration for each examination, with adjustments as appropriate. Creating a well-functioning document starts with a well-formed outline. The examiner can use the outline during the examination and analysis phase to help with documenting the appropriate details and focus on the particular requirements of the outline, which often results in a more detailed report.

Note The information contained within this section is only a recommendation. An examiner can add, remove, or modify these suggestions to fit his or her own needs. Some critical items should always be included in investigatory reports, and these will be noted within the context.

What Right Do You Have?

The initial information in the report should indicate not only how the examiner received the mobile device and conducted subsequent analysis, but also what right the examiner has to collect and analyze its contents. If a search warrant had been obtained to search the device contents, the examiner must indicate this. If an examination does not require a search warrant (for example, consent is given to search, a private investigator is searching, the device is enterprise owned, or the examination is part of a contract), these details must be included in the report to describe why this search and analysis could be legally conducted. Failing to describe the examiner's right to conduct an investigation into mobile device data commonly results in additional questions and concerns from the intended audience.

Documentation that describes the legality of the examination should be included in the Supplemental Documents folder. The text within the rights section of the final presentation will distinctly outline the contents of the supplemental documents and will refer to the location in case the audience needs more detail. Also, the chain of custody form for all exhibits should be included in this folder and should also be documented within the main document. By including this information in the overall presentation, the examiner lays the foundation for the validity of the entire mobile device collection and data analysis. This section should be a mandatory part of all documentation.

The Five W's

Who, what, when, where, and *why* are known as the "Five W's" and are important in all types of writing efforts. Most notably, law enforcement practitioners use these to develop questions to answer when creating reports and also while handling investigations. The answers to these questions should appear at the beginning of the mobile device examination report to set the stage for the processing section of the piece.

The content in the initial portion of the document should clearly introduce the Five W's, setting up the rest of the content and the examination process. By outlining this information first, the examiner helps the audience better understand the rest of the document and supporting materials. When the examiner quickly dives into "This is what I found," readers may be overcome with information overload. Setting the stage for the readers and slowly outlining the necessary materials will give them context for the upcoming content. This section should be a mandatory part of the documentation.

The *who* question is not necessarily "Who dunnit" for an examiner, but a statement of who requested the mobile device processing—often this is the primary investigator, but it may be the person performing the examination. When a request comes from the primary investigator, the examiner should document not only the name of the individual, but also the information surrounding the request. If an investigator has requested that the examiner process "a Samsung SGH-i535 mobile device for documents sent from Bob Kelly to Major Tom sometime between April 1st and April 5th, containing classified materials," this information should be included as part of the *what, when,* and *where* questions. In addition, the *who* may be other persons involved in the case: "Mary Todd, the plaintiff, allowed her iPhone 6 to be examined as part of an investigation surrounding an internal workplace complaint. Ms. Todd stated she had received threatening messages on June 1st, 2015, from Mr. Roger Dokken, her supervisor." The *what* and *when* along with *where* can also be satisfied within this statement. Of course, an examiner should elaborate on each point, making sure every detail is outlined within the processing document completed by the subject who requested the mobile device examination.

The *why* question should explain to the audience the reasons the examiner has been tasked with the collection and examination of the mobile device. Furthermore, it should describe what this particular request for processing has to do with the overall case.

With mobile devices today, just "dumping" a phone, hoping to find something, is like trying to find a needle in a haystack. Massive amounts of data are stored within mobile devices, and an examiner must have a clearly defined objective prior to starting the examination. This objective is the *why* portion of the document.

Tools Used

The next section of the report should outline the tools used throughout the process, including software used to isolate, collect, analyze, view, and report data. The information can be in table form (see Table 14-2) and should include the company that produced the software, a link to the software, the version number used in the analysis, and a comment section. By listing this information within the main documentation, an examiner can duplicate the entire process if necessary.

Usually, two experts are consulted in a trial—one will validate the findings of the other. By listing the specific details for each hardware and software title, along with version numbers,

Examples Using the Five W's

Suppose a mobile device was seized in a drug case, and another device was seized in a case involving a workplace harassment complaint.

In the drug case, the *why* is often defined in the search warrant affidavit that describes how this device was used to communicate via text messages, pictures of drugs, and documents or ledgers stored on the device and used in the sale and purchase of drugs. With this information, the examiner can formulate a plan for the examination and then document this plan within the *why* portion of the report:

> *Detective Ryan indicated the mobile device examined was used to communicate using text messaging and an app known as SnapChat with customers. Detective Ryan also has reason to believe the subject used the mobile device to store and compile records of sales and purchases of drugs using a mobile app and has used the built-in camera to take pictures of drugs and drug paraphernalia as well as receive pictures of drugs.*

In a workplace complaint, examining the *why* portion is similar, with the content again derived from the complaint document. If the document alleges that an employee received messages and photographs of a harassing nature from another employee, the examiner should be able to articulate the *why* using this content and an understanding of what types of data will be examined:

> *Human Resources Director Smith received a complaint from employee Amy Christine, who received nude photographs from another employee, Dale Dummy, along with inappropriate messages in Facebook Messenger, Google Voice, and Tinder in violation of company polices. Ms. Christine relinquished her company-owned mobile device to Director Smith for the examination and recovery of any information involving the complaint.*

TABLE 14-2 Example Table Listing Software Used During the Examination Process

Tool	Version	Download	Notes
UFED Touch	4.2	www.cellebrite.com/Releases/MobileForensics/ReleaseNotes_English.pdf	
Physical Analyzer	4.2	www.cellebrite.com/Releases/MobileForensics/ReleaseNotes_English.pdf	
Oxygen Forensic Analyst	7.4	www.oxygen-forensic.com/en/products/oxygen-forensic-analyst	

a second examiner can set up the same environment used in the original analysis. Another reason for including the software titles and version numbers is to assist the initial examiner. Being able to recall the software used in the examination and the version number, the examiner can resolve problems if current software versions do not provide the same results at a later date. Using the software version, the second examiner can install the exact version that was used for the initial examination to ensure a proper verification and validation platform. This may seem like overkill, but with the constant updates to mobile forensic software, there are bound to be changes that could affect an evidence image. Examiners should maintain all the versions of the software, if possible.

Note Maintaining all versions of the software is not mandatory, because storing many versions can be difficult and expensive. However, most software vendors provide a repository where examiners can download past versions, so maintaining the storage site is unnecessary. An examiner should become familiar with these locations for all software that will be part of his or her mobile forensic toolbox and know how to obtain old versions when needed.

Isolation Methods

As part of the main report, the examiner should include how the device was isolated from the cellular and data network, when it was received, and when it was examined. As covered in several chapters in this book, isolating a mobile device from outside networks is mandatory and should be done as soon as possible. Allowing a mobile device to remain connected can have devastating effects on the data within the device, ranging from altering the file metadata to deleting the entire file system.

When conducting a mobile device collection, the examiner is essentially working with a snapshot of the device data—a picture of the device from a time period leading up to the device's seizure, which in most occasions is right around the time of the event. If a device connects to a network, the probability of data contamination is great and the entire timeline, frozen in time by isolation, could be spoiled. The documentation must include this valuable information.

At the Scene If the examiner seized the mobile device at the scene, the documentation of the isolation technique will be straightforward. The examiner must make sure to include the steps taken at the scene to isolate the device and the state the device was in, along with date and time information when the device was isolated.

At the Lab If the mobile device was seized by someone other than the examiner, the examiner must indicate the state the device was in when he or she received it. This includes whether the device was powered on or off, inside a faraday bag, powered on and in airplane mode, or, in some cases, powered on with no form of isolation.

If the examiner is receiving the device either directly from the field or from a property room, he or she must ensure that clear documentation has been received from the person who seized the device from the location. This information should indicate how the device was isolated (airplane mode, isolation bag), how the device was packaged at the site (faraday box, bag, or container), and the date and time of the isolation. Sometimes this information is difficult to obtain, so the examiner must be diligent and contact the person who seized and isolated the device if this information has not been documented. If it has been documented, the examiner can refer to the report created by the person who isolated the device, which should be placed into the Supplemental Documents folder.

Tip If a device is brought to the examiner powered on and not isolated, the examiner must immediately take steps to isolate the device using his or her standard operating procedure.

Whatever the case, the examiner must outline the details, indicating the removal of the device from the network, how it remained isolated from the network during the examination, and if it was not isolated, the circumstances as to why the device was not isolated. An examiner failing to include this information will often have to explain away the possibility of contaminated data, altered file dates, or other anomalies within the device file system.

Collection Methods

As covered in Chapter 8, examiners can use various collection methods to obtain data from a mobile device, ranging from an invasive chip-off to photographing the mobile device screen. Whatever the technique used, the examiner must outline in detail the way in which the data was collected.

If an invasive chip-off physical collection or JTAG collection occurred, the examiner must document the reasons behind such a technical collection. Typically, these methods are used because gaining access to the mobile device using any other means was impossible—perhaps because the device was password protected, because the device had been destroyed by chemical or mechanical means, or because no mobile forensic solution supported the collection of the device's internal file system.

In most cases, a mobile device will be tethered to a personal computer with a cable during the examination. This cable is the conduit between the software and the mobile device. Mobile devices communicate using protocols and commands that have been outlined throughout the book for both logical and physical collections. The commands used by mobile forensic software and other collection solutions travel via the attached cable, negotiating a backup of the device's internal memory stores or files. This backup can occur either via these commands or after the installation of an application to the mobile device, such as an APK in Android. Of course, communication can occur via other means such as Bluetooth, but the documentation is generally the same; communication to the device using commands causes the device to deliver the requested data to a location specified by the mobile forensic solution.

In all cases, data changes occur within the mobile device, but the examiner must provide a detailed explanation of any system data changes that occurred within the internal store that was not user data. The examiner should be prepared to explain how this is known in case this information is challenged. The explanation of verification and validation does not need to be a part of the final documentation, but it should be a part of the examiner's notes and knowledge base, since this information will surely be brought up in a trial.

An examiner must be confident in detailing the collection methods within the documentation because credibility of the process will often be tested. If an examiner has not documented the details of why an invasive method was employed or not employed, why one software solution collected and displayed a piece of data that another did not, he or she may have to answer to the report audience. This information should be mandatory in the final documentation.

Collected Data

As you know, an examiner should not simply rely on the output from the mobile solution to document the collected data. The examiner must detail the main information within the body of the final document and there refer to the report or reports created by the tool. The audience does not want or need to delve into the thousands of contacts and SMS messages; they need a clear and concise view of the requested data, not a data dump they have to sort through.

The collected data portion of the report should include images and clearly defined, measurable details. If, for example, the UFED Touch was used to complete a physical collection of a Samsung Fascinate SCH-I500 and the userdata.rfs and dbdata.rfs partitions were collected, the report should specify the time of the collection, the size of the binary files, and the overall hash of both binary files within the main body. If possible, and if the tool supports this information, the examiner should list the total number of files in the partition's file system. This information can be valuable when describing the massive amount of data within a mobile device to the audience.

When possible, the examiner should detail the information that was extracted via the automated tool, indicating the number of items that were contained in each user data container and the pertinent information that was recovered for each. If possible, the examiner should include the file from which this data was recovered along with an overall hash of that file. This can ensure that another examiner can duplicate the results using the same file, even if he or she has to use another tool to complete the analysis.

Here's an example of a statement that can be used when describing call history records:

> *500 Call History records were collected from the mobile device. The call history database was located within the file system at \data\com.sec.provider.logsprovider\logs.db. A MD5 hash of the file was obtained: c7da421a8de57e813f947b713f676405. Of the 500 records, 212 calls were made to the mobile number of Ms. Smith and there were no incoming calls from Ms. Smith's mobile number between the dates of June 1, 2015, and June 4, 2015. Of the 212 calls, 15 calls showed a duration of 5 minutes or less, with the balance indicating 1 minute or less.*

The examiner should detail this information for all collected data from a mobile solution as well as information manually collected using advanced methods such as SQL queries or scripting.

When an examiner must use advanced methods, these methods do not need to be explained in detail within the document, but the collected data should include context. Context will help to set the stage to the audience on the process that was taken and the reason why the automated tool was unable to locate all of the important data. This data is often at the center of the audience's attention because the automated tool "didn't find it." As you know, an automated tool not finding app data is a regular occurrence, primarily because of the plethora of available apps. This goes for free file parsing for deleted data from SQLite databases, file carving, and string searching. When using this type of analysis, the examiner should include a section of the report dedicated to outlining this material, apart from what the automated tools collected. This is particularly important when the collected information is relevant to the case requirements and outline.

The collected data portion of the document should reflect all the collected areas that contain valuable data, as requested or as part of the overall data picture. Also, a brief narrative should describe any collected data containers that are void of significant data:

> *Out of the 525 contacts located on the mobile device, the name Ms. Smith, her phone number, e-mail address, or other identifying information was not located.*

If an examiner neglects to include information indicating that something was not located, this missing data is often questioned. Why did the examiner not indicate there was no information? What is the examiner trying to avoid? What other information might be left out? These are all valid questions. This section should be mandatory for the final report.

Tools That Collected and Analyzed the Data Usually, more than one tool is used to collect and examine the data: one tool will be used to collect the device image while other tools are used to parse and dissect the data. The document should distinctly outline the tools used to complete the collection of the image and ensuing analysis. This information should be documented in the collected data section in each area where multiple tools were used. Within the collected data section, examiners can add multiple subsections defined by the tool used, and any data that was analyzed is listed in each subsection. This is often the best method because the information can be easily followed by both the audience and the examiner creating the report.

In the tools section, the examiner can list any discrepancies in the data parsed when using multiple tools. One tool may parse additional fields from a SQLite database that another tool did not, providing a different set of results. When this occurs, this information should be part of the documentation. Again, when this information is not documented, the examiner's report can lead to serious questions on the use of the additional tools. As an examiner who has completed and reviewed hundreds of mobile device examinations and their data, I know that this will happen more often than not. Commonly, the differences in the data result from the queries the tools are using to collect the data from a SQLite database. By outlining this information in the report, an examiner will generally quell any potential challenges. This section should be mandatory for the final report, even if a single tool was used for collection and analysis.

What Does the Data Mean?

The final section of the main report will outline the key points of the case, what was requested, and the information that was located that supports the case. This summary area includes the opinions of the examiner based upon the facts of the case. This section should be supported by the collected data area and should not include any data not already mentioned. The conclusion area of the report should show the audience what the collected data means. Data from a mobile device is fact; it is a snapshot of information from the device's internal store. This data can be confusing if an examiner does not provide a conclusion in the report.

Sometimes the data found within a mobile device does not include the particular information that was requested, or it may include information that contradicts the original hypothesis. This information should be emphasized in this section. An examiner should also use this section to educate the audience on the differences between the types of data collected. The examiner should be prepared to explain the multiple types of digital data to the audience—data on its own and in the context of the examination focus.

This section of the report is often the most powerful one because it provides the big picture, an interpretation of the data collected. Whether multiple devices were collected or data was collected from a single event, including a collective interpretation of the data is recommended, if not mandatory.

Data on Its Own Reports are often spit out by automated tools as single investigations, and this data is interpreted as a singular event, which looks much different from data collectively analyzed. When a mobile device is the only piece of evidence requested and collected, the data is specific to that device only. Mobile devices are seldom used independently, however, and are instead used for communication either directly, with another mobile device, or via an intermediary medium such as a server.

Collective Interpretation Seldom is only a single device involved in a mobile device investigation. The examiner usually creates a report detailing the data collectively. An examiner should create subsections within the overall report that define the individually collected data elements, showing where the data was collected and what data was collected from each piece of evidence as an individual exhibit. This enables the audience to see the data collected from multiple sources, such as mobile devices, computers, servers, and flash media, individually. This is important particularly if one piece of evidence contains unique information not found in the other evidence.

The conclusion should contain the examiner's collective analysis of all the data contained within each device as it relates to the others. The examiner should show relationships among the collected data based on timelines, conversations, and any other artifacts that show collective association.

To Include or Not to Include

Examiners should know what information will be distributed, what will not be distributed, and what will be archived. The documentation should present a list of the included materials to introduce the audience to the contents. This information can be in a README .txt file included with the distributed media. The reader can use this information to identify and refer to the material within the main report. Usually, the materials the examiner includes with the report are governed by the SOP developed by the examiner's sponsoring agency or company.

Some items should not be distributed in the completed report—items that do not provide value to the audience. However, this information should always be available, if requested. No materials should be removed or deleted from the case until directed by the SOP or other authority. Following are some basic suggestions on what to include and what not to include.

Include Media, Documentation, and Screenshots

All media extracted from the mobile device that is part of the case should always be included in the evidence folder within the distributed media. Any pictures, video, and audio taken of the evidence by the examiner or subjects seizing the data does not need to be included. (See the upcoming section "Do Not Include Mobile Device Evidence Images.")

References to screenshots of software or the analysis can also be made, though the actual screenshots themselves need not be included in the main report. Because screenshots are created during the investigation, either during the collection of document settings or during the analysis of document settings and data, references to the screenshots should be included on the distributed media. The screenshot files should be clearly named and referenced in the main report. The actual screenshot files should be placed in the Supplemental Documents folder and a subfolder named Screenshots. The reader can then reference this material, if needed, to support the text in the main report.

Written documentation outlining the process should be included in the case report, clearly indicating the existence of the media. However, media files such as notes do not need to be included unless requested. (See the upcoming section "Do Not Include Examiner Notes.") These files should be saved and archived so that they can be produced if needed.

Include References

It is often important to include reference material for the audience, such as common mobile device terms and acronyms with understandable descriptions, info-graphics showing the number of mobile devices collected, graphics showing the way a mobile device communicates with a network, and breakdowns of data as appropriate. A picture may convey the message better than text. This, of course, will be directed by the type of investigation the examiner is conducting.

For common mobile forensic terms, the examiner should compile a list to be included within every report. As mentioned, the examiner should always strive to avoid technical jargon. This information should be included in the Supplemental Documents folder and referred to within the main report text, if needed.

When imagery or details such as info-graphics or created images outlining the decoding of an artifact are included, the image should be referenced to support a written description within the main documentation. The actual image should not be a part of the main report. This information should be contained with the Supplemental Documents folder.

Do Not Include Examiner Notes

Notes compiled by the examiner, such as the formatted note template discussed earlier, should be used by the examiner to compile the final report and to support any challenges to the reception, condition, and handling of the evidence. Unless the notes are required or requested, they can be left out of the main report. However, all notes and material used to compile the final report should be archived, along with the data and the final submitted report. Each page of written material compiled by the examiner should contain a signature with a date. This security precaution can assist both the examiner and audience if the authenticity of the documents are challenged.

Do Not Include Mobile Device Evidence Images

The examiner should not include the actual forensic images of collected devices used during the investigation and subsequent analysis in the main report. Forensic images are used for collecting intelligence, not for explaining or detailing the evidence recovered. Instead, the original forensic images should be archived with all other data and documents compiled and created for the case. The images will be maintained as outlined in the agency or company SOP.

The forensic images, however, can be requested by the audience if it is determined that the evidence will be examined by a second examiner. At that time, the forensic images should be copied and placed in their own storage media and given to the appropriate persons.

In some cases, if data contained within the image includes criminal images (such as child pornography) or sensitive company information, the images are generally not released for obvious reasons. In such cases, the audience requesting the images often views the information at a designated location; this maintains the legality and sensitivity of the evidence since distributing or making copies of this evidence could technically be a crime. The original examiner should inform the reader of the sensitive content to avoid questions as to why the forensic images cannot be disclosed.

Becoming a Mobile Forensic Device Expert

This book is devoted to the examiner's journey to becoming a mobile forensic expert. Becoming a mobile forensic expert has nothing to do with certifications received for performance on aptitude tests, subjective practical exams, or other written tests. The word *journey* best describes how becoming an expert should feel.

Unfortunately, a lot of individuals who are starting out in the field of mobile forensics would rather it be a called a *sprint*. Most look for certifications as a quick way to find a career and believe that a certification will somehow propel them into becoming an expert. It is this belief that has cast a shadow on a field that is growing at breakneck speed, where the number of examiners considered experts has flat-lined.

The word *certification* has been used not only in this final chapter, but throughout the book. Certifications currently come in two main flavors: vendor created and tool based. A *vendor-created certification* "certifies" that the examiner knows how to use the vendor's product; this is not the same as being an expert in mobile forensics. A *tool-based certification* indicates that the examiner has completed the necessary steps to use the vendor's product; it may simply be a label to attach to a namc on a calling card.

Currently, mobile forensics lacks a *general certification*, which would expose an examiner to processes and procedures, various tools, a variety of methods, and a core set of proficiencies. This should be changing soon, however, with the addition of a general mobile device certification board at the International Association of Computer Investigative Specialists (IACIS). However, an examiner does not become an expert in the field merely by getting certified—it takes a lot of hard work.

A mobile forensic expert is an examiner who never relies completely on an automated tool or process. This examiner resists the temptation to click the "Easy" button in search of the truth within an ever-growing amount of data. The expert examiner is never satisfied but will fine-tune the examination processes and procedures whenever possible. The mobile forensic expert will spend countless hours exploring in an effort to uncover massive amounts of data, including never-before-found artifacts.

The ability to locate data using manual techniques does not on its own define an expert mobile forensic expert, but it is part of the equation. Once the expert examiner locates this data, he or she will research and test to arrive at a conclusion as to why this data is written to the device's storage area. Furthermore, the expert will seek to comprehend the processes that took place or that needed to occur for this type of evidence to be written to the device's storage. Then the examiner can determine what this data might mean to the investigation—by looking at the totality of the evidence, not just a located artifact.

On the road to becoming an expert, the road is full of switchbacks and curves, and examiners must navigate undocumented terrain. Experts do not wait for the instructions; they often write the instructions themselves. One of the most critical aspects of the investigational process is peer review. When instructions, procedures, and methods are created and tested, the examiner should allow for the review of the process and artifacts. This critical stage will not only maintain the process's integrity, but it will help the processes continue to improve. Changes are needed to maintain the most up-to-date and relevant procedure consistently in the ever-changing mobile device environment.

In 1990, psychologist Anders Ericsson determined that 10,000 hours of repetition was the secret to becoming an expert. However, how the 10,000 hours are spent matters. To become an expert means to practice, conform, and evolve to refine the discipline, constantly updating and improving the methods. For a mobile forensic examiner, this includes not only collections but research, documentation, and testimony of findings.

The legal world often describes a forensic expert as an individual who provides an opinion more knowledgeable than that of a typical layperson, based upon specialized knowledge or training. The expert's opinion is deemed more valuable because it is based upon scientific, technical, and specialized training, education, or experience.

Obtaining testimonial experience of the findings of an examiner's mobile device investigation is also extremely important. Whether it be simply explaining the findings to a council, board, magistrate, judge, grand jury, or state or federal juries, providing testimony is critical. This type of practice is essential for an examiner on his or her journey to becoming an expert in the field. Providing testimony will help an examiner discern the value of meticulous research and conscientious documentation—either good or bad. During testimony, the examiner will be expected to support any opinion with facts presented in his or her written documentation, as well as evidence uncovered. If an examiner cannot support his or her examination with insight into the data's existence within the mobile device by documentation or testimony, the data is difficult, if not impossible, to use in a case.

By investigating the mobile device, formulating the documentation, and grasping the principles as outlined in this book, the examiner will have the best chance of success. The more an examiner is able to testify to the findings uncovered in a mobile device examination, the better the testimony will be, and the better the examinations of the data will become.

Importance of a Complete Collection

A *complete collection* is one of the most important considerations for a mobile forensic examiner. A complete collection of a mobile device contains a file system, not just an outputted report with data pulled from the mobile device. Of course, in some situations, an examiner will be unable to produce a collection that includes a file system because of limitations of the mobile device or supported software. However, if the mobile device can be collected to include a file system, which is possible with the majority of today's devices, there is no excuse not to include a file system in each collection.

Unfortunately, mobile forensic examiners often need to collect as much information as possible in the least amount of time. As a result, software vendors often highlight their product's collection speed over other features. But this speed can also result in a partial collection or a partial parsing of the data. Some examiners contend that there is not enough time to complete a collection that includes the file system, but an expert examiner's logical iOS collection *must* include the entire file system. An expert is not the examiner who merely pushes a button to extract data from the mobile device.

Full Examination Importance

In the early years of training federal, state, and local law enforcement officers, while explaining the necessity of understanding where the data came from when conducting a collection using the UFED Classic forensic solution, many instructors used a real-life story to convey the importance of credibility.

The officer who took the stand had performed the collection of an LG VX6100 legacy telephone. The officer was called to testify about the call logs and text messaging that had been recovered from the mobile device and was being used as evidence in the trial. He was asked for his credentials and training, along with his number of years of service. The evidence was then presented to the jury. The officer testified that the call logs and text messages were extracted from the mobile device using a UFED device. The prosecutor had the officer explain how the UFED device is attached to the mobile device and how data is extracted to a flash drive. The drive is then inserted into another computer where the report can be viewed. The report was also presented as evidence. The prosecutor did not have further questions.

The officer was then cross-examined by the defense council, who again asked about the evidence. The officer again explained that the information was obtained from the mobile device using UFED Classic, which extracted the data to the attached flash drive. He was

(Continued)

then asked if any other data was collected from the phone. The officer replied that there were contacts and some pictures. The officer explained that all this information was in the report created automatically by the UFED. The word "automatically" perked up the defense council, who said this:

"So.... Can you explain 'automatically' to me?"

The officer then stated, "The data is pulled from the phone by the UFED unit automatically after I put in the make, model, and the items I want to extract."

"OK, that makes sense," the attorney said. "But, where does the data come from?"

"From the phone," the officer added.

"Yes, I understand it comes from the phone, but where in the phone? Is there a file that the text messages, contacts, or pictures come from?"

The officer responded, "It came from the phone, I pushed the button on the UFED and the data came out."

The attorney finally asked, "So, the data in the report is automatically produced by the UFED after it magically connects to the device to obtain the data, and you have no idea if there are actual files on the device?"

The prosecutor then objected, saying that "the officer is not the manufacturer of the UFED and should not have to testify to how it works." The objection was sustained, but then the defense called its own expert, who had also obtained the mobile device file system. He showed the changes made to the device and pointed out the actual files that contained the call logs and SMS messages. At that point, the credibility of the first officer's testimony was significantly challenged.

This true story is from many years ago, but similar stories are still typical during mobile forensic testimony. By completing a full and complete collection of a device, understanding the methodology, process, and procedures, an examiner can overcome such challenges.

Conforming to Current Expectations May Not Be the Best Approach

Based upon misconceptions of the process and procedures along with the methods of collection, mobile forensics has sometimes been compared to magic. Many software vendors early on believed that ease of use, limited access to device file systems, immediate reporting, and a simple output was what the mobile forensics community needed. The tool would be so easy to use that little or no training would be required. This backward approach to mobile forensics continues to be the current expectation for examinations across the globe.

This book was written to inform the mobile forensic examiner that by conforming to this type of collection expectation, an examiner becomes a person who simply presses a few buttons and pitches a smile when the data materializes on the screen. This type of collection shows zero regard to how that information was obtained, where it was obtained from, and whether or not additional information was collected by the tool. This conforming attitude among examiners will continue unless more examiners seek to become experts in the field of mobile forensics.

Today's mobile forensic examiners must realize that thousands of files are available within a mobile device's file system, and these are often viewable using free open source tools. These files and file systems represent digital gold to the examiner who knows what to look for. An examiner today should be digging into these areas, creating automated scripts, researching the various file types, and discovering new methods. Mobile forensics expert examiners are pioneers who know that the forensic processing of a mobile device and all the associated data should include the application of the methods and theories expressed in this book, instead of conforming to conventional mobile device collection processes.

Additional Suggestions and Advice

This book has provided solid techniques and approaches to mobile device forensics, plus real-life examples from the author's many years of being a practitioner in the field. It has offered suggestions on how to make mobile device collection and analysis a process that can be duplicated when needed.

An examiner should never look for a faster way to perform a collection or complete the parsing and analysis of the collected data. Instead, an examiner should look for the best methods and means that will cost the least amount of time in explaining what was done, or not done, during the examination. Once a report of the examination has been distributed, a good measure of the work can be indicated by the questions that follow. If an examiner shortcuts the examination, the odds are good that he or she will face multiple challenges and questions by the readers and audience.

The following sections provide some additional suggestions for the examiner who seeks to become an expert in the field of mobile forensics.

Constant Research and Testing

An examiner must stay up-to-date with the rapidly changing technology, continuous updating of mobile device software, and massive influx of mobile forensic solutions and features. The diverse and ever-changing mobile device landscape creates a challenge to the dedicated mobile device forensic examiner.

Samsung reported in 2014 that 1 million devices were being sold each day, and Google reported in 2015 that there were more Internet searches completed using mobile devices than personal computers. Moore's law suggests that technological growth doubles every 18 months, but at times the exponential growth of mobile device technology exceeds this estimate. This is compelling information, but unfortunately mobile forensic examiners and software solutions are having a difficult time keeping up. An examiner must take it upon himself or herself to research continually the various devices coming to market, the newest file systems, and the trending apps that will surely make their way on to the next mobile device submitted for analysis. An examiner who relies on forensic solutions alone will only be as good as the tool that he or she is using. By staying in pace with the technology, an examiner will be adapting, practicing, and gaining more time toward the 10,000 hours needed to be an expert in the field.

More Mobile Forensics Information

Compiled in the following table are web sites where an examiner can find an abundance of information to assist on the road to becoming an expert examiner.

Site	Location	Description
Apple Developer	https://developer.apple.com	Main Apple site for iOS developers. Great place to get pre-release versions, if registered, or use the support area to learn about the iOS file system.
iPhone Developers	http://forum.iphone-developers.com/	Run by XDA developers and dedicated to analysis and exploits within the various iOS file systems, apps, and so on.
Android Developers	http://developer.android.com/	Main Android site for developers. Many support areas discuss internal classes, ADB commands, and much more. A must for examiners.
Android Central	www.androidcentral.com/	Up-to-date information on all things Android, including new releases, coming releases, and predictions on technology.
DroidForums	www.droidforums.net/forums/	Much like Android Central, but with hacking, modding, and rooting information.
CyanogenMod	http://forum.cyanogenmod.org/	Leader in custom ROMs for Android devices and frequented by mobile forensic software developers who create non-invasive physical bypass ROMs for Android.
Windows Dev Center	https://dev.windows.com/	Main Windows Phone development site. Using the search bar, many tips on file system locations, files, and more can be found within the forum.
XDA Community Forums	http://forum.xda-developers.com/	This forum is a wealth of information on mobile device internals and contains many repositories used by software solutions in their own tools—for iOS, Android, Windows Phone, BlackBerry, and more.
Forensic Focus	www.forensicfocus.com/Forums/viewforum/f=14/	The mobile phone forum, plus other forums for applicable laws and other digital forensic forums. This active forum includes many experts in the digital forensic field.

Chapter Summary

The path to becoming a mobile forensic expert is an arduous one that does not depend on quick solutions. An expert is defined by the successful presentation of abundant facts, his or her knowledge and training within this specialized field, and his or her constant need for growth within the discipline.

The examiner presents his or her discoveries in a fact-filled document to a predetermined audience—ranging from a single individual to a judge and jury. A skilled examiner prepares the final document to suit a multitude of readers by creating a report that is structured to introduce the reader to the investigation's five W's, present the process workflow, and then define the conclusion reached based upon the evidence. As this chapter explains, an automated report generated by a forensic solution does not provide the big picture. The automated report can contain exceptional data, but it provides no context. A reader needs context to see the big picture of the captured data, and the final document created by the examiner provides this context.

Collecting valuable data from a mobile device and creating a tremendous final document doesn't make an examiner an expert by any means. Becoming an expert in any field requires that an individual constantly adapt to the changing environment, seek to find new ways to solve problems, practice the craft, redirect the course if needed, and become immersed in ideas to improve the discipline. Becoming an expert is not about becoming better than someone else, but involves challenging yourself to become the best you can be. The only way to accomplish such a lofty goal in mobile forensics is to be vigilant in training, research, and testing of new methodologies and ideas. An expert is not made with a certification document, but through hard work and dedication.

The road to becoming an expert in the field of mobile device forensics will be long and often filled with potholes. However, along the way, the examiner will meet many other great examiners and practitioners, and those meetings and conversations will show the examiner the benefits of hard work and perseverance.

Index

B

C

D

E

F

G

H

I

O

P

Q

R

S

T

U

X

Y

Z